The Northern Ireland economy:
A comparative study in the economic
development of a peripheral region

RICHARD HARRIS
CLIFFORD JEFFERSON
JOHN SPENCER

The Northern Ireland economy:

A comparative study in
the economic
development of a
peripheral region

Longman

London and New York

Longman Group UK Limited,
Longman House, Burnt Mill, Harlow,
Essex CM20 2JE, England
and Associated Companies throughout the world.

*Published in the United States of America
by Longman Inc., New York*

© Longman Group UK Limited 1990

First published 1990.

British Library Cataloguing in Publication Data
The Northern Ireland economy: a comparative study in
   the economic development of a peripheral region.
   1. Northern Ireland. Economic conditions
   I. Harris, Richard   II. Jefferson, Clifford   III. Spencer, John Ervine
   330.9416′0824

ISBN 0-582-02924-4

Library of Congress Cataloging in Publication Data
Harris, Richard I. D. (Richard Ian)
   The Northern Ireland economy: a comparative study in the economy development of
a peripheral region/Richard Harris, Clifford Jefferson, John Spencer,
      p.   cm.
   Includes bibliographical references.
   ISBN 0-582-02924-4: £14.95 (est.)
   1. Northern Ireland – Economic conditions. 2. Northern Ireland –
   Economic policy.   I. Harris, Richard (Richard I. D.)
   II. Jefferson, Clifford W. III. Spencer, John E.
   HC257.N58S64 1990
   338.9416—dc20   89–13261
                                                                                    CIP

Set in Times Roman 10pt

Printed and bound in Great Britain
at the Bath Press, Avon

Contents

CHAPTER SIX

The labour market: Clifford W Jefferson 148

CHAPTER SEVEN

Labour force characteristics: Janet M Trewsdale 178

CONTRIBUTORS

CHAPTER ONE
T WILSON
Former Professor of Economics,
The University of Glasgow

CHAPTER TWO
J E SPENCER
Professor of Economics,
The Queen's University of Belfast

J M WHITTAKER
Lecturer in Agricultural Economics,
University of Exeter

CHAPTER THREE
R I D HARRIS
Senior Lecturer in Economics
University of Waikato

CHAPTER FOUR
R T HARRISON
Senior Lecturer in Applied Economics,
University of Ulster at Jordanstown

CHAPTER FIVE
I P ENDERWICK
Professor of Management Studies,
University of Waikato

G H GUDGIN
Director,
Northern Ireland Economic Research Centre

D M W N HITCHENS
Lecturer in Economics,
The Queen's University of Belfast

CHAPTER SIX
C W JEFFERSON
Senior Lecturer in Economics,
The Queen's University of Belfast

CHAPTER SEVEN
J M TREWSDALE
Lecturer in Economics,
The Queen's University of Belfast

CHAPTER EIGHT
J B H BLACK
Lecturer in Economics,
The Queen's University of Belfast

CHAPTER NINE
R I D HARRIS
Senior Lecturer in Economics,
University of Waikato

CHAPTER TEN
M A McGURNAGHAN
Senior Lecturer in Economics,
The Queen's University of Belfast

CHAPTER ELEVEN
R W HUTCHINSON
Senior Lecturer in Economics,
University of Ulster at Coleraine

D G McKILLOP
Lecturer in Economics,
University of Ulster at Coleraine

CHAPTER TWELVE
R T HARRISON
Senior Lecturer in Applied Economics,
University of Ulster at Jordanstown

CHAPTER THIRTEEN
V N HEWITT
Lecturer in Economics,
The Queen's University of Belfast

CHAPTER FOURTEEN
P R SIMPSON
Lecturer in Economics,
The Queen's University of Belfast

M P TRAINOR
Research Officer in Economics,
The Queen's University of Belfast

CHAPTER FIFTEEN
M J TRIMBLE
Lecturer in Economics,
The Queen's University of Belfast

CHAPTER SIXTEEN
J F BRADLEY
Senior Lecturer in Economics,
The Queen's University of Belfast

ACKNOWLEDGEMENTS

We are grateful to the following for permission to reproduce copyright material:

Basil Blackwell Ltd. for table 8.5 (Black, 1987); Cambridge University Press and the author, B. Black for fig. 9.3 (Black, 1985); Coal Advisory Service for fig. 10.11 (Coal Advisory Service, 1988); Commission of the European Communities for tables 12.2 (Green, 1985), 15.8, 15.9 (Eurostat, 1987), 15.11 (ERDF, 1985) & 15.12 (Harris, 1988); Department of Economic Development for tables 7.10 (DED, 1987), 12.3, 12.7, 12.9, 12.10 & Appendix 12.1 (DED, 1985); Department of Energy, Dublin for fig. 10.3 (Depart. of Energy, Dublin); Department of Finance & Personnel, Belfast (Policy Planning & Research Unit) for tables 3.12, 14.6 (PPRU) & 13.5 (DFP, 1988) © Crown copyright; The Economic & Social Research Institute for tables 16.10 & 16.11 (FitzGerald et al., 1988); the Controller of Her Majesty's Stationery Office for figs. 3.1 (HMSO), 3.2 from Centrality, Peripherality & EEC Regional Development (Keeble, Owens & Thompson, 1982), 9.1, 9.2, 9.4, 9.6, 9.21 (HMSO, 1981), 10.1 (HMSO, 1980), 10.2 (HMSO, 1988) & tables 2.1 (MAFF, 1988), 2.8, 2.12 (HMSO, 1988), 4.4 (Moore et al., 1986), 5.10, 5.11, 5.12 (HMSO, 1987), 6.8 (HMSO, 1987), 6.9 (HMSO, 1987 & 1988), 10.2 (HMSO, 1988), 14.11, 14.14 (HMSO, 1988) & 15.13 (HMSO, 1988); Industrial Development Board for Northern Ireland for table 12.12 (IDB, 1985); Northern Ireland Economic Council for fig. 4.3 from report 40 (NIEC, 1983b) & tables 4.2, 12.11 from report 60 (NIEC, 1986b) © 1983 & 1986 Northern Ireland Economic Council; the editor, Petroleum Review for fig. 10.6 (Petroleum Review, 1986); the Controller, Stationery Office, Dublin for tables 7.16 & 7.17 (LFS, 1985); University of Edinburgh (Depart. of Geography) for fig. 4.2 (Bull et al., 1982); University of Reading (Depart. of Agricultural Economics & Management) and the author, Prof. A.K. Giles for table 2.15 (Ansell et al., 1988).

EDITORS' PREFACE

Much has been written about the Northern Ireland economy since Isles and Cuthbert produced their seminal study in 1957. It is opportune now, after 30 years of substantial social and economic change, to provide a comprehensive update on the local economy.

It is important to place Northern Ireland within a wider economic setting and this book has accordingly been written with a strong emphasis on regional comparisons. This approach should strengthen the account and analysis of developments that have taken place, and it may interest those who have not previously considered Northern Ireland as a 'case study' in regional economics.

It is not intended that this book should be solely a study of one particular region, but rather that it should be seen as a general contribution to the literature on regional economics. The book is written to provide the reader with information on how a regional economy develops, what distinguishes it from a national economy, and how the government uses particular policies to try to influence growth and well-being in different geographical areas. The material is particularly relevant to an understanding of the economic development of a peripheral regional economy and it is aimed not only at students in higher education taking courses in regional economics or economic geography, as a useful supplementary text, but also at businessmen, trade unionists, government and a wide cross-section of economists.

The book is in the main a conventional study of the economic development of one region, Northern Ireland, seen in comparison with that of other British regions and the Republic of Ireland. However, it also contains topics and material which are not normally studied at the regional level owing to a lack of information. Thus, there are chapters dealing with the regional banking system, the energy sector, social services and industrial relations. These inclusions have been possible because of the relatively rich database that is available in Northern Ireland and, indeed, contributors to the book have in general been able to cover more material than would be possible in a study of any other United Kingdom region. It is, therefore, hoped that this book will prove to be a valuable reference, given the scope and depth of analysis covered.

This study has brought together economists from several institutions in Northern Ireland. The majority were from the Economics Department at Queen's University, two of whom have now moved to the University of Waikato, but there were also contributions from the the University of Ulster, the University of Exeter and the Northern Ireland Economic Research Centre. Special mention must be made of Professor Tom Wilson who, as adviser to the Northern Ireland Government, was responsible for the 1965 Wilson Report on local economic development. In this present volume he introduces and sets the scene for later contributions. The writing, in the main, was completed by September 1988 and the manuscript was delivered to the publisher by June 1989. As usual, full responsibility for the views expressed in each chapter rests with the authors.

The book has benefited greatly from the diligent research assistance and guidance on style provided by one of the book's contributors, Mary Trainor, assisted by Ann Toman. We also wish to record our appreciation of the efficient work of departmental secretaries, Georgina Holmes and Carol Richmond, who typed the manuscript.

We gratefully acknowledge the considerate and professional cooperation which we have received in all our dealings with the publisher. We also would like to record our thanks for the encouragement and financial assistance of TSB Northern Ireland, without whose support the book might not have been written.

Richard I D Harris
Clifford W Jefferson   The Queen's University of Belfast
John E Spencer   June 1989

Editors' Note

In September 1989 the summary results of the 1987 Census of Employment for Northern Ireland were released. They revealed that the official estimates of employees in employment based on the Quarterly Employment Survey had been substantially understated. Overall, in September 1987, some 14,000 employees had been missed from the quarterly estimates, the majority of whom were employed in private sector services. The details of the figures over the years affected (1985 to 1989) are not yet available but it seems likely that the error has been increasing over time. For this reason and because the book was in the final stages of printing when the summary data became available it has been decided not to incorporate these revised data.

The change in the estimates of employees in employment principally affects Chapters 6, 7 and 12. In order to advise the reader on the extent and nature of the changes we have added Appendix 6.3 to the Labour Market chapter and inserted footnotes in the text where the analysis is affected.

ABBREVIATIONS

AAS	Annual Abstract of Statistics
b	billion
BEQB	Bank of England Quarterly Bulletin
BES	Business Expansion Scheme
BSU	Business Size Unit
CAP	Common Agricultural Policy
CHS	Continuous Household Survey
COP	Census of Population
CSO	Central Statistics Office
DAFS	Department of Agricultural and Fisheries for Scotland
DANI	Department of Agriculture (NI)
DED	Department of Economic Development (NI)
DFP	Department of Finance and Personnel (NI)
DG	Directorate-General
DHSS	Department of Health and Social Services (NI)
DMS	Department of Manpower Services (NI)
EAGGF	European Agricultural Guidance and Guarantee Fund (FEOGA)
EC	European Community
ECU	European Currency Unit
EEC	European Economic Community
EG	Employment Gazette
EMS	European Monetary System
ERDF	European Regional Development Fund
ESF	European Social Fund
ESRI	Economic and Social Research Institute
ESU	European Size Unit
ET	Economic Trends
EUA	European Unit of Account
Eurostat	Statistical Office of the European Communities
FBI	Farm Business Income
FBS	Farm Business Survey
FES	Family Expenditure Survey

FI	Farming Income
GATT	General Agreement on Tariffs and Trade
GB	Great Britain
GDP	Gross Domestic Product
GHS	General Household Survey
GNP	Gross National Product
HBS	Household Budget Survey
HMSO	Her Majesty's Stationery Office
IDA	Industrial Development Authority
IDB	Industrial Development Board
ISB	Irish Statistical Bulletin
LEDU	Local Enterprise Development Unit
LFA	Less Favoured Areas
LFS	Labour Force Survey
LGS	Loan Guarantee Scheme
m	million
MAFF	Ministry of Agriculture, Fisheries and Food
MCA	Monetary Compensatory Amount
MDS	Monthly Digest of Statistics
MIES	Meat Industry Employment Scheme
MMB	Milk Marketing Board
na	not available
NACE	General Nomenclature of Economic Activities in the European Communities
NES	New Earnings Survey
NESC	National Economic and Social Council
NFI	Net Farm Income
NI	Northern Ireland
NIAAS	Northern Ireland Annual Abstract of Statistics
NIDS	Northern Ireland Digest of Statistics
NIEC	Northern Ireland Economic Council
NIERC	Northern Ireland Economic Research Centre
NIHE	Northern Ireland Housing Executive
NIHS	Northern Ireland Housing Statistics
OECD	Organisation for Economic Cooperation and Development
OPCS	Office of Population Censuses and Surveys
RGAR	Registrar General's Annual Report
RI	Republic of Ireland
RPI	Retail Price Index
RT	Regional Trends
SIC	Standard Industrial Classification
SITC	Standard Industrial Trade Classification
SMUK	Supplementary Measures United Kingdom
ST	Social Trends

UK	United Kingdom
UKDES	Digest of United Kingdom Energy Statistics
UKHS	United Kingdom Housing and Construction Statistics
VAT	Value Added Tax
VP	Variable Premium

N

Scotland

Northern
Ireland

North

REPUBLIC
OF
IRELAND

Yorkshire
and
Humberside

North
West

East
Midlands

Wales

West
Midlands

East Anglia

South East

South West

0   k m   200

FIG 1 Standard regions of the United Kingdom and the Republic of Ireland

CHAPTER ONE

Introduction

Thomas Wilson

'The practical objective of the report is to assess Northern Ireland's economic condition, and to examine the factors limiting its economic development, in order to throw light upon the broad problems of economic and industrial policy.' In these words Isles and Cuthbert (1957) described their pioneering and authoritative *An Economic Survey of Northern Ireland*. A large number of investigations, both official and private, have been carried out in the intervening years as the situation has changed and policies have evolved. The need for a new survey, up-to-date and comprehensive in its range, has become increasingly apparent. The purpose of the present volume is to meet that need.

Northern Ireland, at one time respected as a thriving industrial centre, has fallen on evil days, and some are inclined to the view that an elegy should now suffice. For it is common enough to hear it said that the province is not economically 'viable' and cannot conceivably be made so. That the situation is difficult is beyond question, but the use of the term 'viable' is scarcely appropriate; for 'viability' suggests a sharp borderline between success and failure whereas the real question is always one of degree. Northern Ireland's performance needs to be tested by various measurements, both as to how its own economy has changed over time and how it compares with that of other areas. These six counties have maintained their historical position as the poorest region in the United Kingdom with the lowest level of output per head and the highest level of unemployment but, as one would expect, important changes have nevertheless taken place. Between 1926 and 1938, output per head fell from just over two-thirds to just over half that of the United Kingdom as a whole, with Northern Ireland one of the regions worst affected by the decline in the older industries. The Second World War then saw a vast improvement as the region's industries were brought up to something like full capacity and remained prosperous during the immediate post-war years. By 1947, the ratio of provincial gross domestic product per head to the national figure had risen to over 70 per cent, but the need for a substantial change in the industrial structure soon became plain once more. By 1960, per capita output had dropped to 63 per cent of the national average but another period of relative advance was then to lift the proportion to 73 per cent by 1973 and to 78 per cent by 1980 where, more or less, it has remained to date. In both the Republic of Ireland and Northern Ireland, output per head rose more rapidly than in the United Kingdom from the early 1960s until the first oil crisis in 1973. In the Republic of Ireland this ratio went up from half of the United Kingdom figure in 1960 to two-thirds in 1973, and to about three-quarters by 1987. As these figures imply, the Republic of Ireland had also gained some ground relatively to Northern Ireland with the result that the two parts of the island had similar levels of GDP per head by the mid-1980s. Owing to outflows of profits, however, GNP is substantially lower than GDP in the Republic of Ireland and, per capita, amounted to just two-thirds of the United Kingdom level in 1987.

Over the years both parts of the island have demonstrated some ability to adjust their economies and to expand their output. In both cases, conditions in the world economy are of crucial importance, as is only to be expected. Northern Ireland has always had a very open economy and, in the post-war period, the Republic of Ireland also moved decisively away from the more protectionist position it had previously adopted. To this openness both have clearly owed an advance in living standards that could never otherwise have been achieved, but the cost has been vulnerability when the external environment has become difficult. Both did well during the long period of well-sustained growth in the world economy between the late 1940s and the mid-1970s. Both were badly affected when the second oil crisis of 1979 brought general recession, and both have regained a little of the lost ground during the subsequent recovery, although unemployment still stands at high levels. With the further steps towards a single European market that will be taken in 1992, there will be new opportunities, but there may also be some new threats to the peripheral areas as well.

In broad outline, economic development in Northern Ireland has followed a pattern that is familiar throughout the developed world, with a relative decline in agriculture's contribution to both employment and output, with jobs in manufacturing falling in line with the international trend, with rising productivity generally, and with the service industries providing most of the demand for additional manpower.

As Spencer and Whittaker show in Chapter 2, agriculture contributes about 4.5 per cent of provincial output, as compared with 2 per cent in Great Britain and 3.5 per cent in the EC as a whole. It therefore remains an important industry, and is still more so in providing occupations for about 8 per cent of the labour force with another 3 per cent in related industries such as food-processing. It is true that the larger contribution to jobs than to output implies productivity per head of about half the provincial average. With incomes also lower, there is an incentive to leave the land but its force must be blunted by the shortage of jobs at the higher levels of income extracted elsewhere in the economy. Moreover, an allowance must be made for the perceived advantages of a rural occupation that are not included in conventional comparisons of real income.

As is well known, the movement from lower productivity agriculture to higher productivity industry has been one of the factors contributing to the growth of total output in a number of countries, but it would be unwise to anticipate any large future effect of this kind in Northern Ireland. This is so, not only because the agricultural labour force has already been reduced to a small fraction of the total, but also because the disparity in productivity, large though it is, is probably well below what it is in some other European countries.

If some industries have suffered from competition in the market place which they have been unable to meet, agriculture has suffered, in certain respects at least, from the official policies of the European Community. Spencer and Whittaker conclude that Northern Ireland's balance of gains and losses under CAP is hard to strike, but they have no doubt that the intensive livestock industry has been damaged by the artificially high price for feedstuffs. The profitable dairy industry has been curbed by quotas designed to check over-production in response to CAP support prices, but any comparison with the situation as it might have been without CAP is necessarily hazardous. Beef production should, in their view, continue to prosper.

What continues to be particularly interesting is the possibility of substituting more income support for some price support. In this way it might be possible to provide those who are working marginal farms throughout the Community with whatever help was thought to be socially desirable – or politically expedient – and to do so at less cost to the taxpayer and consumer than that of running CAP in its present form. Perhaps this now familiar proposal will be adopted more fully in the future. The incentive to leave the land would then be weakened, and this might be a pity if higher-productivity jobs were available elsewhere. If, however, the effect was simply to be less unemployment, a different view might be taken.

In 1987 manufacturing industry employed 21 per cent of the labour force. Together with other regions, Northern Ireland had suffered severely from the contraction in manufacturing over the preceding decade. Thus in 1986, output was at 97 per cent of its 1979 level and 75 per cent of its 1973 level. It was a bitter experience, though not unique, as the authors of Chapter 5 demonstrate. The drop in manufacturing employment between 1975 and 1983 came to 48,000 jobs, or 32 per cent of the manufacturing labour force, as compared with a national loss of 2.1 million or 30.5 per cent (Table 5.5). For Scotland and Wales the outcome was a little worse; for England, a little better.

In Chapter 3, Harris compares the difference in growth rates for net output in manufacturing in the eleven British regions over long periods of years, 1963–79 and 1963–85. Northern Ireland's record is about the top of the lower half and close to the national average. When the effects of differences in industrial structure are distinguished from other effects, it would appear from his analysis that Northern Ireland's industrial mix was the handicap that offset what would otherwise have been a performance slightly above the average. There may be a grain of comfort in these figures, but those for the levels of productivity confirm that the province has still failed to catch up.

It may seem surprising that the fall in manufacturing employment was not much worse, as compared with the rest of the United Kingdom. The explanation must largely lie in the higher subsidies provided. The general case for, and the case against, the subsidisation of industry in the less prosperous areas will be discussed at a later stage. At this stage, however, it is right to ask whether industrial development, as shaped by such subsidies during the earlier years of strong expansion until the mid-1970s, had been of such a form as to leave the province particularly vulnerable to recession. The question is of more than historical interest, for the lessons thus learned may be relevant in determining future measures. Was the expansion of a kind likely to be appropriate in the longer term? To what extent was the ground gained subsequently lost during the recession? How far can the remaining weaknesses be attributed to deficiencies in public policies? Was too much reliance placed on branch factories? What were – or are – the alternatives? If mistakes were made, has there been an appropriate response in more recent formulations of policy? How have small firms fared and what success has attended the efforts made over almost twenty years to provide them with special assistance? These are some of the questions that are taken up in subsequent chapters. The relevance of the answers is by no means confined to regional policy in Northern Ireland, for the regional problem is common to most countries.

After the war, Northern Ireland's heritage of manufacturing industry was highly specialised, and the specialisation was in industries that did not offer much prospect of expansion. The industrial structure needed to change and, if it could also be made more diversified, it might be made less vulnerable. As Harris records in Chapter 3, substantial changes did take place but, as judged by his coefficients, the degree of specialisation was little altered, partly because there was a good deal of specialisation within the new industries themselves. This was, in particular, the consequence of the establishment of the man-made fibre industry which was to suffer so severely during the subsequent recession that it has virtually disappeared in Northern Ireland.

It has been a familiar criticism of regional policy, in Great Britain as well as in Northern Ireland, that subsidies for investment in fixed capital were particularly inappropriate in labour surplus areas. In so far as such grants led to an increase in capacity rather than an increase in capital intensity, this objection did not hold, but a bias towards capital-intensive methods was present. Safeguards could indeed be introduced when the capital grants were selective – that is to say, dependent upon certain conditions being met. Indeed these grants could then be turned into assistance with capital expenditure based on each new job to be created – together with any appropriate variations in order to allow for other considerations, such as the ratio of male to female employment. However, selectivity can encounter two difficulties. First, potential newcomers who are choosing between different locations like to know, as definitely and as soon as possible, what assistance they can expect, and negotiations about selective assistance can take time. A double tier system, with standard grants supplemented by selective assistance, has therefore been a familiar feature. In Northern Ireland, however, even selective negotiations could be conducted quickly because authority had been devolved to a provincial parliament. The Ministry of Commerce could act with a speed and authority that the regional offices of the Whitehall ministry could not achieve –

and it was partly their failure to do so that led to standard capital grants in Great Britain that were essentially conditional only on the investment being carried out. Moreover, in Northern Ireland, other departments could arrange with greater speed for the provision of complementary services, such as special supplies of electrical power or additional housing. Such gains in resource management could be substantial and it is interesting to note in passing that the usual textbook list of considerations that should determine when sub-central government would, or would not, be appropriate often leaves out the effect of efficiency in administration – X-efficiency, to use the jargon.

What has just been said would seem to constitute an argument for devolved government, but it has now been shown in practice that effective decentralisation does not necessarily require an elected regional assembly. Similar administrative results can be achieved by the modern forms of administrative devolution, as in Scotland – or, for that matter, in Northern Ireland. Allocative efficiency in matching the use of resources to local preferences, as explained in Chapter 13 is, of course, another matter.

In assessing the case for directing assistance to labour rather than capital, it must be recognised that subsidies for running costs would be still more likely to subsidise inefficiency. Even when capital grants are unselective, there is at least some presumption of a *net* increase in investment and this may bring with it some changes in products and processes. Nor is it really so obvious that labour subsidies must be appropriate in a labour-surplus area, for ordinary market forces should ensure that labour is relatively cheap. If the answer is that the proper market response is prevented by restrictive practices, can we then be sure that a subsidy – such as the old Regional Employment Premium – will not be absorbed in still higher factor incomes? For these reasons, the case against directing subsidies towards investment rather than labour is not so conclusive as is often implied. To concede as much is not, of course, to underestimate the importance of assistance with labour costs when it is specifically designed to help with training.

The earlier expansion before 1969 largely took the form of branch factories in both Northern Ireland and the Republic of Ireland, and even in those British development areas that had a larger initial industrial base. This way of achieving expansion has often been denounced as fatally flawed. It is indeed true that, when a firm is obliged to contract in bad times, the branch factories will obviously be the ones to be closed down. It is a danger that was perceived in the past, but it was also observed that the branches had survived the recessions of the 1960s rather well, with management planning for the trend, right across the small cyclical disturbances. A deep recession would be a different matter – but was it not the case that, with Keynesian policies to hand, any grim eventuality of that kind could be forestalled? An unpleasant lesson had to be learned about the limitations of macro-economic policy. Undoubtedly it would be better, as a general rule, to have more firms that were locally based rather than branches. The former should not only be less vulnerable but would also provide experience in top management and in R & D of a kind that branches cannot offer. Moreover, there would be some likelihood – though not a certainty – that a larger proportion of profits would be reinvested in the region. The Republic of Ireland has experienced in a very marked way the effect of having such profits transmitted abroad. These are important points, but it cannot be assumed that the expansion of indigenous firms would have sufficed in the past or will do so in future. As Enderwick, Gudgin and Hitchens observe in Chapter 5: 'Evaluation of the prevailing manufacturing structure must be placed within the context of feasible alternatives.' The branch factories made a contribution to output and employment that could not have been obtained without them. Moreover the fact that these factories were the principal source, first of gain and then of loss, should not obscure the continuing availability of government assistance to local industry as well. Substantial assistance was available but its effectiveness depended upon local entrepreneurship.

In Northern Ireland, as elsewhere, the importance of small firms was only tardily conceded and there was a long debate before the Local Enterprise Development Unit (LEDU) was established in 1971 with the responsibility of assisting firms with up to 50 employees. In the late 1980s, a quarter of all manufacturing employment was in such firms, which is slightly above the Great Britain average. During the expansion from 1981 to 1988 LEDU job promotions came to 24,000 out of a provincial total of 50,000 jobs promoted in government sponsored industry (NIEC 1989). Some of these jobs may be short-lived but nevertheless large firms can grow from small beginnings. Will a 'William Morris' one day appear in Northern Ireland – or should one say 'reappear'? For Northern Ireland has already produced a 'William Morris' in the person of Harry Ferguson; but he took his tractor to the USA after the war, ignoring the blandishments of Stormont. Perhaps another innovating entrepreneur of his stature will one day emerge. Meanwhile firms that are still small make a valuable total contribution.

It may be tempting to infer that the contraction of employment in large firms was one of the main reasons for the setting up of small ones but the evidence does not fully support this view, for the latter were usually established by persons who voluntarily left employment in order to do so. Obviously it will be a help if, in that previous employment, they have acquired some experience of management, even at branch factory level, or experience in an R & D department. Indeed one of the several reasons for seeking to induce incoming firms to bring their R & D is the hope that some clever boffins, in search of independence, may later decide to set up their own concerns. But the inducements have had only a limited appeal to the incoming firms – and are not likely to evoke much response so long as it is feared that a casual terrorist bomb might destroy the work of years of skilled investigation and assessment.

Northern Ireland is a little area with a population of just 1.5 million situated on Europe's western edge. It may therefore appear that we must accept, as a disagreeable fact, that its performance will be hampered both by smallness and remoteness. Differences in rates of growth between different areas are notoriously hard to explain with large questions inadequately answered. Size is one of the factors but it can be said with confidence that

Northern Ireland's labour force is big enough for a reasonably diversified industrial structure. For, at the plant level, the main economies of size can often be obtained with a labour force of 200–300, with probably only a limited number requiring 500 or more (see Lyons 1980). The average size of immigrant plant in Northern Ireland was 175 workers. It must be emphasised that the reference is to static economies at the level of the plant – static in the sense that products and processes are assumed to be given, with size the only determining variable. It is a quite different matter at the level of the firm where decisions must be made about changes in techniques, about the product cycle, about marketing strategy and so on. The economies of scale may, of course, require much larger units for the firm as a whole. It would be absurdly unrealistic to expect much success in persuading non-indigenous firms to move to Northern Ireland. The now almost routine condemnation of expansion with branch factories needs, therefore, to be tempered by a realistic acceptance of what is feasible.

In looking ahead, one can anticipate that fixed capital will constitute a smaller part of costs, with more emphasis on training and software. The large multinationals, for their part, will be able to choose the location of their plants from a wide range of possibilities – the 'economies of scope'. The less developed British regions, together with the Republic of Ireland, can offer the attraction of access to the large European market, but the inadequate training of the labour force may be a continuing handicap in this highly competitive field.

About two-thirds of those in civil employment in Northern Ireland are in the service industries, a fact that need occasion no surprise. The figure for the United Kingdom as a whole is much the same and a similar proportion is found in some other EC countries – though the German figure, at a little over one-half, is substantially lower. It has come to be widely accepted, as I have observed above, that the service industries will continue to be the main source of additional employment in the developed world, with the number in manufacturing likely to be roughly unchanged. Admittedly this sweeping forecast need not hold in all the smaller areas for, in some, good fortune or outstandingly good performance could conceivably lead to a substantial rise even in manufacturing employment. Northern Ireland might, just conceivably, be made one of those areas with sufficient effort, sufficient resourcefulness and sufficient luck – but this is scarcely something to be confidently anticipated! It is far more prudent to assume that a strong effort will be required even to maintain manufacturing employment. Indeed if massive Exchequer support were to be gradually reduced and industry left to stand on its own feet, an immense effort would be required in both parts of Ireland to prevent a further significant decline in manufacturing industry.

The service industries, on which so much reliance must be placed, are sometimes described contemptuously as merely a way of 'taking in one another's washing'. This, of course, is a nonsensical view which seems to rest on the assumption that there is no scope for a beneficial division of labour within this large and manifestly diverse collection of activities. On more serious grounds, a heavy reliance on these industries is held to entail two disadvantages, as Harrison explains in Chapter 12. The first of these is that technical progress is believed to be slower than in manufacturing. This may be true of the mixed bag of service industries taken as a whole, as identified by Harrison, although marked changes have occurred in some of them. Moreover it is necessary to allow for the fact that the difficulty of measuring service 'output' may lead to dubious conclusions. The second characteristic, often cited as a disadvantage, is that relatively to output or employment, these industries do not make the same contribution to the balance of external payments as do manufacturing industries. Once more qualification is required, for some service industries do in fact make a large contribution. The financial services provided by the City of London are the obvious example. Scotland has also benefited in this way and the Republic of Ireland is hoping to do so on a greater scale than in the past. From this particular point of view however, Northern Ireland's financial sector is less well placed, as Hutchinson and McKillop are forced to conclude in Chapter 11. Tourism makes a contribution which could be increased if political stability were restored. It would then be possible to resume the attempt started many years ago, just before the current 'troubles' began (in 1969), to have a 'tourist circuit' for the whole of the island. There is a further area where Northern Ireland, like other parts of Britain, may have a comparative advantage in the new Europe. That is in the field of higher education.

It should go without saying that many service industries (eg transport and banking) contribute indirectly to the performance of other industries that make a more direct contribution to the balance of payments. Thus a distinction is drawn by Harrison between consumer services and producer services. Indeed the distinction between services and manufacturing is arbitrary in some cases. For example, a fleet of lorries owned by a manufacturing concern will belong to manufacturing; if however the same services are performed by a transport contractor, the function will be classified as part of the service sector. Moreover, local services sometimes compete for the consumers' pound with imported manufactures. These complications are important, but it remains true that the service sector cannot be expected to make as large a contribution as manufacturing industry to the provincial balance of payments.

A further distinction has to be made between services that are provided through the market and those provided without charge by public agencies. When this distinction is made, an interesting feature of economic development in Northern Ireland becomes apparent. This is the lowness of the ratio of employment in *marketed* services to employment in the production industries, as compared with that ratio in other parts of the United Kingdom. Thus, as Jefferson shows in Chapter 6 (Table 6.8 and Appendix 6.3), the number so employed in Northern Ireland in 1986 was only 100 per cent of the number employed in the production industries (including agriculture), as compared with 114 per cent in Wales, 118 per cent in Scotland and 130 per cent in England. A detailed explanation would have to take account of various other differences such as the relative importance of agriculture, but it may be interesting to observe that if even the Scottish ratio were to be achieved in Northern Ireland, the increase in employment in the service industries would be over 22,000. Of course this is only a statistical adjustment and the outcome would be more complicated in reality. A substantial rise in jobs could nevertheless be expected. The slow rate of growth of the marketed service industries is not a new puzzle. For example, we over-estimated the prospective rise in service employment in the first development plan (1965–70) (HMSO 1965). Harrison now draws attention to slow growth in more recent times.

By contrast, the proportion in the non-marketed service activities – 'public administration and other services' – is high by comparison with those for England, Scotland or Wales. Part of the explanation is the large number employed in the security services. There are also differences in other 'needs' as these are assessed for the purposes of public finance, as discussed in Chapter 14 by Simpson and Trainor.

Unemployment has always been high in Northern Ireland relatively to the position in other areas of Britain, but there have been substantial changes over the years in the assessment of what would constitute 'full employment'. Keynes himself was sceptical about the possibility of keeping even the national figure down to 5 per cent and, by that standard, even Northern Ireland was close to 'full employment' in the 1960s but well above the national average of rather less than 2 per cent. To put the point differently, Northern Ireland used to provide employment for 93–94 per cent of the labour force, but can now do so for only slightly more than four-fifths. Moreover even this four-fifths depends upon heavy support from the public sector. One measure of the scale of this support is the proportion of GDP at factor cost that is derived from the public sector. As can be seen in Table 13.1, this proportion – defined to include publicly owned industry – has risen from 33 per cent in 1974 when it was already slightly ahead of the proportion of the United Kingdom to 44 per cent in 1986 when it was 10 per cent ahead. The reason was only partly the relatively greater expansion of the public sector which rose by 14.5 per cent as compared with 14.1 per cent in the United Kingdom. The main explanation was the relatively greater fall in private sector GDP. Another important measure is public expenditure relative to GDP and in Northern Ireland total public expenditure on goods and services, subsidies and transfers, amounted to the staggering proportion of 69 per cent in 1985/86 as compared with 38 per cent in Great Britain (Table 13.2). This contrast is startling.

It may be tempting to say that Northern Ireland's dependence on financial support is nothing new. Is it not the case that the province has always been subsidised? There is a misunderstanding here that needs to be cleared up, not only in order to set the record straight but in order to understand the current position. Under the Government of Ireland Act which established legislative devolution in Northern Ireland, the province was expected to meet all its domestic expenditure and to make a specified contribution to such central costs as defence. It soon became clear that, with taxes at the same rates, this obligation to contribute to national costs could not be met unless the public services were to be run at levels far below those of the rest of Britain. The financing of social security transfers proved particularly troublesome for the responsibility for these benefits, retained by Westminster in the 1914 Home Rule legislation, had for some reason been devolved in 1920. Northern Ireland was thus at a severe disadvantage compared with other poor regions in the United Kingdom – and Northern Ireland was the poorest of the lot. For example, no one expected Clydeside to finance its own social security transfers. Any such idea would have been rejected as absurd for it was universally agreed that revenue should be pooled. More generally there was – and is – no relationship between the sums contributed as taxation by any region in Great Britain and central government expenditure in that region. Indeed no official calculation is made even today, except for Northern Ireland. Throughout the whole of the inter-war period, the province, far from being specially subsidised, was placed at a disadvantage compared with other regions. The explanation lay at least partly in the fact that the modern principles which determine inter-regional transfers had not been developed in the 1920s and progress in doing so was slow. It was only towards the end of the 1930s that the principle of 'parity' was conceded, not only in Britain with regard to Northern Ireland, but also in Australia and Canada with regard to federal–state financial relationships. The broad principle then accepted, though with variations between different countries in its precise interpretation, was that the payment of taxation at the same rates across regions would imply an entitlement to expenditure on a common scale, related to needs and to the cost of meeting them which may vary regionally. It was also subsequently conceded that special provision should be made for the accumulated deficiencies in Northern Ireland's social capital. But, for many years, these principles were only imperfectly implemented. Even in the early 1960s public expenditure per head was below the figure for England as a whole although the latter included much more prosperous areas where the 'need' for social transfers and for improvements in social capital was substantially less (Wilson 1989).

One of the aims of the development programmes of the 1960s and 1970s was to make good the backlog in social capital and expenditure per capita. Northern Ireland then began to pull ahead of the English figure, though still lagging well behind the figures for expenditure in Scotland and Wales. It was in the early 1970s, after devolution had been replaced by 'direct rule', that expenditure rose so sharply, with Westminster now directly responsible for meeting the deficiencies and hopeful that, if this were done as fast as possible, the social tensions in the province might be greatly eased.

It has sometimes been said that during the half-century of devolution, Northern Ireland was self-governing but not self-financing. This is almost the reverse of the truth. The Northern Ireland taxpayer paid for much the greater part of provincial expenditure, though without contributing much, except in wartime, to national expenditure. But provincial expenditure was tightly controlled, item by item, by the Treasury and self-government was fully exercised only when no money had to be spent – for example in the law relating to divorce or to the local government franchise. Under 'direct rule', there has been much more to spend and greater freedom to spend it – though that freedom has been exercised by a Secretary of State, not by an elected government.

Two questions must now be asked. First, has the wheel come round full circle so that Northern Ireland, formerly deprived, is now being pampered? This is a difficult, as well as an important, question, partly because there is a lack of comparable statistics for the different British regions and partly because 'need' cannot be determined with precision. Secondly, even if the province is being treated no better than equity requires, can it be right for any area to be so heavily dependent on assistance from other areas? This is a still more difficult question which raises some basic questions of social policy.

The subvention, as it is now called, amounted to about 5–10 per cent of public expenditure in the 1960s which, we may infer, was well below the proportion for some of the regions or sub-regions of Great Britain. Under 'direct rule' a large increase then began until a peak was reached in real terms in 1986/87 which has been followed by some decline. The support received in the later years of that decade came to about a third of public expenditure and to rather more than a fifth of personal income before tax. Can assistance on so large a scale really be justified when regard is paid to taxation on the one hand and the need for public expenditure on the other? The answer with regard to taxation is clear in principle. Apart from local rates, the taxes are the same as those levied in Great Britain, and differences in yield should simply reflect differences in taxable capacity. In practice, various assumptions have always to be made in calculating the amount of taxation paid, and the difficulties are held to be so formidable in the case of the regions within Great Britain that no official assessments are made and hardly any private ones. These difficulties are less in the case of Northern Ireland, but some broad assumptions about incidence are still required. On the expenditure side serious difficulties are encountered, for 'need' cannot be assessed in a fully comprehensive and fully objective way and approximations have to be attempted with the aid of simplifying rules. Calculations of this kind – which are a normal feature of the annual public expenditure reviews – were presented in 1978 in a special Treasury report on Scotland, Wales, England and Northern Ireland in order to throw light on the financial implications of the legislation for devolution in the first two countries. The services covered were only those to be devolved. The outcome of this investigation is reviewed by Simpson and Trainor in Chapter 14. A number of more comprehensive assessments have been made from time to time by the Northern Ireland Economic Council from which it has been concluded that the higher expenditure per capita in Northern Ireland, as compared with the other countries in the United Kingdom, can be satisfactorily explained by greater needs. The factors stressed are 'different administrative arrangements, the greater incidence of public sector housing, a quite distinct demographic structure, the size of the agricultural sector, the exceptional demands of law and order provision and various other matters' (NIEC 1989). Their calculations suggest that, as compared with Great Britain, expenditure over the years 1980–86 has sometimes been marginally above 'parity' (from 1.7

to 2.6 per cent) and sometimes marginally below (from 0.5 to 1.7 per cent). In view of the uncertainties, these differences are trivial.

The subvention can be regarded as largely a consequence of the welfare state on the one hand and the progressiveness of the tax system on the other. The effect of this combination is usually discussed from the point of view of persons or households within the nation with no particular reference to location, but the effect is given a particularly sharp focus when attention is directed to a poor region. If then the subvention is held by some critics to be excessive, does this mean that, in their view, the net fiscal package in Britain – benefits less taxation – is too favourable to those with lower incomes? It is a searching question.

What is not in doubt is that the people in an area so heavily dependent upon transfers are in a vulnerable position and will feel the effect, in geographically concentrated form, of any national reduction in benefits or in the progressiveness of the tax structure. It is also true that this insecurity may simply be ignored for a long time and there may be an inclination to assume that, in so far as their own efforts are inadequate to meet their 'needs', the deficiency will always be made good by Whitehall. Apart from this 'psychology of dependence' on which much stress is sometimes laid, there are other problems. In particular, with benefits provided at levels thought appropriate for the country as a whole, the 'poverty trap' will be deeper and wider in the poorer areas. Furthermore, the effect of a large public component in the services sector, where pay is much more influenced by powerful national unions, has also been suspected of having an inflationary effect on wage demands in the market sector. These points are taken up by Harris in Chapter 9 and by Hewitt in Chapter 13.

The possible psychological consequences of dependence can, per-haps, be better appreciated by comparing the position of Northern Ireland with that of the Republic of Ireland, as described in Chapter 16 by Bradley. As the former became increasingly dependent on subsidisation, the latter became increasingly dependent on debt – partly as a consequence of a big increase in social benefits that was unaccompanied by a much-needed reform of an exceedingly inefficient tax system. Thus the public debt had risen by the mid-1980s to the equivalent of nearly sixteen months' GNP, or roughly IR£21,000 per employed person, with about 40 per cent owed abroad (Table 16.2). As Bradley shows, Northern Ireland would have had a still heavier burden of debt, per capita, if it had had to borrow the sums received as subventions – although it should be added that this excess would also have been the reflection of social expenditure at a still higher level than in the Republic of Ireland.

Indebtedness cannot be increased indefinitely, and the Republic of Ireland has been obliged to embark upon a policy of fiscal austerity. Some may maintain that it is better for a people to have to get themselves out of a mess of this kind mainly, if not entirely, by their own efforts, instead of remaining dependent on assistance from elsewhere. Others may defend that assistance as an expression of social solidarity. Here we are approaching, perhaps from a somewhat unfamiliar angle, the old controversy about the welfare state. We can recognise it as such without, however, venturing too far into it.

In order to avoid misunderstanding, however, it is of some importance to stress that it is not only the lower income groups that benefit from the fiscal package. Obviously the benefits derived from the provision of education and the health service, and from such public goods as roads, extend much more widely throughout the community. Moreover, in so far as a debilitating sense of dependence is created by industrial subsidies, its effect will extend to management as well as to the workforce.

In this context it should also be noted that the distribution of income in Northern Ireland is more unequal than in Great Britain. Unearned income cannot provide an important explanation, for it is only a small proportion of the total. Heavier unemployment must be part of the reason but only part. This whole question appears to merit further detailed investigation.

Although the net fiscal transfers within the United Kingdom – which flow mainly from the south-east to other regions – are very large, these transfers have attracted little criticism, or even attention. The main reason is presumably the complexity of the fiscal process and the paucity of statistical information. There is, however, one part that has come under sustained fire, although only a modest part of the total. This is the assistance given to industry in the development areas of Great Britain and in Northern Ireland. Is this concentrated attack warranted? In order to gain a sense of proportion it is necessary to look at the ways in which public money, swollen by the subvention, is spent in the province. As in the United Kingdom by far the largest item is expenditure on social transfers such as pensions and unemployment benefit which accounted for about 30 per cent of the total in 1987/88. If expenditure on health, education and housing is added, the cost of the 'welfare state' – thus delineated – came to 70 per cent of total public expenditure, and law and order accounted for another 12 per cent. By comparison, industry, energy, trade and employment cost 8 per cent of the total. Of this latter total the part directed particularly towards industrial development was the expenditure by the Industrial Development Board and by the Local Enterprise Development Unit, and their combined outlays came to 2.5 per cent. This is the expenditure which, in intention at least, is meant to foster some of the changes needed to strengthen the economy and make it less dependent on outside assistance. Of the help thus given to industry, part is always liable to be wasted on unsuccessful projects, or wasted by being spent on projects that would have been financed anyway without assistance. Experience has taught some disagreeable lessons, but a case can be made for helping firms during difficult periods of expansion so that they can stand later on their own feet – as is stressed for example in the official 'Pathfinder' statement of policy (DED 1987). A further and more contentious line of defence – but one which economists cannot properly dismiss – is that industry in the province faces so many obstacles that assistance is warranted in order to prevent a further deterioration of the social and political situation.

We are now touching on the controversial issues of regional development policy which, of course, extend far beyond the affairs of Northern

Ireland. It is a large topic which cannot be adequately treated here but one further point at least must be made. This is the important fact that the country as a whole may benefit from such policies if well designed. Thus it used to be customary to observe that, by these means, it should be possible to reduce the danger of overheating in the more prosperous areas at a time when there are still idle resources in the less prosperous. Unfortunately this regrettable contrast between different regions was clearly evident in the late 1980s – and was so at a national average rate of unemployment far above what had been experienced before regional development policies fell out of favour. It is true that migration has always been the more important factor in checking the growth of regional unemployment in the less prosperous regions of the United Kingdom, as well as in the Republic of Ireland, but it does not follow that nothing was ever achieved by attempting to bring work to the workers. Moreover, if the workers themselves are to move, there must be houses available in the areas to which they go and the general infrastructure in those areas must be appropriately expanded. When a weak regional policy is combined with an inadequate expansion of social capital in the reception areas, inflationary pressures are only to be expected even when the level of unemployment in the nation as a whole is still at a high level.

The establishment of a single market in Europe in 1992 will bring new opportunities and new problems. The probable effect on the poorer areas of the European Community, which may also be the more peripheral, remains a controversial question. It has been maintained that the free movement of goods, people and capital will be the cause of greater prosperity throughout the whole of the Community, including these difficult areas. The sceptics, for their part, hold that whatever benefit accrues will be largely confined to the richer central areas to which an increasing proportion of mobile capital will be drawn. To those that have shall be given; those that have not will lose even that which they had! This conflict of views is probably made more sharp by a certain vagueness in delineating the less developed areas that may suffer. Spain, with relatively low income per head, has been doing well as a member state even before 1992, and may continue to do so thereafter. Should we, however, be concerned with member states or with areas within them? In the context of the present volume the answer must be the latter, and the pessimists among the forecasters may then insist that their gloomy verdict is likely to hold all the more firmly, for these less developed areas are usually still more peripheral as well. Even from a more cautious standpoint, it may be pointed out that, if income per head should in the event rise faster in the difficult areas than it would otherwise have done, it may also be the case that the gap between these areas and the richer areas will be further increased. To use the now familiar jargon, 'absolute poverty' may fall everywhere, but 'relative poverty' may remain or may actually be magnified.

A good many years ago, attention was directed to the fact that wide differences between different areas in real disposable per capita income could impose a continuing‘strain on social cohesiveness within the Community, and the possibility of reducing these differences by means of fiscal transfers was examined in some detail by an EC committee. The results were presented in a report (EC Commission 1977) which contained several suggestions. The silence with which these proposals were then received did not bode well for the future. We can assume that, for an indefinitely long period, the assistance provided through Brussels to areas such as Northern Ireland will be far below that received from the national government.

The assistance already provided through Brussels to the poorer areas – as described by Trimble in Chapter 15 – will continue and could be enlarged, even with an unchanged total budget, if the still vast agricultural subsidies could be further reduced for the benefit of other programmes. Moreover, this total budget can be expected to increase over time. A special case for expenditure in Northern Ireland can, of course, be made and has already been accepted. A good deal of stress has been laid on the need to ensure that any such EC assistance is in fact additional to what would otherwise have been received – the principle of 'additionality'. The difficulty is, of course, to determine 'what would otherwise have been received' – a hypothetical figure that might become increasingly elusive with the passage of time.

Important though these issues are, it would be a great mistake, in assessing future possible benefits from the EC, to confine attention too narrowly to financial assistance. Northern Ireland is already heavily dependent upon public expenditure and the longer-term objective must be a rise in relative productive efficiency which will have the incidental effect of reducing that dependence. A great deal of what is said in subsequent chapters relates to the causes of Northern Ireland's difficulties and to the means of meeting them. How will both the problems and the possible solutions be affected by 1992? What are the new opportunities and the new hazards that may reasonably be anticipated? Financial assistance, whether as a means of assisting industrial development by an improved infrastructure or as a contribution to special social needs may indeed be important, but must not be allowed to overshadow these wider issues.

There is another important factor which will alter the economic environment. This is the ageing of the population in Northern Europe and North America. The numbers in the age-groups classified as 'active' will decline markedly by comparison with the number of dependants. There will then be a growing pressure to raise participation rates, ie the proportion in each age-group of those in paid employment or in search of it. Various ways of fostering increased participation can be followed, of which one has been the abolition of compulsory retirement as a condition for obtaining a state pension. Another possible suggestion would be a rise in the female participation rate – that is to say, in the proportion of women of working age who are in gainful employment. As Jefferson's statistics show, there would be scope for a large increase in the Republic of Ireland if the social implications were acceptable, for the rate there is only about two-thirds of the rate in Northern Ireland which is not greatly different from the average British rate. Or, to look at the matter the other way round, the numbers available for paid employment in Northern Ireland in the 1980s would have been less, by as much as 100,000 – with some marked effect on unemployment – if the female participation rate had been as low as it was in the Republic of Ireland. The scope for a further rise in Northern Ireland is therefore much less.

What can be anticipated is that an increased demand for labour – with other things equal – will greatly improve the prospect of reducing unemployment throughout the developed world. In the 1950s and 1960s when output was rising at fairly steady rates in the developed countries and unemployment was very low, the availability of labour was one of the attractions to industry of regions such as Northern Ireland. That attraction was lost when recession raised unemployment everywhere, but it should be gradually restored under the pressure of demographic change. The outlook for the unemployed should then become less bleak even in the more difficult areas.

Unemployment could be reduced by various combinations of, on the one hand, a further increase in outward migration and, on the other, of an enhanced domestic demand for labour. Historically, in most of the less prosperous regions, the movement of workers in search of work has been of much greater quantitative importance than the bringing of work to the workers, and there is no reason to anticipate that this will cease to be the case. In both parts of Ireland, realism warrants the assumption that outward migration – however much deplored on political grounds – will continue to be the more important factor. But it is also realistic to anticipate a welcome rise in the numbers of jobs at home. All that has been said about industrial development policy both in previous paragraphs, and by Harrison in Chapter 4, is relevant at this point. Indeed, in the circumstances envisaged, the various measures to attract new industry and to assist indigenous industry should acquire a sharper edge, and the industrial change that takes place ought not only to provide new jobs but ought also help to raise the rate of growth of output.

How can Northern Ireland take full advantage of these changes in the wider environment? This is clearly a question of central importance. Various answers have already been given. Others lie beyond the scope of this general introduction. There are, however, some important issues not so far discussed that call for mention in these concluding paragraphs.

The first is the need for flexible wages and salaries that will respond to supply and demand in the labour market. The very use of the word 'market' is a reminder that the situation there can never be understood without reference to price. It will not do to refer to a 'labour surplus' area without making it clear that the surplus has emerged at some particular price for labour. It would be wrong to say that Northern Ireland has failed to generate a sufficient demand for jobs unless it were understood that the outcome might have been different at different rates of pay. For the terms 'surplus' or 'shortage' have no clear meaning without reference to price. To say this is not to introduce some new theory of doubtful monetarist parentage. It is simply to recall what lies at the very core of economic theory.

The fixing of wages and salaries at uniform national levels that take no account of differences in regional conditions is one of the causes of regional unemployment. The explicit reference to salaries as well as wages is appropriate at this point, not only as a reminder that what is said in general terms about the labour market applies to the higher incomes as well as the lower, but also because in the immediate context public-sector salaries are particularly relevant. The insistence upon uniformity – apart from fairly modest London allowances – is particularly effective in the public sector where the taxpayer is forced to meet the financial cost. But it also appears that pay in some private occupations is nationally uniform, or close to it, and in others, is higher in the labour-surplus areas than would be the case if determined by bargaining on a local basis. The fact that 'parity' is accepted in public financial transactions between London and Belfast can be represented – wrongly but with insidious force – as a reason for attempting to achieve, or maintain, parity in pay with more prosperous areas.

To suggest that pay should be lower in Northern Ireland than in the more prosperous areas may be taken to reflect a callous indifference to the fact that this is a poor area. This protest may still be sustained, though perhaps with less force, even if it is made clear that what is contemplated is a lower relative rate of growth of pay rather than any absolute cut. There are, however, two points to be kept in mind. The first is that the reference is to the rate of growth of gross earning before account has been taken of the tax structure or of the various welfare benefits in cash and kind. The second is that excessive gross earnings can cause unemployment, thus opening up a gap between the 'insiders' who have jobs at the higher wage level and the 'outsiders' who have not, with a corresponding rise in relative poverty in the region.

Average male earnings in Northern Ireland were in fact about 10 per cent below the national average in the 1980s. When adjusted, however, for differences in the cost of living between different regions, Northern Ireland appeared – perhaps a little surprisingly – to be close to the middle rank for the British regions. The information given in Chapter 9 also shows that London and the South East region as a whole were at the bottom, largely because housing costs were so large. As Harris also observes, East Anglia has combined moderate increases in pay with strong relative increases in employment. It is an example that may, perhaps, deserve some further attention in Northern Ireland.

In any regional economy that is even modestly dynamic, a gradual adjustment of costs relative to the costs incurred in other regions could be brought about gradually without cuts in actual earnings. This could be achieved if any gradual rise in earnings, though positive, was less relative to the rise in productivity than was the case in other areas. That is to say, the objective is a relative reduction in wage-cost per unit of output. Obviously relative wage-cost per unit can be reduced both by means of a slower rate of growth of money wages and by a faster growth in productivity – or, of course, by some combination of the two. It may be recalled that for the United Kingdom, there was a long record of wage-cost per unit in manufacturing rising at a high rate relative to that of many other OECD nations, in particular, West Germany and Japan. Then, as the 1980s progressed, Britain achieved a remarkable improvement which owed much to an accelerated growth in productivity as well as to greater moderation in wage demands. A similar outcome might be achieved in Northern Ireland. There is plenty of scope for improvement. It can be inferred from the statistics given by Harris (Table 9.10) that wage-cost per unit in the production industries was almost a fifth above what it was in the United Kingdom in 1983. With the need to offset higher transport costs and the other disadvantages of remoteness, wage-cost per unit should have been *lower* in Northern Ireland, not higher as these figures show. It is possible, of course, that the figures mislead, for the unfavourable comparison may really reflect differences in the industrial mix which would be revealed and corrected by a shift-share adjustment. In so far, however, as the contrast remains seriously unfavourable to Northern Ireland, it may be asked how such an uncompetitive position could be maintained. Was this really an unstable position about to be corrected by a further fall in output and employment as the economy moved towards some sort of equilibrium at a still lower level of activity? Or was an otherwise unstable position made stable by means of industrial subsidies?

So far the main comparison has been with other British regions but, of course, it is necessary to take a wider view and to allow for competition from the rest of the world, in particular from other parts of the Community. The need for responsiveness in costs and prices would be still greater if Britain were to join the exchange rate mechanism of the EMS, and greater still if there were ever to be a single European currency. For, if the possibility of achieving some measure of adjustment by means of changes in the national exchange rate were to be completely removed, or even strictly limited, more reliance would then have to be placed on a competitive labour market as a means of protection against a loss of jobs. In a previous paragraph, we have conceded that the creation of a single market could possibly widen the productivity gap between the central and the peripheral regions of the Community, even if there were to be some improvement everywhere. It does not follow, however, that unemployment would also have to rise in the latter areas. Whether or not that further disadvantage would follow would depend substantially upon the behaviour of local labour markets.

Ideally, wages and salaries should rise more slowly in Northern Ireland than in other less handicapped regions until the province had achieved sufficient competitive edge to bring about a fall in its above-average level of unemployment. The practical question is to know how such moderation might be achieved. It is a very familiar problem at the national level, and it has also a regional dimension. It may be objected that, even if attainable, this moderation would only produce a low-wage region from which the skilled would flee. But this is not so. For a more freely competitive market would not only reduce the rate of growth of money earnings and thus produce a lower average level of costs at any point in time than that which would have emerged with restrictive practices unimpaired. Competition would also produce a wider dispersion around this reduced average. Unfortunately there would be other difficulties, in particular a widening and deepening of the poverty trap for those with low earning power, unless the tax-benefit system could also be further reformed.

The problem may be approached, as we have seen, from the other end by seeking to raise efficiency. Some of the many topics that fall under this heading have already been mentioned but there are two that must be given at least a brief mention in these concluding paragraphs.

The first is the need to improve industrial relations. As Black records in Chapter 8, Northern Ireland has a worse record for industrial disputes than Great Britain, even when a shift-share adjustment has been made. It is true that some northern British regions have also a bad record, and that the Republic of Ireland is still worse, by a quite spectacular margin. The fact remains that a remote region faced with so many handicaps cannot afford the further gratuitous addition of bad industrial relations. Moreover, it is significant that many of the disputes have been about parity with Great Britain in wage settlements. That is to say, the aim has been to prevent or remove precisely the kind of differential required for a higher level of employment.

A second way of raising efficiency would be to reform and improve education and training at all levels. It is an old and valid complaint that, as compared with countries such as West Germany, Britain has been and is a laggard. Fortunately some large reforms have now been started although Britain remains backward. (*The Oxford Review of Economic Policy,* Vol 4, No 3, Autumn 1988 was entirely devoted to this issue.)

Even by British standards, Northern Ireland's position is weak, as Trewsdale shows in Chapter 7. Two-fifths of the workforce have no educational qualification at all as compared with the United Kingdom fraction of one-third (Table 7.1). If attention is now directed to school leavers, it will be seen that there are some marked contrasts. In the A-level category, as measured in Table 14.11, there has been a splendid record with Northern Ireland in the first place in the league table for the British regions. But about a fifth of the school leavers have had no qualifications at all compared with around 10 per cent in England and Wales (Chapter 14). Some interesting questions may then be raised. How far could administrative or legislative devolution be used in order not only to catch up but even, perhaps, to follow a different and a more ambitious path? What other programmes might then have their budgets trimmed in order to make this possible? Or, if some special schemes were to be devised under this general heading, might their financing not be an appropriate form of assistance to be partially provided by the Community? As a first step, should such assistance be sought in reducing the number of children without qualifications? How can attention also be directed to the high-level technical training that has for long been inadequately provided throughout Britain? How far, however, is it possible to make satisfactory progress with an industrial base now so limited as to restrict severely the scope for training on the job in Northern Ireland? The exploration of such possibilities would carry us into one of those important but difficult areas where economic issues are closely intertwined with many others. It is an area that calls rather urgently for further attention but it is also one that lies well beyond the scope of these introductory observations.

References

Department of Economic Development (1987) *Building a Stronger Economy: The Pathfinder Process* (Pathfinder Report).

EC Commission (1977) *Report of the Study Group on the Role of Public Finance in European Integration, I and II* (MacDougall Report).

HMSO (1965) *Economic Development in Northern Ireland*, Cmd 479 (Wilson Report).

Isles, K S and Cuthbert, N (1957) *An Economic Survey of Northern Ireland*, HMSO, Belfast.

Lyons, B S (1980) A new measure of minimum efficient plant size in UK manufacturing industry, *Economica*, 47, 19–34.

Northern Ireland Economic Council (1989) *Economic Strategy: Overall Review*, Report 73, March.

Wilson, T (1989) *Ulster: Conflict and Consent*, Blackwell, Oxford, ch 9, Fiscal constraints and the subvention.

Agriculture

John E Spencer and Julie M Whittaker

1. Introduction

The prosperity of the agricultural sector in Northern Ireland is closely interrelated with the prosperity of the whole regional economy. In the first instance, this is because agriculture employs a major proportion of the employed civilian workforce, currently around 8 per cent[1] (DANI 1989). Therefore the level of earnings in the sector, which tends to be affected by farm size, natural conditions, access to markets, and the extent of financial subsidy, has consequences for aggregate demand in the province. In addition, it is estimated that around 3 per cent of the civilian workforce are employed in agriculture related industries in Northern Ireland, while employment is also supported in areas such as banking, insurance and machinery supply and repair (Stainer 1985). Concurrently the degree of economic activity in other sectors acts upon agriculture by influencing the rate of outmigration from this primary sector, which is typically in relative decline. Outmigration permits farm amalgamations and improved incomes for those remaining in farming, while a paucity of jobs in other sectors tends to leave agriculture as the residual employer of labour, and the associated disguised unemployment results in depressed incomes on the land.

Although the agricultural sector in Northern Ireland has accounted for a falling proportion of total activity in the region over the years, it still contributes 4 or 5 per cent of the province's GDP (MAFF 1988). Agriculture is therefore of greater significance within the province's economy than in the United Kingdom as a whole where the sector accounts for no more than 2 per cent of GDP (HMSO 1988). In fact along with Germany, the United Kingdom has the lowest national percentage of GDP attributable to agriculture within the European Community. Taking all member states together (but excluding Portugal owing to lack of data) agriculture contributes 3.5 per cent of the GDP in the Community's economy (EC Commission 1987a). There is, nevertheless, considerable variation within the Community, with the proportion ranging up to almost 17 per cent in Greece.[2] Variation within the United Kingdom is less marked but still notable.[3]

The minor position of agriculture in the United Kingdom can be explained largely by its historical commitment to industrialisation which established a policy of low level protection for agriculture compared with the rest of Europe prior to its membership of the European Community. The greater importance of agriculture in Northern Ireland may be partly attributable to natural conditions giving it a comparative advantage in agriculture, but it would also appear that a deficiency in the number of other economic activities in the region has also been contributory. Heavy unemployment is indicative of this, as are the low levels of incomes in farming in the province compared with those on the mainland (for evidence of this see later), and the extent of the disparity between these and other earnings in the economy.

There is a tendency for income disparity between agriculture and non-agriculture sectors to occur in even the most buoyant economies. This is frequently attributed to insufficient labour mobility in a declining sector owing to a lack of appropriate skills, old age (the least efficient farmers tending to be the more elderly), geographical remoteness from alternative employment opportunities, or the existence of non-pecuniary benefits from farming for which labour is willing to forgo a larger income. Labour immobility is further reduced when there is a high degree of owner-occupation rather than cash rent tenure, a condition which prevails in Northern Ireland (see below). However, accentuations in income disparities between farming and other sectors can perhaps largely be attributed to differences in the number of alternative economic opportunities.

A broad indicator of income disparity is the divergence between the percentage of GDP attributable to agriculture, and the percentage of the total civilian manpower employed in agriculture.[1] In most cases, the latter percentage, although progressively falling, is the greater, denoting below national average incomes in the sector. Taking the United Kingdom as a whole, the divergence is small with around 2.5 per cent of total employment working in agriculture generating almost 2 per cent of GDP (HMSO 1987, 1988) while in Northern Ireland the divergence is more notable with 8 per cent of labour employed producing around 4.5 per cent of GDP (DANI 1989). The situation in the province is, in fact, more akin to that in the rest of Europe than the United Kingdom. Statistics are not fully comparable but analogous figures suggest that in the Republic of Ireland around 16 per cent of the labour force are in agriculture which contributes about 10 per cent of GDP, while in the EC-12 around 8 per cent of the civilian workforce are on the land and agriculture is 3.5 per cent of GDP (EC Commission 1987a). There is a propensity for the disparity in incomes between agriculture and other sectors to be greater where agriculture has a high profile in the economy, not least because its continued prominence often results from the lower level of development of other economic activity. However, this need not be the situation where natural advantages favour agriculture, as in East Anglia. East Anglia is the only region in the United Kingdom where agriculture's contribution to the local economy is greater than in Northern Ireland,[4] with Gross Agricultural Product (GAP) accounting for 6–9 per cent of GDP, the variation resulting from weather conditions (MAFF 1987, 1988). The GAP in

East Anglia tends to be more than double that in Northern Ireland in absolute terms yet the total number of persons employed in agriculture in East Anglia is less than the number employed in Northern Ireland's agriculture indicating that earnings are substantially higher than in the province.

It is primarily on the social grounds of income disparity between agriculture and other sectors that governments have intervened to support the agricultural industry, although other concerns such as maintaining a rural population, and achieving a certain level of self-sufficiency either for political reasons or to improve the balance of payments, have also been expressed. Public intervention has thus reduced, though not necessarily eliminated, both income disparities and the rate of outmigration from agriculture.

The rest of this chapter is organised as follows. Section 2 examines the structure of the farming sector and examines recent changes in the composition of output. In Northern Ireland the most notable changes, absolute and relative, are the growth in grassland enterprises and decline in the intensive livestock sector, in particular pigs and eggs. Section 3 describes the principles underlying the Common Agricultural Policy and summarises how Northern Ireland agriculture has fared since 1973. Section 4 looks at this in more detail by examining the main sectors in turn. Section 5 then examines income and concludes with a brief discussion of recent EC proposals on income supports. The chapter ends with some concluding comments.

2. The structure of the farming sector and composition of output

SIZE STRUCTURE OF FARMS

With unemployment in Northern Ireland above the national average at around 18 per cent in 1988, and 35 per cent in some rural areas, labour immobility is particularly acute and this has inevitably restricted farm structural change, thus constraining income improvements through increased farm acreage and economies of scale. Also contributing to farm structure rigidity is the fact that virtually all farmers in Northern Ireland, in common with those in the Republic of Ireland, own at least the majority if not all their land. Thus farms have a greater tendency to stay within the family rather than be amalgamated. Some flexibility in farm structures is, however, achieved through the leasing of around 20 per cent of the land under a system known as conacre. This is the region's tradition of seasonal letting for eleven months of the year without the usual tenancy rights. Although legal provision for long leasing of land in Northern Ireland was made in 1956, it has been little used until recent years since higher rents have usually been realised by letting under conacre.

By contrast in England and Wales, only 59 per cent of the farms are fully owner-occupied, 19 per cent are wholly rented on long leases and 22 per cent are of mixed tenure (MAFF 1988). In terms of land area, around a third

TABLE 2.1   Distribution of agricultural land and average size of holdings, June 1987[1]

	United Kingdom	England	Wales	Scotland	Northern Ireland
Total agricultural area (000 hectares)	17,620.18	9,419.85	1,500.0	5,299.14	1,056.48
Total agricultural area within LFAs (000 hectares)	8,108.58	1,604.9	1,158.3	4,599.1	752.25
% land in LFAs	47.0	17.0	77.2	86.8	71.2
Total number of agricultural holdings (000)	254.2	155.7	30.0	25.9	42.6
Number of agricultural holdings in LFAs	89.4	21.6	19.8	18.5	29.5
% of holdings in LFAs	35.2	13.9	66.0	71.4	69.2
Average size of all agricultural holdings (hectares)	67.9	60.5	50.0	204.6	24.8
Average size of agricultural holding in LFAs (hectares)	90.7	74.3	58.5	248.6	25.5

[1] Provisional.
Source: MAFF (1988).

of the agricultural land is let commercially (Hill and Ray 1987). The difference in the situation on the mainland results from differing land legislation. At the turn of the century the great majority of farms throughout the British Isles were tenanted. Then, through a series of Land Acts passed at the end of the 19th and beginning of the 20th century, culminating in the Land Purchase Act 1925, Irish tenants were given the rights to purchase the land they farmed from the landlords with the aid of government loans. In the rest of the United Kingdom different land legislation has led to a more gradual demise of the landlord tenant system.

When in 1925 the landlord tenant system ceased in Northern Ireland, farms were on average smaller than in Great Britain. Although farm sizes have increased in the province during this century, they still remain considerably smaller than in the rest of the United Kingdom. This is rather to be expected given the higher degree of owner occupation. The average size of holdings throughout the United Kingdom is given in Table 2.1 which includes data for the Less Favoured Areas (LFAs) (see below), as well as overall data. It shows that the average size of holdings in Northern Ireland is at least 50 per cent below that in other regions. But an agricultural holding refers to a unit of ownership rather than a farming unit. A farm may consist of more than one holding if the farmer leases additional land. A comparison of the average area of farms can be made only for defined full-time farm businesses, however. Farm businesses are currently categorised according to British Size Units (BSUs) which are based on standard gross margins (output less variable costs) calculated on a regional basis.[5] Farms below 1 BSU are termed minor holdings and are not included in the following. A full-time farm is defined as one above 4 BSUs, although a farm of less than 4 BSUs, while considered as part-time may well be the sole source of income for the occupant. Throughout the United Kingdom, in 1987, 43.3 per cent of farms were below 4 BSUs, while in Northern Ireland the proportion was 65.9 per cent. The average size of full-time farm businesses in the United Kingdom was 29.0 BSUs, but in Northern Ireland this was halved at 14.5 BSUs (HMSO 1988; DANI 1988). In 1986, the average area of a full-time farm in the United Kingdom was 106.3 hectares (HMSO 1987) and in Northern Ireland 43.7 hectares (DANI 1987), while in Scotland average area was 272 hectares (communication with DAFS). Although there is not a strict correlation between farm acreage, BSU size and farm income owing to different intensities of land use which in turn depend upon type of enterprise and farming practice, it would be expected that if farms in Northern Ireland were of a larger acreage then not only would average farm incomes improve but also the province's GAP would increase given the same total acreage and factors employed owing to economies of scale. This is supported by the results of a study which compared the technical efficiency of farms in Northern Ireland with those in Great Britain (DANI 1981). The study came to the conclusion that technical performance on farms of 8 BSUs and over was at least as good in Northern Ireland as in Great Britain. However, smaller farms tended to have a lower level of technical performance,[6] and since Northern Ireland has a high proportion of small scale farms, the overall average level of technical performance for Northern Ireland farms usually compared unfavourably with Great Britain. Whilst improved technical efficiency would be achieved through amalgamations, this would no doubt result in a loss of direct jobs in agriculture, which might only to some extent be compensated by the multiplier effects of spending from increased total agriculture income.

NATURAL CONDITIONS FOR FARMING IN THE PROVINCE

Profits generated from farm businesses are more highly dependent upon the natural environment than is the case in other sectors of the economy. Natural conditions are an important determinant of the cost structure of farm production, and can cause variations in output from one year to the next.

Being adjacent to the sea Northern Ireland experiences moderate summer temperatures and mild winters. The oceanic influence also causes cloudiness and high relative humidity throughout the year. Consequently, in most parts of the province conditions tend not to be advantageous for cereal

TABLE 2.2   Percentage distribution of graded agricultural land within regions of the
United Kingdom, 1976

	United Kingdom	England	Wales	Scotland	Northern Ireland
Grade 1	1.8	3.3	0.2	0.3	—
Grade 2	9.8	16.7	2.3	2.4	3.3
Grade 3	36.4	54.0	17.5	13.6	42.0
Grade 4	18.2	15.7	44.2	10.2	49.0
Grade 5	33.7	10.3	35.8	73.5	5.7
	100.0	100.0	100.0	100.0	100.0

Source: Agriculture EDC (1977) quoted in Hill and Ray (1987).

growing but are particularly suited to pasture, and so livestock production is
favoured. This climatic effect is compounded by the small farm and field size
which are less appropriate for the use of large scale machinery required in
modern arable production. In Northern Ireland in 1987 only 1.4 per cent of
holdings growing cereals had more than 50 hectares of land devoted to cereals.
By comparison throughout the United Kingdom, 26.6 per cent of cereal
holdings had over 50 hectares, these farms being chiefly in England.

Soil type and topology are also important environmental determinants. Since the early 1960s agricultural land has been classified into five grades
according to physical criteria such as height, slope, climate and soil, with grade
1 indicating top quality land. Table 2.2 gives the distribution of grades
throughout the United Kingdom. England contains 52 per cent of all
agricultural land and most of the best land with 80 per cent of all grade 1 and 2
land. Although Northern Ireland has very little of the top two grades of land,
the average quality does appear to be higher than in Scotland and Wales.

Recognition that unfavourable natural conditions (a combination of
disadvantageous topology, soils and climates) constrain agricultural production
in certain parts of Europe, resulted in the European Community designating
Less Favoured Areas (LFAs) in 1975. Farmers in LFAs are eligible for
additional grants and subsidies because it has been politically accepted in
Europe that there is a need to support the population in these difficult farming
areas. In 1984 LFAs were extended. The original LFAs are now referred to as
Severely Disadvantaged Areas, with the extensions referred to as Disadvantaged Areas, receiving a lower level of financial support than the former.

In Northern Ireland 71 per cent of land is within the LFAs. This is
less than the proportion in Scotland and marginally less than the Welsh
proportion. Notably though, in both Scotland and Wales, the average area of an
LFA holding is substantially greater than in Northern Ireland (Table 2.1). On
farms sampled for the 1986/87 MAFF Farm Business Survey, the total number
of livestock units (a common denominator for aggregating different types of
livestock) averaged around 110 for full-time livestock farms in LFAs in
England, Wales and Scotland but only 80 in Northern Ireland (MAFF 1988).

Since a greater proportion of Northern Ireland farms are not full-time farms, if consideration were given to all farms then the contrast may be even greater.

ACCESS TO MARKETS

With a large agricultural sector relative to the population of the province, a large proportion of agricultural produce is 'exported' chiefly to Great Britain. Whilst there is no data on the level of exports from the region, DANI estimate that around 60 per cent of Northern Ireland's agricultural produce, measured at farmgate values, is exported (Stainer 1987). In common with many other industries in Northern Ireland, the agricultural industry's prosperity is reduced owing to its geographical remoteness from the main markets in the United Kingdom. As a result of additional transport costs there is a tendency for prices received by Northern Ireland producers for produce exported from the province to be lower than those received by farmers in Great Britain for the same products; similarly the cost of inputs which have to be imported into the region tends to be greater. Of particular note is cereals since only a small quantity can be grown in the province. These points are developed more fully in Section 4 below.

THE COMPOSITION OF AGRICULTURAL OUTPUT

The composition of agricultural output in the province is influenced not only by the natural environment, but also by socio-economic factors and agricultural policy. The composition is shown in Table 2.3 with comparisons made with other parts of the British Isles and through time. Notable is the small proportion of crop cultivation in Northern Ireland compared with the United Kingdom, Scotland and Republic of Ireland, the importance though declining, of intensive livestock production, and the rising predominance of grassland enterprises. The significance of pastoral based products and relative insignificance of crops, particularly cereals, is not surprising given the environmental conditions in Northern Ireland. More remarkable is the standing of intensive livestock enterprises in total output in a grain deficit region, compared with Scotland where a substantial proportion of cereals is grown and yet the intensive livestock sector is small. The explanation for this lies in the size structure of farms. Although margins in intensive livestock production are relatively low, intensive pig and poultry enterprises gave farmers in Northern Ireland the opportunity to develop full-time work and an income from just a small acreage. Unfortunately, with accession in 1973 to the European Community and the adoption of the Common Agricultural Policy (CAP), intensive livestock became less profitable throughout the British Isles but particularly in Northern Ireland since the transport price differential on imported grain increased significantly. The detail and consequences of this are described later.

Geographical and environmental similarities between Northern Ireland and the Republic of Ireland are greater than between Northern Ireland

TABLE 2.3   Comparison of percentage contribution of each enterprise to total output between regions

	United Kingdom		Northern Ireland			Scotland		Republic of Ireland	
	1972	1986	1961/62	1972	1986	1972	1986	1972	1986
Grassland enterprises									
Cattle	17.3	15.3	23.0	33.3	38.5	32.1	27.5	35.5	39.1
Milk	23.0	21.4	16.3	21.4	28.3	20.2	18.6	36.2	36.4
Sheep	4.8	5.5	6.4	2.8	4.7	11.9	11.4	3.4	3.8
Sub-total	45.0	42.2	45.8	57.5	71.5	64.2	57.5	75.1	79.3
Intensive livestock enterprises									
Pigs	11.4	8.1	28.8	19.7	11.0	6.8	4.3	7.4	5.5
Poultry	6.1	6.4	1.7	3.2	6.6	4.3	5.3	2.6	3.0
Eggs	6.9	4.0	13.6	11.4	3.7	4.5	2.7	1.1	0.9
Sub-total	24.4	18.5	44.2	34.3	21.3	15.7	12.3	11.1	9.4
Arable enterprises									
Cereals	10.7	18.2	1.6	0.8	1.0	10.2	18.3	7.0	4.7
Other	19.8	21.1	8.4	7.4	6.1	9.8	11.8	6.8	6.6
Sub-total	30.5	39.3	10.0	8.2	7.1	20.0	30.1	13.8	11.3

Sources: AAS 1983, 1989; DANI (1968, 1988); DAFS (1987) and communications with DAFS; Correspondence with CSO, Dublin.

and Great Britain. A notable difference though is the Republic of Ireland's ability to grow more cereals, and the lack of concentration on intensive livestock production. Since 1973 both parts of Ireland have received a more similar level of financial support and this has resulted in a greater identity in the composition of output over the years of membership of the European Community. The accession of the United Kingdom to the Community and the adoption of the Common Agricultural Policy has had marked consequences on the pattern and profitability of output (detailed below), and has in effect increased the peripherality of the province.

3. The EC and the Common Agricultural Policy

With the accession of the United Kingdom and the Republic of Ireland to the EC in 1973, agriculture in Britain and both parts of Ireland became subject to the operation of the Common Agricultural Policy (CAP). Under the CAP substantial support is given to various commodities including dairy products, beef, sheepmeat and cereals. Details of the support mechanism differ between the various products but, broadly, prices are supported at levels determined by agricultural ministers in annual bargaining sessions. Cheap imports are kept out by variable levies and any excess domestic supplies are stored in intervention, to be released on to the domestic or world market at a later date. Typically, the surpluses are supplied to the international market at world prices and the gap between the domestic and world price, the export refund, is financed by the Community Budget, Guarantee Section. The costs of this system can be high, especially at times of low world prices and for perishable goods such as beef and butter where storage involves refrigeration.

The costs of the CAP have indeed been high in practice and have typically accounted for around 70 per cent of the EC's budget. EC revenues are made up of 90 per cent of each member state's tariff and levy revenue augmented with VAT contributions up to a specified maximum. In practice, the costs have had a persistent tendency to outstrip the revenues and in early 1987, agreement was reached to augment the resources and change the VAT-based formula to one based on GNP.

For many years the CAP has come under strong pressure for reform. The high proportion of Community funds allocated to agriculture has generated much criticism from the European Parliament, for example, and the fact that the CAP system in no way guarantees equity in the cost–revenue balance between member states has been a source of persistent complaint in the United Kingdom since at least 1975. These internal pressures for reform aimed at reducing the costs of the CAP have been augmented by pressures from without. The external pressures emanate chiefly from agricultural exporters whose prices are undermined by the EC export refunds. Such exporters include the USA, where many farmers have been in serious financial difficulties since the early 1980s, and a pressure group, known as the Cairns Group, formed in 1986 and including Australia, Argentina, Brazil, Canada and New Zealand, aimed at developing a common position in the current GATT negotiations (the Uruguay Round) (see Kain 1988). While agriculture has not, in practice, been subject to GATT rules of liberal trade, there are strenuous efforts on the part of the USA and the Cairns Group to change this. Pressures towards reform of the CAP, aimed especially against EC subsidised exporting, can be expected to remain intense.

In fact, these strains have already generated some reform despite opposition from the EC agricultural lobby. A prime example is the introduction of milk quotas (see below) and the introduction of stabilisers in the grain sector, whereby guarantee prices would be reduced if specified output targets were overshot.

There is little doubt that the internal budgetary pressures and the pressures from traditional exporters and GATT will continue to affect CAP policy and, thereby, agriculture in the member states and the regions, including Northern Ireland.

Any attempt to compare how agriculture in Northern Ireland would have developed since 1973 had the United Kingdom stayed out of the EC would be very speculative and would depend on various crucial assumptions including what United Kingdom policy would have been and what would have been the position in the Republic of Ireland. Stainer (1985), recognising the difficulties of such speculation, considers that the Northern Ireland industry may on balance be better off, though with a different composition of output (see Table 2.3) and facing considerable uncertainties as further measures are developed to combat the EC budget problem. The dairy and sheepmeat sectors have fared rather well under the CAP but the intensive livestock sector, especially pigmeat and eggs, has declined. This decline is related to the high price of imported feed under the CAP and while the intensive livestock sector was under pressure from world market factors in 1973–75, Stainer points to EC membership as a major factor preventing its recovery.

4. The main products

MILK

Milk has for many years been the most important product of British agriculture, the 'cornerstone of our agriculture' (Astor and Rowntree 1939). Rivalling beef production, it has formed a major part of agriculture in Ireland, north and south (Gillmor 1977; O'Connor and Guiomard 1985 and Table 2.3).

Table 2.4 shows the population of dairy cows in Great Britain, Northern Ireland and the Republic of Ireland since 1972. The Scottish proportion of the Great Britain total has varied over the period between about 9 and 11 per cent. The differing directions of trend between Ireland and Great Britain during the 1970s is apparent, with the strongly increasing numbers in Northern Ireland particularly notable. The differing responses to the rise in milk product prices consequent on joining the EC in 1973 are explained by the natural and climatic factors in Ireland favouring grassland enterprise, by the lack of alternative opportunities in Northern Ireland and by the scope for increased cereal production in parts of Great Britain, notably East Anglia. It seems clear that Northern Ireland was not in a position to expand cereal output significantly, owing to the unsuitable wet climate, small size of fields and small farm structure (see below). The milk output of the dairy herd is also given in Table 2.4.

From Table 2.4 it can be seen that milk yields tend to be higher in Great Britain than in Northern Ireland while yields in the Republic of Ireland are lower still. Yield is an imperfect productivity measure and will depend on cow type (Friesian, Holstein etc), weather, capital equipment used (cowshed, milking parlour), amount of feed etc. It is correlated with herd size owing to economies of size and the justifiability of more capital intense milking-techniques associated with modern milking parlours. Table 2.5 shows relevant data on these issues. Yields are similar between Scotland and England and Wales, although the highest yielding area is Aberdeen and District where the

TABLE 2.4 Dairy herd size and milk output, Northern Ireland, Great Britain and the Republic of Ireland, 1972–1987

	Dairy herd size (June, 000 head)			Output of milk (m litres)		
	Northern Ireland	Great Britain[1]	Republic of Ireland	Northern Ireland	Great Britain	Republic of Ireland
1972	224	3,101	1,405[2]	866	12,346	na[3]
1973	236	3,200	1,445[2]	900	12,568	3,328
1978	257	3,017	1,594	1,134	13,960	4,554
1983	294	3,039	1,636	1,416	15,026	5,333
1984	299	2,982	1,642	1,362	14,084	5,564
1985	294	2,856	1,633	1,339	13,924	5,655
1986	292	2,846	1,582	1,324	14,136	5,452
1987	289	2,753	1,527	1,340	13,289	5,362

[1] Figures from 1978 onwards include estimates of number of animals on minor holdings in England and Wales.
[2] Derived from number of total cows and estimate of beef herd by Kearney, B in Agriculture in the Republic of Ireland and Northern Ireland, Co-operation North Paper III, 1981.
[3] Means of measuring milk output have changed and there is no corresponding figure for 1972.
Sources: AAS 1985, 1987, 1989; Dairy Facts and Figures 1976, 1986; NIAAS 1982; DANI (1989); ISB various issues; Annual Review and Outlook of CBF (Irish Livestock and Meat Board) 1987, 1988.

average herd size is largest. Herd size is low in Northern Ireland (Wales is next lowest) and a considerable proportion of systems there still milk in the cowshed as opposed to the milking parlour. In the Republic of Ireland, average herd size is lowest of all, at around half of the Northern Ireland figure (see Sheehy et al 1981).

The marketing of milk in the United Kingdom is the responsibility of the Milk Marketing Board (MMB). There are five regional Boards (England and Wales, Scottish, Aberdeen and District, North of Scotland, Northern Ireland) with Aberdeen and District and North of Scotland very small. Producers, unless exempt, must sell their milk to the MMBs whose responsibility it is to find a market for all milk produced. The income from sales to the separate liquid and manufacturing markets is pooled and the total net returns distributed to all producers in proportion to the amount they sold to the Board, regardless of the end use of their milk. The price received by the Board for liquid milk is higher than that for manufacturing. The detailed mechanism for determining these prices has varied over time but currently each Board area has a Joint Committee consisting of representatives of the MMB and the buyers. In agreeing prices, relevant considerations include changes in manufacturing and marketing costs, the prevailing market prices for the various milk products and changes in the EC Target Price. This is the price which the CAP seeks to create by means of import levies, export subsidies, intervention buying for butter and skimmed milk powder. The negotiations are

TABLE 2.5 Structure of dairy sector, Northern Ireland, England and Wales, and Scotland

Average size of milk producing farms, (hectares of crops and grass)			
	1978	1982	1986
Northern Ireland	33	35	40
England and Wales	65	67	69
Scotland	84	90	94

Average size of dairy herd (cows per herd)				
	1970	1975	1980	1987
Northern Ireland	14	20	28	37
England and Wales	33	46^1	58^1	69^2
Scotland	57	71	82	91

Percentage of systems using milking parlour				
	1978	1981	1984	1987
Northern Ireland[3]	29.0	39.9	46.6	53.6
England and Wales[3]	54.1	64.4	70.3	74.6
Scotland[4]	32.5^5	54.0	60.5	64.8

[1] Excluding herds of 1 or 2 cows.
[2] Excluding herds of 1–9 cows.
[3] December.
[4] May.
[5] 1975 figure.
Source: Dairy Facts and Figures.

designed to produce a milk price which varies according to the product made from it. Should the negotiations fail, as they often do, an independent arbiter can be involved. These arrangements are currently under review.

Over time the consumption of liquid milk has declined and the proportion of output going to manufacture has increased. This proportion is particularly high in Northern Ireland at about 85 per cent compared with some 50 per cent in Great Britain. Since, as mentioned, the manufacturing price is lower, producers in Northern Ireland receive a lower pooled price. A proportion of the gap, currently around one quarter, was made up by Government aid in the form of a consumer milk subsidy (introduced in 1981–82) but this aid ceased in 1988.

The EC system of support for the dairy sector has generated substantial surplus supplies, particularly of butter and skimmed milk powder. The resulting storage and export subsidy costs became intolerable despite various attempts at reform and in March 1984 it was agreed by the Council of Ministers to introduce a quota system for a five year period, recently extended for a further three years, from 2 April 1984. Member state quotas were to be based on 1981 deliveries (apart from the Republic of Ireland, Italy and, later, Spain where the base was 1983). In terms of 1983 wholesale deliveries, the EC total represented a cut of 4.1 per cent, the United Kingdom total a 6.2 per cent cut (despite an allocation of 65,000 tonnes extra for Northern Ireland from the

EC reserve, an allocation based on an EC acceptance of the argument that dairying was of crucial importance in Northern Ireland and that there had been substantial growth in output between 1981 and 1983) and the total for the Republic of Ireland an increase of 4.6 per cent. Further amounts for 'direct sales quotas' and quotas for the rest of the five year period are listed in Commission Background Report ISEC/B12/84, 26 October, 1984. These involved further cuts in the wholesale quotas of about 1 per cent, though not for the Republic of Ireland or Italy. Production above quota was to be subject to a heavy fine.

The United Kingdom quota was divided by the United Kingdom authorities into regional allocations, corresponding to the regions of the MMB. In fact, the resultant Northern Ireland and total Great Britain quotas were both some 5.8 per cent below total 1983 sales, suggesting that the extra allocation for Northern Ireland had been allocated across the United Kingdom, a suggestion denied by the United Kingdom authorities. A further 3 per cent cut was imposed on producers to create a national reserve from which additional quota could be given to (a) producers whose 1983 output was adversely affected by certain exceptional events and (b) producers who had committed themselves to investments in dairying prior to 1 March 1984. Various Outgoers' Schemes have also been set up under which quota may be bought and allocated to (c) exceptional hardship cases and (d) small producers. These schemes have operated regionally in that the reserve and quota released from the Outgoers' Schemes have in the main only been available to producers in the region whence they originated. Since dairying is so important in the province and alternative opportunities scarce, little quota has become available there while the demands for the categories of extra quota have been correspondingly great. Thus, despite some subsequent transfers from Great Britain, many individual producers possess less quota than their counterparts in similar positions in Great Britain (see recent Annual Reports of the Milk Marketing Board for Northern Ireland).

In practice, surpluses in any MMB region are allowed to offset deficits in another so that no levy is payable by producers in any region unless the United Kingdom as a whole has over-produced. Similarly, any excess wholesale deliveries can be offset by any deficiency in the much smaller direct sales sector. Given a net excess in the United Kingdom, this is allocated to over-producing MMB regions and then to over-producers within the region.

The actual outcomes with respect to wholesale deliveries are given in Table 2.6. It should be noted that the original scheme did not lead to the abolition of surpluses and further cuts of some 8.5 per cent on 1986/87 quotas were imposed at the December 1986 Council meeting, 6 per cent for 1987/88 and a further 2.5 per cent for 1988/89 (see *Dairy Facts and Figures*, 1987 Edition). While these cuts have been slightly less for Northern Ireland owing to the transfers from Great Britain mentioned above, it is clear from the table that Northern Ireland is having difficulty adjusting to quota. Table 2.4 confirms this where the small decline in the dairy herd since the introduction of quotas is apparent. There is no doubt that reducing milk production is particularly

TABLE 2.6   Wholesale deliveries relative to quota, 1984/85–1987/88 (+ = % above quota)

	2/4/84–31/3/85	1/4/85–31/3/86	1/4/86–31/3/87	1/4/87–31/3/88
Northern Ireland	+4.9	+1.2	−1.4	+1.2
England and Wales[1]	−1.8	+0.2	+0.9	+1.0
Scotland[2]	−0.5	−1.8	+0.3	+1.2
United Kingdom	−1.5	+0.1	+0.7	+1.1
Republic of Ireland	+0.0	+0.1	−1.3	+0.3[3]

[1] Excludes Scilly Isles.
[2] Excludes Shetland Isles.
[3] Provisional.
Sources: Dairy Facts and Figures, 1988; Personal communication with Department of Agriculture and Food, Dublin.

painful in the province where the intensive livestock section is in decline and cereal production unlikely to expand (see below).

BEEF AND SHEEPMEAT

Beef production has traditionally been the main sector in Irish agriculture and an outstanding part of agriculture in Great Britain. There are two main divisions in the sector, (a) breeding and rearing which is largely carried on in the remoter parts of the country where land is cheap and access to markets difficult and (b) finishing. Broadly, breeding and rearing takes one to two years and finishing takes a further six months. Beef output is also augmented by the culling of old dairy cows and the output of male calves from the dairy herd. The two divisions of the sector are often carried on by separate groups of producers. Cattle can be fattened in the summer on grass but may need to be housed in winter and fed on conserved grass, roots or barley. Such feed is costly so the prices of calves and store cattle tend to be lowest in the autumn.

Table 2.7 gives the beef cow herd and beef output in Great Britain and both parts of Ireland and Table 2.8 gives the percentages of the United Kingdom herds to be found in the standard regions. Table 2.7 shows an expansion in the herds in the early 1970s with a decline thereafter. In Ireland, the peak year was 1974 while in Great Britain the peak year was 1975. The herd size in Scotland has moved in line with that in England and Wales, at around 60 per cent of the latter. Table 2.9 shows that the decline has been markedly greater in both parts of Ireland than in Great Britain. Table 2.8 shows the high proportion of beef cows located in the remoter regions of the United Kingdom, with some 60 per cent in Wales, Scotland and Northern Ireland. Average herd size tends to be much smaller than in the dairy sector.

During the 1960s beef production was encouraged in the United Kingdom in various ways including rising guaranteed prices under the Deficiency Payments Scheme. The fall in herd size in the 1970s was initiated by the beef crisis of 1973–74 when prices slumped following the energy crisis and

TABLE 2.7 Beef cow herd size and output of fat cattle, Northern Ireland, Great Britain and the Republic of Ireland, 1972–1987

	Beef cow herd size (June, 000 head)			Output of fat cattle (000 head)		
	Northern Ireland	Great Britain[1]	Republic of Ireland	Northern Ireland	Great Britain	Republic of Ireland
1972	285	1,191	490[2]	417	3,064	na[3]
1973	324	1,354	651[2]	362	2,932	1,762
1974	339	1,548	732	479	3,703	1,830
1975	327	1,570	637	547	4,281	1,892
1978	262	1,326	502	539	3,337	1,851
1983	194	1,164	421	479	3,332	1,684
1984	196	1,155	436	541	3,639	1,805
1985	201	1,132	446	550	3,606	1,764
1986	198	1,110	443	523	3,305	1,756
1987	196	1,147	456	506	3,541	1,727

[1] Figures from 1978 onwards include estimates of animals on minor holdings in England and Wales.
[2] Derived from estimate of beef herd by Kearney, B. See note 2 Table 2.4.
[3] Owing to changes in definition, no comparable figure for 1972.
Sources: As for Table 2.4 and correspondence with CSO, Dublin.

TABLE 2.8 Regional distribution of cow herd, June 1986 (percentage)

	Dairy herd	Beef herd
North	6.3	9.9
Yorks and Humberside	5.7	4.3
East Midlands	5.5	3.4
East Anglia	1.6	1.8
South East	8.2	4.4
South West	24.5	8.9
West Midlands	9.8	4.4
North West	8.8	1.8
England	70.5	39.6
Wales	11.6	13.2
Scotland	8.6	32.0
Northern Ireland	9.3	15.1

Source: Derived from RT No 23, 1988.

the abandoning of Deficiency Payments consequent on EC membership and full provision for intervention buying was not available. In November 1974 the United Kingdom Government introduced the Variable Premium Scheme as an emergency measure, though it operated until April 1989. Under the scheme a variable premium (VP) was payable to bring the average market price up to an EC determined target price, although an upper limit was placed on the VP.

TABLE 2.9   Ratio of 1987 beef herd size to 1974 or 1975 size (percentage)

		Ratio
Northern Ireland	1987/1974	58
England and Wales	1987/1975	71
Scotland	1987/1975	76
Republic of Ireland	1987/1974	62

Source: Table 2.7 and Dairy Facts and Figures, 1987.

Intervention is also available.

As with most products under the CAP, official prices are announced in ECUs and these are translated into domestic prices by application of the green rates of exchange. Should the green rate differ from the market rate, border taxes and subsidies (MCAs) are applied to prevent arbitrage movements of commodities.

Following the beef crisis described above, the history of the Northern Ireland beef industry is dominated by interactions with the Republic of Ireland, where prices have been maintained through the standard intervention system and which has been a traditional supplier to Britain. Owing to differences in green rates, prices in the Republic of Ireland have tended to be above those in Northern Ireland from 1974 to 1980 and from mid-1986. These differentials should be sustainable through MCA payments and receipts but in practice smuggling has emerged, from north to south in the periods mentioned. An undesirable effect is the starving of meat plants of supplies with adverse effects on unemployment and this was countered in the earlier period, though not recently, with the introduction of the Meat Industry Employment Scheme (MIES). Under this scheme a headage payment equivalent to the MCA was paid to presenters of cattle (and pigs) for slaughter at Northern meat plants, bringing Northern Ireland prices up to those of the Republic of Ireland and removing the incentives for smuggling. Other complicated movements of animals, often illegal and linked with VP and MCA interactions, are described in Norton (1983) and Whittaker and Spencer (1986).

As with the dairy sector, the EC regime has given rise to massive surpluses, which are expensive to store and costly to unload on world markets, especially at a time of declining consumption of red meat. Accordingly, increasingly restrictive rules on eligibility for intervention have come into effect in the last few years. The problem has, of course, been exacerbated with milk quotas, as a side effect of the latter has been to increase short run output, as dairy cows are culled, and to direct heifers to the beef herd. From June 1983 to June 1987 the total number of cows in the EC has declined by over 8 per cent despite an increase of over 2 per cent in the beef herd. In Northern Ireland there has been rather little change in the size of either herd, the small adjustment reflecting the lack of alternative opportunities in the province. Nevertheless, as the EC beef regime adapts to the changing circumstances, the Northern Ireland beef industry, along with that in the Republic of Ireland, should prove relatively strong with its cheap and efficient grass-based production methods.

Sheep remains a small enterprise in the United Kingdom and Ireland (see Table 2.3) but has been growing in the 1980s in response to the emergent CAP regime of price support. These countries are suited to sheep production with climatic advantages favouring grass and considerable areas of hills and uplands favouring sheep browsing but little else. Half of the United Kingdom sheep population are found in Scotland and Wales (in roughly equal proportions) and sheep are numerous in the mid-west of Ireland. The number of breeding ewes and sheep and lamb output have risen particularly sharply in Northern Ireland where, to prevent illegal crossborder movements of animals, the system of support has been aligned to that in the Republic of Ireland since 1982–83. Northern Ireland has been successful in exporting to both the Republic of Ireland and France.

INTENSIVE LIVESTOCK ENTERPRISE AND CEREAL PRODUCTION

The pig and poultry industry has been important in Great Britain and Ireland since pre-war years. Both pigs and poultry have short breeding and finishing cycles, have little requirements in terms of space, are subject to no striking geographical pattern and have production costs dominated by feed requirements.

Table 2.10 charts the numbers of breeding pigs since 1973, numbers which have fallen rather steadily in Great Britain and both parts of Ireland but

TABLE 2.10 Breeding pigs herd size, Northern Ireland, Great Britain and the Republic of Ireland, 1972–1987 (June, 000 head)

	Northern Ireland[1]	Great Britain[1,2]	Republic of Ireland[3]
1972	109	851	129
1973	112	903	130
1974	70	819	93
1978	78	767	122
1983	70	786	118
1984	63	737	113
1985	64	764	112
1986	62	762	117
1987	60	760	112

[1] Sows plus gilts in pig.
[2] Figures from 1978 onwards include estimates of animals on minor holdings in England and Wales.
[3] Sows plus gilts in pig (including gilts not yet served from 1978).
Sources: AAS 1984, 1987, 1989; NIAAS 1983; DANI (1986, 1987, 1988); ISB, various issues; correspondence with CSO, Dublin; Agricultural Statistics, June 1987, CSO, Dublin.

most notably in the north. These declines have occurred against a background of more than self-sufficiency in the EC and a CAP system of rather light support.

The situation deteriorated for producers in the early 1970s when feed prices rose dramatically in 1973 owing to a world grain scarcity. While the scarcity was temporary, prices remained high owing to EC support for cereals. Output of cereals expanded in Great Britain and the Republic of Ireland in response to these high prices to the extent that they became more or less self-sufficient, but such an expansion was not feasible in Northern Ireland owing to its less suitable climatic and structural characteristics (see Table 2.11). Table 2.12 shows the regional outputs and yields in the United Kingdom and the poor showing of Northern Ireland with its wet summers is apparent. Since with EC membership in 1973, cheap imports of grain were no longer available, pig producers had to pay the high EC price of barley. This was a particular problem in Northern Ireland where a further amount of some 10 per cent had to be added to cover the transport costs of the imported grain (and, as an exporting region, the transport costs of shipping the product out of the province had also to be met). This feed price differential pushes feed costs up to over 80 per cent of total costs of pig production, compared with some 75 per cent in Great Britain (HMSO 1984b). While there is some concentration of pig production in areas of barley production in England and the Republic of Ireland, such concentration in Northern Ireland would be of little help since even locally produced barley must fetch the price of feed barley imports plus transport costs. This feed cost disadvantage has undoubtedly been the major factor in the decline of the Northern Ireland pig industry, an industry of great significance in the province before 1973 when cheap imports of grain from North America were available.

While barley is not suitable for poultry feed, the latter relies mainly on imports also. Accordingly, producers in Northern Ireland face a disadvantage in broiler meat and egg production, similar to that faced in the pig industry. Both poultrymeat and eggs receive minimal support under the CAP

TABLE 2.11   Production of barley, Northern Ireland, Great Britain and the Republic of Ireland, 1972–1986 (000 tonnes)

	Northern Ireland	Great Britain	Republic of Ireland
1972	174.6	9,069	982
1973	176.6	8,830	904
1974	197.0	8,936	1,040
1978	219.9	9,630	1,568
1979	175.4	9,350	1,558
1983	199.1	9,781	1,503
1984	222.0	10,848	1,770
1985	161.8	9,578	1,494
1986	192.4	9,818	1,428

Sources: AAS 1984, 1988, 1989; NIAAS 1983, DANI (1986, 1987, 1988); ISB September 1986, June 1987; Correspondence with CSO, Dublin.

but the consumer demand for eggs has been steadily declining in contrast with the increasing demand for poultrymeat. Output of poultrymeat in the province has about doubled since 1973, contrasting with increases of little over 20 per cent in Great Britain and the Republic of Ireland over the same period.

TABLE 2.12 Production and yield of crops, regions of the United Kingdom, 1981–1985 averages

	Wheat		Barley	
	Production	Yield	Production	Yield
North	260	6.5	530	4.8
Yorks and Humberside	1,220	6.7	1,230	5.1
East Midlands	2,250	6.5	1,170	5.0
East Anglia	2,250	6.7	1,210	5.0
South East	2,990	6.4	1,620	5.1
South West	1,060	6.2	1,110	4.9
West Midlands	800	6.0	720	4.8
North West	60	5.7	220	4.4
England	10,920	6.5	7,840	5.0
Wales	60	6.0	240	4.5
Scotland	380	7.0	2,120	4.8
Northern Ireland	10	5.2	190	4.0

Note: Production is in units of thousand tonnes and yield is in tonnes per hectare.
Source: RT No 23, 1988.

This marked increase in Northern Ireland poultrymeat output is surprising given the feed cost disadvantage. While there is steadily rising demand for poultrymeat worldwide, the growth in production in the province must be partly due to outstanding efficiency gains. Certainly the Northern Ireland industry is extremely highly concentrated and vertically integrated (Whittaker and Spencer 1986).

5. Income

REGIONAL AGRICULTURAL INCOMES UNDER THE CAP

Of fundamental concern within the agricultural industry is the significance of changes in market conditions on income. Importance is attached to both the aggregate agricultural income from the 'provincial' farm and incomes at the farm level. The former is significant as a broad measure of prosperity in the industry whilst the latter is a more specific indicator of the economic welfare of those employed in agriculture.

The level of income in agriculture depends on the volume of production, output prices, input costs and productivity. Owing to agriculture's allegiance to the weather, the volume of production can vary between years. Product prices depend upon supply and demand conditions and the level of support given under the CAP, whilst input costs are particularly influenced by inflation, exchange rates, and the cost of energy. Over time, with technological change, agriculture has become progressively more dependent on inputs produced outside the agricultural sector and thus more vulnerable to changes in macro-economic variables. Productivity within the sector tends to be dependent upon technical knowledge, the existing farm structure and farmer response to relative output and input prices.

Despite increased returns for most agricultural products upon United Kingdom accession to the EC in 1973, the agricultural industry has had to contend with an almost unremittant cost–price squeeze since then. This began in 1974 with the sudden increase in the cost of feed due to a world grain scarcity and a rise in the price of energy following the oil price rise. Inflation accelerated in the 1970s, intensifying the cost–price squeeze and, because of the Community's commitment to a prudent product price policy, the squeeze continued into the 1980s even though inflation slowed. Consequently incomes in Northern Ireland have been under persistent price pressure, bar a few years, 1975, 1981, 1982 and 1986 when product prices did actually rise more than input costs.

AGGREGATE AGRICULTURAL INCOME

As a result of longstanding government involvement in agriculture a large data base on farming incomes exists. There are several measures of agricultural incomes and details of these are given in Appendix 2.1. Following Stainer (1987), focus in this study on aggregate agricultural income is given to Farm Business Income (FBI).[7]

Stainer (ibid) compared Northern Ireland's annual proportion of total United Kingdom FBI with Northern Ireland's annual proportional contribution to United Kingdom gross agricultural output between 1970 and 1986 and found that the ratio of Northern Ireland's income proportion to gross output share was always less than 1, thus denoting that at all times during that period the income position of farmers in Northern Ireland has been unfavourable compared with the national average.

Indices of FBI in real terms for the United Kingdom and Northern Ireland graphed in Figure 2.1 show that real income variability has been greater in the province than for the whole of England and Wales. To a degree this is to be expected when comparing a small region with a much larger region. The variations in Scottish FBI were greater than those in Northern Ireland, but notably there were larger divergences in a favourable direction from the national average. Figure 2.1 also prominently illustrates a decline in real FBI throughout the United Kingdom. A comparison of real FBI in 1970–72 with the 3-year average 1984–86, suggests that the decline has been most severe in Scotland, followed by Northern Ireland. However, as indicated above, there has been greater variation in Scottish FBI, and from observation it would appear that the downward trend in income has been most persistent in the province.

FIG 2.1 Indices of farm business income,[1] real terms, 1970–86.
[1] Farm business income deflated by RPI.
Sources: Derived from data in HMSO (1984); HMSO (1988); Stainer (1985); DANI (1987) and DAFS. Figures for England and Wales calculated from UK, NI and Scottish data.

CAUSES OF REGIONAL INCOME VARIATIONS

In an analysis of regional income variations, Furness (1982) attributes the disparities in prosperity to three major factors:

(i)   differences in the main types of farming which have differing rates of technical progress;

(ii)   different rates of structural change and growth in technical efficiency;

(iii) differing economic vulnerability under the CAP.[8]

Whilst differing rates of technical progress in different product enterprises would undoubtedly have an effect on income variations it has not been feasible to test whether these have been markedly detrimental to Northern Ireland. It is possible, however, to identify reasons for disadvantageous rates of structural change in Northern Ireland (see Section 2 above), and to analyse the impact of the CAP on the province's agriculture. It is probably this third factor which has been most important in explaining the more marked deterioration in income at the aggregate level, in Northern Ireland. The implementation of the CAP led to particularly significant changes in relative prices and costs in the province, the change in cereal prices being the most notable. This led to a substantial change in the composition of output which had effects on the volume of net product.

Furness (ibid) records that when net product (gross output less material and service inputs and depreciation) in volume terms in the years 1970 and 1971 was compared with years 1980 and 1981 it was seen to have declined in Northern Ireland by 12 per cent while for the United Kingdom net product rose by 25 per cent with a 9 per cent increase in Scotland.[9] The fall in net product in the early 1970s in Northern Ireland was probably largely attributable to the squeeze on margins and the subsequent decline in production in intensive livestock and beef rearing. Some relief was given to these sectors through national insurance subsidies to the intensive livestock processing industries and MIES payments on pigs, but these were both discontinued at the end of the decade. Net product recovered substantially in the following two years owing to low output prices, high input prices and a low volume at output. In the early years of the 1980s net product in Northern Ireland increased dramatically[10] and this has been attributed to increased productivity resulting from farmers' response to the cost–price squeeze which was most severe in 1979 and 1980 (Stainer 1987). Exceptionaly favourable weather in 1984 was reflected in particularly high net product and incomes. This was followed by a very wet summer in 1985 which significantly affected the province necessitating the purchase of additional feed in 1985 and 1986, leading to a fall in net product and incomes.

AGRICULTURAL INCOMES AT THE FARM LEVEL

In an analysis of incomes received at the farm level, Stainer (1987) compared the index of average earnings in 'real' terms of full-time male employees in all industries in Northern Ireland with the average 'real' FBI per farm.[11] While the former has been rising steadily, FBI per farm has been subject to considerable variation and since 1974 has been constantly below the index of average earnings in other industries. Stainer (ibid) notes that even in 1984 when aggregate FBI was at its highest level since 1973, average income in farming was £5,800 and still compared unfavourably with earnings elsewhere which averaged £8,500.

Inevitably the prosperity of individual farms is varied and tends to depend on farm acreage, land quality, product enterprises and farming expertise. Although a farm of 4 BSUs is defined as full-time it is considered that a farm of 8 BSUs is needed to provide a reasonable living for a farming family (Stainer, ibid). The average business size of a farm in Northern Ireland, including part-time farms but not those below 1 BSU, is 7.7 BSUs. Farms below 1 BSU account for only about 2 per cent of output in the province and are excluded from the following. Statistics show that 70 per cent of all farms are below 8 BSUs with beef and sheep farms in the LFAs accounting for just over half of this category. In fact, 90 per cent of all LFA beef and sheep farms are less than 8 BSUs (Table 2.13). The total number of farms below 8 BSUs produce only 30 per cent of gross margins in the province (derived from Table 48, DANI 1987). If income is taken to be proportional to gross margins then

TABLE 2.13   Number of farms between 1 and 8 BSUs by type,[1] Northern Ireland, June 1986

	Number of farms	% of type[2]	% of all farms between 1 and 8 BSUs
Specialist dairy	1,715	31.4	9.9
Other dairy	719	43.0	4.1
LFA beef and sheep	9,584	90.8	55.1
Non-LFA beef and/or sheep	2,176	88.0	12.5
Pigs and/or poultry	276	54.3	1.6
Mixed livestock	334	74.4	1.9
Crops and livestock	1,286	73.6	7.4
Cropping	941	64.5	5.4
Horticulture	352	69.3	2.0
All types	17,383		100.0

[1] Details on the classification scheme is provided in DANI (1987).
[2] Number of farms between 1 and 8 BSUs as a percentage of the number of all farms (over 1 BSU) by type.
Source: DANI (1987).

the data suggest that the average agricultural incomes on these farms in the province were just under £1,800 in 1986.[12]

There is more detailed information on farm incomes from the Farm Business Survey (FBS). This survey, conducted annually, by the Ministry of Agriculture is a stratified random sample representative of all full-time farms in the United Kingdom. From these data typical Net Farm Incomes (NFIs) on farms classified according to type, size and region are published.[13]

In Table 2.14 NFI by farm type, size group and region for the year 1986/87, is shown along with the average NFI over the five years 1982/83 to 1986/87. The data indicate that on small dairy farms (defined according to acreage) NFI is marginally higher in Northern Ireland than in England and Wales. More outstanding is the performance of medium-sized dairy farms in the province which is substantially better than elsewhere in the United Kingdom with NFI averaging £16,000, whilst the second best performance was in Wales where NFI averaged £12,000 over the five years. However the average income for dairy farms across all farm sizes in Northern Ireland, though greater than those in Scotland, was below those in England and Wales. This results from the higher proportion of small dairy farms in Northern Ireland.

In the case of LFA livestock farms, NFI on small farms in Northern Ireland were on a par with those in other parts of the United Kingdom, but since again the average size of farm in Northern Ireland is relatively small, overall average income on LFA farms is lowest there, being less than half the average income on an English LFA farm. Data on other types of farms in Northern Ireland are not available owing to their low numbers.

While the Farm Business Survey gives information on farm incomes on full-time farms, a recent study, initiated by the Ministry of Agriculture

TABLE 2.14 Net farm income by farm type, size group[1] and country, 1986/87 and average 1982/83–1986/87 (£ 000)

	England		Wales		Scotland		Northern Ireland	
	1986/87	Average	1986/87	Average	1986/87	Average	1986/87	Average
Small								
Dairying	5.5	5.2	5.3	5.1	—	—	3.7	5.6
Hill and upland (LFA)	2.2	4.5	3.2	3.6	2.4	4.3	2.2	4.9
Lowland livestock	−1.5	—	—	—	1.3	—	—	—
Specialist cereals	0.5	1.6[2]	—	—	—	—	—	—
Other cropping	3.7	2.5[2]	—	—	—	—	—	—
Medium								
Dairying	13.1	10.6	13.2	12.0	2.8	7.1	11.8	16.0
Hill and upland (LFA) livestock	9.4	10.9	13.1	13.4	3.6	7.5	3.9	—
Lowland livestock	2.0	5.0	—	—	0.2	3.9	—	—
Pigs and poultry	19.6	17.8	—	—	—	—	—	—
Specialist cereals	5.9	7.2[2]	—	—	3.5	0.9[2]	—	—
Other cropping	8.4	7.4[2]	—	—	1.6	−0.3[2]	—	—
Large								
Dairying	28.4	23.6	29.3	26.0	13.9	14.1	—	—
Hill and upland (LFA) livestock	18.2	24.2	24.7	23.6	8.3	12.3	—	—
Lowland livestock	20.7	18.1	—	—	13.2	—	—	—
Pigs and poultry	28.9	33.9	—	—	—	—	—	—
Specialist cereals	21.7	26.4[2]	—	—	13.9	—	—	—
Other cropping	31.1	26.5[2]	—	—	22.1	3.7[2]	—	—

[1] Size Groups: Small 4–15.9 BSUs (8–15.9 in Scotland except LFA farms), Medium 16–39.9 BSUs, Large 40 BSUs and over.
[2] Average of 3 years 1984/85–1986/87.
Sources: HMSO (1984a, 1985); MAFF (1987, 1988).

(Ansell et al 1988) has thrown light on those farms defined as part-time (ie above 1 BSU but below 4 BSUs) in England, Wales and Northern Ireland. This showed that in 1986 the average income on these very small farms was around £400 with variations according to type of farm and region (see Table 2.15). With respect to type of farming, income was highest on cropping farms at £2,900 and lowest, with an average loss of £100, on LFA livestock farms. For all types, average incomes were £600 in England, £500 in Wales and – £300 in Northern Ireland. Inevitably in many cases income was supplemented from a non-farm source. Frequently in England and Wales, and particularly in the former, the farm was peripheral as a provider of income with instances of the farm having a hobby status. By contrast in Northern Ireland, where average farm incomes were lower, there was a tendency for non-farm income to be also much lower (£3,800 compared to £11,200 in England and Wales). Hence 'the farms appeared to provide an important, albeit very modest, contribution to family incomes'. In addition, a Labour Input Inquiry conducted by the Ministry

TABLE 2.15   Net farm income on very small farms,[1] England, Wales and Northern Ireland, 1986 (£)

	Net farm income	Non-farm income
By type		
Dairying	507	4,364
Livestock in LFAs	−91	6,581
Lowland livestock	210	10,834
Cropping	2,872	7,169
Pigs and poultry	772	9,911
Horticulture	861	11,323
Others	−688	13,793
All types by region		
England East	1,221	16,056
England West	−7	10,145
England North	672	8,150
Wales	455	4,995
Northern Ireland	−323	3,792

[1] Farms between 1 and 4 BSUs.
Source: Ansell et al (1988),

of Agriculture as part of the 1983 European Community Structure Survey showed that 'other gainful activities' (OGAs) are most prominent on farms below 4 BSUs. In the United Kingdom, 42 per cent of farms below 4 BSUs had an OGA, but in Northern Ireland, where proportionally more farms are under 4 BSUs, only 29 per cent had an OGA. With respect to all holdings, 32 per cent in the United Kingdom have an OGA, compared to 26 per cent in Northern Ireland (MAFF 1986).

From an analysis of data on farming income a picture of the province's agricultural sector emerges as one which has had to undergo considerable adjustment to adapt to the new economic environment imposed by the CAP. This has led to a decline in aggregate farming income. However within the aggregate, certain enterprises, notably dairy, have fared relatively well. In spite of distance from markets, farms of comparable size and type to those in Great Britain have managed to achieve comparable or even better incomes. This must result from natural advantages or greater efficiency. But, overall, average farm incomes tend to be lower than in Great Britain as a result of smaller farm businesses with expansion constrained chiefly by land. Thus although farms may be technically efficient within their size group, the preponderance of small farms means that average efficiency is reduced. Severe unemployment within the region has kept people in farming even though, to some, the return for their labour is very low. It would therefore appear that the economic welfare of farmers in Northern Ireland, while considerably affected by the CAP, is also significantly influenced by the lack of prosperity in the regional economy.

DIRECT INCOME AIDS

Given the persistence of high unemployment in the region, it would appear unlikely that farm incomes will be improved by significant structural change in the near future. The component of CAP's structural policy which is concerned with encouraging migration from the land has been singularly unsuccessful throughout the Community in the past, and is unlikely to be any more successful whilst employment prospects are poor, particularly in the weaker, frequently peripheral regions.

The Quigley Report (1976) voiced the opinion that in view of the difficulties of maintaining and creating jobs in other industries in Northern Ireland there was a case for stalling the rate of outmigration from agriculture through extra support to the farming industry. To an extent, Quigley's recommendations have been taken up, as special assistance has been given to Northern Ireland from the United Kingdom government (as outlined above) and more recently from Community sources. Nevertheless, this has not been so great as to alleviate substantially income disparities between the province and the rest of the United Kingdom.

Policies which either nationally or regionally differentiate the level of support are in principle contrary to the fundamental basis of the CAP, which aims to allocate production throughout the Community on the basis of comparative advantage.[14] The United Kingdom government has consequently had to be imaginative in finding means by which to channel extra support to agriculture in the province. Regional measures that have been introduced under the auspices of the CAP have been largely of a structural nature and have been justified on the grounds that certain regions receive inadequate help through price support because their productivity, and hence output, is low (EC Commission 1987b). Northern Ireland has benefited from two of the regional agricultural programmes. First, since 1982 there has been a programme to stimulate agricultural development in the LFAs in the province. As a result land has been improved and roads built, but little use has been made of the provision of aid to reorientate production. Secondly, between 1983 and 1986 there has been a programme to improve drainage in the areas bordering with the Republic of Ireland.

With the present reductions in agricultural prices, the Commission recognises that the commonness of the CAP is particularly threatened as national governments seek means to alleviate the price effects where the potential social hardship is greatest.[15] The threat is apparent as member states look for ways to (a) implement national or regional price support levels, (b) maintain production quotas at existing levels, (c) grant national subsidies (EC Commission, ibid). Whilst the Commission has been willing to accept some additional aid to specific groups, eg extra support to small grain producers, additional milk quota to the Republic of Ireland and Northern Ireland, it argues that there are definite limits to this kind of approach. Not only does it weaken the unity of the CAP but it moves regional economies further away from the Community mainstream (rather than integrate them) (EC Commission 1987c). However, aware that there has to be some response to the social and political forces the Commission has advocated the introduction of direct income support (EC Commission 1987b, c). The advantage of income support is often claimed to be that it can help targeted groups of farms with less distortions to the price system than price support and thus less distortion to production and trade. Accordingly, it could be acceptable to foreign competitors and GATT and could make CAP reform more acceptable to those EC farmers badly affected by it.

Should such a policy be brought into effect, it is highly probable that many small farmers in a poor region such as Northern Ireland would stand to gain, at least in the short run. Outmigration from the land would diminish and the rate of structural change towards larger farm size would be reduced. The effect on the input and processing industries is hard to assess a priori. Perhaps the volume of output for processing might not be affected very much although the composition would probably be more varied with the poorer farmers in the difficult sectors, such as the pig industry, continuing to supply. Certainly, it is likely that the input and processing industries would be more influenced by the other aspects of reform which tend to reduce supplies (quotas, price cuts, stabilisers, set-asides) and it should also be noted that the opening of the internal market in 1992 could also have important implications for the processors.

6. Conclusion

In common with other poorer regions of the Community, agriculture is a large sector in the Northern Ireland economy, but agricultural incomes are low. The economic environment within which farming operates is heavily determined by the CAP, and this, by its common nature, is not tailored to meet the needs of specific regions.

It is difficult to be confident about what the effects of the CAP on the industry have been over the last 15 years but expansion has certainly been curbed in the profitable dairy industry (although that sector would most likely have been less profitable without the CAP) and the recovery of parts of the intensive livestock industry following the difficult conditions of 1973–74 has not been helped. Indeed it seems reasonable to attribute that sector's continued decline to high feed prices consequent on EC policy. The important beef sector, while undergoing change as CAP reform tightens, should remain strong in the long run, however, owing to the suitable natural conditions favouring such enterprise in the province.

Perhaps the most efficient means of improving the welfare of farmers would be to encourage the development of other industries and thus increase migration from the land, but this, if it were to be effective, would be likely to bring benefits only in the long run. In recent years with increasing political importance given to maintaining the socio-economic equilibrium in areas vulnerable to the CAP, more attention has been placed on giving immediate help to certain regions through the maintenance of employment and income in agriculture. This may result in the introduction of direct income support for farmers. Since a significant number of jobs are dependent on agriculture in the secondary industries, however, the effect of all CAP measures on input and food industries should also be taken into consideration in agricultural policy decisions. This point is especially important in a region like Northern Ireland with its persistent tendency towards high levels of unemployment.

Appendix 2.1 Definitions of income measurements

Farming Income: Return to farmers and spouses for their labour, management skills and own capital invested after providing for depreciation.

Farming income = Gross output less gross input, depreciation, labour (other than farmer and spouse), interest payments and rent.[16]

Farm Business Income: Return to farmers, spouses, non-principal partners and directors for their labour and management skills and on all capital (own or borrowed) invested in the industry after providing for depreciation.

Farm business income = Gross output less gross input, depreciation, labour (other than farmer, spouse, non-principal partners and directors) and rent.[16]

Cash-Flow: The pre-tax revenue accruing to farmer and spouse less cash outlays in the specific year.

Net Farm Income: Return to the farmer and spouse for their manual and managerial labour and return on tenant-type capital.

Farm net income = Gross output less gross input, labour (other than farmer and spouse), depreciation on tenant-type capital and rent.

Notes

1. Civilian manpower employed in agriculture includes all regular and part-time workers, all seasonal and casual workers, plus all farmers, partners and directors whether whole-time or part-time. Thus the definition is extremely broad.
2. The percentage contribution of agriculture to GDP throughout the EC in 1985 was as follows: EC-11 (Total EC less Portugal) 3.5 per cent, Belgium 2.5 per cent, Denmark 5.0 per cent, France 3.7 per cent, Germany 1.8 per cent, Greece 16.6 per cent, Ireland 10.2 per cent, Italy 5.0 per cent, Luxembourg 2.6 per cent, Netherlands 4.2 per cent, Spain 6.1 per cent and the United Kingdom 1.8 per cent. Source: EC Commission (1987a).
3. The percentage contribution of agriculture to GDP in United Kingdom regions in 1986 was as follows: England 1.7 per cent, North 1.7 per cent, Yorkshire and Humberside 2.1 per cent, East Midlands 3.2 per cent, East Anglia 6.3 per cent, South East 0.9 per cent, South West 2.8 per cent, West Midlands 1.8 per cent, North West 0.9 per cent, Wales 2.6 per cent, Scotland 2.1 per cent and Northern Ireland 4.7 per cent. Source: MAFF (1988).
4. The definition of 'region' is critically important. Here definitions as for the Farm Business Survey have been used.

5. For Northern Ireland 1 BSU = 2000 ECUs of standard gross margins averaged at 1978–80 prices in the region. Prior to June 1986 farm size was measured in ESUs with standard gross margins averaged at 1972–74 prices. For details see DANI (1987).

6. Stainer (1987) suggests that there is probably an underutilisation of fixed assets on many Northern Ireland farms.

7. FBI is a more suitable definition than Farming Income (FI), which was predominantly used for many years, since with FBI partners and directors are more realistically treated as self-employed whereas in FI they are considered as wage earners. In addition, with FBI there is no deduction of interest payments which gives greater consistency with statistics for other industries.

8. Papers by Henry (1981), Plascosivitis (1983) and Cuddy (1984) are some of the work suggesting that the CAP may have accentuated regional income disparities.

9. Being volume index numbers, these figures should be interpreted with caution, especially since substantial changes in relative prices took place over the 1970s.

10. In the early 1980s, net product (at 1980 prices) rose continuously, increasing by 70 per cent between 1980 and 1984.

11. Average 'real' FBI per farm was calculated by dividing FBI by the number of farms with more than 50 standard man-days of labour between 1970 and 1980. From 1980 to 1984 a series on the number of farms was estimated by applying the annual percentage change in the number of farms of more than 1 ESU (see note 5), and of farms of more than 1 BSU for 1985 and 1986 (Stainer 1987).

12. The total gross margins for all farms of at least 1 BSU but less than 8 BSUs can be derived from Table 47 of the Statistical Review of Northern Ireland Agriculture 1986 (DANI 1987). The gross margin for this group is expressed as a proportion of gross margins from all farms above 1 BSU. This proportion was applied to FBI and the resulting figure divided by number of farms of at least 1 BSU but less than 8 BSUs, to give an average FBI for farms in this group for 1986. (The authors acknowledge Stainer (1987) for suggesting this approximation.)

13. A full definition of Net Farm Income is given in the appendix. Net Farm Income (NFI) is akin to Farm Business Income except that an imputed value for rent (landlord's capital) is applied to owner-occupied farms. Thus it can tend to underestimate the income position on owner-occupied farms, while no allowance for interest on loans can lead towards over-estimation.

14. Note that in fact, a policy which places a floor on market prices limits the relocation of production from the high cost to the low cost region because the returns to the less efficient producer are not undercut. In addition the CAP gives greater support to some products than others so that the resulting allocation of production is distorted.

15. The degree of social hardship within a region will depend upon the importance of agriculture in the economy, the relative share in output of products most vulnerable to CAP adjustments, and the proportion of weaker farms in the region (EC Commission 1987b).

16. In Northern Ireland Accounts no allowance is made for rent payments even though 20 per cent of the land is held under conacre.

References

Agriculture EDC (1977) *Agriculture into the 1980s: Land Use*, NEDO, London.
Ansell, D J, Giles, A K and Rendell, J R (1988) *Very Small Farms, An Economic*

Study, Special Studies in Agricultural Economics Report No 1, University of Reading.

Astor, Viscount and Rowntree, B S (1939) *British Agriculture, The Principles of Future Policy*, Penguin Books: Harmondsworth, Middlesex.

Cuddy, M (1984) Community policy and the periphery, Paper presented at the Irish Association of European Studies Conference on 'Prospects for the European Periphery', Wexford.

DAFS (1987) *Economic Report on Scottish Agriculture 1986*, DAFS: Edinburgh.

Dairy Facts and Figures (1987) (and various dates) The Federation of United Kingdom Milk Marketing Boards.

DANI (1968) *Statistical Review of Northern Ireland Agriculture (June 1967–May 1968)*, DANI, Belfast.

DANI (1981) A comparison of technical efficiency on farms in Northern Ireland and Great Britain, in the *Annual Report of Research and Technical Work in Northern Ireland*, DANI, Belfast.

DANI (1986, 1987, 1988, 1989) *Statistical Review of Northern Ireland Agriculture 1985, 1986, 1987, 1988*, DANI, Belfast.

EC Commission (1985, 1986, 1987a) *The Agricultural Situation in the Community, 1985, 1986, 1987 respectively*, European Community Commission, Brussels.

EC Commission (1987b) *Direct aids to incomes, in The Agricultural Situation in the Community, 1987*, European Community Commission, Brussels.

EC Commission (1987c) Newsflash, *Green Europe* No 4, European Community Commission, Brussels.

Furness, G W (1982) Some features of farm income and structure variations in the regions of the UK, *Journal of Agricultural Economics,* 33 (3), 289–309.

Gillmor, D A (1977) *Agriculture in the Republic of Ireland*, Akademiai Kiado, Budapest.

Henry, P (1981) *The Regional Impact of the CAP*, Regional Policy Series No 21, EC Commission, Brussels.

Hill, B and Ray, D (1987) *Economics for Agriculture*, Macmillan Education, Hampshire.

HMSO (1984a, 1985, 1987, 1988) *Annual Review of Agriculture*, Command Paper: 9137, 9423, 67, 299, for each year respectively, HMSO, London.

HMSO (1984b) *Report on the Effect of Feedstuff Prices on the UK Pig and Poultry Industries*, House of Commons, Select Committee on Agriculture, Cmnd Paper 539, HMSO, London.

Kain, M (1988) Recent trends in world agriculture trade, *National Westminster Quarterly Review*, May 1988, 14–24.

MAFF (1986, 1987, 1988) *Farm Incomes in the United Kingdom*, 1986, 1987 and 1988 editions, HMSO, London.

Norton, D A G (1983) *Ireland and the CAP: Trade Distortion and Induced Smuggling Activity 1974–1981*. European League for Economic Co-operation (Irish Section), Dublin.

O'Connor, R and Guiomard, C (1985) Agricultural output in the Irish Free State area before and after independence, *Irish Economic and Social History, XII*, 89–97.

Plascosivitis, I (1983) A critique on the study of the regional impact of the CAP, *European Review of Agricultural Economics*, 10, 141–50.

Quigley Report (1976) *An Economic and Industrial Strategy for Northern Ireland*: Report by a Review Team (Chairman: W G H Quigley), HMSO, Belfast.

Sheehy, S, O'Brien, J T and **McClelland, S D** (1981) *Agriculture in the Republic of Ireland and Northern Ireland*, Co-operation North Paper III.

Stainer, T F (1985) An analysis of economic trends in Northern Ireland agriculture since 1970, *Studies in Agricultural Economics*, DANI, Belfast.

Stainer, T F (1987) Trends in Northern Ireland farm incomes, Paper presented to the Annual Conference of the Northern Ireland Institute of Agricultural Science.

Whittaker, J M and Spencer, J E (1986) *The Northern Ireland Agricultural Industry: Its Past Development and Medium Term Prospects.* ESRC financed study; The Queen's University of Belfast.

Manufacturing industry
Richard I D Harris

1. Introduction

This chapter deals with the production sector of the economy. The emphasis will be on manufacturing industries, since it has been traditionally argued that manufacturing plays a leading role in generating wealth and income which in turn can support an expansion in other sectors of the regional economy (see Fothergill and Gudgin 1982, Chapter 3; Brown 1972, Chapter 6; and Harris 1987). For this reason manufacturing has been the major recipient of financial aid from Government in attempting to combat the 'regional' problem (see Chapter 4). Therefore, it is a matter of some concern when, in considering the recent fortunes of the manufacturing sector, we find evidence to support the notion of a recent deindustrialisation of the Northern Ireland economy. Following on from this, changes within manufacturing are studied at a detailed level, and this includes a discussion of the differing industrial structures of various regional economies since it is a commonly held view that peripheral regions such as Northern Ireland are over-dependent on 'older, heavy' industries, while the central regions have a more diverse industrial base. This chapter will look at several problems that are considered to be a constraint on manufacturing growth, especially in peripheral regions. Finally, an attempt is made to consider the future importance of manufacturing, as a source of employment and output, and whether there is a critical size to the manufacturing base, which regions such as Northern Ireland may fast be approaching.

2. Output and employment in manufacturing

The emphasis in this chapter will be on output growth, rather than employment growth. The distribution of output between 'labour' and 'capital' within any sector is partly the result of this output growth, but it is also due to the relative costs of factor inputs and their substitutability. Hence, up to the mid-1970s, total manufacturing output was increasing or maintaining its share of total regional GDP, but capital was displacing labour at a rapid pace; however, since the first oil crisis in 1973, the relative importance of manufacturing has declined. Some evidence for this (for certain selected regions) is given in Figure 3.1, which shows manufacturing's share of output in certain years.[1] The decline in the relative importance of manufacturing has been most marked in Northern Ireland, with a 11.0 per cent fall in its share of real GDP over the period 1971–86 (14.3 per cent in the case of employment). A fall in the share of regional GDP would not be so serious if output levels had increased, or at least remained the same. However, in 1986, manufacturing real GDP in the province was 97 per cent of its 1979 level, and 75 per cent of the peak level reached in 1973. Hence, manufacturing has declined in both absolute and relative terms.[2] While manufacturing has declined in relative importance in Northern Ireland it has become more important in the Republic of Ireland. In

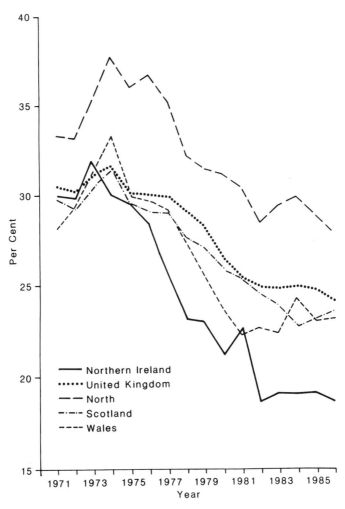

FIG 3.1 Manufacturing's share of gross domestic product in certain regions of the United Kingdom, 1971–1986
Source: Economic Trends, HMSO.

1965, the share of GDP (at 1968 prices) attributable to the production industries (ie including energy, water and construction) was 44.5 per cent in Northern Ireland and 32.6 per cent in the Republic of Ireland. By 1985 these shares had changed to 30.8 and 36.5 per cent respectively (at 1980 prices). Therefore, the Republic of Ireland's manufacturing base is now larger than its counterpart in Northern Ireland, and much of this growth has been as a result of inward investment in export-based high growth industries (see the discussion in the next section).

There are good reasons for concern about the decline in manufacturing in Northern Ireland, especially since there is evidence to suggest that this sector is the most important source of 'self-sufficient' growth, especially in a regional economy. Arguments (and evidence) to this effect have been presented in Harris (1987), where it was shown that manufacturing is the sector most likely to provide the economy's exports, technological advances, productivity gains, and new products (with high income elasticities of demand). In addition, it is regarded as being best suited to passing on growth impulses through its strong input–output linkages, that result from the high level of intermediation that takes place in manufacturing processes.

3. Structural changes and growth

This section begins by examining which industries have dominated Northern Ireland (and compares the situation with other regions of the United Kingdom). However, it is useful to start any discussion of industrial structure by examining the extent to which the region is dominated by consumer or capital-goods producing industries. With the help of the 1974 United Kingdom Input–Output tables, each industry at the Minimum List Heading (MLH) level of the 1968 SIC (Standard Industrial Classification) was allocated to the consumer or capital good sectors. This was done by examining the sources of Final Demand and if more than 50 per cent of output went to final consumption, rather than fixed investment, then the industry was classified as belonging to the consumer good sector. Industries were then further classified as capital intensive or labour intensive, with the aid of regional measures of these variables. Two measures were available on capital intensity;[3] the first measure was based on annual average gross investment per unit of net output (in 1975 constant prices) for the period 1973 to 1979, taking the mean across all industries nationwide as the benchmark for allocation. The second measure was based on the hours worked by shiftworkers in different industries and regions, as recorded in the 1975 Labour Force Survey. If it is assumed that shiftworkers are employed outside the 'normal' working day, and therefore capital equipment is in operation for a longer period than the hours worked by day-shift workers, an approximate estimate of 'capital-hours' is obtained.[4] The end result of using either measure of capital intensity (having allocated industries to the consumer or capital goods sectors) is a four-way classification of industries in each region. When regional net output in 1963 and 1985 is

TABLE 3.1 Percentage distribution of net output between sectors, regions of the United Kingdom, 1963 and 1985[1]

Sector[2]	Regions										
	North	Yorks–Humberside	East Midlands	East Anglia	South East	South West	West Midlands	North West	Wales	Scotland	Northern Ireland
Consumer goods:											
Labour intensive	9.1 (15.1)	11.4 (20.0)	7.1 (12.2)	30.5 (31.3)	8.4 (8.8)	25.0 (20.4)	8.6 (14.6)	6.9 (9.6)	9.6 (12.5)	7.8 (8.4)	18.1 (17.8)
Capital intensive	39.1 (42.7)	41.0 (41.8)	45.2 (52.8)	33.4 (36.5)	49.4 (49.4)	31.2 (34.2)	30.9 (33.5)	55.3 (54.2)	31.0 (40.6)	49.4 (49.3)	48.7 (52.9)
Total	48.2 (57.8)	52.4 (61.9)	52.3 (64.9)	63.9 (67.8)	57.8 (58.2)	56.2 (54.6)	39.5 (48.1)	62.2 (63.9)	40.6 (53.0)	57.2 (57.8)	66.8 (70.7)
Capital goods:											
Labour intensive	5.7 (4.9)	4.6 (4.0)	10.0 (9.2)	11.1 (13.0)	7.7 (12.2)	7.1 (13.2)	8.7 (13.2)	1.4 (2.5)	5.4 (8.0)	4.1 (7.3)	3.2 (6.5)
Capital intensive	46.1 (37.4)	43.0 (34.1)	37.7 (25.9)	25.0 (19.2)	34.5 (29.7)	36.7 (32.2)	51.9 (38.7)	36.4 (33.6)	54.0 (38.9)	38.8 (35.0)	30.0 (22.8)
Total	51.8 (42.2)	47.6 (38.1)	47.7 (35.1)	36.1 (32.2)	42.2 (41.8)	43.8 (45.4)	60.6 (51.9)	37.8 (36.1)	59.4 (47.0)	42.9 (42.2)	33.2 (29.3)
Net output (£m, 1975 prices)	1,304 (2,007)	2,483 (2,974)	1,616 (2,811)	507 (1,224)	7,946 (9,980)	1,163 (2,443)	3,648 (3,890)	3,931 (4,461)	1,047 (1,509)	2,078 (2,863)	405 (554)

[1] 1985 figures in parentheses.
[2] See text for details.
Source: Census of Production databank.

divided between these sectors it is possible to compare their relative importance at the start and end of the period. The results are given in Table 3.1.

Northern Ireland was dominated by consumer goods industries to a much larger extent than any other United Kingdom region, whereas the North, Yorkshire–Humberside, East Midlands, West Midlands and Wales were particularly dependent on the capital goods industries in 1963. Over time, capital goods industries have been displaced, with only the West Midlands and Wales still (in relative terms) dominated by producers of capital goods by 1985. Within each sector the importance of labour and capital intensive industries varies. For instance, consumer goods producers in East Anglia, the South West and to a lesser extent Northern Ireland, were more likely to use labour intensive techniques, reflecting the importance of certain food processing industries in these regions. The large capital intensive consumer goods sector in the North West was dominated to some extent by general chemicals in both 1963 and 1985.

Having considered industrial structure at an aggregated level, it is useful to list those industries that dominated in Northern Ireland at the beginning and end of the period.[5] Table 3.2 shows, in descending order of importance, those manufacturing industries which had standardised net output values greater than 1. The method of standardisation is to convert estimates of real net output (£ million, 1975 prices) into Z-scores by subtracting the mean value of net output for the region and dividing by the associated standard deviation. As can be seen, tobacco, textile machinery, shipbuilding and aircraft manufacture were the largest industries in 1963, with certain textile and food industries also featuring strongly. By 1985, several industries were no longer as prominent, especially shipbuilding and those industries related to traditional textile manufacture, whereas clothing industries were more important, along with newspapers, motor vehicles and synthetics. (Note, inward investment over the period has much to do with explaining these changes – see Chapter 4.) This information shows that there were substantial structural changes in manufacturing over the period, which is confirmed by the low rank correlation coefficient of -0.16 between the standardised net output values of those industries listed in Table 3.2 for 1963 and 1985.

Table 3.2 also indicates whether those industries that dominated in Northern Ireland were also important in other United Kingdom regions. In 1963, only shipbuilding and aircraft manufacture dominated across five or more other regions, and nearly every industry listed had a location quotient greater than 1 (which indicates that the region specialised in the industry to a greater extent than did the nation).[6] This suggests that Northern Ireland manufacturing industry was highly specialised in 1963 (a fact confirmed later on), although by 1985 specialisation had declined since fewer industries had location quotients above 1. Even so, the dominant industries in 1985 were not typically large (in relative terms) in other United Kingdom regions, with the exception of aircraft and motor vehicles. Some of those industries which tended to dominate across the regions of the United Kingdom are listed in Table 3.3. The

TABLE 3.2 Dominant manufacturing industries[1] in Northern Ireland, 1963 and 1985

1963			1985		
Industry (MLH)	UK regions dominated[2]	Relative net output (%)	Industry (MLH)	UK regions dominated[2]	Relative net output (%)
*Tobacco (240) ..	3	8.6	*Tobacco (240) ..	1	7.4
*Textile machinery (335) .	1	8.5	*Milk products (215) ..	2	5.1
* Shipbuilding (370) .	5	6.3	*Abrasives (469) ..	3	4.2
Aircraft (383) .	8	5.0	Aircraft (383) .	5	3.6
*Weaving (413) ..	2	4.4	Newspapers (485) ..	2	3.6
*Bread (212) ..	2	4.1	*Dresses, etc (455)	2	3.4
*Spinning (412) ...	2	4.0	Motor vehicles (381) .	8	3.2
*Milk products (215) ..	2	3.6	* Animal and poultry foods (219) ..	3	3.1
* Animal and poultry foods (219) ..	3	3.2	*Man-made fibres (411) ..	1	3.0
*Made-up textiles (422) ..	2	3.1	Synthetics (276) .	3	2.6
*Telephones (363) .	1	3.0	*Male outwear (442)	1	2.5
*Bacon, meat and fish (214) ..	2	2.5	Pumps, valves (333)	1	2.4
			Bread (212) ..	1	2.4
			Timber (471) .	1	2.3
		Total 56.3			Total 48.8

Notes: Dots on each MLH code indicate whether the industry was: · capital goods/labour intensive; ·· capital goods/capital intensive; ··· consumer goods/labour intensive; ···· capital goods/labour intensive. See Table 3.1 for details.
An asterisk denotes that the industry had a location quotient greater than 1 in the relevant year (see text and note 6 for details).
[1] Industry (1968 MLH) with standardised (Z-score) net output (in 1975 prices) greater than 1. Industries are shown in descending order of importance.
[2] Number of regions (maximum of 11) dominated by same industry.
Source: As Table 3.1.

TABLE 3.3   Most dominant industries[1] across regions of the United Kingdom, 1963 and 1985

1963	1985
Iron and steel (311)	Bacon, meat and fish (214)
Other machinery (339)	General chemicals (271)
Shipbuilding (370)	Other machinery (339)
Motor vehicles (381)	Industrial plant and steel (341)
Aircraft (383)	Motor vehicles (381)
Other metals (399)	Aircraft (383)
Other printing (489)	Other metals (399)
	Other printing (489)

Note: Figures in brackets are SIC 1968 Minimum List Headings.
[1] Dominant in 5 or more UK regions, see Table 3.2 for definition of dominance.
Source: As Table 3.1.

following features are worth noting. The iron and steel (MLH 311) and/or other metals (MLH 399) industries dominated in every region except the two smallest, East Anglia and Northern Ireland. The vehicle industries (primarily motor vehicles (MLH 381) but also aircraft (MLH 383)) were also dominant with only the Northern region as the exception. Chemical industries, especially general chemicals (MLH 271) and pharmaceuticals (MLH 272), also featured strongly in the regions, as did other machinery (MLH 339).

The information in Table 3.2 is now supplemented with details on the degree to which different regions specialised (relative to the nation) in various manufacturing industries. To begin with, overall coefficients of regional specialisation are presented in Table 3.4. Net output (£ million, 1975 prices)

TABLE 3.4   Coefficients of regional specialisation in manufacturing,[1] 1963, 1979 and 1985

	Indices[2]					
	National average measure			Ogive measure		
Region[3]	1963	1979	1985	1963	1979	1985
Northern Ireland	1.14	1.03	0.92	1.14	1.09	0.93
Wales	0.85	0.59	0.62	1.09	0.91	0.96
East Anglia	0.84	0.72	0.69	1.07	1.01	1.00
North	0.83	0.62	0.64	1.05	0.95	0.99
East Midlands	0.77	0.60	0.58	0.95	0.85	0.84
West Midlands	0.75	0.70	0.72	1.12	1.03	0.98
South West	0.75	0.58	0.56	1.02	0.94	0.99
Yorks–Humberside	0.73	0.59	0.59	0.98	0.84	0.83
Scotland	0.55	0.54	0.57	0.91	0.87	0.92
North West	0.50	0.50	0.49	0.84	0.89	0.85
South East	0.48	0.41	0.42	0.86	0.87	0.97

[1] Revised definition based upon a reconciliation of the 1968 and 1980 SIC.
[2] See text and note 7 for definitions.
[3] Ranked from most to least specialised according to the data in first column of figures.
Source: As Table 3.1.

was used in the calculation of two different measures of specialisation, with one based upon deviations from the national average, while the other (the ogive measure) based the norm upon equal concentration of output in each sector. A major weakness of the national average measure, as explained in Brown (1972, pp 39–40), is that measured specialisation tends to decrease in proportion to the size of the region, irrespective of the true pattern of specialisation.[8] Nonetheless, the two measures give similar results; the correlation between the data in columns (1) and (4) in Table 3.4 is 0.83.

According to Table 3.4, Northern Ireland was by far the most specialised region in 1963, 1979 and 1985, on the basis of most of the measures used, although the 1985 ogive measure suggests that by the end of the period the province had become as diversified as other regions.[9] Next in line was Wales (if we consider the national average measure) or the West Midlands (if the ogive measure is used). Proceeding down through the list, the most diverse regions were generally the North West and South East. Of the Development Areas, Scotland had by far the lowest degree of specialisation and overall compares favourably, *if* it is assumed that diversification is an advantage, and that the national economy is diversified (the underlying assumption of the national average measure).

As to the changes in regional specialisation that occurred between 1963 and 1985, Table 3.5 presents estimates of the Coefficient of Regional Redistribution (CRR) for each region,[10] whereby the larger the coefficient, the greater the change in the distribution of output over the period. The results have two interesting facets: firstly, that, in general, the most specialised regions (and especially Northern Ireland) were becoming more diverse, ie closer to the distribution of industry at the national level. (The correlation coefficient between the data in the first columns of Tables 3.4 and 3.5 was 0.71.) The West Midlands was the major exception; the region experienced a level of redistribution which was unexpectedly small considering the level of specialisation

TABLE 3.5   Changes in regional specialisation in manufacturing,[1] 1963–1979 and 1963–1985

Region[2]	1963–79	1963–85
Northern Ireland	0.64	0.71
Wales	0.61	0.70
North	0.54	0.50
East Anglia	0.53	0.74
Scotland	0.45	0.51
South West	0.44	0.55
North West	0.44	0.44
East Midlands	0.43	0.51
Yorks–Humberside	0.39	0.53
West Midlands	0.31	0.42
South East	0.27	0.40

[1] Based on net output data, see text for definition, also footnote 1, Table 3.4.
[2] Ranked from most to least according to the data in column 1.
Source: As Table 3.1.

in 1963. Moreover, although there was a certain amount of convergence towards the national average, the rankings of regions changed very little between 1963 and 1985 (the correlation between the 1963 and 1985 national average measures is 0.83).[11] The second interesting result to be found in the table is the confirmation that there have been rapid changes in industrial structures since 1979, especially in those regions that have typically been the more diverse (eg the South East region). The large increase in the CRR for the 1963–85 period, when compared to the 1963–79 period, indicates the extent to which structures have altered in the six years following 1979.

Turning now to consider specialisation in more detail, Table 3.6 presents correlation coefficients between the value of real net output (£ million, 1975 prices), and net output location quotients having values greater than or equal to 1. These indicate whether regions (including Northern Ireland) actually specialised in their largest industries. In 1963, there were significant correlations for all but the South East and North West (these being the least specialised regions – see Table 3.4). Generally the values of the coefficients were not large in magnitude, except for the West Midlands and Northern Ireland. By 1979, the correlation between industry size and specialisation had diminished significantly, especially in the North, East Midlands and South West. Specialisation declined even further over the period 1979–85 (see the last column of figures in Table 3.6), with a particularly large fall in Northern Ireland being a principal feature of the table. Generally these results confirm our earlier findings that specialisation was decreasing over the period (and no more so than in Northern Ireland), especially during the recent restructuring of manufacturing.

Having presented evidence on the changes in industrial structure that took place in Northern Ireland (and the other United Kingdom regions) over the period 1963–85, we now examine the relative (net output) growth

TABLE 3.6 Spearman rank correlation coefficients of net output with net output location quotients, by industry, 1963, 1979 and 1985[1]

Region	1963	1979	1985
North	0.43***	0.24*	0.22
Yorks–Humberside	0.36**	0.43***	0.31**
East Midlands	0.37**	0.07	0.25**
East Anglia	0.34**	0.31**	0.33**
South East	0.03	0.03	0.16
South West	0.39***	0.18	0.06
West Midlands	0.48***	0.46***	0.34**
North West	0.19	−0.01	−0.03
Wales	0.38**	0.27*	0.05
Scotland	0.42***	0.28**	0.27**
Northern Ireland	0.56***	0.54***	0.27**

Note: *** Significant at the 1% level. ** Significant at the 5% level. * Significant at the 10% level.
[1] Only industries with a location quotient above 1 were included in the correlations.
Source: As Table 3.1.

experience of the province during the same period. Overall output growth rates are likely to have been affected by industrial structures, as the results obtained by others have shown (Fothergill and Gudgin 1982; Brown 1972; Lee 1971; Law 1980). The basic argument is that differing regions are dependent to a greater or lesser extent upon industries that are nationally in decline with the result that the more dependent a region is upon such industries, the lower will be its aggregate rate of growth. The converse holds for those regions that are dominated by industries experiencing above average rates of national growth. To measure the importance of this 'structural' influence, the industries in each region are weighted by either national growth rates (applied to regional shares of these industries) or national shares (applied to regional growth rates) and the resulting 'expected' aggregate growth rates are then compared with actual growth rates in order to establish the relative importance of 'structural' and 'residual' influences. The approach has various limitations which have been discussed in the literature (see Fothergill and Gudgin 1979 for a review), but for our present purposes the results of the shift-share are assumed to be a convenient weighting exercise that seeks to show if any region had an above (or below) average share of nationally growing (or declining) industries. No explanatory (or statistical) *significance* is imputed from the results that have been obtained.

Table 3.7 presents the results from applying the shift-share technique to growth rates based upon net output data for each industry (at the MLH level of classification) in the regions of the United Kingdom. The overall performance of each region can be gauged from its position in the first column. Generally, it appears that those regions with the lowest levels of urbanisation,

TABLE 3.7   Estimates of the 'structural' and 'growth' components of net output growth in manufacturing, regions of the United Kingdom, 1963–1985

Region[1]	% Annual growth[2]	Difference with national growth	'Structural' effect[3]	Growth or 'residual' effect[3]
East Anglia	4.09 (5.29)	+2.79 (+2.97)	−0.83 (−0.61)	+3.62 (+3.58)
South West	3.43 (4.15)	+2.13 (+1.82)	−1.66 (−1.74)	+3.79 (+3.56)
East Midlands	2.55 (3.36)	+1.25 (+1.03)	−0.79 (−1.00)	+2.04 (+2.03)
North	1.98 (3.63)	+0.68 (+1.31)	−1.47 (−2.07)	+2.15 (+3.38)
Wales	1.67 (2.29)	+0.37 (+0.00)	−1.79 (−2.44)	+2.16 (+2.44)
Scotland	1.47 (2.59)	+0.17 (+0.27)	−0.78 (−0.68)	+0.95 (+0.95)
N. Ireland	1.43 (2.29)	+0.13 (−0.03)	−2.11 (−1.85)	+2.24 (+1.82)
South East	1.04 (1.96)	−0.26 (−0.36)	+0.44 (+0.24)	−0.70 (−0.60)
Yorks– Humberside	0.82 (2.04)	−0.48 (−0.28)	−1.83 (−1.80)	+1.35 (+1.52)
North West	0.58 (1.45)	−0.72 (−0.87)	−0.72 (−0.47)	0.00 (−0.40)
West Midlands	0.29 (1.24)	−1.01 (−1.08)	−1.21 (−1.00)	+0.20 (−0.08)

Note: Figures in parentheses refer to the 1963–79 period.
[1] Ranks from highest to lowest according to the data in column 1.
[2] Geometric average of net output at constant prices.
[3] Based upon the mean of regional and national weights – see Equation 8.7 in Dixon and Thirlwall (1975) for the formula used.
Source: As Table 3.1.

TABLE 3.8 Rapidly growing industries[1] in Northern Ireland, 1963–1979 and 1979–1985

Industry	1963–79		Industry	1979–85	
	Growth rate[2] (%)	Relative[3] size (%)		Growth rate (%)	Relative[4] size (%)
MLH 411 – Man-made fibres	11.5	8.7	MLH 381 – Motor vehicles	14.9	3.2
MLH 417 – Hosiery	6.4	2.8	MLH 442 – Male outwear	13.5	2.5
MLH 469 – Abrasives	5.7	3.3	MLH 445 – Dresses and	13.0	3.4
MLH 444 – Male clothing	5.7	3.8	infants' clothing		
MLH 471 – Timber	4.9	2.2	MLH 485 – Printing, publishing		
MLH 482 – Paper packaging	4.3	1.7	newspapers	10.2	3.6
MLH 215 – Milk products	4.3	4.8	MLH 336 – Construction equip	9.0	1.7
MLH 278 – Fertilisers	4.1	1.6	MLH 469 – Abrasives	3.2	4.2
MLH 445 – Dresses and			MLH 219 – Animal foodstuffs	2.9	3.1
infants' clothing	3.8	1.5	MLH 240 – Tobacco	2.1	7.4
MLH 485 – Printing, publishing			MLH 419 – Carpets	0.9	1.7
newspapers	3.0	1.9	MLH 496 – Plastics	0.9	1.5
			MLH 361 – Electrical machinery	0.8	1.0
		32.2			33.2

[1] Only those industries with output levels higher than the mean across all industries in the base year and with output growth above the mean are included in this table.
[2] Average annual compound growth rates (£m, 1975 prices).
[3] Percentage of total manufacturing output in 1979.
[4] Percentage of total manufacturing output in 1985.
Source: As Table 3.1.

and/or those which experienced the highest levels of regional aid, performed in an above average manner over the period 1963–85 (the figures in parentheses refer to the 1963–79 period, when growth rates were higher; note, the simple correlation between growth rates across regions over the two periods is 0.97). Northern Ireland does rather poorly, in comparison with the other smaller regions of the United Kingdom, given that it was such a large benefactor from regional aid. To what extent these results are due to industrial structure, or 'mix', can be seen by comparing the columns relating to structural and residual effects. Structure *dominates* only in Northern Ireland, Yorkshire–Humberside, and the West Midlands (and in the North West and Wales in the 1963–79 period), and exerts proportionately less influence the better the growth performance of the region.[12] Regions that do seem to have had relatively poor industrial structures include the North, Wales, the South West, Northern Ireland, Yorkshire–Humberside, and the West Midlands, while the South East had the most favourable structure. Overall, these results suggest that growth rate differences cannot be entirely attributed to differing structures, but that it was an important factor in many regions like Northern Ireland (especially in terms of restricting growth rates during a period when, overall, growth was quite high).

This section concludes with a closer look at which industries grew the fastest over the period 1963–85, including a discussion of some of the likely determinants of relative growth. Table 3.8 lists those industries that grew fastest (excluding those industries that were not in operation in the base year, and those that were small[13] in size). It is useful to compare the list of industries in Table 3.8 with the information given in Table 3.2 on those industries which dominated Northern Ireland. The dominant industries in 1963 were typically not the fastest growing industries (this is confirmed by the first row of results given in Table 3.9), but during the 1979–85 period many large industries did perform in an above average manner (eg motor vehicles, abrasives, animal foodstuffs, tobacco and certain clothing industries), although overall there was a (weak) negative correlation between industry size and growth (see Table 3.9). These differences between the two periods can be partly explained by noting a fairly strong link between the number of new plants setting up in Northern Ireland during the period 1966–78 (the period for which data were available)[14] and industrial growth rates for 1963–79. Obviously, these new plants tended to add significantly to the relative importance of what were typically underdeveloped local industries (eg man-made fibres, motor vehicles and various clothing industries). Unfortunately, these growth industries, resulting from inward investment, did particularly badly during the 1979–85 period (as evidenced by the −0.24 correlation coefficient given in Table 3.9). Various determinants of these growth rates can be considered, although little adequate data exist with which to test hypotheses.

However, Table 3.9 presents information on the results of correlating output growth (by industry) and some of the various likely influences on growth. The first, the size of the industry in the base year, has already been examined; smaller industries tend to grow faster, because there are dynamic

TABLE 3.9 Simple correlations between output growth and certain determinants,[1] Northern Ireland and the United Kingdom, 1963–1979 and 1979–1985

Determinant[2]	Northern Ireland		United Kingdom[3]	
	1963–79	1979–85	1963–79	1979–85
Net output in base year	−0.29*	−0.20	−0.06	−0.01
Change in location quotient	0.72***	0.92***	0.95***	0.77***
Inward moves of plants into region	0.30**	−0.24*	0.08*	0.12***
Capital/consumer goods	−0.28	0.13	0.01	−0.07*
Capital intensity	0.15	0.01	−0.07*	−0.05
Technology status	−0.17	0.03	0.04	0.21***
Growth of net output in UK industry	0.59***	0.11	0.22***	0.55***

Note: *** Significant at 1% level. ** Significant at 5% level. * Significant at 10% level.
[1] Only manufacturing industries with output levels higher than the mean across all industries in the base year were included in the calculations.
[2] See text for details.
[3] Industries in each standard region of the UK.
Source: As Table 3.1.

economies of scale to be exploited as the industry grows over time. The change in the location quotient is included as a proxy for the growth of exports;[15] this variable is highly correlated with output growth, which is to be expected given that exports are a major source of autonomous demand in a small regional economy. Inward investment has already been discussed, but it is interesting to note that this factor was relatively less important for the United Kingdom as a whole, although the positive link between growth and inward investment in the United Kingdom during 1979–85 contrasts strongly with the results that were obtained for Northern Ireland for the same period. Consumer goods industries tended to grow faster than capital goods industries, although the link is weak (it was stronger in Northern Ireland during the 1963–79 period), and capital intensity had relatively little effect on growth. The next variable in Table 3.9 represents the importance to growth of those industries classed as being technologically advanced;[16] there was little evidence of a positive relationship between technology and growth in the 1963–79 period, although the link was fairly strong in the United Kingdom as a whole for the 1979–85 period (when technological advances have been particularly rapid). However, industry in Northern Ireland has not benefited, mainly because it has fewer of these industries (their share of manufacturing output in 1985 was 10.4 per cent, compared to a United Kingdom figure of 17.6 per cent), and because local industry is generally less technologically advanced than in Great Britain (see below). Finally, and as expected, industrial performance in each region, especially the smaller regions, tends to be heavily influenced by industrial growth at the national level. However, what is surprising is that this relationship was not in evidence in Northern Ireland during the 1979–85 period.

TABLE 3.10 Manufacturing output growth rates, Northern Ireland and the Republic of Ireland, 1978–1985[1] (percentage)

Industry[2]	Northern Ireland	Republic of Ireland
Non-metallic minerals	−8.3	−0.7
Chemicals[3]	0.5	8.8
Metals and engineering	2.4	9.5
Food	−0.7	1.8
Drink, tobacco	−0.1	2.0
Textiles	−1.1	−3.2
Clothing and footwear	0.0	−2.9
Timber and wooden furniture	−1.6	−4.4
Paper and printing	−0.9	−1.0
Miscellaneous manufactures	−5.6	2.2
Total manufacturing	−1.2	4.3

[1] Annual compound growth rates.
[2] 1980 SIC.
[3] Man-made fibres included in chemicals in the Republic of Ireland; only industry division 25 included for Northern Ireland, since man-made fibres (class 26) included in non-metallic minerals.
Source: NIAAS No 5, 1986; Economic Review and Outlook (Dublin).

As to a comparison of growth rates between the two parts of Ireland (Table 3.10), the Republic of Ireland has experienced high relative growth in those export-based industries that have been at the forefront of its inward investment strategy (ie chemicals, computers and office equipment, and other electrical and instrumental engineering industries). Overall it substantially outperformed Northern Ireland over the period 1978–85. As will be seen later (Table 3.14), the high growth industries in the Republic of Ireland tend to be relatively large (when compared to overall manufacturing net output), while the low growth industries (textiles, clothing and footwear, and timber goods) account for a much smaller proportion of manufacturing output than in Northern Ireland.

4. Growth problems

The last section concluded by considering some of the determinants of intra-regional growth in manufacturing industries. However, despite large-scale assistance to industry for over 40 years, manufacturing in Northern Ireland has not performed particularly well. Table 3.7 shows that, of the traditional peripheral areas in the United Kingdom, the province achieved the lowest rate of industrial growth. Furthermore, manufacturing in Northern Ireland has experienced the fastest absolute and relative decline when compared to any other region (see Figure 3.1). Therefore, in this section an attempt is made to outline some of the causes of inter-regional differences in growth, and so explain Northern Ireland's poor performance. The problems of industry 'mix' and over-specialisation have already been discussed, so in this section several other important factors are considered.

PERIPHERALITY

Being positioned at the edge of major concentrations of population and economic activity acts as a disadvantage to a region such as Northern Ireland. Transport costs are higher for both goods that need to be shipped into the region, and goods that are exported. However, these additional costs are unlikely to be particularly high (in pecuniary terms) since most recent studies suggest that transport costs account for between 2 and 4 per cent of gross output and vary only to a limited extent between regions (about 1 per cent of gross output). Table 3.11 presents evidence that is drawn from the Census of Production in 1979, confirming that such costs are quite small. Only for industries that need to ship bulky goods (eg bricks and cement) are there significant transport costs to be met. Table 3.11 also shows that while costs incurred by companies in Northern Ireland are higher, the differential is not large. It is also worth pointing out that the cost figures for Scotland are not significantly different from national average costs. Moore, Rhodes and Tyler (1986), in contrast, suggest that these figures understate the problems faced in the peripheral regions, since no attempt is made to control other factors that affect the comparisons being made. For instance, firms in regions such as Northern Ireland will often adapt to reduce higher costs by, for example, supplying more of their output to local markets, and such measures reduce the cost element in gross output. Moreover, these writers suggest that 2–4 per cent of gross output is not insignificant; for example, if profits are 10 per cent of gross output, reducing transport costs from 4 per cent to 2 per cent would increase profitability by 20 per cent. Finally, the non-pecuniary effects on peripheral firms need to be considered, since many firms operating away from

TABLE 3.11   Transport costs as a percentage of gross output, Northern Ireland and Scotland, 1979

Industry[1]	Northern Ireland	Scotland
Food, drink, tobacco	4.1	2.9
Chemicals	2.8	1.8
Mechanical engineering	4.6	1.6
Electrical engineering	2.3	1.3
Miscellaneous engineering	2.5	1.9
Textiles	3.0	1.9
Clothing	2.8	1.4
Glass, pottery, cement	19.5	12.9
Timber, etc	7.7	1.5
Paper, printing	4.7	3.7
Other manufacturing	2.1	6.6
All manufacturing	4.2	2.6

[1] 1968 SIC.
Source: Census of Production.

TABLE 3.12 Percentage of firms regarding transport costs as a competitive disadvantage, 1984

Northern Ireland		Scotland		South East England	
Clothing	82	Furniture	70	Furniture	22
Furniture	66	Mechanical engineering	38	Electrical engineering	8
Electrical engineering	63	Electrical engineering	27	Mechanical engineering	6
Mechanical engineering	48	Clothing	27	Clothing	0

Source: PPRU Occasional Paper No 7, Table 4.11.
Crown Copyright.

major markets perceive transport costs to be a substantial competitive disadvantage (see Table 3.12). *Distance* costs (pecuniary and non-pecuniary) may therefore have quite a large impact on manufacturing performance in the peripheral regions.

Locational disadvantages also stem from small local populations with low purchasing power, since this will constrain growth unless an industry exports (thereby incurring distance costs). In an attempt to measure overall locational disadvantage, researchers have defined measures of 'economic potential', usually obtained by dividing total regional income by the total distance from the region to all other regions. The greater the total purchasing power of a region, the larger its economic potential, while greater isolation from the major centres of population decreases potential. Using such a measure, Keeble, Owens and Thompson (1982) have been able to map the economic potential of the regions of the EC (see Figure 3.2 and Chapter 15). In 1977, Northern Ireland came seventh from the bottom of an economic potential league table comprising some 108 regions (the Republic of Ireland was two places above), while those regions near or at the top of the table were located in the 'golden triangle' formed from joining up Paris, London and Hamburg.[17] The study repeated the exercise for 1965, and was therefore able to show a worsening of economic potential between 1965 and 1977 in the peripheral regions of the EC.

TECHNOLOGY AND PRODUCTIVITY

The importance of technical change, through the innovative activity of industry, has been stressed in recent literature on regional development (Goddard et al 1983; Gibbs and Edwards 1985). Product innovations help regions to improve their product range and therefore industrial structure, while process innovations lead to greater efficiency and/or improved quality. There is, therefore, a natural link between technological change and productivity which can be considered in formal models of regional growth (see, for example, Kaldor 1985, Dixon and Thirlwall 1975, both of which make use of

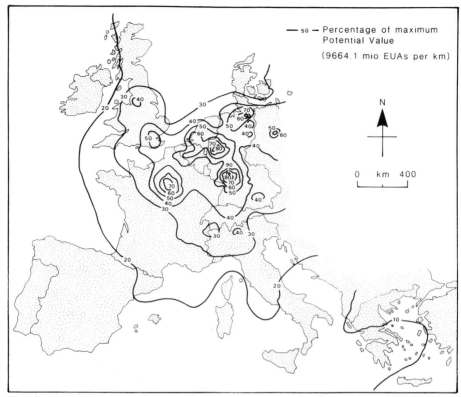

FIG 3.2 Regional economic potentials, 1977
Source: Keeble, Owens and Thompson (1982, Fig 3.7)

the Verdoorn cumulative causation model based upon technological change).
The aims of this sub-section are, however, more modest, seeking simply to
show that technological advance in Northern Ireland has been relatively low
and then presenting evidence which confirms that relative productivity levels
are low in the province.

The number of innovations recorded in the Science Policy Research
Unit's (SPRU) database on significant innovations[18] in the United Kingdom,
1945–83, attributable to Northern Ireland is small. Given the size of the
province, this is not surprising. However, when a measure of relative
innovation intensity is considered, it is found that Northern Ireland and the
other peripheral regions of the United Kingdom have fewer innovations per
unit of net output than the United Kingdom average (see Table 3.13 and
Harris 1988a). Moreover, the poor performance of these regions cannot be
attributed simply to 'structural' effects. Table 3.13 indicates that these were
generally outweighed by 'residual' effects (ie influences not reliant upon a poor
industry 'mix'). For instance, Northern Ireland had the lowest innovation
intensity during the 1964–79 period, which was primarily due to a very large
(negative) residual effect. Part of the explanation for these spatial differences

TABLE 3.13 Shift-share analysis of innovations per unit of net output[1] in manufacturing, regions of the United Kingdom, 1945–1979

Region	1945–63				1964–79			
	Actual[1]	Differential[2]	Structural[3]	Residual[4]	Actual	Differential	Structural	Residual
North	7.41	2.00	-7.20	9.20	3.22	-1.85	-5.07	3.23
Yorks–Humberside	3.66	-1.75	-1.34	-0.41	5.65	0.58	-0.41	0.99
East Midlands	6.64	1.23	-2.49	3.72	5.49	0.41	-0.60	1.01
East Anglia	8.67	3.12	-0.16	3.28	5.19	-0.14	-0.58	0.44
South East	6.69	-1.28	0.09	1.19	6.79	1.72	-2.87	4.59
South West	7.79	2.33	0.37	1.96	5.00	-0.10	-4.01	3.91
West Midlands	5.29	-0.13	-0.43	0.30	3.95	-1.13	-3.47	2.35
North West	4.15	-1.27	-0.39	-0.88	5.61	0.53	0.58	-0.05
Wales	2.17	-3.20	-0.25	-2.95	2.51	-2.24	0.85	-3.08
Scotland	2.92	-2.48	-0.80	-1.68	2.89	-2.16	-7.16	4.99
Northern Ireland	3.42	-1.99	-0.15	-1.84	1.22	-3.85	3.56	-7.41

[1] The total number of innovations in the period 1945–63 and 1964–79, divided by constant-price net output (£ hundred million, 1975 prices in 1963 and 1979).
[2] Difference between the average in each region and the national average.
[3] Defined as 0.5 (A–B) + 0.5 (C–D) where

$$A = \sum_i \sum_r \frac{I_{ir}}{Y_{ir}} \qquad B = \sum_i \sum_r \frac{I_{ir}}{Y_{ir}} \cdot \frac{Y_i}{\sum_i Y_i} \qquad C = \sum_i \sum_r \frac{I_i}{Y_i} \cdot Y_{ir} / \sum_i \sum_r Y_{ir} \qquad D = \sum_i \frac{I_i}{Y_i}$$

and I refers to the number of innovations, Y_{ir} refers to net output in industry i in region r.
[4] Defined as 0.5 (A–C) + 0.5 (B–D).
Source: SPRU and as Table 3.1.

in innovation intensity (which, as shown above, are not simply due to the industrial composition of the regions) can be found in the literature on 'core–periphery models. Over time companies have tended to concentrate control (and therefore R&D functions) in centrally located plants, leaving the (externally controlled) peripheral regions to produce output in branch plants geared more to assembly and sub-assembly functions (Harris 1988b). This has affected the innovativeness of regions such as Northern Ireland, which have (more and more) been developing into production bases since the early 1960s. The effect of this shortfall in technology has had important implications on productivity (both labour and capital productivity).

Figure 3.3 shows that in each of the three years, 1963, 1973 and 1985, Northern Ireland's labour productivity (net output per head) was lower than in all other regions of the United Kingdom. The province achieved a substantial rate of productivity growth for the period 1963–73 (6.9 per cent per annum[19]), which helped it to catch up with productivity levels in the East and West Midlands in 1973. However, over the 1973–85 period, manufacturing productivity growth was relatively poor in the province (1.3 per cent per annum[20]), so that by 1985 Northern Ireland's level of labour productivity was 88.2 per cent of the level obtained in the next lowest region (the West

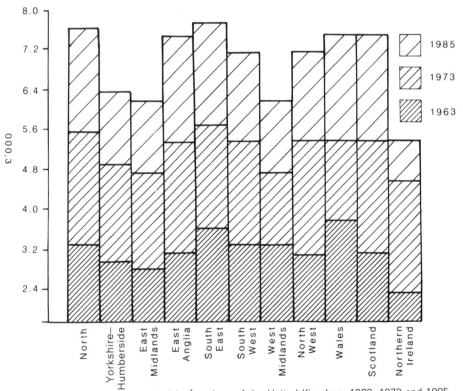

FIG 3.3 Labour productivity,[1] regions of the United Kingdom, 1963, 1973 and 1985.
[1] Manufacturing output per head, £000 1975 prices.
Source: Census of Production.

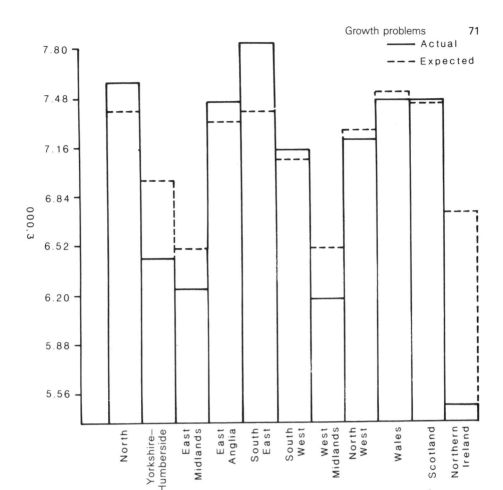

FIG 3.4 Actual and expected labour productivity,[1] regions of the United Kingdom, 1985.
[1] Manufacturing output per head £000 1975 prices.
Source: Census of Production.

Midlands), and 69.4 per cent of the level achieved in the South East. Unfortunately, the province's problem in the later period cannot be attributed to 'industry mix'. Figure 3.4 shows the actual and 'expected' levels of productivity in 1985 in the United Kingdom regions, where the 'expected' levels are obtained by weighting net output in each industry in a region by the national level of productivity in that industry, to show what regional productivity levels would have been with the region's own industrial structure and industry productivity levels prevailing at the national level. For Northern Ireland in 1985, the 'expected' level is 23 per cent higher than the actual level, which suggests that most industries in the province had low productivity, rather than the problem being too great a dependence on a few large low productivity industries.[21] Finally, comparing Northern Ireland's productivity levels with those in the Republic of Ireland in 1983 (Table 3.14), two major facts stand out: firstly, there is much higher labour productivity in the Republic of Ireland and, secondly, the gap between industries was highest in those industries in

TABLE 3.14 Labour productivity (net output per head), Northern Ireland and the Republic of Ireland,[1] 1983 (£000, current prices)

Industry[2]	Labour productivity		% Relative net output	
	NI	RI	NI	RI
Non-metallic minerals	23.6	17.4	7.1	8.8
Chemicals	22.4	45.7	5.5	15.4
Electrical and instrumental engineering	3.7	27.2	6.4	18.2
Other engineering and vehicles	9.4	11.2	16.4	8.1
Food, drink, tobacco	19.4	19.9	28.6	23.7
Textiles	9.4	10.2	7.9	2.7
Clothing and footwear	6.5	6.7	7.7	2.7
Timber and wooden furniture	11.2	8.3	2.6	1.7
Printing and publishing	14.6	13.3	5.3	4.3
Other manufacturing	10.7	14.6	2.1	3.6
All manufacturing	12.9	19.0	100.0	89.2
Correlation coefficient r	0.66***		0.65***	

[1] The net output data for the Republic of Ireland was converted to sterling at the exchange rate £1 = IR£0.822.
[2] 1980 SIC – industrial definitions are equivalent.
Source: As Table 3.11.

which growth rates were very different (cf Table 3.10) and in which the Republic of Ireland now tends to specialise.

As to capital productivity (ie gross value added per unit of net capital stock in plant and machinery), information on the largest sectors in Northern Ireland is presented in Figure 3.5.[22] When compared to the Development Areas in Great Britain, Northern Ireland's productivity is relatively good (even though capital stocks were growing at a faster rate in the province), although it is 12 per cent behind the South East's all manufacturing productivity level. It is also worth noting the low capital productivity of the engineering and textile sectors.

In general, this sub-section has been able to show that technology and productivity are two areas for concern in Northern Ireland, and that there is an important link between the two. It is also possible that low productivity levels have resulted from the inability of plants in the province to exploit the economies of scale which result when companies and plants grow larger.[23] The next sub-section will examine this issue.

RETURNS-TO-SCALE AND GROWTH

The importance of returns-to-scale in the process of economic growth is linked to 'cumulative causation' models (Kaldor 1985). Developed by Myrdal (1957), this approach has been formalised by Kaldor (1970), Dixon and Thirlwall (1975) and Thirlwall and Dixon (1979). Essentially, production is subject

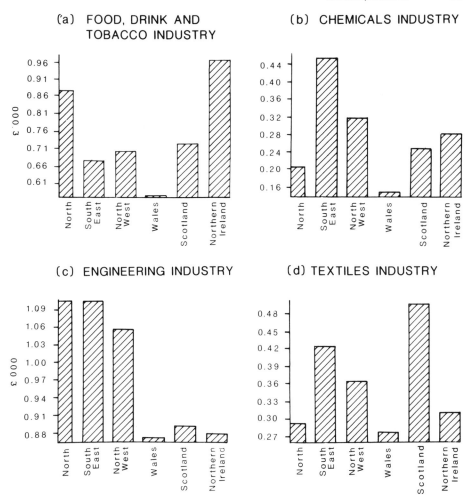

(a) FOOD, DRINK AND TOBACCO INDUSTRY

(b) CHEMICALS INDUSTRY

(c) ENGINEERING INDUSTRY

(d) TEXTILES INDUSTRY

FIG 3.5 Capital productivity[1] in certain regions of the United Kingdom, 1978.
[1] Gross value added per unit of net capital stock, £000 1975 prices.
Source: Harris (1982a)

to increasing returns-to-scale because of internal, external and agglomeration economies. Hence, via the Verdoorn equation, the scenario is one of increasing productivity of labour as output grows so that regions with increasing output levels will have higher productivity, correspondingly lower export prices (these being a mark-up on unit labour costs) and increased competitiveness, with the result that output increases at a faster rate. The presence of returns-to-scale can be measured in various ways: by estimating the parameters of a production function (or its equivalent); by constructs based upon economic data on firms (or plants) of different sizes; and by the 'engineering' approach. The first technique is beyond the scope of this chapter, since it typically involves using aggregated time series data, which sets it apart from the other approaches.[24] The engineering approach involves collecting information on the methods of producing a good and the cost conditions involved in doing so, from which it is possible to construct a picture of how average costs *might* vary with size. That is, technological information is obtained (eg by asking practitioners) about the likely effect on average costs of producing a good(s) at different levels of output with the associated levels of inputs that this would entail. The approach was used by Pratten (1971) for the United Kingdom, and several other attempts have recently been surveyed in Wibe (1984). The strengths and weaknesses of the engineering approach are surveyed in the latter. For our present purposes it is sufficient to note that Pratten (1971) found that the minimum efficient scale (MES) of operations (ie the minimum point of the average cost curve) was substantial for United Kingdom industries in the 1960s. Of the 35 industries covered, the MES was well above the scale at which output was produced, and for nearly a quarter of industries the MES was greater than the total market size. The other approach to measuring scale economies involves using data on the distribution of firms and plants across different size-bands. In this present study, data from the Business Monitor series are used to obtain estimates of the average plant size in Northern Ireland industries relative to average plant size in the United Kingdom. The presence of smaller plants in Northern Ireland can then be taken as evidence of a failure of industry to exploit internal economies of scale. Figure 3.6 shows the average size of plants in Northern Ireland industries relative to those in the United Kingdom, where average plant size is calculated by dividing total employment by the Herfindahl index of the number of 'equal-sized' plants operating in each industry. The 'other transport' industry (Class 36 of the 1980 SIC) has much larger average sized plants, because of the dominating presence of plants belonging to Harland & Wolff and Shorts (companies which, unfortunately, do not enjoy high productivity/profitability levels), while textiles and rubber and plastics are above the national average. In general, though, average plant size is substantially lower in Northern Ireland[25] with industries such as chemicals, electrical engineering, motor vehicles and paper products operating much smaller plants than in the rest of Great Britain,[26] even though economies of scale are likely to be more important in these manufacturing industries.

EXTERNAL CONTROL OF MANUFACTURING

Since 1945, and especially during the 1960s and early 1970s, Northern Ireland, in common with the other peripheral regions, has attracted a large number of new manufacturing plants which are controlled externally, ie the headquarters of the plants are located outside the region (typically in the South East of England, or in the USA if the plant is owned by a foreign multinational company).[27] It has been argued that external control means that plants in the peripheral regions are more likely to be used as assembly and sub-assembly units, while plants in the headquarters' regions have higher proportions of

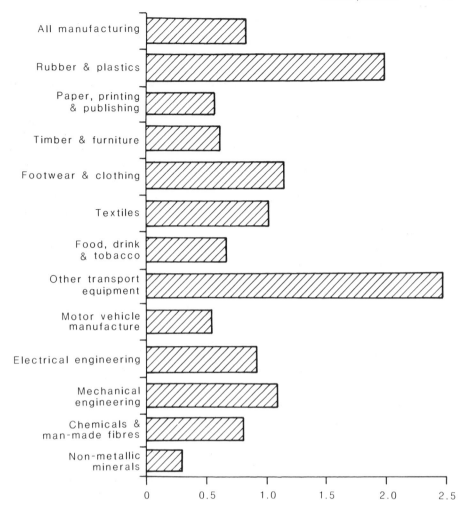

FIG 3.6 Average plant size, Northern Ireland relative to the United Kingdom, 1984. Source: Census of Production, 1984.

white-collar workers and R&D functions. There are therefore implications for job skills, for the quality of work, for local linkages and for the propensity for plant closures in regions such as Northern Ireland. This may affect entrepreneurship in the regional economy (which is linked to the socio-economic structure) and hence the potential for new firm formations (see Chapter 5), and in general enhance any tendency towards regional dualism, ie where the 'core' continues to improve its economic position relative to the 'periphery'. Many of these issues are discussed and analysed at greater length in Harris (1988b), where evidence is presented for the regions of Great Britain which suggests that external control is indeed detrimental to regional development. This present sub-section will consider the position of Northern Ireland.

To begin with, Table 3.15 shows the extent to which manufacturing in Northern Ireland is dominated by production-based activities; the ratio of non-manual to manual employment is lower in every sector (but one) in the province, and especially in those industries that are subject to higher levels of technological advance (chemicals; mechanical engineering; office equipment and electronic engineering; motor vehicles; instrumental engineering; and other manufacturing). In order to gauge the impact of external ownership on these figures, we need information on the location of company headquarters. Table 3.16 uses data drawn from Hart and D'Arcy (1988),[28] which show that some 41 per cent of manufacturing workers were employed in externally owned companies, many of which are concentrated in those industries listed above. Furthermore, Table 3.17 aggregates industries and examines the division of the workforce between manual and non-manual occupations. The general pattern shows (perhaps a little surprisingly) little difference in the proportion of white-collar workers across industry groups and location of headquarters.[29] However, major differences are apparent when manual workers are split on the basis of skilled to unskilled occupations. For foreign-owned companies, there is a marked tendency for the workforce to be predominantly unskilled, confirming the branch-plant status of these firms. This is even more apparent when industry group B, representing those industries where technological advance is more important, is examined. In this instance, there is a wider gap between Northern Ireland and externally owned (including, this time, Great Britain owned) plants, with the former having a much larger percentage of skilled manual workers. These results seem to confirm the idea that in those sectors where external ownership is highest, plants are more likely to concentrate on production-based activities only.

TABLE 3.15 Proportion of non-manual employees in manufacturing industries, Northern Ireland and the United Kingdom, 1983

Industry (Class)[1]	NI	UK
Minerals, etc (21–24)	22.8	26.6
Chemicals (25–26)	35.3	43.4
Other metals (31)	27.8	25.6
Mechanical engineering (32)	27.5	38.2
Office equipment and electrical engineering (33–34)	24.9	41.6
Motor vehicles (35)	15.5	27.0
Other transport (36)	37.6	38.3
Instrumental engineering (37)	30.7	39.7
Food, drink, tobacco (41–42)	21.9	22.6
Textiles (43)	17.2	20.6
Leather, clothing and footwear (44–45)	15.9	16.8
Timber (46)	21.6	24.7
Paper industries (47)	36.3	39.0
Other manufacturing (48–49)	20.5	29.2
All manufacturing	24.1	31.7

[1] 1980 SIC.
Source: As Table 3.11.

TABLE 3.16   Proportion of employees in Northern Ireland manufacturing by location of company headquarters, 1986

| Industry (Class)[1] | Total employment | Location of headquarters (percentage[2]) | | | |
		Northern Ireland	Great Britain	Other EC	Other country
Minerals, etc (21–24)	4,030	71.2	22.6	6.2	—
Chemicals (25–26)	2,696	29.6	7.4	25.7	37.4
Other metals (31)	2,326	72.1	11.3	5.5	11.1
Mechanical eng (32)	6,415	64.6	8.1	2.3	25.0
Office equip and electronic eng (33–34)	6,803	24.9	37.7	9.4	28.0
Motor vehicles (35)	3,179	24.7	3.3	—	72.0
Other transport (36)	12,690	98.6	1.4	—	—
Instrumental eng (37)	888	34.1	33.7	—	32.2
Food, drink and tobacco (41–42)	20,247	61.3	24.1	5.6	9.0
Textiles (43)	12,978	49.6	44.1	0.9	5.5
Leather, clothing and footwear (44–45)	16,481	46.2	48.2	2.7	2.9
Timber (46)	4,297	89.8	9.5	0.7	—
Paper industries (47)	5,174	76.2	18.3	4.4	1.1
Other manufacturing (48–49)	4,868	39.9	18.7	31.1	10.2
All manufacturing	103,072	59.2	25.1	5.2	10.6

[1] 1980 SIC.
[2] The row percentages sum to 100% which is equivalent to the figure for total employment.
Source: NIERC Manufacturing Databank.

The implications for Northern Ireland of being a branch plant economy are serious. Firstly, the most important R&D functions are not located in the region and this has consequences for the number of product and process innovations that emanate from the local economy (see the discussion above). Secondly, externally owned plants tend to belong to large companies that are operating branch plants in several locations. During periods of recession, these companies rationalise their operations by restructuring, which generally results in closing down production capacity in peripheral regions such as Northern Ireland. Evidence to support this contention is not complete, although *The Financial Times* database shows that during the period 1976–86, of the 44,045 job losses attributable to (large) United Kingdom companies operating in Northern Ireland, only 8,884 job losses were due to large companies which had their headquarters in the province. The remainder were from job-shedding by companies located in, for example, Greater London (accounting for 59.8 per cent of the 44,045 job losses), or the West Midlands (accounting for a further 16.4 per cent of the losses). A third major impact of external ownership has recently been experienced in the Republic of Ireland. Because of the large degree of foreign ownership of high growth industries, profits have been flowing out of the country on a large scale. By 1986, the

TABLE 3.17 Proportion of employees in Northern Ireland manufacturing by occupation, industry and location of company headquarters, 1988 (percentage)

Occupation group	Location of company headquarters									
	Northern Ireland		Great Britain		USA/Japan		Other country		All plants	
	A[1]	B[2]	A	B	A	B	A	B	A	B
Managers	6.9	6.9	6.6	6.0	20.0	7.4	10.3	7.2	7.3	6.8
Technical staff	6.1	7.6	5.9	17.3	5.0	6.0	3.9	6.7	6.0	9.8
Sales staff	5.0	4.6	5.5	0.4	0.0	1.1	1.8	3.4	4.9	2.5
Clerical	8.9	8.1	7.9	8.6	8.0	8.9	9.4	4.7	8.6	7.7
Skilled manual	49.3	50.6	41.1	26.3	21.0	2.6	35.1	5.5	45.6	24.5
Unskilled manual	24.2	22.2	33.3	41.4	45.0	74.0	39.7	72.5	28.0	48.8

Note: Column percentages may not add to 100 because of non-response to survey question.
[1] 1980 SIC Classes: 21–24, 31, 36, 41–47.
[2] 1980 SIC Classes: 25–26, 32–35, 37, 48–49.
Source: Harris (1989).

TABLE 3.18 Proportion of local purchases in Northern Ireland manufacturing by industry and location of company headquarters, 1988 (percentage)

Purchases from	Location of headquarters									
	Northern Ireland		Great Britain		USA/Japan		Other country		All plants	
NI companies of	A[1]	B[2]	A	B	A	B	A	B	A	B
Materials[3]	29.3	29.4	35.6	5.9	5.0	4.5	22.6	5.3	30.2	12.6
Business services[4]	76.8	73.9	55.1	45.9	25.0	51.2	15.9	36.8	68.0	53.8

[1] 1980 SIC Classes: 21–24, 31, 36, 41–47.
[2] 1980 SIC Classes: 25–26, 32–35, 37, 48–49.
[3] Excluding fuel and wholesale imports.
[4] Accountancy, banking and general business services.
Source: As Table 3.17.

problem was such that the net balance of trading income as a percentage of the Republic of Ireland's GDP was 11.3 per cent (O'Malley and Scott 1987). It is not possible to obtain comparable figures for Northern Ireland, but the problem may potentially be as bad if companies in Great Britain operating in the province are included as a major source of profit outflow. A further major impact on the local economy of a high degree of external control relates to linkage effects. Plants that are externally owned tend to be integrated into a larger corporation which requires them to purchase and sell internally. This truncates backward linkages, via purchases from local suppliers, which then reduces local demand for goods and services and the ability of externally owned firms to pass on what are termed 'growth impulses' to the local economy. Table 3.18 presents evidence that shows that purchases of both materials (excluding fuels and wholesale imports) and business services produced in Northern Ireland companies are generally much lower in the externally owned sector.

5. Conclusion

This chapter has considered the manufacturing sector in Northern Ireland, finding a higher degree of specialisation during the post-war period (although this has been decreasing) and a generally poor 'mix' of industries that experienced lower growth rates than their national counterparts. Indeed, the contrast is especially poignant when manufacturing performance in Northern Ireland is compared with the structure and growth of the Republic of Ireland's manufacturing industry. The latter did much better in the 1970s and early 1980s.

Many of the problems faced by industry in the province can be attributed to four major areas: the peripherality of the region (which lowers economic potential through higher distance costs); lower productivity and technological advance in the region; lower exploitation of returns-to-scale (because smaller markets make it impractical to expand plant and company size); and a high degree of external control (which lowers economic linkages, makes industry vulnerable to high levels of plant closures during periods of (inter)national restructuring, and lowers the potential for entrepreneurial activity, partly because of the effect on the region's occupational structure). These problems are complex, and there are no simple solutions that can be offered. The industrial development policy of the 1960s, which concentrated on inward investment, appeared to offer a quick and relatively easy solution (a large number of new jobs in industries under-represented in the region), but many of the early successes, such as the setting-up of the man-made fibres, electronics and rubber and plastics industries, have faltered over time so that now the emphasis seems to be more on indigenous industry.

Because of the continuing contraction (in both output and employment terms) of the manufacturing base, it is important to ask whether the sector will continue to decline and what effect this would have on the economy as a whole. It is likely that employment will continue to fall in manufacturing, but then this is a well-established long run trend that is by no means peculiar to Northern Ireland. What is more important is a possible slower rate of growth in manufacturing output (see NIERC 1987) such that the sector declines in relative importance when compared to other sectors. This has implications for growth in these other sectors and leads to continuing dependence on the rest of the United Kingdom to maintain the high level of subvention that is already present. Northern Ireland currently produces only a small proportion of the goods and services that it consumes and, unfortunately, the high levels of imports of tradable goods that have to take place to satisfy local demand are not balanced by a high volume of exports, because of the small size of the manufacturing base. Thus, Northern Ireland is only able to pay for these imports because employment in public services (and other subsidies from government) is relatively high, and thus incomes are sufficient to meet expenditure. If manufacturing declines further, more and more dependence will be placed on the government which will reduce the province's ability to generate self-sufficient growth, as well as tying the development of the economy to government expenditure decisions (and political influences). Moreover, manufacturing, unlike many other sectors, has a greater ability to foster economic growth, because of its export orientation; its high level of intermediation of production (and therefore, the potential for spreading 'growth impulses'); its ability to gain from technological innovation and exploit returns-to-scale. It would seem, therefore, that a continuing high priority should be placed on manufacturing in order for the province to improve its economic position and standard of living.

Notes

1. Fuller details are given in Harris (1987), especially Tables 1 and 2.
2. A gradual decline in employment within manufacturing would give less cause for concern, if in fact manufacturing was becoming more productive and efficient and so able to boost overall regional growth levels.
3. Two measures are necessary because in some industries gross investment per unit of output is relatively small, and yet these industries would normally be classified as capital intensive. Prominent examples include many metal manufacturing industries in various regions, the pumps, valves and compressors industry and aerospace in all regions. Hence, if an industry was classified as capital intensive on either measure, it was allocated to the capital intensive sector. In practice, very few industries showed up as capital intensive on the first measure (gross investment per unit of output) but as labour intensive on the second measure (based on shiftworking).
4. The actual approach used was to weight the hours worked by shiftworkers by a factor of 2, while day-time worker-hours were unweighted. Then average 'capital hours' were calculated as the mean hours worked by all employees in each industry and region. Hence, we are assuming that capital is in operation for twice as long as

the hours worked by the average shiftworker, since shiftworkers are 'covered' during the day by day-time workers. Finally, an industry in each region was designated as capital intensive, on the basis of this second measure, if it had 'capital hours' above the mean across all industries in the nation.

5. The pattern of specialisation is considered in detail later in the chapter.

6. Defined as:

$$\left| \frac{x_i}{x} - \frac{X_i}{X} \right|$$

   See note 7 for definitions.

7. The two indices are defined as:

   (a) National Average $(NA) = \sum_i \left| (x_i/x) - (x_i/x) \right|$

   (b) Ogive $(OG = \sum_i \left| (x_i/x) - (1/N) \right|$ where x_i = regional output/employment in industry i; x = total regional output/employment; X_i and X are the national counterparts to x_i and x; N = the number of industrial sectors in the region/nation. Note, for the NA measure the coefficient can vary between 0 and 2; the nearer it is to the former, the closer the industrial distribution of output/employment is to the nation. For the OG measure the interpretation of the coefficient is similar; the nearer it is to zero, the more diverse the industrial structure of the region.

8. That does not mean that with the ogive measure the size of the region and specialisation are not linked; there are good grounds for expecting that larger regions are more able to support a more diverse industrial base. The point being made is that the National Average measure has 'built-in' to it a statistical bias towards demonstrating an inverse relationship between size and specialisation.

9. The 1985 ogive figures give rise to the biggest differences in rankings cross regions when compared to any of the other results. This suggests that the dramatic changes in manufacturing, as a result of the 1980–82 recession, have had a large effect in restructuring the spatial distribution of industry. Specifically, since the recession disproportionately affected the largest plants and industries, this would tend to increase the value of the ogive measure, *vis-à-vis* the National Average measure.

10. Defined as $CRR = \sum_i \left| (x_i/x)_t - (x_i/x)_{t-1} \right|$

    See note 7 for definitions.

11. Law (1980) presents very similar results for the period 1921–71, suggesting that the economic forces affecting regional structures have been operating consistently for a considerable period of time.

12. When the effects of the 1979–85 period are included, it would seem that structural effects became relatively more important in those regions that had the lowest growth rates throughout the entire period; see, for example, the increase in the negative structural effect in Northern Ireland in Table 3.7.

13. That is, had standardised net output values less than 0.

14. Note, these data refer to moves (branches and transfers) into Northern Ireland for each industry MLH, obtained from the Record of Openings and Closures, and supplied in an unpublished form by the Department of Industry, London.

15. Harrigan (1982) found that for Scotland in 1973, the correlation coefficient between location quotients and relative Scottish *net* exports was 0.913. Other studies have used the location quotient to identify which activities form the export base. See Norcliffe (1983) for a survey.

16. The definition of which industries are technologically advanced is based on the 'official' classification given by Butchart (1987).

17. Northern Ireland's 'economic potential', measured in EUAs per kilometre, was only 16 per cent of the potential of the top region, Rheinhessen-Pfalz.

18. See Harris (1988a) for a discussion of this database from a spatial perspective.
19. This compares with 5.4 per cent for the North, which had the next highest rate, and 3.8 per cent for Wales, the region with the lowest growth rate.
20. Compared to 2.2 per cent in the East Midlands, the next poorest rate, and 2.8 per cent in Scotland, which topped the productivity growth league.
21. This is confirmed by a 'shift-share' analysis which shows that the 'structural' component was −0.37 per cent while the 'residual' component was −1.28 per cent (the sum of the two components equals the difference between the regional and national productivity levels). There is also other evidence (that is not dependent upon the shift-share approach) that suggests that low productivity is a Northern Ireland problem; a Kruskal–Wallis test of the null hypothesis that productivity levels in (MLH) industries across regions were the same is rejected at the 1 per cent level of significance for each of the years 1963, 1968, 1973, 1979 and 1985. In each of these years the mean rank for industries in Northern Ireland was much lower than that in every other region.
22. Data are taken from Harris (1982a); see also Harris (1983).
23. Ball and Skeoch (1981) found that in most manufacturing there was a significant relationship between the size of plants in the industry and labour productivity.
24. For an example of the results that can be obtained from the production function approach, see Harris (1982b).
25. Average company size is also much smaller in Northern Ireland; using the *Northern Ireland Trade Directory* for 1987, and the UK Census of Production for 1985, manufacturing employment was distributed as follows across company size-bands:

(percentage)

Size-band	1–99	100–499	50–999	1000+
Northern Ireland	20.3	432.3	10.01	27.4
United Kingdom	23.4	16.5	7.4	52.7

26. This conclusion is not reached simply on the basis of the evidence given in Figure 3.6; comparisons with 10 Great Britain regions were made, with industry in Northern Ireland having the lowest or next to lowest 'average' plant size in 10 out of 14 industries for which data are available.
27. Some of the growth in external control has probably resulted from existing indigenous companies being taken over by firms with headquarters in the South East. There is a growing body of evidence that shows this has happened in the Great Britain peripheral regions (Leigh and North 1978; Smith 1979; Goddard and Smith 1978; Ashcroft et al 1987).
28. The source of these data is the manufacturing databank that has been developed at the NIERC. Ownership of plants have been identified from various sources including the Cabinet Lists, the Industrial Training Board and the Census of Employment. Note, the data used in the remaining tables in this chapter are based on a special survey of manufacturing industry carried out by the present author (Harris 1989). However, the NIERC data were preferred for Table 3.16 since it is based on more comprehensive 'official' data sources.
29. It is interesting that multinational companies have proportionately more managers, but fewer technical and sales staff.

References

Ashcroft, B K, Love, J H and Scouller, J (1987) *The Economic Effects of the Inward Acquisition of Scottish Manufacturing Companies*, Industry Department for Scotland, ESU Research Paper, 11.

Ball, J M and Skeoch, N K (1981) *Inter-plant Comparisons of Productivity and Earnings*, Government Economic Service Working Paper, 38, London.

Brown, A J (1972) *The Framework of Regional Economics in the United Kingdom*, NIESR, Cambridge University Press.

Butchart, R L (1987) A new UK definition of the high technology industries, *Economic Trends*, 400, February, 82–88.

Dixon, R J and Thirlwall, A P (1975) *Regional Growth and Unemployment in the United Kingdom*, Macmillan, London.

Fothergill, S and Gudgin, G (1979) In defence of shift share, *Urban Studies*, 16, 303–19.

Fothergill, S and Gudgin, G (1982) *Unequal Growth: Urban and Regional Employment Change in the UK*, Heinemann Educational Books, London.

Gibbs, D C and Edwards, A (1985) The diffusion of new production innovations in British industry, in Thwaites, A T and Oakey, R P (eds), *The Regional Economic Impact of Technological Change*, Frances Pinter, London.

Goddard, J B and Smith, I J (1978) Changes in corporate control in the British urban system, *Environment and Planning A*, 10, 1073–84.

Goddard, J B et al (1983) *Technological Innovation in a Regional Context: Empirical Evidence and Policy Options*, Centre for Urban and Regional Development Studies, Discussion Paper No 55, University of Newcastle upon Tyne.

Harrigan, F J (1982) Revealed comparative advantage and regional industrialisation: the case of Scotland, *The Fraser of Allander Institute Discussion, Paper 22*, University of Strathclyde.

Harris, R I D (1982a) *A Data Bank of Regional Economic Time Series for UK Manufacturing Industries*, Department of Economics Occasional Paper, 18, The Queen's University of Belfast.

Harris, R I D (1982b) Estimates of rates of return on capital employed in UK regions, 1968–78, *Scottish Journal of Political Economy*, 29, 298–309.

Harris, R I D (1983) The measurement of capital services in production in UK industries, 1968–78, *Regional Studies*, 17, 3, 169–80.

Harris, R I D (1987) The role of manufacturing in regional growth, *Regional Studies*, 21, 4, 301–12.

Harris, R I D (1988a) Technological change and regional development in the UK: evidence using the SPRU database on innovations, *Regional Studies*, 21, 5, 361–74.

Harris, R I D (1988b) Market structure and external control in the regional economies of Great Britain, *Scottish Journal of Political Economy*, 35, 334–60.

Harris, R I D (1989) *Industrial Development in Northern Ireland, 1945–88*, Policy Research Institute, Belfast, forthcoming.

Hart, M and D'Arcy, E (1988) *External Control and Manufacturing Employment Change in Northern Ireland, 1973–86*, Northern Ireland Economic Research Centre, Working Paper, 3.

Kaldor, N (1970) The case for regional policies, *Scottish Journal of Political Economy*, 17, 337–48.

Kaldor, N (1985) *Economics without Equilibrium*, University College Cardiff Press, United Kingdom.

Keeble, D, Owens, P L and Thompson, C (1982) *The Influence of Peripheral and Central Locations on the Relative Development of Regions*, Department of Geography, University of Cambridge, Cambridge.

Law, C M (1980) *British Regional Development since World War I*, David & Charles, Newton Abbot.

Lee, C H (1971) *Regional Economic Growth in the United Kingdom since the 1880s*, McGraw-Hill, London.

Leigh, R and North, D J (1978) Regional aspects of acquisition activity in British manufacturing industry, *Regional Studies*, 12, 227–45.

Moore, B C, Rhodes, J and Tyler, P (1986) *Geographical Variations in Industrial Costs*, Department of Land Economy Discussion Paper, University of Cambridge.

Mydral, G (1957) *Rich Lands and Poor*, Harper & Row.

NIERC (1987) *Regional Economic Prospects: Analysis and Forecasts to the Year 2000*, NIERC, October 1987.

Norcliffe, G B (1983) Using location quotients to estimate the economic base and trade flows, *Regional Studies*, 17, 3, 161–68.

O'Malley, E and Scott, S (1987) Profit outflows from Ireland. Paper read to the first annual conference of the Irish Economics Association, Kilkenny.

PEIDA (1984) *Transport Costs in Peripheral Regions*, Policy and Planning Research Unit Occasional Paper, 7, Department of Finance, Belfast.

Pratten, C K (1971) *Economies of Scale in Manufacturing Industry*, Cambridge University Press, Cambridge.

Smith, I J (1979) The effect of external takeovers on manufacturing employment change in the Northern region between 1963 and 1973, *Regional Studies*, 13, 421–37.

Thirlwall, A P and Dixon, R J (1979) A model of export-led growth with a balance of payments constraint, in Bowers, J K (ed), *Inflation, Development and Integration: Essays in Honour of A J Brown*, Leeds University Press, England.

Wibe, S (1984) Engineering production functions: a survey, *Economica*, 51, 401–413.

Industrial development policy

Richard T Harrison

1. Introduction

There can be little doubt that Northern Ireland has experienced, and continues to experience, severe economic and social disadvantages within the United Kingdom context (Review Team 1976; Bull and Hart 1987; Damesick and Wood 1987). The post-war Northern Ireland economy has been characterised by a persistent imbalance between the supply of and demand for labour. Higher than average birth rates have been accompanied by a correspondingly rapid growth in the population of working age, which has only partially been alleviated by net migration. At the same time the demand for labour has been reduced by a substantial fall in employment in the region's staple industries of agriculture, shipbuilding and textiles, on which the regional economy was, and still is, unduly reliant (see Chapter 6). In the last decade this has been reinforced by significant labour shedding and restructuring in the externally owned sector of the Northern Ireland economy as branch plants established in the post-war period have contracted and closed (Bull et al 1982; Harrison 1982, 1986a). The consequence has been a level of unemployment which has been persistently higher than the national average, and on almost every measure of economic welfare Northern Ireland emerges as the poorest region of the United Kingdom and one of the poorest regions in the EC (Commission of the European Communities 1981a). The response of a succession of regional and national governments to this problem of manufacturing industry decline and rising unemployment has been the development and implementation of a considerable programme of industrial development in Northern Ireland, generally based on United Kingdom regional policy but administered locally and including provisions unique to Northern Ireland to meet the perceived needs of the region (Hoare 1981).

2. The development of policy

REGIONAL POLICY IN GREAT BRITAIN

Since the 1930s the British Government has recognised the existence of a regional problem. This in part reflects structural problems arising out of the pattern of late nineteenth century industrialisation in the United Kingdom and is manifest in levels of regional unemployment that are deemed to be unacceptably high compared with the national average. The main policy response to this situation has emphasised the creation of new employment opportunities in the peripheral areas to redress the apparent imbalance in the labour market. Up until the mid-1970s the development of regional policy in the United Kingdom was fairly steady and there was a good deal of continuity of attitude and approach, based on four major identifiable themes (McCallum 1979). First, unemployment discrepancies have been the basic (almost exclusive) justification for regional policy, and inter-regional equalisation has accordingly emerged as of overriding importance. Secondly, regional economic problems have been viewed as a reflection of an unfavourable industrial structure. Thirdly, the primary focus has been on the welfare of geographical areas rather than people – what McCallum (1979, 36) refers to as 'place prosperity' – and consequently the emphasis on 'work to the workers' has remained almost totally unchallenged. Finally, a relatively passive public posture was assumed in which government's role was to induce private industry to take an initiative, both by providing incentives (financial and infrastructural) to attract investment to the assisted areas and by imposing controls on industrial development outside those areas (Armstrong and Taylor 1986).

Reflecting these basic themes, which characterised regional policy nationally up to the end of the 1970s, British regional policy came to have an almost exclusive emphasis on capital mobility and investment in manufacturing. This was based on the assumption, valid for the most part up to the 1973–74 oil shock, that there was a secular growth trend in the post-war national economy that would generate a continuous flow of new industrial investment. Major strategies, therefore, have included the movement of manufacturing facilities from the south of England and the Midlands, through the use of Industrial Development Certificate controls and the provision of an extensive package of financial and infrastructural incentives, to encourage the development of both indigenous and non-indigenous manufacturing enterprises in the regions. This policy, nationally and regionally, was based on the fundamental premise that the attraction of mobile British investment and new foreign direct investment to a region such as Northern Ireland would provide a necessary broadening of the industrial base of the regional economy and offer the prospect of stable or expanding employment opportunities in manufacturing industry (Department of Trade and Industry 1983).

REGIONAL POLICY IN NORTHERN IRELAND

Although industrial development policy in Northern Ireland dates back to the 1932 New Industries Development (NI) Act (NIDA 1932), it was not until the introduction of the Industries Development (NI) Act in 1945 (IDA 1945) that ID policy in Northern Ireland became firmly established (Murie et al 1974). This Act represented a major step forward in ID legislation in the province. It was modelled on the Great Britain Distribution of Industry Act of 1945, which was in turn the outcome of the report of the Royal Commission on the Distribution of the Industrial Population (Barlow Report 1940). The Industries Development (NI) Act established the basis for the provision of selective financial assistance for employment creation, mainly in new industrial undertakings, and subsequent legislation in the 1950s enabled government to grant-aid existing firms to re-equip and modernise with no employment test. In 1971 the ID legislation was extended to enable the Government to provide financial assistance for the maintenance as well as the creation of employment. Throughout the 1970s a number of new institutions were established to assist industrial development in Northern Ireland. The Local Enterprise Development Unit (LEDU) was set up in 1971 with special responsibility for employment creation in firms employing not more than 50 people. The Northern Ireland Finance Corporation (NIFC) was established in 1972 and succeeded in 1976 by the Northern Ireland Development Agency (NIDA), which was closely modelled on the industrial banking functions of the National Enterprise Board and the Scottish and Welsh Development Agencies (Harrison 1989a). In September 1982 NIDA and the Industrial Development Organisation arm of the then Northern Ireland Department of Commerce, which had hitherto been responsible for the provision of financial assistance to ID projects, were amalgamated to form the new Industrial Development Board (IDB).

In late 1983 the Government published its regional development White Paper (HM Government 1983), which reviewed the operation of the Regional Development Grant (RDG) scheme in Great Britain. This paved the way for the introduction of a revised RDG scheme in November 1984, in conjunction with a revision of the map of assisted areas in Great Britain (Martin 1985). The nature of this review highlights two major differences between the regional policy incentives package on offer in Northern Ireland and that available in Great Britain (Harrison 1986b).

First, the existing incentives package available in Northern Ireland, established in 1945 and modified in 1971, is heavily biased towards the provision of selective, employment-related assistance for capital investment. As Murie et al (1974) point out, this difference can be traced back to the 1945 Act, which introduced a selective, employment-related, grant package in Northern Ireland, compared with the loans-based package originally introduced in Great Britain. The Northern Ireland package, therefore, also differed from the situation in Great Britain pre-1984, where the package was predominantly automatic in nature. Indeed, one of the major proposals of the 1983 White Paper in Great Britain was that there should be a shift away from automatic schemes of assistance such as Regional Development Grant towards selective assistance which would only be awarded to projects demonstrating that employment was being created or safeguarded which would not exist in the absence of assistance. In 1983/84, for example, in Great Britain the automatic, capital investment related, Regional Development Grant accounted for 82 per cent of expenditure of regional policy incentives (excluding the provision of sites and premises) and only 18 per cent went on the provision of selective, employment related incentives. In Northern Ireland, however, the proportions were very different: 65 per cent of ID expenditure in 1983/84 was accounted for by selective employment related assistance (paid largely in the form of capital grants) and only 35 per cent by automatic Standard Capital Grants (equivalent to the Regional Development Grant in Great Britain). Examination of the Northern Ireland industrial development experience, therefore, provides a useful case study of the impact and effectiveness of selective assistance as a regional policy instrument.

The second feature of the incentives package which distinguishes Northern Ireland from Great Britain is the relationship between automatic and selective assistance. In Great Britain regional selective assistance has been available either as the only form of assistance (in the outer tier of designated areas in the pre-1984 map of assisted areas) or as a top-up or supplement to Regional Development Grant which was available on a more spatially restricted basis and formed the core of the grant system. In Northern Ireland, on the other hand, automatic Standard Capital Grant and selective assistance are alternative channels of assistance offered under different legislation until 1982. Accordingly, a project qualifying for and claiming selective assistance cannot, at the same time, receive Standard Capital Grant. As grant rates for plant, machinery and buildings have generally been higher under selective assistance (ranging from 30 per cent to 50 per cent depending on location within Northern Ireland) than under Standard Capital Grant (30 per cent before the 1984 review, subsequently reduced to 20 per cent), selective assistance has been the primary instrument in the drive to attract inward investment under the region's industrial development programme. On the other hand, Standard Capital Grant has been used primarily by companies already operating in Northern Ireland, including inward investment projects originally established with selective assistance, to assist them to modernise and re-equip (Harrison 1986b; Harris 1988).

THE RETREAT FROM REGIONAL POLICY

In both Great Britain and Northern Ireland regional policy has continued to evolve. The shift nationally from automatic to selective financial assistance has been taken further in the 1988 White Paper (HM Government 1988). Department of Trade and Industry policy now emphasises the centrality of encouraging the creation of enterprise and an enterprise culture in the regions. The focus has been shifted away from the provision of the 'hard' forms of assistance, such as financial inducements, on which post-war regional policy has been based, towards the provision of 'soft' assistance in the form of training and advice to enable existing businesses to become more efficient and competitive. This has been reflected in a general downgrading of expenditure on regional policy, the redrawing of the map, and hence coverage, of the assisted areas, and most recently, the abolition of Regional Development Grants in Great Britain (Martin 1985, 1989). This is part of a wider reorientation of regional development strategies in most advanced industrial economies (Bachtler 1988; Albrechts et al 1989) and reflects, in the United Kingdom context at least, the playing down of regional policy issues in favour of national policies designed to improve macro-economic performance, stimulate deregulation and develop an enterprise culture. One consequence of this has been a progressive reduction in regional policy expenditure, in constant 1985 prices, from around £1.5 billion at its peak in 1973/74, and almost £1.0 billion in 1979, to a planned £400 million in 1988 (Martin 1989).

In Northern Ireland there has been a similar evolution in official thinking. The Pathfinder report published by the Department of Economic Development in 1987 emphasised the role of self-reliant economic growth as the primary aim of economic development policy and identified the stimulation of enterprise and competitiveness as major strategies (Department of Economic Development 1987; Stutt et al 1988). Much of the discussion in Pathfinder has been general comment of a ground-clearing nature rather than formulation of detailed strategies. In particular there is little discussion of the particular instruments of industrial development policy beyond identification of the over-dependency of the private sector on public sector funds as a constraint on the achievement of self-reliant development (Teague 1989).

However, some of the specific instruments of industrial development policy have come under specific official scrutiny in Northern Ireland. In particular, preceding Pathfinder, but clearly part of this evolution of policy, the Department of Economic Development announced a review of the automatic Standard Capital Grant in Northern Ireland in the light of the national review of the Regional Development Grant (Department of Economic Development 1985). As a consequence of this, the rate of grant available was reduced to 20 per cent and certain sectors were excluded from aid. Subsequent reviews led to further reductions in both the grant rate and the sectoral coverage of the scheme, culminating in the decision in 1987, following a review of the additionality and economic impact of the scheme, to withdraw it completely on the grounds that much of the investment supported by Standard Capital Grant would have taken place in any case. This decision has, however, come in for criticism recently on the basis of survey evidence on the utilisation of the scheme (Harris 1988).

The industrial development incentives package now available in Northern Ireland is therefore based primarily on the provision of selective financial assistance for employment creating projects through either indigenous or new inward investment. In addition, however, between 1985 and 1988 assistance was available to assist small and medium-sized firms to acquire expert outside advice and consultancy on business organisation, management, marketing, product quality and development. This assistance was funded from the non-quota section of the European Regional Development Fund under a programme to stimulate restructuring in areas affected by decline in the textiles and shipbuilding industries. The schemes have not been renewed following expenditure of the original budget allocation. Although no formal announcement has yet been made it is likely that the shift of emphasis signalled in the 1988 White Paper (HM Government 1988) towards the provision of 'soft' forms of assistance (in the form of training and advisory services) rather than 'hard' assistance, such as the provision of sites and financial incentives, will be reflected in the future evolution of regional industrial development policy in Northern Ireland.

Overall, the scale of expenditure on industrial development assistance in Northern Ireland has been considerable. In the two decades 1967/68 to 1986/87 £886 million (at constant 1984 prices) was spent on automatic investment grants and Standard Capital Grants. A further £1,335 million was paid out in selective financial assistance for the creation and maintenance of employment over this period. Reflecting the emphasis in the industrial development programme placed on the provision of infrastructure, and the development of sites and factory construction in particular (Murie et al 1974), some £650 million (1984 prices) was spent on site and factory provision.

In recent years there has been a shift of emphasis within the selective financial assistance package in Northern Ireland. Firstly, the overwhelming bias within the package towards grants for capital which (with the exception of Regional Employment Premium in the late 1960s and early 1970s) has been characteristic of the post-war incentives package, has been reduced somewhat: between 1967/68 and 1971/72, for example, less than 6 per cent of total selective financial assistance grants were paid in the form of employment grants; between 1977/78 and 1981/82, however, employment grants accounted for over 20 per cent of total selective assistance grant payments (Harrison 1986a), largely reflecting the growing significance of assistance to maintain, rather than create, employment in a deteriorating regional economy (NIEC 1985b). Secondly, and more generally, the structure of expenditure on regional policy in Northern Ireland has changed in recent years (Table 4.1). Total expenditure on site development and factory provision has fallen, reflecting the rundown of the advance factory programme in the light of lower levels of mobile investment relative to the 1960s, and the Industrial Development Board is now following a policy of divesting itself of its industrial property holdings.

TABLE 4.1   Industrial development expenditure, Northern Ireland, 1979/80–1987/88 (£m, current prices)

	Land and buildings	Selective assistance	Other services	Local enterprise	Capital grants
1979/80	20.7	76.2	na	6.2	17.5
1980/81	16.2	91.6	0.5	5.6	39.8
1981/82	18.0	78.8	0.6	6.0	41.7
1982/83	15.6	104.1	1.3	7.8	53.7
1983/84	12.7	76.6	1.6	11.0	37.2
1984/85	14.1	63.5	2.9	14.4	54.7
1985/86	13.3	80.3	3.3	17.7	55.7
1986/87	14.8	84.8	3.2	20.2	30.0
1987/88	10.8	79.7	3.5	21.2	18.3

Source: Northern Ireland Estimates.

Selective financial assistance continues to remain important, but the level of provision fluctuates from year to year in line with actual and anticipated levels of investment activity. However, it does appear that in real terms there has been a downward drift in this category of expenditure since the early 1970s (NIEC 1984). Expenditure on automatic capital grants has reduced sharply following the decision to reduce the rate of grant and coverage of the scheme and the subsequent abolition of the scheme. There is little evidence to suggest that this reduction will be compensated for by an increased provision for selective financial assistance, suggesting that there is a substantive cut in total public sector support for industry in Northern Ireland. Finally, and significantly, there has been a very significant increase in the budget allocation to support local enterprise development through the work of LEDU. This involves not only the direct job promotion activities of LEDU itself (see below) but also support for local and community enterprise development through the Local Enterprise Programme in Northern Ireland (Harvey 1987). At the regional level this is the clearest illustration of the changing shift of emphasis towards 'enterprise' as the basis for national and regional policies (HM Government 1988).

In the remainder of this chapter the impact of this assistance will be assessed in three stages. Firstly, the impact of job-related selective assistance will be discussed, with particular reference to its impact on employment generation and stability in Northern Ireland. Secondly, the impact of selective assistance specifically for small enterprises, which has become much more important in recent years, will be assessed. Finally, the impact of automatic capital grants will be evaluated with particular reference to their impact on manufacturing investment in the region.

3. Impact of selective assistance

Since 1932, financial assistance for industrial development in Northern Ireland has been made available with the specific aim of attempting to overcome the region's unemployment problem by expanding and restructuring the industrial base of the region, primarily through the attraction of new inward investment as the basis for stimulating self-generating regional economic growth (Wilson Report 1965; Northern Ireland Development Programme 1970; Review Team 1976; Harrison 1989a).

The impact of this ID programme has been considerable. Between 1946 and 1982 over 170,000 jobs were promoted in manufacturing industry in Northern Ireland, representing around 1.4 million man-years of employment actually created (NIEC 1983b). Around 40 per cent of these job promotions are accounted for by new inward investment from Great Britain and overseas. From Figure 4.1 it is clear that throughout the 1950s there was a steady but fairly slow increase in the level of ID activity in Northern Ireland, reflecting the generally weak application of regional policy throughout the United Kingdom at that time (Armstrong and Taylor 1979). After 1960, however, the rate of job

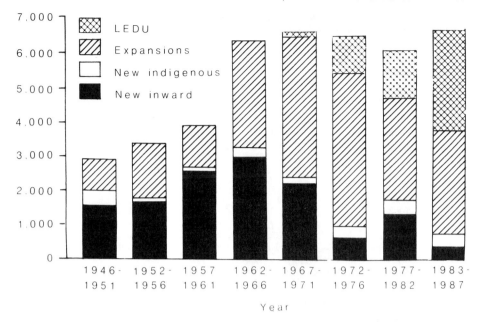

FIG 4.1 Average annual ID and LEDU job promotions, Northern Ireland, 1946–1987.
Source: Harrison (1986a).

promotion increased sharply as regional policies were applied more strongly and the Northern Ireland economy entered a major growth phase, stimulated in part by this increase in capital investment in manufacturing (NIEC 1983a). After 1974, however, the ID effort lost momentum in the wake of continued civil unrest and the oil shock induced recessions of 1973–74 and 1979 (Harrison 1982).

From Figure 4.1 it is also clear that the main effect of ID policy in the 'successful' period between the early 1960s and the mid-1970s, when job promotions[1] (though not necessarily net new jobs created) exceeded 6,000 per annum, was concentrated on inward investment. Before 1951 indigenous Northern Ireland owned enterprises accounted for 30 per cent of total job promotions. Between 1952 and 1971, however, job promotions by indigenous (Northern Ireland owned) companies were negligible; fewer than 3 per cent of total job promotions were in new companies from within Northern Ireland and, even if jobs promoted in expanding indigenous enterprises are included, the indigenous sector accounted for less than 13 per cent of all job promotions (Harrison 1986a). In the decade after 1972, by contrast, 26 per cent of all promotions (including those supported by LEDU in the small firm sector) were in indigenous companies and, for the first time, exceeded jobs promoted in companies new to Northern Ireland (Figure 4.1).

In general, jobs in small industry (LEDU assisted projects with an employment potential of under 50) have cost less to promote than those in inward investment and larger indigenous projects (which include reinvestment

TABLE 4.2 Industrial development selective assistance, average cost per job promoted, 1975–1985 (£m, constant 1983 prices)

	Inward investment	Larger indigenous[1]	Small business
1975	4,013	13,186	4,292
1976	19,586	4,723	3,490
1977	5,129	8,862	3,176
1978	19,083	11,546	5,283
1979	24,855	7,931	4,331
1980	9,143	9,595	3,229
1981	4,163	6,902	3,919
1982	2,939	8,290	na
1983	6,297	7,053	3,511
1984	10,253	11,484	3,977
1985	13,456	13,519	4,017

[1] Includes expansions by externally owned projects originally established as new inward investment in Northern Ireland.
Source: NIEC (1986b).

projects in Northern Ireland undertaken by companies originally established in Northern Ireland as new inward investment under the ID programme) (Table 4.2). These estimates are, of course, based only on the cost of promoting new employment opportunities. As such, they underestimate the real net cost of job creation through the industrial development programme, for four main reasons. Firstly, these figures take no account of deadweight effects, that is, the promotion and grant-aiding of jobs which companies would have created in any case in the absence of assistance. Secondly, they make no allowance for displacement effects, as grant-aided establishing or expanding companies displace employment in non-grant aided or other companies serving similar markets, through the encouragement of subsidised competition. Thirdly, not all jobs promoted actually convert into employment opportunities on the ground: it appears that jobs created represent around 60 per cent of total jobs promoted (ITC 1982, 38). Finally, not all jobs created survive. From an analysis of projects grant-aided between 1951 and 1980 Simpson (1984) has shown than on average peak employment was reached after six years, after which project employment levels began to fall. Project closure has also been significant: of the 325 entirely new manufacturing projects established between 1945 and 1979 in Northern Ireland, 43 per cent had closed by 1979, and almost 30 per cent of these closures had been recorded in the period 1975–79 (Bull et al 1982). As a result of the combined influence of contraction and closure, the average duration of employment in grant-aided projects up to 1982 has been estimated at 6.8 years in closed projects and 8.1 years in projects which were still in production (NIEC 1983b). While data on the cost per job created are not available, estimates suggest this ranges from £880 per job year in LEDU assisted businesses (NIEC 1985a, 26) to around £1,500 to £2,000 per job created per year in larger ID projects (DED 1985) and around £4,000 per job per year created in the synthetic fibres industry (NIEC 1983b, 42).[2]

INDUSTRIAL DEVELOPMENT PROJECTS IN NORTHERN IRELAND

It is possible to compare the temporal trend of project openings (new externally owned projects) in Northern Ireland and the Department of Trade and Industry's data on inter-regional industrial movement held on the Record of Movement (ROM) and Record of Openings and Closures (ROC) (Nunn 1980; Pounce 1981). In general, it appears that the temporal patterns of United Kingdom inter-regional moves and new externally owned openings in Northern Ireland follow broadly similar courses over the post-war period (Figure 4.2). There are, however, a number of important differences. Firstly, the immediate post-war fall-off in activity in Northern Ireland is much more pronounced than the national figure, which is a reflection of considerable inter-regional variations in mobile investment in the post-war period (Armstrong and Taylor 1979, 214–15). Secondly, although the 1950s is generally recognised, in regional policy studies, as a period of weak policy application in Great Britain (Moore et al 1978, 1986) and a strong regional policy continued to apply in Northern Ireland, the region does not appear to have benefited significantly from this differential: there is no evidence of an upward trend of new in-moves to

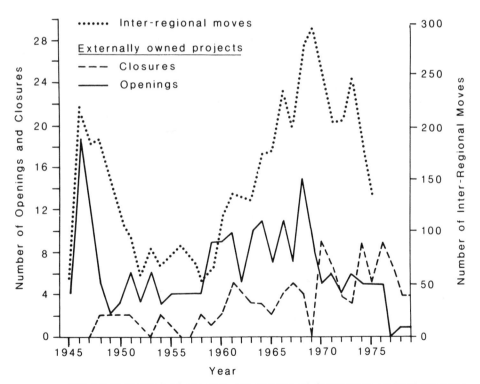

FIG 4.2 Comparison of openings and closures of Government assisted externally owned manufacturing projects in Northern Ireland with inter-regional moves in the United Kingdom.
Source: Bull et al (1982).

Northern Ireland relative to the national inter-regional mobility pattern in the 1950s (Bull et al 1982).

Thirdly, following the resumption of a strong regional policy in Great Britain in 1960, which may be expected to have increased the relative attractiveness of other assisted areas *vis-à-vis* Northern Ireland, the region began to lose out in terms of share of total inter-regional movement. Based on comparison of the data in Nunn (1980) and Bull et al (1982), for example, it appears that the level of new externally owned openings in Northern Ireland was equivalent to around 10 per cent of total inter-regional movement in the United Kingdom in 1960: by 1968, when movement was at a peak, this figure had fallen to 5 per cent and by the early 1970s it had fallen further to between 2 and 3 per cent, as the fall-off in investment in Northern Ireland was more severe than nationally (Figure 4.2). While the post-1968 experience suggested that the political violence has had a discouraging effect on potential inward investment (Rowthorn 1981, 1987; Harrison 1982), it does appear that Northern Ireland was losing its competitiveness and attractiveness in the early 1960s as the regional policy framework nationally was modified and strengthened (Black et al 1967).

This pattern of movement has implications for estimates of the employment impact of regional policy in Northern Ireland and nationally. The impact of regional policy on the immigrant sector (ie excluding any intra-regional impact on existing or new indigenous enterprises) in the United Kingdom Development Areas is shown in Table 4.3 for the period 1960–81. In employment terms Northern Ireland was a major beneficiary of industrial movement in the United Kingdom in the 1960s, due in part to inward investment activity in the late 1950s and early 1960s. However, the region has entirely lost out in this respect in the 1970s as the volume of inter-regionally mobile investment fell (Nunn 1980; Pounce 1981). Northern Ireland's image problem intensified (Harrison 1982) and project closures increased (Bull et al 1982).

TABLE 4.3   Estimated net employment[1] impact of regional policy, United Kingdom development areas, 1960–1981 (000)

	1960–71	1971–81
Net employment in policy induced moves in British development areas	144	48
Net employment in policy induced moves to Northern Ireland	26	0
Total employment in policy induced moves in United Kingdom development areas	170	48
Northern Ireland as percentage of total	15.3	0

[1] Net employment is defined as employment in openings during the period minus closures in the same period, in policy induced moves to the United Kingdom Development Areas.
Sources: Moore et al (1986); Canning et al (1987).

Northern Ireland's progressive difficulties in maintaining the flow of new inward investment in the late 1960s and 1970 is reinforced from an analysis of Department of Trade and Industry data on factory movement (Moore et al 1986). Of the 1,200 or so factory moves to Development Areas (14 per cent of total industrial movement in the United Kingdom) recorded for the period 1966–78, around 4 per cent were attracted to Northern Ireland (Table 4.4). However, confirming the evidence presented above, there was a very sharp fall in the regional share in the period 1972–78. In employment terms, Northern Ireland has attracted the smallest number of jobs (around 7,000) through policy induced industrial movement (Table 4.4). However, this is likely to underestimate the employment effects of industrial movement to the region for two reasons (Moore et al 1986): firstly, significant numbers of projects were attracted to Northern Ireland in the late 1950s and have not been included in the employment estimates in Table 4.4 (NIEC 1983b); secondly, many of the projects attracted to Northern Ireland in the late 1950s and early 1960s (notably in synthetic fibres) were very much larger than average, and this has not been allowed for in the estimating methodology (Moore et al 1986, 58).

TABLE 4.4   Industrial movement to the development areas

| Development areas in | Factory moves into the development areas | | | | | | Employment associated with policy-induced movement to development areas 1960–76 | |
| | 1966–71 | | 1972–78 | | 1966–78 | | | |
	Number	%	Number	%	Number	%	(000)	%
Northern region	149	22.9	120	21.4	269	22.1	65	32.5
Wales	206	31.6	208	37.1	414	34.0	59	29.5
Scotland	146	22.4	130	23.2	276	22.6	39	19.5
South West	80	12.3	89	15.9	169	13.9	24	12.0
Merseyside	24	3.7	16	2.9	40	3.3	6	3.0
Northern Ireland	47	7.2	3	0.5	50	4.1	7	3.5
Total	652	100.0	566	100.0	1,218	100.0	200	100.0

Source: Moore et al (1986, pp 56–59).

The comprehensive employment analyses quoted above are estimates of the regional policy effect. It is possible, however, to extend the discussion to include actual employment data (unadjusted for any deadweight or displacement effects) generated in Northern Ireland through industrial movement. From the data in Table 4.5 the fall in Northern Ireland's share of industrial movement to the peripheral regions of the United Kingdom in the 1970s is confirmed. With the exception of the 1971–75 period, Northern Ireland's share of employment in industrial moves exceeded the region's share of projects, indicating a particular attractiveness of the region to larger than average projects, and an investment category in which Northern Ireland had a particularly competitive incentive package (Plant Location International 1983). Of greater significance, however, is the evidence that Northern Ireland attracted almost no mobile investment from Great Britain between 1976 and 1980 but continued to be successful in attracting foreign investment. The region attracted 16 per cent of such projects and 30 per cent of the related employment between 1976 and 1980, and although the Northern Ireland share fell in the 1980s it was still higher than the overall share of moves to peripheral regions in the late 1960s (Table 4.5). However, in interpreting these figures it must be noted that between 1981 and 1986 there were fewer than 20 foreign origin projects in total attracted to the peripheral regions of the United Kingdom, with employment of under 18,000 in 1986. Although Northern Ireland has been relatively successful in attracting these projects, the small scale of the investment and employment they represent calls into question suggestions that inward foreign investment can and should remain a major element in an industrial development strategy for Northern Ireland (Teague 1987, 1989).

TABLE 4.5   Industrial movement to the peripheral regions of the United Kingdom,[1] 1966–1986

	NI as % total peripheral regions	
Origin	Number of moves	Employment in moves
1966–70 (GB and foreign origins)	11.1	15.0[2]
1971–75 (GB and foreign origins)	5.6	5.8[2]
1976–80 (GB and foreign origins)	5.2	10.1[3]
of which:		
GB origins only	0.7	0.1
Foreign origins only	16.1	28.6[3]
1981–86 (foreign origins only)	13.4	19.6

[1] Northern Ireland, Northern, Scotland, Wales.
[2] Based on 1975 employment.
[3] Based on 1980 employment.
Sources: British Business, 17 June 1983; Hansard, 13 April 1988; DTI.

THE EMPLOYMENT CONTRIBUTION OF ID PROJECTS

Reference has already been made above to the estimated employment contribution of regional policy, in particular through the stimulation of industrial movement, in Northern Ireland within the United Kingdom context. It is possible to analyse in greater detail the direct employment impact of industrial development policy in Northern Ireland using detailed unpublished employment records. This data source is not available for other development areas with the same degree of temporal coverage as in Northern Ireland, and has been used in a number of other studies of the industrial development process in the region (Harrison 1986a; Hoare 1982; Simpson 1984). Between 1945 and 1982, 673 projects were assisted to establish or expand their operations in Northern Ireland and had created 1.428 million man years of employment (Harrison 1986a). This is equivalent to an average of 37,570 jobs in existence in each of the 38 years of this period. While this employment creation has been insufficient to overcome or redress the imbalance between the supply of and demand for labour in Northern Ireland, it does represent a significant achievement which has prevented the exacerbation of the region's economic malaise. Over half of all projects (55 per cent) created fewer than 500 job years each. These represent only 4 per cent of the total job years created. By contrast, two-thirds of total job years created were provided in 73 projects (11 per cent of the total) each of which created more than 5,000 job years during the period as a whole, indicating clearly the dependence of the regional economy on a relatively small number of multinationals (Teague 1987).

Indigenous projects accounted for almost half of all project openings but only provided 20 per cent of total job years. Conversely, the relative importance of British (33 per cent of projects and 54 per cent of job years) and foreign (18 per cent of projects and 25 per cent of job years) owned projects was correspondingly higher (Table 4.6). The very much smaller employment potential of indigenous projects re-emphasises the problems inherent in relying on this source of investment and employment as the basis for the encouragement of self-sustaining regional economic development on a scale sufficient to preserve or improve the employment position of Northern Ireland. More generally this implies that regional development policies which are premised on the mobilisation of indigenous potential (rather than relying on an increasingly uncertain flow of inter-regionally and internationally mobile investment), such as have been proposed for Ireland (O'Farrell 1980), Great Britain (Goddard et al 1979) and the European Community (Commission of the European Communities 1981b) and are now being implemented in Northern Ireland (Stutt et al 1988), will only have a significant impact on the employment situation in the long term.

IMPACT OF CLOSURE

The impact of project closure on employment creation has been considerable (Table 4.6): almost half a million job years were created in projects which had ceased production by June 1982. This, however, represents only 34 per cent of all job years created during the period. Table 4.7 compares the percentage incidence of project closure and job loss in Northern Ireland by ownership group. For all ownership groups, with the exception of West German projects, project closures account for a lower proportion of total job years than they do of projects, and this is reflected in surviving projects (Table 4.6).

From the analysis of grant-aided industrial projects in Northern Ireland, it is clear that their recent employment performance reflects a sharp rise in the number of project closures in the 1970s: the severe recessions in the

TABLE 4.6 Employment creation in ID projects by nationality of ownership, Northern Ireland, 1945–1982 (job years)

Origin	Total	Percentage	Average per project
Openings			
Northern Ireland	290.4	20.3	883
Great Britain	775.2	54.3	3,476
North America	175.6	12.3	2,853
West Germany	38.4	2.7	2,398
Other foreign	148.1	10.4	3,526
Total	1,427.7	100.0	2,121
Closures			
Northern Ireland	84.4	17.4	703
Great Britain	284.1	58.7	2,153
North America	341.8	6.6	2,117
West Germany	23.5	4.9	3,913
Other foreign	60.3	12.5	2,739
Total	484.1	100.0	1,636
Survivors			
Northern Ireland	206.0	21.8	986
Great Britain	491.1	52.1	5,397
North America	143.8	15.2	3,060
West Germany	14.9	1.6	1,490
Other foreign	87.8	9.3	4,390
Total	943.6	100.0	2,503

Source: Harrison (1985).

periods 1973–74 and 1979–82 have not, apparently, affected the flow of new project openings (Bull et al 1982). However, there has been an increased reliance on new and expanding smaller indigenous projects rather than the new inward investment in large and medium-sized projects which characterised the period 1960–74 (Harrison 1982, 1986a; NIEC 1983b; Bull et al 1982). The employment performance of these more recent openings also suggests that the industrial development agencies have been prepared to accept more risky projects (typified by De Lorean and Lear Fan) in the face of increased international competition for a declining flow of internationally mobile investment against a background of an unattractive location for such investment in Northern Ireland due to the violence (Teague 1989; Harrison 1986a).

Against this, however, over half of all ID projects which have closed between 1945 and 1982 have done so since 1972 and the annual incidence of project closure, which has been rising since the 1950s, has more than doubled since 1974, reflecting the severe impact of regional, national and worldwide recession on the regional economy (Bull and Hart 1987). In the longer term the high incidence of plant closures in the current recession, rather than *in situ* contraction, as a means of adjusting to changing economic circumstances, represents a serious eroding of productive capacity which significantly reduces the potential of the Northern Ireland economy to respond to any recovery in the national and international economy (Black 1981).

These plant closures reflect the operation of at least three factors: the branch plant syndrome (Watts 1981), variations in economic conditions in both the source nation and the host region (Torneden 1975; Forsyth 1972) and the age of the project (Bull et al 1982). American companies investing in Northern Ireland since the early 1950s, as is true of much of US direct investment throughout Europe in the post-war period, was primarily motivated by the need and desire to develop ready access to the British and European markets (Hood and Young 1983). As such, their commitment to stay in production may have been rather greater than that of a British company (and to a lesser extent one from Europe) which established a branch plant in Northern Ireland primarily to take advantage of the financial assistance available and which, therefore, may have been more susceptible to rationalisation and restructuring during a recession (Bull and Hart 1987).

This aspect of the branch plant syndrome (which may be reinforced by differences in the level of devolved functional and decision-making autonomy) has been intensified by the fact that the British economy has been very much weaker than the United States and West European (particularly West German) economies throughout the 1970s and early 1980s when most project closures took place. Although the relatively low incidence of closure among indigenous projects appears to indicate a greater commitment to production and employment in the region, reflecting the fact that the principal decision makers are based in the region, and offers some encouragement for future regional development, these projects have tended to be smaller, in employment terms, than inward investment projects and their long term stability has yet to be adequately demonstrated. Certainly, on the basis of one recent study, there appears to be no significant difference in the durability of employment in small indigenous ID assisted enterprises and in larger indigenous and externally controlled ID projects after making allowance for project age (NIEC 1985a).

Finally, in accounting for the observed differences in the incidence of closure among projects of different nationalities of ownership, it is important to note that there have been a number of distinct phases in ID investment in Northern Ireland. Projects from Great Britain dominated ID in the late 1940s and 1950s, while foreign direct investment only became significant in the 1960s (Bull et al 1982). It is recognised that the potential for divestment increases with an increasing stock of ID investment (Boddewyn 1979; Van den Bulche et al 1979), and in particular that the probability of plant closure and divestment increases with the age of the plant (Bull et al 1982). This increases the likelihood of structural change necessitated by technological advances and changing comparative cost structures (Frobel et al 1980), and in the absence of reinvestment programmes, leaves the regions' dependency on externally controlled direct investment progressively more exposed to the contraction,

TABLE 4.7 Project closure and job loss in ID assisted firms by nationality of ownership, Northern Ireland, 1945–1982

| | Closures as percentage of all openings | |
	Projects	Job years
Northern Ireland	36.5	29.1
Great Britain	59.2	36.7
North America	24.2	18.1
West Germany	37.5	61.2
Other foreign	52.4	40.7
Total	43.9	33.9

Source: As Table 4.6.

rationalisation and ultimate closure of plants producing products at the end of the product life cycle (Vernon 1966).

OWNERSHIP AND EMPLOYMENT

Within the Northern Ireland economy, projects assisted under the industrial development programme have made a significant contribution to regional manufacturing employment, and since the mid-1960s actual manufacturing employment in Northern Ireland has exceeded that expected on the basis of manufacturing industry performance in Great Britain (Canning et al 1987). In terms of direct employment, in 1950 ID employment represented 5 per cent of total manufacturing employment. By 1960 this had grown to 17 per cent (32,000 jobs) and at its peak in 1974 ID employment accounted for 71,400 jobs, equivalent to almost 43 per cent of manufacturing employment. Despite the loss of 26,600 jobs between 1974 and 1982 this sector still accounted for 42 per cent of manufacturing employment in the region (Harrison 1986a). This change in the performance of the ID sector in the mid and late 1970s reflects the operation of two factors (NIEC 1983b). Firstly, there is a general tendency for employment in any project or cohort of projects to build up to a peak over time before declining again (SEPD 1983; Simpson 1984). In the absence of a continued inflow of new projects, therefore, there will be a natural fall in employment in the ID assisted sector. Secondly, superimposed on this 'rise and fall' profile is the impact of recession on employment as firms either reduce their employment or close completely. From the detailed analysis of employment profiles carried out by the Northern Ireland Economic Council it appears that the post-1973 recessions have accelerated the tendency for employment to decline from a peak with the result that actual ID employment in 1982 has been reduced considerably, compared with what would have been expected in the absence of recession, as job losses in more recently established projects have been brought forward (NIEC 1983b).

From an analysis of the contribution of indigenous, British, American and other foreign inward investment to employment change in Northern Ireland, it is clear that since the mid-1950s there has only been a marginal

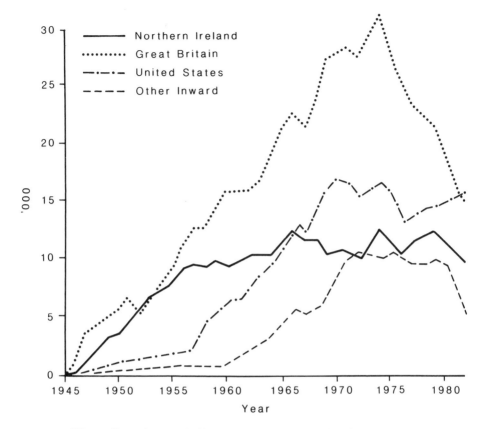

FIG 4.3 ID employment in Northern Ireland by nationality of ownership, 1945–1982.
Source: NIEC (1983b).

increase in employment in indigenous projects, which collectively employed just under 10,000 in both 1956 and 1982 (Figure 4.3). Employment growth in externally owned projects was significant in the 1950s (British owned projects) and 1960s (US and other foreign owned projects), and employment peaked in 1974. However, by 1982 almost 40 per cent of that peak employment had been lost as companies restructured to meet the changed economic climate of the mid and late 1970s.

Indeed, it appears that externally controlled industry may have been more susceptible to recession than indigenous industry, whether ID assisted or not (Table 4.8). Between 1950 and 1979 indigenous non-ID assisted employment in Northern Ireland fell fairly steadily at a rate of between 2.5 per cent and 3 per cent annually; the post-1974 recession appears to have led to no more than a marginal increase in the rate of job loss. However, between 1979 and 1982 the rate of employment loss in the non-assisted sector more than trebled to 9.5 per cent. Indigenous ID assisted employment, which initially had grown rapidly from a very small base in 1950, grew more slowly in the 1960s and early 1970s, reflecting the general absence of new and expanding ID projects in the 1950s, and then also fell sharply after 1979. There was continued rapid growth in total non-indigenous ID employment up to 1974, with the major growth phase for employment in American owned projects during the period 1950–59 and for other foreign controlled employment between 1959 and 1974. Between 1974 and 1979, however, it appears that externally controlled industry was in general more susceptible to recession than was the indigenously controlled sector. This position contrasts with the Scottish experience, which suggests that the post-1974 net employment performance of overseas incomer openings has been stronger than that of other openings and has not been due to either industry structure or size differences (Scottish Economic Planning Department 1983). However, the poor Northern Ireland performance is largely due to the very poor employment performance of projects originating in Great Britain, employment which fell by over 7 per cent per annum during the period. Indeed, while these projects accounted for 44 per cent of total ID employment in Northern Ireland in 1974, they contributed 78 per cent of all ID assisted jobs lost between 1974 and 1979.

TABLE 4.8   ID industry and manufacturing employment change, Northern Ireland, 1950–1982 (% per annum)

| | Employment change | | | |
	1950–59	1959–74	1974–79	1979–82
Indigenous non-ID	−2.8	−2.6	−2.9	−9.5
Indigenous ID	13.0	1.8	−0.3	−8.4
Total indigenous	−2.3	−2.3	−2.6	−9.3
Total non-indigenous ID	12.6	7.3	−4.6	−8.8
Great Britain	11.5	5.4	−7.2	−12.6
North America	20.6	8.3	−2.7	1.9
Other foreign	3.4	18.8	−0.6	−24.6
Total manufacturing (ID and non-ID)	−1.3	0.2	−3.3	−9.2

Source: As Table 4.6.

After 1979 there was a general increase in rates of job loss for all ownership groups with the exception of projects of American origin: this reflected the build-up of employment in a small number of large American investments which were only coming into production in the late 1970s, including the now defunct De Lorean sports car project. British-owned projects continued to shed labour rapidly in the period 1979–82, although not quite as rapidly as did the non-assisted sector. However, projects of predominantly European origin have recorded the most dramatic employment losses: in 1979 this group of projects accounted for 17 per cent of total ID project employment; by 1982 employment in this group had fallen by almost half, representing 34 per cent of the total net loss of employment in the ID sector in Northern Ireland. This very poor employment performance reflects the impact of two major plant closures, those of the Grundig audio products plant and the British Enkalon synthetic fibres production facility, which together at their peak had employed almost 4,000 workers.

INDUSTRIAL STRUCTURE AND DIVERSIFICATION

The contribution made by the ID programme to industrial diversification has been widely discussed (Steed and Thomas 1971; NIEC 1983b; Bull 1984). From the data in Table 4.9 it is clear that ID employment has been concentrated in textiles, instrument and electrical engineering and, to a lesser extent, vehicles and aircraft, food, drink and tobacco, and clothing and footwear. In recent years, other manufacturing (predominantly rubber products) has become increasingly significant (Table 4.9a). To a large extent this reflects not only the predominance of light engineering in growth-induced industrial mobility in the United Kingdom (Steed and Thomas 1971) but also the concentration in Northern Ireland during the 1960s and 1970s of the United Kingdom man-made fibres industry, which was dominated by a few very large multinationals (Northern Ireland Office 1974). Within each industry the relative importance of ID employment varies considerably (Table 4.9b). Some industries, notably instrument and electrical engineering, other manufacturing (rubber) and (although not shown separately on the table) man-made fibres production and automotive components have been almost entirely the creation of ID policy. In other sectors, such as textiles other than man-made fibres, mechanical engineering and clothing and footwear, the importance of ID employment has

TABLE 4.9 Employment in ID assisted industry by industrial sector,[1] Northern Ireland, 1959–1982

	a Percentage of total ID employment			b ID as % of total industry employment		
	1959	1974	1982	1959	1974	1982
Food, drink and tobacco	15.3	9.4	11.2	22.3	25.5	26.3
Coal and petroleum products	—	1.6	2.9	1.8	40.9	47.2
Metal goods	2.0	3.1	2.0	41.3	46.2	34.1
Mechanical engineering	4.0	6.7	6.5	14.9	38.9	40.7
Instrument and electrical engineering	24.3	19.5	15.4	95.9	91.8	85.9
Vehicles and aircraft	13.0	5.0	14.1	27.2	33.1	58.1
Textiles	21.9	31.7	17.9	11.7	57.4	57.1
Clothing and footwear	11.6	9.7	12.5	13.7	30.1	40.1
Miscellaneous[2]	5.3	3.7	4.5	10.6	14.9	14.7
Other manufacturing	2.7	9.8	13.6	84.7	89.2	93.6
Total	100.0	100.0	100.0	17.3	42.6	42.1
Total ID employment (000)	(30.1)	(71.4)	(44.8)			

[1] 1968 SIC.
[2] Bricks, pottery, glass and cement; Timber and furniture; Paper, printing and publishing.
Source: Based on data supplied by DED and IDB.

been broadly comparable to that in manufacturing as a whole. In the remaining sectors the ID employment proportion has been much lower – 26 per cent in food, drink and tobacco and 15 per cent in miscellaneous manufacturing in 1982.

Between 1959 and 1974 total ID employment rose steadily at a rate varying between 3 and 7 per cent per annum, compared with declining non-ID employment. Between 1974 and 1982, however, ID employment began to fall also, and in the period 1974–79 in particular ID employment was lost at a faster rate than non-ID employment. Although there are some sectoral variations in the temporal pattern of employment change before 1974 (notably in aircraft and vehicles and textiles) which may reflect sectoral differences in cyclical reactivity, most interest attaches to the profile of change in the post-1974 period.

Between 1974 and 1979 ID employment fell more rapidly than did non-ID employment in manufacturing industry. To a large extent this reflects the poor employment performance of three industries – mechanical engineering, instrument and electrical engineering and textiles – in which the net loss of ID employment was higher, both relatively and absolutely, than the loss of non-ID employment. In other sectors, notably coal and petroleum products, aircraft and vehicles and miscellaneous industries, ID employment continued to increase; and in the remaining industries ID employment declined less rapidly than did non-ID employment. The most striking feature of the 1979–82 period is the almost universal increase in the rate of employment loss – the most noticeable exception is ID employment in aircraft and vehicles, which grew by over 10 per cent per annum during this most recent period, reflecting in part the build-up of employment in the De Lorean sports car project which was still in production in June 1982, the cut-off date for this analysis (Table 4.10).

The greatest relative and absolute loss of employment, in both the ID and non-ID sectors, has occurred in the textiles sector. Between 1979 and 1982 over 8,600 ID jobs were lost in this sector, representing 61.3 per cent of the net fall in ID employment in the period. To a large extent this reflects the collapse of the man-made fibres industry in Northern Ireland following the withdrawal of major producers such as ICI, Courtaulds and British Enkalon from the province (NIEC 1983b), and re-emphasises the openness of the Northern Ireland economy to changes in the international conditions of demand and production.

Over much of the post-war period the rate of growth of the Northern Ireland economy (measured as the rate of growth of GNP per head at constant prices) has been similar to that of the United Kingdom as a whole (NIEC 1983a). There have, however, been two exceptions to this pattern: in the period 1958–68 the Northern Ireland economy expanded by 3.5 per cent per annum compared with a national rate of 2.8 per cent and between 1979 and 1981 the Northern Ireland economy contracted almost twice as rapidly as the national economy (−5.0 per cent per annum compared to −2.6 per cent per annum). A major source of the high average growth rates in the 1960s was increased capital investment, particularly by manufacturing industry. This is, of course, reflected in the job promotions and industrial movement statistics discussed earlier which show a significant increase after 1960. Closer examination of the figures demonstrates that a substantial proportion of this growth in manufacturing investment is accounted for by two sectors: shipbuilding and textiles. Between 1964 and 1974 the textiles industry (which includes both natural and man-made fibres) represented 40 per cent of total manufacturing investment. Much of this was accounted for by a relatively small number of large inward investment projects by man-made fibres producers in the mid-1960s (NIEC 1983b). The attraction of these projects reflected not only the renewed drive to attract new investment to Northern Ireland but also the rapid expansion of synthetic fibres producing capacity worldwide (Shaw and Shaw 1980).

In retrospect this component of regional growth strategy was risky, as it depended to a considerable extent on sustained demand for products which historically had exhibited a cyclical pattern. Following the sharp increase in oil prices in late 1973 the competitive position of the world synthetic fibres industry (which depended on oil feedstock as a basic raw material) *vis-à-vis* natural fibres deteriorated. Subsequent recessions in the mid-1970s led to a general reduction in world demand for textile and clothing products which, together with the loss of competitiveness, depressed demand for synthetic fibres. The result was considerable over-capacity in the industry (Shaw and Shaw 1983). The position of the United Kingdom fibres producing industry was not helped in the late 1970s by an increase in synthetic fibre imports from developing countries and then, particularly in 1980 as a consequence of the strength of sterling against the dollar and the United States Government's cheap energy policy, from the United States. The impact on Northern Ireland was dramatic – during 1980 alone, when United Kingdom synthetic fibres capacity was reduced by 26 per cent (compared with a 4 per cent fall in Western Europe), 73 per cent of capacity in Northern Ireland was lost (Sector Working Party 1981). By 1982 the industry had all but disappeared from Northern Ireland, which at its peak represented one quarter of United Kingdom fibres producing capacity: employment had fallen from a 1974 peak of over 10,000 to less than 1,350 by June 1982, and most of these jobs were lost after 1979. Largely as a consequence of the collapse of the man-made fibres industry ID employment in textiles fell by 14,000 between 1974 and 1982 and ID employment in textiles as a proportion of total ID employment in Northern Ireland fell from 32 per cent in 1974 to 18 per cent in 1982 (Table 4.10).

4. Impact of selective assistance to small firms

The preceding discussion of the impact of ID policy has been based on the analysis of the impact of that part of the package administered by the IDB and its predecessors. From the analysis, it is clear that indigenous industrial

TABLE 4.10 Employment change in ID and non-ID assisted industry,[1] Northern Ireland, 1959–1982 (% per annum)

		Employment change					
		1959– 1964	1964– 1969	1969– 1974	1974– 1979	1979– 1982	1959– 1982
Food, drink and tobacco:	ID	−1.4	4.8	4.0	−0.9	−7.7	0.3
	non-ID	3.5	0.7	−0.5	−2.7	−6.2	−0.6
Coal and petroleum products:	ID	112.7	6.7	−6.5	5.0	−3.1	18.5
	non-ID	8.9	0.8	−6.9	−5.5	6.0	0.0
Metals and other metal goods:	ID	19.2	7.4	2.5	−3.4	−19.7	2.3
	non-ID	11.7	9.5	0.5	−5.0	−2.2	3.7
Mechanical engineering:	ID	8.1	12.7	8.1	−6.7	−2.3	4.3
	non-ID	9.9	0.5	−8.0	−3.3	−12.2	−2.1
Instrument and electrical eng.:	ID	8.6	1.4	2.8	−8.8	−7.4	−0.3
	non-ID	7.2	20.3	2.1	4.8	−9.8	5.8
Aircraft and vehicles:	ID	−5.4	8.1	−2.7	4.2	10.5	2.1
	non-ID	−2.1	−1.7	−3.6	−6.0	−4.7	−3.5
Textiles:	ID	7.7	10.7	7.2	−5.8	−21.8	0.8
	non-ID	−4.5	−6.6	−9.8	−4.6	−16.5	−7.8
Clothing and footwear:	ID	12.2	4.7	−3.2	−2.3	−2.3	2.0
	non-ID	−3.8	−0.4	−2.6	−2.8	−15.5	−4.2
Miscellaneous industries:[2]	ID	7.7	4.2	−1.6	2.6	−12.2	1.0
	non-ID	0.7	1.7	−0.6	−1.0	−6.5	−0.7
Other manufacturing:[3]	ID	19.1	25.3	3.8	0.0	−4.5	9.3
	non-ID	—	—	—	—	−	—
Total manufacturing:[4]	ID	7.2	7.2	3.3	−3.5	−8.7	1.8
	non-ID	−2.7	−1.8	−5.4	−2.9	−9.5	−3.6

[1] 1968 SIC.
[2] Bricks, pottery, glass and cement; Timber and furniture; Paper, printing and publishing.
[3] As almost all employment in this industry has been ID assisted, it is not possible to calculate meaningful rates of employment change for the non-ID sector.
[4] Excluding shipbuilding and marine engineering.
Source: As Table 4.9.

development has provided a more stable source of employment opportunities in Northern Ireland but on a scale insufficient to make a significant impact on the regional economic problem. Discussion of this aspect of policy in the chapter, however, has been incomplete. Since 1971 LEDU has had specific responsibility for job creation among small businesses in Northern Ireland (see Chapter 5). In particular, the agency was set up with the objectives of promoting employment in small businesses, encouraging the establishment of new enterprises and fostering craft industry (Busteed 1976; Cooley 1976; Hart 1984). Although initially intended to concentrate its activities on the support of small (under 50 employees) firms in manufacturing in the rural west of Northern Ireland, LEDU's remit was broadened in 1980 to include service industries and problem inner city areas in Belfast, to safeguard employment in viable companies and seek out mobile small industry from the United Kingdom mainland (Hart 1984).

Between its establishment in 1971 and 1981/82 LEDU was involved in the promotion of almost 12,800 jobs in 1,160 separate projects (Table 4.11).

Since then the scale of LEDU's activities has expanded rapidly: between 1982/83 and 1987/88 almost twice as many jobs and projects were promoted as in the preceding period through selective assistance for employment creation. If the Enterprise Grant Scheme, introduced in the early 1980s to support individuals with business ideas in the move into self-employment, is included, the expansion of LEDU's activities in the 1980s appears even more dramatic. On average, indigenous small business projects have provided over 4,000 job promotions annually since 1983: this is almost equivalent to the total jobs promoted annually through selective financial assistance to inward investment and existing medium to large ID projects by the IDB and represents a very marked contrast to the pre-1971 period, which was dominated almost exclusively by the attraction and subsequent expansion of inward investment projects.

The number of jobs actually created and surviving in LEDU assisted small business projects in Northern Ireland grew steadily from around 400 in 1973 to almost 5,500 in 1980 before falling slightly to just under 5,000 in 1982, reflecting the impact of widespread recession in the regional economy (NIEC 1985a, 11). However, the dramatically increased level of promotional activity in the small firm sector by LEDU in the 1980s is reflected in a corresponding increase in actual jobs created and surviving in LEDU assisted businesses: by the end of 1987 there were over 10,000 such jobs on the ground, representing the equivalent of almost 10 per cent of total manufacturing employment in Northern Ireland (Table 4.11).

As recent research by the Northern Ireland Economic Council indicates, the employment created in small business projects assisted by LEDU is no less stable than that created in IDB assisted projects over a similar time period (NIEC 1985a). Furthermore, it appears that indigenous LEDU sponsored projects are more likely to source their purchases of both raw

TABLE 4.11   LEDU job promotion activity, 1971–1987/88

	Employment related[1]		Enterprise grant[2]		Total promotions		Actual employment created[3]
	Projects	Jobs	Projects	Jobs	Projects	Jobs	
1971–1981/82	1,160	12,784	—	—	1,160	12,784	4,993[4]
1982/83	270	2,425	114	125	384	2,550	6,177
1983/84	408	3,392	233	266	641	3,658	7,896
1984/85	387	3,583	381	426	768	4,009	na
1985/86	325	3,403	441	485	766	3,888	na
1986/87	342	3,770	607	773	949	4,543	9,329
1987/88	336	3,804	566	766	902	4,570	10,335
Total 1971–1987/88	3,228	33,161	2,342	2,841	5,570	36,002	

[1] Selective financial assistance for employment creation in new and expanding projects.
[2] Assistance to individuals with a basic project to set up in business on their own account.
[3] Based on projects in receipt of employment related assistance only, excluding enterprise grants.
[4] Figure for February 1982.
Source: LEDU.

materials and components and business services from suppliers in Northern Ireland than are other ID assisted projects: in 1983, for example, 57 per cent of the expenditure of LEDU assisted projects on raw materials and components was spent within Northern Ireland compared with only 36 per cent for ID assisted projects as a whole. The equivalent figures for services expenditure were 80 per cent and 59 per cent respectively (NIEC 1986a). This suggests that support for local enterprise will have a rather greater direct inter-industry regional multiplier impact than will support for other forms of industrial development. Against this, however, LEDU assisted projects were also less likely to sell to customers outside Northern Ireland (NIEC 1986a).

Given concern about the quality of many of the businesses established with LEDU support, in terms of their general reliance on a purely local market with the potentially high displacement effects this implies (Hart 1984; Harrison 1987; Harvey 1987), LEDU has recently acknowledged the need to devote more attention to identifying and concentrating assistance on those services and support which will increase the survival rate and ultimate growth of small firms rather than simply promoting increasing numbers of new small companies (LEDU 1986). While this change of emphasis, if followed through, may reduce the number of projects and jobs promoted annually it should ultimately lead to further increases in the net job creation impact of the assistance offered. In the absence of new inward investment on anything like the scale of the 1960s and early 1970s, and in the light of the massive wave of firm closures among externally owned plants in the early 1980s which has reduced the base from which economic regeneration and employment growth can come (Black 1981; Bull and Hart 1987), maximising the employment contribution of the small firm sector, while not a panacea in view of the magnitude of the economic problems of Northern Ireland, must play an important part in any future industrial development strategy (NIEC 1986b).

IMPACT OF AUTOMATIC CAPITAL GRANTS

Earlier in this chapter it was noted that industrial development policy in Northern Ireland was until recently based on two separate schemes of assistance: selective financial assistance for employment creation (discussed above in terms of its impact on inward investment and medium to large indigenous projects and on small businesses), and automatic Standard Capital Grants. The Standard Capital Grant scheme, as an automatic non-employment related scheme, dates back to 1951 in Northern Ireland (Harrison 1989a). It was originally introduced to stimulate the modernisation of existing industry in Northern Ireland and thereby complement the selective financial assistance introduced in 1945, which was primarily geared to the attraction of new inward investment from Great Britain and overseas (Murie et al 1974). As Harris (1988) has recently pointed out, the original capital grants scheme in Northern Ireland was initially introduced to help indigenous industry modernise and improve efficiency, with an implicit acceptance that short-run substitution effects (of capital for labour) thus encouraged would give way to an output effect and hence a higher demand for labour. The efficiency criterion, however, was dropped in 1954 and was also absent from the 1966 investment grant scheme (Harrison 1989a). However, in Northern Ireland as in Great Britain, the 1966 investment grants scheme linked the payment of grant not to replacement investment and modernisation of the capital stock but to boosting net investment and increasing productive capacity. Nationally, this was to lead to increased exports and an improved balance of payments position; regionally, it was designed to facilitate the redistribution of industry to areas where there was excess capacity (Harris 1988, 4). The effects of capital subsidies, therefore, may include: the modernisation and improved efficiency of the capital stock in the region; and increased levels of net investment by indigenous enterprises, leading to higher output and export levels, the introduction of new products and, depending on the relative magnitude of the output and substitution effects, increased employment.

The scale of investment under Standard Capital Grants in Northern Ireland has been significant. Between 1966 and 1987 a total of £885 million had been paid under the investment and Standard Capital Grant schemes in Northern Ireland in support of total investment of almost £3 billion (constant 1984 prices) (Department of Economic Development 1985). Take-up of the scheme has been dominated by three sectors; food, drink and tobacco (19 per cent), engineering and metal goods (18 per cent) and textiles (16 per cent). Comparing expenditure in the periods 1968/69 to 1975/76 and 1976/77 to 1983/84 there has been a sharp fall in the share of payments going to the engineering sector: this accounted for 22 per cent of total payments before 1977 and only 13 per cent in the later period. This largely reflects the fact that in the period 1969/71 the figures are distorted by a very high level of Standard Capital Grant payments in support of a major investment in the shipbuilding industry in the region (Harrison 1989b). In the textiles industry, by contrast, there was a substantial increase in payments between the two periods, despite the major difficulties faced by this sector in the late 1970s. To a large extent this increase reflects the short term behaviour of multinational synthetic fibre producers: this industry received around 70 per cent of all Standard Capital Grant payments to the textiles sector between 1976/77 and 1982/83 as the industry attempted to restructure and adapt, unsuccessfully, to changing market and competitive conditions (NIEC 1983b).

These differences in the sectoral take-up of Standard Capital Grant reflect in part the relationship between Standard Capital Grant and selective financial assistance in Northern Ireland discussed above. As alternative rather than supplementary schemes of assistance, the balance between Standard Capital Grant and selective assistance may vary depending on the nature and purpose of the investment being undertaken. Two sectoral examples – textiles and food, drink and tobacco – illustrate the point (Harrison 1986b). During the 1960s and early 1970s the synthetic fibres industry received substantial selective assistance for employment creation: between 1968 and 1972, for example, this industry received £182 million (at constant 1982 prices) in selective assistance (NIEC 1983b), and it is likely that this considerable expenditure has contributed to the very low level of Standard Capital Grant payments in the textile sector as a whole relative to overall sectoral investment performance. In food, drink and tobacco, by contrast, the proportion of total Standard Capital Grant payments received has been higher than expected on the basis of the investment record of the sector. This sector, and in particular the capital intensive tobacco industry, has continued to invest heavily while reducing employment. Under such conditions of jobless growth, with investment associated with a process of capital–labour substitution, automatic Standard Capital Grants, made available without employment conditions, are likely to be more important than employment related selective assistance. Indeed, between 1981 and 1984 the two main tobacco companies in Northern Ireland received almost £7 million in Standard Capital Grant payments and nothing in selective assistance, and have since then continued to restructure, close plants and shed employment (Harrison 1986b).

There is some evidence to suggest that the output effects of capital subsidies may outweigh the substitution effects, particularly in capital intensive sectors (Harris 1988: see also Swales 1981; Woodward 1974; Guccione and Gillen 1982; Armstrong and Taylor 1986, 195–203). Furthermore, there is considerable evidence to suggest that companies are more likely to take into account, through formal investment appraisal, automatic Standard Capital Grants where the eligibility criteria are known in advance than is the case with selective assistance (Begg and McDowall 1987; Allen et al 1986), although this does not necessarily imply that the availability of such grants determines the investment decision (Walker and Krist 1980).

In principle, therefore, there may be economic justification for the retention of automatic capital grants. However, recent experience in Northern Ireland suggests that, despite the apparent objectives of the Standard Capital Grant scheme to increase net investment rather than simply fund replacement investment, the latter has come to dominate in the utilisation of the scheme (Harrison 1986b). Therefore, while the considerable expenditure on Standard Capital Grants may have encouraged at least some inward investment projects to reinvest and re-equip in Northern Ireland rather than disinvest from the region (Harris 1988), the apparent lack of additionality and correspondingly high level of deadweight associated with the scheme (according to reports of an unpublished Department of Economic Development evaluation) suggest that the scheme has not made a major contribution to the restructuring and diversification of the Northern Ireland economy. Following the review of the national Regional Development Grant scheme in 1983 and later evidence from an internal review of Standard Capital Grants that much of the investment supported by Standard Capital Grant payments in Northern Ireland would have been undertaken in the absence of assistance, the scheme was terminated in 1987, leaving the package of industrial development incentives on offer in Northern Ireland entirely job related and selective.

5. Conclusion

Regional industrial development policy in Northern Ireland has evolved over the last fifty years in the context of the development of British regional policy as a whole. As such, and in keeping with the wider emphasis of regional policies in other developed economies, this policy has relied on the encouragement of industrial mobility and the attraction or redirection of new manufacturing capacity (McCrone 1969; Klaassen and Molle 1983). The particular form that regional policy has taken in Northern Ireland has, however, reflected the actual and perceived special needs of the region within the context of the separate administrative arrangements which have obtained there since 1921 (Harrison 1989a). Accordingly, the incentives package available in Northern Ireland has always been much more heavily orientated to the provision of selective employment related assistance than to automatic Regional Development Grants as in Great Britain, and much higher levels of assistance have been available to prospective investors in the regional economy.

From the Northern Ireland experience it appears that a policy of diversification through inward investment, supported by selective financial assistance for capital investment in employment generating projects and investment in infrastructure for industrial development, has not led to self-sustaining regional economic growth. The creation in Northern Ireland of a dual economy – a traditionally orientated indigenous sector onto which is grafted an externally owned and controlled, externally orientated and regionally unintegrated sector – has led to increased openness to variations in the international economic climate and changes in the global corporate strategies of multinational corporations and has intensified the impact of corporate restructuring policies in the face of changing international conditions of production and markets.

Given the reduction in the volume of new inward investment in the 1970s and 1980s, reflecting the reduced volume of internationally mobile investment, the increasing share of foreign direct investment taken by newly industrialised countries at the expense of Western Europe and the negative impact of political violence on the image of Northern Ireland as an investment location, divestment decisions by earlier cohorts of investments have contributed to the decline of the regional manufacturing economy in Northern Ireland over the last decade.

This chapter has discussed the Northern Ireland experience of regional policy in the United Kingdom context. Relative to the debate in regional policy within the United Kingdom and other European countries over the relative merits of selective versus automatic assistance (Bachtler 1988), this experience does not suggest that selective financial assistance will necessarily lead to a more favourable outcome than automatic incentives. Indeed, in the light of the continued evolution of regional policy in the United Kingdom, this case study is likely to reflect a historically specific stage in the development of policy.

Although the degree of commitment to and enthusiasm with regional policy has varied in the post-war period, the fundamental aims and form of regional policy have only recently become the focus for radical reassessment and political conflict (Martin 1989), in a trend which has characterised other advanced industrial economies (Albrechts et al 1989). One common theme underlying this reassessment is the recognition that the spatial configuration and underlying nature of the regional problem is changing, and as a result 'regional policies conceived and designed for the structural conditions and problems of prior decades are now generally considered to be neither appropriate nor applicable to this new and rapidly changing situation' (Martin 1989, 28).

The response to this existing situation, within the countries of the European Community, is crystallising around two sets of trends (Bachtler 1988). The first is the greater targeting of regional aid by area, sector and project type, combined with greater selectivity in the design of incentives packages. This reflects both a reduction in regional policy budgets through general cutbacks in the growth of public expenditure and in response to pressure from the European Commission for the reduction or elimination of state aids to industry. The second set of trends relates to attempts to improve the relevance of policy measures to the conditions of the late 1980s by reorientation of the sectoral emphasis (in favour of the service sector), support for innovation as a key theme and increased support for new and small firms both at national level and as part of a local economic development strategy (Albrechts et al 1989). One of the most significant emerging themes of regional policy in the late 1980s, therefore, is the indigenisation of policy, partly in response to a vacuum created by the withdrawal of central government support (Armstrong 1988). Within Northern Ireland, this indigenisation of regional policy can be seen in four respects. Firstly, the IDB is increasingly placing its emphasis on the development of a sectoral focus to its development strategy to maximise the contribution made by firms already operating in Northern Ireland (IDB 1985), a strategy clearly adopted from that followed by the Scottish Development Agency (Danson et al 1988). Secondly, continued support for the development of the small business sector in Northern Ireland has emerged as an increasingly important element of policy both through the work of LEDU in supporting the formation and development of small businesses and through the network of local enterprise organisations focused on the economic regeneration of particular areas in Northern Ireland (Harvey 1987). Thirdly, there has been an attempt to shift the focus of ID policy away from the exclusive reliance on manufacturing to include the development of employment opportunities in the service sector (IDB 1985). Fourthly, and in line with recent developments in Great Britain (HM Government 1988), attention is increasingly being focused on the provision of 'soft' assistance in the form of training, information and advice rather than financial assistance, with a view to strengthening and improving the competitiveness of local industry and thereby providing a springboard for long-term development.

This strategy represents a major break with the post-war regional policy consensus and clearly arises out of the particular political framework within which regional policy in the United Kingdom now exists (Martin 1989). There does appear to be wide acceptance of the arguments that the economic adaptability of traditional industrial areas needs to be improved, mature industries need to be rejuvenated, the regional production and employment base restructured around new technologically advanced industries, processes and services and that endogenous rather than exogenous development will be the way to regional economic revitalisation. However, this general consensus (allowing for differences of emphasis across the political spectrum) is accompanied by a fundamental debate over what constitutes the best mode of intervention for securing these goals. Regional development policy is now, more than at any other time in its fifty-year history, caught up in a fundamental debate over the politics of economic intervention (Chisholm 1987; Martin 1985).

As developed in the United Kingdom over the decade since 1979, regional policy is increasingly based on a micro-economic interpretation of the regional problem which highlights lack of competitive adaptation caused by local inefficiency and socio-economic inflexibilities in work structures, wages and management practices (HM Government 1988; Department of Economic Development 1987). Economic dynamism, it is argued, will be achieved not through large-scale regional investment and capital subsidies but by a combination of macro-economic and special policies which will create the conditions under which competitiveness and enterprise can flourish. Nationally, this emphasis has been reflected in: firstly, a reduction in the scale of traditional regional aid; secondly, a greater reliance on national rather than spatially restricted schemes to promote enterprise, reduce or eliminate socio-institutional rigidities and improve the macro-economy; and thirdly, the encouragement of free market economic recapitalisation through 'central government localism' initiatives such as enterprise zones, free ports and urban development corporations. The minimalist regional policy which results from this approach has been signalled in the substitution of social for economic justifications for the existence of a regional policy (HM Government 1983), reinforced by the subsuming of regional policy as one relatively minor differentiation of the national enterprise initiative (HM Government 1988) and reflected in the evolving role and remit of regional development agencies (Danson et al 1988; Harrison 1989a). Given the continued drift towards greater regional inequality in contemporary Britain there is widespread concern that the present policy may reinforce rather than redress these spatial inequalities. If an effective regional policy is to be designed in the United Kingdom it will only be effective to the extent to which the powers of planning and implementation are delegated to the local and regional level (Martin 1989). In this respect, Northern Ireland, with its historically separate administrative arrangements, may be able to maintain much of the traditional regional policy framework. However, if this is to make an effective contribution to economic regeneration in the region in the 1990s there will be a closer strategic integration of the traditional approach, represented by the IDB, and the new initiatives flowing from the Pathfinder process than is so far evident.

Notes

1. Jobs promoted are those which companies have contracted to use their best endeavour to provide as a condition of receiving selective financial assistance. Jobs actually created, on the other hand, are jobs which materialise on the ground. From research carried out by the Department of Economic Development it appears that jobs created represent approximately 60 per cent of jobs promoted (ITC 1982, 38). From Northern Ireland Economic Council analyses it appears that jobs created have had an average lifespan of between 6 and 8 years (NIEC 1983b).

2. These cost per job estimates are likely to significantly understate the real costs of net employment creation in the region. Firstly, they make no allowance for deadweight in regional assistance, which arises when financial assistance is given to projects which would have been implemented in any event. The existence of high levels of deadweight was a major factor underlying the decision to abolish the Standard Capital Grant scheme in Northern Ireland (Harris 1988). Secondly, these cost per job estimates do not fully identify the net additional job creation in Northern Ireland. In particular, they ignore the existence of displacement effects as the employment and output of assisted firms displaces that in competitive firms elsewhere in the regional economy, thereby reducing the overall net employment impact of the policy. Against this, however, there may be additional indirect employment created in the region through regional multiplier effects (NIEC 1986a). Furthermore, the Department of Economic Development has argued that in the case of new inward investment in particular both deadweight and displacement effects are likely to be zero, as in the absence of financial incentives mobile investment would be unlikely to consider Northern Ireland as an investment location, and a high degree of export orientation reduces the potential displacement effects in the regional economy (ITC 1982; Northern Ireland Assembly 1983). However, one recent estimate suggests that, after making allowance for these various influences, the cost of job creation through regional policy in Northern Ireland has been about £10,000 per net job created per year, around three times as high as the equivalent figure for Great Britain (Canning et al 1987).

References

Albrechts, L, Moulaert, F, Roberts, P and Swyngedouw, E (eds) (1989) *Regional Policy at the Crossroads: European Perspectives*, Jessica Kingsley, London.

Allen, K, Begg, H M, McDowell, S and Walker, G (1986) *Regional Incentives and the Investment Decision of the Firm*, Department of Trade and Industry, London.

Armstrong, H (1988) The conflict between district councils and regional policy in England and Wales. Paper presented to Regional Studies Association Conference 'Divided Nation: Regional Policy in Britain's Periphery', Belfast, September 1988.

Armstrong, H and Taylor, J (1979) *Regional Economic Policy and its Analysis*, Philip Allan, Oxford.

Armstrong, H and Taylor J (1986) *Regional Economics and Policy*, Philip Allan, Oxford.

Bachtler, J (1988) Regional policy: European perspectives and the comparative experience. Paper presented to the Regional Studies Association Conference 'Divided Nation: Regional Policy and Britain's Periphery', Belfast, September 1988.

Barlow Report (1940) *Report of the Royal Commission on the Distribution of Industrial Population*, Cmnd 6153, HMSO, London.

Begg, H M and McDowell, S (1987) The effect of regional investment incentives on company decisions, *Regional Studies*, 21, 459–70.

Black, W (1981) The effects of the recession on the economy of Northern Ireland, *Irish Banking Review*, December, 16–23.

Black, W, Cuthbert, N and Simpson, J V (1967) Investment incentives and the 1965 Act: regional implications, *Scottish Journal of Political Economy*, 14, 12–29.

Boddewyn, J (1979) Divestment: local vs foreign, and US vs European approaches, *Management International Review*, 18, 21–28.

Bull, P J (1984) The impact of government policy on industrial diversification: The Northern Ireland case, in Barr, B M and Waters, N M (eds), *Regional Diversification and Structural Change*, Tantalus Research, Vancouver.

Bull, P J, Harrison, R T and Hart, M (1982) Government assisted manufacturing activity in a peripheral region of the United Kingdom: Northern Ireland 1945–1979, in Collins, L (ed), *Industrial Decline and Regeneration: Proceedings of the 1981 Anglo-Canadian Symposium*, University of Edinburgh, Edinburgh.

Bull, P J and Hart, M (1987) Northern Ireland, in Damesick, P and Wood, P (eds), *Regional Problems, Problem Regions and Public Policy in the United Kingdom*, Clarendon Press, Oxford.

Busteed, M A (1976) Small scale economic development in Northern Ireland, *Scottish Geographical Magazine*, 3, 172–81.

Canning, D, Moore, B and Rhodes, J (1987) Economic growth in Northern Ireland: problems and prospects, in Teague, P (ed), *Beyond the Rhetoric: Politics, the Economy and Social Policy in Northern Ireland*, Lawrence and Wishart, London.

Chisholm, M (1987) Regional development: the Reagan–Thatcher legacy, *Environment and Planning C: Government and Policy*, 5, 197–218.

Commission of the European Communities (1981a) *The Regions of Europe. First Periodic Report on the Social and Economic Situation of the Regions of the Community*, COM (80) 816 Final, European Commission, Brussels.

Commission of the European Communities (1981b) *The Mobilisation of Indigenous Potential*, Internal Documentation on Regional Policy in the Community 10, European Commission, Brussels.

Cooley, A (1976) Approaches to encouraging small indigenous industrial development, in Clubley, R (ed), *Indigenous Industrial Development*, Aycliffe and Peterlee Development Corporation.

Damesick, P and Wood, P (eds) (1987) *Regional Problems, Problem Regions and Public Policy in the United Kingdom*, Clarendon Press, Oxford.

Danson, M, Lloyd G and Newlands, D (1988) The changing priorities of Development Agencies in Scotland. Paper presented to the Regional Studies Association Conference 'Divided Nation: Regional Policy in Britain's Periphery', Belfast, September 1988.

Department of Economic Development (1985) *Review of Standard Capital Grants, Information Paper by the Department of Economic Development*, Department of Economic Development, Belfast.

Department of Economic Development (1987) *Building a Stronger Economy: The Pathfinder Initiative*, HMSO, Belfast.

Department of Trade and Industry (1983) *Regional Industrial Policy: Some Economic Issues*, Department of Trade and Industry, London.

Forsyth, D C (1982) *US Investment in Scotland*, Praeger, New York.

Frobel, F, Heinrich, J and Krege, O (1980) *The New International Division of Labour*, Cambridge University Press, Cambridge.

Goddard, J B et al (1979) *The Mobilisation of Indigenous Potential in the United Kingdom: A Report to the Regional Policy Directorate of the European Community*, Centre for Urban and Regional Development Studies, University of Newcastle upon Tyne.

Guccione, A and Gillen, W (1982) The optimality of labour subsidies in a regional context: a skeptical note, *Regional Science and Urban Economics*, 12, 381–386.

Harris, R I D (1988) Automatic capital incentives and company investment decisions in Northern Ireland. Paper presented to Regional Studies Association Conference 'Divided Nation: Regional Policy in Britain's Periphery', Belfast, September 1988.

Harrison, R T (1982) Assisted industry, employment stability and industrial decline: some evidence from Northern Ireland, *Regional Studies*, 16, 267–85.

Harrison, R T (1985) The stability of indigenous and foreign owned ID assisted industry in Northern Ireland (mimeo).

Harrison, R T (1986a) Industrial development policy and the restructuring of the Northern Ireland economy, *Environment and Planning C: Government and Policy*, 4, 53–70.

Harrison, R T (1986b) The standard capital grants scheme in Northern Ireland: a review and assessment, *Regional Studies*, 20, 175–182.

Harrison, R T (1987) Enterprise development in a peripheral regional economy: a medium term perspective. Paper presented at the Northern Ireland Enterprise Convention: European Opportunity, Cascais, Portugal, September.

Harrison, R T (1989a) Industrial development in Northern Ireland, the Industrial Development Board, in Connolly, M and Loughlin, S (eds), *Public Policy in Northern Ireland: Adoption and Adaptation*, Policy Research Institute, Belfast.

Harrison, R T (1989b) The politics of industrial decline and restructuring in Northern Ireland shipbuilding industry, in Gibbs, D (ed), *Government Policy and Industrial Change*, Routledge, London.

Hart, M (1984) Local agencies and small firm formation: the case of Northern Ireland 1971–81, in Barr, B M and Waters, N M (eds), *Regional Diversification and Structural Change*, Tantalus Research, Vancouver.

Harvey, S (1987) The local enterprise programme: an overview. Paper presented at the Northern Ireland Enterprise Convention: European Opportunity, Cascais, Portugal, September.

H M Government (1983) *Regional Industrial Development*, Cmnd 9111, HMSO, London.

H M Government (1988) *DTI – The Department for Enterprise*, Cm 278, HMSO, London.

Hoare, A G (1981) Why they go where they go: the political imagery of industrial location, *Transactions, Institute of British Geographers*, 6, 152–75.

Hoare, A G (1982) Problem region and regional problem, in Boal, F W and Douglas, J N H (eds), *Integration and Division: Geographical Perspectives on the Northern Ireland Problem*, Academic Press, London.

Hood, N and Young, S (1983) *Multinational Investment Strategies in the British Isles: A Study of MNEs in the UK Assisted Areas and Republic of Ireland*, Department of Trade and Industry, London.

IDA (1945) Industrial Development (NI) Act, *Public General Acts – George VI*, Chapter 12, HMSO, London.

IDB (1985) *Encouraging Enterprise: A Medium Term Strategy for 1985–1990*, Industrial Development Board, Belfast.

ITC (1982) Reports (1981–82). Government Support for Trade and Industry in Northern Ireland, Industry and Trade Committee, *House of Commons Papers – Session 1981–82*, 500, 398-i-ii, HMSO, London.

Klaassen, L H and Molle, W T M (eds) (1983) *Industrial Mobility and Migration in the European Community*, Gower, Aldershot.

LEDU (1986) *A Better Job, The Small Business Agency's Strategy for 1986–89*, Local Enterprise Development Unit, Belfast.

McCallum, J D (1979) The development of British regional policy, in MacLennan, D and Parr, J B (eds), *Regional Policy: Past Experience and New Directions*, Martin Robertson, Oxford.

McCrone, G (1969) *Regional Policy in Britain*, George Allen and Unwin, Hemel Hempstead.

Martin, R (1985) Monetarism masquerading as regional policy? The Government's new system of regional aid, *Regional Studies*, 19, 379–88.

Martin, R (1989) The new economics and politics of regional restructuring: the British experience, in Albrechts, L et al (eds), *Regional Policy at the Crossroads: European Perspectives*, Jessica Kingsley, London.

Moore, B, Rhodes, J and Tarling, R (1978) Industrial policy and economic development: the experience of Northern Ireland and the Republic of Ireland, *Cambridge Journal of Economics*, 2, 99–114.

Moore, B, Rhodes, J and Tyler, P (1986) *The Effects of Government Regional Economic Policy*, HMSO, London.

Murie, A S, Birrell, W D, Roche, D J D and Hillyard, P A R (1974), *Regional Planning and the Attraction of Manufacturing Industry in Northern Ireland*, Centre for Environmental Studies, London.

NIDA (1932) New Industries Development (NI) Act, *Public General Acts – George V*, Chapter 2, HMSO, London.

NIEC (1983a) *Economic Strategy: Historical Growth Performance*, Northern Ireland Economic Development Office, Belfast.

NIEC (1983b) *The Duration of Industrial Development Assisted Employment*, Report 40, Northern Ireland Economic Development Office, Belfast.

NIEC (1984) *Public Expenditure Priorities: Overall Review*, Northern Ireland Economic Development Office, Belfast.

NIEC (1985a) *The Duration of LEDU Assisted Employment*, Northern Ireland Economic Development Office, Belfast.

NIEC (1985b) *The Duration of Industrial Development Maintained Employment*, Northern Ireland Economic Development Office, Belfast.

NIEC (1986a) *Economic Strategy: Industrial Development Linkages*, Northern Ireland Economic Development Office, Belfast.

NIEC (1986b) *Economic Strategy: Industrial Development*, Report 60, Northern Ireland Economic Development Office, Belfast.

Northern Ireland Development Programme 1970–75, HMSO, Belfast.

Northern Ireland Office (1974) *Finance and the Economy*, HMSO, Belfast.

Nunn, S (1980) The opening and closure of manufacturing units in the United Kingdom. Government Economic Service *Working Paper 36*, Department of Industry, London.

O'Farrell, P N (1980) *The Mobilisation of Indigenous Potential: Towards a Complementary Regional Strategy*, Department of Town Planning, University of Wales Institute of Science and Technology, Cardiff.

Plant Location International (1983) *A Comparative Analysis of the Incentives Offered to Industry in the EC Countries*, Plant Location International, Brussels.

Pounce, R (1981) *Industrial Movement in the United Kingdom, 1966–1975*, HMSO, London.

Review Team (1976) *Economic and Industrial Strategy for Northern Ireland*, HMSO, Belfast.

Rowthorn, R C (1981) Northern Ireland: an economy in crisis, *Cambridge Journal of Economics*, 5, 1–31.

Rowthorn, R C (1987) Northern Ireland: an economy in crisis, in Teague, P (ed), *Beyond the Rhetoric: Politics, the Economy and Social Policy in Northern Ireland*, Lawrence and Wishart, London.

Scottish Economic Planning Department (1983) *Employment Performance of Overseas Owned Manufacturing Units Opening in Scotland 1954–77*, Scottish Economic Planning Department, Edinburgh.

Sector Working Party (1981) *Man Made Fibre Production SWP Progress Report*, National Economic Development Office, London.

Shaw, R W and Shaw, S A (1980) Synthetic fibres, in Johnson, P S (ed), *The Structure of British Industry*, Granada, London.

Shaw, R W and Shaw, S A (1983) Excess capacity and rationalisation in the West European synthetic fibres industry, *Journal of Industrial Economics*, 32, 149–68.

Simpson, J V (1984) An investigation into the employment generated by new industry locating in Northern Ireland, 1951–80. Paper presented to the Statistical and Social Inquiry Society of Ireland, Belfast.

Steed, G P F and Thomas, M D (1971) Regional industrial change: Northern Ireland, *Annals, Association of American Geographers*, 61, 344–60.

Stutt, C, Haire, W and Graham, B (1988) The Pathfinder process in Northern Ireland, *Public Money and Management*, 8, 75–77.

Swales, J K (1981) The employment effects of a regional capital subsidy, *Regional Studies*, 15, 4, 263–73.

Teague, P (1987) Multinational companies in the Northern Ireland economy: an outmoded model of industrial development? in Teague, P (ed), *Beyond the Rhetoric: Politics, the Economy and Social Policy in Northern Ireland*, Lawrence and Wishart, London.

Teague, P (1989) Economic development in Northern Ireland: has Pathfinder lost its way? *Regional Studies*, 23, 63–69.

Torneden, R L (1975) *Foreign Divestment by US Multinational Corporations*, Praeger, New York.

Van den Bulche, D, et al (1979) *Investment and Divestment Policies of Multinational Corporations in Europe*, Saxon House, Farnborough.

Vernon, R (1966) International investment and international trade in the product cycle, *Quarterly Journal of Economics*, 80, 190–207.

Walker, G and Krist, H (1980) *Regional Incentives and the Investment Decision of the Firm: A Comparative Study of Britain and Germany*, Centre for the Study of Public Policy, University of Strathclyde.

Watts, H D (1981) *The Branch Plant Economy: A Study in External Control*, Longman, London.

Wilson Report (1965) *Economic Development in Northern Ireland*, Cmnd 479, HMSO, Belfast.

Woodward, R S (1974) The capital bias of DREE incentives, *Canadian Journal of Economics*, 7, 161–73.

CHAPTER FIVE

The role of the firm in manufacturing

Peter Enderwick, Graham H Gudgin and David M W N Hitchens*

1. Introduction

The aim of this chapter is to survey the role of two classes of manufacturing firm. Firstly, large establishments employing more than 200 people are reviewed. These plants account for the great majority of all output and employment in manufacturing, and their success or failure is the major influence on the performance of the manufacturing sector in Northern Ireland. Secondly, special attention is given to small firms in manufacturing employing less than 50 people. Although much less quantitively significant, small firms are important because they have provided virtually the only source of employment stability within Northern Ireland manufacturing in recent years. While a considerable collapse has occurred in employment within the largest plants, small firms have in many cases been able to expand, and even high closure rates have not prevented them from maintaining their employment. In discussing large plants, we refer mainly to establishments since the units in Northern Ireland are usually (although not always) parts of multinational or multi-regional companies. For small plants this is not the case. Here the Northern Ireland units are normally whole firms.

The reasons for concentrating on the manufacturing sector are partly those of data availability, but also importantly because of the role played by manufacturing in the overall local economy (eg, see Harris 1987). This role has already been outlined in Chapter 3 and will not be repeated here. The next four sections of the chapter are concerned with large plants, discussing their significance and importance, and also the consequences of regional dependence on them. The remaining sections describe the importance and characteristics of small firms in Northern Ireland. A good deal is now known about the relative performance of small firms and this is contained in Section 9. Finally, small firms policy is discussed in Section 11.

* Section 1 was written by Dr Gudgin, Sections 2–5 by Professor Enderwick and the rest of the chapter by Dr Gudgin and Dr Hitchens.

2. The significance of large plants

The importance of large plants in the Northern Ireland economy reflects the economic significance of such plants in the United Kingdom in general. At the aggregate level the United Kingdom has one of the most highly concentrated economic structures in the world. In 1983 the largest 100 private sector firms accounted for 40 per cent of manufacturing net output. Dependence on large units has always been particularly strong in the peripheral regions. Table 5.1 shows the relative importance of large plants in the peripheral regions of Northern Ireland, Scotland, Wales and the Republic of Ireland in 1983. For comparative purposes similar data are also provided for England. Table 5.1 reveals three major findings. Firstly, the data confirm the high level of economic concentration within the United Kingdom with plants employing 200 or more accounting for around two-thirds of all manufacturing employment. Secondly, with the exception of Northern Ireland the peripheral regions of the United Kingdom do display a marginally higher dependence on large plants than the English regions. Thirdly, large plants are less important to the economy of the Republic of Ireland accounting for only around 10 per cent of the total number of plants in industry and 45 per cent of employment. There are a large number of very small establishments in the Republic of Ireland.

TABLE 5.1   The relative importance of large manufacturing[1] plants in areas of the British Isles, 1983

	Large plants as % of all plants[2]	Large plant employment as % of all employment
Northern Ireland	14.4	61.9
Scotland	16.2	67.6
Wales	17.1	68.2
England	15.5	65.7
Republic of Ireland	9.8	45.4

[1] For the Republic of Ireland the data are for all industry.
[2] Excludes plants employing less than 20.
Sources: UK Census of Production 1983; RI Census of Industrial Production 1983.

The importance of large plants to the peripheral regions of the United Kingdom is partly a result of the success of regional policies which operated in the late 1950s and the 1960s. Through the attraction of mobile plants Northern Ireland was able to maintain its manufacturing employment between 1965 and 1969. The boost to regional policy after 1966 resulted in an increase in longer distance manufacturing plant moves between the United Kingdom regions. Of the resulting 79,300 jobs created in peripheral regions in the period 1966–71 Northern Ireland attracted 10,000 which is a larger proportion than would be expected from the size of the province's manu-facturing sector (Keeble 1976).

Migrant plants displayed two principal characteristics. Firstly, they tended to be large with average employment in mid-1971, for plants established in the assisted areas, being 115. In the Northern Ireland case the comparable figure was significantly higher, averaging 175. Secondly, the majority (60 per cent) of establishments created in the assisted areas were 'branch plants' (additional capacity concentrating on assembly/manufacturing operations) and not simply inter-regional transfers of capacity. The pattern of shifts to adjacent regions in the core of the economy (West Midlands, South East and East Anglia) was very different with branches accounting for only 24 per cent of moves (29 per cent of employment). The result of this is a truncated industrial structure in peripheral economies, with an under-representation of managerial and technical functions and occupations, within both establishments and the regional population as a whole (see Chapter 3). In addition, there is a high degree of external control. While the data in Table 3.17 do not control for plant size it is apparent that externally controlled companies do account for a significantly larger employment share in those industries characterised by above average plant sizes (chemicals, motor vehicles).

Foreign-owned firms have also made a significant contribution to manufacturing employment creation within the peripheral regions. A comparative perspective on their importance is presented in Table 5.2.

Three important conclusions emerge from Table 5.2. The first is the dominance of the Republic of Ireland's manufacturing sector by foreign-owned firms which, in 1983, accounted for nearly 38 per cent of all manufacturing employment. The Republic of Ireland has been very successful over the last twenty years in attracting such investment. It has increased its share relative to the assisted areas of the United Kingdom and Northern Ireland in particular (Bull and Hart 1987). Secondly, foreign-owned firms are more important in the peripheral regions of the United Kingdom than in the more central English regions. This finding is consistent with the widely held view of a high level of locational flexibility for foreign-owned affiliates (Dunning 1981). In addition, it may indicate a greater sensitivity of such plants to the level or structure of regional incentives. Thirdly, in all the areas considered in Table 5.2 the contribution of overseas based firms to net output invariably exceeds their employment or numerical significance. This might be interpreted as an indication that such plants are likely to be of above average size (enjoying

TABLE 5.2 The relative importance of foreign-owned manufacturing plants in areas of the British Isles, 1983

	Foreign-owned establishments as % of total	Foreign-owned employment as % of total	Foreign-owned net output as %of total
Northern Ireland	7.4	16.3	19.5
Scotland	11.0	15.7	21.0
Wales	11.9	19.4	26.3
England	8.4	14.1	18.4
Republic of Ireland	14.8	37.9	58.1

Sources: As Table 5.1.

economies of scale), of above average productivity, or located in the most productive manufacturing industries.

Table 5.3 presents some evidence of structural differences between foreign-owned and indigenous plants with regard to these issues. It is clear from this table that foreign-owned plants are absolutely much larger than domestic plants, being on average more than two and a half times larger in employment terms. Interestingly, the very largest plants are found in Northern Ireland. This finding, which is consistent with evidence on the size of domestically owned branch plants located in the province, may reflect the impact of regional policy, as it has operated in Northern Ireland, encouraging large-scale projects.

TABLE 5.3 Structural differences between foreign and domestically owned manufacturing plants in areas of the British Isles, 1983

	Average unit size[1] (employment)			Net output per head (£)		
	Foreign owned	Domestic owned	FO/DO	Foreign owned	Domestic owned	FO/DO
Northern Ireland	386	117	3.30	15,389	12,383	1.24
Scotland	268	139	1.93	22,070	15,492	1.43
Wales	283	138	2.05	22,531	15,239	1.48
England	291	134	2.17	20,743	15,093	1.37
Republic of Ireland	103	33	3.12	34,200	15,100	2.27

[1] Includes plants with 20 or more employees.
Source: As Table 5.1.

It is also apparent that foreign-owned plants have higher productivity (as measured by net output per head). The difference is very considerable in the case of the Republic of Ireland. Plants operating in Northern Ireland record the lowest levels of net output per head; for foreign-owned firms this occurs despite the largest difference in average unit size. These contrasts in productivity levels are largely attributable to differences in the industrial distribution of inward investment (see also Table 3.14).

Sectoral analyses at the regional level reveal a considerable degree of industrial concentration. Foreign-owned firms in the Republic of Ireland are clustered into a small number of sectors which they tend to dominate. Typically, these are sectors producing newer and more technically advanced products. The metals and engineering sector accounts for 46 per cent of all overseas-controlled employment. These firms are also important in chemicals, artificial fibres and footwear. The evidence for Northern Ireland suggests a similar concentration with foreign firms employing significant numbers in engineering, textiles (particularly man-made fibres) and areas of food, drink and tobacco.

Inward investment has brought only a modest degree of diversification to the Northern Ireland manufacturing base with investments in consumer electronics and automotive components for example (Bull 1984). The limited degree of diversification achieved is due to the fact that a large number of the new projects were attracted to traditional sectors such as textiles and, in the case of man-made fibres for example, simply served to reinforce an already high degree of specialisation. In addition, many have closed in recent years (Bull and Hart 1987). The result is that the Northern Ireland economy has the smallest and most specialised manufacturing sector of all the standard regions of the United Kingdom (see Table 3.4).

The above discussion suggests a degree of homogeneity with regard to inward investment in the assisted areas which may not be justified. In fact there appear to be important regional contrasts in the role and likely impact of foreign-owned firms. Table 5.4, using data drawn from a survey of some 140 foreign affiliates in the United Kingdom, highlights some of the distinguishing characteristics of multinational manufacturing plants in Northern Ireland. The comparisons are made in terms of other multinational plants in the remaining assisted areas of the United Kingdom (broadly Wales, Scotland and the North West of England). Two important points emerge from Table 5.4.

Firstly, the direct employment creation effect of inward investment in Northern Ireland appears to be considerable. This follows from the above average incidence of 'green field entry' (the setting up of a new plant) and

TABLE 5.4   Some inter-regional contrasts in multinational activity: Northern Ireland in comparison with other assisted areas of the United Kingdom

AA = above average; BA = below average	
Affiliate characteristics	
Level of employment	AA
Output per head	BA
Incidence of green field entry	AA
Incidence of administrative functions at plant	BA
Number of other group plants in Europe	BA
Locational determinants	
Importance of government financial assistance	AA
Importance of opportunities for entry by acquisition	BA
Plant characteristics	
Capital employed per employee	AA
Decline in costs with larger plant size	AA
Direct labour costs as percentage of total costs	AA
Product and market characteristics	
Incidence of single source activity	BA
UK orientation of output	BA
Percentage of inputs from within region	BA
Net export (exports minus imports)	AA
Workforce characteristics	
Ratio of 1980 to peak employment	BA
Percentage of manual workers	AA
Incidence of non-unionisation	BA
Absence of strikes and stoppages	BA

Sources: Tables 5.2 and 5.3, and Hood and Young (1983).

limited opportunities for acquisition. The preference for this method of entry may also be partly the result of generous financial assistance which receives an above-average rating by investors in the province. Secondly, the evidence of declining cost (increasing returns) conditions, limited local sourcing, orientation of output to non-United Kingdom markets, high export propensity and a high percentage of manual workers is consistent with branch plant status. Such a finding is compatible with evidence on the characteristics of mobile indigenous plants located in Northern Ireland.

3. The performance of large plants

Since the recession of 1979 the performance of large firms, particularly in employment terms, has been little short of disastrous. While there has been a general decline in manufacturing employment, between 1975 and 1983 the United Kingdom lost some 2.1 millions jobs, 30.5 per cent of its manufacturing base; employment decline has been sharpest amongst larger plants. As Table 5.5 shows, this tendency is particularly pronounced in the peripheral regions.

TABLE 5.5   Changes in plant numbers and employment for large manufacturing plants, areas of the United Kingdom, 1975–1983

	Change in the number of large plants	% Change	Change in employment within large plants	% Change	Change in all manufacturing employment	% Change
Northern Ireland	−53	−32.9	−35,793	−36.0	−48,313	−32.0
Scotland	−199	−31.8	−147,973	−35.2	−206,697	−33.9
Wales	−110	−32.5	−91,402	−39.2	−104,724	−33.5
England	−1,684	−27.6	−876,438	−24.3	−1,782,782	−30.0
United Kingdom	−2,046	−28.3	−1,151,606	−26.4	−2,142,516	−30.5

Source: UK Census of Production.

It is apparent from Table 5.5 that in relative terms the loss of both plants (closures) and employment (closure and contraction) has been greatest in the peripheral regions of Northern Ireland, Scotland and Wales. Interestingly, the differences are greatest when considering large plants (more than 200 employees) as opposed to all plants and employment. Indeed, employment loss in large plants in Northern Ireland, Scotland and Wales accounted for 74.1, 71.6 and 87.3 per cent of all jobs lost over the period 1975 to 1983 compared with 49.2 per cent in the case of England. For the peripheral regions these percentage figures invariably exceed the share of such plants in manufacturing employment (see Table 5.1). These differences are attributable to both the greater importance of large plants in regions like Scotland and Wales (see Table 5.1) and their industrial distribution as well as a tendency for companies to concentrate their rationalisation within plants located in the peripheral regions (Townsend 1983).

Table 5.6 breaks down the employment change by ownership

nationality. The data allow a distinction to be made between foreign-owned and domestically owned (Great Britain and Northern Ireland) plants. The distinction by ownership nationality reveals a number of interesting findings. Firstly, it is apparent that in the period 1979–83 the majority of large plant closures occurred within the stock of domestically owned plants. Secondly, employment loss within large plants in the regions of England occurred predominantly within indigenous plants. The two regions which departed from this pattern were Scotland, where employment losses within the two types of plants were more comparable and Northern Ireland, where the losses in large foreign-owned plants were proportionately greater. Thirdly, for both types of firm a higher rate of job loss (and often plant closure) was experienced in the peripheral regions of Northern Ireland, Scotland and Wales. The major exception to this is the below average rate of job loss within large domestically owned plants in Northern Ireland.

TABLE 5.6   Changes in plant numbers and employment for large manufacturing plants by area and ownership nationality, United Kingdom, 1979–1983

	Nationality	Change in number of large plants	% Change	Change in employment	% Change
Northern Ireland	Foreign-owned	−7	−20.0	−7,400	−27.6
	Domestically owned	−33	−29.2	−9,749	−18.1
Scotland	Foreign-owned	−3	−2.8	−17,100	−21.2
	Domestically owned	−142	−30.6	−74,831	−26.3
Wales	Foreign-owned	−13	−17.1	−8,900	−19.4
	Domestically owned	−55	−24.9	−56,573	−35.1
England	Foreign-owned	−80	−9.3	−92,100	−14.6
	Domestically owned	−1,147	−24.0	−790,599	−26.5
United Kingdom	Foreign-owned	−103	−9.5	−125,500	−16.0
	Domestically owned	−1,377	−24.7	−931,752	−26.7

Source: As Table 5.5.

The Northern Ireland experience requires further examination. The region experienced the highest rate of plant closure and employment decline within the foreign sector. Three principal reasons for this are suggested. Firstly, for foreign-owned firms Northern Ireland appears increasingly disadvantaged as a location. The overcapacity and excessive competition in industries like man-made fibres and chemicals has encouraged restructuring in the form of plant scrapping and mothballing (Enderwick forthcoming). Why the closures effected by these multiplant firms occurred in Northern Ireland is probably attributable to the declining locational attractions of the province which, in comparison to other regions, suffers high energy and transport costs, social conflict, slow growth and low levels of income. In a period of recession companies, and particularly multi-regional companies, become increasingly sensitive to such locational contrasts. Secondly, the comparatively low rate of job loss within the domestically owned sector of Northern Ireland may reflect favourable aspects of its industrial structure. Unlike Scotland and Wales which have both lost steel, vehicles and mechanical engineering, Northern Ireland has only limited capacity in many of these sectors. Thirdly, contraction of the domestically owned sector may have been retarded by the generous provision of financial assistance. In the year 1986/87 government subsidy to Northern Ireland manufacturing amounted to £204 million (equivalent to £39 per week per manufacturing employee). Government assistance may have had a greater impact on the behaviour of indigenous companies, a number of which are state-owned, because these firms are more effective at lobbying for, and obtaining, support and assistance.

Although grant aid as a proportion of total corporate investment expenditure is falling, it still accounted for over 75 per cent of all investment expenditure in the corporate sector of Northern Ireland over the last four years. Most worrying of all, perhaps, is the fact that over the ten-year period 1976–85, more than half the firms receiving assistance were helped more than once. In the absence of such generous levels of subsidy employment contraction would undoubtedly have been much greater.

With the exception of the foreign-owned sector published data are not available for an examination of the relationship between job loss and the location of ownership of a plant. However, using a data base compiled by the author from announced job losses reported in *The Financial Times*, some light can be thrown on this question. The data, which are for the period 1976–87 and include the largest companies in the United Kingdom, cover some 32,000 job losses within Northern Ireland. Table 5.7 provides a breakdown of job loss in the peripheral regions of Northern Ireland, Scotland and Wales.

TABLE 5.7 Job losses in peripheral regions by regional location of company headquarters, 1976–1987

	Number of reported job losses	Percentage of job losses accounted for by:	
		Companies headquartered in the region	Companies headquartered outside the region (of which in Greater London and South East)
N Ireland	32,231	16.6	83.4 (67.8)
Scotland	128,951	14.9	85.1 (63.1)
Wales	88,233	2.3	97.7 (83.1)

Source: Enderwick (forthcoming).

It is clear from Table 5.7 that, in the majority of cases, responsibility for cutting employment in the peripheral regions of the United Kingdom lies with companies whose headquarters are outside the region in question. Thus, in the case of Northern Ireland more than 80 per cent of job losses occurred within companies based outside Northern Ireland. Not surprisingly the majority (67.8 per cent) of these branch plants were controlled from the 'core' of Greater London and the South East. This tendency is also apparent in Scotland and is particularly pronounced for Wales.

4. Some consequences of dependence on large plants

The preceding discussion has shown the considerable dependence of the Northern Ireland economy upon the operation of large plants, many of which are externally controlled. Such dependence has a number of consequences for the economic position of a region (Healey and Watts 1987; Young, Hood and Hamill 1988). There are four major disadvantages which are particularly relevant in the Northern Ireland context.

Firstly, large plants have been linked with employment instability, displaying high rates of both closure and contraction. Employment instability may be a direct result of large size (large firms may be less responsive to changing market needs or may be subject to higher levels of industrial conflict) or employment decisions may be closely related to the role of the plant within a wider corporate framework depending more on overall corporate performance or strategy than local contribution or prospects (Young, Hood and Hamill 1988).

A second disadvantage is associated with the tendency to locate standardised products in the later stages of their life cycle in the branch plants of peripheral areas. This has implications for both the quantity and quality of employment creation. For Northern Ireland the generous financial assistance (and in many cases continuing subsidisation) necessary to attract such firms accelerates plant write-offs, encourages excessive capital intensity in an economy characterised by a chronic over-supply of labour and adds little to the stock of industrial training and skills formation.

A third disadvantage, the under-development of linkages, is also one associated with branch plant status. In such a case, the plant's input needs (services, intermediate products) are met from related affiliates or the parent, generally based outside the region (Hoare 1978). The underdevelopment of linkages has two major implications for a regional economy like Northern Ireland. Firstly, the low level of local sourcing means that the secondary economic effects of the plant (indirect employment creation, income multipliers etc) could be quite low. Secondly, the 'internalisation' of demand (within the company) limits opportunities for small businesses locally to meet the input needs of large firms.

The fourth consequence of dependence on large plants results from the truncated structure of many branch units. In concentrating on routine assembly such plants are generally devoid of the higher order business functions such as research and development, marketing, strategic planning and finance. This has important implications for the occupational structure of a region, suggesting an under-representation of certain professional occupations in peripheral regions.

It is important to note a significant caveat to these criticisms. Emphasising the disadvantages of branch plant operations implies the existence of a superior alternative position, ie what the industrial structure of Northern Ireland would resemble in the absence of branch plants. The preferred alternative might be a comparable (or expanded) level of employment offered by indigenous enterprises. Whether Northern Ireland would have been capable of generating and sustaining such employment in the absence of incoming investment is debatable. The performance of local firms, the level of outward migration of qualified labour and the parlous state of the economy and society suggest that it is unlikely. Evaluation of the prevailing manufacturing structure must be placed within the context of feasible alternatives.

5. Conclusions on large plants

Our discussion suggests a number of conclusions. Firstly, it is apparent that over the long run a policy of attracting large mobile plants has done little to overcome the problems Northern Ireland faced in having a small and highly specialised manufacturing base. It would be fair criticism to say that policy has over-emphasised the equity effects (employment creation) over efficiency considerations in the development of Northern Ireland.

Secondly, there is a clear link between past policy actions and options for the future. The creation of a branch plant economy has implications for the innovative and entrepreneurial potential of a region (see Chapter 3). The recent change in emphasis in industrial development policy within Northern Ireland placing greater weighting on indigenous development must recognise these policy-created constraints.

Finally, it is important to recognise the more general constraints which impinge upon industrial development within a regional economy like Northern Ireland. The performance of leading companies like Harland and Wolff and Short Brothers implied a continuing drain on resources until their recent privatisation. In industries like electronics, chemicals, vehicles and pharmaceuticals the established global organisation of production means that any role Northern Ireland might play will be strictly determined by company decisions on the spatial allocation of functions. In such industries self-supporting indigenous development is difficult.

It is important to recognise that, for the foreseeable future, the economic health of Northern Ireland manufacturing will depend to a considerable extent on the performance of its large plants. For this reason at least such establishments will remain an important policy issue.

6. The importance of small firms

Small firms have assumed a considerably increased importance in many industrialised countries over the period of slower economic growth since 1973. Several studies in the United Kingdom and elsewhere have found that the relatively few new jobs created in manufacturing in this period have been generated by small firms (Birch 1979; Fothergill and Gudgin 1979; Department of Industry 1981). Evidence within the United Kingdom suggests that small firms were becoming less important during the 1950s and 1960s but that this downward trend has been sharply reversed in the 1970s and 1980s (Gudgin 1984). Registrations for Value Added Tax (VAT) show a steady and substantial increase in the number of manufacturing businesses, the vast majority of which are very small. In 1974 a total of 112,000 manufacturing businesses were recorded within the United Kingdom. By 1987 this number had risen to 159,000. Small firms are partly important as low cost subcontractors to larger firms, but in many industries they also compete directly with larger firms. While most small firms either remain small or eventually close, a minority achieve greater importance as the medium or large firms of the future.

It is difficult to count accurately numbers of small firms and different sources may record significantly differing numbers. The short-lived nature of the smallest firms, and in some cases attempts to avoid or minimise tax, may make detection difficult. In Northern Ireland the VAT register recorded 2,874 small firms (employing less than 50) in 1985. The NIERC Industrial Database, on which figures in this chapter are chiefly based, includes a smaller number. The main exclusions are of the very smallest firms, and employment in the small firms sector as a whole is more fully counted. The NIERC database recorded 1,679 small establishments in 1986 employing 21,000 people. It is estimated that as many as a further 1,200 very small firms may have been omitted from the NIERC database employing a further 5,000 people (Gudgin et al 1989).

As in other areas small firms in Northern Ireland manufacturing have increased their economic importance. In 1973, firms employing less than 50 accounted for only 12 per cent of manufacturing employment in the province. By 1986 this total had risen to 21 per cent (or 24 per cent including those small

TABLE 5.8   Change in numbers of manufacturing establishments, Northern Ireland, 1973–1986

Employment size band	0–49	50–99	100–199	200–499	500+
Percentage change in establishments	7.1	−22.7	−23.8	−29.0	−60.0
Number of establishments in 1986	1,679	174	125	86	22

Source: NIERC Industrial Database.

TABLE 5.9   Employment change in manufacturing establishments, Northern Ireland, 1973–1986

Employment size band	0–49	50–99	100–199	200–499	500+
Percentage change in employment	−3.0	−24.6	−24.4	−30.8	−65.5
Employment in 1986	21,217	11,866	17,624	25,754	26,611

Source: As Table 5.8.

firms not individually identified in the NIERC database). Small firms were the only category of company to increase their numbers (Table 5.8), and also the only category not to suffer a substantial decline in employment (Table 5.9).

Small firms constitute a higher proportion of manufacturing employment in Northern Ireland (24 per cent) than in Great Britain (22 per cent). However, this is a rather limited comparison since Northern Ireland's manufacturing sector is itself proportionately small by British standards. Compared with its population rather than its manufacturing employment Northern Ireland can be seen to be under-endowed with small firms. In 1986 Northern Ireland had 2.1 small manufacturing firms for every thousand people. The equivalent figure for Great Britain was 2.6.

7. The size and sectoral distribution of small firms

Most small firms in Northern Ireland, as elsewhere, are very small indeed. The latest available statistics, based on registrations for VAT, show that 70 per cent of small firms employed less than 10 people (Table 5.10). However, the average employment in this smallest category of firms was only three people, and despite their large numbers they accounted for little over a quarter of employees in Northern Ireland's small firms. In contrast, the 389 largest small firms, employing between 20 and 49 employees, accounted for almost half of the employment.

TABLE 5.10   Size of small firms, Northern Ireland, 1987

Employment size	1–9	10–19	20–49	Total
Number of establishments	2,186	550	389	3,125
Number of employees	7,385	7,541	12,091	27,017

Source: Business Monitor PA 1003, 1987.

Small firms are found throughout the range of manufacturing industries although they dominate some trades more than others. Barriers to entry, caused by high costs of capital equipment required to realise economies of scale, are the major factor causing some industries to be relatively closed to small firms. Another aspect of barriers to entry is distribution costs including the competitive necessity of expensive advertising. Small firms tend to dominate in the production of clothing, timber and furniture, printing and publishing, and in general jobbing engineering and miscellaneous metal or plastic goods. However, in every industry, including those dominated by large firms, there are a number of market niches occupied by small business.

In Northern Ireland 70 per cent of the small firms are in six sectors (Table 5.11). Most important are timber and furniture and non-metallic mineral products, both partly serving local construction trades, and food

TABLE 5.11   Sectoral distribution of small firms, 1987

| | Establishments | | Employment % | |
	Number	%	Northern Ireland	United Kingdom
Non-metallic mineral products	460	13.9	13.3	5.0
Chemicals	98	3.0	3.2	3.5
Metal goods	270	8.2	6.8	12.2
Mechanical engineering	369	11.2	9.3	15.9
Electrical and electronic engineering	120	3.6	2.5	7.5
Motor vehicles	71	2.2	2.1	2.1
Other transport equipment	23	0.7	0.5	1.7
Instrument engineering	49	1.5	0.6	2.2
Food, drink, tobacco	466	14.1	18.7	8.3
Textiles	123	3.7	6.9	4.4
Clothing, footwear, leather	269	8.2	12.0	9.3
Timber, furniture	481	14.6	11.6	7.6
Paper, printing, publishing	289	8.8	7.7	12.2
Rubber and plastics	90	2.7	3.4	4.8
Other manufacturing	120	3.6	1.4	3.3
Manufacturing	3,298	100.0	100.0	100.0

Note: Small firms are defined as local units employing less than 100.
Source: As Table 5.10.

products. Also significant are mechanical engineering, clothing, footwear and leather, and printing and publishing. This distribution reflects the specialisation of Northern Ireland industry in addition to the more general influence of barriers to entry. Employment is proportionately high in the food, textiles and clothing sectors which dominate Northern Ireland manufacturing as a whole (Table 5.11). The most notable positive difference between the sectoral distribution of small business employment in Northern Ireland and that nationally occurs in food processing. On the other hand Northern Ireland has relatively few small firms in the engineering sectors, reflecting the small size of this sector in Northern Ireland.

One simple measure of the impact of high barriers to entry is the number of small firms per thousand employees in each sector. Sectors with high barriers to entry have most of their employment in large firms and thus have few small firms relative to total employment in the sector. To maintain comparability with the United Kingdom, the definition of small firms in Table 5.12 is extended to include firms with up to 100 employees. High barriers to entry in motor vehicles, other transport equipment and chemicals are evident in the United Kingdom figures (Table 5.12). Conversely, low barriers to entry in clothing, printing and especially in timber and furniture and other manufacturing are also clear.

What also emerges from Table 5.12 is that Northern Ireland has a high intensity of smaller firms in some industries which have high barriers to

TABLE 5.12   Number of small establishments per thousand employees, by sector, Northern Ireland and the United Kingdom, 1987

	Northern Ireland	United Kingdom
Non-metallic mineral products	75	20
Chemicals	3	11
Metal goods	86	31
Mechanical engineering	49	39
Electrical and electronic engineering	20	16
Motor vehicles	22	7
Other transport equipment	2	7
Instrument engineering	43	28
Food, drink, tobacco	22	16
Textiles	12	19
Clothing, footwear, leather	15	37
Timber, furniture	90	70
Paper, printing, publishing	49	46
Rubber, plastics	26	22
Other manufacturing	170	107
Manufacturing	30	27

Note: Small firms are as defined in Table 5.11.
Source: As Table 5.10.

entry nationally (eg non-metallic mineral products). Other Northern Ireland industries display a low intensity of small firms in low barrier to entry industries (eg clothing). In some cases the differences are explained by dissimilarities in the detailed composition of industries. In metals and metal goods, for instance, Northern Ireland has no production of iron or steel and hence lacks the large establishments which in Great Britain dominate this sector. Similarly, the restricted size of local markets for building products accounts for the importance of small firms within non-metallic mineral products. Less easy to understand is the relative lack of small firms in the clothing, footwear and leather industries. Northern Ireland's clothing industry is dominated by shirt makers to a larger extent than in Great Britain, and shirt makers tend to be relatively large by the standards of the clothing industry as a whole. Nevertheless, low wages combined with a tradition of clothing manufacturing might be expected to have resulted in a larger population of small clothing firms.

The importance of small firms in Northern Ireland industries already alluded to above is further emphasised by the fact that the ratio of small firms to total employment is above the national average in almost every industry except clothing and textiles. This may reflect the positive influences of local entrepreneurial ability, and the success of LEDU in promoting small firms. Another possibility is that it reflects the enormous decline of employment in large firms since 1979. Most of the latter were externally controlled branch plants and subsidiary companies, many of which closed during the deep recession years of the early 1980s. The contraction of the large firm sector has not led to a concomitant decline of the small firm sector. On the contrary, closures of the large plants may have led to an increase in the formation of new small firms by releasing potential entrepreneurs.

8. Labour market characteristics and employment growth in small firms

The most recent evidence on the labour market characteristics of small firms remains the survey undertaken in 1980 by Hart (1987). The survey included 262 firms in the Belfast urban area. Hart found that males comprised two-thirds of employees in small firms and that this proportion was very similar to that in large firms in the same area. A higher proportion of employment was part-time in small firms, mainly of female workers, although this only amounted to 10 per cent of all small firm employees. There is thus little evidence that small firms in Belfast were systematically using part-time employees to increase labour flexibility. Many of the smallest firms require part-time clerical assistance, and this factor alone might account for the higher rate of part-time working in small firms.

Hart also found that three-quarters of employees in small firms were in manual occupations, 22 per cent were clerical workers and 5 per cent professional and managerial. Most (78 per cent) of the manual workers were described as skilled, although it seems likely from Hart's survey that this would include semi-skilled workers. This picture of small firms employing predominantly skilled workers fits with what is known of small firms elsewhere.

As already seen, small manufacturing establishments in Northern Ireland declined slightly in terms of employment between 1973 and 1986. In the rest of this section we confine attention to locally owned companies and exclude the few small externally owned branch plants and subsidiary companies. In addition, firms in Northern Ireland are compared with those in the Republic of Ireland and with a non-peripheral area in England (Leicestershire). The results reported here are based on Gudgin et al (1989). The firms included in Table 5.13 are those which had less than 50 employees either in 1973 or in their first year in operation if they were founded after 1973. Some of these firms had grown in excess of 50 employees by 1986, and would not thus be classified as small firms at the end of the period.

Looking at the growth in this way it can be seen from Table 5.13 that small firms in Northern Ireland expanded their employment by over 50 per cent between 1973 and 1986. Small firms employed 17,500 people in 1973. By 1986 most of these firms had closed with a loss of 60 per cent of the base-year employment. The survivors however expanded their employment by almost half. In addition, new small firms founded by local people in 1973–86 added a further 17,200 jobs. The substantial job losses in closures were more than compensated for by the expansion of survivors and particularly by the formation of new firms. Even so, it can be seen that the cohort of firms in

TABLE 5.13   Employment change in small locally owned firms, 1973–1986

	Northern Ireland		Republic of Ireland		Leicestershire	
Employment in 1973	17.5		53.3		20.3	
Job losses in closures	−10.5	(−60.0)	−25.5	(−47.8)	−8.5	(−41.9)
Employment change in survivors	3.1	(17.7)	4.2	(7.9)	10.0	(49.3)
Job gains in new small firms	17.2	(98.3)	30.0	(56.3)	19.9	(98.0)
Total change	9.8	(56.0)	8.7	(16.3)	21.4	(105.4)

Note: Employment in thousands. Figures in parentheses are percentages of base year employment in small firms.
Sources: NIERC Industrial Database; IDA Employment Survey.

operation in 1973 underwent a large contraction. Overall decline in the small firm sector was only averted by the creation of new firms. What this suggests is that many of the new firms may have taken local markets previously served by older small firms. The figures in Table 5.13 suggest a mixture of company replacement and of overall growth in the small firm sector.

Compared with the Republic of Ireland, Northern Ireland's small firms performed relatively well in terms of employment growth. Northern Ireland's older small firms (those in operation in 1973) suffered a higher closure rate but the survivors grew faster. Taking the two things together the older firms in both areas lost some 40 per cent of their jobs over the period. The macro-economic environment was more favourable in the Republic of Ireland for small firms serving local industrial markets but less favourable, especially after 1980, for those serving consumer markets. Even so, older small firms in the Republic of Ireland lost fewer jobs than their counterparts in Northern Ireland in every industry except mineral products and chemicals. New firms added large numbers of jobs in both parts of Ireland. The rate of employment increase due to new firms was higher in Northern Ireland as a proportion of base year employment in small firms. However, if jobs in new small firms are expressed as a proportion of base year employment in manufacturing firms of all sizes the rate is higher in the Republic of Ireland. The latter measure is preferable since founders of new firms come from larger firms as well as small firms.

Small firms in both parts of Ireland performed substantially worse than those in Leicestershire. Fewer jobs were lost in closures in Leicestershire than in Northern Ireland but the major difference was in the growth of older surviving small companies (those which had been open in 1973 and survived until 1986). These expanded their employment by 44 per cent in Northern Ireland, by only 15 per cent in the Republic of Ireland, but by 86 per cent in Leicestershire. In Leicestershire the gains in survivors outweighed job losses in closures and as a result the cohort of older firms gained jobs. Additional jobs in new firms thus formed a net expansion of the small firms sector as a whole. There was thus little evidence in Leicestershire of new firms merely displacing older small firms. In the next section we suggest some reasons for the slow growth of surviving Northern Ireland small firms compared to their British counterparts. At this stage we merely note that the faster growth in Leicestershire survivors in 1973–86 occurred in eight of the eleven industrial sectors and in all of the more important sectors.

9. Competitiveness and performance

Job creation is not only concerned with setting up new firms but also with the quality of those firms, in terms both of job duration and company growth. Northern Ireland was one of six regions included in a study of small firm competitiveness and performance by Hitchens and O'Farrell (1987, 1988a, 1988b) and this section summarises some of their results. Their research compared demand and supply side factors between matched manufacturing firms in different regions of the British Isles with the overall aim of singling out the strengths and weaknesses associated with different locations. In addition the purpose was to assess the impact of government assistance available and to form policy prescriptions which might be adopted by the various development agencies to overcome obstacles to growth. The regions included with Northern Ireland were Scotland, Wales, Southern England, the Mid West of Ireland and Dublin.

Companies were randomly matched principally in the engineering and clothing trades though a miscellaneous sector was also included to reflect broadly other characteristics of manufacturing. Direct comparisons were made between about forty Northern Ireland firms and a similar number of companies in South Wales and about half that number in South East England and the Mid West of Ireland.

In comparison with their British counterparts they found that Northern Ireland companies served more geographically immediate markets; for example, 92 per cent of the output of precision engineers was sold within Northern Ireland compared with just 72 per cent of that of their Welsh counterparts (the difference was not related to methods of selling). Since serving wider markets is an important means of growth for firms geographically separated from major markets, the apparent implication of the finding was that Northern Ireland's peripheral location in some way restricts growth. Such a problem was further suggested by the fact that a sample of Mid West companies too served more regional markets than did their Great Britain counterparts. But when they compared transport costs they were found everywhere to be small, of the order of 2 or 3 pence in the £, and while costs in Northern Ireland were found to be greater in comparison with those experienced by Welsh firms the differences were tiny, ranging from 0.01 pence to 1.1 pence in the £ and were therefore unlikely to limit the distance at which goods could be sold.

Differential transport costs on material inputs were investigated in comparison with small firms in South East England and no variation in delivered prices by local stockists was found. Purchasing disadvantages in peripheral localities were more likely to revolve around a restricted choice available at stockists. Logistic problems of supplying customers from a peripheral location were found to be potentially a greater obstacle, for example in engineering where interpretation of drawings and periodic consultations are required, but the experience across a wide range of producers indicated that such problems are not insurmountable provided that the product is competitive on price and quality.

While physical distances and transport costs were not a major constraint, more than half the firms in the Northern Ireland sample reported that a lack of demand for their products was an important impediment to growth compared with one in ten of their British mainland counterparts and despite the fact that the main source of custom outside Northern Ireland was Great Britain. Why then did the Northern Ireland companies have difficulties selling beyond the province?

Hitchens and O'Farrell made an assessment of the prices charged by firms in Northern Ireland and the quality of products produced by inviting matched companies to quote a price and judge the quality of products shown them. Similarly Northern Ireland proprietors assessed mainland British products. Table 5.14 reproduces the main results and shows that Welsh engineering firms were found on average to be cheaper and Northern Ireland clothing firms slightly more price competitive.

TABLE 5.14   Comparison of price and quality of products made by firms in Wales and Northern Ireland, 1986

Welsh products	Judgement by Northern Irish firms			
	Price quotations same or lower %	Number of products	Quality satisfactory %	Number of assessments
Engineering	27	12	93	17
Clothing	56	7	89	14
Total		19	90	31
Northern Irish products	Judgement by Welsh firms			
	Price quotations same or lower %	Number of products	Quality satisfactory %	Number of assessments
Engineering	67	15	18	21
Clothing	40	13	8	25
Miscellaneous	67	5	33	7
Total		33	15	53

Source: Hitchens and O'Farrell (1988a).

On quality, producers in Northern Ireland found fault with fewer than 10 per cent of Welsh products shown them, while Welsh owners considered that only 15 per cent of the Northern Ireland samples were of satisfactory quality as judged by the standards set for their own factories. Taking this finding in conjunction with the prices quoted, the authors concluded that the sample of Northern Irish companies was not competitive on quality and that the lack of demand and poor penetration of extra regional markets was due to that lack of competitiveness.

How then do uncompetitive firms survive? Among other factors, Hitchens and O'Farrell found that companies in Northern Ireland recognised only half the number of direct competitors indicated by their mainland British counterparts, suggesting a lack of exposure to wider British competition. Companies in the Mid West of Ireland were found to recognise fewer competitors than their British counterparts and when samples of their products were compared in the same way, they were found to be uncompetitive especially on price (less so on quality).

A number of further factors were investigated in order to identify underlying reasons for the lack of product competitiveness. The cost and size of premises were found to benefit the Northern Ireland companies in relation to their mainland British counterparts. A comparison of machinery used indicated substantially more modern and more computerised equipment in Northern Ireland. Those purchases were enabled by the generous grants obtainable there, and similarly modern machinery was found at Mid West companies again as a legacy of generous industrial assistance available in that region. However, despite having older equipment the authors found that mainland British companies did not consider themselves under-equipped and capital shortages reported by those companies had more to do with working capital needs than with financial requirements for the purchase of new plant and equipment.

The key, they claim, to understanding differences in product performance between firms in Northern Ireland and their mainland counterparts lay in the characteristics of their respective labour forces. While the cost of labour was found to be similar and the proportion of persons designated skilled was also similar, there was doubt about the level of skill or standard of on-the-job training received. Not only was this the implication of their findings on the comparatively poor product quality of products made by those Northern Ireland firms, but in addition a quarter of the proprietors in Northern Ireland reported an unsatisfactory level of skill on their shop floor. No mainland company said this. More Northern Irish owners also complained of labour force difficulties arising from an unacceptable attitude to work and linked this to trainability and productivity problems.

Productivity in Northern Ireland was measured by Hitchens and O'Farrell to be lower than in Wales in all sectors. It is interesting that they found fewer complaints made by Mid West managers about the attitudes and abilities of their labour forces. In the Mid West the greater lack of price competitiveness (compared with either Northern Ireland or mainland Britain) was traced to higher wages paid and productivity difficulties at sample companies. The better product quality performance by Mid West companies was associated with the proprietor's training background (and by extension to the on-the-job training and standards set for their workforce). They found that significantly fewer criticisms were made of products manufactured by Mid West firms where they were owned, managed or supervised by individuals trained at a foreign owned multinational or who had work experience abroad. In engineering, for example, three-quarters of proprietors at the Mid West companies had received such experience compared with just one-third in the Northern Ireland sample. Similarly, in both the Northern Ireland and Mid West of Ireland samples, companies run by foreign nationals expanded their employment faster than the average for the samples as a whole, and there were twice as many such companies in the Mid West sample as the Northern Irish sample.

Growth performance was measured over the period 1982–86 in terms of both employment and sales. The Northern Ireland companies sampled were found to have grown more slowly than those of any other region studied. While product competitiveness was a clear reason why these firms failed to sell more outside Northern Ireland, the fact that firms in the Mid West registered a better growth performance despite an even greater lack of price competitiveness than the Northern Ireland companies suggested that the level of home demand is also important, given that firms in both these areas of Ireland share a somewhat protected market. Geographical separation, small population size, lack of competition in the distributive sectors and fear arising from the Troubles serve to isolate the markets.

Notwithstanding the findings reported in the comparisons, Hitchens and O'Farrell did not consider that Northern Ireland companies were at a disadvantage because of their geographic location, there being no physical barrier to effective competition by firms in the peripheral region. However a recommendation was made for Development Agencies to move away from grant aiding machinery and equipment towards an emphasis on the human assets of businesses by way of both training and advice.

10. New firm formation

It has already been shown (Table 5.13) that new independent firms founded as small-scale businesses between 1973 and 1986 have contributed a large number of jobs to the manufacturing total in Northern Ireland. These new firms are widely distributed across industries. Northern Ireland is no exception to the general rule that new companies are concentrated in industries with low capital requirements for entry. These include timber products, mechanical engineering, metal goods, plastics and miscellaneous goods including toys. However, the rate of entry is higher than that in either the Republic of Ireland or Leicestershire in two industrial groups, food, drink, tobacco, and non-metallic mineral products. Conversely the number of new clothing firms is relatively low in view of the importance of this industry within Northern Ireland together with its low capital and skill requirement.

In all, an estimated 2,014 new firms founded in 1974 or later were still in operation in 1986. The great majority of these new companies remain small and three-quarters of them employed under ten people in 1986. However, even these smallest companies accounted for over 5,000 jobs. It is sometimes argued that most jobs in new firms are generated by a few high flyers. The contribution of the latter obviously depends on how high flyers are defined. However, if we define them as firms employing more than 50 at the end of the period, then it can be stated that Northern Ireland exhibits the typical pattern, ie the majority of jobs are generated by medium-sized new companies (employing between 10 and 49 people) rather than by high flyers. It is the large number of these medium-sized firms (486) which is more impressive than their individual size. While the 27 largest new companies, with over 50 employees each, employed 2,453 people by 1986, the medium-sized companies employed 9,103.

Harrison and Hart (1983) investigated the extent to which macro-economic constraints operate on the process of new firm formation in Northern Ireland over the period 1950–80. Using annual data on company registrations they demonstrated the importance of unemployment as a stimulus for the formation of new businesses in both the manufacturing and service sectors. However, more detailed work on the motivations of actual founders of new businesses would be desirable to test further the extent to which macro-economic variables have influenced their decision. More importantly, the relationship between the factors influencing the formation decision and the subsequent performance of the business is worthy of much greater study.

11. Small firms policy

The last ten years have seen an explosion of government interest in small firms. A wide range of measures have been enacted in favour of small business including exemptions from existing regulations. Northern Ireland firms potentially benefit from most of the national schemes and in addition have an active and well-funded local agency, LEDU, to promote enterprise. The most important national schemes to improve the flow of finance to small firms have been the Small Firms Loan Guarantee Scheme (LGS) and the Business Expansion Scheme (BES). The most intensive attempts at deregulation have involved the establishment of a series of Enterprise Zones in which firms were exempt from local rates, and most of local planning restrictions. Two Enterprise Zones have been established in Northern Ireland: in Belfast and in Derry. However, the benefits of an Enterprise Zone location are lower in Northern Ireland since most manufacturing industry is derated, and because the pressing need for new industry means that planning restrictions are less likely to hinder industrial development than in some parts of Great Britain.

The Loan Guarantee Scheme was initiated in 1981 in an attempt to improve the availability of medium-term bank finance to soundly based businesses which might otherwise experience difficulty in raising finance. Under the scheme the Government undertook to guarantee 80 per cent of loans (subsequently reduced to 70 per cent) up to a maximum of £70,000 for which firms are charged a premium over normal interest rates. The regional impact of LGS has been investigated by Harrison and Mason (1987). They show Northern Ireland's share of LGS loans was very low in the first phase (1981–84) partly due to a delay of a year in extending the scheme to the province. However, even in the first year of the revised LGS (1984–85) the take-up of loans in Northern Ireland was only three-quarters of what might have been expected given its share of eligible small firms. Harrison and Mason suggest that this below average take-up rate might reflect the availability of cheaper loans from LEDU. Nationally, the impact of LGS has been relatively small. In the first four years, 15,000 guarantees were issued, of which around half were to manufacturing firms and half of which were truly additional (Robson Rhodes 1984). The number of loans issued in Northern Ireland was 198, equivalent to only 1 or 2 per cent of all eligible firms.

The Business Expansion Scheme (originally the Business Start-up Scheme or BSS) was introduced in 1981 and revised and extended in 1983. Its aims were to facilitate investment by private individuals in small businesses through the provision of generous tax relief. To ease the transfer of funds from individuals the Government permitted the establishment of Approved Investment Funds. Watkins and Knowleman (1987) show that 70 per cent of the 26 Funds established were located in the South of England and none in Northern Ireland.

The average size of BES investment in 1984/85 was £160,000, with 234 companies being financed in that year through Funds. The scheme is thus a means of providing substantial investments to a few relatively larger small firms. In Northern Ireland it is likely that this role overlaps significantly with that of LEDU and to some extent also the Industrial Development Board.

12. The Local Enterprise Development Unit (LEDU)

Established in 1971, LEDU has grown rapidly in the 1980s to the position in 1987 when it had a staff of over 100 and an annual budget of £25 million. LEDU exists to promote employment in small business in Northern Ireland. It does so through a combination of administering Government grants and loans to small firms, and through organising a variety of schemes to increase competitiveness in small firms.

LEDU has become a highly active business development organisation. It had supported 4,620 projects by 1987, many of them during the last four years. Enquiries now run at a huge level of over 16,000 a year. In 1986/87

TABLE 5.15   LEDU support for small business, Northern Ireland, 1986/87

	£m	Projects	Jobs promoted and renewed
Employment related grants and loans			
New firms and expansions	16.6	320	3,281
Joint expansion/renewal	1.0	10	190
Job renewal	0.8	na	299
Enterprise Grants Scheme	3.2	607	773
Business support programmes			
R & D	1.0	124	na
Innovation	0.8	na	na
Property development etc			
Local Enterprise Programme	2.0	35	na
Private Developers Scheme	0.2	7	na
Youth Enterprise Scheme	0.3	na	na
Total	25.9	1,710	4,543

Source: LEDU Annual Report and Accounts.

support was given to 1,755 projects under the headings in Table 5.15. Over 4,500 jobs were promoted (ie promised by companies), and LEDU claims that within companies which survive 86 per cent of these promised are realised. Taking account of closures the figures drops to 69 per cent.

Most expenditure is committed to grants, and to a lesser extent loans, to encourage job creation through the setting up of new business ventures or the expansion of existing companies. Over the 16 years of LEDU's existence from 1971 to 1986 £15.5 million has been paid out in loans of which £6.0 million is currently outstanding. The £15 million of loans is in current rather than constant prices and the value (especially in earlier years) of the loans at the time they were issued would thus have been significantly greater. The loans are typically for five years with a two year initial repayment holiday. This scale of lending is likely to explain the lower take-up of LGS loans in Northern Ireland. Moreover, the level of irrecoverable or doubtful loans, at 22 per cent, appears to compare well with the national Loan Guarantee Scheme. Grants and loans are also made to support firms which might otherwise contract or close.

Enterprise Grants up to a total of £5,000 per person help employed people to set up in business, and assist the self-employed to take on an employee. In 1986/87 over 700 jobs were promoted in this way. This scheme is likely to explain the rapid rise in the number of very small manufacturing firms in Northern Ireland over recent years. Back-up support in the form of management training, advice in accountancy, and grants to employ managers, are also available.

One aspect of Northern Ireland's small manufacturing firms which emerges from analysis of the VAT registration data is that new small firms have a higher propensity to survive than in most parts of Great Britain.[1] This is likely to reflect both the generous regime of grants and loans available in Northern Ireland, and the wide range of business support schemes operated by LEDU. The latter include special grants and aid to promote R & D, design, marketing and innovation in small firms. LEDU also operates an Innovation Centre providing stimulus for business ideas, and New Enterprise Workshops to assist new firms to produce prototypes to the point of testing for commercial viability.

Enterprise Agencies promoting small business in local areas within Northern Ireland are now largely organised under the umbrella of LEDU which provides a significant part of their funding. There are 17 Enterprise Centres providing premises, advice, and other support to local businesses and an overall total of 24 Local Enterprise Agencies. In 1986/87 LEDU provided £1.6 million to Enterprise Groups, and this together with £0.4 million from the European Development Fund will provide 262 workshop units for small firms. Several of the Enterprise Centres are located in areas of extremely high unemployment with few alternative sources of employment. LEDU also encourages private provision of premises for small business. In the current year 30 per cent of the cost of a construction programme has been provided. This will provide 84,000 sq feet of space (approximately 60 units).

Finally, LEDU organises a Youth Enterprise Scheme providing grants and practical help to young people starting up in business. It also organises a range of conferences and exhibitions to promote small business and its products.

13. Conclusions on small firms

Small firms are an important part of Northern Ireland's manufacturing sector. The fact that the manufacturing sector is relatively small in comparison to the population of the province makes the small firms an even more important component of the local economy. Unfortunately the evidence suggests a number of shortcomings in the performance of Northern Ireland's small firm sector despite the existence of generous government financial assistance and an active local small firms agency itself employing more than 100 people.

A comparison of employment growth 1973–86 undertaken by Gudgin et al (1989) showed that Northern Ireland's small firms performed much less well than those in a selected non-peripheral area, Leicestershire. Closure rates were higher in Northern Ireland and the growth of survivors lower. Entrepreneurship has however flourished and rates of new firm formation were as high in Northern Ireland as in Leicestershire. Compared with the Republic of Ireland small firms in Northern Ireland performed more favourably.

Some of the reasons for the poorer growth performance have been investigated by Hitchens and O'Farrell (1987, 1988a, 1988b). Their conclusions suggests problems of competitiveness connected with both product quality and price compared with British regions. Capital equipment appeared to be at least as good in Northern Ireland as elsewhere, and lack of labour skills were suggested as a more likely source of the competitive deficiencies.

Note

1. Examination of numbers of registrations for VAT of manufacturing companies between 1981 and 1986 shows that Northern Ireland had a below average rate of new registrations per thousand employees. It also, however, had an even lower level of deregistrations. As a consequence the stock of registered companies rose more rapidly in Northern Ireland than in Great Britain. Nothing is known of the employment in these companies, and hence it is not possible to compare the implications of this evidence with that given in Table 5.13. It should also be noted that the period is different from that used in Table 5.13.

References

Birch, D L (1979) The job generation process, *MIT Program on Urban and Regional Change*, Cambridge, Mass.

Bull, P J (1984) The impact of government policy on industrial diversification: the Northern Ireland case, in Barr, B M and Waters, N M (eds), *Regional Diversification and Structural Change*, Tantalus Research, Vancouver.

Bull, P J and Hart, M (1987) Northern Ireland, in Damesick, P and Wood, P (eds), *Regional Problems, Problem Regions and Public Policy in the United Kingdom*, Oxford University Press, Oxford.

Department of Industry (1981) The components of change by size and region. Mimeo.

Dunning, J H (1981) *International Production and the Multinational Enterprise*, George Allen and Unwin, London.

Enderwick, I P (forthcoming) *The Economics of Multinational Restructuring*, Routledge, London.

Fothergill, S and Gudgin, G (1979) The job generation process in Britain, *Centre for Environmental Studies Research Series* No 32.

Gudgin, G (1984) Employment creation by small and medium sized firms in the UK, in Greffe, X (ed), *Les P.M.E. Créent-Elles Des Emplois? Economica*, Paris.

Gudgin, G, Hart, M, Fagg J, Keegan, R and D'Arcy, E (1989) Job generation in manufacturing industry. A comparison of Northern Ireland with the Republic of Ireland and Leicestershire. NIERC Mimeo.

Harris, R I D (1987) The role of manufacturing in regional growth, *Regional Studies*, 21, 301–12.

Harrison, R T and Hart, M (1983) Factors influencing new business formation: a case study of Northern Ireland, *Environment and Planning A* 15, 1393–1412.

Harrison, R T and Mason, C (1987) The regional impact of the small Firms Loan Guarantee Scheme, in O'Neill, K et al (eds), op cit.

Hart, M (1987) The urban labour market impact of new and small manufacturing firms – some evidence from the Belfast Urban Area, in O'Neill, K, Bhambri, R, Faulkner, T, and Cannon, T (eds), *Small Business Development, Some Current Issues*, Avebury.

Healey, M J and Watts, H D (1987) The multiplant enterprise, in Lever, W F (ed), *Industrial Change in the United Kingdom*. Longman, Harlow.

Hitchens, D M W N and O'Farrell, P N (1987) The performance of small manufacturing firms in Northern Ireland and SE England, *Regional Studies*, 21, 6, 543–53.

Hitchens, D M W N and O'Farrell, P N (1988a) The comparative performance of small manufacturing companies in South Wales and Northern Ireland, *Omega*, 16, 5, 429–38.

Hitchens, D M W N and O'Farrell, P N (1988b) The comparative performance of small manufacturing companies located in the Mid West and Northern Ireland, *The Economic and Social Review*, 19, 3, 177–98.

Hoare, A G (1978) Industrial linkages and the dual economy: the case of Northern Ireland, *Regional Studies*, 12, 2, 167–80.

Hood, N and Young, S (1983) *Multinational Investment Strategies in the British Isles*, HMSO, London.

Keeble, D (1976) *Industrial Location and Planning in the United Kingdom*, Methuen, London.

Robson Rhodes (1984) *Small Business Loan Guarantee Scheme*, DTI, London.

Townsend, A R (1983) *The Impact of Recession on Industry, Employment and the Regions, 1976–1981*, Croom Helm, Beckenham.

Watkins, D and Knowleman, N (1987) The Business Expansion Scheme and the supply of capital to the small firm sector, in O'Neill, K et al (eds), op cit.

Young, S, Hood, N and Hamill, J (1988) *Foreign Multinationals and the British Economy*, Croom Helm, Beckenham.

CHAPTER SIX

The labour market

Clifford W Jefferson

1. Introduction

Northern Ireland has a strong industrial tradition dating back to the middle of the last century but despite this it remains the United Kingdom region with the lowest level of per capita income, the highest rate of unemployment and the highest rate of outward migration. Although the rate of job creation during periods in the past has been among the highest in the United Kingdom, it has still failed to keep pace with the natural growth in the labour force. The region's high rate of natural population increase, lack of natural resources, and remoteness from principal markets have been the basic causes of its economic problems. Writing in 1957, Isles and Cuthbert described the Northern Ireland economy in similar terms and concluded that 'Under-employment is therefore not merely a passing phase but a chronic tendency ...'. Thirty years later, in the wake of the most extensive and sustained programme of regional development in the United Kingdom, and major expansion in the state sector of the economy, unemployment is at its highest level since the 1930s and the prognosis is no more optimistic than when Isles and Cuthbert were writing. The Northern Ireland labour market is still characterised by the inability of the regional economy to generate sufficient employment growth to match the rapid natural growth in the labour force with consequential high outward migration and high levels of unemployment.

An analysis of the forces operating in the labour market requires examination of the factors affecting both the growth of employment and the labour supply. These two variables are not independent and both are affected, one indirectly, the other directly, by demographic factors. A simple methodology which permits analysis of the major variables affecting the labour market is the 'labour market accounts' technique devised by the Cambridge Economic Policy Group (1980). This technique is based on an ex-post identity which attributes the natural increase in the labour force[1] to changes in employment, regional migration of labour and changes in unemployment. In what follows, the technique is used firstly as a vehicle for the historical analysis of the major components of the Northern Ireland labour market over the past three decades and secondly as a framework on which to examine the likely future course of the labour market on the basis of a set of plausible assumptions.

As a purely numerical accounting model the labour market accounts approach is limited in some ways. It cannot take account of qualitative factors such as changes in skill levels or the impact of education or training programmes. In addition, it takes no account of wage rates, the price of the commodity in the regional labour market. These topics are dealt with in later chapters. Chapter 7 considers several qualitative aspects of the Northern Ireland labour market and Chapter 9 examines the major issues associated with local wage rates.

The labour market identity shows the natural increase in the labour force as being equal to the sum of the change in employment and the change in unemployment less net migration as:

$$\Delta L_t = \Delta E_t + \Delta U_t - M_t \qquad [1]$$

where

ΔL_t = the natural increase in the labour force in the region during period t
ΔE_t = the change in employment
ΔU_t = the change in unemployment
M_t = the net migrant labour force (net inward migration is +ve).

With population growth in Northern Ireland tending to be more rapid than growth in employment opportunities, net migration is invariably outward and hence negative to the region. The natural increase in the labour force is thus equal to the sum of the change in employment, the change in unemployment and net outward migration of labour.

The identity can of course be rewritten as:

$$\Delta L_t - \Delta E_t = \Delta U_t - M_t \qquad [2]$$

which implies that any shortfall in job creation in relation to the natural increase in the labour force must result in either an increase in unemployment and/or outward migration.

An alternative rearrangement

$$\Delta L_t + M_t = \Delta E_t + \Delta U_t \qquad [3]$$

could be interpreted as saying that the actual increase in the labour force within the region (ie $\Delta L_t + M_t$) must exactly equal the change in employment plus the change in unemployment.

For the purpose of the present analysis it is convenient to designate the left-hand side of [3] as the supply side of the labour market and the right-hand-side variables as the demand side. Section 2 of the chapter discusses the historical influences on the supply side of the labour market, specifically examining demographic factors, migration and activity rates. Section 3 outlines the major changes in the levels and pattern of employment over the past three decades and the trend and characteristics of regional unemployment. In Section 4 both sets of variables are brought together and summarised in the labour market accounts model. Section 5 examines the labour force outlook for

TABLE 6.1 Northern Ireland population and net migration, 1951–1986 (000)

Year of enumeration	Population (1)	Births (2)	Deaths (3)	Natural increase (4) = (2) − (3)	Intercensal Changes		
					Population change (5)	Adjustment for HM Forces[2] (6)	Net outward migration (7)
1951[1]	1,370.9	402.2	243.7	158.4	+91.2	—	67.3[3]
1961	1,425.0	298.8	152.5	146.3	+54.1	—	92.2
1966	1,484.8	182.5	85.0	97.4	+59.7	—	37.7
1971	1,536.1	148.7	72.6	76.1	+51.3	6.7	31.5
1981	1,532.2	274.8	167.2	107.6	−3.9	—	111.4
1986[4]	1,566.8	144.6	84.0	60.6	+34.6	—	27.3[5]

Note: The population figures are at a point in time at the date shown. All other figures are for intercensal periods ending on the date shown.
[1] The previous COP was in 1937.
[2] Since the COP estimate includes all persons present and enumerated in Northern Ireland on Census night including civilians and service personnel it is necessary to make an adjustment to take account of changes in HM Forces in order to arrive at civilian migration for the intercensal period 1966–71.
[3] Including deaths in HM Forces and Mercantile Marine which occurred outside Northern Ireland.
[4] Mid-year.
[5] This published figure does not correspond exactly to the change in population and natural increase.
Source: The NI COP, 1981 Preliminary Report, with subsequent revisions in official estimates for 1981 published in the RGAR 1984. Figures for 1986 from NIAAS No 6, 1987.

TABLE 6.2 Rates of natural increase per 1,000 population, EC, 1960–1986

Year	NI	Bel	Den	Fr	Ger	Gr	Irl	It	Lux	Neth	Port	Spn	UK	EC12
1960	11.7	4.6	7.1	6.5	5.9	11.6	9.9	8.8	4.1	13.2	13.3	13.1	6.8	8.0
1970	10.1	2.3	4.6	6.1	1.3	8.1	10.4	7.2	0.8	9.9	9.9	11.3	4.5	5.8
1980	7.6	1.1	0.3	4.7	−1.5	6.3	11.9	1.7	0.2	4.7	6.5	7.4	1.6	2.7
1986	7.7	0.6	−0.5	4.3	−1.2	2.4	7.9	0.3	0.9	4.1	3.1	4.4[1]	3.1	1.8

[1] 1984.
Sources: Eurostat, Demographic Statistics, Luxembourg 1988; NI RGAR.

the period 1986 to 1996. The conclusion examines the implications for policy measures which arise from consideration of the labour market accounts.

2. The supply of labour

The size of the labour force depends on the size of the population, its age/sex composition and the level of participation among working age groups, all of which are affected by the level and composition of net migration.

POPULATION

The official estimates[2] of population and migration for Northern Ireland are shown in Table 6.1. They show the rapid increases in population in the 1950s and 1960s as the net results of high rates of natural increase and outward migration. In the 1970s the natural increase in the population, somewhat reduced, though still high by international standards, was more than cancelled out by the greatly increased level of outward migration, so that the population fell by 4,000. The estimated rapid growth in population during the 1980s is due to the low levels of outward migration.

Northern Ireland experiences a high rate of natural increase, compared with other western countries. This is readily confirmed by Table 6.2 where only the Republic of Ireland has a higher rate. In common with most European countries, a fall in the birth rate in the 1970s reduced the rate of natural increase in Northern Ireland (to 7.6 per 1,000 of population in the early 1980s). In contrast, the rate of natural increase in the Republic of Ireland increased in the 1960s and 1970s to a level of 11.9 per 1,000 in 1980 before declining in the early 1980s.

The intercensal estimates of migration show a high level of outward migration (92,000) in the 1950s, a period of relative stagnation in the Northern Ireland economy, followed by a substantial fall in the level of outward migration in the economically buoyant 1960s (69,000). The dramatic increase to 111,000 in the 1970s can be principally attributed to the impact of the civil disturbances. The estimates of migration in individual years given in Appendix 6.1 indicate the exceptionally high levels in the early 1970s during the worst years of the civil disturbances, which peaked in 1972/73 at almost 24,000 emigrants.[3]

At a point in time the supply of labour depends not on the total population but on the population of working age and on the level of labour force participation. Table 6.3 shows numbers in working age groups over the period 1951 to 1986. Corresponding to the school leaving ages, the working age groups include persons aged 14 and over in 1951, 15 and over in 1961 and 1971, and 16 and over in 1981 and 1986. The raising of the school leaving age to 15 in 1957 and to 16 in 1972 had the effect of reducing the size of the population of working age. In addition, the natural rate of population growth and the level of outward migration determine its size. For example, the rapid increase in the working age groups of 52,000 from 1981 to 1986 partly reflects the low level of outward migration over the period and partly the high birth rates of the late 1960s.

WORKFORCE PARTICIPATION

Activity rates for males and females were calculated separately by dividing the workforce in each year by the corresponding population of working age. The data in Table 6.3 indicate that the male workforce remained substantially unchanged from 1951 to 1971 but increased by 17,000 in the 1970s. The female workforce remained static during the 1950s but grew by 21,000 in the 1960s as the expansion in the economy provided opportunities for female labour in

TABLE 6.3   Male and female activity rates, Northern Ireland, 1951–1986

		1951	1961	1971	1981	1986
(1) Number in working age groups[1] (000)						
	Male	485.5	482.6	519.6	521.8	550.2
	Female	528.9	530.2	559.5	567.1	590.7
	Total:	1,014.4	1,021.8	1,079.1	1,088.9	1,140.9
(2) Number in civil employment (June) (000)						
	Male	371.0	371.2	364.8	336.8	313.2
	Female	176.0	168.8	189.9	230.4	236.2
	Total:	547.0	540.0	554.7	567.2	549.4
(3) Numbers unemployed[2] (June) (000)						
	Male	18.5	23.4	27.9	65.3	92.0
	Female	5.2	8.5	6.8	24.6	33.9
	Total:	23.7	31.9	34.7	89.9	125.9
(4) Workforce[3] (000) (2) + (3)						
	Male	389.5	394.6	392.7	402.1	405.2
	Female	181.2	177.3	196.7	255.0	270.2
	Total:	570.7	571.9	589.4	657.1	675.3
(5) Activity rates (4) + (1) × 100						
	Male	80.2	81.8	75.6	77.1	73.6
	Female	34.3	33.4	35.2	45.0	45.7
	Total:	56.3	56.5	54.6	60.3	59.2

[1] Working age groups include persons aged 14 and over in 1951, 15 and over in 1961 and 1971, and 16 and over in 1981 and 1986.
[2] Numbers unemployed in 1971, 1981 and 1986 are 'claimant based'. (Figures supplied by DED.) Figures for 1951 and 1961 are 'registered unemployed'. For comparison between the two measures the level of registered unemployment in 1971 was 37,000.
[3] Working population.
Sources: NI COP; NIDS; NIAAS.

modern light manufacturing industry and in the expanding service industries. In the 1970s the sustained expansion of public sector services, providing part-time employment for females, was largely responsible for the growth of female employment.[4] By 1981 the number of females in civil employment had increased by 40,000 over the decade while female unemployment rose by 18,000. The growth was principally among married women returning to work after their childbearing years,[5] see Chapter 7. The overall growth in the workforce from 571,900 in 1961 to 657,100 in 1981 was substantially due to the expansion of female employment.

The combination of these changes in the workforce and numbers of working age are reflected in the activity rates. The fall in male activity rates from 1961 to 1971 was due to the increase in the number of working age while the increase from 1971 to 1981 is the result of the increase in the workforce, albeit a workforce with a much larger proportion unemployed. The female activity rate altered little between 1951 and 1971 but the major increase in female participation occurred in the 1970s with the rapid increase in female employment throughout the decade and the sharp rise in female unemployment in the 1980–81 recession. As can be seen in Table 6.4 this rise in female participation might be regarded as catching up on levels of participation in Great Britain. Female participation in Northern Ireland is now substantially above that in the Republic of Ireland (one of the lowest in the European Community) which has a low level of participation for married women.

TABLE 6.4 Activity rates[1], Northern Ireland, Great Britain and the Republic of Ireland, 1971–1986

	1971		1981		1986	
	Males	Females	Males	Females	Males	Females
Northern Ireland	75.6	35.2	77.1	45.0	73.6	45.7
Great Britain	80.5	43.9	76.5	47.6	73.4	49.2
England	80.6	44.3	76.7	47.9	73.6	49.7
Scotland	80.5	43.6	76.8	47.6	72.6	47.4
Wales	78.4	36.7	73.3	42.2	68.9	45.0
Rep. of Ireland	79.2	27.3	75.4	29.1	72.3^2	29.4^2

[1] In Great Britain and Northern Ireland activity rates are calculated as the percentage of the home population of working age who are in the civilian labour force. In the Republic of Ireland they are calculated as the percentage of the population of working age (14+ in 1971 and 15+ in 1981 and 1986) who are 'economically active'.
[2] 1985.
Sources: RT No 23, 1988; NIAAS and Employment Supplement 1987. For Republic of Ireland, 1985 LFS and COP, various.

MIGRATION

Migration plays a major role in the Northern Ireland labour market. On the one hand, net outward migration reduces the labour supply while on the other, the emigrants take their expenditure out of the regional economy, thereby reducing regional demand and hence employment. Inflows of migrants into prosperous regions have a cumulative expansionary effect on output and employment while outflows of migrants from depressed regions such as Northern Ireland will tend to have the opposite effects on the regional economy. In the short term, the net effect of outward migration on the Northern Ireland labour market is to reduce unemployment but this may well be at a cost to the longer term growth prospects, especially since migrants tend to be biased towards the younger and more highly skilled members of the workforce.

In common with other peripheral regions in Great Britain, the South East is the principal destination for migrants from Northern Ireland. In the past inter-regional flows have followed national economic fluctuations, falling during recession and rising during periods of expansion (Ogilvy 1982). In Northern Ireland, high levels of unemployment, low incomes and, during the early 1970s, the civil disturbances have provided the major push factors. The influence of the economic factors may well be affected by the availability of social security benefits and their levels relative to average wages. However, the historical migration of labour from the province to Great Britain has been principally due to the lack of employment opportunities in the former and their availability in the latter. In regions with high rates of population increase, such as Northern Ireland and the Republic of Ireland, outward migration has acted as a safety valve which has prevented levels of unemployment from continuously diverging from levels in the more prosperous regions.

The annual estimates of migration given in Appendix 6.1 together with estimates of the age/sex breakdown and age/sex specific death rates[6] were used to estimate surviving migrants of working age at the end of each decade. Multiplying these figures by end-of-decade activity rates for Northern Ireland gives estimates of the potential migrant workforce.

TABLE 6.5   Net civilian migration and potential migrant workforce, 1951–1981 (000)

	1951–1961			1961–1971			1971–1981		
	Male	Female	Total	Male	Female	Total	Male	Female	Total
(1) All migrants	49.1	43.1	92.2	36.1	33.1	69.2	58.7	52.7	111.4
(2) Surviving migrants of working age[1] at end of decade	41.6	36.4	77.9	30.4	27.9	58.3	52.5	48.3	100.8
(3) Potential migrant workforce at end of decade	34.0	12.2	46.2	23.0	9.8	32.8	40.4	21.7	62.1
(4) Percentage of total potential workforce at end of decade[2]	7.9	6.4	7.5	5.9	4.7	5.3	9.1	7.8	8.6

[1] Working age is taken as 14 and over in 1951, 15 and over in 1961 and 1971, and 16 and over in 1981.
[2] Calculated as (3) ÷ [(3) + working population in Northern Ireland at end of decade].

Table 6.5 indicates, for example, that of the 69,200 net emigrants from 1961 to 1971, 58,300 aged 15 and over would have survived to 1971 (after applying age specific mortality rates). If the 1971 activity rates for Northern Ireland are applied to these surviving migrants this would give an estimated potential migrant workforce of 32,800 in 1971. Similarly, the 111,400 emigrants in the decade to 1981 imply a potential migrant workforce of 62,100 in 1981.

These figures of the potential migrant workforce must of course be regarded as somewhat speculative since activity rates are unlikely to be independent of the level of migration.[7] Nevertheless it seems a reasonable working hypothesis that intercensal migration in the decade to 1971 reduced the supply of labour by 32,800 (5.3 per cent of the total workforce) and in the decade to 1981 by 62,100 persons (8.6 per cent).

3. The demand side

EMPLOYMENT

After remaining relatively static in the 1950s the total in civil employment rose almost continuously throughout the 1960s and 1970s to a peak of 598,000 in 1979 before falling back to 567,000 in 1981 and stabilising between 560,000 and 550,000 in the early and mid 1980s (see Table 6.3).[8]

The patterns for male and female employment are quite different. Apart from the 1950s when it remained constant over the decade, male employment in the province has been in long term decline punctuated by cyclical fluctuations over the period. The most recent cyclical peak was in 1979 with male employment at 359,000 but more than 30,000 male jobs were lost over the next three years in the recession and numbers continued to fall to 313,000 in 1986.

Female employment began to grow in the 1960s with the introduction into the province of the light manufacturing industries and the expansion of services. This expansion of services accelerated in the 1970s and only contracted in 1981 because of the recession and the cutbacks in the growth of

TABLE 6.6   Civil employment, Northern Ireland, 1951–1986

	(000)					% of total employment				
	1951	1961	1971	1981	1986	1951	1961	1971	1981	1986
Primary	124	89	65	48	47	22.3	16.5	11.6	8.5	8.6
Manufacturing	203	174	174	123	103	36.5	32.2	31.4	21.7	18.8
Construction	34	43	48	37	32	6.2	8.0	8.7	6.5	5.8
Services	195	234	268	359	367	35.0	43.3	48.3	63.3	66.8
Total	556	540	555	567	549	100.0	100.0	100.0	100.0	100.0

Sources: 1974–1986, NIAAS Employment Supplement, April 1987 (based on 1980 SIC). 1951–1973, DMS Gazette, No 3, 1979 and various issues of NIDS (based on 1968 SIC).

public expenditure. Since then it has grown continuously, if rather slowly. Female employment which constituted 31 per cent of total employment in 1961, accounted for 43 per cent in 1986.

The growth of sectoral employment over the period is illustrated in Figure 6.1 and Table 6.6. There are several obvious long term trends: the decline of agricultural and manufacturing employment, the rise and eventual decline of construction and the rapid growth of services in the 1960s and especially the 1970s. The overall picture is one of massive structural change. In the first part of this century, shipbuilding, linen and agriculture were the cornerstones of the local economy. In 1951 these three industries employed some 239,000 persons, about 43 per cent of total employment. By 1981, changes in technology and changes in world markets had reduced employment in these three industries to 64,000, 11 per cent of the total.

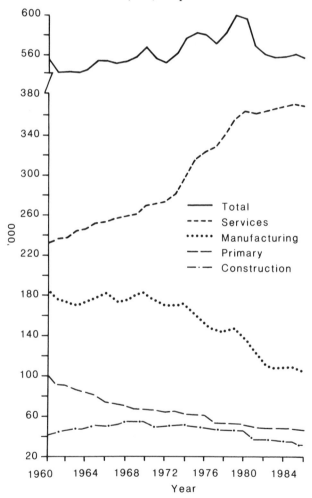

FIG 6.1 Civil employment, Northern Ireland, 1960–1986.
Source: as Table 6.6.

In the 1960s the decline in the traditional manufacturing industries was largely offset by employment created in the new science-based industries attracted to the province by the Government sponsored industrial development programme (see Jefferson 1987). During this period Northern Ireland was probably the most successful region in the British Isles in attracting mobile investment.[9] However, with the worsening national and international climate of the 1970s, the 'oil crisis' and the civil disturbances, manufacturing employment fell steadily in the second half of the decade and plunged dramatically in 1980 and 1981 as national and regional economies went deep into recession. Manufacturing employment, which in 1971 was 174,000 (not far below the post-war high) had fallen to 123,000 by 1981 and many of the firms regarded as the successes of the Industrial Development Policy had contracted or closed down (see Chapter 4).

Surprisingly, the civil disturbances had relatively little direct impact on existing manufacturing industry.[10] The major damage to the manufacturing sector was due to the adverse effects on the perceived image of Northern Ireland presented in Great Britain and abroad during a period when internationally mobile investment was contracting. As a result, the inflow of viable investment projects from outside the province fell to a trickle in the early 1970s and, despite successive initiatives on the part of the various Government agencies to change the situation, it has remained small and quite insufficient to revitalise the manufacturing sector. Rowthorn (1981) has estimated the net loss of manufacturing jobs between 1970 and 1980, as a consequence of the disturbances, at 25,000.

After the recession years of 1980–82 manufacturing employment in Northern Ireland has continued to decline and in 1986, at 103,000, provides only 19 per cent of total employment.

Employment in the construction industry reached a peak of 54,000 in the late 1960s as a result of the expansion in the public sector building programme and the rising level of prosperity. However, it has contracted slowly and fitfully since then, principally reflecting the cuts in the public sector building programme, which traditionally has accounted for the major part of construction work in the province. There was a gradual contraction throughout the 1970s but a massive fall of 8,000 in 1981 as the recession bit hard in the private sector and the Conservative Government's policy of cutting back on the growth of public expenditure began to take effect. The slow decline in employment in the construction industry has continued throughout the 1980s.

Civil employment in services grew rapidly throughout most of the period under consideration so that while it accounted for about one-third of all employment in 1951, by 1986 two out of every three jobs in the province were in services. Although there is evidence of employment growth in a number of private sector services, for example, banking, insurance and business services, marketed services as a whole grew relatively little. The major area of service growth was in the public sector where, for example, employment[11] increased between 1961 and 1981 by 164 per cent from 73,000 to 193,000. This rapid growth was due, in part, to the increased emphasis on the provision of public services within the United Kingdom, but the expansion in Northern Ireland in the 1960s and 1970s was much more rapid than in the rest of the United Kingdom reflecting the drive to achieve parity of standards in the provision of social services in areas where Northern Ireland lagged behind.[12] This is discussed in more detail in Chapter 14.

Public sector employment, as shown in Table 6.7, grew from 13.5 per cent of total civil employment in 1961 to 36.1 per cent in 1986. As part of the Government's Medium Term Financial Strategy, expressed in the March 1980 Budget Statement,[13] the growth of public expenditure has been curtailed throughout the 1980s so that the growth of public sector employment, which was the principal engine of growth of the regional economy in the 1960s and especially the 1970s, virtually ceased in the 1980s. With Government policy firmly set against the growth of public spending and Northern Ireland's public expenditure (relative to need) now having caught up with the rest of the United Kingdom, major growth in public sector employment is unlikely in the foreseeable future.

TABLE 6.7   Civil employment in private and public sector services,[1] 1961–1986

	Private sector (000)	Public sector (000)	Public sector services as % of total employment
1961	161	73	13.5
1971	167	117	21.1
1981	166	193	34.0
1986	167	198	36.1

[1] For the definition of public sector services used here see Note 9.
Source: As Table 6.6 and DED.

The regional comparison of the distribution of employees in employment in 1986 in Table 6.8 strongly suggests that the pattern in Northern Ireland is out of line with the rest of the United Kingdom with the very high proportion in public sector employment, a very low proportion in the grouping referred to as 'marketed services' and a relatively low proportion employed in manufacturing.

UNEMPLOYMENT

Any analysis of unemployment faces conceptual and statistical problems of measurement. Though the conceptual definition is far from precise it is generally accepted that to be regarded as unemployed, a person must be without a job, and be actively seeking and be available for work at the going wage. This still leaves some rather difficult grey areas, for example, in distinguishing between the unemployed and the economically inactive. The statistical measurement of the unemployment concept is usually dependent on administrative procedures or policy decisions. Thus for example, in the United

TABLE 6.8   Industrial distribution of employees in employment, Northern Ireland and Great Britain, June 1986 (percentage)

	Agriculture, forestry and fishing	Manufacturing	Construction	Marketed services	Public admin and other services
Division	0	2, 3, 4	5	1,6,7,8	9
N Ireland	2.1	21.3	4.5	28.0	44.3
England	1.4	24.7	4.4	39.5	29.9
Wales	2.4	23.9	5.1	35.8	32.9
Scotland	1.6	22.0	7.4	36.5	32.5

Source: RT No 22, 1987.

Kingdom unemployment was measured by the National Insurance card count up until April 1975 but from then until October 1982, the count of persons 'registered' as unemployed at Job Centres was used. From October 1982 onward there have been several changes in the statistical definition,[14] most of which have tended to reduce the size of the category of unemployment, but the major change has been to count only those unemployed persons actually claiming benefit.

Measured unemployment in Northern Ireland has continuously been the highest of all the regions of the United Kingdom. Even while Great Britain was enjoying low levels of unemployment around 2 per cent in the 1960s, the unemployment rate in Northern Ireland rarely fell below 6 or 7 per cent. Figure 6.2 shows that the unemployment rate[15] reached a post-war low of 4.2 per cent (25,500) in 1974 but from then it rose almost continuously. By June 1979 claimant based unemployment had grown to 60,000, 9.1 per cent of the

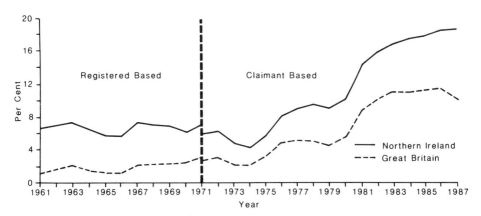

FIG 6.2   Unemployment rates,[1] Northern Ireland and Great Britain, 1961–1987
[1] Figures are for June each year. From 1961 to 1971 unemployment rates are based on registered unemployment as a percentage of insured employees. From 1971 to 1981 they are calculated as claimant based unemployment as a percentage of the working population.
Sources: DNS Gazette, No 1, Spring 1978; NIASS; British Labour Statistics; E9; AAS.

working population. The numbers unemployed increased dramatically through-out the recession of 1980–82 to stand at 106,000 (15.9 per cent) in June 1982 and while the rate of increase slowed thereafter, by June 1986 it had reached 126,000 (18.6 per cent).

The high level of correlation between the national and regional rates of unemployment is evidenced by the similarity of the cyclical movements of the two series. There is ample evidence that this cyclical relationship is common to all regions of the United Kingdom but recent work (Forrest and Naisbitt 1987) suggests that the peripheral regions, and especially Northern Ireland, are prone to larger than average fluctuations. Although Northern Ireland's unemployment rate has persistently been the highest in the United Kingdom, Table 6.9 confirms that other regions, most obviously the North, but also the North West, Wales and Scotland, have rates well above the national average. Currently, Northern Ireland's unemployment problem should be seen in the context of the level of national unemployment, high historically and in comparison with other national economies, and at its most severe in the peripheral regions. As can be seen in Table 6.10, substantial regional variation in unemployment is common in Europe. The Republic of Ireland has a similar unemployment rate to Northern Ireland and the second highest national rate in Europe. It suffers from the same basic economic problems as Northern Ireland, namely the inability of a small open economy with limited natural resources, on the periphery of Europe, to grow fast enough to absorb the rapid natural growth in the labour force.

Appendix 6.2 shows that the changes in the method of counting unemployment reduced the count by almost 19,000 between October 1982 and March 1986. Measured on the basis in operation prior to October 1982

TABLE 6.9   Regional unemployment rates in the United Kingdom, 1979, 1982 and 1986

	Unemployment rates[1] (annual average) %			
	1979	1982	1986	Deviation from United Kingdom rate, 1986
United Kingdom	4.9	10.9	11.8	0.0
North	7.9	15.5	16.3	4.5
Yorks and Humberside	5.1	12.2	13.5	1.7
East Midlands	4.0	9.9	10.6	−1.2
East Anglia	3.7	8.5	8.7	−3.1
South East	3.0	7.7	8.6	−3.2
South West	4.8	9.1	10.1	−1.7
West Midlands	4.8	13.6	13.5	1.7
North West	6.1	13.6	14.9	3.1
Wales	6.5	13.8	14.9	3.1
Scotland	6.9	13.0	14.6	2.8
Northern Ireland	9.1	16.1	18.6	6.8

[1] Percentage of working population.
Source: RT No 22, 1987 and No 23, 1988.

TABLE 6.10   European unemployment rates,[1] 1979 and 1986 (percentage)

	1979[2]	1986[2]	Minimum and maximum regional rates, 1986 (April)			
Belgium	8.4	11.8	West-Vlaanderen	7.2	Hainaut	14.2
Denmark	5.8	5.8	Hovedstadregionen	7.9	Ost for Storebaelt	8.3
West Germany	3.3	6.6	Stuttgart	3.3	Bremen	13.3
Greece	na	8.2	Thraki	3.6	Kentriki Ellas Kai Evia	10.2
France	6.0	10.4	Alsace	7.1	Languedoc-Roussillon	13.9
Ireland	7.4	18.5	Ireland[4]	18.7		
Italy	6.7	10.6	Valle d'Aosta	4.6	Sardegna	19.3
Luxembourg	0.7	2.7	Luxembourg[4]	2.5		
Netherlands	5.5	10.2	Zeeland	6.5	Groningen	13.2
United Kingdom	4.7	11.5	East Anglia	9.8	Northern Ireland	18.7
Spain	na	21.3	Galicia	14.0	Andalucia	30.2
Portugal	na	8.7	Portugal[4]	8.7		
Eur 12	5.5[3]	10.8	Luxembourg	2.5	Andalucia	30.2

[1] Registered unemployed as a percentage of civilian working population.
[2] Annual averages.
[3] Estimate.
[4] No regional breakdown available.
Sources: Eurostat, Eurostatistics 6/1988 and Eurostat Review 1976–1985 Eurostat Regions – Statistical Yearbook 1987.

unemployment could have amounted to around 145,000 at June 1986.

Persons undergoing training in a Government sponsored scheme or in a special employment scheme are not officially counted as unemployed though, in general, it may not be unreasonable to assume that the majority are in these schemes because they have been unable to find suitable employment. At the end of June 1986 there were almost 11,000 adults in employment and training schemes run by the Department of Economic Development and over 9,000 young people engaged in the Youth Training Programme. If these persons on special employment and training programmes are added to the estimated unemployment on the pre-October 1982 basis it would suggest a total of 165,000 persons looking for work at June 1986.

4. Labour market accounts 1951–1986

The labour market accounts for the three decades 1951 to 1981, and for the five year period 1981 to 1986 are summarised in Table 6.11. The method of calculation can readily be appreciated by examining the figures for one time period, for example 1961–71.

The natural increase in the population of working age is made up of those who remained in the province and those who migrated. If the home

TABLE 6.11   Labour market accounts for Northern Ireland, 1951–1986 (000)

	1951–61	1961–71	1971–81	1981–86
Natural increase in working age				
groups	76.5	125.6	110.6	75.7
Apply activity rates at start of period	44.0	74.2	61.1	47.2
Due to change in activity rates	3.4	−23.9	68.8	−14.6
Increase in workforce (working				
population)	47.4	50.3	129.9	32.6
Change in civil employment	−7.0	14.7	12.5	−17.8
Shortfall in employment				
opportunities	54.4	35.6	117.4	50.4
Outward migration of labour	46.2	32.8	62.1	14.4
Increase in unemployment	8.2	2.8	55.2	36.0

Note: Details may not sum to totals because of rounding.

activity rates at the end of the period, ie in 1971, are applied to the potential population of working age surviving in 1971 this will give an estimate of the potential workforce in 1971. Thus the natural increase in population of working age (at home and migrating) of 125,600 is accompanied by a potential increase in the workforce of 50,300.

This can be seen as the result of natural increase and a change in activity rates. The effect of the change in activity rates can be calculated by subtracting the increase in the potential workforce based on 1961 activity rates (74,200) from the figure based on activity rates at the end of the decade (50,300). Thus the change in activity rates between 1961 and 1971 was responsible for a fall of 23,900 in the potential workforce.

The excess of the increase in the potential workforce over the change in civil employment (14,700) leaves a shortfall in employment opportunities of 35,600. This shortfall in jobs, which is simply the left-hand side of equation [2] in the introduction, is exactly equal to the change in unemployment and net migration of labour. Outward migration of labour accounted for 32,800 of the shortfall and the remainder 2,800 is the increase in unemployment.

In the decade 1971–81, the reason for the large increase in the potential workforce (129,900) was partly the increase in the numbers of working age but even more important was the effect of the increase in female activity rates. The rise in civil employment of 12,500, which is the result of a loss of 28,000 male jobs and a gain of 40,500 female jobs, left a major shortfall in employment opportunities of 117,400. This shortfall resulted in outward migration of 62,100 potential workers and an increase in unemployment of 55,200.

Labour market accounts have also been calculated for the period 1981–86 though it is recognised that the official estimates of population and migration for 1986 are not based on a Census of Population and consequently must be regarded as less reliable. The high natural increase in working age groups principally reflects the high rate of increase of the age group 16–24. The increase of 32,600 in the workforce was accompanied by a major fall in civil employment of 17,700 thus causing a shortfall in employment opportunities of 50,400. The relatively low level of outward migration in the first half of the 1980s resulted in the loss of 14,400 potential workers, leaving an increase in unemployment of 36,000 between 1981 and 1986.

Other studies have compared labour market accounts for United Kingdom regions (see Moore, Rhodes and Tyler 1986; Cambridge Econometrics and NIERC 1987). The latter study covers the period 1971–86 and uses somewhat different statistical definitions for some of the principal variables; however it provides an interesting comparison for Northern Ireland with other regions.

The information given in Table 6.12 has been extracted from the more extensive and more detailed Table 3.7 'Employment Accounts for UK Regions, 1971–1986', in that study. The data show that the 28.9 per cent increase in the labour force in Northern Ireland, due partly to natural increase and partly to an increase in participation, was almost twice the national percentage increase. Northern Ireland experienced a very similar lack of change in the numbers employed over the period and consequently had around twice the national percentage shortfall. Of the 28.9 per cent shortfall in jobs in Northern Ireland 2.1 per cent were accounted for by the increase in numbers on Government schemes, 12.2 per cent by net outward migration and 14.6 per cent by increased unemployment.

Employment shortfalls in some regions are principally due to relatively rapid growth in the labour force as opposed to poor employment growth. Northern Ireland and Scotland are in this category with rates of natural increase in the labour force well above the national average. In addition, Northern Ireland experienced substantial increases in participation particularly in jobs in the public services, many of which were for part-time married females.

Perhaps the most remarkable region shown in Table 6.12 is East Anglia where the increase in the indigenous labour force was outpaced by the change in employment by 4.2 per cent. However high inward migration of 15.6 per cent meant that despite the rapid increase in employment, unemployment rose by 8.9 per cent of the 1971 labour force. Unlike the situation in national labour markets where international migration is relatively small (1.3 per cent from 1971–86), net regional migration whether outward or inward is a major influence on regional labour markets.

5. Labour force outlook 1986–1996

Detailed forecasts of the components of the labour market are clearly beyond the scope of this chapter,[16] though on the basis of several working assumptions it is possible to usefully examine the trends in the labour force over the

TABLE 6.12 Labour market accounts for regions of the United Kingdom, 1971–1986 (percentage of 1971 labour force)

	Northern Ireland	Scotland	North	Wales	South East	East Anglia	South West	East Midlands	United Kingdom
Change in labour force due to:									
natural increase	18.6	15.1	8.7	5.8	6.0	9.0	4.8	10.3	8.1
change in participation	10.3	6.4	4.1	4.0	7.8	14.6	14.9	13.4	7.0
Less:									
Change in employment due to:									
full-time	−5.5	−8.2	−14.3	−11.7	−0.6	19.4	10.5	5.2	−4.6
part-time	5.5	5.6	5.1	5.8	3.9	8.6	8.0	7.5	5.1
Equals:									
employment shortfall	28.9	24.0	22.2	15.7	10.5	−4.2	1.2	11.0	14.7
Of which:									
rise in numbers on Government schemes	2.1	4.1	4.4	5.0	2.0	2.4	3.8	−4.1	3.4
net outward migration	12.2	9.6	5.5	−1.4	0.8	−15.6	−12.5	−3.5	1.3
rise in registered unemployment	14.6	10.4	11.9	12.4	7.7	8.9	9.9	10.7	10.0

Source: see text.

medium term. As the previous analysis indicates, the growth in the labour force can be attributed to the natural increase in the working age population, the change in activity rates and the amount of outward migration.

Unpublished population projections for the period 1986–96 were obtained from the Department of Finance and Personnel, Northern Ireland and the natural increase in the population of working age was obtained from the projections of the 16+ population on the assumption of zero migration. All those who will be in the labour force from 1986 to 1996 have already been born and consequently the working age population projection with zero migration depends only on the application of assumed death rates. Since death rates change very slowly the projected natural increase should provide an acceptable base.

TABLE 6.13 Working age civilian population projections for Northern Ireland with zero migration, 1986–1996 (age 16+, 000)

	Male	Female	Total
1986	539.9	590.3	1,130.3
1991	572.9	619.3	1,192.2
1996	602.4	644.8	1,247.2

Note: Details may not sum to total because of rounding. The differences between the figures given here for 1986 and those given in Table 6.3 are due to the exclusion of the numbers in the armed forces from the above figures.
Source: Figures based on unpublished projections from DFP.

The projections for working age population with zero migration for 1991 and 1996 are given in Table 6.13. Annual projections for different age categories are shown in Figure 6.3.

It is of interest to note that although the population aged 16+ increases continually throughout the decade, the 16–24 age group is expected to peak in 1988/89 at 251,000 before falling to 234,000 by 1996. The fall in this age group reflects the fall in the birth rates in the latter part of the 1970s and is responsible for the reduced rate of growth in the total working age population in the latter quinquennial, ie from an expansion of 61,900 during 1986–91 to 55,000 in the period 1991–96.

No official projections of activity rates for Northern Ireland are available so the trends in projected activity rates in Great Britain were used for guidance. Projected civilian activity rates for Great Britain for the years 1986 to 1991 are given as part of a feature on labour force projections in the *Employment Gazette*.[17] In earlier projections of activity rates (1984 based) three main factors were identified as affecting male activity rates: the level of long term unemployment; the numbers of men aged 60–64 taking early retirement under the job release scheme; and for men aged 60 and over a trend towards earlier retirement. However, the Labour Force Surveys of 1985 and 1986 suggest that these relationships may have changed. The overall projection for male activity rates is for a small fall of 0.6 per cent over the period 1986 to

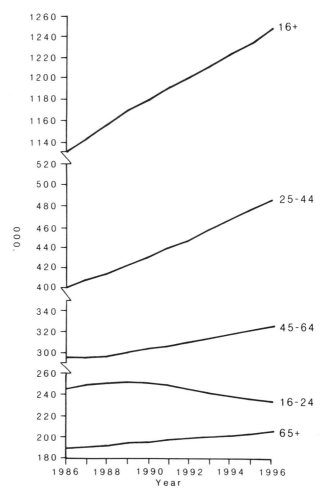

FIG 6.3 Civilian population projections, zero migration, persons 16+, Northern Ireland, 1986–1996
Source: DFP.

1991, principally due to the continued decline in activity rates of males 60 years and over.

A different set of factors influence female activity rates; apart from economic conditions, various studies have emphasised the importance of demographic and social factors. Women are less likely to be economically active if they have had children and especially if they are currently bringing up young children. Social change has had the effect of increasing the attachment of women to the labour force. A model based on these factors projects a rise in the overall female activity rates by about 1 percentage point from 1986 to 1991. This is the net result of assumptions regarding the continuing rise in the age at which women have children, the continuing rise in activity rates among women aged 35 to 59 years, despite being partly offset by earlier retirement and the

TABLE 6.14   Workforce projections[1] with zero migration, 1986–1996 (000)

	Workforce[2]	Projected		Natural increase in workforce		Average annual increase in workforce	
	1986	1991	1996	1986–91	1991–96	1986–91	1991–96
Male	405.2	429.7	451.8	24.5	22.1	4.9	4.4
Female	270.2	283.7	295.3	13.5	12.4	2.7	2.5
Total	675.3	714.4	747.1	38.0	34.5	7.6	6.9

[1] Using constant 1986 activity rates.
[2] Working population.

long term decline in activity rates of those over the retirement age of 60.

For Northern Ireland it has been assumed, as a starting point, that activity rates will remain constant at the 1986 values[18] throughout the projection period. Estimates of the natural increase in the workforce between 1986 and 1996 based on the assumption of constant activity rates are given in Table 6.14. The assumption of zero migration permits the calculation of the natural increase in the workforce. With constant activity rates, the natural increase in the workforce between 1986 and 1991 would be 38,000 and from 1991 to 1996, 34,500; an average of 7,600 per annum and 6,900 per annum in the respective periods.

It may be a useful simplification to assume that there is no increase in employment opportunities. Given the long term trends in the different sectors of the Northern Ireland economy discussed in Section 3, the poor success rate of the industrial development policy in recent years in attracting international investment, and the Conservative Government's attitude to the public sector, the assumption of zero employment growth may well be optimistic at least in the earlier period.

With employment remaining constant at the 1986 level, the shortfall in employment opportunities will thus equal the full natural increase in the workforce. In the labour market accounts this shortfall must be allocated between migration and the increase in unemployment. Thus with zero migration, zero employment growth and no change in government training or special schemes unemployment would rise by the full amount of the natural increase in the workforce. With constant 1986 activity rates this would mean annual increases in unemployment of 7,600 and 6,900 over the periods 1986–91 and 1991–96.

Official population projections are made for different annual levels of migration and these have been used to project the resident workforce. For example, outward migration of 5,000 per annum, with the assumed age/sex structure derived from past experience, would reduce the projected increase in the Northern Ireland working population by approximately 2,700 per annum. Under this scenario with no increase in employment or government schemes, unemployment would be expected to increase by around 4,800 per annum from 1986 to 1991 and by 4,100 per annum from 1991 to 1996. In a scenario with constant 1986 activity rates, zero employment growth, no growth in government schemes and emigrants with the historical age/sex distribution, it would require annual total outward migration of around 13,000 to 14,000 persons per annum to entirely remove the natural increase in the labour force and leave the level of unemployment unchanged. In the scenario approach it is clearly possible to vary the assumptions about projected activity rates, the change in employment and government schemes and outward migration to obtain a range of projections of the change in unemployment. However, the variable which is fundamental to all such projections and which cannot be altered in the short or medium term is the natural growth in the working age population. With knowledge of this variable, the labour market accounts technique can be useful in scanning changes in labour market conditions.

6. Conclusion

The fundamental problem in the Northern Ireland labour market is that the long term natural growth in the labour supply continually outstrips the growth in the demand for labour at prevailing wage rates. Since the problem is concerned with an imbalance in growth rates any lasting solution must be aimed at equating or at least reducing the differential in growth rates. One-off measures to increase the stock of job opportunities or reduce the pool of unemployment are merely short-term palliatives.

Employment growth may be regarded as a function of the growth of demand for the region's output whether from indigenous producers or from those encouraged to establish there, and the state of technology, which relates output to employment. The natural growth in the labour force is determined by economic, demographic and social factors of which the most important is likely to be the natural growth in population. However, there is no natural mechanism which ensures that a region's growth in employment opportunities will match the natural growth of its labour force. Indeed, empirical observation suggests that imbalance may be the norm. This seems to be particularly the case in peripheral regions.

Even if a nation achieves a situation where its long term growth in employment opportunities is broadly in line with the natural growth in the labour force one would expect to find some regions with above average growth in employment opportunities and others with below average. Similarly there will be regions with above and below average natural growth in the labour force. In general it is likely that peripheral regions which are less likely to achieve high growth rates in employment, will be the regions with the most rapid population growth and hence the most rapid rates of growth of the labour force.

In the long run, even in the absence of successful policy measures, some kind of dynamic equilibrium across regional labour markets will be brought about through regional migration. In a modern economy with wage rates inflexible downwards, regional migration is the main mechanism which prevents regional unemployment rates from continuously diverging.

Government policy to achieve a balance in the labour market can approach the problem from the demand side or from the supply side. Clearly the politically most attractive option is to expand the demand side of the labour market by creating new employment opportunities, especially if this can lead to self-sustaining growth. Historically the major thrust of regional and industrial development policy in the province has been directed towards this end. For the future, under the present Government's philosophy, such employment growth must be sought in the traded goods sector. The recent Pathfinder initiative (DED 1987) emphasised the continuing importance of this approach together with the need to scrutinise its cost-effectiveness and improve the general levels of productivity, marketing and quality.

Currently there is much interest and debate, both in academic and official circles, in the main alternative policy which affects the demand side, namely regional incomes policy designed to reduce the real wage. The argument, based on neo-classical theory, is that the labour surplus exists because the price of labour is too high. With lower real wages, or more specifically, lower wage costs per unit of output, profitability in the traded goods sector should increase, leading to expansion of investment, output and employment. In addition, production techniques should become more labour intensive as firms substitute the relatively cheaper factor of production. Theoretically it should be possible to achieve these same potential benefits from reducing wage costs per unit by raising labour productivity while avoiding the adverse effects of reduced real incomes. Indeed, raising Northern Ireland's relatively low levels of productivity in the production industries (Table 9.10) is a major aim of the Pathfinder initiative.

One can readily accept that there would be some positive employment effects, particularly in the exporting sector, from a policy which reduced wage costs, however the extent of the wage cuts required to achieve a substantial increase in employment or the overall effect on employment and output in the regional economy is not clear. In addition to being dependent on various unknown elasticities of demand, its impact would be greatly influenced by policy decisions in the public sector. For example, if wages were lowered in the public sector as well as the private sector, would this result in reduced real incomes and expenditure in the province with negative employment effects, especially in induced services? There is no convincing economic model which can demonstrate that the regional trade-off between the potential increase in employment and the reduction in income would necessarily benefit the region, even if it could be implemented politically.

In the 1950s and early 1960s wages of manual workers in the production industries in Northern Ireland were more than 20 per cent below the national average (see Chapter 9, Table 9.7). In the 1950s, despite this wage advantage in a period of political stability, employment in the production industries fell and there was no substantial flow of inward investment. It was only after the introduction of active regional policy at the end of that decade that mobile investment was attracted to the province and that was mainly capital intensive. By the early 1980s manual wage rates in the production industries had risen relatively to 92 per cent of the national level as more and more firms and groups of workers came under the ambit of national wage agreements.

One major drawback of a policy of overall regional wage reduction is that it could lead to increased outward migration of the more highly skilled and qualified workers, the people on whom economic regeneration should depend. Against this it could be argued that wider dispersion of earnings is needed with skilled workers retaining or even improving their real incomes but incomes coming down for unskilled workers who form the majority of the labour surplus. The obvious costs are increased poverty and hardship for those at the lower end of the employment hierarchy in what is the region with by far the highest levels of poverty in the United Kingdom (see Chapter 9).

As a policy measure, implementing a reduction in the real wage is fraught with difficulty and if it were implemented the potential benefits are unclear and are likely to be mixed. Nevertheless it would be quite erroneous to conclude that wage costs can be ignored in the operation of the labour market. Wage costs per unit are a major element in determining the competitiveness of our products and reducing wage costs by improving efficiency or reducing real wages should make industry more competitive. As a measure to increase the demand for labour, real wage restraint cannot be ruled out. The present Government's philosophy is sympathetic to this type of 'market' measure and perhaps partly in response to the limited success of industrial development policy in recent years, the local administration has shown more interest in its possibilities.

Policies designed to alter the supply of labour in Northern Ireland must attempt to affect the natural rate of increase in the population of working age, lower participation rates, encourage outward migration or alter the quality of the labour force. The first option is to adopt policies to reduce the rate of natural increase of the population; effectively to reduce the birth rate. Such a policy is essentially a long term remedy since it would take 16 years for a change in the birth rate to begin to work its way into the potential labour force. In the meantime it could have the opposite effect of increasing the activity rates of married females freed from child care. There are social and moral issues involved in attempting to implement policies designed to reduce the birth rate, issues for the sociologist and the political scientist to consider. It is the role of the economist to point out the causes of economic problems and suggest policies for economic reform. Excess supply of labour relative to demand will almost inevitably lead to low incomes, unemployment and/or outward migration. Reducing the supply will tend to alleviate these symptoms of imbalance in the regional labour market.

It is possible to reduce activity rates by such methods as raising the school leaving age or reducing the age of retirement. However these would be costly methods to reduce the labour supply if that were their sole purpose. Activity rates may also fall because of lack of employment opportunities, as individuals, especially females, fall out of the labour force. From a statistical point of view the authorities can and indeed have reduced activity rates by altering the methods of counting numbers unemployed, however this seems to be largely a cosmetic exercise which does not alter the actual numbers seeking work. In general reducing activity rates in real terms results in raising the proportion of dependants to workers in the region. Activity rates in Northern Ireland are already relatively low and here, as in the other less prosperous regions of Great Britain, this contributes to and is partly caused by low levels of regional economic activity. Reducing activity rates cannot be regarded as an acceptable option.

It is unlikely that encouraging outward migration would ever become an explicit Government policy for reducing the regional labour supply since it is principally seen as an indication of the failure of other positive policies. Nevertheless it remains the most effective element in reducing the labour supply in a region such as Northern Ireland. Emigration is not without its negative effects. On average, migrants tend to be from among the younger, more active and more skilled members of the labour force so that the regional economy is losing above average workers and is left with a higher ratio of dependants to workers. In addition, emigration, even of unemployed persons tends to reduce the level of expenditure in the region and hence the demand for labour. Nevertheless historically outward migration has operated as an effective escape valve on the Northern Ireland labour market.

Throughout the early 1980s, estimated outward migration has been relatively low despite the dramatically high levels of unemployment providing more than adequate push factors. However, the major pull factors associated with employment opportunities in the south east of England and other traditional destinations appear to have been relatively weak. As the prospects for job opportunities improve in Great Britain, outward migration from Northern Ireland will pick up considerably, though the high house prices in the south of England may be an important adverse factor.

Demographic trends in Great Britain in the 1990s are likely to encourage migration from Northern Ireland. The number of people of working age is projected to remain broadly stable at a little over 34 million for most of the 1990s. The labour force is expected to grow much more slowly than in the 1980s. The most radical change is in the number of young people in the labour market with the numbers aged under 25 projected to fall by 1.2 million between 1987 and 1995 (see Department of Employment, 1988, 5–9). Similar demographic trends are expected in most countries of Western Europe and the USA, reflecting the reductions in birth rates in the 1970s discussed earlier. It seems likely that as labour becomes scarcer in Great Britain and abroad, Northern Ireland's labour force will be able to find more opportunities through emigration or, indeed, more firms will be attracted to the province to take advantage of its abundant labour supply. In either event, the quality and skill levels of our workers will be a key element in determining the ease with which they obtain employment and the quality of that employment.

The labour market accounts technique is essentially a numerical accounting identity which says nothing about changes in the quality of the labour force. The model has nothing to say about manpower training, a major plank of Government policy, designed to provide a better matching of supply and demand in the labour market and lead to an improvement in competitiveness and efficiency. The labour market accounts will be affected directly because persons undergoing training in a Government supported scheme are not included in the count of the labour force, and indirectly because increases in efficiency should lead to increased output and employment. However, while manpower training is taken to be an essential policy for underdeveloped and developed regions alike, the perception of its need and potential benefits stems from other models and methods and not from an analysis of labour market accounts.

In the Northern Ireland labour market the natural increase in the labour force will continue to outstrip the growth rate in employment opportunities for the foreseeable future. While alterations in the statistical methods of counting unemployment, increasing numbers on training and other one-off measures, may bring about short term reductions in unemployment, the prospective lack of growth in employment opportunities suggests that unemployment will go on increasing in the medium to long term unless checked by a major expansion in outward migration. Examination of the history of the Northern Ireland labour market and its relationship to the national economy leads to the conclusion that outward migration will expand sufficiently to prevent the level of unemployment continuously diverging from national levels.

Appendix 6.1 Registrar General's annual estimates of net outward migration, 1951–1986 (000)

Year	Net outward migration	Year	Net outward migration
1951/52	11.1	1969/70	6.2
1952/53	4.8	1970/71	8.2
1953/54	10.8	1971/72	20.4
1954/55	6.1	1972/73	23.9
1955/56	11.9	1973/74	13.7
1956/57	13.1	1974/75	9.9
1957/58	10.9	1975/76	9.7
1958/59	9.6	1976/77	7.7
1959/60	4.2	1977/78	8.7
1960/61	8.5	1978/79	5.6
1961/62	8.7	1979/80	5.3
1962/63	6.5	1980/81	6.1
1963/64	6.5	1981/82	9.9
1964/65	8.0	1982/83	5.3
1965/66	8.0	1983/84	4.0
1966/67	5.9	1984/85	4.5
1967/68	5.9	1985/86	3.5
1968/69	5.3		

Note: The annual estimates from 1972–73 onwards have recently been extensively revised and are published in NIAAS No 6, 1987.
Source: RGAR.

Appendix 6.2 Recent changes in the basis of measuring unemployment

Until October 1982 the official unemployment figures were based on registrations at Employment Offices. Since then there have been several changes in definition which have substantially altered the unemployment count. The main changes and their effects on the count were as follows:

October 1982 Effect in N. Ireland	
1) Exclusion of unemployed persons not claiming benefit	−5,400
2) Inclusion of severely disabled persons not previously in count	+300
3) Closer monitoring of unemployment position on day of count	−5,300
Total	**−10,400**

June 1983

1) Men aged 60 and over no longer have to sign on at Social Security Offices	**−1,600**
2) June school leavers now unable to claim benefit until September (impact on figures only in June-September)	−

August 1985

Reconciliation on computer records of unemployment in
DE and DHSS (specific to Northern Ireland)   **−5,150**

March 1986

Delaying the computation of unemployment statistics by
two weeks to avoid over-recording   **−1,600**

Total:	**−18,750**

In June 1986 the basis for calculating the unemployment rate was changed from expressing the number unemployed as a percentage of all employees (employed and unemployed) to expressing it as a percentage of the working population, ie the sum of employees in employment, unemployed, self-employed and armed forces. In June 1986, unemployment was 18.6 per cent of the working population compared to 21.5 per cent of all employees on the old basis.

Appendix 6.3 Revised estimates of employees in employment

The results of the 1987 Census of Employment for Northern Ireland indicate that the number of employees in employment in Northern Ireland at September 1987 was 507,312. This figure is 14,232 (2.9%) higher than the previously published estimate for September 1987 which has been used elsewhere in this book.

The change in the Census of Employment estimates of employees in employment from September 1984 to September 1987 is shown below in Table 6.3.1A together with the difference between the original estimates for September 1987 based on the Quarterly Employment Survey and the revised estimates.

TABLE 6.3.1A   Employees in employment, 1984 and 1987

	Census of Employment			Original estimate[1] September 1987 (4)	Difference from COE estimate (2)–(4)
	September 1984 (1)	September 1987 (2)	Change (3)		
Agriculture, forestry and fishing	19,993	19,445	−548	19,540	−95
Energy and water supply	9,123	8,325	−798	8,560	−235
Manufacturing industries	108,401	103,702	−4,699	101,470	+2,232
Construction	27,943	25,762	−2,181	25,000	+762
Services	334,986	350,078	+15,092	338,510	+11,568
All industries	500,446	507,312	+6,866	493,080	+14,232

[1] Based on Quarterly Employment Survey.
Sources: Census of Employment Results 1987, DED Statistics Notice, September 1989; DED Statistics Notice, September 1988.

The revised estimates show that the increase in service employment between 1984 and 1987 was substantially more than originally estimated while the fall in manufacturing was not as severe. Discussion with DED indicates that the underestimation in services occurred principally in the private sector. The Statistics Notice shows that the increase in employment from 1984 to 1987 was principally in part-time employment and especially for part-time females as shown in Table 6.3.2A. Comparison of the actual charge and that based on the original estimates shows the error was fairly evenly divided between males and females.

TABLE 6.3.2A   Employees in employment, full-time and part-time, 1984 and 1987

		September 1984	September 1987	Change	Change based on original 1987 estimate
Males:	Full-time	245,607	239,505	−6,102	na
	Part-time	26,069	28,824	+2,755	na
	Total	271,676	268,329	−3,347	−11,116
Females:	Full-time	147,318	149,283	+1,965	na
	Part-time	81,452	89,700	+8,248	na
	Total	228,770	238,983	+10,213	+3,750

Source: As Table 6.3.1A.

Notes

1. The natural increase in the labour force in a region is defined as the increase in the labour force which would have occurred if there had been zero migration over the period and the end-of-period actual regional activity rates applied to the entire end-of-period population of working age.
2. The population and migration estimates for 1981 are revised figures, published in the RGAR, 1985. Because a proportion of households did not make returns to the 1981 COP, the Census Office was obliged to estimate the population associated with the non-respondents. Evidence provided subsequently from other official sources indicated the need for revision. See Morris and Compton (1985).
3. Annual estimates of migration are published in the RGAR. These figures are principally based on a count of the transfer and issue of medical cards and lagged to take account of administrative delay. These figures are often adjusted to take account of the fact that not all medical cards are returned by migrants. At the end of the decade the total of annual estimates are compared with the decennial estimates from the COP and adjusted pro-rata to achieve consistency. Given the limitations in the estimates of annual net migration it is necessary to be careful in using or interpreting these data.
4. The numbers of female employees in employment were as follows:

	1971	1981
Part-time	34,700	77,600
Full-time	148,100	147,300
Total:	182,800	224,900

Sources: DMS, Spring 1987 and DED for 1981.

5. Figures from the 1971 COP and the 1981 EC LFS suggest that between 1971 and 1981 the number of married females in employment in Northern Ireland rose by 36,000 while the number of other females fell by 16,000.
6. The estimated age/sex breakdown of migrants was obtained from the RGO. The age specific mortality rates were taken from the RGAR.
7. The relationship between migration and activity rates is complex. Migration affects not only the regional labour supply but also the level of employment through its effects on aggregate demand and as a consequence the level of participation can be affected. See for example, Armstrong and Taylor (1985, Ch 6).
8. Throughout this chapter the figures of employees in employment for 1985 and after are the official estimates based on the Quarterly Employment Survey. The 1987 Census of Employment Summary results published in September 1989 show that the figures for 1987 were underestimated by some 14,000. Consequently the employment figures from 1985 onwards will all have been underestimated to some degree. See Appendix 6.3 for details.
9. See Moore, Rhodes and Tyler (1977) and Rowthorn (1981).
10. According to the Report of the Industrial Development Organisation for Northern Ireland (1980), between 1968 and 1975 (the worst years of violence) only 16 manufacturing companies with fewer than 1,000 employees, in total, closed down as a result of physical damage due to the civil disturbances.
11. To facilitate comparison between public sector employment in 1961 and 1971 on

SIC 1968, and 1981 and 1986 on SIC 1980 the following categories have been included. In 1981 and 1986: Public Administration and Defence (Class 91), Education (93), Health Services (95), Other Services to Public (96) and Recreation and other Cultural Services (97). In 1961 and 1971: Order 27, MLHs 872, 874, 882 and 899.

12. For discussion of the pattern and levels of public expenditure in Northern Ireland relative to other parts of the United Kingdom see HM Treasury (1979) and NIEC (1981).

13. 'Financial Statement and Budget Report 1980/81' HC500, HMSO March 1980, pp 16–19.

14. See Appendix 6.2 for a summary of the changes in the statistical definition and the magnitude of the effects on the unemployment count in Northern Ireland from October 1982.

15. Unemployment rates from 1971 onwards have been calculated from the most recent official series of 'claimant based' unemployment as a proportion of the working population. Prior to 1971 the figures are taken from the old official sources with registered unemployment expressed as a proportion of all insured employees.

16. Regional projections to the year 2000 can be found in Cambridge Econometrics and NIERC (1987).

17. Labour Force Outlook for Britain, *Employment Gazette*, May 1987, pp 253–263.

18. The activity rates used here are based on the 1986 civilian population of working age estimates, ie excluding armed forces.

References

Armstrong, H and Taylor, J (1985) *Regional Economics and Policy*, Philip Allan.

Cambridge Econometrics and The Northern Ireland Economic Research Centre (1987) *Regional Economic Prospects*.

Cambridge Economic Policy Review (1980) *Urban and Regional Policy with Provisional Regional Accounts, 1966–1978*, 6, 2 July, Gower.

Department of Economic Development (1987) *Building a Stronger Economy: The Pathfinder Process* (Pathfinder Report).

Department of Employment (1988) *Employment for the 1990s*, HMSO, Cm 540.

DMK Consultants (1987) *Ireland's Changing Population Structure*, September, Dublin.

Forrest, D and Naisbitt, B (1987) The sensitivity of regional unemployment rates to the national trade cycle, *Salford Papers in Economics*, 4.

HM Treasury (1979) *Needs Assessment Study*, Report of an Interdepartmental Study.

Isles, K S and Cuthbert, N (1957) *An Economic Survey of Northern Ireland*, HMSO, Belfast.

Jefferson, C W (1987) Economy and employment, Chapter 10 in Buchanan, R H and Walker, B M (eds), *Province, City and People: Belfast and its Region*, Greystone Books Ltd.

Moore, B C, Rhodes, J and Tyler, P (1977) The impact of regional policy in the 1970s, *CES Review*, I, 67–77.

Moore, B C, Rhodes, J and Tyler, P (1986) *The Effects of Government Regional Economic Policy*, Department of Trade and Industry, HMSO.

Morris, C and Compton, P (1985) Census of Population in Northern Ireland, *Population Trends*, 40, Summer.

Northern Ireland Economic Council (1981) *Public Expenditure Comparisons between Northern Ireland and Great Britain*, 18.

Ogilvy, A A (1982) Population migration between regions of Great Britain, 1971–1979, *Regional Studies*, 16, 1, 65–73.

Rowthorn, R E (1981) Northern Ireland: an economy in crisis, *Cambridge Journal of Economics*, 5, 1–31.

CHAPTER SEVEN

Labour force characteristics

Janet M Trewsdale

1. Introduction

This chapter looks in detail at a number of aspects of the Northern Ireland labour market. Chapter 6 dealt with the major aggregate variables in the labour market using a labour market accounts analysis. The main conclusions from that analysis were of a regional macroeconomic nature, namely that job creation has been unable to match the rapid natural growth in the Northern Ireland labour force, a growth which would have been even greater had it not been for a significant reduction in the labour supply through migration. The direct consequence has been a continuously high level of unemployment which has been exacerbated by the economic recession of 1980–82.

The purpose of this chapter is to examine the characteristics of the Northern Ireland labour force, including the unemployed, to see if microeconomic examination of the labour market can yield further insights into its problems. For example, one might question the suitability of the labour force in relation to the changes in the demands of modern industry. Is it well qualified, highly skilled and sufficiently well trained? These are questions of major importance for manpower policy. In a chapter of this kind one cannot attempt to explore all such issues or indeed achieve useful conclusions for major policy purposes. Indeed, given the number of topics included it has only been possible to highlight some of the main characteristics in each area. Section 2 comprises a brief analysis of the educational qualifications, skills and training background of the Northern Ireland labour force. Section 3 looks at the nature of unemployment, and several characteristics of the unemployed including age, duration and health are covered in Section 4. Section 5 contains a detailed analysis of female and part-time employment, its extent and growth in importance. Section 6 briefly examines training policy within Northern Ireland and Great Britain. An analysis of unemployment in Northern Ireland by religious affiliation is given in Appendix 7.1.

In order to illustrate the situation in Northern Ireland, comparisons with the regions of Great Britain and, where comparable data are available, the Republic of Ireland, are provided throughout the chapter.

2. The quality of the employed labour force

The people of Northern Ireland constitute the province's principal natural resource. At a time of major industrial structural change involving falling employment in traditional sectors such as manufacturing, agriculture and construction, with little prospect of growth in the services, and the existence of high unemployment, further growth in the labour force might be regarded as a liability. But other countries such as Japan, Hong Kong and Singapore have shown how economies can develop and prosper if the labour force is skilled and educated to meet the challenge of new technology.

Northern Ireland, in common with the rest of the United Kingdom, has not proved successful in developing its human resources. Within the boundaries of the United Kingdom, Northern Ireland's record of education and training of the workforce is amongst the worst. As shown in Table 7.1, in 1986, 6.2 per cent of the Northern Ireland workforce were graduates or equivalent compared to a United Kingdom average of 8.9 per cent; only 12.4 per cent had 'A' levels as their highest qualification compared to 20.5 per cent in Scotland and just under 17 per cent for the United Kingdom as a whole. However, the proportion of the workforce involved in recognised apprenticeships was 12.2 per cent in Northern Ireland against a United Kingdom figure of 7.1 per cent. At the other end of the scale, 40 per cent of the workforce in Northern Ireland were completely lacking in any qualification compared to 32.6 per cent for England and 33.3 per cent for the United Kingdom.

In a report published in 1984, P A Management Consultants predicted that by the mid 1990s the numbers employed in manufacturing in Northern Ireland would have fallen to below 90,000 and to maintain current employment levels would require the development of industries producing high-technology products and services. To further these developments, they predicted an increase in the demand for mental skills and a decline in the need for manual skills. The report forecast a doubling in the demand for computer and related technicians and an increase by a half in the demand for technologists. On the other hand, the demand for engineering craftsmen and construction workers was expected to fall by a tenth and a quarter respectively. The report concluded that training and retraining should be the priority as the rate of change will be constrained by the speed at which the workforce can accommodate the necessary changes and adopt the new skills which are required.

It is clear that training forms a fundamental part of any development in employment policy in Northern Ireland and an analysis of training policy in the province is given in Section 6 of this chapter.

3. Unemployment

The accepted international definition of unemployment is that people are counted as unemployed if they are seeking work but do not have it. Being out

TABLE 7.1 Educational qualifications[1] of the workforce,[2] 1986 (percentage)

	Degree or equivalent	Other higher education	GCE 'A' level or equivalent	Apprenticeship	GCE 'O' level or equivalent	CSE below Grade 1	None	Other[3]	Total
United Kingdom	8.9	5.9	16.9	7.1	16.5	5.5	33.3	5.9	100.0
England	9.2	5.9	16.9	6.5	16.7	6.0	32.6	6.2	100.0
Wales	8.1	7.1	14.5	6.9	17.3	5.1	35.7	5.2	100.0
Scotland	7.0	5.6	20.5	11.1	14.3	0.5	37.3	3.8	100.0
Northern Ireland	6.2	6.4	12.4	12.2	14.4	4.8	40.0	3.6	100.0

[1] Figures relate to highest qualification.
[2] Economically active persons of working age.
[3] Includes not known or not stated.
Sources: LFS 1986; RT 1988.

of work is a straightforward and easily observed concept, but seeking work is more nebulous in that it can vary in intensity. It can range between the two extremes of a young male consciously looking for work and the married woman who has not been working but who would take a job should a suitable one arise. Male unemployment is more readily defined than female unemployment.

Unemployment is conventionally divided into three types – demand, frictional and structural. In this chapter the analysis is centred on frictional and structural forms of unemployment. Frictional unemployment is classified as being the result of employees changing jobs and hence is usually short-term. Structural unemployment is the consequence of changes in the industrial structure of the economy and varies in duration. The precise duration is determined by the speed at which the labour force is able to adapt to such changes. The basic cause of structural unemployment is a mismatch between the skills and location of the unemployed and the skills and location of the vacancies available. This mismatch has long been accepted as a powerful cause of unemployment but evidence in Great Britain from Layard (1986) suggests that mismatch today is no greater a problem than it was in the past; Layard's detailed analysis is based on nine regions in Great Britain and does not include Northern Ireland.

Chapter 6 suggests that historically high unemployment levels in Northern Ireland owe much to rapid natural growth of the labour supply. For example, all of the growth in unemployment during the period 1971–81 could be attributed to the increase in the workforce, a conclusion which is supported by work done by MacKay and Jones (1988). From the onset of the recession in the early 1980s, persistent problems with the demand side were exacerbated and what had been a state of virtual zero growth in employment up to that time changed to a state of falling employment levels. The result of the continuing rise in the numbers seeking work and a rapid decline in the number of jobs was an increase of over 25,000 in the number unemployed and claiming benefit between 1981 and 1986.

The problems of the Northern Ireland labour market are only too apparent when one considers the unemployment and vacancy statistics. The U–V analysis as described by Armstrong and Taylor (1985) is an accepted framework for analysing regional unemployment. However, one of its major drawbacks is the unreliability of the data on vacancies, in the form of under-recording. Vacancy data in Northern Ireland are particularly unreliable for two reasons which are unique to the province. First, public sector vacancies in Northern Ireland, unlike the rest of the United Kingdom, are not notified to Job Centres. Secondly, a high but unquantifiable number of vacancies are filled through informal recruitment procedures.

These problems make the comparison between Great Britain and Northern Ireland data more difficult than between other regions in the United Kingdom. With these problems in mind, a simple unemployment–vacancy ratio has been calculated and is set out in Table 7.2. In common with other studies the vacancy data have been multiplied by three (in itself a fairly arbitrary number) in order to allow for the recognised problems with under-recording

TABLE 7.2   Unemployment–vacancy ratios, regions of the United Kingdom, 1966–1987

	1966	1973	1979	1984	1987
South East	0.23	0.27	0.82	3.99	2.38
East Anglia	0.49	0.38	1.19	4.44	2.81
South West	0.60	0.47	1.73	4.36	2.67
West Midlands	0.25	0.70	2.67	9.21	4.11
East Midlands	0.30	0.51	1.56	7.36	4.51
Yorks and Humberside	0.37	0.89	2.33	9.45	5.21
North West	0.49	1.38	3.21	8.89	4.91
North	1.11	1.54	3.48	9.37	4.52
Wales	1.05	1.41	2.71	7.04	3.84
Scotland	1.43	1.92	2.71	6.90	5.19
Northern Ireland	5.57	3.48	15.45	26.98	21.08
United Kingdom	0.47	0.68	1.79	6.36	3.73

Note: The U–V ratio is calculated as $U/(V \times 3)$.
Sources: RT; EG.

(Armstrong and Taylor 1985).

The U–V ratio for Northern Ireland is considerably and consistently higher than any other region in the United Kingdom. Even in the cyclical peak year of 1979 the Northern Ireland ratio stood at 15.45 compared to 1.79 for the United Kingdom as a whole and 3.48 for the North, the highest of all the Great Britain regions. By 1986 the Northern Ireland figure had risen to 26.98 and the United Kingdom figure to 6.36. This unenviable position of the province is not only a phenomenon of the 1970s and 1980s – in 1966, before the present civil unrest, Northern Ireland returned a ratio of 5.57, some eleven times the United Kingdom figure of 0.47.

The measurement of unemployment is often controversial and nowhere more so than in the measurement of the numbers of the female unemployed. The Labour Force Survey (based on a sample of 1 per cent of households in Northern Ireland) allows a detailed analysis of the unemployed in the province. Of the 101,000 persons classifying themselves as unemployed in the Spring of 1985, 83.5 per cent were claiming benefit. This compares with 73 per cent for the LFS in Great Britain (based on a sample of 0.5 per cent of households in Great Britain). In Northern Ireland, 70 per cent of the total were males of whom 93 per cent were claiming benefit. Females accounted for 30 per cent of the unemployed and 62 per cent were claiming benefit. Hence 38 per cent of females who classified themselves as unemployed were not claiming benefit.

The Department of Employment issued figures comparing the official claimant count of unemployment and the Labour Force Survey results for Great Britain for the Spring of 1985 (*Employment Gazette*, October 1986). The LFS estimated that there were 2.81 million people without jobs and seeking work compared to an average of 3.13 million included in the claimant count during the survey period. The number of men included in the labour force measure was less than those in the claimant count while for women the survey

TABLE 7.3 Labour force estimate of unemployment compared with the claimant count, Northern Ireland and Great Britain, April 1985 (000)

	Northern Ireland			Great Britain		
	Males	Females	Total	Males	Females	Total
Labour force estimate of unemployed persons seeking work[1]	70.8	30.7	101.5	1,720	1,100	2,810
of which:						
not claiming benefits	8.4	15.7	24.1	180	580	760
claiming benefits	62.4	15.0	77.4	1,530	520	2,050
Claimants not unemployed[2]	26.1	18.1	44.2	640	440	1,080
of which:						
inactive[3]	23.4	15.9	39.3	530	350	880
in employment	2.7	2.2	4.9	110	90	200
Claimant count	88.5	33.1	121.6	2,170	960	3,130

[1] Includes those waiting to start a new job or who were prevented from seeking work only by temporary sickness or holiday.
[2] Not unemployed on conventional labour force definition.
[3] Pesons not in work nor unemployed on labour force definition (see note 1).
Sources: DED (unpublished); EG.

figure exceeded the claimant count[1]. The British results along with comparable data for Northern Ireland are set out in Table 7.3.

Using the claimant count and the LFS results for Northern Ireland it was estimated by the Department of Economic Development (DED) that 44,000 persons were claiming benefit but were not 'unemployed'. Of those 39,000 were economically inactive and 5,000 were in employment. For females it was estimated that 18,000 of the claimants were not unemployed. Of these 16,000 were inactive and 2,000 were in employment. The actual claimant count for women in the Spring of 1985 was 33,000. It appears that of the 33,000 who were classified as unemployed, 18,000 were not actually seeking work and hence were not strictly unemployed and that this more than compensates for the 15,000 'extras' which the LFS estimated as being unemployed but not claiming benefit.

The data for males in Northern Ireland follow the same pattern as those for males in Great Britain; the LFS estimate is lower than the claimant count. The data for females are the exact opposite, in that the LFS data are also lower than the claimant count. One of the main reasons for this difference was that just under 35 per cent of all inactive claimants believed that no jobs were available. This compares with 26 per cent in Great Britain. Only 8.2 per cent of women gave this reason for being economically inactive compared to 52.4 per cent of men, while in Great Britain the corresponding figures were 12 per cent and 36 per cent respectively. The second most common reason given by the economically inactive was 'looking after family or home' which accounted for 65 per cent of all women and only 1.0 per cent of all men. In Great Britain the equivalent figures were 53 per cent and 6 per cent. The long term sick or disabled accounted for 13 per cent compared to 16 per cent in Great Britain with over three times as many men as women. Interestingly, 10 per cent of men claimed they did not want/need employment. This compares with 4 per cent in Great Britain and 4.7 per cent of women in Northern Ireland. This result is somewhat surprising: it was the third most popular reason for male claimants not seeking work. It could be an indication of the so called 'poverty trap' whereby low wages result in men on supplementary benefit finding that taking a job makes them worse off. In Northern Ireland, as in Great Britain, the main reason men gave for not seeking work was that they thought no jobs were available. For women almost two-thirds reported they were 'looking after family or home'. It is important to keep these differences between the male and female labour markets in mind when considering the characteristics of the unemployed in Northern Ireland.

4. Characteristics of the unemployed

AGE STRUCTURE

The analysis of the age breakdown of the wholly unemployed in the official count shown in Table 7.4 demonstrates quite clearly that unemployment is concentrated in the younger age groups. In Northern Ireland over 60 per cent of unemployed males were less than 35 years old compared with just over 50 per cent in both Great Britain and the Republic of Ireland. The data for

TABLE 7.4 Unemployment by age groups, Northern Ireland, Great Britain and the Republic of Ireland, 1981, 1985 and 1987 (percentage)

Age	1981		1985		1987	
	Male	Female	Male	Female	Male	Female
Northern Ireland[1]						
16–24	39.4	55.3	35.2	47.6	32.6	44.3
25–34	24.3	22.5	26.9	25.3	28.2	25.9
35–44	15.8	9.7	18.5	12.5	19.2	13.9
45+	20.5	12.5	19.4	14.6	20.0	15.9
Great Britain[1]						
16–24	34.7	55.8	33.1	45.9	29.9	41.3
25–34	21.5	19.7	23.5	23.9	24.3	24.5
35–44	13.6	9.5	16.3	11.4	16.9	12.9
45+	30.2	15.0	27.1	18.8	28.9	21.3
Republic of Ireland						
16–24	23.3	38.4	25.9	44.7	25.7	41.3
25–34	29.2	28.1	28.6	28.0	28.2	30.7
35–44	19.6	14.2	20.8	12.5	22.1	13.4
45+	27.9	19.3	24.7	14.8	24.0	14.6

[1] 1981 figures are based on registered unemployment, 1985 and 1987 are claimant based.
Sources: DED; EG; CSO (Dublin).

females show an even greater bias towards the younger age group with 70 per cent being under 34 in both Northern Ireland and Republic of Ireland compared with 66 per cent in Great Britain. These results are a reflection of the fact that married women tend to leave the labour force for five to ten years in their mid-twenties to raise a family and hence disappear from the official statistics. The rate and age at which these women return to the labour force differ dramatically between the three regions, with women in Great Britain showing a much higher rate of return at an earlier age than those in Northern Ireland and women in Republic of Ireland tending to leave the labour force permanently on the birth of their first child (Trewsdale 1980).

That the pattern of unemployment is concentrated in the younger age groups is confirmed by the figures on unemployment rates. For both men and women in the United Kingdom[2] and Republic of Ireland, unemployment rates are highest among the youngest age groups (see Table 7.5). For men in the United Kingdom the 1985 estimate shows an average rate of 21.4 per cent among the under 20 year olds, falling progressively to 9.2 per cent for those aged 50–64. In the Republic of Ireland although the pattern is similar the rates are somewhat higher, ranging from 33.6 per cent for the under 20 year olds to 11.5 per cent for the 50–64 age group. Female rates in the United Kingdom follow a similar pattern. In the Republic of Ireland there is a fall from 34.3 per cent in the youngest age group to 17.8 per cent for the 20–24 year olds which is then followed by a slight rise to 18.3 per cent for the 25–49 age group.

DURATION

The increase in the numbers of unemployed persons during the late 1970s and the 1980s up to the summer of 1987 has been accompanied by a substantial increase in the proportion of the long-term unemployed. In the first quarter of 1977 just over 25 per cent of the registered unemployed in Northern Ireland had been out of work for more than one year compared to 22 per cent in Great Britain. In the same quarter in 1987 just over 51 per cent of claimants in Northern Ireland and 41 per cent of those in Great Britain fell into this category. Thus in both cases the proportion of long-term unemployed has approximately doubled. The doubling of the proportion represents, in each case, a more than fivefold increase in the actual numbers involved. In complete contrast the number of newly unemployed people with less than two weeks unemployment experience remained relatively constant between 1977 and 1987. The age breakdown of these long-term unemployed shows that the majority (well over 50 per cent) are in the 18–34 year band. Hence not only are the young more prone to unemployment but once they become unemployed they are more likely than the older age groups to remain unemployed for at least a year.

Data for the Republic of Ireland are only available from 1980 and are shown along with the Great Britain and Northern Ireland figures in Table 7.6. The experience of the three areas is broadly similar, although it differs in degree. In 1980 just under 35 per cent of the Republic of Ireland's unemployed

TABLE 7.5 Unemployment by age groups, United Kingdom and the Republic of Ireland, 1983 and 1985 (percentage)

Age	United Kingdom						Republic of Ireland					
	1983			1985			1983			1985		
	Male	Female	Total	Male	Female	Total	Male	Female	Total	Male	Female	Total
19 and under	27.7	23.4	25.7	21.4	19.4	20.4	30.0	28.9	25.9	33.6	34.3	33.9
20–24	19.1	13.2	16.6	18.5	14.6	16.8	19.5	13.6	16.9	22.7	17.8	20.5
25–49	9.5	8.3	9.1	9.9	10.2	10.0	13.2	15.6	13.9	16.6	18.3	17.1
50–64	9.2	4.6	7.5	9.2	6.3	8.1	8.8	9.4	8.9	11.5	11.7	11.6

Source: Eurostat.

had been out of work for a year or more. By 1987 the figure had risen to 44.4 per cent. The increase in Northern Ireland was more dramatic from 29.6 to 51.3 per cent, a rise of 21 percentage points. In Great Britain, the increase was from 23 to 41.3 per cent during the same period. Thus, the recession had a more profound effect on long-term unemployment in the United Kingdom than in the Republic of Ireland.

The data in Table 7.6 represent the stocks in the unemployment equation. As would be expected, an analysis of the flows on and off the official count show clearly (see Table 7.7) that in Northern Ireland from 1983 until 1988 the flow on to the claimant based count has exceeded the flow off. In Great Britain, 1987 saw a reversal of this trend with the outflow exceeding the inflow resulting in a fall in British unemployment which has continued into 1988. A more detailed analysis of the data for both areas shows that, over time, the inflow has remained relatively constant, in contrast to a steady decrease in the outflow.

TABLE 7.6 Duration of unemployment, Northern Ireland, Great Britain and the Republic of Ireland, 1980, 1984 and 1987 (percentage)

Duration (weeks)	1980	1984	1987
Northern Ireland			
Less than 13	33.6	19.5	18.4
13 – 52	36.7	33.0	30.3
52 and over	29.6	47.5	51.3
Great Britain			
Less than 13	40.0	23.6	23.5
13 – 52	37.0	37.5	35.2
52 and over	23.0	38.9	41.3
Republic of Ireland			
Less than 13	33.0	26.8	22.4
13 – 52	32.1	34.1	33.2
52 and over	34.8	39.1	44.4

Source: As Table 7.4.

TABLE 7.7 Unemployment flows,[1] Northern Ireland and Great Britain, 1983–1988 (April, 000)

	Northern Ireland		Great Britain	
	Inflow	Outflow	Inflow	Outflow
1983	13.7	10.9	350.8	329.9
1985	8.9	8.2	332.5	303.9
1987	9.9	9.5	346.4	350.5
1988	11.9	11.2	313.5	329.9

[1] Standardised monthly flows (not seasonally adjusted).
Sources: DED; EG.

The relatively high duration figures in Northern Ireland compared with Great Britain and the Republic of Ireland is a simple reflection of the much higher levels of unemployment in the province. The relatively higher number of long-term unemployed in Northern Ireland represents a higher level of wasted resources, which is exacerbated by the fact that the longer people are unemployed, the more difficult it becomes for them to find work as they tend to lose their skills and their work habits and to give up hope (Layard and Bean 1988). Unemployment as a whole can perform an economic function by exerting some downward pressure on wage rates. But the long-term unemployed account for very little of this effect; in this respect they can be regarded as 'outsiders' to the labour market. Layard (1986) discusses various solutions to the problem, arguing that the cost in social security payments is such that the government should consider extending the then Manpower Services Commission remit to include the employment of the long-term unemployed on basic repair and maintenance projects. Layard also suggests that private employers, not involved in construction, should be paid for hiring the long-term unemployed for one year.

INDUSTRIAL AND OCCUPATIONAL STRUCTURE

The data sources on the industrial and occupational structure of the unemployed are notoriously unreliable for two reasons. First, a high proportion (36 per cent in the case of Northern Ireland in 1987) of the unemployed are not classified. Secondly, Moylan et al (1984) showed that only 33 per cent of the unemployed go back to the industry in which they were formerly employed. With these reservations in mind, it can be seen from Table

TABLE 7.8 Unemployment by industry, Northern Ireland and Great Britain, 1977 and 1982 (percentage)

	Northern Ireland		Great Britain	
	1977	1982	1977	1982[1]
Agriculture, forestry and fishing	2.9	2.5	1.7	1.6
Mining and quarrying	0.3	0.3	1.6	1.4
Manufacturing	18.9	21.8	25.4	29.6
Construction	20.6	19.4	14.6	13.4
Gas, electricity and water	0.3	0.4	0.7	0.5
Transport and communication	2.6	2.6	4.3	4.4
Distributive trades	7.8	8.3	10.2	10.4
Financial, professional and misc services	11.2	13.5	16.6	17.5
Public administration and defence	5.4	5.2	5.5	4.8
Others, not classified	30.0	26.0	19.5	16.4
Total	100.0	100.0	100.0	100.0

[1] 1982 is the last date for which data are published for Great Britain.
Sources: DMS Gazette; EG.

7.8 that of those unemployed who were classified by industry in Northern Ireland in 1977 just under 21 per cent were former construction workers compared to just under 15 per cent in Great Britain.

Changes in the industrial structure do play an important part in determining the level and extent of unemployment. This can be seen by examining the changing pattern of employees in employment (Layard 1986). In all three areas there has been a dramatic fall in the number of employees in employment from 1979 to 1987. In Northern Ireland 49,300 jobs were lost (9.2 per cent of the total). In Great Britain the loss was approximately 1.3 million, equivalent to 5.7 per cent and in the Republic of Ireland (since 1981) 64,000 jobs (5.6 per cent of the total) have been lost. The majority of these job losses have occurred in the manufacturing sector. In Northern Ireland manufacturing employment fell by 45,600 (31.3 per cent) from 1979–1988, in the Republic of Ireland it fell by 34,000 (14.2 per cent) and in Great Britain the comparable figure was a fall of 2.03 million (28.6 per cent) over the same period.

Employment in the services sector followed a different pattern and varied in the three areas, remaining roughly level in Great Britain and increasing slowly but steadily in both Northern Ireland and the Republic of Ireland. The vast majority of job losses in manufacturing were in what might be termed 'male' occupations while the jobs gained in the service sector were taken up predominantly by female part-time workers. Hence one would expect a high proportion of the unemployed in Northern Ireland to be former manufacturing workers.

The decline in the manufacturing base of the United Kingdom economy was widespread and universal, but the industrial structure of a particular region played an important part in the extent to which manufacturing employment fell within that region. The economic structure of Northern Ireland is such that it has been particularly hard hit by the decline in certain manufacturing industries, such as shipbuilding and man-made fibres. The numbers employed in shipbuilding fell by 27.5 per cent from 1977 to 1982, while those employed in the man-made fibre industry fell by 82 per cent over the same period. These two industries accounted for 26.4 per cent of the total fall in manufacturing employment between 1977 and 1982, compared to a fall of 3.1 per cent in the same industries in Great Britain. Historically some industries have been more prone to unemployment than others. An obvious example is the construction industry. In Northern Ireland a higher proportion of employees have been employed in the construction industry than in either Great Britain or the Republic of Ireland. In 1979, 11.7 per cent of the male employees in Northern Ireland were employed in construction but by 1987 some 11,000 jobs had been lost, a decline of 23.7 per cent over the period. The main reasons for this decline, apart from the general recession, were the cutback in public sector civil engineering projects and the contraction of the budget of the Northern Ireland Housing Executive (NIHE). The NIHE is the sole authority administering public housing in the province and consequently one of the largest employers in the construction industry. In 1982, the last date for which figures are available, the unemployment rate for construction in

Northern Ireland stood at 42 per cent compared to 25 per cent in Great Britain. The Northern Ireland economy has proved to be particularly vulnerable to the dramatic decline in both manufacturing and construction employment which has been experienced by all three areas.

Although official data on the occupations of the unemployed in the United Kingdom have not been published since 1982, Layard (1986) estimates that for the past ten to fifteen years in Great Britain semi-skilled and unskilled workers were roughly four times as likely to be unemployed as non-manual workers. Data such as are available indicate very little difference between Northern Ireland and Great Britain, in that 56.8 per cent of the unemployed in Northern Ireland in 1982 were classified as general labourers or other manual occupations, compared to 56.6 per cent for the same category in Great Britain.

SICKNESS

The relative health of the labour force has both a direct and an indirect effect on the levels of unemployment. Studies by Disney (1976), Townsend (1979) and Smith, R (1987) have shown that prolonged or frequent sickness can lead to unemployment and, in turn, long-term unemployment can lead to prolonged or frequent sickness. Hence illness is recognised as contributing to both the level and the duration of unemployment of the individual.

Northern Ireland holds the unenviable position at the top of the unemployment league for the United Kingdom and it also has a higher than average proportion of long-term unemployed. This is reflected in the number of absences due to sickness among the labour force, both employed and unemployed. As Table 7.9 shows, between 1980 and 1985 the average number of days of certified incapacity per head of working population in Northern Ireland was over 6 days greater than Great Britain for males and just under 9 days greater for females. The high morbidity of the population of Northern Ireland compared to that of Great Britain was officially recognised in a report of HM Treasury (1979). It is widely accepted that these data underestimate the actual number of days lost through sickness, but they are available on the same basis for the two regions and thus make comparison possible.

TABLE 7.9 Days of certified incapacity per head of working population, Northern Ireland and Great Britain, 1980/81–1985/86

	Northern Ireland		Great Britain	
	Male	Female	Male	Female
1980–81	23.1	17.5	16.5	8.1
1983–84[1]	21.4	14.7	15.3	6.6
1985–86	22.1	16.2	16.6	7.3
1980/81–1985/86 (average)	22.5	16.7	16.4	7.7

[1] Introduction on 6 April 1983 of SSP.
Sources: DHSS (unpublished); NIAAS No 6, 1987; Social Security Statistics.

The data for males show that the highest number of claims was in the 20–34 age group in Northern Ireland up until the introduction of the Statutory Sick Pay scheme (SSP) in 1983. From 1983/84 onwards the largest number of claims was in the 35–49 year old age group with over one-third of the total compared to one-fifth of the total for the same group in Great Britain. The age distribution of certified sickness in Northern Ireland is in complete contrast to that of Great Britain. In Great Britain it is the older age groups (50+) which account for the majority (72 per cent) of the days lost through sickness; the comparable figure for Northern Ireland was 33.8 per cent. Hence the economy of Northern Ireland demonstrates the twin phenomena of high unemployment and relatively high levels of sickness, which tends to support the findings of the studies carried out in Great Britain.

GEOGRAPHICAL DIVISIONS

There is considerable variation in the levels of unemployment within Northern Ireland. One can examine the local unemployment rates or the proportions of total employment located in the different areas.

In Northern Ireland the river Bann provides a geographical division between those areas of the province experiencing low and medium rates of unemployment in the north and east and those experiencing relatively higher rates in the south and west. Table 7.10 shows that, in June 1987, travel-to-work

TABLE 7.10   Unemployment by travel-to-work areas, Northern Ireland, June 1987

		Unemployment rate[1](%)	Unemployed as % of NI total
I	East of the Bann		
	Ballymena	13.9	2.7
	Belfast	17.8	49.3
	Coleraine	22.5	5.8
	Craigavon	18.7	9.0
	Total		66.8
II	West of the Bann		
	Cookstown	30.9	2.1
	Dungannon	26.0	3.1
	Enniskillen	24.5	3.5
	Londonderry	27.6	10.0
	Magherafelt	28.6	2.4
	Newry	30.2	6.1
	Omagh	22.4	2.9
	Strabane	33.9	3.1
	Total		33.2
	Northern Ireland	20.4	100.0

[1] Unemployment as a percentage of employees in June 1986.
Source: DED, 1987.

areas east of the Bann reported rates varying between 14 and 28.6 per cent compared to between 22.4 and 33.9 per cent west of the Bann. The individual unemployment rates increase as one moves west and south from Belfast. This pattern of unemployment has not changed through time; the areas included in Group I have always experienced the lowest individual rates, and as far back as 1974 the highest in Group I was below the lowest in Group II. However, within the relatively low Group I there are wards and streets in West Belfast where male unemployment is between 50 and 80 per cent, representing pockets of high unemployment where two generations of the same family have never held a permanent job (Rolston and Tomlinson 1988).

Examining the percentage of total Northern Ireland unemployment located in individual travel-to-work areas presents a different picture from the local unemployment rates. The Belfast area with its relatively low unemployment rate of 17.8 per cent in fact contains just under one-half of all the unemployed in Northern Ireland. At the other extreme, Strabane, which recorded an unemployment rate of 34 per cent, accounted for only 3 per cent of the unemployed.

The disparity between the rural and urban rates compared to the proportion of the unemployed is not unique to Northern Ireland. In Scotland the Strathclyde region recorded an unemployment rate of 18.4 per cent in 1987 compared to 20.3 per cent in the Western Isles. However, just under 54 per cent of the total unemployed in Scotland lived in the Strathclyde area compared to 0.6 per cent in the Western Isles. Table 7.11 shows that the unemployment pattern was similar in the Republic of Ireland where the rural north west recorded the highest unemployment rate of 24.2 per cent which accounted for 6.8 per cent of the total unemployed, whereas the urban east (Dublin and its environs) accounted for 40 per cent of the unemployed which resulted in an unemployment rate of 19.3 per cent. An industrial breakdown of the unemployed by travel-to-work areas in Northern Ireland for June 1987 shows that all areas west of the Bann, except Londonderry, demonstrate a common factor, namely the proportion who reported construction as the industry in which they held their last job was well above the Northern Ireland average. For example, in the area of Dungannon the proportion was as high as 39.6 per cent – over double the overall rate of 17.5 per cent. This relatively large pool of unskilled labour reflects the historical development of the two industrial ports of Belfast and Londonderry which are in stark contrast to the traditional rural areas west of the Bann.

5. Female and part-time employment

The relatively recent development of the substantial part-time component of the Northern Ireland workforce requires more detailed analysis. In what follows we move away from the characteristics of the unemployed and concentrate on the female labour force and its characteristics, including the important part-time element.

TABLE 7.11 Intra-regional rates of unemployment,[1] Northern Ireland, Republic of Ireland and Scotland, April 1987

Northern Ireland

County	Unemployment as % total	Unemployment rate (%)
Belfast DC	24.2	15.7
Antrim	15.6	18.6
Armagh	9.4	17.2
Down	21.1	18.9
Fermanagh	3.1	21.4
Londonderry	15.6	24.8
Tyrone	10.9	25.0
Northern Ireland	100.0	19.0

Republic of Ireland

Planning area	Unemployment as % total	Unemployment rate (%)
East	40.2	19.3
South East	10.8	19.5
North East	6.0	22.1
Midlands	6.0	16.1
South West	13.7	18.0
Mid West	8.4	18.3
West	8.0	19.4
North West & Donegal	6.8	24.2
Ireland	100.0	19.3

Scotland

Region	Unemployment as % total	Unemployment rate (%)
Borders	1.0	9.4
Central	5.1	16.7
Dumfries & Galloway	2.2	13.3
Fife	6.2	15.9
Grampian	6.4	9.6
Highland	3.8	14.9
Lothian	13.2	12.6
Strathclyde	53.9	18.4
Tayside	7.2	14.8
Orkney	0.2	12.5
Shetland	0.2	8.0
Western Isles	0.6	20.3
Scotland	100.0	15.5

[1] In Northern Ireland and Scotland the unemployment rate is calculated as claimant based unemployment as a percentage of total employees in employment and the unemployed; in the Republic of Ireland the unemployment rate is calculated as the numbers on the live register as a percentage of the labour force.
Sources: DED; CSO (Dublin); Scottish Economic Bulletin.

TABLE 7.12   Employees in employment by industry and sex, Northern Ireland and Great Britain, 1975, 1979 and 1987 (June, 000)

		Northern Ireland			Great Britain		
		1975	1979	1987	1975	1979	1987
Manufacturing	Male	104.1	94.2	63.8	5,175.2	5,001.1	3,569.8
	Female	55.0	51.3	36.1	2,189.3	2,106.2	1,501.1
Construction	Male	38.0	35.7	22.5	1,124.9	1,096.5	870.2
Services	Male	135.8	148.2	146.9	6,017.2	6,194.1	6,638.7
	Female	142.3	172.0	185.9	6,504.5	7,065.8	7,887.7
All industries	Male	296.0	303.8	257.4	13,242.0	13,183.0	11,714.8
	Female	201.1	230.8	227.9	8,974.0	9,455.1	9,662.0

Sources: NIAAS No 6, 1987; EG.

From 1979 until 1987[3] the total number of employees in employment fell from 534,600 to 485,000. The number of male employees fell consistently over the nine year period but the number of female employees increased by over 3,000 during the period. Table 7.12 provides more detailed data on employment in the three major industrial groups. Employment in manufacturing fell by 28,550 for males and 14,350 for females between 1979 and 1986. There was a small increase in female employees during 1984 and 1985 which can be linked to the increase in clothing industry output.

The service sector, on the other hand, has seen a steady increase in the number of female employees but little change in male employment. The relative importance of this sector has, however, changed markedly. In 1979, males employed in the service industries accounted for 48.8 per cent of all male employees. By 1986 this figure had risen to 57 per cent although it represented an increase of only 400 actual jobs. For females, the figures were 74.5 per cent and 81.3 per cent respectively, representing an increase of 14,050 jobs.

In common with the rest of the United Kingdom, the rise in female employment in Northern Ireland can be almost wholly attributed to a rise in part-time employment within the service industries. The latest official data available for Northern Ireland (1984) show that the proportion of part-time employees to total employees increased from 11.5 per cent in 1972 to 21.5 per cent in 1984. The proportion of male part-time employees showed an increase from 6.5 to 9.6 per cent and female part-time employees increased from 19.6 per cent to 35.6 per cent of all female employees in employment. A breakdown of the 1984 data by industry showed 26.8 per cent of all employees in the service sector working part-time with 40.8 per cent of female employees classified as part-time. Around 92 per cent of the 81,500 female part-time employees in the Northern Ireland economy worked in the service sector.

In order to put the increase in female employment into perspective, the data for 1972 and 1984 can be adjusted to a full-time equivalent basis by treating a part-time worker as one-half of a full-time worker.[4] In terms of full-time equivalents, the 1972 figures would be: males 292,000; females 167,000; total 459,000, which is 28,000 less than the unweighted official employment figures. For 1984 the full-time equivalent figures are: males 255,000; females

TABLE 7.13   Female economic activity by marital status, Northern Ireland, 1981 and 1985 (percentage)

	Single		Married		Other[1]		Total	
	1981	1985	1981	1985	1981	1985	1981	1985
Paid employment and self-employed	48.0	48.1	38.2	40.2	17.8	16.8	37.3	37.9
Unemployed	9.4	8.6	5.2	4.6	3.4	3.3	5.9	5.3
Full-time student	20.1	18.7	na[2]	na[2]	na[2]	na[2]	5.1	4.5
Retired	13.8	14.6	7.6	11.4	48.5	57.8	16.0	20.6
Housewife	4.9	3.9	46.1	36.7	27.3	15.2	32.7	25.2
Long-term sick or disabled	3.0	3.7	1.6	2.4	2.3	2.7	2.1	2.8
Other	0.7	2.4	1.1	4.5	0.6	4.0	0.9	3.9
Total	100.0	100.0	100.0	100.0	100.0	100.0	100.0	100.0

[1] Divorced, widowed or separated.
[2] Not available because of small sample size.
Source: LFS.

186,000; total 441,000. Thus female full-time equivalent employees accounted for 34.3 per cent in 1972 and 42 per cent in 1984. In both weighted and unweighted figures there was a four percentage point difference between the two years.

The 1985 LFS estimated the female activity rate in Northern Ireland to be 43.2 per cent, representing no change from 1981 (see Table 7.13). The proportion employed was 37.9 per cent of the relevant population, the unemployed 5.3 per cent. This can be compared with the LFS activity rate for females in Great Britain for 1985 of 48.7 per cent and 32.6 per cent in the Republic of Ireland. The activity rate for married females in Northern Ireland was 44.8 per cent compared to 52.2 per cent in Great Britain and 20.4 per cent in the Republic of Ireland.[5] The much lower rate in the Republic of Ireland compared to Northern Ireland reflects different cultural attitudes to the employment of married women and the prevailing job opportunities in the two areas. For single and 'other' women the Northern Ireland figure was 40.8 per cent compared to 44.4 per cent for Great Britain. It has long been recognised that Northern Ireland has one of the lowest female activity rates of any region in the United Kingdom. What has not been so clearly recognised is that compared with other areas of 'special need' within Europe the female activity rate in the Northern Ireland is amongst the highest (see Table 7.14).

The activity rate for single women in Northern Ireland fell slightly to 56.7 per cent in 1985 compared to 57.4 per cent in 1981. Indeed, the overall figures have changed very little since 1979. The unemployed component remained fairly stable between 1981 and 1985, with a fall of less than one percentage point. In 1985, of the 57 per cent of the female population who classified themselves as economically inactive, over 45 per cent recorded that they were younger than the statutory retirement age of 60 or were housewives. When asked why they were not seeking work, 43.2 per cent said they were housewives and retired, despite the fact they were under the statutory

TABLE 7.14   Female activity rates in selected regions, 1981 and 1985 (percentage)

	1981	1985
Great Britain	47.6	48.7
North	46.2	45.4
Yorkshire and Humberside	47.7	47.5
East Midlands	48.3	49.2
East Anglia	46.3	48.1
South East	48.8	51.1
South West	44.0	47.6
West Midlands	48.8	48.8
North West	48.9	48.9
England	47.9	49.2
Wales	42.2	43.0
Scotland	47.6	47.6
European Community Areas of 'special need':		
Northern Ireland (highest)	43.2	43.2
Abruzzi-Molise (next highest)	32.2	34.4
Republic of Ireland	29.0	32.6
Sicily (lowest)	21.6	22.0

Source: As Table 7.13.

retirement age of 60. As would be expected, of the 43.2 per cent, 37.5 per cent were married (representing almost two-thirds of all married females who answered the question). If married women who classify themselves as retired and who are over 60 years of age are included, the percentage rises to 87.3 per cent.

The overall pattern of occupations carried out by women in Northern Ireland and Great Britain is broadly similar with the majority in both areas employed in low status, low paid jobs in catering, cleaning etc (IX) or clerical and related (VI), see Table 7.15. There is, however, a difference in the proportion of Great Britain women employed in Group I, managerial and professional, 3.8 per cent compared to 1.3 per cent for Northern Ireland, which reflects the differing opportunities available in the two regions for this type of work.

The LFS data for the Republic of Ireland are presented (Table 7.16) using the Republic of Ireland's own occupational definitions which are not directly comparable with the United Kingdom data. Where comparison is possible, it can be seen that the occupational pattern in the Republic of Ireland in 1985 is broadly similar with the largest proportion of female employees, 27.5 per cent, employed in clerical and related (VI). There were, however, only 15.3 per cent employed in catering, cleaning, etc (IX) in 1985 compared to 24.5 per cent in Northern Ireland. The proportion of women involved in farming, fishing, etc (X) was 5.4 per cent in 1985. This is more than ten times the figure for Northern Ireland, reflecting the relative importance of agriculture in the

TABLE 7.15   Occupational analysis of female civil employment, Northern Ireland and Great Britain, 1979 and 1985 (percentage)

	Occupation	Northern Ireland		Great Britain	
		1979	1985	1979	1985
I	Managerial and professional and related supporting management and administration	1.1	1.3	2.2	3.8
II	Professional and related in education, welfare and health	15.3	18.1	12.1	14.5
III	Literary, artistic and sports	0.4	0.4	0.7	1.0
IV	Professional and related in science, engineering and technology	0.3	0.4	0.8	0.7
V	Managerial (excluding general management)	3.8	5.2	4.3	5.5
VI	Clerical and related	25.9	25.3	31.1	30.1
VII	Selling	7.8	9.5	9.2	10.1
VIII	Security and protective service	1.2	0.3	0.4	0.4
IX	Catering, cleaning, hairdressing and other professional services	23.6	24.5	22.2	26.6
X	Farming, fishing and related	0.4	0.5	0.5	0.7
XI	Material processing (excluding metal)	12.7	7.7	6.6	4.8
XII	Processing, making and repairing (metal and electrical)	0.7	1.3	1.7	0.8
XIII	Painting, repetitive assembling, product inspection etc	4.7	3.6	5.7	4.1
XIV	Construction, mining etc	0	0	0	0
XV	Transport operating, moving and storing materials	0.3	0.5	1.0	0.5
XVI	Miscellaneous	0.3	0.1	0.4	0.3
	No reply/inadequately described	1.5	1.3	1.1	0.1
	Total	100.0	100.0	100.0	100.0

Note: Republic of Ireland data not compatible with United Kingdom data, see Table 7.16.
Source: As Table 7.13.

Republic of Ireland and the lack of other alternative opportunities for rural female workers.

The industrial analysis of employees in employment as defined by the LFS emphasises the importance of the service sector in Northern Ireland, with just over 80 per cent of all female employees and 57 per cent of all male employees employed there in 1985 (Table 7.17). These figures represent a 5 percentage point increase in female employees in services and a 6 percentage point increase for males since 1981. For the first time, over one-half of the male employees in employment are involved in service industries. The 'other services' category requires further explanation as it accounts for the largest proportion of both male and female employees. 'Other services' comprises such public services as health, education and public administration. The

TABLE 7.16 Occupational analysis of female civil employment, Republic of Ireland, 1979 and 1985 (percentage)

	1979	1985
Agricultural workers	6.2	5.4
Producers, makers and repairers	12.5	10.8
Labourers and unskilled	0.4	0.2
Transport and communication	3.2	2.6
Clerical workers	28.2	27.5
Commerce, insurance and finance	12.8	13.1
Service workers	14.8	15.3
Professional and technical workers	20.6	23.6
Others	1.2	1.4
Total	100.0	100.0

Source: LFS, CSO Dublin, 1985.

proportion of women working in this sector has fallen slightly since 1981, but despite this just under 50 per cent of all female employees and 28 per cent of all male employees still work in the public services. This compares with 40 per cent and 18 per cent respectively for Great Britain, and 48 per cent and 19.8 per cent for the Republic of Ireland.

PART-TIME WORKERS

The 1985 LFS estimated that out of a total of 256,000 male employees only 6,000 (2.6 per cent) were working part-time. This compared to a figure of

TABLE 7.17 Industrial analysis of civil employment by industry, Northern Ireland, Great Britain and the Republic of Ireland, 1985 (percentage)

Industrial order (NACE)	Northern Ireland		Great Britain		Republic of Ireland	
	Male	Female	Male	Female	Male	Female
Agriculture, forestry and fishing	1.8	0.7	3.0	1.3	20.3	5.4
Energy and water	3.0	0.3	4.3	1.0	1.8	0.01
Extraction/processing of minerals	2.5	0.7	4.4	1.8	1.3	0
Metal manufacture/ mechanical engineering	10.3	2.8	14.8	5.1	5.5	5.0
Other manufacturing	13.1	13.8	10.9	10.1	14.5	13.5
Building/civil engineering	11.9	1.0	11.4	1.6	9.8	0.01
Distributive trades	15.5	21.7	16.1	25.4	15.1	17.1
Transport and communication	7.5	2.4	8.3	3.0	7.5	3.6
Finance/insurance	6.1	6.6	8.6	10.2	2.9	5.6
Other services	27.8	49.8	17.9	40.3	19.8	48.0
No reply	0.6	0.2	0.3	0.2	1.5	1.8
Total	100.0	100.0	100.0	100.0	100.0	100.0

Source: LFS, 1985.

209,000 female employees of whom 75,000 were part-time workers, representing 37 per cent of all female employees.

The Department of Employment estimated[6] that just under 44 per cent of female employees and 7.6 per cent of male employees were working part-time in Great Britain in June 1987. In the Republic of Ireland the latest figures available (1984) record that 14 per cent of female employees stated their main occupation to be part-time compared with 2.5 per cent of male employees.

The 1985 LFS[7] estimated that the majority (73 per cent) of female part-time workers in Northern Ireland worked in the two industrial sectors of distributive trades and other services, the latter accounting for 55 per cent of the total. In Great Britain the corresponding figure was just over 48 per cent. However in both regions just over 90 per cent of all female part-time workers worked in the service sector compared with over 80 per cent of all male part-time workers. There can be no doubt that the high participation rate of female employees in Great Britain and Northern Ireland is due to the higher levels of part-time jobs in the service sector and in particular 'other services' available in the United Kingdom compared to the Republic of Ireland.

From the LFS data we are able to establish that the typical female part-time worker in Northern Ireland is married, aged over 35, working in the service sector in 'other services' in a catering or cleaning occupation for between 8 and 21 hours per week.

6. Training

Manpower policy recognises training and education as vital ingredients for the current and future economic success of the United Kingdom. In recent years numerous changes and developments have been introduced by governments in an attempt to ensure that both the potential and existing workforce receive the training necessary to enable industry to operate efficiently.

In Great Britain, the Manpower Services Commission[8] and the Department of Employment were primarily responsible for the organisation of government sponsored training schemes. The main thrust of training policy has been towards increasing the responsiveness of training schemes to demand, to maintaining opportunities for young people to enter skills training and to promote adequate vocational training for the young person lacking qualifications. In Northern Ireland the present system of training embodies both youth and adult training and is extensive and diverse. At present DED is responsible for Training Centres (GTC), training grants, schemes for the training and employment of the unemployed and the administration of the Youth Training Programme (YTP). In addition there are eight Industrial Training Boards (ITBs) with specific responsibility for the particular sectors of industry to which they are related. The Northern Ireland Training Authority (NITA) administers the Boards, encourages cross-sectional training and develops and promotes new techniques of training and training in new technology.

In April 1988 the DED published a policy document on the reorganisation of the training facilities in the province with a single training organisation. The proposed single organisation is to include the entire range of training functions undertaken by DED, the ITBs and NITA and will extend to all training relevant to Northern Ireland industry and commerce including both youth and adult training.

The Republic of Ireland amalgamated its three main training bodies in January 1988 with AnCO, the National Manpower Service and Youth Employment Agency combining to become An Foras Aiseanna Saothair (FAS). The reasons for the amalgamation were similar to those of the proposed merger in Northern Ireland – namely to provide a more co-ordinated and integrated approach to the whole area of training and employment.

In both the United Kingdom and the Republic of Ireland, the employment and training measures have been developed as a direct response to the rise in unemployment during the late 1970s and the 1980s. There have been a series of changes in Great Britain. For example, the Community Enterprise Programme was replaced by the Community Programme in 1982 which in turn was phased out in 1988. The Temporary Short-Time Working Compensation Scheme was phased out in 1984 and the Restart Programme, aimed at the long-term unemployed, was introduced in 1986. In 1983 the Youth Training Scheme (YTS) in Great Britain replaced the Youth Opportunities Programme and in 1985 the YTS was extended to include certain 18 year olds who had been unable to join the scheme earlier due to personal circumstances. The scheme initially provided one year of training and work experience for the participants but was expanded in 1986 to offer two years' training for 16 year olds.

The Community Programme was set up to provide temporary employment for the long-term unemployed adult (aged 18 and over). In addition the Enterprise Allowance Scheme, which became nationally available in 1983, was designed to help the unemployed set up a business of their own by providing a weekly allowance for up to a year.

There are other, smaller schemes operating, but in Great Britain the YTS and the CP were by far the largest of the schemes administered by the then Manpower Services Commission. In 1985 the two schemes accounted for 443,000 or 78 per cent of the number supported; by 1987 the figure had risen to 563,000 or 83 per cent of the total. The two main schemes run by the Department of Employment – the Job Release Scheme and the Young/New Workers Scheme – are much smaller in size. In 1985, they accounted for approximately 20 per cent of the total and by 1987 their relative importance had fallen to just over 6 per cent. The participants in the Enterprise Allowance Scheme have more than doubled from 43,000 in 1985 to 93,000 in 1988.

There are differences between the structure of training provision in Northern Ireland and Great Britain, although the overall ethos is very similar. In Northern Ireland, the Youth Training Programme (YTP) was introduced a year earlier than YTS in Great Britain and from the beginning was a two year scheme. For the first two years of operation 1982–84 the second year was project-based full-time training which has subsequently been replaced by Workscheme. The guaranteed first year of YTP also differs from YTS in that the main training providers are the Training Centres, Community Workshops and Further Education Colleges whereas the first year of YTS is almost exclusively employer-based. The main difference between the two schemes lies in their organisation, mode of operation, funding and their development from YOP, which manifests itself in the amount of employer participation. The Northern Ireland schemes have been characterised by lack of employer participation in the first of the two years compared to the schemes run in Great Britain; only 8 per cent of first-year entrants to YTP in Northern Ireland are in employer-based schemes compared with 76 per cent to YTS in Great Britain. However, estimates show that in the second of the two years of the YTP two-thirds of the trainees are involved in the employer-based Workscheme.

Industrial training for adults in Northern Ireland, as indicated earlier, is carried out under the organisation of the NITA, GTCs, Attachment Training Schemes, Training on Employers' premises (TOEPS) and the Management Training Unit. In addition, special employment measures, unique to Northern Ireland, include Enterprise Ulster and Action for Community Employment (ACE). The ACE scheme was set up in 1981 to provide temporary employment for the long-term unemployed on community-based projects and as such is similar to the Community Programme in Great Britain. Enterprise Ulster is a direct labour scheme set up in 1973 to provide temporary employment for the long-term unemployed in construction and environmental projects. The very nature of such projects has resulted in the scheme benefiting the unemployed male, rather than affording equal opportunity to all.

As can be seen from Table 7.18, YTP and ACE form the major planks of employment and training measures in Northern Ireland, the ACE scheme having grown rapidly since its introduction in 1981 to include over 8,800 young adults by 1988. There were 8,700 YTP places in 1988.

The training schemes in Northern Ireland and Great Britain are broadly similar, with the emphasis on the training of the potential workforce to assist both industry and commerce, to meet their training skills and to assist

TABLE 7.18 Employment and training measures, Northern Ireland, by industry March
1982 and 1988

	1982	1988
Adults	4,600	na
Training on employers' premises	800	550
Government Training Centres	800	450
Attachment Training Scheme	50	2,600[1]
Other training schemes	1,450	1,300
Enterprise Ulster	1,500	8,850
Action for Community Employment	12,300	13,800
Youth Training Programme		

[1] Including 2,000 on the Enterprise Allowance Scheme.
Sources: NIAAS; DED.

individuals to achieve their vocational and personal development goals. The main differences lie within the organisation and funding of the two youth programmes, with the YTS in Great Britain being until recently somewhat more strongly employer-based than the YTP.

7. Conclusion

Northern Ireland is a peripheral region of the United Kingdom in which the development of opportunities for employment has for many years fallen short of the natural growth of the labour force. This has been the main factor influencing the characteristics of the labour market which have been discussed above. The most significant characteristics include higher rates of unemployment than in any other region of the United Kingdom, particularly high rates of unemployment for young workers, lower levels of female participation than in Great Britain (but substantially higher than in the Republic of Ireland) and higher rates of absenteeism because of sickness than in Great Britain.

These characteristics are largely the consequence of the problems which confront the economy of Northern Ireland; they are effects rather than causes. Amongst the characteristics which may contribute to poor performance are the low levels of educational attainment in the labour force. Forecasts suggest that in the 1990s there will be a substantial increase in the demand for mental skills at the expense of manual skills. This implies a formidable task in the fields of education and training. However, Northern Ireland's present form of government and education system allows for such a development and implementation of training measures which are closely geared to the demands of the local economy. Far-reaching changes in industrial structure during the past two decades have brought in their train changes in the pattern of employment. The demand for female workers has increased over a period when the demand for male workers has fallen continuously. Within the female labour market part-time employment has become increasingly important. These trends are changing the character of the labour force and will have far-reaching consequences for the labour market in Northern Ireland, in the form of a shift from the dominance of male manual employment to female part-time service employment.

Appendix 7.1 Unemployment and religion

Religion and its effects on the economic and social life of the province is well documented. Numerous studies have been made of the religious mix of the population and its influence as it pertains to employment, unemployment, education etc (Aunger 1975; Compton 1981; Cormack and Osborne 1983; Rolston and Tomlinson 1988).

In what follows we briefly analyse the religious affiliation of the unemployed in Northern Ireland and consider possible causes of the different unemployment rates experienced by the two communities. The main sources of data are the Census of Population for 1971 and 1981, both of which included a question on religious affiliation.

Exact comparisons between the two dates are virtually impossible for various reasons. The first was the problem of non-enumeration in the Census of 1981. The estimates of the scale of this non-enumeration vary, although most is thought to have taken place in predominantly Roman Catholic areas (see Osborne and Cormack 1987). Secondly, and equally important, was the problem of non-response to the voluntary religious affiliation question. In 1971 the non-response was just over 9 per cent, and in 1981 it was almost 20 per cent.

Since 1981 an additional source has been made available in the form of the Continuous Household Survey which is akin to the General Household Survey for Great Britain. In 1985 the Policy Planning and Research Unit (PPRU) of the Department of Finance published data based on a combination of the 1983 and 1984 surveys.

Although the data are subject to reservations the broad thrust is one of substantial differences in the unemployment rates among the two communities as set out in Table 7.1A.

The 1981 Census data show an unemployment rate for all Roman Catholics of just over twice that for all Protestants; the unemployment rate for male Roman Catholics is approximately two and a half times that for male Protestants. The same relative difference is found in the CHS results for 1983/84 and moreover the results are consistant with the figures reported in the 1971 Census of Population.

TABLE 7.1A   Unemployment rates[1] by religion, Northern Ireland, 1981 and 1983/84 (percentage)

	Protestant			Roman Catholic		
	Male	Female	All	Male	Female	All
1981	12.4	9.6	11.4	30.2	17.1	25.5
1983/84	15.0	11.0	13.0	35.0	17.0	28.0

[1] Bases on economically active persons 16+.
Sources: NI COP 1981; CHS Monitor (PPRU) 2/85.

The figures show that unemployment is consistently higher amongst Roman Catholics than amongst Protestants. Other characteristics such as rate of population growth, geographical location, education and age structure also differ between the two communities (Compton 1981, 1985) and these may serve to explain much of the difference in the totals.

Amongst the more obvious differences between the two communities which was evident until the mid-1980s was the relationship between unemployment, social class and the number of dependent children per economically active male head of household. The correlation between high levels of unemployment and family size has been explored for both Great Britain (Townsend 1979) and Northern Ireland (Trewsdale 1980). Compton showed that in 1971, 17.6 per cent of Roman Catholic households contained 5 or more dependent children compared with 3.3 per cent for similar Protestant households. Furthermore, 72.6 per cent of Roman Catholic households were headed by economically active males in the three lowest social classes, compared with 62 per cent of Protestant households. A combination of these two characteristics was associated with unemployment rates as high as 61 per cent for Roman Catholics with 9 children in the lowest social class (the overall rate for the class was 38.7 per cent).

Since 1971 average family sizes in both religious groupings in Northern Ireland have been falling. For Roman Catholics it fell from 3.64 in 1971 to 3.24 in 1983. Protestant family size fell only slightly from 2.37 to 2.29 over the same period (Compton 1985).

A recent study by the Policy Studies Institute (Smith, D 1987) using data from the Continuous Household Survey, concluded that, in spite of the importance of the other factors, a significant proportion of the differences in unemployment rates can be attributed to discrimination. This conclusion is, however, still subject to considerable controversy. A more cautious approach to the problem suggests the following: unemployment rates differ between the two communities, but this in itself cannot be regarded as prima facie evidence of discrimination because we do not know whether they differ because of discrimination or because of social, geographical and cultural factors. Whatever the reasons for the differences they have led to the 'religious problem' in Northern Ireland, which has been recognised by successive United Kingdom governments since the late 1960s and has subsequently moved into the international arena with the acceptance of the MacBride Principles[9] by several states of the United States of America, bringing an influential American input into the domestic employment practices of the province.

This recognition has manifested itself in the creation in 1976 and development of the Fair Employment Agency, whose powers are now strengthened by The Fair Employment (Northern Ireland) Act 1989. The key points of the new legislation are that all public sector employers and private sector employers employing more than 10 employees will be required to register with the newly named Fair Employment Commission. Registered employers will have to submit annual monitoring returns showing the religious composition of their workforce; applications to employers with more than 250 employees will also be monitored. It is a requirement for all employers to review their recruitment, training and promotion practices to ascertain whether affirmative action measures are required to meet set goals and timetables. Failure to comply with the legislation will be a criminal offence.

Notes

1. The explanation for these differences was cited as the net effect of the difference between two partly offsetting groups. The first group were either not seeking work during the reference week of the survey or had some form of paid employment. Those in paid employment were defined as working part-time and available for full-time work and claiming at Unemployment Benefit Offices because they were either entitled to supplementary benefit in that they had low incomes and were working less than 30 hours per week; or were claiming unemployment benefit for days they earned £2 or less provided any paid work was of a temporary nature; or were claiming national insurance credits if they worked no more than one day or eight hours a week, with weekly earnings below the lower earnings limit for paying national insurance contributions. The second group consisted of those without jobs and seeking work but not claiming benefit.
2. The Department of Economic Development does not estimate rates for Northern Ireland because the sample size is such that the results would be statistically invalid.
3. See Appendix 6.3.
4. The factor of one-half takes into account double counting, ie one person having

two part-time jobs as well as the proportion of hours worked and has been used in other labour market studies (Townsend 1986).

5. 'Married' in the Republic of Ireland includes separated and divorced – these categories are classified under 'other' in Great Britain and Northern Ireland along with widowed.
6. Estimates of employees in employment include an allowance based on LFS to compensate for persistent undercounting in the regular sampling enquiries. Individuals with two jobs as employees of different employers are counted twice.
7. The author wishes to thank the Equal Opportunities Commission for Northern Ireland for permission to use the data from the LFS (1985) for Northern Ireland.
8. The Training Commission replaced the Manpower Services Commission (set up in 1974) in the Autumn of 1988. The White Paper, *Employment for the 1990s*, published in January 1989 proposes that the Training Commission be replaced by the Training Agency which will continue to operate as did its predecessor.
9. For a statement and discussion of the MacBride Principles see Rolston and Tomlinson (1988).

References

An Roinn Saothair (1987), Department of Labour, *Annual Report*, Dublin.

Armstrong, H and Taylor, J (1985) *Regional Economics and Policy*, Philip Allan.

Aunger, E A (1975) Religion and occupational class in Northern Ireland, *The Economic and Social Review*, 7, 1–23.

Blackwell, J (1986) *Women in the Labour Force*, Equal Employment Agency, Dublin.

Compton, P A (1981) Demographic and geographical aspects of the unemployment differential between Protestants and Roman Catholics in Northern Ireland, in Compton, P A (ed) *The Contemporary Population of Northern Ireland and Population-Related Issues*, Institute of Irish Studies, Queen's University of Belfast.

Compton, P A (1985) An evaluation of the changing religious composition of the population of Northern Ireland, *The Economic and Social Review*, 16, 3, 201–224.

Cormack, R J and Osborne, R D (eds) (1983) *Religion, Education and Employment*, Appletree Press, Belfast.

Department of Economic Development (1987) *Methodology to Evaluate Training Assistance*.

Department of Economic Development (1988) *The Organisation of Training in Northern Ireland – Proposals for the Future*.

Department of Education (Northern Ireland) (1988) *Education in Northern Ireland – Proposals for Reform*.

Department of Finance and Personnel (1985) *PPRU Monitor 2/85, Religion*.

Disney, R (1976) *The Distribution of Unemployment and Sickness Among the UK Population*. University of Reading Discussion Paper, 87.

HMSO (1988) *Fair Employment in Northern Ireland* Cm 380.

HMSO (1989) Fair Employment (Northern Ireland) Act 1989.

H M Treasury (1979) *Needs Assessment Study*.

Layard, R (1986) *How to Beat Unemployment*, Oxford University Press.

Layard, R and Bean, C (1988) *Why does Unemployment Persist?* Centre for Labour Economics, LSE Discussion Paper, 321.

MacKay, R R and Jones, D R (1988) The Northern Ireland labour market, chapter 11, mimeo PPRU Seminar.

Moylan, B, Millar, J and Davies, R (1984) *For Richer for Poorer? DHSS Cohort Study of Unemployed Men.* DHSS, Security Social Research Branch, Research Report 11.

Osborne, R D and Cormack, R J (1987) *Religion, Occupations and Employment 1971–1981*, Fair Employment Agency Research Paper 11, Belfast.

P A Management Consultants (1984) *The Future Demand for Skilled Manpower in Northern Ireland.*

Rolston, B and Tomlinson, M (1988) *Unemployment in West Belfast: The Obair Report*, Beyond the Pale Publications, Belfast.

Smith, D (1987) *Equality and Inequality in Northern Ireland, Part I.* Policy Studies Institute.

Smith, R (1987) *Unemployment and Health: A Disaster and a Challenge*, Oxford University Press.

Townsend, A (1986) Spatial aspects of the growth of part-time employment in Britain, *Regional Studies*, 20, 4, 313–330.

Townsend, P (1979) *Poverty in the UK*, Pelican Books.

Trewsdale, J M (1980) *Unemployment in NI 1974–1979*, Northern Ireland Economic Council, Paper 14, Belfast.

Trewsdale, J M (1988) *The Aftermath of Recession: Changing Patterns in Female Employment and Unemployment in Northern Ireland.* Equal Opportunities Commission for Northern Ireland, Belfast.

Industrial relations
J Boyd H Black

1. Introduction

The regional dimension in industrial relations has been largely neglected until recently. Most standard treatments of British industrial relations take the system as a uniform whole and ignore regional variations within the system to the extent that these exist. These variations may be in matters such as collective bargaining structure, trade union recognition, trade union membership, density and organisation, industrial action and, in the case of Northern Ireland, the constitutional and statutory framework of industrial relations. The Workplace Industrial Relations Surveys (Daniel and Millward 1983; Millward and Stevens 1986) did include a regional coding, but this dimension was not analysed in the preliminary reports.[1] Other major surveys such as that reported by Brown (1981) on manufacturing industry and the Royal Commission under Lord Donovan (1968) also ignored the regional dimension. The tendency has been to assume regional homogeneity in industrial relations and that the determinants of industrial relations at the regional level will be the same as for the country as a whole.

There has been a recent upsurge in interest in the regional dimension. A study by Smith et al (1978) provided an analysis of strike activity in Great Britain at the sub-regional level and concluded that the regional dimension was of relatively little importance. On the other hand, studies by Elshiekh and Bain (1980) and Bain and Elias (1985) found the regional variable to be significant in explaining trade union membership patterns. Both Millward and Stevens (1988) and Beaumont and Harris (1988a) found a North/South divide in British industrial relations, with trade union membership and density and collective bargaining coverage being higher in the North. After adjusting for industrial structure, Beaumont and Harris also found what they called a residual regional 'proximities' effect which they thought reflected an industrial relations culture specific to the region.

Most of these studies cited confined their research to Great Britain, so that even where a regional analysis was carried out, Northern Ireland data were not included. There were exceptions to this; eg the Commission on Industrial Relations (1973) survey of industrial relations at establishment level included Northern Ireland establishments in its sample as did a CIR report on industrial relations training (1972). To date, the only survey work published on Northern Ireland industrial relations is that of Tipping and McCorry (1988).

Northern Ireland industrial relations is of particular interest for two reasons. First, because of the constitutional arrangements applying in Northern Ireland, the Department of Employment and its predecessors have not had direct responsibility for industrial relations in Northern Ireland since 1920. Under the Government of Ireland Act 1920, legislative and executive responsibility for industrial relations in Northern Ireland was devolved to the Northern Ireland Parliament at Stormont. Thus, from 1920 to 1972, industrial relations in Northern Ireland evolved under devolution. In addition, in the absence of the Conservative and Labour Parties which have refused to seek an electoral mandate in Northern Ireland from 1920, industrial relations developed from 1920 to 1972 under the political hegemony of the Ulster Unionist Party which held power at Stormont throughout the period.

When the Northern Ireland Parliament was prorogued in 1972 and Direct Rule introduced, responsibility for industrial relations was assumed by the Secretary of State for Northern Ireland and has remained with the Secretary of State since then, apart from a brief period in 1974 when a Northern Ireland Executive held power under the provisions of the Northern Ireland Constitution Act 1973. This authority is currently exercised through the Department of Economic Development for Northern Ireland (DED).

Industrial relations in Northern Ireland are also of particular interest because of the trade union links with the Republic of Ireland at congress level. The Irish Congress of Trade Unions (ICTU) with its headquarters in Dublin, is the officially recognised trade union centre for Northern Ireland, rather than the TUC.

The Report of the Review Body on Industrial Relations (1974) treated industrial relations arrangements in Northern Ireland as constituting a distinctive separate industrial relations system, related to, and with close links to the system in Britain, but separate nonetheless. For reasons that were never very explicit, it favoured the development of an even more distinctive regional system of industrial relations in Northern Ireland, a theme which was taken up at a Labour Relations Agency seminar by Professor Sir John Wood who had been the sole independent member of the Review Body (Labour Relations Agency 1984, 95).

In what sense can we talk in terms of a separate regional industrial relations 'system' or 'sub-system' in Northern Ireland? Benson and Hince (1984) have argued that the issue is whether and to what extent the key determinants of industrial relations behaviour in the region differ from the broad explanatory variables operative in the industry or in the economy as a whole.

This chapter will examine to what extent industrial relations behaviour in Northern Ireland is influenced by the same factors as the rest of the United Kingdom and to what extent regional factors unique to Northern Ireland influence that behaviour. The impact of the industrial relations system on economic performance will be assessed. Comparisons will be drawn, where appropriate, with the Republic of Ireland.[2]

Section 2 examines the constitutional and statutory framework of industrial relations which has influenced the collective bargaining structure treated in Section 3. Section 4 analyses trade union membership and organisation including the role of the ICTU. The incidence of industrial conflict is examined in Section 5. Section 6 assesses the impact of the particular characteristics of the Northern Ireland industrial relations system on the performance of the Northern Ireland economy. In Section 7 we draw some conclusions and consider the implications for industrial relations policy.

2. The statutory framework

A separate Northern Ireland statute book was established in 1921 and existing United Kingdom legislation was incorporated in it. Although, after 1921, the Stormont government possessed the constitutional powers to develop a distinctive approach to industrial relations legislation, it chose in practice to follow closely legislative practice in Britain. This policy of keeping legislation in Northern Ireland broadly in line with that in Great Britain has continued under Direct Rule, although there has tended to be some years delay in introducing the relevant legislation by Order in Council or Statutory Rule.

The Trade Union Act 1871, the Conspiracy and Protection of Property Act 1875 and the Trade Disputes Act 1906 established the basic framework of trade union immunities throughout the United Kingdom. The Trade Disputes and Trade Unions Act (Northern Ireland) 1927 followed the Trade Disputes and Trade Unions Act 1927 very closely in its provisions. While the Westminster Parliament repealed the 1927 Act in its entirety with the Trade Disputes and Trade Unions Act 1946, the 1927 Act remained on the Northern Ireland statute book until 1958. Then the Trade Disputes and Trade Unions Act (Northern Ireland) 1958 repealed those sections of the 1927 Act which had removed immunities confirmed under the 1906 Act.[3]

The provisions of the Trade Disputes Act 1965 and the Industrial Relations Act 1971 did not extend to Northern Ireland,[4] but most of the major provisions of legislation such as the Trade Union and Labour Relations Acts, 1974 and 1976 (which, amongst other enactments, repealed the 1965 and 1971 Acts while retaining some of their provisions), the Employment Protection Act 1975 and the Employment Acts 1980 and 1982 have been enacted in Northern Ireland through Orders in Council. The important legislation has been the Industrial Relations (Northern Ireland) Order 1976, the Industrial Relations (No 2) Northern Ireland Order 1976, the Industrial Relations (Northern Ireland) Order 1982 and the Industrial Relations (Northern Ireland) Order 1987.

Part III of the Trade Union Act 1984, which contains provisions relating to expenditure by trade unions on political objects, extends to Northern Ireland, although unions were not obliged to ballot their Northern Ireland membership over the continuance of their political funds (Black 1984). The government is currently considering whether or not to extend Parts I and

II of the 1984 Act, which contain provisions for the election of voting members of trade union executives and for secret ballots before industrial action, respectively, and the Employment Act 1988 to Northern Ireland.

If government does extend this legislation to Northern Ireland, the areas in which there will remain important differences in legislation will be relatively few. In the area of collective labour law, the main differences will be that most of the functions which the Certification Officer carries out in Great Britain will still be carried out in Northern Ireland by the Registrar of Friendly Societies. Also, Northern Ireland still has statutory procedures for trade union recognition which resemble those which applied in Great Britain under Sections 11–16 of the Employment Protection Act 1975 and which were repealed in 1980.[5]

In the area of individual employment rights, the main difference is that while the race relations legislation has not been extended to Northern Ireland, there is legislation to outlaw discrimination on grounds of religion or politics. The Fair Employment (Northern Ireland) Act 1989 aims to eliminate what is termed indirect as well as direct discrimination in employment. Employers are required to monitor their employees by religion. Employers may also be required to engage in affirmative action and meet employment goals and timetables as directed by a newly established Fair Employment Commission. Whether this is consistent with the merit principle in employment remains to be tested in the courts.

Increased legislation on employment rights has been accompanied by a growth in state agencies to implement and enforce these rights, many of them established on a tri-partite basis with their governing bodies composed of representatives of both employers and trade unions as well as independents. These statutory bodies usually exist as separate bodies from their Great Britain equivalents, having been established under parallel legislation with broadly equivalent powers, eg Equal Opportunities Commission for Northern Ireland, the Health and Safety Agency for Northern Ireland and the Northern Ireland Wages Councils. Nine of the latter exist, operating under the terms of the Wages (Northern Ireland) Order 1987, setting statutory minimum remuneration for some 36,000 employees in 1988, about 7 per cent of the employed workforce. There is also an Agricultural Wages Board.

In some instances bodies equivalent to those established in Britain have not been set up in Northern Ireland. Thus, while industrial tribunals adjudicate on the employment rights of individuals, there has been no legislation to establish an Employment Appeal Tribunal in Northern Ireland, so that appeals go directly to the Northern Ireland Court of Appeal. Similarly, while the Labour Relations Agency performs the same functions as the Advisory, Conciliation and Arbitration Service in the field of arbitration and conciliation, the Northern Ireland Industrial Court has not been replaced by a Central Arbitration Committee. Also, the functions performed in Britain by the Training Commission in the areas of manpower forecasting and the encouragement of training and the administration of labour exchanges are performed in Northern Ireland by a government department, the Department of Economic Development.

Nevertheless, given that the statutory framework of industrial relations in Northern Ireland has developed within the parameters laid down by the Government of Ireland Act 1920 and the Northern Ireland Act 1974, the extent to which it has developed in parallel with that in Great Britain is its most remarkable feature. The 'devolved' legislative framework has not been used to develop a distinctive legal system for industrial relations.

The Irish Free State (later to become the Republic of Ireland) inherited the British system of statutory immunities when it was established in 1922 and these have remained intact ever since. Trade unions thus currently have more protection under statute in the Republic of Ireland than they do in the United Kingdom since there has been no equivalent of the Employment Acts 1980 and 1982, the Trade Union Act 1984 and the Employment Act 1988, which have narrowed these immunities, passed in that jurisdiction.[6]

3. Collective bargaining structure

In the latter part of the nineteenth century collective bargaining was predominantly local or regional in character. The 1897 engineering agreement was the first national agreement to apply to Belfast, but it still left wages to be settled on a district basis. It was not until the First World War that national wage determination became widespread, especially following the recommendations of the Whitley Committee in 1917. By 1921, a growing number of trades were regulated by United Kingdom-wide machinery, but bargaining was still conducted on a local, district or area basis for a large number of occupations. In a number of industries there were agreements covering the whole of Ireland.

Two developments interrupted this evolving pattern and influenced subsequent arrangements. First, the onset of the interwar depression put pressure on these national arrangements, causing a number of them to collapse. Second, the establishment of a Parliament and Government at Stormont with legislative and executive responsibility for a range of devolved functions, including industrial relations, had a significant impact on the development of collective bargaining structure. It encouraged the establishment of separate Northern Ireland machinery in parts of the private sector which would otherwise in many cases have been covered by United Kingdom-wide machinery. It also resulted in the development of separate Northern Ireland machinery in those parts of the public sector for which Stormont had responsibility (Black 1985a).

As a result, major collective agreements in Northern Ireland today fall into three main types (see Appendix 8.1). First, in many parts of both the private and public sectors, national agreements cover the whole of the United Kingdom or, in some instances, England, Wales and Northern Ireland where separate machinery exists for Scotland. Second, in parts of the private sector, industry-wide machinery covers just Northern Ireland. Third, in those parts of the public sector which fall within the remit of the Northern Ireland Office, formal Northern Ireland machinery is closely linked to a bargaining arrangement covering the rest of the United Kingdom. Cross-border collective bargaining machinery is now of negligible importance.

Recent developments in collective bargaining structure in the private sector have included the tendency for Northern Ireland machinery to be replaced by wider, usually United Kingdom machinery (Black 1985a).[7] Even so, private sector industry-wide agreements covering Northern Ireland alone affect 15.0 per cent of employees in employment.[8] Administrative convenience may be one reason for this. Also, the geographical concentration of an industry in Northern Ireland may be an influence in some cases, as with linen. Another likely determining factor is the level of earnings. If earnings in an industry are below the United Kingdom average, then employers will wish to maintain separate Northern Ireland bargaining structures, eg as in the furniture industry. As earnings levels approach parity with Great Britain, often, in part, as a result of pressure from trade unions, then both employers and unions may prefer United Kingdom machinery to replace local arrangements, as happened in the flour milling and tobacco industries. In building and civil engineering, the local machinery established in 1977 resulted in basic rates rising above levels in Great Britain.

Individual establishment and company bargaining are important in determining terms and conditions of employment in the private sector. Thirty-two per cent of employees in the private sector were covered by establishment/company agreements in 1984.[9] Where company-wide bargaining occurs this can take place at the United Kingdom corporate or divisional level. Great Britain/foreign-based multi-establishment firms employed 32 per cent of all employees in Northern Ireland in 1984.[10] The same factors influencing their choice of bargaining unit in Great Britain presumably apply in Northern Ireland (Deaton and Beaumont 1980).

The main determinants of bargaining structure in the public sector have been the various constitutional and statutory arrangements, so that in those 'reserved' areas where Westminster retains control and in United Kingdom public corporations, United Kingdom machinery applies. Northern Ireland machinery has been established in those parts of the public sector over which powers were transferred to the Stormont Parliament in 1920. Many of these bodies have reached agreements which provide parity or equivalent pay and conditions of service with comparable groups in the public sector in Great Britain. In certain parts of the public sector, eg the Fire Service and the Prison Service, United Kingdom machinery has replaced Northern Ireland machinery.

The establishment of the principle of parity in pay and conditions of service with comparable grades of employees in Great Britain for employees in those parts of the public sector in Northern Ireland covered by local agreements has generated considerable problems. Usually, neither employers nor unions in Northern Ireland are represented on the key negotiating machinery which covers only Great Britain (or in some cases England and Wales). This has not prevented public sector unions here participating in industrial action in support of a claim lodged with the appropriate Great Britain machinery on which they are not represented. It does, however, mean that industrial relations practice in many parts of the public sector has outgrown the framework of the Northern Ireland bargaining machinery. There is a strong case for the replacement of Northern Ireland Joint Industrial Councils by United Kingdom machinery on both functional and democratic grounds. At the very least, Northern Ireland public sector employers and unions should be represented on the national negotiating machinery.

Overall, collective bargaining coverage, defined as the percentage of employees covered by collective agreements, is higher in Northern Ireland than in Great Britain (Table 8.1, Col 4). This is true for both males and females and holds across most industry groups with the notable exceptions of agriculture and the extractive industries (there is no coal mining in Northern Ireland). The main reason for this is the greater coverage of national/industry agreements in Northern Ireland (Cols 1 and 2). Bargaining coverage is also higher in Northern Ireland within each socio-economic group for both males and females with the exception of female skilled manuals (Table 8.2).

Harris and Wass (1988) found that, in manufacturing, country of ownership was an important determinant of collective bargaining coverage, with employees in firms owned in Great Britain being more likely to have their earnings affected by a collective agreement than those working in foreign or Northern Ireland owned firms. They also found establishment and company size to be important influences on the extent of collective bargaining coverage.

Collective bargaining in the Republic of Ireland has been dominated in recent years by national pay agreements. From 1970 to 1978, the main collective bargaining machinery was the Employer/Labour Conference, a voluntary body composed of 26 representatives of employers (from both the public and private sectors), 26 trade union representatives nominated by the ICTU and an independent chairman. The Irish Government was represented at the Conference only in its capacity as a public sector employer. Seven National Wage Agreements were negotiated between 1970 and 1978 under its aegis.

In 1979, the Irish Government became involved for the first time in national pay talks as a Government. These tripartite talks resulted in the negotiation of two National Understandings, which covered issues such as taxation, social welfare, employment creation, health and education as well as pay over the years 1979–81. They were followed by a year-long Public Sector Pay Agreement negotiated in 1982, and an immediate return to free collective bargaining in the private sector, which spread to the public sector in 1983. Free collective bargaining lasted until the tripartite negotiation of a three-year Programme for National Recovery in September 1987, which included the terms for pay increases over the following three years.

Unlike in Northern Ireland, bargaining structures in the Republic of Ireland have no links with those in Great Britain. Bargaining is conducted either at national level, industry level, or at the level of the individual enterprise.

TABLE 8.1 Percentage of full-time adults affected by types of collective agreement by industry, Northern Ireland, 1984, Great Britain, 1985

Industry SIC 1980	National[1] plus supplementary company/ workplace Col 1		National[1] only Col 2		Company/ workplace only Col 3		Any collective agreement Col 4	
	NI	GB	NI	GB	NI	GB	NI	GB
0–9 All industries								
Males	14.2	14.2	46.5	37.7	14.5	12.0	75.2	64.2
Females	7.7	10.4	64.3	45.8	8.7	7.8	80.7	64.0
0 Agriculture								
Males	0.0	7.1	0.0	28.8	11.1	3.0	11.1	38.9
Females	—	—	—	—	—	—	—	—
1 Energy and water								
Males	85.2	15.9	14.8	69.9	0.0	4.8	100.0	90.4
Females	88.9	27.8	11.1	52.0	0.0	3.3	100.0	83.1
2 Extractive industries								
Males	6.5	23.3	9.7	12.3	16.1	25.4	32.3	61.0
Females	20.0	13.0	0.0	9.3	0.0	3.3	20.0	46.6
3 Engineering and vehicles								
Males	12.6	20.8	19.0	13.7	48.6	22.0	80.2	56.5
Females	42.9	16.5	28.6	8.4	0.0	21.5	71.4	46.4
4 Other manufacturing								
Males	27.5	17.5	15.3	19.7	23.5	19.9	66.3	57.0
Females	17.9	14.7	17.9	22.8	32.8	15.8	68.7	53.3
5 Construction								
Males	17.5	16.8	45.6	46.8	1.8	2.6	64.9	66.3
Females	0.0	2.8	25.0	11.0	0.0	3.0	25.0	16.8
6 Distribution								
Males	7.0	6.2	16.7	17.3	23.7	10.4	47.4	33.9
Females	5.7	5.0	8.6	21.5	20.0	9.9	34.3	36.5
7 Transport and communications								
Males	1.7	9.7	92.8	60.1	8.6	13.1	93.1	83.0
Females	0.0	4.7	81.3	54.3	0.0	11.3	81.3	70.4
8 Business services								
Males	0.0	7.7	57.7	19.2	7.7	10.6	65.4	37.5
Females	2.6	8.1	57.9	21.6	7.9	7.8	68.4	37.6
9 Other services								
Males	4.3	14.4	86.3	74.5	0.8	1.4	91.4	90.3
Females	1.8	10.7	93.2	78.3	1.4	0.9	96.4	89.9

[1] National includes Northern Ireland industry-wide agreements.
Source: Harris and Wass (1988), Tables 1 and 2.

TABLE 8.2 Percentage of full-time adults affected by collective agreements by socio-economic group, Northern Ireland, 1984, Great Britain, 1985

| | Percentage affected by collective agreement | | | |
| | Males | | Females | |
Socio-economic group 1–8	NI	GB	NI	GB
1 Managers	51.3	42.9	87.5	44.0
2 Professionals	77.5	56.6	95.0	78.2
3 Intermediate non-manual	74.4	65.6	95.4	68.2
4 Junior non-manual	68.0	65.8	76.5	62.2
5 Foreman	78.3	64.9	74.9	61.9
6 Skilled manual	78.7	74.3	56.5	66.2
7 Semi-skilled manual	76.7	70.3	79.3	58.8
8 Unskilled manual	89.5	71.1	84.9	62.0

Source: Harris and Wass (1988), Tables 3 and 4.

4. Trade union growth and organisation

By the end of the nineteenth century, the great majority of trade unionists in the north of Ireland were members of national (Great Britain-based) unions. This meant that trade unionism in Northern Ireland developed within the context of British trade unionism. Aggregate trade union membership growth followed the broad historical trends that have been identified for Great Britain. However, membership growth in Northern Ireland has increased faster than the Great Britain average since the 1930s depression. In particular, membership continued to increase in Northern Ireland between 1974/75 and 1983, a period in which aggregate membership fell in the United Kingdom as a whole (Black 1986). Membership has fallen since 1983.

The great majority of trade unionists in Northern Ireland (77 per cent) are in Great Britain-based unions, with the remainder mostly in Northern Ireland-based unions (Table 8.3).[11] Only a small minority (7 per cent) are in unions with their headquarters in the Republic of Ireland. The pattern of union membership by occupation is similar to that in Great Britain. The main exception is that most local government officials and white collar staff employed in the Northern Ireland Civil Service, Education and Library Boards and Health and Social Services Boards are members of the Northern Ireland

TABLE 8.3 Trade union membership in Northern Ireland, 1987

Union headquarters	Number of trade unions	Membership (000)	Percentage of total
Great Britain	83	201.7	77.1
Northern Ireland	5	41.4	15.9
Republic of Ireland	5	18.3	7.0
Total	93	261.4	100.0

Source: Author's survey.

Public Service Alliance (NIPSA) rather than the National Association of Local Government Officers (NALGO). NIPSA has over 80 per cent of the membership of Northern Ireland-based unions. The development of a separate Northern Ireland public service union was a result of the existence (up to 1972) of a devolved legislature and government at Stormont, with responsibility for much of the public sector.

Over the period 1974/75–87, individual union growth in Northern Ireland has closely mirrored the United Kingdom pattern. The unions showing the largest membership gains were public sector unions such as the Royal College of Nursing (RCN), the National Union of Public Employees (NUPE), the Confederation of Health Service Employees (COHSE), and the National Association of Schoolmasters/Union of Women Teachers (NAS/UWT). The main exception was that NIPSA substituted for NALGO as the union with the largest absolute growth in membership. The union experiencing the biggest membership loss in Northern Ireland was the Amalgamated Transport and General Workers Union (ATGWU) (the name in Ireland of the TGWU), which had most of its membership in the rapidly contracting manufacturing sector. The ATGWU remains the union with the largest absolute membership in Northern Ireland with 18 per cent of total membership, but it has lost the predominance it had in 1953, when it accounted for as much as 36 per cent of the total.

In assessing the determinants of Northern Ireland aggregate trade union growth between 1953 and 1983, Black (1986) found that potential union membership (employees in employment plus the unemployed) had grown more rapidly in Northern Ireland than in Great Britain, particularly between 1974/75 and 1983. Also, a much higher proportion of employees in employment were trade union members in Northern Ireland in 1983 (60.9 per cent compared to a United Kingdom average of 53.5 per cent). Trade union density, defined as total trade union membership as a percentage of potential membership, was slightly higher in Northern Ireland in 1983 (48.9 per cent compared to 46.9 per cent for the United Kingdom) despite the higher level of unemployment in Northern Ireland which would tend to reduce density.

Changes in the sexual composition of potential union membership in Northern Ireland between 1953 and 1983, resulting from increased female employment, worked against the maintenance of aggregate union density. However, changes in the occupational and industrial composition of potential union membership in Northern Ireland actually worked to increase aggregate union membership. This was because of changes in the employment structure, particularly the rapid growth in public service employment between 1974/75 and 1983, where unionisation is on average much higher than in private sector services (though lower than in public services in Great Britain). The membership expansion in public services was more than enough to offset the large losses incurred in manufacturing. As a result, both the proportion of employees in employment who are trade union members and overall trade union density were above the United Kingdom average in 1983. This rate of public sector expansion is unlikely to be sustained. In so far as the public sector share of employment declines in the future, this may bring union density into line with the Great Britain average.

A number of other factors may have influenced Northern Ireland membership growth. Trade unions may have played some part in raising average earnings in Northern Ireland as a proportion of the United Kingdom average through their policy of bargaining for parity in earnings with similar occupations in Great Britain.[12] This additional 'credit' effect may have increased membership. Against this, once parity was achieved, so that pay settlements negotiated for Great Britain were automatically implemented in Northern Ireland, then the perceived advantages of union membership may have fallen. This 'free rider' effect would help explain the relatively low union density in public services in Northern Ireland compared to Great Britain.

Also, the fact that different statutory provisions regarding trade union recognition have applied in Northern Ireland over much of the post-war period may have influenced trade union membership growth in different ways at different times. In particular, Beaumont (1984) has argued that the current procedures established under the Industrial Relations (Northern Ireland) Order 1976 may have contributed significantly to union membership growth between 1977 and 1983, because of the higher union success rate achieved.

Although Northern Ireland is part of the United Kingdom and the great majority (93.3 per cent) of trade unionists are members of unions with their headquarters in the United Kingdom, its trade union affairs are under the authority of a trade union centre in the Republic of Ireland.

The existence of a single trade union centre for Ireland has a long tradition, dating back to the establishment of the Irish Trades Union Congress (ITUC) in 1894 based in Dublin. The ITUC was intended to complement the work of the TUC.

Following an upsurge of Irish nationalist sentiment in the trade union movement in the early decades of this century, a number of Dublin-based unions left the ITUC in 1945 to form a separate body, the Congress of Irish Unions (CIU) whose aim was to secure a wholly Irish-based and controlled trade union movement. The ICTU was established as a result of a merger between the ITUC and the CIU in 1959.

The ICTU is the recognised trade union centre for Ireland. A subordinate Northern Ireland Committee (NIC) of the ICTU, elected annually by block vote at an annual Northern Ireland Conference of affiliated unions with membership in Northern Ireland, is the official voice of the trade union movement in Northern Ireland and is recognised as such by Government. The NIC is responsible for implementing ICTU policy in Northern Ireland. It is responsible for dealing with matters relating solely to Northern Ireland and implements its own decisions and the decisions of the annual Northern Ireland Conference on such issues, subject to the overall control of the ICTU Annual Delegate Conference. It has a representative role to the ICTU Executive Council and to the TUC concerning policy matters relating to Northern Ireland. Because the ICTU in Dublin is the recognised trade union centre for Ireland, the TUC handles the trade union affairs of Northern Ireland through its international department!

Clause 2b of the ICTU constitution lays down certain conditions which Great Britain-based unions must fulfil before they can affiliate to the ICTU. Clause 2b(ii) requires that such a union must provide for a certain amount of autonomy for its Irish members, a requirement that was incorporated into Section 17(2) of the Trade Union Act 1975 in the Republic of Ireland. Certain unions, eg the EETPU, AUEW (TASS), AEU and ASTMS, have made special provision in their rules for some sort of autonomy for their membership resident in Ireland.

Given the existing organisation of trade unions in Northern Ireland, the existence of the ICTU is a trade union anomaly which creates a number of practical difficulties for the conduct of industrial relations (Robertson and Sams 1976). Many of these difficulties would be overcome and an improvement in the functioning of the trade union movement achieved by the TUC taking full responsibility for trade union affairs in Northern Ireland by establishing a Northern Ireland Trades Union Congress, constituted as part of the TUC's regional machinery along the same lines as the Wales TUC, to replace the ICTU. Northern Ireland-based unions should be allowed to affiliate their membership to the TUC, from which they are presently barred as a result of the ICTU arrangement. In particular, there is a strong case for NIPSA being allowed to affiliate to the TUC. Trade unionists in Northern Ireland live and work in the United Kingdom economy and are affected by the Government's economic and industrial relations policies. The TUC would be much more relevant and effective in representing their needs and interests to Government than the ICTU.[13]

5. Industrial conflict

As Table 8.4 shows, average working days lost per 1,000 employees in Northern Ireland have been slightly above the United Kingdom average during the period 1941–86. Northern Ireland's relative performance has improved considerably in the 1980s recession, partly because it was not affected by the national steel strike in 1980 or by the national coal strike of 1984–85. Looking

TABLE 8.4 Working days lost in trade disputes per 1,000 employees, Northern Ireland and the United Kingdom, annual average, 1941–1986

Period	Northern Ireland	United Kingdom
1941–45	523	153
1946–73	297	265
1974–79	562	535
1980–86	126	400
1941–86	330	309

Sources: Isles and Cuthbert (1957), p 232; Durcan et al (1983), p 186; EG; NIAAS.

at the overall picture, however, it is not possible to justify claims that Northern Ireland has a particularly good industrial relations record (Tipping and McCorry 1988, 174).

Black (1987) found that when the working days lost figures were adjusted to take account of the fact that Northern Ireland has a different industrial structure from the United Kingdom average, eg no coal mining or steel industries, the Northern Ireland figure was as much as 30 per cent above the United Kingdom average over the period 1966–84. The number of recorded stoppages per hundred thousand employees (unadjusted) was also found to be 30 per cent above the United Kingdom average over the period 1958–84.

Detailed analysis (Black 1987) of returns filed with DED for the period 1980–84 showed that 12 per cent of strikes, accounting for 45 per cent of working days lost, occurred in strikes which were either part of, or linked to, strikes in the rest of the United Kingdom (Table 8.5). It confirmed that Northern Ireland has been particularly prone to small disputes at the level of the individual establishment. The local single-establishment stoppage was by far the most numerous, accounting for 79 per cent of all strikes and 47 per cent of working days lost between 1980 and 1984.

The majority of these single-establishment stoppages were in the private sector where they accounted for 72 per cent of total working days lost; 89 per cent of them involved manual workers and 56 per cent were unofficial; 67 per cent occurred in the Belfast travel-to-work area; 52 per cent involved the ATGWU. These strikes were concentrated in a number of particularly strike-prone establishments and, at the same time, were fairly widespread.

These findings are consistent with those of Knowles (1952) who found Northern Ireland to be the second equal most strike-prone United Kingdom region over the period 1911–47, after adjusting for industrial structure. They are also consistent with the results of Isles and Cuthbert (1957) who found strike incidence in Northern Ireland to be very much higher than the United Kingdom average during World War II and the immediate post-war period. Northern Ireland, with 2 per cent of the United Kingdom population, had 10

TABLE 8.5 Percentage distribution of strike activity in Northern Ireland by type, 1980–1984

Type	% of strikes	% of working days lost
UK national/industry	1	5
NI–GB parity[1]	6	38
UK single employer (multi-establishment)	5	2
NI single employer (multi-establishment)	8	8
Single establishment	79	47

[1] By NI–GB parity is meant a strike in solidarity with a stoppage in Great Britain where the settlement in Great Britain will more or less automatically apply in Northern Ireland.
Source: Black (1987).

per cent of major United Kingdom strikes between 1946 and 1952, spread across thirteen different industry groups (Durcan et al 1983, p 47).

While the historical record in no way puts Northern Ireland in the Merseyside category (Bean and Stoney 1986) and while the recent performance in recessionary conditions has much improved, there is little justification for the widespread public complacency which exists about the state of industrial relations in Northern Ireland.

Part of the explanation for the relatively high strike incidence in Northern Ireland may lie in the fact that there is greater collective bargaining coverage and a higher proportion of employees in trade unions than the national average (Sections 3 and 4). Differences in the statutory framework over the period (Section 2) are unlikely to have made a significant difference to the relative strike performance, at least up to 1984 when strike ballots were introduced in Great Britain, but not in Northern Ireland.

The most plausible explanation for the persistent (until recently) residual relative strike proneness of Northern Ireland is one consistent with Clifton and Creigh's (1977) preferred hypothesis that regions with a faster rate of increase in earnings than the national average tend to have a higher level of strike activity. Wage levels in Northern Ireland caught up rapidly with the United Kingdom average during periods of relatively full employment such as World War II and its aftermath (Isles and Cuthbert 1957, pp 214–15) and the period between 1960 and the mid to late 1970s (Black 1985b). In each of these periods, strike activity in Northern Ireland has been well above the United Kingdom average (Isles and Cuthbert 1957, 232; Black 1987). Northern Ireland's strike record tends to approximate or fall below the United Kingdom average during times of acute depression, as in the 1930s (Isles and Cuthbert 1957, 232) and the early 1980s (see Table 8.4).

The relatively high incidence of local single-establishment disputes occurring between 1980 and 1984, a time of high unemployment, suggests that other factors may be at play. Bean and Stoney (1986) have acknowledged that militant workforce attitudes, stemming from the historical experience of the casual labour markets which were for long predominant in the port-based community of Merseyside, may have contributed to the poor strike record of that area. Belfast's industrial relations traditions have also developed around port-based industries, such as the docks and shipbuilding. It would seem possible that practices developed in these industries, possibly among both management and unions, may have spread to other industries – the 'proximities' effect (Beaumont and Harris 1988a).

TABLE 8.6 Percentage of full-time employees on adult rates whose pay was affected by absence, Northern Ireland and Great Britain, annual average, 1984–1987

	Manual males	Non-manual males	Manual females	Non-manual females
NI	11.5	4.0	16.2	5.7
GB	12.5	3.5	15.3	4.8

Source: NES.

Strike statistics may not, in themselves, be an adequate indicator of the quality of industrial relations. Other factors which might be taken into account would include indicators of possible individual conflict at work such as absenteeism. The evidence here is somewhat mixed. Table 8.6 shows that absenteeism rates for non-manual males and all females in Northern Ireland were slightly above the Great Britain average between 1984 and 1987. The absenteeism rate for manual males was slightly less than the Great Britain average. The absenteeism rate for manual men in manufacturing, however, has been higher in Northern Ireland in most years since 1971 (see Figure 8.1), a possible confirmation of the picture of above average conflict in manufacturing found in the strike statistics. Unfortunately, figures on labour turnover are not available for Northern Ireland.

On an unadjusted basis, working days lost in the Republic of Ireland were about twice as high as in Northern Ireland over the period 1975–84, even though it has a much larger agricultural sector (see Table 8.7). Also, the number of stoppages per 100,000 employees in the Republic of Ireland was

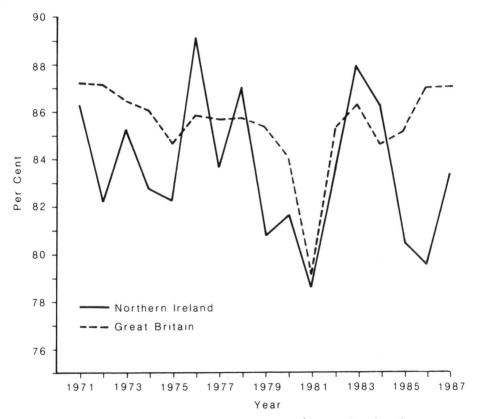

FIG 8.1 Percentage of manual men on adult rates[1] in manufacturing whose pay was not affected by absence, Northern Ireland and Great Britain, 1971–1987.

TABLE 8.7 Number of working days lost and the number of recorded stoppages, Northern Ireland and the Republic of Ireland, annual average, 1975 – 1984

	Working days lost per 1,000 employees	Stoppages per 100,000 employees
Northern Ireland	354	12.3
Republic of Ireland	680	13.3

Sources: Black (1987), Tables 1 and 3; Kelly and Brannick (1986), Table 3; EG (1986).

higher than in Northern Ireland over the same period (Kelly and Brannick 1986).

This picture of the Republic of Ireland as strike prone when compared with Northern Ireland was noted by Hood and Young (1983). They sampled the experience of multinational enterprises with establishments in the Republic of Ireland and in the United Kingdom assisted areas, including Northern Ireland. They found that for the years 1976–80, while the sample establishments located in Northern Ireland experienced an annual average of 7.0 working days lost, above the average for the United Kingdom assisted areas of 4.3 working days lost, the establishments located in the Republic of Ireland lost, on average, 17.1 working days per annum, more than twice the Northern Ireland figure.

6. Economic performance

Recent research has cast some light on the influence that trade unions and industrial relations have on economic performance. Metcalf (1988) has summarised the British evidence as follows. Union presence in a workplace or company is associated with lower productivity and higher pay relative to non-union firms. Consequently, financial performance and profitability are lower where unions are recognised for collective bargaining. In the last decade, unionised workplaces have been less likely than non-union workplaces to experience job gains and more likely to suffer job losses. Furthermore, strong unions, indicated by the existence of the closed shop or very high union density, have a bigger impact on labour productivity, pay, profitability and employment than does weak unionisation where unions are recognised for collective bargaining but density is lower. On the other hand, unions produce greater pay equality among individuals and reduce pay differentials by race, sex, and occupation. (It is likely that this would also be so by religion although there is no evidence on this.)

Black (1986) estimated that union density in manufacturing in Northern Ireland in 1983 was about the same as that in Great Britain in 1979. It must therefore have been higher in Northern Ireland than in Great Britain in 1983 given the fall in density occurring in the latter in the intervening years. Reliable evidence of the extent of the closed shop in Northern Ireland does not exist, but there is little reason to believe it has been less pervasive than in Great Britain. In addition, collective bargaining coverage is much higher in the Northern Ireland manufacturing sector than in Great Britain (SICs 3 and 4, Table 8.1, Col 4) and, as has been seen (Table 8.4), the incidence of industrial action has been somewhat above the United Kingdom average.

Taken together, these facts would suggest that the industrial relations system in Northern Ireland is likely to have had an adverse impact on labour productivity, which continues to lag behind the United Kingdom average (see HMSO 1988, Table 10.1). The overall scale of this impact may well be greater than the United Kingdom average given the higher union density and collective bargaining coverage in Northern Ireland.

From the early 1960s until the mid-1970s average hourly earnings levels in Northern Ireland rose rapidly as a percentage of the United Kingdom average (from about 83 per cent to about 96 per cent for manual workers). This convergence in pay levels occurred even after the earnings figures were adjusted for changes in industrial structure (Black 1985b). There is evidence of a widening of the regional earnings differential during the later 1980s (*New Earnings Survey* (NI) 1988). (For further information, see Chapter 9, Section 5, Table 9.7 and Figure 9.3.)

There were many reasons for the rise in Northern Ireland relative earnings over this period. Government policies which helped to generate a relatively high demand for labour and a fall in the regional unemployment rate up to the mid-1970s undoubtedly contributed to the earnings acceleration.

It is more difficult to assess the impact of the industrial relations framework on earnings levels. The 'earnings-spread' hypothesis developed by Thirlwall (1970) and Hart and MacKay (1977) suggests various ways in which earnings increases in leading markets where there is excess demand can be passed on to other regional markets where employment conditions may be very different. This transmission can occur either through competitive market pressures or through the institutional process of collective bargaining. In the latter instance, trade unionists use 'coercive comparisons' to achieve increases in earnings similar to those in other regions where employment conditions may be more favourable. This process can occur independently of industry-wide collective bargaining agreements. The earnings-spread hypothesis, however, was used to explain the stability of the regional earnings structure in Great Britain. In itself, it does not explain the narrowing of the Northern Ireland earnings differential, which involved a catching-up process.

A more plausible possible contributory factor is a feature of collective bargaining in Northern Ireland over this period which was the effort made by trade unions to obtain parity in pay and conditions of employment with comparable grades of workers in Great Britain. Many industrial disputes were about achieving parity. The extent to which parity has been achieved is evident from the number of workers in Northern Ireland whose pay is determined as a result of either a national agreement at industry or company level, or a Northern Ireland–Great Britain parity agreement (see Appendix 8.1). In addition, many employees are covered by United Kingdom company-wide agreements.

Harris and Wass (1987) found the union wage premium in Northern Ireland in 1973 to be 6.8 per cent for manual males and 16.8 per cent for manual females. A similar study for Great Britain in the same year found the wage premium for manual males to be 4.2 per cent and for manual females 7.0 per cent (Beaumont and Harris 1986). The union wage premium would seem to be considerably higher in Northern Ireland (especially for semi-skilled manual males and for females) and to have contributed to the regional earnings convergence.

Metcalf (1988) found that union presence is 'certainly associated' with lower profits, a conclusion which would probably hold even more strongly for Northern Ireland given the bigger pay premiums noted above. If, as a result, unionised firms invest less in physical and human capital and in research and development this is likely to adversely affect the performance of the economy and in particular to damage employment prospects.

The British evidence suggests that unionised workplaces have been more likely to experience job losses and less likely to experience job gains (Blanchflower and Oswald 1988) and that militant union activity over wages cost around 400,000 jobs between 1951 and 1979 (Nickell and Andrews 1983). The impact of trade union wage bargaining activity on employment in Northern Ireland may well have been at least as significant (Geary 1986).

The link between pay levels, productivity and employment is one of considerable controversy and complexity (Metcalf and Nickell 1985). One might expect that a rise in relative earnings in Northern Ireland would make it less attractive as an investment location for foreign firms. But Hood and Young (1983) found relative labour costs (and industrial relations matters generally) to be of little significance in influencing the locational decisions of multinational enterprises.

The author has examined some data from a 1988 survey of manufacturing industry in Northern Ireland conducted by R I D Harris. 500 manufacturing companies were asked if high or rising labour costs posed an obstacle to their expansion plans. Of the 196 respondents to the survey, 29 per cent said they were not a relevant factor, but 25 per cent said they were either the most important or the second most important obstacles to their expansion and therefore their employment plans. (Lack of orders, uncertainty about future demand and high materials and energy costs were often considered more important.)

When asked if poor industrial relations posed an obstacle to expansion of their production, 57 per cent of respondents said industrial relations did not inhibit the growth of the firm. However, 5 per cent of respondents said it was either the most important or the next most important in a list of nine possible obstacles to further expansion. Also, while 41 per cent of respondents thought low productivity was not a relevant factor in their expansion decisions, 2 per cent thought it was either the most important or the next most important constraint on expansion.

It would appear from these results that for a small minority of companies, perceived problems of industrial relations and low productivity are a major constraint on expansion and thus employment, while high or rising labour costs are a significant constraint for a larger minority of manufacturing firms.

The present Government has on a number of occasions hinted that it would like to see a widening of regional pay differentials as part of its strategy for reducing regional unemployment differentials.[14] This strategy has been advocated with considerable force as the solution to Northern Ireland's unemployment problems by *The Economist*.[15] The continued existence of separate bargaining arrangements for Northern Ireland in much of the public sector, together with the separate existence of NIPSA, offer something of a hostage to fortune in that it would be administratively relatively easy to re-establish regional pay bargaining and restore a Northern Ireland–Great Britain pay differential in much of the public sector. Interestingly, however, both the Report of the Interim Advisory Committee on the Pay of Teachers in England and Wales (1988) and the Report of the Nurses Pay Review Body (1988) have come down strongly against regional pay bargaining.

According to Metcalf (1988), the changed industrial relations climate of the 1980s has transformed labour productivity growth in manufacturing, a transformation based on fear of redundancy, increased competition and the decentralisation of collective bargaining leading to the introduction of more flexible working practices and increased efficiency. Northern Ireland has been particularly hard hit by the wind of change in terms of job losses, despite the continued high levels of Government financial support. While union membership and collective bargaining coverage have so far remained relatively intact (Tables 8.1 and 8.3), the impact of the changed climate has been particularly marked on the falling level of strike activity and the widening regional earnings differential. While productivity growth in manufacturing has been substantial it still lags behind that for the United Kingdom as a whole (see NIAAS 1988, Table 12.3).

The impact of the 1980s industrial relations legislation on local economic performance is likely to have been, if anything, less than in Britain, given that not all the legislation, eg on strike ballots, has so far been implemented, and that which has been implemented has only been introduced after a considerable delay.

Wage levels in the Republic of Ireland rose particularly rapidly relative to those in Great Britain (Bacon et al 1982) during the 1970s under a series of National Wage Agreements and National Understandings. The demand for labour was high in the period following entry into the European Community when the Republic was attracting a high level of foreign investment and running large budget deficits. Since 1980 real pre-tax incomes have declined and an accompanying increase in productivity in manufacturing industry has resulted in the Republic of Ireland increasing its international competitiveness measured in terms of unit wage costs (Bacon 1986).

Thus, while in Northern Ireland real wages advanced in the early to mid 1980s slightly behind those for the United Kingdom as a whole, despite the high unemployment, the return to free collective bargaining in the Republic of

Ireland in 1982 was accompanied by a period of real wage adjustment to its even more severe unemployment crisis. Even so, employers in the Republic of Ireland complained in 1987 (Confederation of Irish Industry 1987) that in many industries, particularly the more labour-intensive ones, wage rates and unit wage costs were higher than in some regions of Great Britain. (For further information about relative earnings and productivity in the Republic of Ireland, see Chapter 9, Section 5 and Tables 9.10 and 9.11.)

7. Conclusion

The broad conclusion of this chapter is that despite the fact that industrial relations developed in Northern Ireland under unique constitutional and party political arrangements, the Northern Ireland system is governed, for the most part, by the same determinants as other United Kingdom regions. As we have seen, although there is a separate Northern Ireland statute book, the outstanding differences in legislation are of limited importance (particularly if the outstanding provisions of the Trade Union Act 1984 and the Employment Act 1988 are extended to Northern Ireland). Also, while separate statutory bodies have been established in Northern Ireland, these normally have equivalent or similar powers to their Great Britain counterparts.

Certain anomalies have emerged as a result of the treatment of industrial relations as a transferred function under the post-1920 constitutional arrangements, particularly in the public sector. It has resulted in the existence of separate collective bargaining machinery in those parts of the public sector which were under Stormont control. It may also be said to have encouraged the establishment of NIPSA. However, the impact of these developments on wages and, to a lesser extent, conditions is negligible because of the fact that parity is now the accepted principle. The constitutional arrangements may also have led to the establishment of some separate Northern Ireland bargaining structures in parts of the private sector which would otherwise have been covered by national machinery, but the growth of plant and company bargaining is offsetting the importance of this.

The existence of the ICTU and its recognition by the Northern Ireland Government is again probably an indirect result of the 1920 settlement. While this has resulted in some minor organisational changes within some Great Britain-based affiliated unions, its impact on the formal conduct of industrial relations is minimal.[16] Its main significance is that it distances Northern Ireland trade unionists from the TUC, the congress of their state, and subjects them to the authority of the essentially irrelevant all-Ireland ICTU.

Thus, while it is possible to talk of a distinctive Northern Ireland system of industrial relations (Review Body 1974; Labour Relations Agency 1984) for the most part these distinctions are superficial. Northern Ireland's industrial relations can be more accurately categorised as a regional part of the British system.

When the extent of collective bargaining coverage and trade union membership is examined, the evidence suggests that Northern Ireland's industrial relations bears more resemblance to the Northern rather than the Southern part of any North/South British divide. Tables 8.1 and 8.2 have shown that collective bargaining coverage (all industries) in Northern Ireland is higher than in Great Britain for both males and females. Table 8.8 suggests that for SIC Divisions 2–4 (manufacturing) coverage is higher in Northern Ireland than in any other region of the United Kingdom.

It was established in Section 4 that a higher proportion of employees in employment in Northern Ireland were trade union members than the United Kingdom average in 1983 (60.9 per cent compared to 53.5 per cent). Although lack of data prevents direct regional comparisons, Table 8.8 suggests that the Northern Ireland figure for trade union membership is at least comparable to that in the Northern regions of Britain.

The evidence on industrial action (Table 8.4) has demonstrated that Northern Ireland has experienced a higher level of working days lost in industrial disputes than the United Kingdom average in every period since the Second World War, except the most recent. This relative strike proneness is even more apparent when allowance is made for Northern Ireland's different industrial structure.

The evidence in Table 8.8, however, shows that while Northern Ireland is more strike prone than the South East or South West of England on an unadjusted basis, its record compares favourably with that of most Northern regions. Table 8.7 suggests its industrial relations record is much better than that of the Republic of Ireland.

TABLE 8.8   Collective bargaining coverage, trade union density and strike activity, regions of the United Kingdom

	CB coverage, 1984[1] (%) SIC 2–4	Employees in trade unions[2] (%) SIC 0–9	Working days lost per 1,000 employees (annual average), SIC 0–9		
			1946–73	1974–86	1968–84[3]
North	76	61	372	976	693
Yorks–Humberside	80	51	301	683	605
West Midlands	75	45			480
East Midlands	70	59			367
East Anglia	56	35	149	183	276
South East	60	36			248
South West	66	36	157	220	293
North West	80	57	337	512	666
Wales	76	64	545	1,056	658
Scotland	78	56	384	575	736
Northern Ireland	83	57	297	323	476

[1] Employees in establishments with 25 or more employees. Figure for Northern Ireland refers to employees in establishments with 20 or more employees.
[2] Average for years 1984, 1985 and 1986. Northern Ireland figure is average for 1983 and 1987.
[3] Adjusted for industrial structure. Data for 1983 not available.
Sources: Millward and Stevens (1988); RT; NES (NI) (voluntary return) 1984; Black (1986) and author's survey.

There is, however, little evidence to support the suggestion (Sholl 1980) that Northern Ireland has a more harmonious industrial relations climate than that in Great Britain. Indeed, it is possible that since industry here has been dominated by shipbuilding for so many years, the industrial relations culture of that and other port-based industries may have spread out into 'Laganside' and may be reflected in the incidence of stoppages and absenteeism and in general management and workforce attitudes – the 'proximities' effect.

It is difficult to estimate what impact this local industrial relations culture and the industrial relations system generally have had on relative regional economic performance. However, the discussion in the previous section suggests it is unlikely to have been insignificant.[17]

What is clear is that rapid structural change is changing the face of employment in Northern Ireland. The Northern Ireland economy is increasingly dominated in the services as well as the manufacturing sector, by enterprises controlled from outside the region, usually Great Britain. It is increasingly becoming a branch office, a branch plant or a branch outlet economy with a trade union, collective bargaining and earnings structure largely common with that in Great Britain. This being so, there is limited scope for industrial relations experimentation and for the development of a more regionally distinctive industrial relations system.

Appendix 8.1 Major collective bargaining agreements in Northern Ireland

	Coverage (approx.)		Coverage (approx.)
UK MACHINERY		General Printing (Eng, Wales and NI)	2,000
BBC	1,000	Govt Industrial Establishments	3,000
British Telecommunications	3,000	Heating, Ventilating and	
Brush and Broom NJC	350	Domestic Engineering	600
Cement Manu NJIC	370	Iron and Steel Scrap JCC	250
Cinema Theatres	200	Local Authorities Fire Brigades	
Civil Air Transport NJC	500	JNC	1,500
Civil Service	3,000	Mastic Asphalt NJIC	300
Clothing Manufacturing	2,000	Merchant Navy	560
Electrical Contracting JIB (Eng,		Motor Vehicle Retail and Repair	200
Wales and NI)	1,000	National Pharmaceutical	
Environmental and Engineering		Association NJIC	500
Staff Assoc NJC	1,500	Newspaper Printing (Eng, Wales	
Engineering	12,600	and NI)	3,000
Flour Milling NJIC	100	Paper Making, Paper Coating,	
Footwear Manufacture	600	Paper Board and Building Board	n/a
Ford Motor Co	600	Plumbing JIB (Scotland and NI)	1,000

	Coverage (approx.)		Coverage (approx.)
Post Office	3,500	Stewarts Supermarkets	1,100
Prison Services	3,100	Trustee Savings Bank	550
Production of Man-Made Fibres	2,250	Ulsterbus	3,000
Ready Mixed Concrete NJC	250	Wholesale Hardware Trades JIC	400
Retail Cooperative Societies	1,800		
Retail Multiple Footwear	200	**NI–GB PARITY MACHINERY**	
Sawmilling (NI and Scotland)	300		
Seed Crushing, Compound and		AECP and Functional Council	2,000
Provender NJIC	1,500	Electricity Supply Industry	6,000
Timber Containers JIC (Eng,		Forestry and Agriculture	450
Wales and NI)	200	Functional Committee Ancillary	
Tobacco NJNC	7,000	and General Staff	8,000
Universities Committee A and B	1,500	Gas Industry	1,100
Universities Negotiating Comm		Government Industrial	
(Non-teaching)	3,500	Establishments	3,000
Vehicle Building JWB (England		Health and Personal Social	
and NI)	200	Services	46,000
Woolworths	1,500	Local Authority Services	11,500
		NI Civil Service Whitley Council	22,000
NI MACHINERY		Negotiating Committee (College	
		of Education)	1,200
Bacon Curing JC	1,000	Negotiating Committee (Schools)	18,000
Belfast Harbour Commissioners		Negotiating Committee (FE)	1,680
(ITGWU)	200	Water Industry	2,200
Belfast Port Employers (ATGWU)	350		
Belfast and Ulster Licensed		**WAGES COUNCILS**	
Vintners	700		
Builders' Merchants	300	Bakery	550
Building and Civil Engineering	22,000	Boot and Shoe Repair	60
Flax Preparation, Spinning,		Catering	14,330
Weaving and Finishing	4,000	Clothing Manufacturing	8,013
Furniture	700	Laundry	334
Harland and Wolff	4,000	Linen and Cotton Handkerchief	
Irish Banks	6,500	and Household Goods and	
Irish Linen Merchants	200	Linen Piece Goods	1,260
Milk Processing JIC	4,000	Paper Box	720
NI Coal Importers	450	Road Haulage	5,831
NI Railways	900	Sugar, Confectionery and Food	
Plant Bakeries JIC	3,500	Preserving	203
Quarrying JIC	3,750		
RUC Regulations	12,500	**WAGES BOARD**	
Retail Meat	1,500		
Road Asphalt JIC	500	Agricultural	4,200
Short Bros	6,000		

Source: Black (1985a), and authors survey.

Notes

1. For a follow-up report on regional trade union membership see Millward and Stevens (1988).
2. For a useful survey of industrial relations in the Republic of Ireland, see: Department of Industrial Relations, University College Dublin (1987).
3. S 4 of the Trade Disputes and Trade Unions Act (Northern Ireland) 1927 which established the principle of 'contracting in' to a trade union's political fund, remains on the Northern Ireland statute book (Black 1984).
4. As a result, S 4 of the Conspiracy and Protection of Property Act 1875 remains on the statute book. This makes it unlawful for an employee of a municipal authority or of a company or contractor required by statute to provide gas or water to break their contract of employment.
5. For a detailed comparison of the procedures see: *Industrial Relations Review and Report* (1979). The future of these provisions is currently under consideration by Government.
6. However, the Republic of Ireland courts have interpreted the law on picketing in S 2 of the Trades Disputes Act 1906 very narrowly in a series of judgments with the result that a large number of workers are excluded from S 2 of the 1906 Act. Also, trade unions in the Republic do not have immunity in respect of commercial contracts as under the Trade Union and Labour Relations Act 1974 in Britain and under the Industrial Relations (Northern Ireland) Order 1976, Article 64.
7. There are exceptions to this, eg the building and civil engineering agreement covering just Northern Ireland, replaced national agreements for the building industry and civil engineering construction in 1977.
8. Based on the results of a voluntary survey included with the 1984 New Earnings Survey.
9. Ibid.
10. Ibid.
11. By contrast 13.8 per cent of trade union members in the Republic of Ireland are in GB-based unions (ICTU Membership Survey, 1987). The remainder are in Republic-based unions.
12. See Chapter 9.
13. Trade unionists in Northern Ireland could remain affiliated to the ICTU if they so desired. A fairly minor problem would remain concerning the small Northern Ireland membership of unions based in the Republic of Ireland. There is no reason why this membership should not also be affiliated to the TUC. The membership of GB-based unions in the Republic of Ireland would remain affiliated to the ICTU.
14. See, eg, Mr Kenneth Clarke, the then Secretary of State for Employment, quoted in Income Data Services *Report* 495, April 1987.
15. 31 March 1988. For a discussion of the issue in the Scottish context see Beaumont and Harris (1988b).
16. Disputes between trade unions affiliated to the TUC may be handled by the ICTU disputes procedure rather than that of the TUC.
17. Wadhwani (1989) finds no evidence for the views that unions either reduce investment or productivity growth and queries their alleged negative impact on employment.

References

Bacon, P (1986) *Medium Term Outlook 1986–1990*, ESRI, Dublin.

Bacon, P et al (1982) *The Irish Economy: Policy and Performance 1972–1981*, ESRI, Dublin.

Bain, G S and Elias, P (1985) Trade union membership in Britain: an individual level analysis, *British Journal of Industrial Relations*, XXI, 2, 71–92.

Bean, R and Stoney, P (1986) Strikes on Merseyside, *Industrial Relations Journal*, 17, 1, 9–23.

Beaumont, P B (1984) Trade union recognition in Northern Ireland, *British Journal of Industrial Relations*, XXII, 3, 364–71.

Beaumont, P B and Harris, R I D (1986) The effects of collective bargaining on pay: some recent evidence from the 1970s, Queen's University of Belfast, Department of Economics, mimeo.

Beaumont, P B and Harris, R I D (1988a) Sub-systems of industrial relations: the spatial dimension in Britain, *British Journal of Industrial Relations*, XXVI, 3, 397–407.

Beaumont, P B and Harris, R I D (1988b), The government case against national pay bargaining: an analysis for Scotland, in McCrone, D and Brown, A (eds) *Scottish Government Yearbook 1988*, Unit for the Study of Government in Scotland, Edinburgh University, Edinburgh.

Benson, J and Hince, K (1984) Regional industrial relations systems, *Labour Studies Working Paper*, 12, Faculty of Economics and Commerce, University of Melbourne, Victoria 3052.

Black, B (1984) Trade union democracy and Northern Ireland – a note, *The Industrial Law Journal*, 13, 4, 243–50.

Black, B (1985a) Collective bargaining structure in Northern Ireland: dimensions, determinants and development, *Journal of the Statistical and Social Enquiry Society of Ireland*, XXV, II, 1984–85, 159–93.

Black, B (1985b) Regional earnings convergence: the case of Northern Ireland, *Regional Studies*, 19, 1, 1–7.

Black, B (1986) Against the trend: trade union growth in Northern Ireland, *Industrial Relations Journal*, 17, 1, 71–80.

Black, B (1987) Collaboration or conflict? – Strike activity in Northern Ireland, *Industrial Relations Journal*, 18, 1, 14–25.

Blanchflower, D and Oswald, A (1988) The economic effects of Britain's trade unions, *Centre for Labour Economics, Discussion Paper*, 324, London School of Economics.

Brown, W (ed) (1981) *The Changing Contours of British Industrial Relations*, Blackwell, Oxford.

Clifton, R F and Creigh, S W (1977) Regional strike-proneness: a research note, *Regional Studies*, 11, 2, 79–86.

Commission on Industrial Relations (1972) *Industrial Relations Training*, Report No 33, London.

Commission on Industrial Relations (1973) *Industrial Relations at Establishment Level: A Statistical Survey*, Study 2, London.

Confederation of Irish Industry (1987) *Newsletter*, 46, 17.

Daniel, W W and Millward, Neil (1983) *Workplace Industrial Relations in Britain*, Heinemann Educational Books, London.

Deaton, D R and Beaumont, P B (1980) The determinants of bargaining structure:

some large scale survey evidence for Great Britain, *British Journal of Industrial Relations*, XVIII, 2, 202–216.

Department of Employment (1986) *Employment Gazette*, 94, 7, 267.

Department of Employment, *New Earnings Survey*, HMSO, London.

Department of Industrial Relations, University College Dublin (1987) *Industrial Relations in Ireland*, UCD, Dublin.

Durcan, J W, McCarthy, W E J and Redman, G P (1983) *Strikes in Post-War Britain*, Allen and Unwin, London.

Elsheikh, F and Bain, G S (1980) Unionisation in Britain: an inter-establishment analysis based on survey data, *British Journal of Industrial Relations*, xviii, 2, 169–78.

Geary, P T (1986) The determinants of employment in Northern Ireland 1959–83: an empirical investigation, Department of Economics, Maynooth College, mimeo.

Harris, R I D and Wass, V (1987) The effect of collective bargaining on earnings in Northern Ireland in 1973, *The Economic and Social Review*, 19, 1, 1–14.

Harris, R I D and Wass, V J (1988) The structure of collective bargaining in Northern Ireland 1973–84, *The Economic and Social Review*, 19, 2, 99–122.

Hart, R A and MacKay, D I (1977) Wage inflation, regional policy and the regional earnings structure, *Economica*, 44, August, 267–81.

HMSO (1988) *Regional Trends*, London.

Hood, N and Young, S (1983) *Multinational Investment Strategies in the British Isles*, HMSO, London, 221–74.

Income Data Services (1987) *Report* 495.

Industrial Relations Review and Report (1979) 214, December.

Interim Advisory Committee on the Pay of Teachers in England and Wales (1988) *Report*, HMSO, London.

Isles, K S and Cuthbert N (1957) *An Economic Survey of Northern Ireland*, HMSO, Belfast.

Kelly, A and Brannick, T (1986) The changing contours of Irish strike patterns: 1960–84, *Irish Business and Administrative Research*, 8, 1, 77–88.

Knowles, K G J C (1952) *Strikes – A Study in Industrial Conflict: With Special Reference to the British Experience 1911–47*, Blackwell, Oxford.

Labour Relations Agency (1984) *Industrial Relations in Northern Ireland – A New Strategy?* LRA, Belfast.

Metcalf, D (1988) Trade unions and economic performance: the British evidence, *Centre for Labour Economics, Discussion Paper*, 320, London School of Economics.

Metcalf, D and Nickell, S (1985) Jobs and pay, *Midland Bank Review*, Spring, 8–15.

Millward, N and Stevens, M (1986) *British Workplace Industrial Relations 1980–84*, Gower, London.

Millward, N and Stevens, M (1988) Union density in the regions, *Employment Gazette*, 96, 286–95.

Moore, B and Rhodes, J (1981) The convergence of earnings in the regions of the United Kingdom, in Martin, R L (ed), *Regional Wage Inflation and Unemployment*, Pior, London.

Nickell, S and Andrews, M (1983) Unions, real wages and employment in Britain 1951–79, *Oxford Economic Papers*, 35, 507–530.

Review Body for Nursing Staff, Midwives, Health Visitors and Professions Allied to Medicine (1988) *Report*, HMSO, London.

Review Body on Industrial Relations (1974) *Industrial Relations in Northern Ireland, Report of the Review Body 1971–74*, HMSO, Belfast.

Robertson, W and Sams, K I (1976) The role of the full-time trade union officer, *The Economic and Social Review*, 8, 1, 23–41.

Royal Commission on Trades Unions and Employers' Associations 1965–68 (1968) *Report*, Cmnd 3623, HMSO, London.

Sholl, R K (1980) An analysis of Northern Ireland statutory trade union recognition procedure. Unpublished MA Dissertation, University of Warwick.

Smith, C T B, Clifton, Richard, Makeham, Peter, Creigh, S W and Burn, R V (1978) *Strikes in Britain*, D. Emp. Manpower Paper 15, HMSO, London.

Thirlwall, A (1970) Regional Phillips curves, *Oxford Bulletin of Economics and Statistics*, 31, 1, 19–32.

Tipping, B and McCorry, P (1988) *Industrial Relations in Northern Ireland, The LRA Survey*, Labour Relations Agency, Belfast.

Wadhwani, S (1989) The effects of unions on productivity growth, investment and employment: a report on some recent work. *Centre for Labour Economics, Discussion Paper*, 356, London School of Economics.

Income

Richard I D Harris

1. Introduction

This chapter[1] covers the important topic of income distribution, poverty, earnings and expenditure in Northern Ireland. The emphasis is on the relative position of the province within the United Kingdom and compared to the Republic of Ireland. The analysis begins by examining the composition of income in 1981. This is followed by measuring the distribution of income and the incidence of poverty which includes an attempt at highlighting the principal causes of poverty. Since low income from employment plays an important role in creating a poverty trap (and wages and salaries are the dominant source of income anyway), a large proportion of the study will look at the extent and causes of both inter-regional and intra-regional differences in earnings.

2. The composition of earnings

Information on the make-up of earnings in regions of the United Kingdom is available from the Family Expenditure Survey (see, for example, FES 1981); comparable data for the Republic of Ireland are collected as part of the Household Budget Survey (HBS). The most recent comparable data (1981) referring to household income is given in Table 9.1. Northern Ireland stands out because of its relatively large dependence on income from state pensions and state benefits; by contrast, the share of income from self-employment, investments, occupational pensions and owner occupation is relatively lower than in most regions. This partly explains the lower level of household incomes in the province (column 1 in Table 9.1), although, as we shall see later, wages and salaries are also significantly below the national average. In general, Table 9.1 shows that the United Kingdom can be crudely divided into a relatively prosperous 'South', where owner occupation and investment incomes (and to some extent self-employment incomes) are important, and a less prosperous 'North', which is more dependent on state aid. The Republic of Ireland is particularly dependent on income from self-employment[2] and, despite the low level of average household income and high unemployment, state benefits are surprisingly low. This highlights the difference that exists between the Republic

TABLE 9.1 Composition of household incomes, regions of the United Kingdom and the Republic of Ireland, 1981[1] (percentage)

	Average income[2] (£)	Wages and salaries[3]	Self-employment	Investment income	Occupational pension	State pensions	State benefits	Owner-occupation[4]	Other
Northern	147.6	69.1	4.6	2.7	3.0	7.4	9.3	3.3	0.5
Yorks–Humberside	145.7	70.1	3.9	2.7	2.6	7.6	8.4	3.6	1.1
East Midlands	149.9	72.3	4.9	2.4	2.3	6.5	6.4	4.4	0.8
East Anglia	155.4	65.8	7.4	3.8	2.8	6.9	7.1	5.3	1.0
Greater London	193.5	69.4	6.2	5.8	2.5	5.2	4.5	4.9	1.6
Rest of South East	195.1	70.1	6.5	3.6	3.3	5.5	4.4	5.7	1.0
South West	162.8	58.5	6.7	7.0	5.3	8.8	5.3	5.4	3.0
Wales	153.5	63.9	6.4	3.4	4.2	7.7	9.9	3.7	0.6
West Midlands	161.2	70.2	4.7	3.0	2.6	6.0	7.1	5.7	0.7
North West	170.1	68.2	6.0	3.3	2.9	6.3	7.1	5.1	1.2
Scotland	158.1	66.4	9.8	3.0	3.3	7.1	7.7	1.9	1.0
N Ireland	120.0	60.1	4.6	2.9	2.2	11.4	15.6	2.8	0.5
Republic of Ireland	121.5	63.1	15.0	2.4	2.4	6.2	6.8	1.8	2.4

[1] Results for the Republic of Ireland are not strictly comparable.
[2] Per household per week.
[3] Including income from subsidiary employment.
[4] For UK regions, this refers to imputed rent; for RI this item refers to own garden/farm produce.
Sources: FES, HBS (CSO, Dublin).

of Ireland and the United Kingdom with respect to the role of government provision of social security (Appendix 9.1).

3. The distribution of incomes

Both parts of Ireland experience not only the lowest level of earnings, but household income is also more unevenly distributed. The most usual way to analyse the distribution of income is by drawing a Lorenz curve from which it is possible to compute a Gini coefficient measuring the degree to which the curve differs from that which would be obtained if incomes were evenly distributed throughout the population.[3] Figure 9.1 shows Northern Ireland's 1981 Lorenz curve for the cumulative proportions of total household income and cumulative proportions of the population (of households). This diagram also shows Lorenz curves for certain other United Kingdom regions, most noticeably East Anglia (which had the lowest level of United Kingdom inequality in 1981) and Greater London (with the second highest level of inequality). The underlying values of the Gini coefficient are given in Table 9.2 (column 1).[4] If income from state benefits are excluded from household income, the resultant Lorenz curves and Gini coefficients are those shown in Figure 9.2 and Table 9.2. These show (i) a much greater unequal distribution of income in the province, when government transfer payments are excluded; and (ii) the extent of the redistributional effect that state benefits have on incomes in each region, but more especially in those regions with the greatest levels of inequality (this can be gauged by comparing columns 1 and 3 in Table 9.2). Hence, a fairly large proportion of households in certain regions (and most especially Northern Ireland) would find themselves with particularly low relative incomes if it were not for government attempts at reducing inequality. The major exception to the above is the Republic of Ireland, where income inequality is greater but the gap between actual inequality and the inequality that would exist if state benefits are removed is less than in United Kingdom regions. Again, the different emphasis in the Republic of Ireland on state provision of social security helps to explain these results.

Given these results on income inequality, the extent to which regions suffer from a high incidence of poverty is now examined, since there is a strong link between income inequality and poverty (Atkinson 1987).

4. The incidence of household poverty in United Kingdom regions

There is no single satisfactory measure of poverty; attention is usually focused upon the proportion of the population with incomes below the 'official' poverty line (ie the Supplementary Benefit level), but this measure is insensitive to how far below the poverty line the incomes of the poor fall. Hence, and following

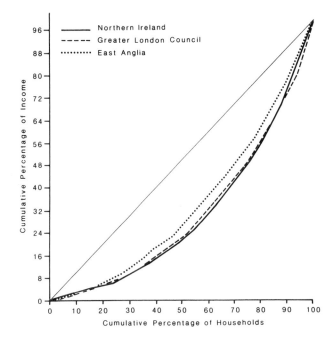

FIG 9.1 Lorenz curves for household incomes, Northern Ireland, GLC and East Anglia, 1981.
Source: FES, 1981.

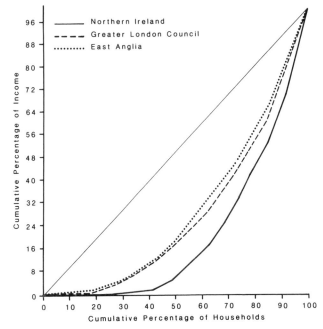

FIG 9.2 Lorenz curves for household incomes, excluding social security income, Northern Ireland, GLC and East Anglia, 1981.
Source: FES, 1981.

Clark, Hemming and Ulph (1981), this section will provide information on several alternative indices for comparisons. The first index is the *head count ratio*:

$$H = q/n \qquad\qquad [1]$$

here q is the number of households with incomes below z, the level of income that would be payable through Supplementary Benefit (given the composition of the household); and n is the total number of households. A second related index is the *poverty gap ratio*:

$$I = \sum_i (z-y_i)/qz, \quad (z-y_i) > 0 \quad i = 1 \dots q \qquad\qquad [2]$$

where y_i is the income of household i.[5] Unfortunately, both of these indices have undesirable properties. Neither index satisfies the 'transfer axiom' which states that (*ceteris paribus*) a transfer of income from a household below the poverty line to a richer (although possibly still poor) household must increase the poverty index (see Sen 1976 for a fuller discussion). An index that satisfies the transfer axiom (as well as having other desirable properties outlined below) is the *Sen index*:

$$S = H(1-(1-I)\{1-G[q/(1+q)]\}) \qquad\qquad [3]$$

here G is the Gini index of the distribution of income among the poor. This index also has the desirable properties that it is increasing in H, I and G; and it lies in the closed interval (0,1), ie between there being no poor and when all households have zero incomes. The results obtained for each United Kingdom region using 1981 FES data are set out in Table 9.3; the H index suggests that some 25 per cent of households in Northern Ireland had incomes below the Supplementary Benefits level, which was a much higher percentage than in any other region (some 7 per cent higher than in the North, the region with the next highest incidence of poverty). The I index confirms the province at the top of the poverty league, but the gap between Northern Ireland and the other regions is substantially lower with this particular measure. However, the preferred index (the Sen measure) shows that poverty is indeed much higher in Northern Ireland.

This section concludes by looking at some of the variables associated with household poverty in the regions of the United Kingdom. Table 9.4 splits the 1981 FES data into those households that were in poverty as opposed to those with incomes above the poverty line. There was an obvious concentration of 'poor' households living in council dwellings in both Northern Ireland and the United Kingdom as a whole. Households where the chief economic supporter (CES) was retired were more likely to suffer poverty, although this was slightly less true for Northern Ireland. Households where the CES was economically inactive or unemployed experienced higher poverty levels, while households with older and less skilled heads of households (HOH) had the expected positive bias towards being in poverty. Average net hourly earnings of the HOH also showed an expected, large difference when households are

TABLE 9.2   Gini coefficients relating to the distribution of household income, regions of the United Kingdom, 1981, and the Republic of Ireland, 1980

	All households	Rank[1]	All households excluding state benefit incomes	Rank[1]
Northern	36.5	4	50.4	3
Yorks–Humberside	35.5	6	48.1	4
East Midlands	32.8	11	43.2	10
East Anglia	31.3	13	41.6	13
Greater London	37.9	3	45.0	8
Rest of South East	34.9	8	41.9	11
South West	36.2	5	46.7	6
Wales	34.9	8	48.1	4
West Midlands	31.9	12	41.7	12
North West	34.2	10	44.1	9
Scotland	35.2	7	46.2	7
Northern Ireland	38.3	2	58.5	1
Republic of Ireland	39.3	1	47.6	2

[1] Ranking from highest to lowest values.
Source: Based on calculations using FES and Murphy (1985, Table 1).

separated on the basis of poverty. The remaining determining variable had a different effect in Northern Ireland and the United Kingdom as a whole: larger households were associated with poverty in the province but not in the United Kingdom. To see how each of these variables are associated with poverty, regression equations were estimated with poverty status as the dependent variable.[6] The results for each region, using 1981 data, are presented in Table 9.5.

The results confirm that poverty is strongly associated with those households in which the CES is either retired, unemployed or economically

TABLE 9.3   Household poverty indices, regions of the United Kingdom, 1981

	Head count index (H)		Poverty gap ratio (I)		Sen index[1] (S)		Gini index (G)	
Northern	0.18	(2)	0.14	(9)	5.16	(3)	0.17	(8)
Yorks–Humberside	0.17	(3)	0.14	(9)	5.30	(2)	0.19	(4)
East Midlands	0.11	(8)	0.20	(2)	3.70	(9)	0.17	(8)
East Anglia	0.11	(8)	0.15	(5)	3.32	(10)	0.20	(3)
Greater London	0.12	(6)	0.18	(4)	3.84	(6)	0.16	(11)
Rest of South East	0.08	(12)	0.15	(5)	2.36	(11)	0.17	(8)
South West	0.09	(11)	0.15	(5)	2.31	(12)	0.15	(12)
Wales	0.13	(5)	0.14	(9)	4.04	(5)	0.19	(4)
West Midlands	0.10	(10)	0.19	(3)	3.81	(7)	0.22	(2)
North West	0.12	(6)	0.15	(5)	3.77	(8)	0.19	(4)
Scotland	0.15	(4)	0.14	(9)	4.38	(4)	0.18	(7)
N Ireland	0.25	(1)	0.21	(1)	10.07	(1)	0.26	(1)

Note: Ranks from highest to lowest are shown in parentheses.
[1] Index has been multiplied by 100.
Source: Based on calculations using FES.

unoccupied. In Northern Ireland, the (*ceteris paribus*) effect of being unemployed increases the probability of being in poverty by over 60 per cent,[7] while those households with a retired CES are nearly 29 per cent more likely to experience poverty. (The effect of the CES being economically unoccupied increases the probability of poverty by 25.7 per cent.) Similar results are obtained for other United Kingdom regions. The regression results confirm that the poor are also more likely to live in council (Housing Executive) accommodation, and have relatively large numbers in the household. Furthermore, households with older HOHs had a greater probability of being in poverty (typically, parameters have values of around −0.018, which means that households with HOHs over 70 were at least 18 per cent more likely (*cet par*) to be in poverty when compared to those households where the HOH was 30 years old). However, both of the last two effects (household size and the age of the HOH) were not statistically significant in Northern Ireland. Low occupation status had the expected effect in a few regions (the North, Yorks–Humberside, East Anglia, Wales and Scotland), and low earnings were positively associated with poverty in every region except the North.[8] In general, it would seem that poverty is more closely associated with economic status and housing type than it is with other variables,[9] although these other effects tend to be important.[10]

Overall, these results have important implications for the workings of the labour market; in particular, low household income in Northern Ireland, coupled with high levels of unemployment and retirement, and relatively generous social security payments, may act as a disincentive to labour supply and, thus, render the labour market inefficient as a means of matching supply

TABLE 9.4 Mean values of determining variables cross-classified on the basis of household poverty, 1981

Variable	United Kingdom		Northern Ireland	
	Not in poverty	In poverty	Not in poverty	In poverty
% Council dwellings	29.7	79.8	41.8	81.3
% Retired	14.6	40.3	22.4	31.3
% Unoccupied	7.1	29.7	15.3	28.1
% Unemployed	3.2	18.7	2.0	28.1
Average number of persons in households	2.81	2.19	3.16	3.22
Average age of head of household	49.3	57.8	50.5	52.1
% HOH in low status occupation	4.0	5.8	5.1	12.5
Average net hourly earnings of HOH (£)[1]	0.88	0.16	0.78	0.23

[1] The average includes a substantial proportion (43% for the UK) for all households where the HOH received no income from employment. The mean average hourly wage for households where the HOH was in employment was £1.40 (after tax and superannuation had been deducted).
Source: FES 1981.

TABLE 9.5 Estimated regression results for the Logit model of the causes of poverty, 1981

Variable[1]	North	Yorks–Humberside	East Midlands	East Anglia	Greater London	Rest of SE	South West	Wales	West Midlands	North West	Scotland	Northern Ireland
COUNCIL	1.006	0.954	1.274	1.889	1.148	1.664	1.306	0.830	1.320	1.297	1.076	1.025
	(5.3)	(6.2)	(6.2)	(4.9)	(7.2)	(11.0)	(6.7)	(4.2)	(6.9)	(8.4)	(5.1)	(3.3)
RETIRED	1.857	1.394	1.248	0.995	2.006	1.186	1.012	0.507	1.488	1.280	1.537	1.149
	(5.9)	(4.7)	(3.6)	(1.8)	(6.6)	(4.8)	(3.0)	(1.5)	(4.7)	(4.4)	(5.5)	(1.9)
UNOCC	1.753	1.771	1.281	0.499	1.902	0.942	0.732	0.929	2.027	1.081	1.898	1.026
	(5.9)	(6.1)	(4.0)	(0.9)	(6.6)	(3.7)	(2.2)	(3.0)	(6.1)	(4.1)	(7.0)	(1.9)
UNEMP	1.253	1.794	1.516	2.225	2.498	1.827	0.815	1.476	1.980	2.020	1.550	2.404
	(4.2)	(7.0)	(3.6)	(3.8)	(8.1)	(7.1)	(1.6)	(4.4)	(7.7)	(7.5)	(5.7)	(3.8)
NUM	-0.025	-0.046	-0.063	-0.384	-0.171	-0.112	-0.094	-0.287	-0.067	-0.131	-0.139	0.054
	(0.3)	(0.7)	(0.6)	(2.5)	(2.2)	(1.7)	(0.9)	(3.0)	(0.8)	(2.0)	(2.2)	(0.5)
AGEHOH	-0.016	-0.006	-0.017	-0.005	-0.011	-0.019	-0.016	-0.011	-0.023	-0.019	-0.022	-0.008
	(2.3)	(1.0)	(2.1)	(0.4)	(1.8)	(3.0)	(2.0)	(1.4)	(3.1)	(3.0)	(3.5)	(0.7)
LOCC	0.958	0.945	-2.183	1.380	0.331	-0.205	0.159	0.972	0.405	-0.051	0.673	0.166
	(2.9)	(3.0)	(0.5)	(1.6)	(0.7)	(0.5)	(0.3)	(2.4)	(1.0)	(0.1)	(2.0)	(0.2)
AHE	-0.001	-0.005	-0.008	-0.019	-0.003	-0.011	-0.009	-0.003	-0.002	-0.008	-0.006	-0.005
	(0.8)	(3.1)	(2.8)	(2.5)	(1.5)	(5.8)	(2.8)	(1.9)	(2.0)	(4.1)	(3.4)	(1.6)
Intercept	3.467	3.198	3.845	3.710	3.104	3.802	3.967	4.464	3.613	4.109	4.034	3.325
	(6.9)	(6.9)	(6.6)	(3.7)	(7.1)	(8.9)	(6.8)	(7.7)	(7.0)	(9.9)	(8.6)	(3.4)
χ^2	467.2*	455.5	418.1	69.5	853.7**	695.3	489.1	591.1***	564.1	453.6	728.4***	87.6
n	431	595	468	265	768	1153	470	380	627	757	603	123

Note: Households in poverty are coded 1, households not in poverty are coded 0. Asymptotic t-values in parentheses. *** denotes significance at the 1% level, ** at the 5% level, * at the 10% level.
[1] Definitions of these variables are provided in Appendix 9.2.

with demand. There is now a well-established literature[11] that suggests that high replacement ratios (the ratio of unemployment benefits to net income) tend to prolong spells of unemployment (and thus, consequently, increase the stock of unemployed). Evidence is not generally available to consider this question at the United Kingdom regional level; however, Table 9.6 provides some indications by using the previous results on entitlement to Supplementary Benefits and household incomes[12] to calculate ratios for those households where the CES was employed. The ratios are calculated for different occupation groups in order to give some idea of the likely relative disincentive effects operating across regions. As can be seen, ratios often have the highest values in Northern Ireland (especially for teachers and manual workers), which coincides with the province having higher levels of unemployment (and unemployment duration) and poverty than in most other United Kingdom regions.

TABLE 9.6   Ratios of supplementary benefit income entitlement[1] to actual net household income for certain occupations where the chief economic supporter is working, regions of the United Kingdom, 1981

	Occupation of chief economic supporter							
	I	II	III	IV	V	VI	VII	VIII
Northern	0.33	0.42	0.37	0.47	0.53	0.48	0.55	0.66
Yorks–Humberside	0.51	0.49	0.36	0.44	0.61	0.50	0.50	0.58
East Midlands	0.43	0.41	0.40	0.48	0.60	0.48	0.49	0.58
East Anglia	0.50	0.50	0.37	0.45	0.48	0.50	0.59	0.56
Greater London	0.41	0.34	0.29	0.43	0.47	0.44	0.46	0.54
Rest of South East	0.38	0.36	0.35	0.41	0.43	0.48	0.45	0.53
South West	0.39	0.44	0.37	0.45	0.37	0.50	0.50	0.49
Wales	0.42	0.37	0.36	0.43	0.53	0.50	0.51	0.58
West Midlands	0.39	0.44	0.35	0.45	0.52	0.54	0.54	0.54
North West	0.41	0.41	0.39	0.41	0.49	0.47	0.51	0.55
Scotland	0.39	0.43	0.31	0.46	0.47	0.53	0.53	0.56
Northern Ireland	0.46	0.48	0.49	0.42	0.56	0.54	0.54	0.71

[1] This was calculated separately for each household unit before aggregation.
Occupations: I   Professional and technical
               II   Administrative and managerial
               III   Teachers
               IV   Clerical
               V   Shop assistants
               VI   Skilled manual
               VII   Semi-skilled manual
               VIII   Unskilled manual.
Source: As Table 9.4.

5. Relative earnings differences

Labour income (ie wages and salaries) is the most important source of total household income; for the vast majority of people their earnings will determine such key economic issues as expenditure patterns and the probability that a family will suffer from poverty. Therefore, this section will look at relative earnings in Northern Ireland (and other regions). Differences in earnings will be analysed both in terms of nominal values and after taking account of the effect of variations in the cost of living across regions. This section will also consider the causes of earnings differentials; more specifically, both inter- and intra-regional differences will be considered and explained (where possible).

Earnings in Northern Ireland have historically been relatively low when compared to the United Kingdom average. This can be seen from the data presented in Table 9.7, which shows that earnings in production industries were generally much lower in the 1950s and early 1960s (as much as 22 per cent lower overall for manual workers in 1963). The relative dependence on textile and clothing industries in these years, in which earnings were particularly low, plays a part in explaining Northern Ireland's relative position. However, earnings were also lower in other production industries, which suggests that factors other than 'industry mix' were important; Isles and Cuthbert (1957) argued that '... other general causes of the lower average earnings than in Great Britain are: the relatively high proportion of unskilled workers; the comparative absence of incentive schemes supplementing minimum wage rates; the comparative lack of need for bonus systems as a means of retaining workers' services; and probably a tendency for capital equipment to be relatively deficient and for shortages in the supply of materials to be more prevalent, with the result that earnings from given piece rates may tend to be depressed' (pp 229–30). A lack of data for this earlier time period would make it difficult to test these views, but it is worth noting that many of them are not pertinent for non-manual workers (unless skill-mix is taken to mean that Northern Ireland had relatively fewer managers and technical staff), and yet 'white-collar' earnings were equally low when compared to the national average. During the 1960s and early 1970s, Northern Ireland experienced a period of 'catch-up' whereby the earnings gap with Great Britain narrowed substantially. Figure 9.3 shows this for all industries and services; the 'adjusted' line shows what relative earnings levels would have been if the province had had the national employment structure, and therefore this pattern of regional convergence in earnings cannot simply be explained by the advent of a more favourable mix of (higher paying) industries.[13] Much of the relative growth in earnings may have resulted from the inward movement of foreign (and often Great Britain-owned) companies that were willing to negotiate wage rates comparable to those paid in their other plants outside the province.[14] The growth in earnings by industry over the period 1961–71 tended to be highest in those sectors that experienced the largest increase in foreign-owned (usually ID-assisted) employment (eg vehicles, textiles, transport and communications) and in the public sector.[15] Since the mid-1970s relative earnings have been more stable; for males, relative earnings in the province during the period 1972–82 were typically around 88 per cent of the United Kingdom average, 74 per cent of earnings in the Greater London Council (GLC) (which has the highest average hourly earnings), and 96 per cent of earnings in East Anglia (which has the lowest average hourly wage for a region of Great Britain); for females, the comparable relative values were 88–90 per cent, 74 per cent and 94 per cent (see Harris 1989b). However, even though there was this stability after a period of rapid catch-up, there is some evidence that suggests that relative earnings have fallen back in the province, after reaching a peak in 1976 (most notably for males, although movements have been somewhat erratic). Lastly, it is worth noting that the influence of both 'industry mix' (or 'structure') *and* socio-economic occupation 'mix' on relative earnings has been small during the 1970s and 1980s (typically less than 1 per cent for males and a much smaller percentage for females – see Harris 1989b for a fuller discussion).

TABLE 9.7 Wages and salaries (per head) in the production industries, Northern Ireland relative to the United Kingdom

	Non-manual workers				Manual workers			
	1951	1963	1973	1983	1951	1963	1973	1983
Food, drink, tobacco	0.73	0.83	0.99	0.94	0.93	0.99	1.06	1.13
Chemicals and allied	0.75	1.18	1.07	1.11	0.92	1.06	1.18	1.11
Mechanical engineering	0.75	0.87	1.06	0.96	0.88	0.86	0.91	0.94
Electrical engineering	1.23	0.91	0.94	0.93	0.99	0.94	0.97	0.91
Ships and vehicles	0.98	0.99	0.89	0.88	0.94	0.85	0.79	0.95
Textiles	0.70	0.93	1.04	1.06	0.74	0.80	1.03	0.98
Clothing and footwear	0.66	0.81	0.96	0.96	0.70	0.78	0.87	0.89
Bricks, pottery and glass	0.87	0.85	0.89	1.00	0.87	0.89	0.86	0.95
Timber, furniture etc	0.62	0.82	0.90	0.94	0.77	0.78	0.80	0.79
Printing and publishing	0.76	0.80	0.89	0.96	0.80	0.75	0.83	0.91
Other manufacturing	0.89	0.84	1.09	1.06	0.78	0.79	1.11	1.11
Gas, electricity and water	0.88	0.85	0.98	0.97	0.89	0.85	0.85	1.00
Construction	0.82	0.84	na	na	0.92	0.73	na	na
Total	0.83	0.87	0.96	0.95	0.80	0.78	0.89	0.92

Note: Based on 1968 SIC.
Source: Census of Production.

Thus, earnings tended to be lower in the province which suggests that firms may have experienced a cost-advantage over rivals in more centrally located regions. This may be a factor in explaining the relative attractiveness of the province to inward investors during the 1960s and 1970s, especially if transport costs are not prohibitive (and thus acting as a counter-balance to lower labour costs – see Chapter 3 for a discussion of the importance of transport costs). On the supply side in the labour market, relatively lower earnings might act as a disincentive to workers; however, since real earnings are more relevant in this instance, we need to consider the effect of different regional costs of living on earnings levels. When real earnings are compared (Harris 1989b), the relative differences across regions are much narrower than before. More importantly, the rankings of the regions alter; from being at the bottom of the earnings league, Northern Ireland moves up to mid-way while the GLC and South East have the lowest real earnings, primarily because of the higher costs of living (especially housing) in the GLC and Southern regions.[16] This may have important consequences for the operation of the labour market, since it suggests, for example, that relative lower nominal earnings in the province may not be such an incentive for outward migration of labour.

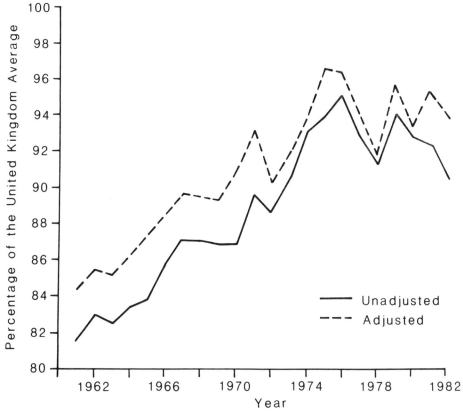

FIG 9.3 Average hourly earnings[1] for male manual workers, Northern Ireland, 1961–1982.

[1] Including overtime pay and overtime hours in October each year. The adjusted series has been calculated using UK employment weights and is expressed as a percentage of the UK average (all industries and services).
Source: Black (1985).

INTER-REGIONAL EARNINGS DIFFERENCES

Differences in relative earnings across regions are the result of several factors. In this sub-section the influence of the differing composition of earnings; plant and/or company size, productivity; and collective bargaining structures will be examined in an attempt to explain these differences.[17] The 'mix' of high and low paying industries/occupations has already been mentioned as being unlikely to provide an overall, simple explanation of earnings differences. Therefore, given that there is a positive earnings–size relationship (especially on the basis of company size), an over-dependence on small units in Northern Ireland may play an important role.[18] Tables 9.8 and 9.9 present the relevant data. They confirm that there is a positive gradient to the earnings–size

TABLE 9.8 Average weekly pay by size of company and sector, Northern Ireland, April 1979 (£)

Employment size	Males				Females			
	Private sector	Public sector	Total		Private sector	Public sector	Total	
0–49	81.46	—	81.46	*89.56*	45.95	103.50	47.80	*53.95*
	(258)		(258)	*(4,689)*	(90)	(3)	(93)	*(1,761)*
50–99	86.50	101.10	88.13	*95.06*	48.37	—	48.37	*54.87*
	(72)	(9)	(81)	*(1,227)*	(30)		(30)	*(486)*
100–499	89.03	95.98	90.63	*99.61*	49.92	61.77	52.52	*57.05*
	(171)	(51)	(222)	*(3,632)*	(96)	(27)	(123)	*(1,428)*
500–999	79.15	98.55	83.62	*101.98*	62.42	117.75	66.38	*59.42*
	(30)	(9)	(39)	*(1,871)*	(39)	(3)	(42)	*(698)*
1000–4999	98.96	98.56	98.76	*104.84*	68.21	77.88	74.42	*62.61*
	(161)	(162)	(323)	*(4,303)*	(82)	(147)	(229)	*(1,729)*
5000+	90.81	102.46	100.56	*104.73*	44.38	62.64	62.22	*68.01*
	(60)	(309)	(369)	*(10,976)*	(6)	(252)	(258)	*(5,786)*

Notes: Only full-time adult workers, without loss of pay, are included in these figures.
Sample size is given in parentheses. Figures in italic refer to comparable all industry data for Great Britain in the same pay-week.
Sources: NES (NI); NES (GB); Harris (1989b).

TABLE 9.9 Average weekly pay by size of plant and sector, Northern Ireland, April 1979 (£)

Employment size	Males				Females			
	Private sector	Public sector	Total		Private sector	Public sector	Total	
0–49	84.83 (552)	98.68 (501)	91.42 (1,053)	99.78 (18,910)	52.59 (90)	68.19 (3)	62.98 (665)	63.47 (9,680)
50–99	89.23 (43)	—	89.23 (43)	95.58 (609)	49.71 (27)	—	49.71 (27)	52.43 (216)
100–199	84.46 (58)	—	84.46 (58)	96.89 (878)	52.98 (42)	—	52.98 (42)	54.53 (352)
200–499	91.93 (73)	103.23 (3)	92.38 (76)	98.23 (1,610)	53.78 (42)	—	53.78 (42)	57.18 (595)
500–999	89.92 (45)	—	89.82 (45)	101.63 (1,204)	58.74 (32)	—	58.74 (32)	61.20 (391)
1000+	112.20 (62)	116.10 (57)	114.07 (119)	108.75 (3,487)	70.13 (27)	58.57 (3)	69.01 (30)	66.56 (654)

Note: See notes on Table 9.8.
Source: As Table 9.8.

relationship, especially on the basis of company size, and that this gradient exhibits a steeper slope using Northern Ireland data.[19] The figures also confirm the dependence on smaller units in the province; only about 29 per cent of workers were employed in companies in Northern Ireland with 5,000 or more workers, compared to over 41 per cent in Great Britain (these comparisons are based on the sample sizes for male workers), while the comparable figures for the largest plants are 8.5 and 13.1 per cent. Tables 9.8 and 9.9 show that an earnings differential is apparent for each size-band, which suggests that dependence on smaller units helps to explain only a very small proportion of the overall differential. For males, weighting average weekly pay by the percentage of workers in each Great Britain (company) size-band closes the gap in earnings by only 0.5 per cent. The influence of the public sector is given separately for the Northern Ireland data, and this shows that for all size-bands earnings were higher in this sector.[20] The growth of the public sector in the province during the 1960s and 1970s (see Chapter 13) may therefore have pushed up private sector pay levels (and consequently raised unit-labour costs in private industry). However, an overall differential in earnings (for all company and plant sizes) is apparent despite the fact that public sector workers in Northern Ireland are just as highly covered by nationally negotiated collective agreements, and that something in the order of 60 per cent of workers in the private sector work for companies that are based in Great Britain.

As to productivity differences, Table 9.10 lists average annual earnings and productivity levels in various production industries in Northern Ireland, the Republic of Ireland and the United Kingdom, with the expectation that those industries with the greatest difference in relative earnings should also have the largest differences in productivity levels. For Northern Ireland, the Pearson correlation between earnings per person and productivity differences (with the United Kingdom) was 0.50 across all industries, while the correlation coefficient for the Republic of Ireland (with the United Kingdom) had a lower value of 0.21. Differences between earnings and productivity levels in both parts of Ireland would also seem to be unimportant, since the correlation coefficient in this instance is −0.06. Therefore, the existence of higher productivity in (higher wage) United Kingdom industries would seem to be important in explaining the earnings differential between Northern Ireland and the United Kingdom, but the relationship is not well established for explaining inter-regional earnings levels in the two parts of Ireland. This is despite the fact that in Northern Ireland and the Republic of Ireland the correlation between productivity and wage levels across industries is 0.63 and 0.71 respectively; ie in both areas wages are higher in those industries that experience relatively high productivity. This might suggest that the Northern Ireland labour market is more closely linked to the United Kingdom labour market in other ways, eg institutional factors (such as collective bargaining arrangements) may weaken the inter-industry link that exists between productivity and wage levels in both parts of Ireland. Before pursuing this point, Table 9.11 shows what has happened to relative earnings in Northern

TABLE 9.10 Average annual earnings and productivity in the production industries, Northern Ireland, Republic of Ireland[1] and the United Kingdom, 1983 (£ 000, current prices)

Industry (1980 SIC)	Earnings per person			Productivity levels		
	NI	RI	UK	NI	RI	UK
Energy and water (1)	9.25	8.72	8.91	16.14	26.76	25.31
Chemicals and man-made fibres (21, 22, 25–26)	10.29	9.08	8.55	22.44	45.67	24.04
Extraction of minerals (23)	6.14	7.55	7.69	23.87	15.61	41.05
Non-metallic minerals (24)	6.97	7.63	7.31	23.56	18.63	19.69
Metal goods (31)	6.28	5.85	6.46	10.95	10.89	12.58
Mechanical engineering (32)	7.09	5.94	7.64	12.33	13.84	15.03
Electronic engineering (33–34)	6.15	6.52	7.15	11.73	29.20	15.67
Motor vehicles (35)	7.89	6.94	7.78	12.79	7.94	14.49
Other transport (36)	7.31	8.29	7.81	6.77	11.62	13.42
Instrumental engineering (37)	7.21	6.65	6.90	16.08	21.02	13.80
Meat and fish products (412, 415)	5.06	5.90	5.49	11.12	14.33	12.57
Milk and milk products (413)	6.89	7.96	7.31	18.66	15.99	23.23
Bread, etc (419)	6.38	5.36	5.07	11.40	8.63	10.07
Other food. drink and tobacco (411–429 excl above)	8.77	8.15	7.60	28.34	28.82	27.51
Hosiery and knitted goods (436)	4.81	4.57	4.46	7.92	7.24	7.77
Carpets (438)	6.61	5.90	6.44	14.23	12.82	13.37
Other textiles (43 excl above)	4.82	5.94	5.43	8.77	11.52	10.57
Leather, footwear and fur (441–442, 451, 456)	5.93	5.95	5.20	8.45	7.59	9.61
Clothing (453)	6.21	3.85	4.00	10.26	6.32	7.30
Household textiles (455)	3.86	4.77	4.56	7.09	7.75	9.65
Timber (461–462)	5.98	4.91	6.28	13.27	10.31	15.89
Other timber products (463–466)	4.47	4.55	6.23	8.81	8.43	12.68
Furniture (467)	5.24	4.16	6.61	10.40	7.32	12.53
Paper products (471–472)	6.52	6.98	7.46	15.04	13.94	15.37
Printing and publishing (475)	7.57	7.46	8.74	14.19	13.12	18.32
Other manufacturing (48–49)	6.41	6.16	6.60	10.69	14.57	14.20
All industries	6.59	6.81	7.28	12.89	18.98	16.87

[1] Converted to £ sterling at IR£1 = £0.8222.
Sources: Census of Production (NI), (UK); Census of Production (RI) (CSO, Dublin).

Ireland and the Republic of Ireland for the period 1949–83; the catch-up in relative earnings in production industries in Northern Ireland does not seem to have been linked to a similar growth in productivity, which is in contrast to the much greater growth in relative earnings *and productivity* in the Republic of Ireland during this period. This result still holds when differences in (wholesale price) inflation are taken into account.

Turning now to collective bargaining structures, Tables 9.12 and 9.13 compare these in Northern Ireland and Great Britain.[21] The primary interest is in whether relative differences in earnings (the figures in column 1) are correlated with differences in the percentage of workers covered by collective agreements (since it is assumed that covered workers in Northern Ireland will

TABLE 9.11   Relative earnings and productivity[1] in the production and construction industries, Northern Ireland and the Republic of Ireland, 1949–1983

	Northern Ireland		Republic of Ireland			
			Nominal		Real (1980) prices	
	Relative annual earnings	Relative productivity	Relative annual earnings	Relative productivity	Relative annual earnings	Relative productivity
1949	0.742	0.713	0.764	0.745	na	na
1963	0.745	0.770	0.743	0.795	0.786	0.840
1978	0.887	0.758	1.036	1.158	0.925	1.034
1983[2]	0.905	0.764	0.935	1.125	0.869	1.007

[1] Relative to UK figures.
[2] Figures based on production industries only, derived from Table 9.10.
Source: As Table 9.10.

both receive higher earnings *vis-à-vis* non-covered workers, and that earnings negotiated nationally will tend to raise wage levels in the province). For non-manual males, the correlation is −0.39 and for manual males the figure is 0.41.[22] The former result suggests that non-manual workers in Northern Ireland have lower earnings if they are covered by a collective agreement (in fact the correlation between earnings and coverage levels is −0.25, whereas the same figure for Great Britain is 0.22), and therefore bargaining does not have the expected effect. This can be explained by the fact that we have not controlled for a host of other relevant factors that determine non-manual pay, and such factors (especially those that tend to lead to higher pay) are linked to lower levels of coverage by collective bargains. For manual workers, where collective bargaining has traditionally played a much greater (and direct) role, there is evidence to suggest that low relative earnings in the province are related to relatively low coverage levels.[23] Examples include agriculture, metals and chemicals, food etc, paper and publishing, construction and other services. It is therefore possible to suggest that differences in levels of collective bargaining coverage accounts for some of the difference in relative earnings for male manual workers.

Finally, to return to some of the reasons for inter-regional differences put forward by Isles and Cuthbert (1957); Table 9.14 presents details on the composition of earnings for male manual workers in the regions of the United Kingdom for 1982. It can be seen that Northern Ireland experienced a particularly low level of dependence on shift-premium and overtime pay relative to other United Kingdom regions, while normal basic hours and pay were relatively more important. This helps to explain the lower level of average weekly earnings in the province, especially when *relative* gross weekly earnings are correlated across regions with the *relative* composition of pay. Results (see the correlation coefficients reported in Table 9.14) show that there was a strong and positive statistical relationship between 'other' pay and relative gross pay, and a negative relationship between relative gross pay and high levels of relative basic pay. Since manual male workers in Northern

TABLE 9.12 Coverage by collective agreement by industry,[1] male manual workers, Northern Ireland, 1987 and Great Britain, 1985

	Relative average hourly earnings 1987 (%)	Percentage covered by			
		Any collective agreement	National and supplementary agreement	National agreement only	Supplementary agreement only
Agriculture (1–3)	85	10.0 (41.5)	10.0 (7.4)	0 (31.4)	0 (2.7)
Energy (11–17)	82	93.1 (96.0)	70.7 (14.6)	22.4 (76.9)	0 (4.5)
Metals and chemicals (21–25)	86	36.8 (71.5)	0 (29.7)	21.1 (15.3)	15.8 (26.5)
Other metals (31)	119	100.0 (58.6)	50.0 (28.7)	0 (14.1)	50.0 (15.8)
Mechanical engineering (32)	91	73.7 (63.1)	21.1 (29.4)	5.3 (19.4)	47.4 (14.3)
Electrical engineering (33–34, 37)	88	55.6 (58.7)	11.1 (27.5)	0 (10.4)	44.4 (20.8)
Motor vehicles (35)	104	100.0 (75.0)	25.0 (16.3)	0 (10.6)	75.0 (48.1)
Other transport (36)	88	90.2 (86.7)	2.4 (39.8)	0 (36.4)	87.8 (10.5)
Food, etc (41–42)	75	50.0 (64.0)	9.4 (9.7)	12.5 (18.9)	28.1 (35.4)
Textiles (43)	110	51.9 (70.4)	3.7 (22.1)	0 (29.1)	48.2 (19.2)
Footwear and clothing (44–45)	94	37.5 (63.0)	25.0 (18.2)	12.5 (37.7)	0 (7.1)
Paper and publishing (47)	85	55.6 (78.8)	33.3 (42.9)	22.2 (30.5)	0 (5.4)
Construction (50)	82	50.0 (76.7)	7.6 (19.3)	27.3 (55.3)	15.2 (2.1)
Distribution (61–67)	95	34.3 (43.0)	3.0 (9.0)	7.5 (21.5)	23.9 (12.5)
Transport and communication (71–79)	103	70.8 (85.3)	2.1 (11.4)	64.6 (60.5)	4.2 (13.4)
Banking and finance (81–85)	80	64.3 (44.1)	0 (14.4)	64.3 (19.0)	0 (10.7)
Public admin (91)	94	95.7 (85.9)	26.1 (19.9)	69.6 (63.6)	0 (2.4)
Education and health (93, 95)	90	66.8 (93.3)	4.2 (12.2)	62.5 (80.1)	0 (1.0)
Other services (92, 94, 96–98)	84	64.1 (74.2)	12.8 (25.8)	51.3 (44.0)	0 (4.4)
All industries	87	61.7 (70.6)	15.3 (19.3)	26.2 (37.6)	20.2 (13.7)

Note: Figures for Great Britain in parentheses.
[1] 1980 SIC.
Sources: NES (NI); NES (GB).

TABLE 9.13 Coverage by collective agreement by industry,[1] male non-manual workers, Northern Ireland, 1987 and Great Britain, 1985

	Relative average hourly earnings 1987 (%)	Percentage covered by			
		Any collective agreement	National and supplementary agreement	National agreement only	Supplementary agreement only
Energy (11–17)	72	90.3 (77.6)	51.6 (18.9)	38.7 (53.3)	0 (5.4)
Metals and chemicals (21–25)	99	70.0 (36.3)	0 (8.4)	10.0 (5.2)	60.0 (22.7)
Mechanical engineering (32)	86	80.0 (27.2)	0 (6.9)	0 (5.4)	80.0 (14.9)
Electrical engineering (33–34, 37)	75	50.0 (33.3)	0 (4.6)	0 (3.2)	50.0 (25.5)
Other transport (36)	71	100.0 (65.6)	0 (12.2)	0 (15.3)	100.0 (38.1)
Food, etc (41–42)	82	10.0 (34.3)	10.0 (2.5)	0 (6.4)	0 (25.4)
Paper and publishing (47)	65	100.0 (47.0)	75.0 (19.6)	0 (17.7)	0 (9.7)
Construction (50)	138	11.1 (31.5)	11.1 (8.4)	0 (18.7)	0 (4.4)
Distribution (61–67)	85	25.5 (24.4)	2.0 (3.3)	2.0 (12.9)	21.5 (8.2)
Transport and communication (71–79)	77	76.0 (77.0)	0 (5.5)	68.0 (59.2)	8.0 (12.3)
Banking and finance (81–85)	73	44.4 (36.4)	2.2 (6.6)	17.8 (19.2)	24.4 (10.6)
Public admin (91)	89	89.9 (91.8)	0.9 (11.7)	88.8 (79.1)	0 (1.0)
Education and health (93,95)	122	87.9 (94.6)	16.7 (9.0)	71.2 (85.4)	0 (0.2)
Other services (92, 94, 96–98)	97	47.8 (68.8)	8.7 (16.4)	39.1 (47.2)	0 (5.2)
All industries	85	67.8 (56.1)	8.7 (8.4)	47.0 (37.9)	12.1 (9.8)

Note: Figures for Great Britain in parentheses.
[1] 1980 SIC.
Sources: As Table 9.12.

percentages)

	Relative average hourly earnings	Relative gross weekly pay	Relative proportion of gross weekly pay due to				Relative normal weekly hours worked	Relative overtime hours worked
			Basic pay	Incentive pay	Shift pay	Overtime pay		
(1) Skilled and semi-skilled males								
GLC	110	110	103	72	101	98	98	105
South East	99	100	102	74	85	107	99	106
East Anglia	93	96	100	88	79	111	101	113
South West	94	93	102	80	95	100	101	99
West Midlands	99	97	99	136	86	86	101	87
East Midlands	99	99	97	129	97	98	100	98
Yorks–Humberside	99	99	95	137	115	101	101	103
North West	99	98	101	95	111	96	101	94
North	104	102	97	128	117	93	100	91
Wales	102	102	97	116	127	101	101	100
Scotland	100	102	100	79	100	114	99	111
Northern Ireland	92	91	103	91	81	91	102	88
r^1	0.93	1.00	−0.66	0.31	0.59	0.34	0.12	0.39
(2) Unskilled males								
GLC	108	109	98	83	151	110	99	119
South East	99	100	101	87	85	109	100	107
East Anglia	92	96	97	104	96	114	97	111
South West	93	91	103	93	77	91	100	93
West Midlands	97	96	101	106	77	97	100	97
East Midlands	102	101	101	90	108	101	99	97
Yorks–Humberside	100	98	98	122	103	92	102	90
North West	99	97	100	101	93	101	101	95
North	102	100	97	126	113	97	101	92
Wales	102	100	100	124	100	84	102	87
Scotland	102	107	101	102	83	99	98	104
Northern Ireland	87	84	107	83	61	77	103	72
r^1	0.91	1.00	−0.70	0.42	0.50	0.41	0.02	0.54

[1] A correlation coefficient was calculated between relative gross weekly pay (column 2 of data) and each other variable in the table using data disaggregated by 12 regions with 10 industry divisions, i.e. 120 data observations.
Source: As Table 9.12.

Ireland were particularly dependent on basic pay, their relative gross weekly earnings were generally much lower than in other United Kingdom regions.

INTRA-REGIONAL DIFFERENCES IN EARNINGS

This sub-section looks at the causes of differences in earnings between workers in Northern Ireland. Both demand and supply influences are important, and later statistical analysis attempts to incorporate factors that comprehensively represent both sides of the labour market. To begin with, it is interesting to consider the extent to which relative differentials across industries and socio-economic groups have changed in the period 1972–82; the *a priori* expectation is that institutional forces (largely linked to collective bargaining) will have maintained a fairly rigid industrial and occupational pay structure over time. Table 9.15 presents the results from comparing movements over time in earnings across industry divisions (10 under the 1980 SIC) in each region, with comparable movements at the national level.[24] A strong correlation signifies that relative pay differentials were maintained and/or mirrored those changes that were occurring nationally. Only in Northern Ireland was the expected relationship absent (for males) or much weaker (the case of females). This suggests that relative industrial pay structures within the province were undergoing quite rapid changes during the period (and especially up to 1979), which is in marked contrast to what took place in other United Kingdom regions. When this exercise is repeated for socio-economic occupations, stability exists for all regions *including* Northern Ireland. Therefore, on the industrial front, the local labour market does seem to have shown more flexibility towards changes resulting from the pressures of demand and supply.

TABLE 9.15 Partial correlation[1] coefficients of relative earnings across industry divisions[2] for each region with relative earnings across industry divisions for Great Britain, 1972–79 and 1980–82

	Males		Females	
	1972–79	1980–82	1972–79	1980–82
GLC	0.97	0.96	0.94	0.93
South East	0.97	0.97	0.97	0.95
East Anglia	0.95	0.97	0.90	0.91
South West	0.96	0.96	0.91	0.94
West Midlands	0.95	0.95	0.94	0.92
East Midlands	0.94	0.96	0.95	0.95
Yorks–Humberside	0.96	0.97	0.94	0.96
North West	0.97	0.98	0.95	0.94
North	0.95	0.97	0.93	0.87
Wales	0.94	0.94	0.86	0.80
Scotland	0.96	0.98	0.93	0.87
Northern Ireland	−0.17	0.29	0.40	0.74

[1] Correlations control for time.
[2] Ten divisions of the 1980 SIC.
Source: As Table 9.12.

As a result of a special voluntary return which accompanied the 1987 Northern Ireland New Earnings Survey, detailed information on pay and certain characteristics of individuals are available. Tables 9.16 and 9.17 show the results of dividing male and female full-time workers into various sub-groups and testing whether there was a statistically significant difference in average hourly earnings between categories of workers. Four industry and two occupation groupings were used, and workers were then further sub-divided, eg on the basis of whether they were covered or not by a collective agreement. The results indicate that coverage by agreements did lead to higher wages in manual occupations and for non-manuals in private services; the ratio of covered to non-covered earnings was usually much higher for female workers, and generally more important in the private sector for all workers (reflecting the high coverage levels existing in the public sector – see Tables 9.12 and 9.13). Earnings were also generally higher in non-Northern Ireland owned and/or multi-plant firms (the exception to this being non-manual workers in public services). As expected, larger plants and/or companies paid higher wages, especially for manual workers in the private sector (or non-manual males working in public utilities). These results probably reflect the ability of these units to achieve higher productivity from exploiting economies of scale. The remaining sub-groups in Tables 9.16 and 9.17 are intended to highlight the 'human capital' invested in individuals: higher earnings are positively linked to a worker being older (especially non-manual earnings, and generally workers not employed in the public utilities); to a worker having been with the same employer for a longer time (although this relationship was weaker for non-manual workers in production industries, and manual workers employed in public services); and for those workers with qualifications (female manual workers are the exception, as many do not possess any qualifications). As to the effects of an individual receiving shift and/or incentive pay, there was a positive effect on earnings for manual workers (especially in production industries), and some tendency towards a negative effect for male non-manual workers (except in the case of workers receiving incentive payments in private services). Overall, the ratios reported in the tables were generally higher for female workers, and were more likely to conform to prior expectations in private sector industries (rather than for those working in public services).

Since these results do not take into account interactions between the various sub-categories listed and pay levels, it is necessary to employ more sophisticated statistical techniques that delineate between the various determinants of earnings across workers. Therefore, regression analysis was used, and the results obtained are reported in Table 9.18. The Lewis-type equations estimated[25] were of the following form at the level of the individual:

$$\ln W_{ij} = a + a_x X_{ij} + a_y Y_j + (a_u - a_n) U_{ij} \qquad [4]$$

here i refers to the i-th individual in the j-th industry (21 industry groups were used[26]); W denotes hourly earnings; X is the vector of explanatory variables; Y is the 'extent of coverage' variable and refers to the percentage of workers

TABLE 9.16 Ratios of average hourly earnings of male full-time workers in various sub-groups to those not in the sub-group, Northern Ireland, 1987

	Non-manual industry				Manual industry			
	I	II	III	IV	I	II	III	IV
Covered by collective agreement	1.31*	0.92	0.92	1.63*	1.21*	1.21*	1.07	1.14
Employed in non-NI firm	1.26*	1.02	0.97	na	1.38*	1.14*	na	na
Received incentive pay	1.26*	0.89	0.94	0.63*	1.00	1.10*	1.16*	0.95
Aged less than 37 years	0.82*	0.78*	0.83*	0.91	0.86*	0.90*	0.88	0.97
Employed by same firm more than 4 years	1.47*	1.12	1.21*	1.43*	1.24*	1.19*	1.00	1.13*
Received shift pay	0.98	na	1.00	0.77	1.10	1.23*	1.16*	1.12*
Employed in multi-plant firm	1.30*	1.05	0.85*	na	1.34*	1.05	1.02	na
Employed in plant with > 200 employees	1.27*	1.04	0.98	1.34*	1.29*	1.20*	1.09	1.06
Employed in company with > 1,000 employees	1.26*	1.00	0.90	1.63*	1.34*	1.18*	1.06	1.09
Employees with qualifications	1.25*	1.17*	1.24*	1.40*	1.01	1.16*	1.37*	1.08

Note: Industries (1980 SIC): I Private services (DIV 6–8, plus SIC 92, 94–99), II Agriculture, manufacturing, construction (DIV 0, 2–5), III Public services (SIC 91 and 93), IV Public utilities (DIV 1), na: not available due to small sample size or all workers in only 1 sub-group. The t-test algorithm available in SPSSX 2.1 was used. *t-test is significant at 5% level.
Source: NES (NI).

TABLE 9.17 Ratios of average hourly earnings of female full-time workers in various sub-groups to those not in the sub-group, Northern Ireland, 1987

	Non-manual industry				Manual industry			
	I	II	III	IV	I	II	III	IV
Covered by collective agreement	1.31*	1.27	0.98	na	1.74*	1.36*	1.24	na
Employed in non-NI firm	1.34*	na	0.98	na	1.95*	1.33*	na	na
Received incentive pay	1.57*	1.09	1.04	na	1.74*	1.08	0.94	na
Aged less than 37 years	0.77*	1.01	0.88*	1.00	0.79	0.88	1.31	na
Employed by same firm more than 4 years	1.56*	1.25	1.19*	1.21*	1.36	1.22*	1.14	na
Received shift pay	na	na	1.12*	na	1.66	1.41*	0.75	na
Employed in multi-plant firm	1.36*	1.00	0.95	na	1.65*	1.35*	1.09	na
Employed in plant with > 200 employees	1.37*	1.17	1.03	na	1.64*	1.35*	0.76	na
Employed in company with > 1,000 employees	1.43*	1.16	0.90	na	1.75*	1.38*	1.28*	na
Employees with qualifications	1.58*	1.53*	1.21*	1.08	na	0.87	na	na

Note: See notes and source on Table 9.16.

TABLE 9.18 Regression equations of individual log hourly earnings, 1987

Variable	Males		Females	
	All	Manual	All	Manual
UNION	0.012 (0.3)	−0.006 (0.2)	0.025 (0.5)	0.104 (1.4)
COVER	0.002 (2.2)	0.002 (2.2)	0.002 (1.4)	0.006 (2.2)
YGROWTH	−0.792 (1.5)	−0.022 (0.1)	0.611 (0.5)	5.675 (2.4)
EMPG	0.349 (0.5)	0.135 (0.2)	−1.059 (0.8)	−5.253 (1.9)
PROD	−0.001 (0.3)	−0.001 (0.5)	−0.001 (0.3)	0.001 (0.1)
NCOMPANY	−0.008 (0.9)	0.031 (2.8)	0.047 (3.7)	0.030 (1.5)
NEST	0.036 (4.2)	0.001 (0.1)	−0.002 (0.2)	−0.004 (0.2)
LOC	0.083 (3.0)	0.102 (3.6)	0.127 (3.3)	0.044 (0.9)
MULTI	−0.135 (2.9)	−0.015 (0.3)	0.075 (1.1)	−0.069 (0.8)
STRIKES ($\times 10^3$)	2.156 (2.3)	2.751 (3.0)	−0.001 (0.7)	−7.021 (1.0)
QUAL	0.251 (8.9)	0.163 (5.3)	0.244 (4.5)	−0.020 (0.2)
YBIR	−0.005 (3.8)	−0.005 (3.7)	−0.002 (1.1)	0.004 (1.5)
NYR	0.009 (5.3)	0.002 (1.2)	0.016 (5.4)	0.023 (4.1)
OCC	−0.031 (10.2)	0.002 (0.3)	−0.058 (8.8)	0.012 (0.7)
PBR	0.008 (0.2)	0.036 (1.2)	−0.063 (1.0)	0.054 (0.8)
SHIFT	−0.127 (3.2)	−0.184 (4.9)	−0.067 (1.3)	0.086 (1.1)
O/TIME	−0.336 (9.0)	−0.238 (5.7)	−0.476 (6.1)	−0.277 (1.3)
TPUB	0.049 (0.9)	−0.147 (2.3)	−0.151 (2.0)	−0.094 (0.8)
Const	1.696 (11.6)	1.227 (7.8)	1.303 (5.5)	−0.368 (1.0)
$\bar{R}^2$	0.50	0.47	0.51	0.49
n	698	361	365	100

Note: Variables are defined in Appendix 9.2. t-values in parentheses.

covered by a collective agreement in the j-th industry; U is a dummy variable (0,1) indicating whether the individual is covered by a collective agreement.[27] The vector of explanatory variables, X, are those used in Table 9.16 and 9.17 plus the following: the number of overtime hours worked by an individual; the number of working days lost in each industry (average over the period 1980–86); output and employment growth in each industry (average for 1980–86); and productivity levels in each industry (average for 1980–86). Full details of the variables used are given in Appendix 9.2.

The results show that whether an individual was covered by a collective agreement or not was generally unimportant (except for female manual workers), which is contrary to expectations based upon earlier results (Tables 9.16 and 9.17, and Harris and Wass 1987). However, the explanation for this probably lies with two econometric problems encountered: firstly, the collinearity between firm and/or plant size and bargaining structures. Harris and Wass (1988) found that unit size is a strong determinant of bargaining structure, while with the data used in this study the (Pearson) correlation between UNION and NEST/NCOMPANY is generally around 0.5. Secondly, it is likely that coverage by a collective agreement leads to higher wages *and* the mark-up on wages resulting from coverage affects the individuals' decision as to whether to belong to a trade union (see Lee 1978). Clearly, the use of ordinary least squares is inadequate since both wages and coverage are endogenous and are both determined by company and plant size. Ideally, a simultaneous equations model is required, but this is complicated by the fact that the endogenous variable UNION is a dichotomous variable. Hence, and for simplicity, we keep to a single-equation linear model, even though the results are statistically biased.[28] The 'extent-of-unionism' variable, COVER, which indicates if high coverage industries obtain higher earnings, is also very small (although generally statistically significant) at around 0.2 per cent. The next set of variables relate to the demand side of the labour market; output and employment growth were not particularly important in determining earnings, except for female manual workers where there is some evidence to suggest that productivity growth was influential (given the size and signs of the coefficients). Company size or employment size were important (but not both, because of collinearity between these two variables), and earnings were (ceteris paribus) higher in non-Northern Ireland plants. Multi-plant status was generally unimportant on its own, except for all male workers where a negative relationship existed. On the supply side, those industries with the worst strike records had higher male earnings; this confirms that trade unions had considerable bargaining power to influence earnings levels during this period, even though the economy was in recession. Human capital variables were all influential: qualifications and age were particularly important for non-manual workers; the number of years with a company was also important, although more so for female workers (the effect was relatively weak for manual males); and occupation group was predictably influential. As to the effect of an individual being paid by results, this seemed to have little independent influence on earnings, whereas shift and overtime payments were quite strongly related to lower average *hourly* earnings.[29] Finally, male manual employees in public services received 13.7 per cent lower earnings overall (for females working in public services, earnings were around 14 per cent lower).

To conclude the results on intra-regional earnings, Table 9.19 gives the correlation coefficients between earnings growth (across 21 industries) and changes (over the period 1980–86) in some of the variables from the previous table. It can be seen that strikes were positively associated with male manual

TABLE 9.19 Pearson correlations between earnings growth and certain determinants across industries, Northern Ireland, 1980–1987

	Male		Female
Determinant	Non-manual	Manual	Non-manual
Average working days lost per worker 1980–86	−0.13	0.56*	−0.19
Employment growth 1980–86	−0.57*	−0.16	−0.11
GDP growth 1980–86	−0.67*	−0.16	0.03
Productivity growth 1980–86	−0.34	−0.06	0.19
% workers covered by collective agreement 1987	−0.20	0.68*	0.29
Earnings levels in 1980	−0.60*	−0.81*	−0.82*

Note: *Significant at the 5% level.
Sources: NES; NIAAS No 6, 1987.

earnings growth, while falls in employment *and output* were strongly correlated with the male non-manual growth in wages. Male manual workers in highly unionised industries received proportionately higher earnings by 1987, and for all three categories of workers earnings grew fastest in those industries with the lowest levels of earnings in 1980.

6. Expenditure

Differences in income levels *and* the relative distribution of income should have important consequences for the pattern of regional expenditure on goods and services. Furthermore, any differences across regions in income elasticities of demand for various commodities will have potentially important effects on regional growth and fluctuation, as industrial output and employment adjusts to changes in income levels over time.[30]

Therefore, this chapter concludes with a brief look at the relative composition of regional demands for goods and services, as well as attempting to estimate expenditure elasticities for each commodity group.

Table 9.20 splits the 1981 FES sample of households into those that received sufficient income to render them above the official poverty line, and those households that fell below; relative expenditure on various commodities is then presented for each sub-group. Several salient features are noticeable: households in Northern Ireland (in both categories) spend proportionately less on housing and more on fuel, light, power, and food than do households in Great Britain, although there is evidence of a 'North–South' correlation between relative costs of living (which is heavily influenced by housing costs) and relative expenditure levels across regions. A similar spatial pattern exists for drink and tobacco, clothing and services, although relative expenditure levels are also influenced by the socio-economic composition of the population in different areas. There is a greater likelihood of poorer, more working-class households purchasing relatively larger quantities of drink, tobacco and clothing, while less is spent on services and, to some extent, household durables; this can be attributed to what is known as Engel's law. In general, household expenditure patterns in Northern Ireland do not appear to differ substantially from expenditure patterns on the mainland: more is spent on essential commodities. The Republic of Ireland stands out as being different; expenditure on housing is very low, even lower for poorer households (which is an unexpected departure from the results obtained for United Kingdom regions). As with Northern Ireland, expenditure on food is proportionately high, while there is evidence to suggest that poorer households spend a larger relative proportion of their incomes on fuel and light, and drink and tobacco.[31]

Given that Table 9.20 shows that peripherally located regions with the lowest incomes tend to spend larger proportions of their incomes on more basic goods, it is useful to estimate total expenditure elasticities for each region. The expenditure model that was estimated is based upon linear Engel curves:

TABLE 9.20 Relative expenditure on various commodities, regions of the United Kingdom and the Republic of Ireland, 1981[1] (percentage)

	Average weekly expenditure (£)	Housing	Fuel, light, power	Food	Drink, tobacco	Clothing	Durables	Transport	Services
Northern	131.6 (52.6)	13.5 (19.6)	5.5 (11.2)	21.4 (27.8)	9.2 (9.0)	8.1 (6.5)	14.8 (12.1)	17.5 (6.6)	10.1 (7.3)
Yorks–Humberside	120.5 (50.8)	13.4 (19.8)	5.8 (10.0)	22.8 (29.4)	10.2 (9.4)	8.8 (4.8)	14.5 (12.2)	13.9 (5.6)	10.6 (8.3)
East Midlands	120.9 (60.6)	13.9 (18.4)	5.7 (12.5)	21.3 (28.2)	7.4 (6.6)	6.4 (7.0)	19.5 (11.3)	14.8 (7.0)	11.0 (8.7)
East Anglia	128.7 (56.8)	14.7 (19.9)	6.0 (10.2)	22.2 (29.5)	5.9 (5.9)	7.4 (2.6)	15.7 (12.9)	16.3 (11.7)	11.9 (7.1)
Greater London	156.0 (56.5)	17.7 (27.5)	4.5 (8.8)	19.7 (28.3)	7.7 (6.3)	7.2 (4.1)	15.3 (10.4)	14.8 (5.1)	13.1 (9.1)
Rest of South East	146.6 (65.1)	17.1 (20.8)	5.4 (8.5)	19.9 (28.8)	6.8 (7.2)	6.6 (4.5)	16.0 (13.0)	15.7 (9.0)	12.4 (8.1)
South West	127.5 (60.1)	17.2 (19.0)	6.7 (11.9)	20.4 (26.5)	6.4 (7.0)	6.7 (9.0)	14.4 (11.1)	15.6 (7.8)	12.7 (7.5)
Wales	131.6 (59.8)	13.3 (19.3)	6.8 (11.2)	22.2 (29.2)	7.6 (6.8)	7.6 (6.5)	15.6 (14.0)	16.2 (6.4)	10.7 (6.5)
West Midlands	129.0 (70.6)	17.0 (18.1)	5.2 (9.2)	22.0 (28.3)	7.7 (7.4)	7.8 (6.7)	14.1 (9.8)	16.0 (10.1)	10.0 (10.5)
North West	132.6 (55.9)	15.7 (23.4)	5.7 (9.6)	21.9 (26.8)	8.0 (7.9)	8.0 (4.0)	14.4 (10.4)	14.7 (7.8)	11.7 (10.1)
Scotland	131.0 (55.1)	11.5 (16.1)	6.5 (10.3)	23.2 (29.1)	9.6 (8.4)	8.0 (8.5)	14.3 (12.8)	15.0 (6.0)	11.8 (8.9)
Northern Ireland	116.2 (64.3)	10.3 (15.5)	9.6 (15.9)	25.7 (34.2)	8.2 (7.6)	8.7 (7.4)	10.9 (6.1)	14.8 (4.6)	11.9 (9.0)
Republic of Ireland	133.5 (39.9)	7.1 (4.8)	7.3 (15.0)	27.3 (39.1)	7.2 (9.3)	7.1 (6.6)	11.0 (7.4)	14.8 (7.1)	18.4 (10.7)

[1] For the UK, the first set of figures refer to expenditure by all households except those with income below the Supplementary Benefit level, which are given in parentheses. For the Republic of Ireland, figures in parentheses refer to those families that received less than £48 (IR £60) gross weekly household income.

Sources: FES; HBS (CSO, Dublin).

$$e_{ij} = a_i + b_iE_j + c_iH_j + d_iA_j + u_{ij} \qquad [5]$$

here e_{ij} represents the expenditure on the i-th commodity (i = 1, . . . , 8) in the j-th household in a region; E_j represents total expenditure in the j-th household; H_j represents the number of persons living in the household; A_j represents the age of the head of household; and u_{ij} is an error term assumed to have the usual desirable properties. Because the sum of expenditures (e_{ij}) on various commodities equals total expenditure E_j, estimation of [5] requires the use of a simultaneous equations approach; hence, two-stage least squares was used with household income entering as the exogenous instrument for total household expenditure.[32] Individual household data were used, taken from the 1981 FES, and in general the estimated equations gave significant parameter values. The complete set of results are not presented here, but rather Table 9.21 presents the expenditure elasticities for each commodity by region.[33] These results confirm prior expectations that commodity groups such as durables, transport and services tend to be income-elastic (ie more than proportionately increase their shares of total expenditure as economic growth causes incomes to increase), while fuel, light and power, and food tend to be broadly inelastic. There do not appear to be any major differences across the regions of the United Kingdom, except for the Northern region, which had the largest degree of difference in the value of its elasticities.[34] Comparing the results for Northern Ireland with those obtained by Geary (1977) using 1967 FES data, it can be seen that expenditure elasticities have remained fairly stable over the 14-year period, and any changes that have taken place may be more to do with differences in estimation (Geary used OLS and did not include the age of the head of household as a regressor).

Therefore, in conclusion, households in the province would appear to have similar expenditure patterns to those displayed in each United Kingdom region, but the greater problem of poverty tends to curtail the relative volume of demand for income-elastic goods and services. This means that Northern Ireland industries must look to other (export) markets in order to be able to expand their sales of those commodities that will grow at a relatively faster pace.

7. Conclusion

This chapter has shown that Northern Ireland has the lowest level of household income of any region in the United Kingdom and, partly in consequence, it suffers from the highest incidence of poverty. Although earnings have 'caught up' to a large extent during the period since the Second World War, and even though pay bargaining levels are comparable to United Kingdom levels, the province still suffers from the consequences of the lower levels of economic activity that largely cause a lower level of earnings in the region. That is, much of the analysis of this chapter points to the fact that income levels are usually a consequence of past economic development, and are likely to only marginally

TABLE 9.21 Total expenditure elasticities for various commodities, regions of the United Kingdom, 1981

	Housing	Fuel, light, power	Food	Drink, tobacco	Clothing	Durables	Transport	Services
Northern	0.53	0.34	0.49	0.61	0.70	0.88	2.86	0.86
Yorks–Humberside	0.56	0.20	0.63	1.15	1.74	1.28	1.53	1.07
East Midlands	0.45	0.03[1]	0.43	0.89	0.86	1.85	1.43	1.51
East Anglia	0.85	0.39	0.58	1.45	1.19	1.13	1.50	1.12
Greater London	0.64	0.30	0.96	1.00	0.64	1.18	1.40	1.37
Rest of South East	0.80	0.34	0.56	0.91	1.09	1.44	1.14	1.57
South West	0.83	0.15[1]	0.51	0.73	1.10	1.07	1.38	2.07
Wales	0.85	0.15[1]	0.44	0.87	1.42	1.47	1.38	1.51
West Midlands	0.78	0.18	0.54	0.95	1.36	1.30	1.41	1.54
North West	0.68	0.36	0.59	0.85	1.30	1.29	1.56	1.40
Scotland	0.68	0.34	0.45	0.84	0.97	1.20	1.66	1.92
Northern Ireland[2]	0.53	0.32	0.57	1.04	0.99	1.92	1.58	1.58
	(0.90)	(0.00)	(0.52)	(0.83–1.94)	(0.89)	(1.50)	(2.02)	(1.85)

[1] The estimated parameter value was not significantly different from zero at the 5% level.
[2] Figures in parentheses refer to those elasticities presented in Geary (1977) and refer to 1967 FES data for Northern Ireland.
Source: FES, 1981.

affect future growth. This should, therefore, guard the unwary from listening to the siren call of the new classical economist, who claims that cutting or holding back wages in the province would contribute to future economic growth. Cutting back on wage levels would probably increase poverty, act as a disincentive to work, and, anyway, the present differential has not induced a higher rate of economic growth than in the rest of the United Kingdom. In fact, some proportion of the narrowing of the wage differential in the 1960s and 1970s was probably as a result of growth.

Appendix 9.1 Social security in the Republic of Ireland

In this appendix, the differences in the social security systems that operate in Northern Ireland and the Republic of Ireland are briefly examined, principally in an attempt to explain the high levels of state pensions and benefits in total household income in Northern Ireland, and the relatively lower levels in the Republic of Ireland (see Table 9.1).

The social security systems that were in operation in the United Kingdom and the Republic of Ireland in 1981 are quite similar (a detailed comparison for 1984 can be found in Evason 1985). Combining state pensions and state benefits (in Table 9.1) gives the following comparisons (Table 9.1A) of the value of different categories of transfers to the average household. The differences shown in the table reflect the influence of various (potential) effects: demographic, rates of benefit, economic conditions in each region, and the take-up of means-tested aid. The different rates of benefit are dealt with first. Children's allowances were more generous in the South, since for the first child £4.80 was available (£4.75 in the United Kingdom for each and every child), but for each subsequent child, benefit was £7.20 per child. State retirement pensions were paid at similar rates throughout Ireland. In Northern Ireland the contributory pension was £27.15 for a single person (£43.45 for a married couple, and £16.30 for a non-contributory widow's pension), while in the Republic of Ireland

TABLE 9.1A   Average household income from state transfers, Northern Ireland and the Republic of Ireland, 1981 (£ sterling)

	Northern Ireland	Republic of Ireland
Children's allowance	6.70	1.89
Old age and retirement pensions	12.64	5.93
Widows' and orphans' pensions	1.78	1.55
Unemployment benefit and assistance	2.41 ⎫	3.61
Supplementary benefit	3.57 ⎭	
Family income supplement	0.13	—
Education grants/scholarships	0.20	0.15
Other transfers[1]	4.97	2.65
Total	32.40	15.78

Note: Exchange rate IR£ = £0.8002.
[1] Sickness benefits are the largest proportion in this total for both NI and RI.
Sources: FES; HBS (CSO, Dublin).

contributory pensions were paid at £24.53 (and £42.85 for a married couple; widows received £22.53). However, unlike the situation in Northern Ireland where almost everyone would have been on a contributory-based pension, only about 34 per cent of pensioners in the Republic of Ireland would have belonged to the state contributory scheme. Hence, the remainder received non-contributory pensions valued at £21.00 for a single person (£31.57 for a married couple and £21.00 for a widow). Therefore, and except for the pension paid to widows claiming a non-contributory pension based on their husband's insurance (about 24 per cent of pensioners in both parts of Ireland in 1981), pensioners in Northern Ireland received substantially higher amounts (eg a married couple received about 22 per cent more income in Northern Ireland).

As to unemployment benefit, the system in the Republic of Ireland is more complicated than in Northern Ireland, since an unemployed person might have claimed unemployment assistance or unemployment benefit (only in the latter case was an earnings-related supplement also paid). There were also two different rates of assistance depending on whether the recipient was living in an urban or rural area (in fact, in 1981 there were roughly equal proportions of claimants in both areas). The different levels of benefit, as well as comparison with Northern Ireland, are given in Table 9.2A.

This table shows that unemployment benefit was generally higher in Northern Ireland, and this is especially important when it is noted that a large proportion of households in Northern Ireland were particularly dependent on supplementary benefit, which becomes payable if an individual has worked insufficient time to accrue the necessary national insurance to qualify for unemployment benefit. (Supplementary benefits, payable at the same rate as rural unemployment assistance, was not an important feature of state payments in the Republic of Ireland.)

TABLE 9.2A   Rates of unemployment benefit (and supplementary benefit), Northern Ireland and the Republic of Ireland, 1981 (£ sterling)

	Single person	Married couple	Married + 3 children	Average payment of earnings-related supplement
(i) Northern Ireland				
Unemployment benefit	20.65	33.40	37.15	9[2]
Supplementary benefit	21.30	34.60	60.10[1]	nil
(ii) Republic of Ireland				
Unemployment assistance				
Urban	16.32	28.09	40.97	nil
Rural	15.80	27.29	40.17	nil
Unemployment benefit	19.56	32.37	47.09	5[2]

[1] Based on children aged 12, 8 and 3.
[2] Approximate.
Sources: Budget statement for RI; Social Security Statistics (UK) for NI.

Therefore, different levels of benefits are a major cause of the differences shown in Table 9.1. Since the unemployment rate in Northern Ireland in 1981 was also higher (14.4 per cent compared to 10.1 per cent in the Republic of Ireland) it can be surmised that higher benefits, and a higher dependence on benefit, largely explain any differences relating to state benefits. The greater dependence on contributory pensions is also relevant in explaining the larger overall dependence on state pensions in Northern Ireland. In addition there was a larger 1981 population of pensionable age

(14.4 per cent in Northern Ireland, compared to 12.8 per cent in the Republic of Ireland). The only finding that it has not been possible to explain is the dependence on children's allowance in Northern Ireland; both parts of Ireland have similar proportions of young children (and similar size of families), and so it is difficult to see why there should have been such a large difference, unless take-up was very much lower in the Republic of Ireland.

Appendix 9.2

1) DEFINITIONS OF VARIABLES USED IN TABLE 9.5

COUNCIL	– dummy variable coded 1 if council tenure
RETIRED	– dummy variable coded 1 if chief economic supporter (CES) in household was retired
UNOCC	– dummy variable coded 1 if CES in household was economically unoccupied
UNEMP	– dummy variable coded 1 if CES in household was unemployed
NUM	– number of persons in household
AGEHOH	– age of the head of household (HOH)
LOCC	– dummy variable coded 1 if CES was a shop assistant or unskilled manual worker
AHE	– net average hourly earnings of HOH (zero if not working), after tax and superannuation

Source: FES 1981.

2) DEFINITION OF VARIABLES USED IN TABLE 9.18

UNION	– dummy variable coded 1 if individual is covered by a collective agreement. Source: NES voluntary return.
COVER	– percentage of workers in the industry covered by a collective agreement. Source: NES voluntary return.
STRIKES	– average number of working days lost per 1,000 employees in industry 1980–86 average annual (compound). Source: NIAAS No 6, 1987.
YGROWTH	– growth in output 1980–86 in industry (based on GDP data). Source: NIAAS No 6, 1987.
EMPG	– average annual (compound) growth in employment in industry 1980–86. Source: NIAAS No 6, 1987.
PROD	– average level of productivity in industry (output per person, using above two variables) over the period 1980–86. Source: NIAAS No 6, 1987.
NCOMPANY	– employment size of company in which individual worked (coded 1 for ‹50 employees and up to 10 for ›100,000 employees)
EST	– employment size of plant in which individual worked (coded 1 for ‹50 employees and up to 10 for ›100 employees)
LOC	– dummy variable coded 1 if location of company head-

	quarters in which individual worked was outside Northern Ireland
MULTI	– dummy variable coded 1 if individual worked in a multi-plant establishment
QUAL	– dummy variable coded 1 if individual had ONC/HNC/degree/completed an apprenticeship
YBIN	– year of birth (last two digits) of individual
NYR	– number of years individual has worked for the company
OCC	– occupation group (coded 1 through 10 from professional to unskilled manual worker)
PBR	– dummy variable coded 1 if individual received incentive pay
SHIFT	– dummy variable coded 1 if individual received shift premium pay
OTIME	– ratio of overtime to normal weekly hours for individual
TPUB	– dummy variable coded 1 if individual worked in public services Classes 91 or 93 (1980 SIC)

Source: All variables from NCOMPANY TO TPUB from NES (1987) voluntary return.

Notes

1. Some of the data used in this Chapter were obtained as the result of an ESRC award (reference A05252006).
2. This reflects the importance of agriculture and a generally higher proportion of casual workers.
3. A Gini coefficient measures the area between the evenly 'distributed income' Lorenz curve (a 45° angled straight line) and the actual Lorenz curve.
4. If incomes were equally distributed across all households, the Gini coefficient would have a value of 0; if all income went to only 1 household, the value of the coefficient would be 100. Note, our calculations of the Gini coefficient are based upon grouped data, and are therefore only an approximation of the true Gini value, although it should be noted that we made use of 10 groupings (in order to increase the accuracy of the Gini measure). Note, the results obtained do not differ substantially with those reported in Borooah and McGregor (1988). The latter use data for 1986.
5. The term in brackets denotes the poverty gap of a poor household i, since it measures the difference between what the law states is the minimum income necessary, and the actual household's income.
6. Since the dependent variable is dichotomous (that is, takes on values 0, 1), a logit regression model is estimated (see Maddala 1983, pp 22–27). This model obtains maximum likelihood estimates of the probability, p, of being in poverty where $p = 1[1 + \exp(-\beta x)]$. In order to interpret the parameter results obtained, note that:

$$\frac{\partial \hat{p}}{\partial x_i} = \hat{p}(1 - \hat{p})\hat{\beta}_i$$

Thus at p = 0.5 the estimated effect on the probability of a unit change in a variable is approximately equal to $\beta_i/4$, eg if variable X_i increased by 10% and β_i = 0.9, then this would amount to a 2.25% increase in the probability of being in poverty.

7. The role of unemployment as a cause of poverty needs to be defined more clearly; for instance, it is likely that unemployment duration, rather than simply being part of the stock of unemployed, plays an important role, especially if the CES of poorer households suffer longer periods (or more frequent periods) of unemployment when compared to better-off households. A more sophisticated model than that used here would be necessary to introduce such distinctions.

8. In order to avoid regressing poverty status on income *per se*, when the latter has been used in a key way to split households into those which are in poverty and those which are not, the determining variable used in the equation is average net hourly earnings of the HOH. Note also, these results suggest that increasing the average HOH hourly wage from 20 pence per hour, for a typical family in poverty, to an average of £1.40 per hour (see the footnote in Table 9.4) would have lowered the probability of poverty (*cet par*) by nearly 24 per cent.

9. Of course, the ability to obtain accommodation is generally not independent of whether the CES is an 'insider' or 'outsider' in the labour market.

10. For the econometrically minded, the chi-squared values in Table 9.5 represent a test of homogeneity of the residuals. A significant value shows that the residuals were not randomly distributed around the regression line, and so a 'homogeneity factor' is used to adjust the confidence intervals on the regression coefficients. Significant chi-squared values often indicate that the model is misspecified (ie lacks a complete set of regressors). Although not reported in the table, the results do have fairly high explanatory power, as evidenced by pseudo R^2 values – see Maddala (1983) for a review of diagnostic tests in models with limited dependent variables.

11. See, for example, Narendranathan, Nickell and Stern (1985) and Hughes and Walsh (1983).

12. Although, in this instance, household income has been adjusted to a net figure, ie minus tax and national insurance.

13. This convergence in earnings was also apparent in other 'peripheral' regions of the United Kingdom and, as with Northern Ireland, cannot be attributed to changes in industrial structures (see Moore and Rhodes 1981 for a discussion). For more up-to-date information for the regions of Great Britain, see Harris (1989a).

14. Black (1985) states that '. . . (the) use by trade unions of "coercive comparisons" to establish "parity" in earnings levels has been a major factor in raising Northern Ireland earnings closer to the United Kingdom average' (p 6).

15. See Black (1985), Table 1, and the discussion in Harris (1989b).

16. The use of regional deflators, heavily influenced by house prices, to obtain real earnings figures assumes that most people are facing high repayment costs from mortgages with long periods to run, when for some people the asset may be largely paid for, which may have a positive wealth effect on consumer expenditure. In any event, the regional price indices may bias downwards real earnings in the 'South'.

17. See also Harris (1989a) for more details relating to regions in Great Britain. The present analysis concentrates upon Northern Ireland.

18. This earning–size relationship is linked to productivity (since larger plants and firms are likely to benefit from returns-to-scale, and hence higher wages) and to collective bargaining structure (coverage is usually higher the larger the size of the

plant and/or company, and this leads to higher wages if there exists a positive mark-up on unionised wages). Therefore, we might not expect plant or company size in itself to account for inter-regional differentials in earnings if, in fact, size acts as the intermediary for productivity and collective bargaining effects. As will be seen, this expectation is confirmed by the data.

19. More up-to-date information is available for 1987 with regard to the province, and this confirms that the positive relationships in 1979 persist. However, comparable Great Britain data are only available for 1979.

20. It is also apparent that the majority of public sector workers belong to large companies which operate comparatively small plants, and that earnings levels vary by much less, both across company and plant-size, when compared to the private sector.

21. For a discussion of relative bargaining structures, and the determinants of bargaining over the period 1973–84, see Harris and Wass (1988).

22. The coefficients do not change greatly if public sector industries are omitted from the calculations.

23. Differences in earnings levels across industries are also correlated with differences in the level of coverage in the province; the correlation for male manuals is 0.75.

24. It is necessary to control for time since there are potentially two changes occurring: changes in relative earnings between industries (eg industry X_i is moving up the pay rankings on all regions) and changes in relative earnings across regions (eg industry X_i is moving up in region Y_j only). Time is used as a proxy for changes in the industrial rankings over time.

25. See Harris and Wass (1987) for full details.

26. The industries listed in Table 9.12, plus timber and wood (Class 46) and other manufacturing (Classes 48–49).

27. For more details on the methodology, see Harris and Wass (1987), p 6.

28. Work is currently being undertaken to estimate a more sophisticated two-stage mixed qualitative/quantitative model (see Harris 1989c).

29. This suggests that lower hourly wage rates are supplemented to some extent by overtime and/or shift work, in order to boost weekly earnings – see Table 9.14.

30. Although, if local industries are mainly export-orientated, low income elasticities may not act as a constraint.

31. Note, these comparisons need to be treated with care because definitions of the two household groups are not identical in the Republic of Ireland and in United Kingdom regions.

32. The correlation between household income and expenditure was rarely above 0.65 but is nevertheless sufficiently correlated to make it a good instrument. Note, the assumption is being made that expenditure takes place out of a given income, rather than individuals plan their employment such as to achieve joint income and expenditure flows.

33. These elasticities are calculated as $b_i/(e_{ij}/E_j)$, and are evaluated at the sample means of the data.

34. For example, it has the lowest elasticity for drink and tobacco; the elasticities on durable goods and services are inelastic; and the high income elasticity of demand for transport is unique. These results are therefore subject to confirmation using another set of FES data.

References

Atkinson, A B (1987) On the measurement of poverty, *Econometrica*, 55, 4, 749–64.

Black, B (1985) Regional earnings convergence: the case of Northern Ireland, *Regional Studies*, 19, 6, 1–8.

Borooah, V K and McGregor, P (1988) Income distribution in Northern Ireland and other regions of the United Kingdom. Presented at the European meeting of the Regional Science Association, Stockholm.

Clark, S, Hemming, R and Ulph, D (1981) On indices for the measurement of poverty, *Economic Journal*, 91, 515–26.

Evason, E (1985) Social security: north and south, *Administration*, 33, 3, 355–77.

Geary, P T (1977) Wages, prices, income and wealth, in Gibson, N J and Spencer, J E (eds) *Economic Activity in Ireland: a Study of Two Open Economies*, Gill and Macmillan, Dublin.

Harris, R I D (1989a) Relative earnings in the regions of Great Britain, 1970–1982, in Thomson, A W J and Gregory, M G (eds) *Portrait of Pay in the 1970s: Using the New Earnings Survey*, Oxford University Press.

Harris, R I D (1989b) Relative earnings in Northern Ireland, 1972–1982, in Jenkins, R (ed) *Northern Ireland: Studies in Social and Economic Life*, Gower.

Harris R I D (1989c) The determinants of collective bargaining coverage and its effect on earnings in Northern Ireland in 1987 (mimeo).

Harris, R I D and Wass, V J (1987) The effect of collective bargaining on earnings in Northern Ireland in 1973, *The Economic and Social Review*, 19, 1, 1–14.

Harris, R I D and Wass, V J (1988) The determinants of collective bargaining structures in Northern Ireland, *The Economic and Social Review*, 19, 2, 99–122.

HMSO (1981) *Family Expenditure Survey*, London.

Hughes, G and Walsh, B M (1983) Unemployment duration, aggregate demand and unemployment insurance: a study of Irish Live Register survival probabilities, 1967–1978, *The Economic and Social Review*, 14, 2, 93–118.

Isles, K S and Cuthbert, N (1957) *An Economic Survey of Northern Ireland*, HMSO, Belfast.

Lee, L F (1978) Unionism and wage rates: a simultaneous equations model with qualitative and limited dependent variables, *International Economic Review*, 19, 415–33.

Maddala, G S (1983) *Limited Dependent and Qualitative Variables in Econometrics*, Cambridge University Press.

Moore, B and Rhodes, J (1981) The convergence of earnings in the regions of the United Kingdom, in Martin, R L (ed) *Regional Wage Inflation and Unemployment*, Pion, London.

Murphy, D C (1985) Calculation of Gini and Theil inequality coefficients for Irish household incomes in 1973 and 1980, *The Economic and Social Review*, 16, 3, 225–49.

Narendranathan, W, Nickell, S and Stern, J (1985) Unemployment benefits revisited, *Economic Journal*, 95, 2, 307–29.

Sen, A (1976) Poverty: an ordinal approach to investment, *Econometrica*, 44, 219–31.

Energy

Michael A McGurnaghan

1. Introduction

The main purpose of this chapter is to examine the major energy issues and developments in Northern Ireland, with particular reference to the situation encountered in the period since the energy crises of the 1970s. While the problems associated with the rapid increases in oil prices and cutbacks in supply were responsible in large part for economic recessions in the world economy over ensuing years, the volatility of the international energy market had especial adverse consequences in a small isolated peripheral region such as Northern Ireland with oil as its dominant fuel. Given the importance of energy costs not only for the purpose of industrial development but also as a significant component of consumer expenditure in a region with income levels below the United Kingdom average, adapting to the changing economics of energy provision and energy management became a prime concern of the local economy. In this way, energy matters in Northern Ireland have been of more strategic importance and evoked greater government responses directly or indirectly than in any other region, until privatisation developments in recent years changed the status of all the energy supply industries throughout the United Kingdom.

The next section outlines two fundamental features which differentiate the province as a region of the United Kingdom with its own distinct and separate energy system and unique problems. Section 3 provides a statistical sketch of the existing energy profile and surveys the principal changes which have taken place in the supply and demand structure since the 1960s. Section 4 identifies the specific priorities of the government's energy policy for the province which is the background to the discussion of the electricity, gas and coal industries respectively. Section 5 deals with better energy efficiency and conservation as key factors in saving scarce resources and controlling costs. While many energy aspects are determined by external and often unpredictable forces not entirely under the province's control, conservation and greater efficiency of fuel consumption are among the main ways of mitigating some of the resulting disadvantages. A brief conclusion to the chapter is provided in Section 6.

2. Regional characteristics

Compared with either the Republic of Ireland or Great Britain, one major difference is the lack of available indigenous fossil fuels in Northern Ireland except for the recently established deposits of lignite which have not yet been developed – see Section 4. There is no production of coal and, unlike the Republic of Ireland, the use of the small peat reserves in Northern Ireland as an energy source is not significant. Exploration activity to date has indicated the possible existence of oil and gas but no proven evidence of viable quantities. The alternative of nuclear power for generating electricity is not a feasible option in a relatively small supply area like Northern Ireland. This option was considered in the past but the minimum scale of a commercially viable nuclear power station is far in excess of foreseeable demand and the option of a specially designed prototype reactor was ruled out as too expensive (NIES 1983). The only practical basis for a nuclear power station is to supply an all-Ireland system. In contrast, the government has given nuclear power a special and preferred position in the impending privatisation of the electricity supply industry in Great Britain (Department of Energy 1988). Other alternative non-fossil sources such as tide and wind power have not developed beyond the experimental stage.

A second key feature is the physical isolation of the province's energy system with no interconnection at present with any adjacent utility. Unlike the fully interconnected system in Great Britain where the grid transmission system in England and Wales has links both with Scotland and France, the province has the smallest isolated electricity system in the European Community. It is also the only region without access to a supply of natural gas. Alternative attempts in the late 1970s and early 1980s to establish a natural gas pipeline link from Scotland or from the Kinsale field off the south west coast of Ireland were unsuccessful and have led to the virtual disappearance of the gas industry in Northern Ireland. The possibility of an interconnecting submarine cable importing surplus coal-based electricity from the larger South of Scotland Electricity Board's system was investigated but ruled out as an economic proposition because of the cost and the uncertainty about excess capacity there after the year 2000 (NIES 1983, 1987; DED 1983). Only a very limited interchange of supplies occurred between 1971 and 1975 by means of an all-Ireland electricity interconnector agreed with the Republic of Ireland's state-owned Electricity Supply Board. This functioned with operational economies for both utilities until its disruption by terrorist action (McGurnaghan and Scott 1981). At present, there is little prospect of the interconnector with the Republic of Ireland being re-established, despite its desirability.

The lack of such networks, which are common internationally, is of considerable disadvantage with regard to the efficiency and security of a small system like Northern Ireland. This is due to the additional costs arising from the need for greater reserve capacity against emergencies. For example, the resulting cost to Northern Ireland Electricity (NIE) arising from the need to maintain a higher spinning reserve amounts currently to approximately £2.5

TABLE 10.1 Primary energy supplies,[1] Northern Ireland and the United Kingdom, 1963–1986 (percentage)

	1963		1968		1973		1981		1986	
	Northern Ireland	United Kingdom	Northern Ireland	United Kingdom	Northern Ireland	United Kingdom	Northern Ireland	United Kingdom	Northern Ireland	United Kingdom
Oil	47.9	30.4	62.4	41.3	79.8	46.5	78.1	35.0	78.4	35.6
Coal	52.1	68.1	37.6	53.3	20.2	37.6	21.9	37.3	21.6	32.8
Natural gas	—	0.1	—	1.5	—	12.5	—	22.7	—	24.7
Nuclear/Hydro-electricity	—	1.5	—	3.9	—	3.4	—	5.0	—	6.9
Total	100.0	100.0	100.0	100.0	100.0	100.0	100.0	100.0	100.0	100.0

[1] Includes use of energy for transport purposes.
Sources: DED (1983); NIAAS No 6 1987; UKDES, 1987.

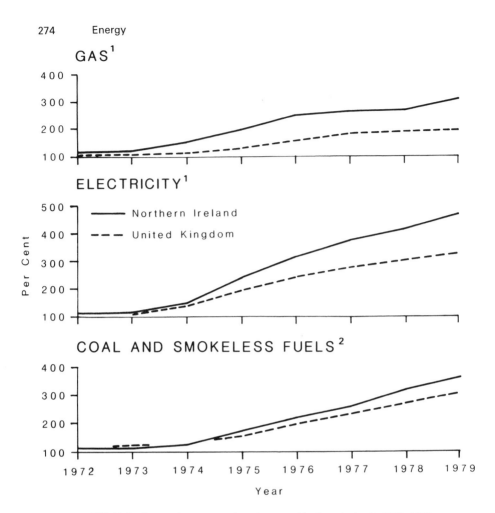

FIG 10.1   Domestic energy price changes, Northern Ireland, 1972–1979.
[1] Average annual price as a percentage of 1971 value.
[2] Price at January each year as a percentage of January 1971.
Source: Social and Economic Trends in Northern Ireland, No 6, 1980 (HMSO).

million a year (House of Commons 1987–88). The benefit of loadsharing through interconnection would help to smooth energy supply and so reduce costs to the system.

In the absence of developed indigenous sources of energy and power transfers, the province has had to import all its primary energy supplies. Together, these factors have made energy provision more expensive than in other regions. As Table 10.1 shows, in 1973 almost 80 per cent of primary energy in Northern Ireland was in the form of oil and this reliance remained virtually unchanged until 1986. With predominantly oil-fired electricity generation and gas derived from oil feedstock, Northern Ireland had benefited from relatively cheap energy in the 1960s and early 1970s. For example, in the decade prior to 1973 the cost of electricity sent out from power stations rose by less than the rate of inflation and the increase was due solely to non-fuel costs as the fuel price element in unit cost was practically the same throughout the period (NIES 1983). However, as Figure 10.1 shows, after 1973 fuel prices in Northern Ireland increased faster than the national average. By the end of 1979, it was estimated that domestic electricity prices were 25 per cent above average Great Britain levels, gas prices 153 per cent higher, coal prices 8 per cent higher, due to transport costs, and domestic fuel oil was similarly priced to mainland levels. On average, domestic fuel prices in Northern Ireland in that year were about 40 per cent higher than those in Great Britain although the price differential has decreased in recent years (Northern Ireland Consumer Council 1980, 1983, 1985; Northern Ireland Assembly 1984). To mitigate these effects, the government has subsidised both electricity and gas prices and is implementing currently a strategy centred on reducing the high dependence on oil as a generating fuel – see Section 4. Before examining the aims of energy policy, the province's existing energy balance will be sketched.

3. Energy profile

Northern Ireland's total primary energy supplies for fuelling power stations, domestic and industrial use, transport and other direct purposes in 1987 is shown in Figure 10.2, which reflects the vulnerability of the province's energy situation. All fuels consumed in the province are based either on oil (including naphtha used in the manufacture of town gas) which contributed 72 per cent of total primary energy needs or, to a much lesser extent, on coal. The electricity industry used the largest proportion, 40 per cent, of the total primary energy input of 4.12 million tonnes of oil equivalent (mtoe), the generating fuel mix being 80 per cent oil and 20 per cent coal. The transport sector used 22 per cent of primary energy supply with the remaining 38 per cent, of which 18 per

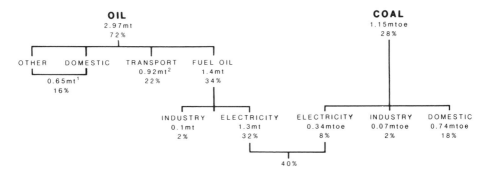

FIG 10.2 Primary energy supplies in Northern Ireland, 1987.
Note: mt = million tonnes; mtoe = million tons of oil equivalent; 1 mt of coal = 0.6 mtoe.
[1] Includes butane, propane, naphtha, burning oil and gas/diesel oil, excluding derv.
[2] Includes aviation spirit, motor spirit, aviation turbine fuel and derv fuel.
Source: UKDES (1988).

cent was oil or oil products, available to meet direct user needs for domestic, industrial and other purposes.

As Table 10.1 shows, the province's high dependence on oil contrasts with the wider range of primary energy sources available to the United Kingdom, where in 1986 oil accounted for 35.6 per cent of the input of primary energy to the economy, coal 32.8 per cent, natural gas 24.7 per cent and hydro- and nuclear energy almost 7 per cent. The Republic of Ireland is also more diversified in its primary energy sources than Northern Ireland, as shown in Figure 10.3. In 1986, oil contributed 53.7 per cent and coal 18.2 per cent of primary energy needs with native fuels accounting for 28.1 per cent.

Energy consumption by main fuel-using sectors in 1987 in Northern Ireland and the United Kingdom is shown in Table 10.2. Oil (66.5 per cent) and coal (23.8 per cent) were the province's most important fuel sources, dominating the non-domestic and domestic sectors respectively. In Northern Ireland, coal accounted for 64.4 per cent of total domestic energy consumption while gas provided only 1.4 per cent. This contrasts with the overall United Kingdom situation where gas had a 64.1 per cent share of domestic energy consumption: virtually the same as the domestic market share of coal in Northern Ireland. Only in relation to electricity is the share of a fuel in all sectors reasonably close regionally and nationally.

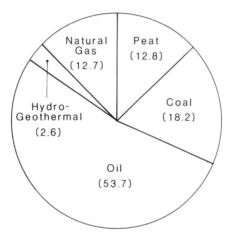

FIG 10.3 Primary energy input,[1] Republic of Ireland, 1986.
[1] Percentage mtoe.
Source: Department of Energy, Dublin.

Information on individual fuels is summarised in Figure 10.4 which shows the principal trends in energy supplied to final users (excluding transport) in Northern Ireland over the period 1965 to 1986. The period pre-1973 was characterised by a steady growth in oil and electricity use and a steady decline in coal. These movements reflected changes in relative prices and were consistent with consumer preferences for clean, convenient and flexible energy sources. In the period 1973 to 1981, total energy demand was

TABLE 10.2   Energy consumption by sector, Northern Ireland and the United Kingdom, 1987 (percentage)

Type of energy	Domestic		Industrial and other		Total	
	Northern Ireland	United Kingdom	Northern Ireland	United Kingdom	Northern Ireland	United Kingdom
Electricity	16.1	19.6	7.1	8.2	9.1	10.5
Public supply gas	1.4	64.1	0.3	13.1	0.6	23.3
Coal	64.4	11.0	11.9	41.8	23.8	35.6
Petroleum products	18.1	5.3	80.7	36.9	66.5	30.6
Total	100.0	100.0	100.0	100.0	100.0	100.0

Source: UKDES, 1988.

fairly constant up to 1979 but fell by almost 25 per cent between 1979 and 1981. The corresponding market shares of oil and coal remained largely unchanged while electricity increased fairly consistently and gas had a market share of just under 3 per cent.

Since 1981, there would appear to have developed a new pattern in Northern Ireland's energy markets with total energy demand increasing significantly between 1981 and 1985, although it fell again in 1986. The market share of oil fell in favour of coal which displaced oil both in 1983 and 1985 as the principal fuel used for heating, light and power, reversing the previous trend of almost 20 years. This was primarily because coal was preferred in the early 1980s as a central heating fuel when oil supplies were interrupted and there was considerable conversion to coal. Given the sharp fall in oil prices in more recent years compared to domestic coal prices, shown in Figure 10.5, it

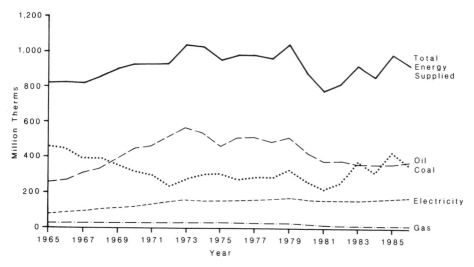

FIG 10.4   Energy supplied[1] to final consumers, Northern Ireland, 1965–1986.
[1] Excluding transport.
Source: DED (1983); NIAAS No 6, 1987.

HEAVY FUEL OIL PRICES (c.i.f.) NW EUROPE

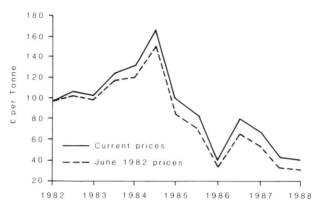

GROUP 2 COAL PRICES (BELFAST)

FIG 10.5 Fuel prices[1], 1982–1988.
[1] Constant price figures derived using RPI.
Sources: *Financial Times*; John Kelly Ltd, Belfast; MDS.

was predictable that oil would re-establish itself and this explains the increase in the demand for oil products in 1986.

Figure 10.6 shows the relative changes in domestic and industrial energy consumption between 1967 and 1985, particularly their contrasting performances since 1973. The decline in the industrial sector can be attributed to an overall poorer economic performance, particularly the recession in manufacturing after 1979 when a number of major factories closed. Increasing real energy prices and greater energy efficiency may also have had an effect. The significant increase in the domestic sector, despite the pronounced price changes, may be attributable largely to increasing personal disposable incomes outweighing the changes in energy prices.

Finally, the energy sector in Northern Ireland, in terms of overall economic activity in 1986, accounted for 4.2 per cent of Gross Domestic Product, 1.8 per cent of employment but approximately 16 per cent (1983 figure) of Gross Domestic Fixed Capital Formation. This made it the industry with the second highest level of investment in the province in that year. The

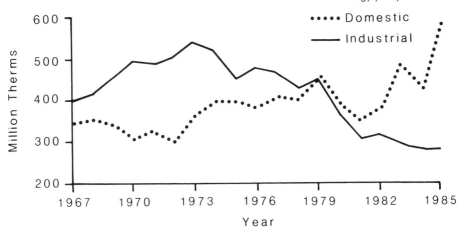

FIG 10.6 Domestic and industrial energy consumption, Northern Ireland, 1967–1985.
Source: *The Petroleum Review* December 1986, Vol. 40, No. 479, p 15.

relative importance of the energy sector in terms of output and employment
was similar to the national shares of 5.1 per cent and 1.4 per cent respectively.

4. Energy policy

In Northern Ireland, responsibility for energy policy is the remit of the
Department of Economic Development (DED), not the Department of Energy
as in other regions. Notwithstanding this separate administrative arrangement,
energy policy objectives in the province are expected to be broadly in line with
national policy of which a major aim is to ensure the efficient operation of
energy markets (DED 1983). While prices and the market mechanism thus
play a major role in the pattern of fuel usage, some intervention has been
deemed to be appropriate on equity and efficiency grounds. One obvious
departure from the market principle on equity grounds has been price
subsidisation in the electricity supply industry where there are strong natural
monopoly elements, particularly in transmission and distribution and where, in
the absence of competition, no true market can be said to exist. The resource
allocation implications of subsidisation have been far from clear.

However, the overriding issue has been the need to widen the
province's energy base by reducing the share of oil in the energy mix, a focal
point of weakness, and thus providing an improved diversity and security of
fuel supply. The strategy to secure this position is: first, and to date the most
important means, the diversification of the fuel mix in electricity generation to
reduce its dependence on oil through investment in capacity to use alternative
fuels; second, greater energy self-sufficiency through the exploitation of
indigenous sources when there would be an economic means of using these;
and, third, a wide range of conservation and energy efficiency measures and,
possibly, the longer term use of renewable sources. Of the various energy

industries, the electricity supply has been perceived as the most important problem and has been given priority by the government (Department of Commerce 1979).

ELECTRICITY

The electricity supply industry in Northern Ireland was brought together in 1973 under the control of a public monopoly, the Northern Ireland Electricity Service (NIES) – renamed Northern Ireland Electricity (NIE) in 1987. The NIES replaced four separate bodies, the Electricity Board for Northern Ireland, the electricity undertakings of Belfast Corporation and the Londonderry Development Commission and the Northern Ireland Joint Electricity Authority. At present, NIE is a vertically integrated entity with statutory responsibility for all aspects of generation, transmission and distribution in the province and as such is similar to the two Scottish electricity utilities. A decision to consider ways of privatising the Northern Ireland electricity system was made in July 1988 but it is not yet known what changes in its structure might result. With around 581,000 customers and a typical maximum demand in 1987 of 1,364 megawatts (MW) compared to the CEGB's peak demand of 46,935 MW, the Northern Ireland system is small and self-contained. A low population density in many parts of the province means that the distribution network is quite widely spread and relatively costly. Together, these factors prevent the fuller exploitation of economies of scale available to larger utilities and in more densely populated areas.

As Table 10.3 shows, there are four power stations in the province, located at Belfast West, Ballylumford, Coolkeeragh and Kilroot (Figure 10.7) with a total nominal installed generating capacity of 1,800 MW currently (1988), of which 86.7 per cent is oil-fired. Belfast West power station (240 MW) is the only coal-fired station. Built in the 1950s, it is probably the oldest functioning power station in the whole of the United Kingdom. This plant has contributed intensively to the economic operation of the system in recent years because the fuel price differential compensated for its relatively poor thermal efficiency and higher maintenance costs due to age. Of the oil-fired stations, Ballylumford is the largest with a capacity of 1,080 MW. Coolkeeragh (420 MW) is the oldest oil-fired plant and has been little used in recent years, having been held largely in reserve to give voltage support to the north west of the province.

Kilroot, the newest plant in the system, was planned in the early 1970s as a 1,200 MW oil-fired power station before the escalation in the price of oil changed a very rapid increase in electricity demand pre-1973 to a severely reduced growth pattern afterwards. As Figure 10.8 shows, growth in electricity consumption increased at a rate of about 9 per cent per annum in the 1960s and early 1970s. On the basis of an assumption of continuing stable oil prices and an accompanying long-term forecast of similar or higher growth (Ministry of Commerce 1971), it was decided in 1971 to construct Kilroot. However, high generating costs after 1973 and the probability of large excess capacity

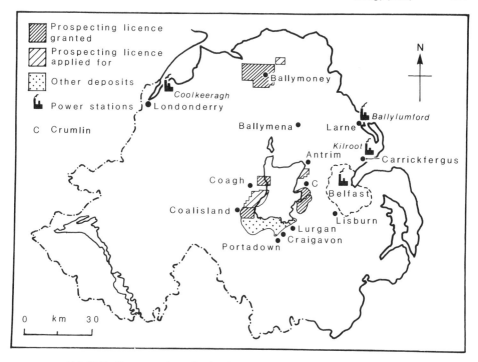

FIG 10.7   Power stations, lignite deposits and prospecting areas, Northern Ireland
Source: Jefferson (1989)

occurring when the new increment was completed led to a review of NIES's
financial position (Shepherd Report 1976). Subsequently, the government
decided to proceed with Kilroot's original oil-fired design and capacity but to
mitigate the industry's difficulties through a capital restructuring, together with
a subsidy of £20 million for each of 5 years, to reduce industrial and
commercial tariffs to average levels in England and Wales. Notwithstanding,
by 1980 there had developed a tariff differential of 22 per cent for domestic and
7 per cent for industrial consumers in Northern Ireland compared with the
average of those in the rest of the United Kingdom. As a result, in 1981 a new
subsidy was introduced which set electricity tariffs at the level of the highest
prevailing in England and Wales. Under this tariff link, the subsidy to NIE has
amounted to almost £350 million over the period 1981 to 1986. With the recent
fall in oil prices, however, there has been no need for subsidisation.

The first two generating sets, Kilroot Phase I, were completed and
operating by 1982. However, the prospect of continued recession following the
second oil crisis of 1979, meant shelving the instalment of the third and fourth
sets, Kilroot Phase II, although the plant for the sets had been purchased. To
achieve greater diversification in the fuel mix, NIES, at the government's
request, undertook a review of its future generation policy (NIES 1983). It was
recommended that Kilroot Phase I should be converted from oil to coal-firing
followed at a later stage by the completion of Phase II. In the event, Kilroot

TABLE 10.3   Generating plant stock in Northern Ireland, 1988

Site	Installed capacity (MW)	Plant load factor (%)	Thermal efficiency (%)	Units sent out (MWh)	Installation period (expected retirement)	Design life (years)
Coal-fired station						
Belfast West	240	49.2	27.2	979.1	1954–1958 (1994–1999)	40
Oil-fired stations						
Ballylumford 'B'	960	54.6	32.3	4,325.5	1968–1974 (1999–2005)	30
Gas turbines	120	0.7	23.0	7.1		
Coolkeeragh	360	17.2	24.0	502.3	1959–1967 (1990–2002)	30
Gas turbines	60	2.0	22.5	10.5		
Kilroot[1]	—	—	—	—	1981–1982 (2011–2012)	30
Gas turbines	60	1.7	25.1	9.1		

[1] Kilroot decommissioned 1986–89 for conversion to dual coal/oil-firing; recommissioning in 1989 with design rating of 520 MW (oil)/360 MW (coal).

Source: Northern Ireland Electricity Annual Report 1988.

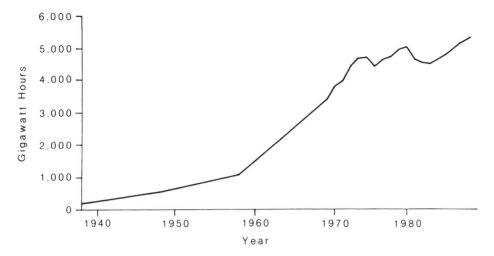

FIG 10.8 Electricity demand, Northern Ireland, 1938/39–1986/87.
Sources: DED (1983); NIAAS No 6, 1987.

Phase I was decommissioned in 1985 for conversion to dual coal/oil-firing. In the interim, its capacity is 60 MW of gas turbine plant but when recommissioned in 1989 it will have a combined design rating of either 520 MW oil-fired or 360 MW coal-fired.

The existing plant stock situation encapsulates the problems of NIE in recent years and its future capacity needs. With the exception of Kilroot, the system is reliant on ageing and predominantly oil-fired plant. Although there will be both a reduced dependence on oil for generation purposes and a surplus of capacity with the recommissioning of Kilroot Phase I in mid-1989, the Belfast West and Coolkeeragh stations are nearing the end of their operational lives and due to be retired in the mid-1990s. With an increase in electricity consumption of over 14 per cent between 1984 and 1988, there was a need for a programme of plant replacement to meet an anticipated growth in demand in the period leading up to the year 2000.

The amount and timing of new generating capacity required in Northern Ireland can be obtained by comparing the retirement of existing plant with forecasts of future maximum demand for electricity, making suitable allowance for a reserve margin of plant to meet the Generation Security Standard (GSS). As Figure 10.9 shows, up to 1995/96 it is assumed that life expired plant is phased out by year of commission and design life and the re-commissioned Kilroot Phase I is operating as an oil-fired station. From 1995/96 onwards the upper graph draws total generating capacity including the oil-fired capacity of Kilroot Phase II. The decision in August 1988 to complete Phase II similar to Phase I, for reasons discussed below, means that the new power station will probably be commissioned around 1995/96 with a combined design rating of 600 MW burning oil and 360 MW burning coal. The lower graph from 1995/96 onwards shows the situation without the planned commissioning of

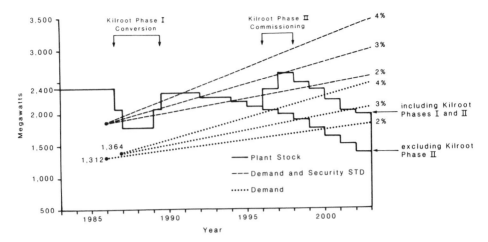

FIG 10.9 Generating capacity required by the Northern Ireland electricity system.
Source: NIEC (1987), Figure 5 (amended).

Kilroot Phase II but includes the oil-fired capacity of Phase I. If the coal-fired capacity for the complete Kilroot station is included instead of the oil-fired capacity, the upper plant stock graph from 1995/96 would be displaced downwards by 400 MW.

Forecasting electricity demand in Northern Ireland has been a risky task historically and previous over-estimation, as in the case of Kilroot where the sudden increase in oil prices was unforeseen, caused excess capacity to be installed with serious financial implications. In line with estimates that electricity demand is expected to increase at a long-term rate of over 2 per cent per annum (NIE 1987), growth of maximum demand from 1986 to 2002 is shown at rates of 2, 3 and 4 per cent per annum: the latter rates may be more realistic assumptions. Unlike other undertakings, the electricity service has a statutory requirement to supply all reasonable demands for electricity from its customers which means a margin of surplus capacity additional to the amount necessary to meet an actual level of demand. The GSS provides the basis for determining required plant margin over expected peak winter demand which, in the case of the Northern Ireland system operating in isolation, has been estimated to be about 40 per cent (NIEC 1987). This has been added to demand.

From Figure 10.9, the 2 per cent growth rate plus the GSS outstrips available capacity by 1994/95 or earlier depending on whether annual demand for electricity grows at higher rates. While there are uncertainties about the possibilities of refurbishment and plant life extension, the forecasts predict that if economic progress was maintained, new generating capacity would be needed, first by 1995, and then further investment by the beginning of the next century. Given the lead times involved, the decision on construction would need to be made well in advance if the form of the additional capacity involved a new power station. Accordingly, the dominant issue in recent years has been the form of the first tranche of new generating capacity and, more significantly, the role of the private sector in future electricity provision.

The two main alternatives were:

(i)   a new 450 MW purpose-built power station, constructed by NIE or by the private sector, alongside the lignite ('brown coal') deposits at Crumlin, Co Antrim;

(ii)   for NIE to maximise the use of its existing plant by completing Kilroot Phase II similar to Phase I.

Knowledge of the existence of lignite in the province goes back to the 18th century but it remained largely unexplored until the changing economics of energy in the 1970s encouraged further investigation. The deposits are in three main sites, Crumlin and Coagh around the Lough Neagh shoreline with a third major seam at Ballymoney, Co Antrim, with proven reserves of lignite sufficient as a feedstock supply for a medium sized power station well beyond the year 2000 (Figure 10.7). Total recoverable deposits at Crumlin, where exploratory mining began first in the late 1970s, are estimated at 420 million tonnes, of which about two-thirds lies offshore (NIEC 1987). Geological survey discovered the Ballymoney site at a later date and thus development has not been as far advanced as at Crumlin. On the basis of available information, it probably has much greater potential with proven reserves of 530 million tonnes, of which 350 million tonnes lie outside the town, with thicker seams nearer the surface (Meekatharra 1987). Coagh is least advanced with detailed exploration work yet to begin but there are geological estimates of 300 million tonnes of lignite to be mined.

As the first major available indigenous energy source, great importance was attached to its exploitation to meet the balance of the province's electricity requirements in the 1990s. Although of a lower calorific value than bituminous coal, lignite is an important energy source in many countries and international experience suggested that its most effective use

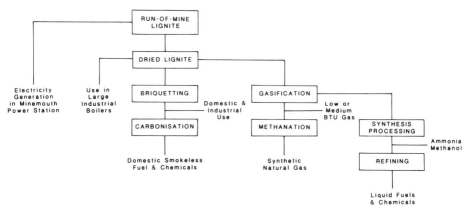

FIG 10.10   Possible uses of lignite
Source: Jefferson (1989).

would be to burn it in a raw state in a power station close to the supply source. As Figure 10.10 shows, it can have other potential economically viable uses through commercial and industrial applications such as carbonising and briquetting to compete with other solid fuels in the domestic market or liquefaction and gasification as an industrial fuel. However, the most immediate substantial market for lignite in Northern Ireland was perceived to be electricity generation with the possibility of further use in a briquetted form. Given the difficulties that overdependence on imported oil had caused in the past, the development of lignite particularly as a means of diversifying the generating fuel mix held out the possibility of reducing both electricity costs and the adverse effects of world energy developments. With the image of a region assured of a long period of self-reliance for power station fuel supply, it would have the potential to attract new industry if it produced the expected cheaper energy.

In 1985, the government authorised NIE to make preliminary planning for a new purpose-built 450 MW lignite-fired station, an optimum size for the province's system and which would be the United Kingdom's first lignite-fired power station. At the same time, a number of private sector consortia were also encouraged to submit bids for evaluation. As information was more advanced about the Crumlin site, proposals were centred there originally although potential operators were later encouraged to consider the Ballymoney deposit. Apart from the appeal of promoting competition into generation, the attraction of a private sector project was the positive impact of what could be the biggest single investment ever made in the region with the highest unemployment rate in the United Kingdom. Antrim Power Company Limited, the consortium set up to develop the Crumlin operation, projected an input of private capital involving about £700 million drawn from national and international sources, creating 2,000 jobs during the construction phase and an estimated 600 long-term jobs involved in mining and operating the new plant. In view of the high capital costs of such a power station, a private sector project had the additional benefit that it would not be constrained by competing for scarce financial resources from the Northern Ireland public expenditure programme as would a public sector programme.

The alternative option was the completion of Kilroot Phase II by NIE with a dual oil/coal-fired capability as a follow-on later stage in the diversification strategy which had commenced in 1985 with the conversion of Phase I. Already virtually completed and costing a further £150 million, it would yield an output of 360 MW coal-fired or 600 MW oil-fired and would give NIE the option of using the cheaper fuel at any time and begin to secure electricity supplies at an earlier date than a green field lignite-fired power station. In the face of the government's intention to consider a privately funded project and the prospect of losing its monopoly status in generation, NIE's preferred option was expansion at Kilroot first, followed at a later date in all probability by a lignite-fired station at the most economic site. Accepting that lignite must be part of any future generating strategy, it argued for delaying development of the Crumlin site until fuller investigation of the viability of all deposits.

Evaluating the rival projects was an exceptionally complex task, finely balanced economically, with a decision in 1988 in favour of completing Kilroot Phase II as the more cost-effective means of providing the new generating capacity. The choice was particularly difficult because the method of appraisal involved comparisons of plant of different sizes using different fuels over a 30-year period and, in the case of lignite, a technology of which there was no experience in the United Kingdom (Hewitt 1988). In the government's view, the fall in oil and coal prices since May 1985 when the appraisal began and their current levels plus lower capital costs were decisive factors in favour of Kilroot Phase II. Although this meant that the original intention of developing the Crumlin site was abandoned at least in the short term, it was nevertheless anticipated that the next major investment after Kilroot would be lignite. Given lead times, this would mean a further decision in the early 1990s about where the next power station should be, with all lignite options open.

Coupled with its preference for the dual-fired Kilroot Phase II, the government also announced that NIE would be privatised for the purpose of introducing competition into the Northern Ireland electricity system. Ahead of this development, the Electricity Supply (Northern Ireland) (Amendment) Order which came into effect in September 1987 had already removed the ban on privately generated electricity supplying the Northern Ireland grid. It is not possible to predict at this stage the form which privatisation might take in the province but the choice lies between transferring NIE to the private sector with its integrated monopoly position in generation and distribution intact, subject to a strong regulatory arrangement on tariff levels, or selling off parts of the system as in the rest of the United Kingdom. In England and Wales generation is to be split between two companies that will run the power stations with control of transmission transferred to a separate grid company owned by the various distribution companies. Given the nature of the industry in Northern Ireland, however, the scope for competition is likely to be more limited and hence the reforms might be expected to be far less than' the Great Britain scheme.

There are a number of fairly obvious questions which arise in privatising the electricity supply industry in Northern Ireland. The first question is whether the system is too small to contemplate any split-up of the assets in generation. There may not be the same presumption of a natural monopoly here as in distribution. The issue, therefore, is whether the existing plant can be split profitably between more than one operator, each of an efficient size. With a relatively limited maximum load in the province, a single electricity station would tend to be dominant and, if running constantly at maximum efficiency, would take the profitable base load function. It may be that competition in generation could be introduced by allowing future expansion in the mid-1990s to be undertaken by a new operator along the lines which had already been explored in relation to the Crumlin project.

Irrespective of this, a second question is whether there are any gains to be made by separating distribution from generation. This has been answered in relation to Great Britain and in particular to Scotland which is perhaps the more obvious comparison with Northern Ireland: the gains from the Scottish system are expected to result from competition between two vertically integrated systems. If technical considerations make it impossible to have competition of this type in Northern Ireland and with the lack of external competition, it is difficult to conclude that there are significant gains to be made from the privatisation process except possibly through pressure from a strong regulatory authority.

Obviously, the development of Kilroot as a modern dual-fired plant would improve the utility's attractiveness to investors and it can be presumed that the government would maximise revenue if NIE was to be sold with its monopoly position undiminished. However, the fundamental question of how much competition will flow from privatisation is more problematic. Finally, there is the practical question of whether the tariff link will be cut with the local industry free to set price to cover cost and the possible implications of this for any significant future increase in tariffs.

GAS

The change-over in gas production in the mid-1960s from carbonising coal to the more efficient continuous catalytic re-forming of naphtha, an oil-based feedstock, led to a growth period for the gas industry in Northern Ireland. Between 1964/65 when the new re-forming plants were introduced initially and 1973/74, gas sales increased by almost 20 per cent in competition with electricity and oil in the traditional cooking and heating markets. However, increasing difficulties in the industry since then culminated during the period between 1986 and 1988 in the closure of all but one small private supplier out of the 13 mostly separate mains gas undertakings. Apart from this sole very small exception, Northern Ireland is the only region in the United Kingdom and within the European Community in which there is no supply of piped gas either as a primary or a secondary fuel.

Initially, the decline of the gas industry was the result of rapidly increasing production costs after 1973 reflected in the consequential effect of higher tariffs and falling sales. A subsequent factor was the uncertainty about the industry's future following the failure to obtain a natural gas supply which induced many potential new gas users to opt for alternative fuels such as electricity or bottled (LPG) gas and caused existing consumers to switch from gas. For example, the manufacturing cost index for the Belfast Gasworks, the largest undertaking and representing 75 per cent of the industry, increased from 100 in 1971 to 323 in 1978 (Brown 1980). In 1988 before closure, gas prices in Belfast were at least three times as high as in Great Britain. The level of consumption fell steadily over the decade from the mid-1970s and by 1986 the number of customers had declined to a third of the 187,000 who were supplied in the early 1970s. To cope with the industry's financial losses, the government intervened from 1974 with subsidies which represented 40 per cent of operating costs by 1982/83 (DED 1983).

This situation compares unfavourably with the gas industry in Great

Britain where wide availability of natural gas by the mid-1970s meant its radical transformation from a relatively minor producer of secondary fuels to a major fuel supplier with economies of scale from an expanding market. As Table 10.1 shows, in 1968 natural gas provided 1.5 per cent of the United Kingdom's primary forms of energy but by 1986 it accounted for almost 25 per cent. As Table 10.2 shows, by 1987 gas accounted for 64.1 per cent of energy consumption by the domestic sector in the United Kingdom and 13.1 per cent of industrial and other sectors: in Northern Ireland the shares were 1.4 per cent and 0.3 per cent respectively.

Government policy has been that Northern Ireland would have access to natural gas only if it could be obtained at a competitive price to ensure a viable industry and as an economic proposition with regard to public expenditure (Energy Statement 1977). The first occasion when the matter was considered was in 1976 when the British Gas Corporation (BGC 1977) was commissioned to evaluate the various options for making gas available to Northern Ireland. As Table 10.4 shows, none of the seven options offered the prospect of a profitable situation developing. Of the alternatives which appeared to have a realistic possibility of implementation, importing North Sea gas by pipeline from Scotland had the lowest projected financial loss and was the preferred choice of the local gas industry. While importing natural gas from the Republic of Ireland was a cheaper (less unprofitable) option, the only proven reserve at that time was the relatively small Kinsale field and this was

TABLE 10.4 Options for the continuation of the Northern Ireland gas industry (£m, April 1977 prices)

Option	Capital costs	Deficits to 1988/89
1 Importation of liquefied natural gas to Belfast, satellite storage at other works	47.4	105.3
2 Importation of liquefied natural gas to Belfast, high pressure mains to other works	51.3	105.9
3 Piped natural gas from Scotland	76.3	85.7
4 Piped natural gas from the Republic of Ireland	55.0	62.2
5 Importation of liquefied petroleum gas to Belfast, satellite storage at other works	45.5	101.5
6 Importation of liquefied petroleum gas to Belfast as synthetic natural gas feedstock. High pressure mains to other works	59.3	135.2
7 Importation of liquefied petroleum gas to Belfast, satellite storage at other works. Distribution as bottled gas	16.9	40.7

Source: British Gas Corporation, 1977.

discounted as not a sufficiently adequate supply source. On the basis of the BGC Report, the government decided that a gas supply by pipeline from Scotland at an economic price did not provide the basis for a viable industry and that it had no choice but to close the industry and assist consumers to change to alternative forms of energy.

An important consideration against the pipeline option was the potential economic cost to the Northern Ireland electricity supply industry with its large surplus capacity. This commitment to the electricity industry is a clear example of the greater inter-linkage between energy industries in a small energy market like Northern Ireland where the impact of additional growth in one energy industry would be of greater significance to the market position of another utility than in a larger supply system.

With regard to the alternative of importing natural gas from the Republic of Ireland, there was a further proposal in 1981 to extend the Kinsale pipeline northwards. From Northern Ireland's point of view, the objective was a transfer price which would be low enough to attract the necessary new domestic, commercial and industrial consumers. For the Republic of Ireland, the basis for determining an appropriate pricing policy was that making gas available was not warranted unless Northern Ireland would be willing to pay a return which represented the real resource cost of natural gas to the Republic of Ireland's economy. This second and final attempt was also unsuccessful because of the Republic of Ireland's insistence on an oil-related supply price and the inadequate demand for gas in Northern Ireland at that relatively high price. As a result, the planned closure of the gas industry in Northern Ireland got under way in 1985. In retrospect, it was ironic that shortly after the Kinsale negotiations had terminated, the price of oil fell decisively by which time the process of closure was irreversible.

Although town gas was only a small supplier of the province's energy needs, its real significance was in providing an extra fuel option. Its failure to establish itself to any great extent in the industrial sector was due mainly to the absence in Northern Ireland of such large users of gas as the iron and steel and heavy chemical industries prevalent in Great Britain. However, companies such as some of the big bakeries and aircraft manufacturing who prefer its use for their processes have chosen to switch to LPG. In the domestic market, the 1988 Fuel Usership Survey indicated that in the cooker market electricity has been the main beneficiary of the closure of the gas industry. On closure of the gas industry in Belfast, present indications in terms of central heating are that 48 per cent of households heated by town gas would opt for coal, 38 per cent for electricity with the remainder shared almost equally between oil and LPG (Coal Advisory Service 1988).

COAL

The general situation for coal used in Northern Ireland over the period 1963 to 1986 is shown in Table 10.5, with much of the principal change having occurred by 1973. In 1963, the domestic sector provided the largest market for coal,

TABLE 10.5 Volume and uses of coal imported into Northern Ireland, 1963–1986[1]

	1963		1973		1981		1984		1985		1986[3]	
	'000 tonnes	%	'000 tonnes	%	'000 tonnes	%	'000 tonnes	%	'000 tonnes	%	'000 tonnes	%
Domestic use[2]	1,178	44	779	55	856	62	1,225	88	1,638	75	1,310	78
Industrial and commercial use	505	19	212	15	28	2	27	2	61	3	91	5
Electricity generation	687	26	437	31	487	36	144	10	496	22	288	17
Manufacture of gas	303	11	—	—	—	—	—	—	—	—	—	—
Total	2,673	100	1,428	100	1,371	100	1,396	100	2,195	100	1,689	100

[1] Figures prior to 1983 relate only to shipments by National Coal Board. From 1983 figures are inclusive of NCB and other sources of coal including foreign imports.
[2] Some of the slack arising from coal shipped for domestic use is sold for industrial or other purposes as the supply exceeds the demand from domestic consumers.
[3] Excludes shipments into NI of petroleum coke; includes coal shipped into NI and re-exported.
Sources: DED (1983); NIAAS No 6, 1987.

accounting for 44 per cent of the total amount imported, while the industrial and commercial sectors took a significant 19 per cent share. Coal's use as a primary fuel in the electricity and gas industries accounted for a further 37 per cent. By 1973, coal had ceased to be used for gas manufacture and its consumption had declined overall. In the period 1973 to 1981, its use in industry and commerce reduced very noticeably although in recent years there are indications of a reversal in this trend. Also in the period up to 1981, coal burnt for electricity generation increased from 31 per cent to 36 per cent but this has since declined and fluctuated erratically. Meanwhile, it consolidated its present position as predominantly a domestic fuel, accounting for 64.4 per cent of domestic energy consumption in 1987 (see Table 10.2).

Regarding the domestic use of solid fuels, Northern Ireland is a very different market situation from the mainland, taking around 21 per cent of United Kingdom domestic coal consumption in 1987/88 for less than 3 per cent of the population. The Continuous Household Survey (Department of Finance and Personnel 1988) found that in 1985, 51 per cent of Northern Ireland households used coal for winter heating and solid fuel in some form was the most commonly used fuel for heating in summer. Of public sector housing with central heating, 80 per cent used solid fuel. In 1985, only 16 per cent of all homes in Great Britain used coal for main heating. This relatively greater level of domestic coal consumption has developed over a considerable period of time, probably because consumers have not had access to low priced natural gas. It may be presumed that their preferences would conform more closely to the national pattern if such a supply had been available at similar prices in the province. In its absence, coal will most likely remain widely used as a domestic heating fuel. As Figure 10.11 shows, a further characteristic of the domestic coal market is the increasing proportion of smokeless fuel sales from 12.6 per cent of total solid fuel sales in 1973/74 to almost 40 per cent by 1987/88. This trend has been due to the creation of smokeless zones combined with the installation of new coal-burning systems, particularly in the public housing sector in anticipation of the closure of the town-gas industry. As the Clean Air programme is extended, especially in the Belfast Urban Area, housecoal sales will reduce further.

The general importance of coal as the dominant domestic fuel in Northern Ireland can be seen from the percentage of household expenditure allocated to energy needs. From Table 10.6 it can be seen that average weekly expenditure on fuel, light and power in 1985/86 was the highest for any region, £15.52 compared with the national figure of £10.20, or 9.4 per cent of total expenditure in Northern Ireland against 5.9 per cent overall in the United Kingdom. Of expenditure allocated to energy needs, coal comprised 48 per cent compared to a national average of just over 10 per cent. In terms of the pattern of household expenditure on fuel, Northern Ireland more closely resembles the Republic of Ireland than any region of the United Kingdom. Given this situation, the supply and price of domestic coal in the province has attracted considerable attention, in particular from consumer organisations, concerning underlying trading practices and pricing policy (Commission of the European Communities 1986).

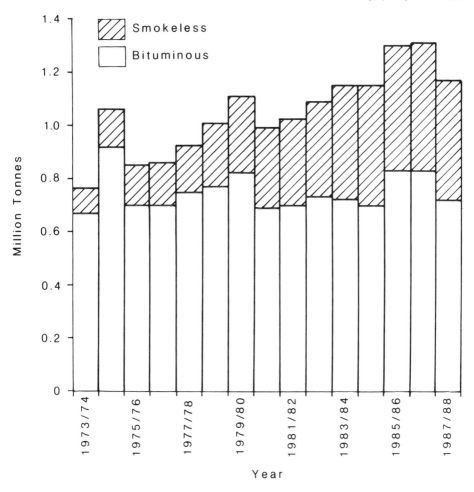

FIG 10.11   Domestic coal sales, Northern Ireland, 1973/74–1987/88.
Source: Coal Advisory Service Annual Report 1987/88, Belfast.

British Coal, previously the National Coal Board, is the main supplier of solid fuel to Northern Ireland. In 1987/88 about 80 per cent of all supplies to the province came from this source: some 93 per cent of all housecoal and 55 per cent of smokeless fuels were supplied by British Coal. The importation and distribution of coal and smokeless fuels are undertaken through a variety of different sized companies. The wholesale market is organised through the Northern Ireland Coal Importers' Association (NICIA), the members of which account for all but a very small tonnage of imports to the province. Although there are 11 importers with significant tonnages, the coal trade is oligopolistic in nature with the two largest companies accounting for some 60 per cent of total imports. These two companies are also involved in shipment. The retail trade is mainly in the hands of a large number of small independent merchants (between 800 and 900) and numerous cash and carry outlets. Most of the importers also sell direct to the public.

Whilst the coal trade is free to import directly from the world market, the major firms have been able to secure significant rebates on housecoal from British Coal to match the price of imports and prevent a shift in demand from this source. As a result, retail prices of British Coal in 1988 were lower in Belfast than in many United Kingdom cities such as Liverpool, London, Plymouth, Bristol and Glasgow (Coal Advisory Service 1988). Only in the main coalfield areas of England were prices lower. Given the additional transport costs incurred, housecoal would appear at this time to be somewhat cheaper in Northern Ireland than might have been expected. Nevertheless, because the coal market in Northern Ireland is dominated by a couple of large companies and given the existence of a rebate and with retail prices aligned with those on the mainland, there is a viewpoint that coal prices in Northern Ireland should be subject to more competitive pressures.

As far as British smokeless fuels are concerned, retail prices vary depending on the fuel. Prices are closer to those in the United Kingdom and relatively more expensive. However, the impact of higher relative prices for British smokeless fuels in Northern Ireland is offset by an increasing demand for the wide range of cheaper foreign smokeless coals available. These now account for 45 per cent of the total smokeless market.

The other main uses of coal in the province are for electricity generation and as an energy source for industry and commerce, 17 per cent and 5 per cent of tonnage in 1986 respectively. The government's preoccupation is directed to the wider use of coal in both these areas as a benefit to the economy in terms of diversification and reduced dependence on oil. Accordingly, priority has been given to coal as an alternative generating fuel. NIE consumed 336,000 tonnes of coal in 1986/87 at Belfast West, which was the only coal-fired station in the system and sent out 678.5 million units out of a total of over 6,000 million or about 10 per cent of the electricity needed. It is difficult to predict the effect of Kilroot Phase I as far as coal usage is concerned. Whether it is used for coal- or oil-fired generation will depend on the respective prices of the fuels and efficiencies. When fully completed, Kilroot Phase I will have an installed capacity of 520 MW oil burning or 360 MW coal burning. In the case of the latter, the percentage of total capacity available by coal burning would increase to around 30 per cent. Coal consumption for electricity generation could, therefore, increase to between two and three times its present figure after 1989, assuming maximum coal-fired generation.

The decision to develop Kilroot Phase II represents a further possible market of 500,000 tonnes of coal a year. As long as NIE or its successor were free to purchase supplies on the world market, it seems likely that British Coal would match this price in respect to any new contracts.

Industry and commerce provide a very small market for coal. The use of coal in these sectors declined from a total of 505,000 tonnes in 1963 to 27,000 tonnes in 1984, or from 19 per cent to only 2 per cent of total coal used.

TABLE 10.6 Average weekly household expenditure on fuel, light and power, regions of the United Kingdom and the Republic of Ireland, 1985/86 (£)

Fuel	Northern Ireland	North	Yorks & Humber	North West	East Midlands	West Midlands	East Anglia	South East	South West	Wales	Scotland	United Kingdom	Republic of Ireland[1]
Coal	7.45	1.29	0.78	0.50	1.11	0.82	1.62	0.47	1.34	2.27	1.28	1.04	3.65[2]
Electricity	4.96	4.01	4.35	4.60	4.20	4.63	4.92	4.53	5.05	4.68	5.26	4.61	2.91
Fuel oil	2.75	0.45	0.33	0.28	0.64	0.48	1.24	0.80	1.12	0.84	0.57	0.65	0.92
Gas	0.35	3.87	4.34	4.50	3.96	4.10	2.92	4.39	3.00	3.18	3.16	3.89	1.02
Total fuel, light and power[4]	15.52	9.61	9.80	9.89	9.91	10.03	10.71	10.06	10.52	10.99	10.27	10.20	8.95[3]
Coal as % of total fuel, light and power	48.0	13.4	8.0	5.1	11.2	8.2	15.1	4.7	12.7	20.7	12.5	10.2	40.8
All expenditure	164.79	146.59	149.16	159.56	161.30	159.81	174.10	207.68	177.66	158.01	161.01	173.89	113.54
Total fuel etc as % of family expenditure	9.4	6.6	6.6	6.2	6.1	6.3	6.2	4.8	5.9	7.0	6.4	5.9	7.9

[1] 1981 latest year for which data are available; figures converted to £ sterling, 1981 prices.
[2] Including turf and briquettes.
[3] Including other fuel and light, mainly wood and kindling.
[4] Details may not sum to total due to rounding.
Sources: FES 1986; HBS 1981 (CSO, Dublin).

A cheap oil price regime prior to 1973 meant a preference for oil-fired plant because of its lower capital cost, ease of maintenance and lower labour requirement. Although coal was a cheaper fuel after 1973, the trend was not reversed due in part to the general depressed energy demand from industry in this period and the closure of a number of major users of coal. In recent years, consumption has increased to 91,000 tonnes, or 5 per cent of total coal usage in 1986. It accounted for only 11.9 per cent of industrial and other energy consumption in Northern Ireland compared with 41.8 per cent in the United Kingdom as a whole (see Table 10.2). The greater non-domestic market for coal in Great Britain arises from the different structure of energy intensive industries in both areas. For example, in Northern Ireland there is no iron and steel industry; the major industrial user of coal at present is the cement industry. The opportunity for assessing the further prospects of any significant industrial switching to coal-fired plant will occur from the late 1980s onwards as the existing boiler stock, much of which was installed in the rapid economic development period of the 1960s, reaches the end of its operational life and requires replacement.

5. Conservation

Northern Ireland shares the prevailing philosophy of the national energy policy which is both to reduce significantly the consumption of depletable fossil fuels, especially oil, and to improve efficiency in energy use so as to maintain reserves for future essential uses. In this strategy, the province has acknowledged the relevant initiatives of the United Kingdom energy conservation programme. Moreover, without the development of either indigenous natural resources or renewable sources of energy, there has been an additional concern for promoting the efficient use of energy in the province because of the cost disadvantage to the economy of having to import its fuel requirements.

In addition to the energy awareness of consumers themselves, an important element has been the government's involvement in supplementing the price mechanism where there may be limited information or means with respect to the relative economic efficiencies of the choices available. Efforts to encourage energy-saving activities are made, through information and exhortation, regulation, advisory and training services and financial incentives aimed at greater home insulation, the installation of more efficient equipment and flexibility in the choice of fuels and industrial processes in all sectors. The main fuel efficiency policies in Northern Ireland have included the following:

(i) The Energy Conservation Scheme (ECS), which operated throughout the United Kingdom between 1983 and 1988 and contributed to the more efficient use of energy in general by offering grants toward replacing or improving inefficient boiler plant, insulating premises, waste heat recovery systems and the more efficient use of existing technology. Up to the end of 1987, over 440 projects were carried out in Northern Ireland with an estimated saving of some £4 million per annum. The ECS scheme was replaced in June 1988 by a new Energy Efficiency Survey scheme under which grants are available for industrial and commercial companies to employ independent consultants to carry out detailed examination of premises or plant to identify the potential for cost-effective improvements in energy efficiency.

(ii) Regarding changes in industrial and commercial coal consumption, the National Coal Firing Scheme which operated between 1981 and 1987 provided assistance towards the cost of approved conversion of boilers to use solid fuel. The uptake was fairly modest with available information showing that during its period of operation 15 projects from Northern Ireland were accepted under the scheme with an estimated coal burn of 101,000 tonnes and oil saving of 55,000 tonnes.

Assessment was also made of a combined heat and power (CHP) system for Belfast to use the waste heat associated with the production of electricity in thermal power stations. CHP's ability to reduce considerably the use of fossil fuels by effectively displacing their burning to heat buildings and the environmental appeal of reduced pollution levels are already recognised in a number of European countries. The idea of such a scheme to produce cheaper power in Northern Ireland was envisaged at the time of the review of future electricity generation strategy and would effectively have provided a large-scale district heating system for the inner city area similar to existing heating schemes in the public housing sector operated by the Northern Ireland Housing Executive.

Following an investigation by the Department of Energy in a number of cities in the United Kingdom, Belfast was identified as offering potential for the development of a CHP scheme. In 1984 the government grant-aided a feasibility study, undertaken by a local consortium Joint Venture for Belfast (JVB). Its report (JVB 1988) showed that the project could be viable in certain circumstances but concluded that the essential risk, especially in developing the market, precluded the funding being provided entirely by private sector investment. Consequently, the government declined further support.

As far as the available data allow adequate conclusions to be drawn about improvements in general energy efficiency, the trends in Figure 10.4 show that between 1975 and 1985 there was a reduced demand for oil with increased coal substitution although there was an upward trend in the total energy supplied to final users after 1981. As might have been expected from the events covered by the period since 1973, there has also been a weakening in the link between energy consumption and economic output. Table 10.7 shows clearly a decline in the energy intensity of economic growth in Northern Ireland, measured in terms of primary energy consumption per £ of real GDP, from a ratio of 0.47 in 1973 to 0.36 in 1987. This was similar to the national experience, although somewhat more erratic in recent years.

TABLE 10.7 Primary energy consumption, gross domestic product and energy ratio, Northern Ireland and the United Kingdom, 1963–1987

	Northern Ireland			United Kingdom		
	Primary energy consumption (m therms)	Gross domestic product at 1980 factor cost (£m)	Energy ratio (1)/(2)	Primary energy consumption (m therms)	Gross domestic product at 1980 factor cost (£m)	Energy ratio (4)/(5)
	(1)	(2)	(3)	(4)	(5)	(6)
1963	975	2,331.5	0.42	70,575	137,186	0.52
1968	1,383	3,059.5	0.45	78,225	161,641	0.48
1973	1,769	3,732.8	0.47	88,550	188,481	0.47
1978	1,778	4,089.7	0.43	84,775	198,820	0.43
1981	1,539	3,985.5	0.39	78,825	196,475	0.40
1983	1,676	4,243.0	0.40	78,400	206,789	0.38
1987	1,771	4,971.7	0.36	83,325	236,483	0.35

Sources: DED (1983); NIEC Paper No 38, May 1983; NIAAS No 7, 1988; UKDES 1988.

6. Conclusion

Northern Ireland is a region with inherent energy problems. These stem from two factors: first, the province lacks developed indigenous energy sources and second, it is a small and isolated system so that secondary energy production is likely to be inherently more expensive because of a widespread distribution network and the lack of economies of scale. However, the ways to deal with the situation are severely limited. It is important to ensure for industrial competitiveness that energy is as cheap as possible. Moreover, in a region that already has lower average income levels, it is particularly unfortunate that domestic consumers are paying electricity tariffs higher than average mainland levels with no access to natural gas. Given these circumstances, it is extremely important to have the energy industries as efficient and cheap as possible with the need to concentrate on energy saving. In the last analysis, the success of any future privatisation has to be judged in terms of its contribution to reducing the costs of electricity production.

One positive aspect is the possibility of developing lignite as a cheap energy source. If lignite does not help and energy costs still remain high, there is a dilemma. Is it acceptable that the economy suffers all the consequences or should the government subsidise? It has not been necessary to subsidise electricity tariffs recently. However, this may be a short-term aberration and, in the long run, prices are not likely to be at desirable levels *vis-à-vis* the rest of the United Kingdom. One possibility that has to be considered is to reduce industry's costs at the expense of other customers. This would create problems of equity but the thought of continued subsidisation of energy in Northern Ireland might not appear so radical or unacceptable when it is realised that in Great Britain these problems are to some extent obscured by substantial cross-subsidisation between regions because of the way the energy industries are organised there.

References

Bailey, R (1988) Privatising electricity in the United Kingdom – problems in store, *National Westminster Bank Quarterly Review*, November 1988, 38–52.
Berrie, T W (1983) *Power System Economics*, Peter Peregrinus Ltd, London.
Borooah, V K and Smyth, M F (1987) *Lignite – Who Benefits*, University of Ulster at Jordanstown.
British Gas Corporation (1977) *The Gas Industry in Northern Ireland*.
Brown, J M (1980) *The Gas Industry – Past, Present and Future in Northern Ireland*. Paper presented to Irish Gas Association in Portrush.
Central Electricity Generating Board (1988) *Annual Report and Accounts for the Year ended 31 March 1988*, London.
Coal Advisory Service (1988) *Annual Report 1987/88*, Belfast.
Commission of the European Communities (1986) *Commission Decision authorising Agreements made in Relation to the Activities of the Northern Ireland Coal Importers' Association (NICIA)*, C(86)431.

Coopers and Lybrand Associates (1980) *Economic and Financial Feasibility Study of a Natural Gas Pipeline from Great Britain*, Belfast.

Department of Commerce (1979) *Energy Policy in Northern Ireland*. Statement by Mr Giles Shaw MP, Northern Ireland Information Service, Belfast.

Department of Economic Development (1983) *Northern Ireland Energy Issues*, Belfast.

Department of Economic Development (1988) *General Assistance (Capital Grants), Local Enterprise Development Unit, Energy Conservation Scheme*, HMSO, Belfast.

Department of Energy (1987) *Energy Policy*, HMSO, London (Cmnd 7101).

Department of Energy (1988), *Privatising Electricity*, HMSO, London (Cm 322).

Department of Finance and Personnel (1988) *The Continuous Household Survey: Heating and Fuel 1983–85*, PPRU Monitor 2/88, Belfast.

Economic Bulletin for Europe (1984) The impact of energy on future economic growth, 36, 157–231.

Hardcastle, R and Evans, R D (1984) *The Changing Pattern of Energy Use in UK Industry*, Energy Technology Support Unit, Harewell (ETSU-L11).

Henry, E (1983) *The Impact of Energy Prices in the Irish Economy 1973–1981*, Economic and Social Research Institute, Paper 112, Dublin.

Hewitt, V N (1988) *The Economics of Electricity Generation Options for Northern Ireland*, Department of Economics Working Paper, The Queen's University of Belfast.

House of Commons (1987–88) *Electricity Supply in Northern Ireland*, Fifth Report of the Select Committee on Energy, HMSO (HC 679).

Jefferson, C W (1989) *Uses of Northern Ireland Lignite*, Department of Economics Working Paper, The Queen's University of Belfast.

Joint Venture for Belfast (1988) *Combined Heat and Power, the Belfast Case*, Belfast.

Lindberg, L N et al (1977) *The Energy Syndrome*, D C Heath and Company, Toronto.

Littlechild, S C and Vaidya, K G (1982) *Energy Strategies for the UK*, George Allen and Unwin, London.

McGurnaghan, M A (1985) Energy in Ireland, *Geopolitics of Energy* (Washington), 7, 2–4.

McGurnaghan, M A and Scott, S (1981) *Trade and Co-operation in Electricity and Gas*, Co-operation North and the Commission of The European Communities, Belfast and Dublin.

Maxwell, M T H (1986) Northern Ireland's energy future, *Petroleum Review*, December 1986, 13–18.

Meekatharra (1987) *Ballymoney Lignite*, Meekatharra (NI) Limited, Belfast.

Ministry of Commerce (1966) *Electricity in Ireland*, Report of the Joint Committee on Co-operation in Electricity Supply on the Scope for Agreement in Cross-Border Co-operation between the Electricity Supply Board of the Republic of Ireland and the Electricity Supply Undertakings of Northern Ireland, HMSO, Belfast.

Ministry of Commerce (1971) *Report of an Enquiry into the Characteristics of the Electricity Supply System in Northern Ireland* (The Marsh Report), HMSO, Belfast.

Monopolies and Mergers Commission (1981) *Report on the Central Electricity Generating Board*, HMSO, London.

National Economic and Social Council (1983) *Irish Energy Policy*, 74, Dublin.

Northern Ireland Assembly (1984) Report, *Social Security Parity*, HMSO, Belfast (NIA 141).

Northern Ireland Consumer Council (1980) *The Cost of Living in Northern Ireland*, Belfast.

Northern Ireland Consumer Council (1983) *The Cost of Living in Northern Ireland*, Belfast.

Northern Ireland Consumer Council (1985) *The Cost of Living for Low Income Households in Northern Ireland*, Belfast.

Northern Ireland Economic Council (1978) *Recommendations on Energy Policy in Northern Ireland*, HMSO, Belfast.

Northern Ireland Economic Council (1980) *Energy Conservation*, No 13, Belfast.

Northern Ireland Economic Council (1983) *Northern Ireland Energy Issues*, Paper 5, Belfast.

Northern Ireland Economic Council (1985) *Economic Strategy: Impact of Lignite*, Paper 9, Belfast.

Northern Ireland Economic Council (1987) *Economic Strategy: Impact of Lignite*, Report 65, Belfast.

Northern Ireland Electricity Service (1983) *Electricity Supply in Northern Ireland. A Strategy for the Future*, Belfast.

Northern Ireland Electricity (1987) The next generation. Background technical brief, News Release, 23 April 1987.

Northern Ireland Electricity (1988) *Annual Report and Accounts 1988 (year to 31 March)*, Belfast.

P A Management Consultants (1977) *Natural Gas for Northern Ireland*, Northern Ireland Gas Employers Board.

Robinson, C (1988) Competition in electricity, *Energy World*, 160, 3–10.

Scott, S (1980) *Energy Demand in Ireland, Projections and Policy Issues*, Economic and Social Research Institute, Policy Series No 2, Dublin.

Shepherd, G T (1976) *Report on the Present and Projected Financial Position of the Northern Ireland Electricity Service* (The Shepherd Report), HMSO, Belfast.

Viggers, P (1988) Address by the Minister responsible for energy matters in Northern Ireland at the annual conference of the Electricity Supply Industry's Joint Co-ordinating Council at Portrush, 27 October 1988, Northern Ireland Information Service, Belfast.

Webb, M G and Ricketts, M J (1980) *The Economics of Energy*, Macmillan, London.

The financial sector

Robert W Hutchinson and Donal G McKillop*

1. Introduction

Regionally based financial institutions can have a major part to play in the transmission of inter-regional capital flows and can provide, within a given region, both a local money transmission mechanism and a potentially important intermediary role between local investment and local savings. The direct impact that these institutions have on the other sectors of the regional economy in which they are located depends crucially on the degree of financial market integration across the regions comprising the national economy. If these markets are fully integrated, trade in national financial assets will be concentrated in the nation's central capital markets and a given region's non-financial sectors will be free to borrow and lend extra-regionally at nationally determined rates of interest. Under these conditions questions about the impact on a regional economy of inefficiencies in local financial institutions and about restrictions on local investment, arising from restrictions on regional supplies of credit, will not arise.

Conversely, to the extent that the other sectors in a regional economy are *restricted* to using locally based financial markets, the efficiency with which these markets operate and their competitive structure will have a bearing on a region's overall ability to undertake profitable investment opportunities. These restrictions (if they exist) result in regionally segmented financial markets and impair inter-regional capital flows. They create the potential for a divergence in both borrowing and lending rates across regions and even the possibility of an absolute limit on the supply of credit in and to a region. These restrictions have their source in, for example, institutional rigidities and regional differences in the cost of obtaining information on the range of borrowing and lending rates throughout the national economy.

Treatment of most of these issues has not, until recently, been given serious attention in either regional economic theory or applied studies of a region's sectoral composition. In the latter case this is in part due to data

* As authors of this chapter we appreciate the assistance received from representatives of a wide range of financial institutions in Northern Ireland. Of particular help were Mr H McDaid, Mr F Adair and Mr R McKinstry. Needless to say we take sole responsibility for the views expressed in this chapter (and any errors).

inadequacies but in an important respect stems from regional economic theory's tendency to assign a residual role to regional financial sectors. Theoretical models, while recognising the importance of inter-regional financial flows in equating rates of return across regions, have in general assumed regionally integrated financial markets with perfectly elastic supplies of capital at the nationally determined interest rate.

Of course even as a residual, a regional financial sector has an important contribution to make to its regional economy. In particular with the rapid advance in financial technology and the global trends in financial market deregulation, there may be greater growth opportunities for regionally based financial institutions through exports of financial services. On the other hand, in regions where these institutions do not adapt quickly to changing market conditions contraction, via import competition, is a possibility.

Given that the degree of regional financial market integration has a key role in the analysis of regional financial market behaviour, the chapter begins with a review of recent theoretical developments in this area. This is followed by a detailed examination of the structure and operation of the Northern Ireland financial sector. This includes a classification of local financial institutions; an analysis of their asset and liability mix through time; consideration of their roles in the local economy; and an assessment of their performance relative to that of their counterparts in the Republic of Ireland and the rest of the United Kingdom. Where possible, observed behaviour will be related to theory in an attempt to discover if there are areas where Northern Ireland's financial markets are regionally segmented and, consequently, whether there are adequate supplies of capital in and to the region. The penultimate section of the chapter deals with possible future prospects for the sector in the context of developments in the United Kingdom's financial markets as a whole. The conclusion includes a discussion on relevant policy issues.

Unfortunately data limitations preclude any worthwhile analysis of inter-regional financial flows and make it difficult to place the analysis in a comparative regional setting. Apart from the South East region of the United Kingdom which includes the cities of London and Westminster (the economy's national or central capital markets), financial statistics relating primarily to clearing bank operations are only available for the Northern Ireland region and, in a more limited form, for Scotland. A comprehensive set of financial statistics is available for the Republic of Ireland and it is this economy's financial sector which forms the primary source of comparison.

Any comparative analysis should include both integrated and non-integrated regional financial sectors. In this respect the Republic of Ireland is the most appropriate choice since, despite political independence in 1921, its financial sector remained fully integrated with the United Kingdom's well into the 1960s. In the last twenty years, however, with the development of Irish government paper, the introduction of exchange controls (1978) and the breaking of the 150 year old punt/sterling exchange rate parity (1979), Dublin's financial markets have become segmented in a fundamental way from those in London.

2. A review of theory

REGIONAL INTEGRATION

The recent growth of theoretical work on regional nnancial sectors has its origins in attempts to incorporate the effects of national monetary policy in regional econometric models. It is important to emphasise, however, that where changes in national monetary policy have differential regional impacts these can be entirely independent of a region's financial sector. This independence occurs where, from a monetarist perspective, perfect inter-regional arbitrage maintains regional interest rates at the national rate. As Bolton (1985) argues:

> '. . . where a regional financial market cannot sustain differentials in the interest rates, then the market need not be modelled – the national model will produce any interest rate that one needs'.

In these circumstances as Fishkind (1977) has shown, the regional effects of monetary policy result where differences in the composition and competitive structure between regional economies induce different elasticities in regional IS schedules. For LM schedules to have distinct regional characteristics there must be some form of regional financial market segmentation. This segmentation has its main source in information and transactions costs. These inhibit inter-regional arbitrage and, depending on the way in which they are modelled, permit not only regional interest rate differentials but forms of regional credit rationing.

INFORMATION COSTS

The starting point for considering possibilities of regional financial market segmentation is information costs. When these differ between regions they allow for the possibility of regional interest rate differentials and different variations in interest rates across regions. An early model which allowed for this was developed by Roberts and Fishkind (1979). In their approach individuals within a regional economy are viewed as having free information on the basic economic activities within the region. There is, however, an opportunity cost in obtaining information on returns outside the region, which is a positive function of the distance (remoteness) of the region from the nation's central capital markets. Thus the region's interest rate can diverge from the national rate by the extent of these information costs.

INSTITUTIONAL SEGMENTATION

In developments of this theme, a more fundamental form of market segmentation has been introduced by Moore and Hill (1982) and Dow (1987). In Moore and Hill's model a region is viewed as containing two classes of borrowers – large businesses, and small businesses and households – and two classes of lenders – the national financial institutions located in the central capital markets and the comparatively smaller regional financial institutions. Once again information costs play a crucial role in inhibiting inter-regional capital mobility. Here, however, they have their source outside the region in the form of large credit evaluation costs experienced by the national financial institutions in respect to lending regionally to small businesses and households. Thus this class of borrowers is restricted to obtaining supplies of credit from their local financial institutions. Credit evaluation costs with respect to the large business sector are minimal, assuming that their shares are traded at the national level in active secondary markets. Consequently, they have access to both national and local financial institutions.

Moore and Hill's model produces predictions on regional interest rate behaviour quite similar to those of Roberts and Fishkind; however, it includes additionally the possibility of local credit rationing. This can occur not only in rapidly growing regional economies but also in regional economies experiencing slow growth or stagnation.

With the regional financial institutions (in particular the regional banks) being autonomous, part of the supply of credit in a region is endogenous and limited by the value of the local bank multiplier. In periods of rapid regional expansion the local demand for credit will exceed the local banks' capacity to lend, based on their deposits. In these circumstances local banks obtain extra supply at the national rate of interest from the central capital markets but charge a mark-up on the national rate to the local small business sector. The possibility of an overall limit to supply enters to the extent that the local banks' own borrowing capacities are limited by their capital bases. Conversely, in periods of low or negative regional growth, activity in the local economy may be such that the regional demand and supply curves for credit, which can be identified because the regional financial market is segmented from the national financial market, have an equilibrium interest rate below the national equilibrium rate.[1] In these circumstances most of the funds available to the local banks will be invested in national assets earning national interest rates. Only a minimum amount will be lent regionally and then only at the national rate, so that the regional demand for loanable funds goes largely unsatisfied when it is weak relative to the regional supply base.

These models are monetarist in character and based solely on the transactions demand for money. In a Keynesian development of Moore and Hill's model, Dow (1987), by introducing speculative demand, allows for liquidity preference. This interacts with the state of confidence (optimism/ pessimism) in the regional economy in a standard multiplier–accelerator framework. Thus, for example, a wave of pessimism about the prospects for the regional economy leads to a much greater down-turn in regional economic activity than the other theories would suggest. A greater up-turn is implied with a wave of optimism but the mark-up and potential credit rationing may have a dampening effect. These themes will be developed at a later stage in the chapter when the impact of the local financial system on the real economy is examined.

While the Roberts and Fishkind model relies purely on information costs as the inhibiting factor in inter-regional capital flows, the Moore and Hill model and its development by Dow places an additional emphasis on institutional segmentation. A very important aspect of this relates to the distinction made between a unit banking structure and a branch banking structure. Applying these concepts in a regional framework, the unit banking structure refers to self-contained or autonomous regional banks which have a network of offices largely confined to a given region. An example here would be the Royal Bank of Scotland in the Scottish region. The standard bank branch structure refers to an inter-regional branch banking system such as that operated by the London clearing banks throughout the regions of England and Wales. It is the unit banking system in the Moore and Hill and Dow models which reinforces any tendency for there to be an unsatisfied regional demand for credit. In a branch banking system regional banks borrow beyond their capacity to lend within their national bank group rather than on the national money markets. In such a system, as Dow points out:

> 'Lending beyond strict capacity should not carry a penalty interest rate. In fact the national rate structure across branches, would normally be uniform'.

In these circumstances while a branch relative to a unit banking system eases the credit availability constraint on growing regions it may increase the constraint on depressed regions, especially if a lending limit is imposed on regional bank branches by their head office.

3. Structure of the Northern Ireland financial sector

FINANCIAL INSTITUTIONS

The financial institutions operating in Northern Ireland are classified under four categories in Table 11.1. The first three encompass maturity transforming institutions where, as Grady and Weale (1986) argue, profits are determined by liquidity premiums. That is, depositors with these institutions accept low returns in exchange for liquidity while borrowers, in exchange for the illiquidity of their debts, pay higher rates of return. In the fourth category institutions are maturity matching (they tend to match the maturity structure of their assets and liabilities) making their profits from mandatory investments and/or tax advantages.

In the context of the wider Northern Ireland economy, the financial sector appears closest to that modelled by Moore and Hill and Dow. There is a distinct small business sector which by and large obtains its funds from local financial institutions. Large companies such as Short and Harlands and the branch plants of multinationals may use local financial institutions for day to day working capital needs but clearly have access to national and indeed international capital markets. Looking specifically at the local financial institutions, the building societies, finance houses, insurance companies and

Giro and Savings Banks are in the main operated in Northern Ireland as an integral part of a national branch system. In the case of the four clearing banks, which have between them the majority shares of local deposits and local lending, the situation is significantly different. Although two of these banks have for a considerable period been subsidiaries of London clearing banks[2] (the other two have head offices in Dublin[3]) they have largely operated as semi-autonomous concerns and appear to have, in regional terms, the characteristics of a unit banking system. Indeed a separate Northern Ireland clearing bank cartel operated up to 1985. The London clearing bank cartel ceased to operate in 1971 with the introduction of the Bank of England's Competition and Credit Control Policy.

TABLE 11.1   Classification of financial institutions operating in Northern Ireland

---

Primary banking sector:
    Northern Ireland clearing banks
    TSB Northern Ireland[1]
    Girobank
    National Savings Bank

Secondary banking sector:
    Merchant banks

Other deposit-taking institutions:
    Building societies
    Finance houses
    Credit unions

Other financial intermediaries:
    Insurance companies
    Pension funds
    Investment and unit trusts
    Venture capital companies

---

[1] The TSB Northern Ireland is now effectively a clearing bank but is not a member of the Northern Ireland Bankers' Association. The four members of this Association are in most literature, by tradition, referred to as the Northern Ireland clearing banks.

In comparative regional terms, the range of financial institutions is broadly similar to that in Great Britain and the Republic of Ireland, with the exception that Northern Ireland's secondary banking sector includes only merchant banks which are subsidiaries of the Northern Ireland clearing banks. Also, while there is activity in the other financial intermediaries sector it is modest in comparison to, for example, activity in this area in the Scottish region. Edinburgh has always been recognised as having expertise in money management stemming historically from its development as an insurance centre (it manages about one-fifth of Britain's life assurance funds). In the 1970s this expertise was used as a basis for development into pension fund and unit trust management. With respect to the latter, there are about one hundred trusts currently managed in Scotland accounting for approximately one-tenth of unit trust business in Great Britain as a whole. An important aspect of these developments is the autonomous nature of many of the Scottish financial institutions. This, as will be seen, is a recurring theme: that the independence of regional financial institutions is an important dimension of regional financial market segmentation.

With respect to the secondary banking sector, it is dominated in Great Britain by three additional sub-categories – overseas banks, consortium banks and other British banks – which owe their development and growth (from the early 1960s) to the central role which London plays in the Eurocurrency and sterling inter-bank markets. The London merchant banks, while involved in these wholesale or parallel money markets, act primarily as term lenders to the corporate sector and advise on, arrange and underwrite new capital issues.

The failure of stock and wholesale money markets to develop on a significant scale at the regional level arises primarily from cost advantages at the centre, where the intensive nature of information flows in these markets and the large volume of transactions enables significant scale economies to be exploited. Indeed as O'Shaughnessy (1987) points out, with the Republic of Ireland's banking system being integrated with the United Kingdom's well into the 1960s the London wholesale money markets serviced the Republic of Ireland's domestic banking sector. There were no recognisable money or foreign exchange markets in Dublin. This position began to alter from 1968 onwards. In 1968 the Republic of Ireland's banks credited £40 million in sterling assets to the Central Bank of Ireland in exchange for a contra credit with the Central Bank. This was to ensure that the provisions of the Basle Agreements – by which the dollar value of officially held sterling reserves was guaranteed – would apply to the unofficially held portion of Irish reserves. In 1969 this transaction was placed on a more formal footing with the transfer of £73 million in sterling assets from the Republic of Ireland's banks to the Central Bank in exchange for certificates of deposit. In turn the initial impetus for the development of wholesale markets in Dublin was thus provided. This developing segmentation fostered the growth of the Republic of Ireland's non-associated banks, the equivalent of Great Britain's secondary banking sector. These non-associated banks comprise merchant and industrial subsidiaries of the associated banks (the Republic of Ireland's equivalent of clearing banks) and subsidiaries of foreign banks: largely United States and European.

EXTRA-REGIONAL COMPETITION

McGowan (1986) argues that the development of the merchant and industrial subsidiaries of the Republic of Ireland's two associated banks was in large measure a competitive response to entry into the Republic of Ireland of the non-associated foreign banks. As a consequence, by the mid-1970s these two indigenous banking groups had a 'strong and competitive base capable of confronting international competition with confidence'. Subsequently, these banks have pursued their own foreign expansion. In addition to their historic roles in Northern Ireland, both have expanded significantly in Great Britain in terms of branch network systems and instalment-credit banking and have become involved in the London capital markets. Expansion has also taken place in the United States, Singapore, Hong Kong and Sydney.

This is in stark contrast to the situation in Northern Ireland. Here the low level of international investment since 1970 implies that foreign banks have not had the incentive to establish in Northern Ireland. Indeed three foreign banks which established themselves in the 1960s – the Bank of Nova Scotia, Citibank and Chase Manhattan – subsequently withdrew from the province. The absence of this type of competitive pressure on the Northern Ireland clearing banks as a whole, coupled with the fact that policy on national and international expansion is the preserve of their parent companies, implies that the environment is not one which would encourage local banks to expand internationally or indeed extra-regionally.[4] This situation is likely to continue while Belfast lacks many of the characteristics necessary for the development of a strong international perspective; unlike Dublin, with its national central bank, its autonomous home-based associated banks and (since the parity break in 1979) its separate currency.

In terms of institutional segmentation the structure of Scotland's banking sector is closer to the Republic of Ireland's than to Northern Ireland's. According to Blanden (1988) while many of the Scottish banks are relatively small, they have retained their independence. Here again independence has played a crucial role enabling most of the Scottish clearing banks to initiate expansion into the English regions, partly in response to the London clearing banks' entry to the Scottish market in the mid-1970s.

This is not to argue that Belfast has no extra-regional dimension. Since the punt/sterling parity break the Northern Ireland clearing banks have developed a considerable foreign exchange business in the former currency, based initially on Northern Ireland's unique trading position with the Republic of Ireland. This has been developed in a wider international context for two reasons. First, as an 'exotic currency' the Irish punt does not attract the same interest from the London clearing banks as, for example, the United States dollar or Japanese yen. Second, Belfast has a foreign exchange transactions cost advantage over Dublin in punt dealings. This arises because of the Republic of Ireland's exchange controls and attendant dealing documentation. An example of the latter is the requirement on the associated banks to produce documentation for all foreign exchange payments in excess of IR£100 thus raising the opportunity cost of dealings with Dublin rather than Belfast.[5]

COMPETITION WITHIN THE REGION

Turning now to the financial structure within the region, the key element is the dominant primary banking sector and within it the four Northern Ireland clearing banks which are 'recognised banks' under the 1979 Banking Act. The first task is to determine the type of competition the clearing bank group as a whole has faced in recent years; the second is to look at the group's role in the region's supply of loanable funds.

In the area of retail banking the Northern Ireland clearing banks have faced some competition from the TSB Northern Ireland. This began in the early 1970s with the TSB gaining a competitive advantage by being the first bank in Northern Ireland to introduce a sophisticated computer network. The four clearing banks had to delay their computerisation until the early 1980s, due to restrictive labour agreements with the Irish Bank Officials Association. The competitive position of the TSB relative to the four clearing banks was, however, more fundamentally enhanced by the TSB Act of 1976. Prior to 1976 the TSB was primarily an intermediary through which personal savings were channelled to the public sector. After the Act the TSB became a fully fledged bank offering a complete range of banking services including loans to individuals and mortgage facilities. Privatisation of the TSB in 1986 has permitted further expansion and has enabled the TSB to become involved in such areas as insurance services, leasing and instalment credit.

The other sources of competition within the primary banking sector, although limited in nature, come from the Giro and Savings Banks. These intermediaries operate through the Post Office chain of outlets in Northern Ireland. With over 50 per cent more outlets than the combined clearing bank branches and longer opening hours, the market shares of these intermediaries are surprisingly small. Gibson (1982) estimates that Girobank, which through the giro system prides itself in offering a simple, swift and economical money transmission mechanism, accounts for only 1 per cent of current account business. The clearing banks appear unconcerned regarding competition from Girobank primarily because of the unprofitability of small current accounts and the limited nature of Girobank lending to the private sector. The anticipated privatisation of the Girobank may, however, change this situation. The National Savings Bank's deposits in Northern Ireland, despite interest being untaxed at source, amount to less than 1 per cent of the National Savings Bank's United Kingdom deposit base. Gibson argues that a figure of 2.7 per cent would have been expected given the population in Northern Ireland relative to the United Kingdom.

In the Republic of Ireland, the public sector intermediaries which compete with the associated banks are: the Post Office Savings Bank, the Trustee Savings Bank and the state-sponsored financial institutions. As McGowan indicates, the competitive pressure exerted by the latter three has diminished considerably over the last twenty years, their share of the total deposit base falling from 20 per cent in 1965 to 10 per cent in 1985.[6]

While the Northern Ireland TSB has presented a competitive challenge to the Northern Ireland clearing banks, the latter face more acute long-term competition from the building societies who as other deposit-taking institutions are outside the primary banking sector. Given that the vast majority of building societies operate branch networks throughout the United Kingdom, it is appropriate to look initially at their activities in a national context.

With building society deposits rising from 50 per cent of the deposits of the London and Scottish clearing banks in 1961, to approximately 110 per cent of their deposits in 1985, building societies have become the dominant financial intermediary in Great Britain's personal deposit market. This has been achieved by societies opening for longer and more convenient hours than banks and by income tax arrangements which have permitted societies to offer more attractive interest rates. The latter competitive advantage has been eroded since 1985 with composite tax arrangements being extended to the clearing banks. This coupled with the latter's earlier entry (1980) into the mortgage finance market does not, however, imply that building societies face a less favourable environment for future expansion, since with the introduction of the Building Society Act (1986) they now have the opportunity to compete in the more traditional retail banking market. This evolving competition is a prime example of what Bain (1986) has identified as the 'most important' trend in the United Kingdom's financial structure: financial market integration by the removal of barriers 'between the business formerly undertaken by specialist categories of (financial) intitution'.

Looking specifically at the Northern Ireland region, with the share of British-based building society deposits increasing from 5 per cent of the Northern Ireland clearing bank deposits in 1961 to 67 per cent in 1985, the increase in building society penetration has not been as great as in Great Britain. Two factors appear to account for this. First, building societies have a lower degree of coverage in Northern Ireland, where bank branches outnumber building society offices by 4:1 compared to 2:1 in Great Britain. Second, lower income per head in Northern Ireland and the relatively large supply of public sector housing, suggests a lower mortgage demand. This in turn implies lower building society deposits, given that until recently it was desirable to be a shareholder or depositor with a society before a mortgage would be granted.

In the Republic of Ireland the progress of the building society movement has also been impressive. Building societies' shares and deposits in 1985 amounted to nearly half of the current and deposit accounts of the associated banks, compared with 7 per cent in 1965. Once again the impressive growth rates are in part a consequence of the societies not having to face very effective competition in attracting savings, due to the benefit of favourable fiscal incentives. Although associated banks have competed in the provision of mortgages for house purchases since 1975, it was only after the fiscal neutral budget of 1986 that they were placed on a competitive par with the building societies. The expectation is that this increase in competitive pressure will eventually lead to the dismantling in the Republic of Ireland of the building societies' cartel arrangements for setting interest and mortgage rates. In the United Kingdom this form of cartel arrangement broke up in 1983.

4. The supply of loanable funds

Having looked at the competitive environment in which the Northern Ireland clearing banks operate, attention is turned to their role in the region's supply of loanable funds. The first task is to assess whether or not there has been any form of absolute credit rationing. Then, given the clearing groups' important role in business and personal lending, an attempt is made at examining interest rate behaviour and in particular the likelihood of a regional mark-up on the national rate. The section is completed by looking at some aspects of lending risks.

The possibility of absolute credit rationing is addressed by comparing the asset and liability structure of the Northern Ireland clearing bank group with that of the clearing bank group in Great Britain. If over the business cycle similar balance sheet structures are observed, there will be no evidence to support regional credit rationing in Northern Ireland. Although not ideal, this is the only available approach in the presence of data limitations.

Selected sterling items in the aggregate balance sheet of the Northern Ireland clearing banks are presented in Table 11.2 from 1977, the first year that reasonably comprehensive data became available. Since it is supply-side factors which are important in assessing whether or not the local financial sector has an inhibiting effect on the rest of the local economy, attention is focused on three areas: the deposit base, liquidity and advances.

THE DEPOSIT BASE

Looking first at the deposit base, in 1985 the Northern Ireland clearing banks' sight deposits, which form the major element in the money transmission mechanism, accounted for 35 per cent of their total sterling deposits as compared to 48 per cent in 1977. Sight deposits are defined as money withdrawable on demand without interest penalty. While data prior to this date are not strictly comparable, the evidence indicates that with current accounts representing 55 per cent of total deposits in 1961, the general trend in the share of sight deposits has been downwards, matching almost exactly that of the London clearing banks. Their relevant shares fell from about 55 per cent in 1960 to approximately 35 per cent in the 1980s.

These trends are explained by two factors which apply generally throughout the United Kingdom. First, the rise in interest rates since the mid-1970s which has increased the opportunity cost of holding funds in low or non-interest bearing accounts. Second, the increased competition which the clearing banks have faced in the area of money transmission, not only from the building societies and the TSB, but also from financial innovations such as credit cards.

The bulk of sterling deposits come under the heading (in Table 11.2) of 'other UK' which to all intents and purposes represent private sector deposits of Northern Ireland residents. These have risen from approximately 50 per cent of the total deposits of the Northern Ireland clearing banks in 1980 to 80 per cent in 1985. By contrast, the private sector deposits of the London clearing banks approximated 80 per cent of their total deposits throughout the 1980s. Two factors in the late 1970s and early 1980s, which indirectly depressed the contribution of private sector funds to total deposits of the Northern Ireland clearing banks and help to explain this contrast, were competition from the building societies and inter-bank borrowing.

While the growth of building society deposits in Northern Ireland started at a later stage than in the rest of the United Kingdom and has not been as marked as in the latter, there was a period when a relative 'catching up' process took place. Between 1977 and 1980 share and deposit balances with the building societies in Northern Ireland increased by 60 per cent compared to the 30 per cent increase in private sector deposits with the clearing banks. For the remainder of the period under consideration both grew in tandem, each increasing by approximately 135 per cent between 1980 and 1985. The other explanatory factor, heavy inter-bank borrowing by the Northern Ireland clearing banks, reached an all time high of 41 per cent of their total deposits in 1980 before gradually trending downwards to 9 per cent in 1985. The latter share approximates the inter-bank borrowing levels of the London clearers throughout the 1980s.

A comparison of market loans to the United Kingdom monetary sector on the asset side of the balance sheet in Table 11.2 with deposits from the United Kingdom banking sector on the liability side, indicates that during the period of heavy inter-bank borrowing the Northern Ireland clearing banks were net debtors to the United Kingdom monetary sector. Traditionally as in 1985 they have been net creditors implying a net outflow of funds to the rest of the United Kingdom. The development of net debtor status, coinciding with the start of a major recession, can be explained as Dow has done from a Keynesian perspective. Here the short-run response to a 'wave of pessimism' about a regional economy is an increase in demand, within the region, for working capital and credit to fund earlier short-term loans. This results in an increase in borrowing outside the region by the local banks. Subsequently, however, as the number of bankruptcies increase and the local demand for credit falls, the regional banks move back into a net creditor position consistent with the region's long-term low growth status.

LIQUIDITY

Alternatively, the behaviour of the Northern Ireland banks in the late 1970s and early 1980s may simply have been a reflection of a more relaxed lending policy; actively encouraged at the national level by the Bank of England in the face of the deepening economic crisis. There is some evidence of this in the behaviour of the liquidity ratios of the Northern Ireland clearing banks which are detailed in the final row of Table 11.2. Liquidity is measured by the ratio of domestic advances to domestic non-bank deposits. A high ratio demonstrates low liquidity and indicates, as Grady and Weale argue, that a bank is exposed to the risk that some of its non-bank deposits may be withdrawn at the same time as funds are scarce in the inter-bank market.[7] As a general rule of thumb prudence dictates that this ratio should not exceed unity.

There was a sharp decline in liquidity in the late 1970s, the ratio peaking at 1.21 in 1980 and remaining in excess of 1 between 1979 and 1981. Ratios at this level raise questions about the portfolio mix of the Northern Ireland clearing banks and suggest that they operated during this period without much regard to liquidity requirements. In this case, however, high liquidity risk did not unduly compound solvency risk, given that ultimately the Northern Ireland clearing banks were backed by their parent companies.

It is interesting to note that the increase in the Northern Ireland

TABLE 11.2   The balance sheet structure of the Northern Ireland clearing banks, 1977–1985 (£ million)

	1977	1980	1982	1985
Liabilities				
UK banking sector	232	553	290	193
Other UK	543	713	1,135	1,684
Overseas	253	73	98	179
(of which sight deposits)	(494)	(468)	(614)	(712)
Other currency deposits[1]	66	17	12	60
Miscellaneous sterling/				
non-sterling liabilities	134	250	331	495
Assets				
Notes and coins	22	30	28	33
Bills	61	72	26	11
Market loans				
UK monetary sector	97	134	367	503
Certificate of deposit	16	11	35	57
UK local authorities	41	53	73	115
Other UK	} 182	14	0	0
Overseas		57	48	145
Advances				
UK public sector	} 474	15	16	21
UK private sector		850	914	1,212
Overseas	11	13	12	10
Investments	51	53	108	174
Other currency assets[1]	37	17	12	66
Miscellaneous sterling/				
non-sterling assets	236	287	227	264
Total assets/liabilities	1,228	1,606	1,866	2,611
Liquidity ratio	0.87	1.21	0.82	0.73

[1] Bank practice is to match closely other currency assets and liabilities. These are relatively small, averaging 1.5% of assets (liabilities) between 1977 and 1985.
Source: NIAAS.

clearing banks' liquidity ratio was much more pronounced in comparison to the increase in the ratio for the London and Scottish clearing banks and reached a much higher level. The latter banks' ratio remained below 1, averaging 0.75 between 1979 and 1981. Subsequently there was a sharp improvement in liquidity among the Northern Ireland clearing banks, their ratio falling below that of the London and Scottish clearers from 1982 onwards.

    Again, however, this could be interpreted from a Moore and Hill and Dow perspective, where following the short-term response to a decline in the state of confidence within a region, there is a medium-term increase in liquidity preference. In the presence of liquidity preference local credit availability is never assured. This causes the non-bank public in a region to exhibit a high preference for holding bank deposits and to prefer to hold long-term investments in national rather than regional assets. With the local banks also exhibiting the latter preference, the value of the local banks' credit multiplier is reduced, reducing the local supply of credit thus reinforcing the non-bank public's liquidity preference.

There is evidence for this in Table 11.2. In addition to the generally more prudent attitude to liquidity exhibited by the Northern Ireland clearing banks since 1982, there has been an increase in the non-bank public's holdings of bank deposits. Similarly the Northern Ireland clearing banks themselves have increased their holdings of national monetary assets.

This interpretation of balance sheet data relies fundamentally on institutional segmentation of the regional banks, implying that they have a direct impact on the regional economy, accentuating the decline in regional economic activity relative to the national economy. Alternatively, under full regional financial market integration the direction of causation would go the other way, with balance sheet changes possibly reflecting underlying changes in the real economy.

ADVANCES

The separate nature of the Northern Ireland clearing banks is underscored when the effects of policy segmentation during the 1970s are considered. Then the Northern Ireland clearing banks were not subject to some of the monetary restrictions placed on the London and Scottish clearing banks. Specifically, the latter group of banks had to operate a supplementary special deposit scheme intermittently over a six and a half year period, starting in December 1973. The scheme, or corset, required non-interest bearing deposits to be made with the Bank of England if these clearing banks allowed their own deposit base to exceed a specified growth rate. The differential impact this had on lending, given that the growth of advances is determined by the growth of deposits, is illustrated below.

Between 1973 and 1979 the nominal growth of advances by the London and Scottish clearing banks to Great Britain's manufacturing and financial sectors was relatively sluggish. The demand for clearing bank credit in the personal and other production sectors seems to have been stronger, with the service sector experiencing the largest increase in advances, at 150 per cent. In contrast, lending by the Northern Ireland clearing banks was relatively uniform across sectors but markedly higher. Nominal growth rates for the manufacturing, other production, personal and financial sectors ranged from 200 per cent to 274 per cent, while lending to the service sector grew by a more modest 175 per cent. At this point, however, a note of caution is necessary since normal banking channels could be bypassed during the corset's operation in Great Britain by 'disintermediation'. This occurred where, for example, companies issued commercial bills which could be sold to other companies. Although bank deposits did not increase as a result, the effect of 'disintermediation' was in many respects similar to an expansion of bank lending and bank deposits.

After 1979 the lending pattern was reversed, with advances by the Northern Ireland clearing banks growing at rates well below those of the London and Scottish clearers. Between 1979 and 1985 the growth in advances in Northern Ireland ranged from 55 per cent for manufacturing to 89 per cent for the personal sector. The range over the same sectors for the London and Scottish clearing banks was 115 per cent to 457 per cent. There are two main reasons for this change. First, since the onset of the last national recession, the Northern Ireland economy has remained in a relatively depressed state and as a region has possibly received least benefit from the subsequent national economic recovery. Second, as Grady and Weale argue, the removal of the corset in 1980 resulted in a relatively rapid rise in the balance sheet activity of the London and Scottish clearers as they looked for new business and sought the necessary deposits.

So far in this section on the supply of loanable funds differences in behaviour between regionally and nationally based banks have been shown. There is consequently the possibility of an endogenous component to the regional money supply although this is not clear, given the possibilities of 'disintermediation' in the presence of monetary restrictions, whether nationally or regionally applied. What is clear is that there is no evidence of an overall limit on the regional supply of credit. The exceptionally high liquidity ratio around 1980 indicates that the local banks' borrowing capacities were not constrained by their capital bases. This points to a 'half-way house' form of institutional segmentation where, as semi-autonomous institutions, the Northern Ireland clearing banks operate in a regional unit banking context but, ultimately, as extensions to national branch networks.

INTEREST RATE DIFFERENTIALS

The absence of an absolute limit on the supply of loanable funds to a region does not of course preclude the existence of some form of interest rate differential. If such differentials exist and can be explained in a Roberts and Fishkind context, then from a policy perspective Northern Ireland's financial institutions would not in themselves be imposing restrictions on investment opportunities in the regional economy. For a given class of assets, any divergence between local and national interest rates would be largely a function of information costs and there would be a natural tendency for these to be eliminated in the developing framework of information technology. On the deposit side, there is some evidence to suggest that during the earlier part of this decade interest rate differentials existed which could be explained from this perspective. For example, Gibson has shown that while interest rates offered by the Northern Ireland clearing banks on deposits in excess of £25,000 were almost identical to those paid by the London clearing banks, interest rates were lower in Northern Ireland for deposits below £25,000 (1 per cent for under £10,000 and 0.5 per cent between £10,000 and £25,000). In other words the opportunity cost of obtaining information on national rates and subsequent transaction costs in dealing with institutions outside the region would have eliminated regional differentials.

On the lending side, interest rate changes through time in Northern Ireland matched those in the nation's central capital markets, implying that there is no evidence of a regional variation in interest rates which is out of line with variations in national rates. This does not, however, preclude absolute interest rate differentials. During the operation of the Northern Ireland bank cartel (1949–85) these appear, at least superficially, to have existed. Taken together with the fact that for most of the period under investigation the Northern Ireland clearing banks have enjoyed net creditor status with the rest of the United Kingdom (investing their surpluses in bills and bonds in the 1960s and early 1970s and in the London inter-bank markets from the mid-1970s) a number of conditions conducive to a Moore and Hill and Dow interpretation are present. Recall that differentials in these models take two basic forms, depending on the state of the regional economy. In an expansionary phase there can be a mark-up to the small business sector over and above the national rate. Alternatively, in a depressed region, like Northern Ireland, local financial market segmentation may imply that the resultant regionally specific demand and supply schedules for loanable funds have an equilibrium interest rate below the national equilibrium rate. Local financial institutions, however, will only lend locally at the national rate, investing any surplus funds in the central capital markets. (Similarly local deposit rates, apart from information cost induced differences, will have to be at least equivalent to nationally offered rates because of the non-bank public's liquidity preference and desire to invest in national assets.) Thus with the actual lending rate above the locally sustainable equilibrium interest rate, the regional demand for credit can be partially unsatisfied.

INTEREST RATES AND RISK

Investigation of this requires an analysis of interest rates in the context of risk since *in practice* what might appear to be above average interest rates (or indeed credit rationing effects) may simply be a reflection of risk differentials. The models reviewed in the theory section were concerned with isolating the effects of market segmentation on interest rate behaviour and consequently abstracted from the risk issue by concentrating on representative assets.

During the operation of the cartel the Northern Ireland clearing banks' standard lending rate was on average 2 per cent above the London clearing bank base rate (the equivalent of the Bank of England minimum lending rate). When, however, borrowing is examined by risk category the mark-up appears to have been superficial. The 'blue chip' rate to large well-capitalised companies with good track records was 0.5 per cent to 1.0 per cent below the standard lending rate, indicating that for this class of borrower banks had to offer rates which were competitive with the central capital markets (where 'blue chip' rates were approximately 1 per cent above base rates). Similarly rates for higher risk borrowers were not excessive. Medium-sized companies which were relatively well capitalised could expect a 1 per cent to 2 per cent mark-up on the standard lending rate while companies with relatively low capital bases and a variable track record could expect a mark-up in excess of 2 per cent. Normally, risks which would have required a mark-up in excess of 4 per cent would not have been undertaken. More recently, with the abolition of the cartel in the face of a highly competitive environment the concept of a Northern Ireland standard lending rate has disappeared. Base rates are now in line with those in London and risk premiums are as before, with appropriate downward adjustments.

While there is therefore no evidence of regional interest rates being levied in excess of national rates, there is still the possibility of a regional interest rate equilibrium, for a given class of assets, *below* the equivalent national rate. It is difficult to obtain a clear view on this since there is no prospect of estimating regional demand and supply schedules for loanable funds. Informal discussions with professional bankers in Northern Ireland have, however, revealed an interesting phenomenon. It would appear that some Northern Ireland companies which are large in regional terms and which are classified by the regional financial institutions as 'blue chip', would not be viewed as having prime lending status in national terms and, consequently, would not receive the 'blue chip' rate in the central capital markets. This suggests either that some risk adjusted regional lending rates are actually below their equivalent national rates or that there are credit evaluation costs experienced by national financial institutions in lending regionally which must be compensated by higher interest rates.

5. Employment

The above has in effect analysed the indirect impact that the Northern Ireland financial sector has, in terms of the provision of financial services, on the other sectors of the local economy. The financial sector has of course a direct impact in that it contributes, as a sector in its own right, to employment and output.

Looking at employment, using the definition of the financial sector implied in the Banks and the Wider Economy (1988) report, gives a favourable picture of employment trends during the 1980s, with total employment increasing from approximately 27,000 in 1983[8] to 29,000 in 1988. This definition, however, is extremely broad in that it includes solicitors, accountants and estate agents amongst others. A more acceptable definition as contained in, for example, Draper et al (1988) excludes these employees and concentrates on banking and finance (SIC 81) and insurance (SIC 82). As can be seen from Table 11.3, this sheds a different light on employment trends. Employment in banking and finance actually fell by 6.1 per cent over the period with the positive growth in insurance employment being insufficient to offset this.

On a United Kingdom regional basis it is impossible to obtain this level of disaggregation. It is interesting to note, however, that even if the

.

TABLE 11.3 Employees in banking, finance and related sectors, Great Britain and Northern Ireland, 1983 and 1988 (March, 000)

SIC 1980 individual class	Great Britain			Northern Ireland		
	1983	1988	Percentage change	1983	1988	Percentage change
Banking and finance (81)	492.7	573.7	16.4	8.4	7.89	−6.1
Insurance excluding compulsory social security (82)	229.7	249.5	8.6	3.04	3.16	3.9
Business services (83)	895.0	1,345.0	50.3	11.16	13.6	21.9
Renting of movables (84)	91.1	112.0	22.9	1.21	1.08	−10.7
Owning and dealing in real estate (85)	102.4	127.6	24.6	3.59	3.69	2.8

Sources: EG; NIAAS.

broader definition is used, Northern Ireland has had the lowest level of employment growth amongst the United Kingdom regions, as can be seen from Table 11.4.

Recruitment by the clearing banks in Northern Ireland has tended to fall off during the 1980s, principally because electronic data processing has tended to displace the need for large staff numbers. Such a trend is likely to continue due to further advances in information technology but also on account of future bank branch rationalisations. Northern Ireland, like many other regions of the United Kingdom, is generally considered to be overbanked. While the Northern Ireland clearers have not as yet implemented a rationalisation policy it is already in force in Scotland where the clearers have

TABLE 11.4 Regional analysis of employees in banking, finance and related sectors,[1] 1983 and 1988 (March, 000)

Standard region	1983	1988	Percentage change	Ranking 1 = best 12 = worst
Greater London	586	736	26.0	8
South East	327	471	44.0	4
East Anglia	46	76	65.2	1
South West	116	173	49.0	2
West Midlands	129	192	48.8	3
East Midlands	80	96	20.0	10
Yorks–Humberside	110	149	35.5	6
North	61	80	31.1	7
Wales	49	67	36.7	5
Scotland	132	165	25.0	9
North West	173	202	16.8	11
Northern Ireland	27.4	29.4	7.3	12

[1] This includes SIC sub-divisions 81–85 as defined in Table 11.3.
Source: EG.

closed some of their less economic branches. A further factor which militates against a growth in bank employment in Northern Ireland is salary levels within the profession. The Irish Bank Officials Association, which has a monopoly union position within the industry, has been able to extract monopoly rents for its members. Although it is difficult to get definitive evidence on salary scales, Davy et al (1984) suggest that between 1971 and 1983:

> 'starting salaries in the Irish banks were well above those in the U.K. . . . The differential has typically been above 60 percent.'

Although over the last number of years the boom in financial services has eroded such a difference, a differential of a smaller order still remains. Such a differential would be unlikely to exist within a free market environment especially with the excess labour supply in Northern Ireland. There has of course been some labour recruitment over the last few years, especially of part-time female workers to service the data-processing element of information technology.

While technology, changing labour requirements and relatively high pay remunerations all have a role to play in the employment decline in banking and finance in Northern Ireland (SIC 81), perhaps the major explanatory factor in this decline has been the sluggish local economy. Slow growth in the economic base has resulted in low demand growth for personal and corporate financial services. This contrasts with the situation in other regional economies of the United Kingdom where, although branch rationalisation and the adoption of information technology is at an advanced stage, the labour saving effects are outweighed by the labour generating effects of the large growth in transactions due to a buoyant economic base.

The insurance industry, which includes the fields of general and long-term insurance and insurance broking, has experienced employment growth in Northern Ireland over the period although at levels lower than that for Great Britain.

6. Future prospects

For most of the first half of this century the financial services industry in the United Kingdom operated in a highly regulated environment and experienced modest change. It was not until the 1960s that major structural changes occurred with the rapid growth of the secondary banking sector, the development of parallel money markets and a bank merger movement. Many of these changes affected Great Britain but had, with the exception of the merger movement, little impact on Northern Ireland.[9] Similarly, the major changes in regulation which occurred after the secondary banking crisis of 1973 had little direct bearing on the Northern Ireland clearing banks.

In marked contrast, during the 1980s the information technology revolution coupled with financial market deregulation has removed the traditional boundaries between markets for different types of financial services both within and across the regions of the national economy. The traditional cartel practices of clearing banks and building societies have disappeared. Clearing banks are now providing investment advice services which were once the preserve of finance houses and are developing their expertise in the insurance and mortgage markets. Similarly, building societies are taking a more active role in the money transmission mechanism and are moving into the non-mortgage personal loan market.

Information technology has through cost reductions increased the efficiency of inter-regional information flows. This combined with deregulation has led to an almost total integration of regional financial markets and has created the potential for regionally based financial institutions to market their services extra-regionally and indeed internationally. The latter in the European context will be given further impetus through the implementation of the Single European Act in 1992. On the other hand, information technology and deregulation have enabled national financial institutions to exploit scale economies thus creating a tendency for increased concentration in and around the United Kingdom's central capital markets. Given this and the present institutional structure in Northern Ireland, there is little prospect of having a locally based financial services industry with strong aspirations to extra-regional growth. Locally based banks are only subsidiaries of financial institutions with headquarters outside the region and building societies and insurance companies operate regional offices as part of integrated national branch networks, again with head offices outside the region.

Within Northern Ireland, competition engendered by deregulation and the new technology may intensify. Both the small size of the Northern Ireland regional economy and its poor medium-term prospects for employment and output growth, imply that without avenues for extra-regional expansion local financial institutions have a limited area within which to exploit their own scale economies. Given the extensive regional branch networks of banks and building societies, the adoption in a competitive but small market of innovations – such as the electronic transfer of funds, automatic teller machines, point of sale facilities and eventually computer home banking – can quickly create excess capacity. Indeed it is in this type of environment that major competitive advantages are conferred on those institutions who can achieve a higher rate of adoption of new cost saving technology than their competitors. Thus in the long run there is a relatively strong likelihood of branch rationalisation with the possibility of mergers.

The Northern Ireland clearing banks in particular have experienced difficulties in implementing new technology, largely as a result of problems in negotiations with the Irish Bank Officials Association. The competitive position of the clearing banks as a whole has and will continue to be further complicated by their unit labour costs which are significantly above those of banks in other United Kingdom regions, as well as the other non-bank financial institutions within Northern Ireland.

Recent changes in legislation – The Insurance Act (1987) – have only begun to impact on the local financial sector. This Act is intended to strengthen investor protection and appears initially to be affecting the structural relationship between banks and insurance companies. The Northern Ireland clearing banks see insurance services as an important market into which they can expand. The Act complicates their market strategy in this area since the regulatory conditions applying to the provision of insurance services are different if a bank decides to operate as an independent intermediary for these services (as the Ulster and Northern banks have decided to do), relative to the position where it ties itself to one insurance company. The two Dublin-based banks have opted to go tied, as they have their own unit trust business; indeed the Bank of Ireland recently bought an option to purchase an insurance company.

As explained in an earlier part of this chapter, the institutional structure in the Republic of Ireland differs significantly from that in Northern Ireland, with the result that prospects for this economy's financial services sector are somewhat more promising. While there is, as Murphy (1988) argues, a cost problem and over-staffing facing the two Dublin-based associated banks and a limited size to their domestic market with 'the local (competitive) scene continuing to look potentially bloody', the independent nature of these banks has and will continue to enable them to 'look abroad to expand their profits'. Further, the Republic of Ireland's government is planning the Custom House Docks development to provide an international financial services centre.

Looking at the Scottish region, somewhat similar conclusions apply as apply to Dublin. While Edinburgh has to compete with London the former's historical development as a financial centre and the independence of a number of Scottish clearing banks places it at a significant advantage. Indeed, under private sector initiative Scottish Financial Enterprise has been established in the last two years to further promote Scotland as a regional financial centre.

7. Conclusion

This chapter has attempted to assess the impact of the Northern Ireland financial sector on its regional economy. Two broad issues have been pursued: the indirect bearing of this sector on the region's overall ability to undertake profitable investment opportunities and its direct contribution in terms of its own growth potential. It was argued that in both cases the degree of regional financial market integration had a crucial role to play. Highly integrated markets would imply, on the one hand, perfectly elastic supplies of capital to the region with no restrictions on local investment. On the other hand, they could result in locally based financial institutions facing stiff extra-regional competition.

Given data limitations which prevented detailed consideration of capital flows to and from the region and the fact that financial institutions such as building societies and insurance companies are in the main parts of integrated national branch networks, attention has focused primarily on the

Northern Ireland clearing banks. They are the dominant group of financial intermediaries and have distinctive regional characteristics.

The available evidence suggests that there are almost no impediments to the free flow of capital to and from Northern Ireland and that within their risk tolerance levels, the Northern Ireland clearing banks do not inhibit the growth of regional investment. The growth of the clearing banks themselves appears under present conditions to be constrained to their local regional markets. With the head offices of their parent companies located outside Northern Ireland, it is unlikely that the local banks will be offered opportunities to expand extra-regionally. If anything, competition within the region is likely to increase, raising the medium- to long-term prospects of bank branch rationalisation. There is even the possibility of further mergers if a given bank falls behind in technological development and/or the Northern Ireland economy does not expand significantly in the long term.

Ironically, if the Northern Ireland financial sector is to benefit in a wider national and international context from the current deregulatory atmosphere and the single European market proposed for 1992 under the Single European Act, a stronger form of institutional segmentation would be necessary. In other words, a policy to establish a distinct autonomous regional banking system akin to the Scottish clearing banks, or even more desirable, the Republic of Ireland's associated banks would be needed. In regional terms, however, given the small size of the Northern Ireland economy this might result in the creation of regional banks with limited capital bases. Consequently, potential benefits from international expansion could be offset within the domestic regional economy by limitations being placed on local supplies of loanable funds. An alternative policy of attempting to attract the head offices of national financial institutions to the Northern Ireland region is feasible, given the information technology revolution. Again, rather ironically, the tendency in such an environment is towards further institutional and market integration with increased concentration of financial institutions in and around the nation's central capital markets.

Notes

1. Note that this model is not dealing with capital market imperfections which would result for a given market in a divergence between borrowing and lending rates in equilibrium.
2. The two Belfast-based banks are the Ulster Bank, a subsidiary of the National Westminster Bank, and the Northern Bank which up to 1987 was a subsidiary of the Midland Bank. The Northern Bank has recently been acquired by the National Australian Bank.
3. The Dublin-based banks are the Bank of Ireland and Allied Irish Banks.
4. Historically the two Belfast-based clearing banks had operations in the Republic of Ireland. In the case of the Northern Bank's Republic of Ireland branches, these now operate as the National Irish Bank which is separate from the Northern Bank, although both have the National Australian Bank as their parent company. The

Ulster Bank continues to operate an all Ireland branch network from Belfast but given its National Westminster Bank link has no prospect of expanding outside Ireland.

5. This cost disadvantage is expected to disappear with freeing of capital movements in the context of the single European market.

6. This conceals small relative improvements in the market shares of the Republic's TSB and state sponsored financial institutions. These were more than offset, however, by the sharp fall in the share of the Post Office Savings Bank.

7. Given that wholesale funds can be withdrawn extremely rapidly and are much less stable than traditional current and deposit accounts, these are excluded from the liquidity measure as are certificates of deposit which are held mainly within the banking system.

8. Employment is analysed from 1983 given that it is generally recognised as being the start of period of employment recovery in the United Kingdom as a whole.

9. During the 1960s a number of bank mergers took place throughout Ireland resulting by the early 1970s in the two Northern Ireland-based clearing banks and the two Dublin-based associated banks.

References

Bain, A D (1986) The British financial structure, in *Bank Strategies for the 1990s*, The Institute of Bankers, London, 1–24.

Banks and the Wider Economy (1988) A discussion document published jointly by the Department of Economic Development and the Northern Ireland Bankers' Association.

Blanden, M (1988) The Scots are coming, the Scots are coming, *The Banker*, April, 77–85.

Bolton, R (1985) Regional econometric models, *Journal of Regional Science*, 25, 4, 495–520.

Davy Kelleher McCarthy Limited (1984) *The Control of Banking in the Republic of Ireland*, Dublin.

Draper, P, Smith, I, Stewart, W and Hood, N (1988) *The Scottish Financial Sector*, Edinburgh University Press.

Dow, S C (1987) The treatment of money in regional economics, *Journal of Regional Science*, 27, 1, 13–24.

Fishkind, H H (1977) The regional impact of monetary policy: an economic simulation study of Indiana 1958–1973, *Journal of Regional Science*, 17, 1, 77–88.

Gibson, N J (1982) *The Financial System in Northern Ireland*, Northern Ireland Economic Council, Report 29, April.

Grady, J and Weale, M (1986) *British Banking, 1960–85*, Macmillan, London.

McGowan, P (1986) Innovation in Irish banking, *Irish Banking Review*, Autumn, 27–54.

Moore, C L and Hill, J M (1982) Interregional arbitrage and the supply of loanable funds, *Journal of Regional Science*, 22, 4, 499–512.

Murphy, P (1988) Seconds out, round one, *The Banker*, February, 42–49.

O'Shaughnessy, K (1987) Changes in the financial services market, *Irish Banking Review*, Winter, 12–25.

Roberts, R B and Fishkind, H H (1979) The role of monetary forces in regional economic activity: an econometric simulation analysis, *Journal of Regional Science*, 19, 1, 15–28.

Private services

Richard T Harrison

1. Introduction

As the manufacturing sector has declined, regionally and nationally, in the United Kingdom since the early 1970s, there has been a considerable resurgence of interest in the actual and potential role of the service sector in national and regional development. This is clearly evident in the rapid expansion of published research on the dynamics of the service sector in the United Kingdom (Producer Services Working Party 1986; Howells and Green 1988) and the European Community (Howells 1988), which complements the already extensive American literature on the service economy (Greenfield 1966; Fuchs 1968, 1969; Stanback 1979; Stanback et al 1981). It is also evident in policy discussion in the United Kingdom. In 1983 the Regional Development White Paper (HM Government 1983) presaged a revision to the framework of regional industrial development policy, including major revisions of the Regional Development Grant scheme which gave significant recognition to the role of the service sector in creating new employment opportunities in the regions in Great Britain by extending eligibility for automatic grant aid to parts of the sector (Marshall 1985).

Services now constitute the dominant form of economic activity in many regional economies in the United Kingdom. The service industries now represent over half of gross domestic product (at factor cost, current prices) in each of the regions of the United Kingdom, and in the South East account for over two-thirds of GDP. In employment terms the service sector is of even greater significance: if service occupations in non-service industries are included, the service sector accounts for around 65 per cent of employment in all regions and for around 75 per cent of employment in the South East (Producer Services Working Party 1986).

Despite the importance of the sector, however, there is no universal acceptance of any single view of the role of the service sector in regional and national economic growth (Wood 1986). As recent commentators have pointed out, there are at least three separate schools of thought represented in the service sector literature (Miles 1985; Gillespie and Green 1987). First, the service sector is seen by some commentators as dependent upon other sectors of the economy, primarily manufacturing, which through exports and the potential for productivity growth and exploitation of economies of scale are at the heart of the economic growth process. This view has been significant in the United Kingdom: it was given influential backing in Kaldor's (1966) emphasis on manufacturing as the engine of growth and in the Bacon and Eltis (1976) discussion of the role of the market and non-market sectors in the economy, which drew attention to the negative effects of the diversion of resources away from the market sector, in particular manufacturing, by the rapidly expanding public service sector. More recently, as Wood (1986) has pointed out, most analyses of the changing spatial pattern of employment in Britain have focused on manufacturing to the neglect of equivalent study of the service sector. This in part reflects the emphasis on export-growth models in regional economics (Dixon and Thirlwall 1975; Thirlwall and Dixon 1979). It also reflects the emphasis on manufacturing as the 'basic' sector of a regional economy, with changes in service sector employment following those in manufacturing or responding to changes in consumer or public expenditure (Fothergill and Gudgin 1982; Cambridge Economic Policy Group 1982).

However, it is increasingly becoming clear that not all services depend for their markets on manufacturing or final demand: slightly more of the output of producer services goes to other service industries than to manufacturing and the increasing indirectness of supply of final consumer demand has stimulated the growth of intermediate services (Producer Services Working Party 1986; McKinnon and Pratt 1984). While the manufacturing sector undoubtedly remains an important influence on regional growth processes (Harris 1987), the traditional relationship between manufacturing and services, in which manufacturing 'demands' and services 'supply' inputs to production, is being replaced by an increasingly interdependent relationship between the two sectors (Wood 1987). It is no longer possible, therefore, to assume that the economic characteristics of a sector (such as high labour productivity) are the product of that sector alone. Manufacturing success and competitiveness now depend on the embodiment within the production process of service inputs such as software (for computer numerically controlled equipment and flexible manufacturing systems), research and development, design and marketing services, and on access to and integration with an efficient and reliable physical distribution network. Services constitute an integral part of the more flexible and integrated systems of production which increasingly characterise modern industry.

A second school of thought on the role of services views the service sector within the context of a stages of economic development perspective. In this view, as developed in particular by Fisher (1945) and Clarke (1940), economic development is seen as a three-stage process, with employment shifting progressively from agriculture to manufacturing and in turn to services. This shift is partly due to a productivity growth lag in services relative to manufacturing (although adequate comparisons are limited by difficulties in the measurement of real output in the services sector: Dewhurst et al 1984), and partly to a consequence of the Engel's Law proposition that the income elasticity of demand for services is higher than that for manufactured goods, with the result that as consumers' affluence increases proportionately more of their income will be spent on services. This stage model of service sector development has been most influentially developed in Bell's (1974) conception of the post-industrial society based on a service sector which is not a low productivity employer of a low skill workforce but rather a knowledge and information based engine of economic growth. As such this school of thought emphasises the 'natural' emergence of an autonomous expanding service sector as the major source of employment in developed economies, belief in which underlies much of the recent policy debate in the United Kingdom.

The third, and final, major school of thought on the evolution of the service sector rejects the explicit emphasis of the stage models of economic development on the autonomous development of the service sector based on its own internal dynamics and rising consumer affluence. In particular, the assumption that higher income elasticities for services relative to goods will drive the service economy forwards has recently been questioned by Gershuny and Miles (1984), who argue that although income elasticities for services may well be high, if price elasticities of demand are also high and if services become relatively more expensive then substitution against services may outweigh the income effect. This, they observe, has in fact occurred in the case of marketed final services, notably personal services. Supporting evidence for this argument comes from an analysis of income and price elasticities which suggests that services do tend to be characterised by both high income and high price elasticities (Deaton 1975) and is reinforced by the suggestion that the price of services has tended to rise relative to manufacturing in the United Kingdom (Harris 1987). Accordingly, the Gershuny/Miles thesis is that consumer goods have been progressively substituted for consumer services as the 'self-service economy' developed (Gershuny 1978). In parallel with this, increased labour demand has been created by the need to market, distribute and service these manufactured goods, or 'intermediate consumer services', and by the development of 'intermediate producer services' as an increasing proportion of service sector employment is involved indirectly in the process of production (Gershuny and Miles 1984). This suggestion that the shift from a goods-based to a service-based economy may not be either inevitable or permanent is reinforced by the suggestion by long-wave theorists that the shift of economic activity to the service sector may be a temporary phenomenon associated with a particular stage in the long-wave evolution of an economic system, which will be reversed as the economy expands on the basis of the production of new types of products in the next Kondratief cycle (Freeman 1986).

Although elements of all three schools of thought coexist in the current debate (Producer Services Working Party 1986; Gillespie and Green 1987), it is possible to identify a number of causes of service sector growth in mature industrial economies (Gershuny and Miles 1984, 28–29; Howells and Green 1988, 6–8). Firstly, there has been an increasing demand for intermediate or producer services as an input to other sectors of the economy (Wood 1984), to the extent that such services now occupy 'a strategic role . . . in the contemporary economy' (Stanback et al 1981, xiv). Secondly, and related to this, is the process of externalisation by manufacturing and other companies of service functions (such as cleaning, catering, public relations and, in particular (Marshall 1982) equipment maintenance) which in the past were undertaken within the firm: this process of externalisation shows up as a redistribution of the balance of economic activity between the manufacturing and service sectors without necessarily involving a net increase in the overall level of economic activity. Thirdly, at least part of the growth in the service sector (particularly in public services and consumer services) reflects an increased demand for services as societies become richer: as Marquand (1979, 1983) has pointed out, growth in consumer services is not autonomous or self-generated but is a function of growth in consumer disposable incomes and general employment growth.

Fourthly, the identifiable rate of increase in labour productivity in the service sector is generally lower than in manufacturing, although the increased diffusion and application of information technology within the sector may increase labour productivity and reduce the rate of employment growth in services (Producer Services Working Party 1986). Fifthly, service activity is increasingly internationalised and provides opportunities for export-multiplier effects on regional and national economies both through invisible export earnings from the direct export of services (Howells and Green 1988, 73–138; Daniels et al 1986) and through the impact of service sector output indirectly exported by being embodied in exported manufactured goods (Wood 1984). Finally, the creation of new service activity itself contributes to overall growth in the sector. While many 'new' services simply represent alternative ways of servicing the same market need and therefore replace existing activities (Howells and Green 1988, 7), some new activities, notably those associated with new forms of technology and the emerging information economy (Porat 1977), do represent an additional stimulus to the development of the service sector.

These six factors underlying the contemporary growth of service sector employment do not, of course, apply with equal force to all parts of the service sector. Indeed, the heterogeneity of the sector and the differing economic roles played by sub-sectors within services have stimulated considerable discussion of the appropriate definition and classification of service sector activities. However, this discussion has not yet yielded any agreed or coherent definition or classification. Stigler's (1956) judgement that there was no authoritative consensus on either the boundary or the classification of services is still unchallenged: 'despite a growth of interest in services since, and the pivotal role of services in some economic analyses, questions of classification and definition remain as problematic as ever' (Producer Services Working Party 1986, 13).

However, these questions of classification and definition are import-ant in developing an understanding of the role of the service sector in economic, and in particular regional, development. Within the United Kingdom, for example, one of the most significant features of the distribution of service industry employment is the high degree of concentration of the sector in London and the greater South East region, one result of which is the general under-representation of service sector activity in peripheral regions such as Northern Ireland. Within this overall pattern there is a fundamental difference in the locational distribution and dynamics of private and public services. In general, public services, provided through non-market mechanisms, are relatively evenly distributed over space, and indeed are over-represented relative to total employment in parts of the periphery, including Northern Ireland (see Chapters 13 and 14). Within the private, marketed, services sector a further sub-division can be made on the basis of market orientation and locational distribution and dynamics. Consumer services are those which serve final consumer demand and the location of such employment closely follows the distribution of population and personal disposable income. Producer services, serving intermediate demand, are much less evenly distributed and are the main contributors to spatial variations in the location of service sector activity. Producer services have been recently defined, and their significance to the process of regional economic development spelt out, in the following terms:

> 'These services supply expertise which enhances the value of other sectors' output at various stages in the production process. They are traded within companies, on the open market and through their contributions to the competitiveness of other sectors. Their demand and supply need not be geographically coincident, and by contributing to the supply capacity of local industry, they may influence uneven development more generally' (Producer Services Working Party 1986, 6).

In the remainder of this chapter the development and importance of the service sector in Europe are reviewed briefly to provide the context for discussions of the sector in Northern Ireland. Following a summary of the inter-sectoral shift of employment in the Northern Ireland economy, the remainder of the chapter examines the quantitative and qualitative aspects of service industry employment growth with particular reference to the private service sector. The chapter concludes with a review of the actual and potential role of the private service sector, and producer services in particular, in industrial development policy in Northern Ireland.

2. Development of the service sector

In terms of employment in service industries, the service sector is now the most important sector in all member states in the European Community (Table 12.1). In 1984, Eurostat data indicated that service industries represented over 60 per cent of total employment in Belgium, Netherlands, Denmark, United Kingdom and France, and only in Greece and Spain did the sector account for 50 per cent or less of total employment. Overall, in the period 1977–83 service industry employment in the Community grew three times as fast as did total employment: by 15.5 per cent compared with growth in total employment of 5.1 per cent (Howells 1988). At national level, service industry growth has

TABLE 12.1   Service industry employment in the European Community

	% change 1977–1983	% total employment in services, 1984
FR Germany	14.1	54.4
France	12.4	60.6
Italy	23.1	55.5
Netherlands	21.1	66.3
Belgium	7.0	68.3
Luxembourg	22.0	58.7
United Kingdom	6.5	65.5
Ireland	26.0	54.8
Denmark	18.8	66.1
Greece	8.7	45.6
Spain	1.6	50.7[1]
Portugal	31.0	43.3
Eur 12	15.5	57.6

[1] 1983.
Sources: Howells (1988, 5–6) and Eurostat.

been fastest in Portugal, Ireland, Italy and Luxembourg over this period and has been lowest in the United Kingdom, Belgium and Spain. Although there are significant exceptions (notably Spain, France, Netherlands and Denmark), there is a tendency for countries with a high percentage share of services in total employment in 1984 to have had low rates of growth of services employment in the period 1977–83.

In terms of output, the service sector as a whole represented an estimated 55 per cent of total gross value added[1] in the Community (excluding Spain and Portugal) in 1978, compared with a 41 per cent share for manufacturing (Howells 1988, 7). In particular, market, or private, services (which covers activities such as wholesale or retail trade; lodging and catering services; transport and communication services; credit and financial services; personal and business services excluding those provided by government) emerge as of particular importance (Green 1985). In the early 1980s these market services contributed 42.3 per cent of gross value added in the Community (Eur 6) compared with 26.7 per cent for manufacturing. Furthermore, this share has been growing relative to manufacturing: in the decade between 1970–72 and 1980–82 the market services share of total gross value added in the Community (Eur 6) rose by 3.5 percentage points while the manufacturing share fell by over four percentage points (Table 12.2a). This improvement in the market services share largely reflects rapid growth in the sector in France and FR Germany: in Italy and the United Kingdom the market services share grew by less than one percentage point (Green 1985, 73) with the result that by the early 1980s the market services share of total gross value added in the United Kingdom had fallen below the European Community (Eur 6) average. This growth trend in the importance of the market services sector in total output is also reflected in the United States and Japan, although in both economies market services have been relatively more

TABLE 12.2   Contribution of market services to gross value added,[1] United Kingdom, Europe,[2] United States and Japan

a. Share of total gross value added[3]

	UK	Eur 6	USA	Japan
Market services				
1970/72	40.1	38.8	47.1	43.5
1980/82	41.0	42.3	49.6	46.2
Manufacturing				
1970/72	31.2	31.0	24.7	32.8
1980/82	24.8	26.7	21.2	28.2

b. Average annual growth rates[4]

	UK	Eur 6	USA	Japan
Market services				
1969/71–1974/76	2.7	4.0	3.8	5.0[5]
1975/77–1980/82	2.0	3.4	3.8	5.1
Manufacturing				
1969/71–1974/76	1.0	3.0	2.7	5.3[5]
1975/77–1980/82	−2.2	1.4	2.1	8.8

[1] Data are based on three year moving averages.
[2] Europe (Eur 6) covers the grouping, FR Germany, France, Italy, United Kingdom, Belgium and Netherlands.
[3] Based on data in current prices.
[4] Based on data in constant 1975 prices.
[5] Data for 1970/72–1975/77.
Source: Green (1985).

important than in Europe (Table 12.2a).

This shift from manufacturing to market services reflects the more rapid growth rates in the market services sector (Table 12.2b). In all countries, with the significant and not unexpected exception of Japan, average annual growth rates of gross value added (at constant 1975 market prices) in the market service sector exceed those in manufacturing, particularly in the late 1970s and early 1980s. Furthermore, although average annual growth rates in market services in Europe and the United States were similar over the period as a whole, in both areas they were lower than in Japan. The data in Table 12.2b also re-emphasise the disadvantageous position of the United Kingdom within Europe: not only has the performance of the British manufacturing sector been much poorer than elsewhere in Europe, but the market service sector has grown at little more than half the rate experienced elsewhere. It is against this background of a relatively sluggish market service sector in the United Kingdom that the structure and dynamics of the private service sector in Northern Ireland will be examined.

3. Private services in Northern Ireland

In terms of output and, in particular, employment, therefore, the service industries have been the most important source of growth within the European

Community, reflecting both rising personal incomes and consumer expenditure and the growing complexity and needs of manufacturing industry. In particular, in the 1970s and early 1980s service employment in peripheral regions of the Community has grown more rapidly than in the more central regions, largely reflecting very rapid employment growth in the Italian regions (Keeble et al 1981, 1986). There are also considerable regional variations in the balance between consumer and producer services which are of importance to long-term regional development prospects: producer services are more likely to form part of the economic base of a region and generate income, as well as strengthening the competitive efficiency of regional production activies (Producer Services Working Party 1986). At the European scale it appears that the relatively more rapid expansion in service sector employment in peripheral regions reflects an increasing relative and absolute specialisation in consumer services (including those in the public sector) while central and highly urbanised regions are characterised by an increased specialisation in producer services (Keeble et al 1981). Within this overall picture, Northern Ireland in the 1970s had one of the lowest rates of growth in total (public and private) service sector employment, recorded one of the lowest ratios between producer and consumer services (and hence a low proportion of producer services in total employment) and experienced one of the slowest rates of change in the balance between producer and consumer services (Keeble et al 1981, 144–46).[2]

SECTORAL CHANGE IN NORTHERN IRELAND

As Table 12.3 indicates, Northern Ireland has shared in the general shift in the occupational and industrial distribution of employment towards the service sector. Between 1971 and 1985 almost 74,000 jobs were lost in the manufacturing sector in Northern Ireland as both indigenous and externally owned industry restructured and contracted (see Chapter 4) with the result that manufacturing accounted for only 22 per cent of total employment in Northern Ireland in 1985 compared with a 37 per cent share in 1971.

Over the same period total employment in service industries increased by over 80,000, accounting for 69 per cent of total employment in 1985 (51 per cent in 1971).[3] As elsewhere in the United Kingdom (Producer Services Working Party 1986) and Europe (Howells 1988), this overall growth in the service industries conceals considerable divergent movements within the sector. The main gains in employment have been in public administration and in financial and business services, particularly in the 1971–78 period. Total employment in transport and communication and distributive trades has fallen over the period.

This is reflected in the changing distribution of output in Northern Ireland (Table 12.4). Between 1978 and 1985 the share of regional GDP accounted for by the manufacturing sector fell by over three percentage points, matched by an even larger proportional fall in employment. By contrast, the service sector as a whole accounted for a rising share of both employment and output. Reflecting the general understanding that productivity improvements in

TABLE 12.3   Employees in employment, Northern Ireland, 1971–1985

SIC 1980 Division		June 1971	June 1978	June 1985	Annual average rate of change (%)	
		(000)	(000)	(000)	1971–78	1978–85
0	Agriculture, forestry, fishing	11.6	9.6	10.0	−2.7	0.6
1	Energy and water supply	8.4	10.0	9.0	2.5	−1.5
2	Extraction of minerals etc	19.5	18.4	9.5	−0.8	−9.0
3	Metal goods, engineering and vehicles	50.3	41.7	30.5	−2.6	−4.4
4	Other manufacturing	105.1	83.1	61.0	−3.3	−4.3
2–4	Total manufacturing	174.8	143.1	101.0	−2.8	−4.9
5	Construction	39.5	37.9	22.9	−0.6	−6.9
6	Distribution etc	72.6	76.1	75.2	0.7	−0.2
7	Transport and communication	23.1	20.9	17.9	−1.4	−2.2
8	Banking, finance, insurance, business services and leasing	17.8	23.5	25.3	4.1	1.1
9	Other services	125.4	182.0	201.9	5.5	1.5
6–9	Total services	239.0	302.6	320.3	3.4	0.8
0–9	Total employment	437.2	503.2	463.2	0.9	−1.2

Source: DED, 1985.

the service sector are disguised by the methods used to measure service sector output (Dewhurst et al 1984), the service sector accounted for a higher proportion of employment than GDP in 1985, and the relative increase in the sector's share of employment was more rapid than for GDP between 1978 and 1985. Within the sector the main increases in output have been in the miscellaneous 'other services' category, largely reflecting developments in the public sector (Chapter 13). Financial and business services also increased their relative share of both GDP and employment in the 1980s, although at a slower rate than elsewhere in the United Kingdom (see Chapter 11; Gillespie and Green 1987). The distribution sector's share of GDP in Northern Ireland increased marginally between 1978 and 1985, and at a lower rate than the sector's employment share. As elsewhere, transport and communication services account for a lower proportion of both employment and output in 1985 than in 1979 (Producer Services Working Party 1986).

EMPLOYMENT CHANGE IN THE SERVICE SECTOR

In interpreting changes in the importance and structure of the service sector it is usual to make a fundamental distinction between public (non-market) and private (market) services. Public services, as defined here, are dominated by health and education services and public administration and defence. As such the definition is rather narrower than the broad definition of public services used in a previous analysis of the service sector in Northern Ireland (NIEC 1982), which included most transportation services, postal services and

TABLE 12.4 Sectoral distribution of gross domestic product and employees in employment, Northern Ireland, 1978 and 1985 (percentage)

		Gross domestic product		Employment	
		1978	1985	1978	1985
0	Agriculture, forestry, fishing	5.6	4.4	1.9	2.2
1	Energy and water supply	3.6	3.9	2.0	1.9
2–4	Manufacturing	22.3	18.7	28.4	21.8
5	Construction	8.1	6.2	7.5	4.9
6	Distribution etc	12.3	12.7	15.1	16.2
7	Transport and communication	5.3	4.7	4.2	3.9
8	Banking, finance, insurance, business services, leasing	13.0	15.2	4.7	5.5
9	Other services	29.9	34.1	36.2	43.6
6–9	Total services	60.5	66.7	60.1	69.2
Total		100.0	100.00	100.0	100.0

Source: Adapted from NIAAS No 7, 1988.

telecommunications in the public service sector category. In keeping with much of the recent research on the service sector, however, these particular services are here treated as private services (Marquand 1979; Hubbard and Nutter 1982; Producer Services Working Party 1986).

Within the private service sector it is also common to classify services by the character of the market served, distinguishing between producer services, primarily serving intermediate demand, and consumer services which serve final demand. In practice, however, the level of aggregation used in the compilation and classification of official statistics makes it difficult to separate clearly those services serving intermediate and final demand, and many classifications introduce a 'mixed' category of services (which includes banking and insurance services, wholesale distribution, property management and legal services). In the analysis in this chapter, however, the argument of the Producer Services Working Party (1986) will be accepted: producer services will be interpreted liberally to include both those services which can be

TABLE 12.5 Employment change in the service sector,[1] Northern Ireland

	June 1971	June 1978	June 1985	% change	
	(000)	(000)	(000)	1971–78	1978–85
Public services	103.0	146.1	161.0	41.9	10.2
Private services	135.9	151.1	159.3	11.2	5.4
Producer services	62.7	67.2	62.3	7.2	−7.3
Consumer services	73.2	83.9	96.9	14.6	15.5
Total services	239.0	302.6	320.3	26.6	5.9

[1] For a definition of service sector categories see Appendix 12.1.
Source: See Appendix 12.1.

unambiguously allocated to the sector together with those, such as banking and insurance services, which straddle producer and consumer markets. As a result, private consumer services are defined as those which largely serve final demand and are not provided from within the public sector.[4]

Using this classification, the employment performance of the service sector in Northern Ireland is summarised in Table 12.5 (for a more detailed analysis, including the allocation of services to each of the categories at the two digit level of the SIC 1980, see Appendix 12.1). As already indicated in Table 12.3 above, substantial employment growth in the service sector was largely a phenomenon of the 1970s in Northern Ireland. This largely reflects the very rapid growth of employment in the public sector, which increased by 42 per cent in the period 1971–78 (Table 12.5). Despite subsequent constraints on public expenditure in Northern Ireland (NIEC 1984), public service employment in the 1980s rose at almost twice the rate of that in private services (see Chapters 13 and 14 for further details).

Within the private service sector the overall pattern of change is similar, with a sharp reduction in growth rates in the 1980s. Within this, however, there is a major and important difference in the employment performance of the producer and consumer service sectors (Table 12.5). In the 1970s employment in consumer services grew at twice the rate of that in producer services. This confirms the observation, already noted above, that in the 1970s employment in services in the peripheral regions of Europe reflected sharp increases in employment in consumer services and a relative shift away from producer services (Keeble et al 1981). In the late 1970s and early 1980s employment in consumer services continued to expand, at a slightly faster rate than did employment in any other subgroup in the sector. However, during this period producer service employment actually fell in absolute terms and by 1985 total employment in the sector was marginally lower than in 1971. As the data in Appendix 12.1 make clear, this poor performance of the producer service sector in the period 1978–85 largely reflects the loss of 3,000 jobs in wholesale distribution (17 per cent of the 1978 total), 1,250 jobs in railways and other inland transport (16 per cent of the 1978 total) and 1,700 jobs in miscellaneous transport services and support services (42 per cent of the 1978 total).

The poor performance of these activities highlights a further distinction within the private service sector, between blue-collar goods handling activities and white-collar information processing activities (Porat 1977; Robinson et al 1982). In the case of the former, the pattern of development has closely paralleled that of manufacturing in the British economy as technical change and competitive pressures have stimulated increased capital intensity and a reduced demand for labour. In the case of information handling activities, Northern Ireland has recorded employment increases in banking and finance and business services in particular (see Appendix 12.1). However, these increases have been lower than elsewhere in the United Kingdom, with the result that the region still has one of the lowest proportions of employment in these activities (NIEC 1982; O'Dowd 1987).

TABLE 12.6   Regional changes in service sector employment, 1971–1981

	Producer services		Consumer services		Public services	
	(000)	(%)	(000)	(%)	(000)	(%)
South East	118.4	11.4	185.7	13.0	99.7	6.8
East Anglia	34.8	41.3	32.3	27.8	21.7	19.1
South West	78.6	42.6	103.0	37.6	67.1	23.9
West Midlands	39.2	15.6	55.7	17.6	53.6	15.9
East Midlands	50.5	34.1	75.6	39.3	59.6	27.8
Yorks–Humberside	43.1	18.1	63.5	20.8	59.4	19.0
North West	−0.8	−0.2	68.1	15.3	48.4	10.6
North	10.7	7.8	23.4	10.5	12.0	5.4
Wales	8.4	7.2	38.0	24.7	42.2	21.1
Scotland	24.8	8.4	74.4	19.7	80.4	21.2
Northern Ireland	4.6	7.9	20.6	26.4	55.8	54.2
United Kingdom	482.3	13.4	740.3	18.9	599.9	14.7

Source: Producer Services Working Party (1986, 80) based on Census of Employment data.

INTER-REGIONAL COMPARISONS

As Table 12.6 indicates, the pattern of employment change in the private service sector in Northern Ireland, and in particular in producer services, occurred within the context of substantial national employment increases in all three groups of services (over 1.2m net increase in private service sector employment and a further 0.6m jobs in public services) and a relative decline in the dominance of the South East region. In the decade 1971–81 for which comparable inter-regional data have been produced, the relative increase in employment in producer services, consumer services and public services in the South East was below the national averages of between 13 per cent and 19 per cent. However, it is also clear that for the most part this relative decentralisation in the distribution of service sector employment was restricted to regions adjacent to the South East (Table 12.6). Over the decade the largest relative increases in consumer service employment were recorded in East Anglia (28 per cent), the South West (38 per cent) and the East Midlands (39 per cent), with Northern Ireland and, to a lesser extent, Wales also recording significantly above average increases.

In the producer service sector the gap between the peripheral regions and other parts of the country is much more pronounced. In both East Anglia and the South West employment in producer services rose by over 40 per cent during the decade 1971–81, and by 34 per cent in the East Midlands, which was still at least twice as high as in any other region of the United Kingdom. More detailed analysis of these data suggests that much of this decentralisation of producer services occurred in the period 1971–78. Between 1978 and 1981 producer service employment in the South East grew by slightly more than the national average rate, and although the highest relative increases were still recorded in the adjacent South West and East Anglia regions, regional variations from the national average were much less pronounced (Producer Services Working Party 1986, 81).

Overall, therefore, Northern Ireland shared with the North West, the North, Wales and Scotland very much lower than average increases in producer service employment: in absolute terms Northern Ireland accounted for less than 1 per cent of the total national increase in producer service employment between 1971 and 1981, compared with figures of 2.8 per cent for consumer services and 9.3 per cent for public services. This poor growth performance of the producer service sector in Northern Ireland has reinforced the already considerable shortfall in such employment relative to the national average: in 1978, for example, only 3.5 per cent of total employment in Northern Ireland was provided by producer services (on the Northern Ireland Economic Council's narrow definition) compared with a United Kingdom average of 5.9 per cent and 8.4 per cent in the South East (NIEC 1982). In the case of tradable producer services (those that are capable of being sold in the market at a price which covers the cost of providing them), including business services and R & D (NIEC 1982, 5), the differential between Northern Ireland and Great Britain is even more pronounced.

The combination of sluggish producer service growth and the very poor manufacturing performance of the Northern Ireland economy emphasises that it is difficult to be optimistic about the prospects for producer service activity in the less favoured regions of the United Kingdom (Green and Howells 1987). As another detailed analysis of the changing geography of producer service employment in Britain concluded (based on a more restrictive definition of producer services than that adopted here), the 'pre-existing spatial disparities between the southern core regions of the country and the northern periphery, in terms of their representation of producer services, were largely maintained during the 1971–81 period. . . . The major spatial shift took place not at the core-periphery regional level but at the intra-regional level' (Gillespie and Green 1987, 409).

4. Nature of service sector employment

These quantitative changes in the structure and importance of the service sector in Northern Ireland have been matched by qualitative changes which are important in the context of the role of the sector in economic development policies at regional and local level (O'Dowd 1987). Two separate but closely related trends are of particular relevance: the growth in part-time and female employment.

PART-TIME EMPLOYMENT

As Table 12.7 indicates, part-time employment in the service sector in Northern Ireland expanded rapidly in the 1970s, the period of most rapid growth for the sector as a whole, and accounted for an increasing proportion of

TABLE 12.7 Growth of part-time employment in the service sector, Northern Ireland, 1971–1978

| | Part-time as % of total employment | | Change in part-time employment 1971–78 | | Part-time workers as % of employment[1] |
	1971	1978	Number	%	1971–78
Producer services	5.1	7.6	1,916	60.6	42.7
Consumer services	24.4	42.4	17,825	100.6	167.2

[1] Growth in part-time workers as percentage of employment growth in the sector 1971–78.
Source: As Table 12.3.

total employment in each part of the sector (see Chapter 7). Although they represented only 5 per cent of the 1971 workforce in producer services, almost half of the net increase in producer service employment up to 1978 was accounted for by part-time workers, who accounted for 5 per cent of employment in 1971 and 7.6 per cent in 1978. As other research confirms, this is in keeping with the situation nationally; in six of the eleven economic planning regions in the United Kingdom at least half of the growth of producer service employment in the 1970s is accounted for by increases in part-time employment (Table 12.8). In Northern Ireland, in fact, part-time workers represent a lower proportion of total employment change in producer services than in most other regions, compensating slightly for the lower absolute and relative growth of producer service employment in the region. In the consumer service sector the number of part-time workers doubled in the 1970s, and by 1978 part-time employees represented more than 42 per cent of total employment in the sector. More significantly, in consumer services part-time employment has displaced full-time employment: part-workers accounted for

TABLE 12.8 Part-time employment growth in producer service industries, regions of the United Kingdom, 1971–1981

	Part-time workers as % of total employment change
South East	64.2
East Anglia	19.9
South West	17.9
West Midlands	50.0
East Midlands	29.0
Yorkshire and Humberside	41.9
North West	109.0
North	56.3
Wales	51.2
Scotland	68.1
Northern Ireland	32.6

Source: Producer Services Working Party (1986, 81).

167 per cent of net employment change in consumer services between 1971 and 1978 (Table 12.7) as a fall of over 7,000 in full-time employees was more than compensated for by an increase of over 17,000 part-time employees.

The significance of part-time employment in the service sector has implications for the measurement of employment growth in the sector. If the overall rates of employment change in the service sector reported in Table 12.5 above are adjusted to a full-time equivalent basis (by adopting the convention that two part-time employees are equivalent to one full-time employee) the apparent employment growth performance of the private service sector is very much reduced (Table 12.9).

TABLE 12.9   Employment growth rates for service industry employment, Northern Ireland, 1971–1978 (percentage)

	Average annual employment growth 1971–78	
	A[1]	B[2]
Producer services	7.2	5.9
Consumer services	14.6	2.7
Total private services	11.2	4.1

[1] Based on unadjusted data on total employees in employment.
[2] Based on adjusted data for full-time equivalent employees in employment (one full-time employee equals two part-time).
Source: As Table 12.3.

FEMALE EMPLOYMENT

This increase in the importance of part-time employment in the service sector in Northern Ireland is matched by a rapid expansion of female employment over the period (see Chapter 7). In all major groups of service industries the importance of female employment has grown. This is particularly true of the 1971–78 period and is less pronounced in the period up to 1985 (Table 12.10). As with part-time employment there is a clear distinction between producer service industries and the rest of the service sector; female employment is twice as important in the latter as in producer services, where it still accounts for only one-third of employees.

TABLE 12.10   Male and female employment in the service sector, Northern Ireland, 1971–1985

	Female as % of total employment			% change in employment				Female workers as % of net employment change	
				1971–78		1978–85			
	1971	1978	1985	M	F	M	F	1971–78	1978–85
Producer services	27.1	30.7	32.8	1.7	21.3	−9.8	−0.8	80.4	2.1
Consumer services	57.9	64.2	66.3	3.7	35.2	2.1	12.2	92.9	91.3

Source: As Table 12.3.

In all sectors, female employment has grown very much more rapidly than has male employment. In producer services male employment was almost static between 1971 and 1978, whereas female employment expanded by one fifth, and between 1978 and 1985 male employment fell by almost 10 per cent (Table 12.10), largely due to employment reduction in 'blue-collar' services in transport, communications and wholesale distribution. In consumer services the growth of female employment was particularly strong in the 1970s, corresponding with a similar increase in part-time employment; between 1971 and 1985 female employment accounted for over 90 per cent of the net increase in consumer service employment.[5]

5. The service sector and industrial development policy

Despite the growing importance of the service sector in Northern Ireland, as in the national economy, the service sector has rarely featured in discussions of industrial development policy in the region; indeed, of 693 identifiable new and expanding indigenous and inward investment projects grant-aided in Northern Ireland between 1945 and 1982 only three were in the service sector (NIEC 1983). To some extent this reflects the truncating effects of inward investment: the relative abundance of nationally and internationally mobile manufacturing investment in the 1960 and early 1970s meant that other avenues, among them the service sector, were simply not considered. It also reflects the view that the scope for encouraging employment in the service sector was small (Report by Review Team 1976, 5). Following the collapse of new inward investment into Northern Ireland in the mid-1970s, however, renewed attention was given to the potential of the service sector, in view of the arguments that the distinction between manufacturing and service industries has become less clear cut, employment in manufacturing has shrunk and developments in telecommunications have increased the array of services which are marketable over a wide area, and which are adaptable to a regional environment (Northern Ireland Office 1981, 31).

In focusing on inward investment in service activity, policy in Northern Ireland was consistent with the general emphasis in United Kingdom regional policy on inter-regional industrial mobility (Harrison 1989). It was also more limited than service industry assistance available in Great Britain, which gave greater emphasis to import substitution and underdeveloped market potential as criteria for assistance (Daniels 1983; Marshall 1985), and which had been in existence in the form of the Office and Service Industries Scheme (OSIS) since 1973 (Kennett and Bamford 1988).

Following the 1984 revisions to regional policy the OSIS Scheme was abandoned in Great Britain, with its main provisions embodied in the new regional selective assistance package. Certain producer services were also included in the revised Regional Development Grant scheme (Harrison 1986).

However, the Department of Economic Development did not make a similar modification to the Standard Capital Grant Scheme in Northern Ireland, on the grounds that all services in Northern Ireland are non-tradable. In particular, the Department argued that the existence of the sea barrier between Northern Ireland and Great Britain protected existing services from competition and hindered the expansion of local firms to national markets. This contrasted with the situation in the assisted areas in Great Britain, where 'there is no physical or psychological barrier to the extension of their activities into neighbouring non-Assisted Areas' (DED 1985, 6). The substantive basis for this argument is unclear. Certainly, from the Economic Council's survey of the linkage patterns of 279 manufacturing businesses in Northern Ireland established with financial assistance from the ID institutions, it appears that only 58 per cent of total expenditure on business services, including some (advertising, computer services, PR consultants, R & D) eligible for Regional Development Grant in Great Britain between 1984 and the abolition of the scheme in 1988 (HM Government 1988), was spent with suppliers in Northern Ireland. A further 35 per cent was spent in Great Britain and 7 per cent was spent with suppliers overseas (NIEC 1986a). In the case of companies of United States origin only 35 per cent of service inputs were sourced within Northern Ireland, with 50 per cent coming from Great Britain and 14 per cent from overseas (Table 12.11).

TABLE 12.11 Service input expenditure by ID assisted manufacturing projects in Northern Ireland (percentage)

| | Source of service inputs | | |
Origin of project	Northern Ireland	Great Britain	Overseas
Small indigenous[1]	80.1	15.6	3.6
Large indigenous[2]	74.2	23.1	2.7
Great Britain	61.8	37.1	1.9
United States	35.4	49.5	14.4
Other foreign	62.7	31.3	5.9
Total	58.6	34.7	7.1

[1] Projects assisted by LEDU.
[2] Projects assisted by IDB.
Source: NIEC (1986b, 34).

Following its establishment in 1982, the Industrial Development Board identified the services sector as one in which Northern Ireland has considerable expertise and competence, and designated the tradable service sector as a target sector for job creation, to be treated on the same basis as manufacturing (IDB 1985, 9). The guidelines for support of a tradable service sector project were defined by the IDB as: viability; additionality (no dependence on local sales at the expense of another company in Northern Ireland); development of new services; development of markets outside Northern Ireland and import substitution. These criteria are similar to those recommended by the Northern Ireland Economic Council (1982) and both the

TABLE 12.12   Possible target tradable services for industrial development policy

Management consultancy
Engineering consultancy
Industrial design consultancy, including computer assisted design
Architectural design including quantity surveying
Energy conservation advice and consultancy
Advertising
Marketing and market research
Personnel recruitment and training services
Data processing services
Software development including computer assisted learning and computer
    managed learning
Industrial and commercial photographic services
Commercial testing laboratories
Technical publishing houses
Mail order houses and mailing services
Television and video scriptwriting, recording, mixing, production and post-
    production services
Music recording, production and publishing
Financial services, especially headquarters and administrative centres for
    locally consumed services (eg hire purchase, leasing, insurance, building
    societies)
Research and development centres both independent and in house
Administrative headquarters marketing centres, and international financial
    centres
Conference, exhibition and trade fair facilities
Holiday tour operators
Health care services

Source: IDB (1985).

range of activities eligible for IDB assistance (Table 12.12) and the criteria for assistance are similar to those applying in Great Britain (Kennett and Bamford 1988).

It is within the small firm sector in Northern Ireland that industrial development support for the service sector has been most evident. Since 1980 the service sector has accounted for an increasing proportion of LEDU's total job promotions and has contributed to the rapid expansion of LEDU's operations (Table 12.13). However, in absolute terms, there was actually a decline in job promotions in the service sector in 1984/85 and, after a sharp recovery in 1986/87, again in 1987/88, and in relative terms the service sector share of total LEDU job promotions is lower now than in the early 1980s. This may be in part a reflection of the introduction by LEDU of an Enterprise Grant aimed as pump-priming assistance for the unemployed person who wants to get into business. In 1983/84 7.3 per cent of LEDU's job promotions were accounted for by this scheme, rising to 19.3 per cent in 1987/88 (Table 12.13). Although no sectoral breakdown is available for Enterprise Grant job promotions, it is likely that a substantial number of them are used to support the creation of service-type businesses where the barriers to entry (knowledge, skills and capital) are lower than in manufacturing. Data on actual employment created through this job promotion activity are rather more limited. However, in March 1983, service sector businesses assisted by LEDU up to March 1982 employed 310 people (5.1 per cent of total employment in LEDU assisted businesses) in 58 firms – an average employment of 5.4 persons per firm (NIEC 1985).

However, this figure is based on employment in projects which received assistance from LEDU before 31 March 1982. As Table 12.13 indicates, the major expansion in LEDU support for the service sector occurred after this date: between April 1982 and March 1988 over 500 service sector projects were approved by LEDU: if the employment performance of these projects is similar to that of the earlier ones, it suggests that somewhere in the region of 2,000 additional service sector jobs could be created in such projects.

TABLE 12.13   Local Enterprise Development Unit job promotions, 1980/81–1987/88

	Services	Enterprise Grant[1]	Manufacturing and craft	Total	Services as % of total
1980/81	66	—	989	1,055	6.3
1981/82	314	—	1,299	1,613	19.5
1982/83	736	na	1,814	2,550	28.9
1983/84	884	226	2,508	3,658	24.2
1984/85	721	426	2,862	4,009	18.0
1985/86	738	485	2,665	3,888	19.0
1986/87	945	773	2,462	4,244	22.3
1987/88	677	766	2,493	3,973	17.0
Total	5,081	2,676	17,092	23,940	21.2

[1] Enterprise Grant cases were not separately identified in 1982/83.
Source: LEDU Annual Reports.

This job creation, however, can be subject to two criticisms. First, the businesses assisted are almost entirely (though not exclusively) locally orientated, and many of them are designed to serve sub-regional or local markets rather than the regional market as a whole. While assistance for this type of service activity can be justified on the grounds that market imperfections mean that there are unmet local needs, it is likely that such assistance, particularly to consumer services, will involve high displacement effects on existing suppliers. The economic case for such assistance, and the quantification of its net benefits, has yet to be made (Harrison 1987). Second, these LEDU supported service sector businesses are small – actual average employment in 1983 in LEDU service business was just over five, and although over 2,700 jobs have been promoted in service sector projects since 1980, the average job promotions per project is less than seven. This is rather less than the average size of manufacturing enterprises in receipt of LEDU job-related assistance (NIEC 1985).

These projects are also considerably smaller than equivalent projects in other regions. Between 1980 and 1985, LEDU service sector promotions represented 8.9 per cent of total IDB and LEDU job promotions. In the

Republic of Ireland, the International Services Programme launched by the IDA in 1981 with a new package of incentives led to the promotion in 1981 and 1982 of 3,233 jobs in 86 internationally mobile service sector businesses, an average of 37.6 jobs per project. This activity represented 5.4 per cent of total IDA job promotions in these years, and was concentrated in inward investment in technical, consulting and computer services (IDA Annual Report). The IDA does not deal with cases with a job potential of under 20 through the International Services Programme on the grounds that the overhead costs for both the IDA and the applicant are too high. In Wales services projects accounted for 11.1 per cent (3,808 jobs) of new employment promoted with regional selective assistance between 1979 and 1983. The average employment promoted per project was 43.8 (compared with over 80 new and safeguarded jobs per manufacturing project) (Committee on Welsh Affairs 1984). Nationally, between 1973 and 1984 the guidelines for the Office and Service Industries Scheme emphasised that a project should demonstrate a job potential of ten or more before becoming eligible for assistance (Marshall 1985). From a recent evaluation of the Scheme it appears that the average outturn employment created per project was just over thirty (Kennett and Bamford 1988).

6. Conclusion

This chapter has reviewed the development of the private service sector in Northern Ireland in the context of developments in Great Britain and the European Community. Whether measured in terms of employment or gross value added, the service sector is now much more significant than manufacturing industry in most of the advanced industrial economies. Furthermore, the service sector has expanded rapidly: in the 1970s, for example, the output of market, or private sector, services (which excludes services provided by government) expanded by between 3 per cent and 4 per cent annually in Europe and the United States and by 5 per cent annually in Japan. However, the United Kingdom experienced a much lower growth rate (of between 2 per cent and 3 per cent annually) over this period, which is only partly explained by the already large size of the sector in the early 1970s.

Within Northern Ireland the shift in employment in favour of the service sector has been significant. In 1971 service industries (including public services) accounted for 50 per cent of employees in employment in the region. By 1985 this proportion had risen to 69 per cent. Much of this employment, and a high proportion of the growth in service industry employment, was in the public sector; private service industries employed 29 per cent of total employees in employment in Northern Ireland in 1971, rising to only 34 per cent in 1985. Within the private service sector, consumer services, supplying final demand, have grown much more rapidly than have producer services which, as 'indirect production inputs' (Gillespie and Green 1987, 409), play a key role in the broader production process as facilitators of adaptation and change (Producer Services Working Party 1986). Indeed, employment in producer services in Northern Ireland actually fell between 1978 and 1985 as employment losses in 'blue collar' services such as transport and communication and wholesale distribution were not compensated for by increases elsewhere, particularly in financial and business services, where Northern Ireland failed to share in the general regional expansion in employment in the rest of the United Kingdom (see Chapter 11). Indeed, the rate of growth of employment in producer services in Northern Ireland was among the lowest regional figures in the United Kingdom and served to maintain the pre-existing regional disparity between the southern core regions of the country and the northern periphery (Gillespie and Green 1987).

The relatively low level of producer service employment in Northern Ireland acts as a constraint on the wider restructuring of the regional economy and reinforces the impact of the decline in manufacturing industry, both because producer services have an important employment and output generating role and because producer services make an important contribution to improving the dynamics and competitiveness of other sectors of the economy (NIEC 1982; Producer Services Working Party 1986). This shortfall reflects a number of factors (O'Dowd 1987). Firstly, the development of producer services within the overall division of labour in production, as specialised extensions of head office type functions, has remained tied to the greater South East region with its concentration of corporate decision making and its well developed professional labour market (Gillespie and Green 1987). Secondly, demand for producer service inputs in Northern Ireland has been depressed by the nature of the manufacturing sector in the region. In particular, externally owned manufacturing enterprises are less likely to source service sector inputs, particularly inputs of high level services, locally than are indigenous enterprises, and indigenous enterprises, particularly small firms, are likely to generate a lower absolute level of demand for producer service inputs from both external suppliers and internal provision (NIEC 1986a).

The growing research interest in the economic significance and locational behaviour of the producer service sector has stimulated discussion of the role of such services in regional development policy (Marshall 1985; Producer Services Working Party 1986; Gillespie and Green 1987). As in the rest of the United Kingdom, the Northern Ireland experience of the service sector in regional industrial development policy has been mixed. On the one hand the institutions involved in the inward investment drive and regeneration of medium and large businesses in the region have been ambivalent at best about the role, if any, to be given to services. The result has been an uncertainty over whether or not such activities should be assisted, arising in part from the absence of a detailed analysis of the locational dynamics of tradable service employment and of the reasons for the relatively low level of such employment in Northern Ireland (NIEC 1982).

At the local level LEDU has had considerable success in the promotion of service sector activities within the small business sector. However, these projects employ hundreds rather than thousands of people, although the figure is likely to rise, reflecting the rapid expansion of this type of activity in recent years. Furthermore, the relative and absolute importance of service sector job promotions within LEDU's overall activities has fallen recently, suggesting that there is a limit to the extent to which a policy based on supporting primarily locally orientated services can be sustained. Indeed, it seems likely from the nature of these businesses and of the markets they serve that the displacement effects of this assistance may have been considerable. Finally, it appears that relative to the experience of other agencies, service sector businesses supported in Northern Ireland have a very much lower average job potential.

In the light of wider political, economic and technological developments, such as the GATT discussions on the liberalisation of international trade in services, investment in information technology (NIEC 1989) and reductions in the cost of computing hardware, the service sector is likely to continue to play an important role in national and regional economic development, and to thereby assume a more prominent place in the targeting of regional assistance in European economies (Bachtler 1988). In designing a policy for the support of private sector services, a number of considerations are relevant. Firstly, local services, serving both final and intermediate demand, merit support if they substitute for imported services or fill a gap in service provision. The emphasis on mobility and export criteria which has characterised service industry policy in the United Kingdom is not necessarily the only basis for assistance. Secondly, if private services are to be adequately supported in a regional policy framework more attention should be given to the design of appropriate policy instruments, to allow for the provision of employment grants, grants for working capital (which is often the major requirement of new service sector projects) and tax incentives, in addition to the capital grants characteristic of support for manufacturing. However, for services to be treated on an equal basis to manufacturing plants, the present distortions in the treatment of capital and revenue grants for taxation purposes would require attention. While the former are tax free (and have their value enhanced by the availability of capital allowances on the full value of the plant and equipment being grant aided) revenue grants, such as employment or interest relief grants, are subject to corporation tax. This reduces the effective rate of grant to non-capital intensive projects (which would include many potential service sector projects) and hinders the marketing cf the overall package of incentives to the service sector.

Thirdly, even if the service sector is treated on exactly the same terms as manufacturing, a regional policy incorporating private sector services should be based on realistic principles. In particular, even with the support of a full range of regional policy measures it is unlikely that employment growth in the service sector, and in producer services in particular, will compensate for the loss of employment in manufacturing and other sectors. A shift of policy emphasis towards the service sector should not, therefore, be at the expense of assistance to other sectors and activities. Finally, and related to the previous point, the rationale for assisting the service sector should be reconsidered. In the light of the sharp reductions in regional aid budgets in the 1980s (see Chapter 4), and the change of emphasis away from providing assistance in the form of financial and infrastructural support towards advisory and training services (HM Government 1988), the primary justification for supporting the service sector can be restated. The view of the late 1970s and early 1980s that private service activities warranted support on the basis of their employment creating potential, is giving way to a more considered view which emphasises the inter-relationships between producer services and other industries (Wood 1984, 1987). Producer services in particular are important not just for their own employment and output contribution, but also for the contribution they make to the dynamics and competitiveness of other sectors (Producer Services Working Party 1986). In this perspective regional assistance for private sector services forms part of a wider programme to improve the competitiveness of indigenous industry. This can be achieved by both stimulating the increased supply of such services and, perhaps more importantly from a development point of view, encouraging a higher level of services demand by firms in the regions. In this respect the availability of government support for the use of expert advice and consultancy services by small businesses in Northern Ireland, funded by the ERDF between 1984 and 1988 under its business improvement schemes, and the emphasis given to assistance of this type nationally in the revised strategy of the Department of Trade and Industry (HM Government 1988), is a welcome development which should, by stimulating demand for particular categories of producer service, ultimately increase their supply and thereby improve the competitiveness of industry in Northern Ireland.

Appendix 12.1 Classification of service sector employment, Northern Ireland, 1971, 1978 and 1985

		June	June	June	% Change	
SIC 1980 Industry Class		1971	1978	1985	1971–78	1978–85
Producer services		62,712	67,200	62,330	7.2	−7.3
61	Wholesale distribution	20,662	21,360	17,670	3.4	−17.3
62	Dealing in scrap etc	394	450	310	14.2	−31.1
63	Commission agents	258	280	240	8.5	−14.3
71	Railways	1,286	1,050	890	−18.4	−15.3
72	Other inland transport	8,058	6,490	5,410	−19.5	−16.6
74	Sea transport	930	410	410	−55.9	—
75	Air transport	603	650	630	7.8	−3.1
76	Supporting services to transport	2,590	2,000	990	−22.8	−50.5

SIC 1980 Industry Class		June 1971	June 1978	June 1985	% Change 1971–78	% Change 1978–85
77	Miscellaneous transport services	1,730	2,010	1,330	16.2	−33.8
79	Postal services and telecommunications	7,909	8,310	8,200	5.1	−1.3
81	Banking and finance	5,268	7,310	7,790	38.8	6.6
82	Insurance services	2,820	2,900	2,640	2.8	−9.0
83	Business services	7,144	9,410	10,120	31.7	7.6
84	Renting of moveables	1,323	1,220	920	−7.8	−24.6
85	Owning and dealing in real estate	1,290	2,690	3,850	108.5	43.1
94	Research and development	452	660	930	46.0	40.9
Consumer services		73,210	89,270	96,930	14.6	15.6
64/65	Retail distribution	37,477	39,320	41,530	−9.5	22.4
66	Hotels and catering	10,328	10,690	12,980	3.5	21.4
67	Repair of consumer goods and vehicles	3,509	4,010	2,430	14.3	−39.4
96	Other services	13,194	24,670	28,880	87.0	17.1
97	Recreation etc	5,163	6,830	8,530	32.3	24.9
98/99	Personal and domestic services	3,539	3,750	2,580	6.0	−31.2
Public services		103,043	146,130	161,040	41.8	10.2
91	Public administration etc	33,647	48,650	52,660	44.6	8.2
92	Sanitary services	2,814	3,490	3,800	24.0	8.9
93	Education	37,900	54,000	57,460	42.5	6.4
95	Medical services	28,682	39,990	47,120	39.7	17.8

Source: DED, 1985.

Notes

1. As Dewhurst et al (1984) have pointed out, measurement of the output of service sector activities and identification of their contribution to value added is complicated by the widespread use of input measures as surrogate for output change and by the limited volume and quality of data collected on the service sector.

2. During the period 1973–79 aggregate services employment in the peripheral regions of the European Community grew by almost 20 per cent, compared with 8 per cent throughout the Community. Within the periphery the Italian regions recorded the fastest rates of growth (33 per cent) and the Northern periphery (Ireland, Denmark, Wales, Scotland, North and Northern Ireland) recorded lower rates of increase in service employment (10 per cent), although this was still above the rate of growth in central regions. From the data presented in Keeble et al (1981, 144), it appears that the growth of service sector employment in Northern Ireland during this period was within the range 6.1 to 9 per cent. The structure of

the service sector in the European Community is measured by Keeble et al (1981) as the ratio of employment in producer services to that in consumer services: the higher the ratio the more favourable the structure of the sector from the point of view of long-term development potential. In both 1973 and 1979 the producer/consumer ratio is highest in the central regions of the European Community (mean 0.292 in 1973 and 0.312 in 1979) than in the periphery (mean 0.216 in 1973 and 0.225 in 1979). In 1973 Northern Ireland had the lowest producer/consumer ratio in the United Kingdom (in the range 0.137 to 0.219) and between 1973 and 1978 recorded (with Scotland) the lowest rate of change in the ratio, indicating that the region was becoming relatively more reliant on consumer service employment.

3. The 1985 employment estimates quoted here and in Table 12.3 slightly overestimate the fall in manufacturing and underestimate the growth of the service sector. On the basis of Census of Employment data the service sector share of total employment has risen from 67 per cent to 69 per cent between 1984 and 1987 (see Appendix 6.3).

4. To ensure consistency of presentation of the Northern Ireland data with the Great Britain analysis of the Producer Services Working Party (1986), the classification of services into public, producer and consumer services follows their recommendations. However, as the PSWP acknowledge, such classifications are far from fully adequate, and may vary over time and over space. In the case of Northern Ireland, for example, it can legitimately be argued that a substantial proportion of employment in SIC (1980) Industry Classes 96 – Other services and 97 – Recreation etc lies within the public sector in the form of publicly financed home helps and leisure services. If these classes are attributed to the public sector (as in Chapter 6) much of the growth of private sector consumer service employment in Northern Ireland disappears.

5. As more recent data make clear, the continued expansion of female part-time employment underlies the growth of the service sector in the mid-1980s (see Appendix 6.3).

References

Bachtler, J (1988) Regional policy: European perspectives and the comparative experience. Paper presented to the Regional Studies Association Conference 'Divided Nation: Regional Policy and Britain's Periphery', Belfast, September 1988.

Bacon, R and Eltis, W (1976) *Britain's Economic Problem: Too Few Producers*, Macmillan, London.

Bell, D (1974) *The Coming of Post Industrial Society*, Heinemann, London.

Cambridge Economic Policy Group (1982) Prospects for the UK in the 1980s, *Cambridge Economic Policy Review* 8, (1), Gower, Aldershot, Hants.

Clarke, C A (1940) *The Conditions of Economic Progress*, Macmillan, London.

Committee on Welsh Affairs (1984) *The Impact of Regional Industrial Policy on Wales*, House of Commons Papers Session 1983–1984, 235–viii, HMSO, London.

Daniels, P W (1983) Service industries: supporting role or centre stage? *Area* 15 (4), 301–09.

Daniels, P W, Leyshon, A and Thrift, N J (1986) *UK Producer Services: The International Dimension*, Working Papers on Producer Services, 1, University of Bristol/University of Liverpool.

Deaton, A (1975) The measurement of income and price elasticities, *European Economic Review*, 6, 261–273.

Department of Economic Development, Northern Ireland (1985) *Review of Standard Capital Grants: Information Paper*, Department of Economic Development, Belfast.

Dewhurst, J H I, Lythe, C M and Peterson, J C (1984) The measurement of output and employment in the Scottish service sector (1962–1980), *ESU Research Papers*, 7, Industry Department for Scotland, Edinburgh.

Dixon, R J and Thirlwall, A P (1975) A model of regional growth rate differences on Kaldorian lines, *Oxford Economic Papers*, 27, 201–214.

Fisher, A G B (1945) *Economic Progress and Social Security*, Macmillan, London.

Fothergill, S and Gudgin, G (1982) *Unequal Growth: Urban and Regional Employment Change in the UK*, Heinemann, London.

Freeman, C (1986) The role of technical change in natural economic development, in Amin, A and Goddard, J B (eds), Technical Change, Industrial Restructuring and Regional Development, Allen & Unwin, London.

Fuchs, V R (1968) *The Service Economy*, National Bureau of Economic and Social Research/Columbia University Press, New York.

Fuchs, V R (1969) *Production and Productivity in the Service Industries*, National Bureau of Economic and Social Research/Columbia University Press, New York.

Gershuny, J (1978) *After Industrial Society: The Emerging Self-Service Economy*, Macmillan, London.

Gershuny, J and Miles, T (1984) *The New Service Economy: The Transformation of Employment in Industrial Societies*, Francis Pinter, London.

Gillespie, A E and Green, A E (1987) The changing geography of producer services employment in Britain, *Regional Studies*, 21 (5), 397–411.

Green, A E and Howells, J (1987) Spatial prospects for service growth in Britain, *Area*, 19, 11–122.

Green, M (1985) The development of market services in the European Community, the United States and Japan, *European Economy*, 25, 69–36.

Greenfield, H I (1966) *Manpower and the Growth of Producer Services*, Columbia University Press, New York.

Harris, R I D (1987) The role of manufacturing in regional growth, *Regional Studies*, 21 (4), 301–12.

Harrison, R T (1986) The standard capital grant scheme in Northern Ireland, a review and assessment, *Regional Studies*, 20, 175–182.

Harrison, R T (1987) Enterprise development in a peripheral regional economy: a medium term perspective. Paper presented at Northern Ireland Enterprise Convention – European Opportunity, Cascais, Portugal, October 1987 (mimeo).

Harrison, R T (1989) Industrial development in Northern Ireland: the Industrial Development Board, in Connolly, M and Loughlin, S (eds), *Public Policy in Northern Ireland: Adoption or Adaption*, Policy Research Institute, Belfast.

HM Government (1983) *Regional Industrial Development*, Cmnd 9111, HMSO, London.

HM Government (1988) *DTI – The Department of Enterprise*, Cmd 278, HMSO, London.

Howells, J (1988) *Economic, Technological and Locational Trends in European Services*, Avebury, Aldershot.

Howells, J and Green, A E (1988) *Technological Innovation, Structural Change and Location in UK Services*, Avebury, Aldershot.

Hubbard, R K P and Nutter, D S (1982), Service employment in Merseyside, *Geoforum*, 209–35.

IDB (1985) *Encouraging Enterprise: A Medium Term Strategy for 1985–1990*, Industrial Development Board, Belfast.

Kaldor, N (1966) *Causes of the Low Rate of Growth of the United Kingdom: An Inaugural Lecture*, Cambridge University Press, Cambridge.

Keeble, D, Owens, P and Thompson, C (1981) *The Influence of Peripheral and Central Locations on the Relative Development of Regions*, Department of Geography, University of Cambridge for the Directorate-General for Regional Policy, Commission of the European Communities, Brussels.

Keeble, D, Offord, J and Walker, S (1986) *Peripheral Regions in a Community of Twelve Member States: Final Report*, Department of Geography, University of Cambridge for Directorate-General for Regional Policy, Commission of the European Communities, Brussels.

Kennett, S and Bamford, P (1988) *An Evaluation of the Office and Service Industries Scheme*, HMSO, London.

McKinnon, A C and Pratt, A C (1984) *Jobs in Store: an Examination of the Employment Potential of Warehousing*. Occasional Papers, 11, Department of Geography, University of Leicester.

Marquand, J (1979) The service sector and regional policy in the UK, *Research Series*, 29, Centre for Environmental Studies, London.

Marquand, J (1983) The changing distribution of service employment, in Goddard, J and Champion, A G (eds), *The Urban and Regional Transformation of Britain*, Methuen, London.

Marshall, J N (1982) Linkages between manufacturing industry and business services, *Environment and Planning*, A14, 523–540.

Marshall, J N (1985) Business services, the regions and regional policy, *Regional Studies*, 19, 353–364.

Miles, T (1985) The service economy and socio-economic development (mimeo).

Northern Ireland Economic Council (1982) *Private Services in Economic Development*, Report No 30, Belfast.

Northern Ireland Economic Council (1983) *The Duration of Industrial Development Assisted Employment*, Report 40, Belfast.

Northern Ireland Economic Council (1984) *Public Expenditure Priorities: Overall Review*, Report 42, Belfast.

Northern Ireland Economic Council (1985) *The Duration of LEDU Assisted Employment*, Report 47, Belfast.

Northern Ireland Economic Council (1986a) *Economic Strategy: Industrial Development Linkages*, Report 56, Belfast.

Northern Ireland Economic Council (1986b) *Economic Strategy: Industrial Development*, Report 60, Belfast.

Northern Ireland Economic Council (1989) *Information Technology*, Report 74, Belfast.

Northern Ireland Office (1981) *Framework for Action*, HMSO, Belfast.

O'Dowd, L (1987) Trends and potential of the service sector in Northern Ireland, in Teague, P (ed) *Beyond the Rhetoric: Politics, the Economy and Social Policy in Northern Ireland*, Lawrence and Wishart, London.

Porat, M (1977) *The Infomation Economy: Definition and Measurement*, Special Publications 77–12 (1), Office of Telecommunications, US Department of

Commerce, Washington, DC.

Producer Services Working Party (1986) *Uneven Development in the Service Economy: Understanding the Location and Role of Producer Services*, Report of the Producer Services Working Party, Department of Geography, University of Birmingham.

Report by Review Team (1976) *Economic and Industrial Strategy for Northern Ireland*, HMSO, Belfast.

Robinson, J A S, Biggs, J M and Goodchild, A (1982) Structure and employment prospects of the service industries, *Research Paper*, 3, Department of Employment, London.

Stanback, T M (1979) *Understanding the Service Economy: Employment, Productivity, Location*, Johns Hopkins University Press, Baltimore.

Stanback, T M, Bearsse, P J, Noyelle, T J and Karasek, R A (1981) *Services: The New Economy*, Allanheld Osmun, Totawa, N J.

Stigler, C J (1956) *Trends in Employment in Service Industries*, National Bureau for Economic Research, Princeton University Press, New York.

Thirlwall, A P and Dixon, R J (1979) An export-led growth model with a balance of payments constraint, in Bowers, J (ed), *Inflation, Development and Integration: Essays in Honour of A J Bowers*, University of Leeds Press, Leeds.

Wood, P A (1984) The regional implications of manufacturing – service sector links: some thoughts on the revival of London Docklands, in Barr, B M and Waters, N (eds), *Regional Diversification and Structural Change*, Tantalus Research, Vancouver.

Wood, P A (1986) The anatomy of job loss and job creation: some speculations on the role of the 'producer service' sector, *Regional Studies*, 20, 37–46.

Wood, P A (1987) Producer services and economic change: some Canadian evidence, in Chapman, K and Humphreys, G (eds), *Technical Change and Industrial Policy*, Blackwell, Oxford.

CHAPTER THIRTEEN
The public sector
Victor N Hewitt

1. Introduction

In common with other regions of the United Kingdom, the functions assumed by government in Northern Ireland have grown dramatically since the Second World War. For much of this period the expansion of the public sector generated little controversy. Indeed the traditional view was that a growing public sector contributed an underlying stability to economic activity and by providing infrastructure, employment and services helped to offset a largely autonomous decline in private sector activity. In recent years, however, this benign view of the influence of the public sector has come under challenge. Aspects of the revisionist approach are implicit in early work by Gibson and Spencer (1981) but more recently have begun to emanate from within the government itself.[1] This approach emphasises the costs as well as the benefits of an expanding public sector both in terms of measurable deficits in the region's public finances and, less tangibly, in the form of a growing dependence on public funds throughout the economy. In addition, while not denying the ability of the public sector to sustain employment in the short term, critics nevertheless point to the longer-term damage to employment prospects which might be caused by excessive public sector intervention. By weakening market disciplines for both firms and workers the government, it is argued, may undermine the ability of the local economy to respond to changing circumstances.

Following Musgrave (1959) it has been conventional to justify government intervention in an economy in terms of promoting allocative efficiency, distributional equity and the stabilisation of economic activity. In a regional context, however, economists have tended to lay greatest stress on the efficiency properties of decentralised government. Few authors are prepared to concede that local administrations have an effective role to play in promoting distribution policy and fewer still in the case of stabilisation policy. The literature on fiscal federalism is dominated by the issue of optimal resource allocation rather than the spatial equalisation of income. This is apparent in both the seminal work by Tiebout (1956) on local public goods and, in a more general context, in the theory of clubs as developed by authors such as Buchanan (1965) and Litvak and Oates (1970). In contrast to these theoretical analyses, however, the development of the public sector in Northern Ireland appears to have been driven by distributional and stabilisation considerations rather than a rational desire to improve the allocation of resources in the province's economy. Since the creation of Northern Ireland in the 1920s the desire for parity with Great Britain in the provision of public services has been the most powerful influence on the growth of the public sector. In the early years of devolved government the ability to adopt common standards for public services was restrained by a lack of resources available to the local administration but over time this constraint was weakened by increasing transfers from central government. With the ending of devolved government in 1972 the availability of resources was no longer an effective constraint to the growth of the public sector in the province. The 1970s therefore saw a spectacular increase in public sector employment and government intervention in the local economy which was partly due to a process of catching up on the level of services available in Great Britain and partly a response to the downturn in industrial activity experienced after the oil price crisis of 1973. A further impetus to public sector employment during this period was the rapid expansion of the police and prison services brought about by the deteriorating security situation in the province. By the early 1980s, however, the expansion of the public sector had peaked and has since remained relatively stable.

2. Size and scope of the public sector

DEFINITIONS AND INSTITUTIONS

In the United Kingdom the public sector is defined to include the economic activities of three distinct sets of institutions. The first of these is central government which encompasses the various departments of state and the non-departmental public bodies which come under their sponsorship. The second is local government and its various agencies while the third set of institutions are loosely known as public corporations of which the nationalised industries are the most important in economic terms. Within official statistics central and local government combined are referred to as 'general government' and together with the public corporations make up the public sector.

The institutions of the public sector in Northern Ireland reflect the constitutional relationship between the province and Great Britain and have changed over time as this relationship has evolved. As a result the form of the public sector in the province differs in some significant respects from its counterparts in the rest of the United Kingdom. Central government in Northern Ireland, for example, consists of the Northern Ireland Office and the Northern Ireland departments and non-departmental public bodies under their aegis. The Northern Ireland Office is a United Kingdom central government department controlled by a Secretary of State with Cabinet rank and is principally responsible for law and order and political matters in the province. This is superficially similar to the arrangements made for Scotland and Wales which also have separate Secretaries of State and administrative departments. The Northern Ireland departments on the other hand are a legacy of the devolved form of government which the province experienced between 1920 and 1972. These departments are responsible for finance, agriculture, economic development, education, environmental services and health and personal social services (including the administration of social security) in the province and are staffed by members of the Northern Ireland civil service which is modelled upon but separate from the United Kingdom civil service. The Northern Ireland departments are unique in that the functions they perform are frequently administered by regional divisions or offices of central government departments in the rest of the United Kingdom.[2] In addition to the Northern Ireland Office and the Northern Ireland departments which are directly responsible to the Secretary of State, other United Kingdom central government departments and organisations including the Ministry of Defence, the Ministry of Agriculture, Fisheries and Food, the Lord Chancellor's Office, the Inland Revenue and Customs and Excise also provide services in the province.

Since 1973 local government in Northern Ireland has consisted of twenty-six district councils which have severely limited functions principally in regard to the provision of recreational facilities and local environmental services. A notable feature of government in the province is the use of statutory agencies for the administration of major public services which would be provided by local authorities in Great Britain. Five Education and Library Boards under the aegis of the local Department of Education administer schools, technical colleges and libraries in the province and four Health and Social Services Boards manage the provision of health and personal social services under the aegis of the local Department of Health and Social Services. The provision of public housing in Northern Ireland is the responsibility of the Northern Ireland Housing Executive which is a public corporation sponsored by the local Department of the Environment.

Northern Ireland did not share in the post-war wave of nationalisation which occurred in Great Britain, partly because the province lacked major extractive or production enterprises such as coal mining or steel production. As a result, the range of state-run industries in the province is limited to public utilities such as electricity and water supply and transport undertakings including the local railway and bus companies and some port and airport facilities. However, special mention should be made of the position of Harland and Wolff, the local shipbuilding company, and Short Brothers, the aerospace firm, which are the largest industrial employers in the province. Short Brothers was nationalised in 1943 and responsibility for the company was transferred from the Department of Trade and Industry in Great Britain to the Northern Ireland Department of Economic Development in 1978. Harland and Wolff was nationalised in 1975. Notwithstanding the fact that both companies are at present wholly owned by the government, their activities have continued to be classified to the private sector in official statistics. This anomaly may be resolved if the government is successful in returning these firms to private ownership.[3]

Despite a brief but unsuccessful flirtation with creating a state owned manufacturing enterprise in the 1970s, the government in Northern Ireland has never favoured public enterprise as a vehicle for developing the economy.[4] In this respect the public sector in Northern Ireland differs significantly from the experience in the Republic of Ireland which in the past has used a variety of state owned companies to develop the economy. Prominent examples of this approach were the formation of the Dairy Disposal Company and the Agricultural Credit Corporation in 1927 and the Turf Development Board in 1934 (later to become Bord na Mona, in 1946) to exploit indigenous peat resources.

MEASURING THE PUBLIC SECTOR

The public sector in Northern Ireland supplies a wide range of goods and services. For example, electricity, water and other essential services are publicly provided and much of the local transport infrastructure is paid for from public funds. With minor exceptions, health care and education services are also supplied or paid for by the public sector and state pensions and benefits are the only source of income for a substantial proportion of the province's population. In addition the public sector interacts with the private sector of the economy at many different levels both through the provision of grants and subsidies and its own purchases. In general therefore it is unwise to attempt to capture the importance of the public sector in the region within the compass of a single dimension measure. It is also the case that all absolute measures of the size of the public sector are of very limited value unless they are set against similar magnitudes for the economy as a whole. Nevertheless, by examining a series of indicators for the public sector it is possible to infer, however imperfectly, its role in the regional economy.

OUTPUT

An obvious measure of the importance of any sector of the economy is the contribution it makes to total output. The standard measure of the output of the domestic economy over a given period is Gross Domestic Product (GDP) which is the value added in the process of converting inputs to final output. There are several methods by which GDP can be calculated but at the regional level the estimates are based upon the sum of all factor incomes. Northern Ireland GDP is therefore taken to be the total value of the sum of income from employment and self-employment, the profits of both public and private sector trading enterprises, rent and an imputed charge for capital consumption by non-trading bodies less stock appreciation.[5] While official statistics provide a breakdown of the composition of regional GDP by industry they unfortunately do not distinguish between private and public sector components which therefore have to be estimated by other methods. The most straightforward approach is to use employment shares as the basis for apportioning GDP by industry groups between the private and public sectors. This is appropriate where the output of the public sector is not marketed and effectively values that output in line with the value of the inputs used up in its production. The principal drawback in this case is that there is an implicit assumption that labour productivity in the provision of public services is constant, which in many cases is far from the truth.

Table 13.1 shows the results of applying this methodology to GDP estimates for Northern Ireland and the United Kingdom as a whole for the period 1974 to 1986. As the table indicates, public sector output is of considerably greater importance in the province compared to the national situation. Comparisons of the public sector share of GDP between Northern Ireland and the Republic of Ireland are not straightforward because of differences in classifications. However, public administration and defence, which is a broadly similar category, in each case accounted for about 6 per cent of GDP at factor cost in the Republic of Ireland in 1986 compared to 15 per cent in Northern Ireland.

TABLE 13.1 Public sector GDP as a percentage of total GDP, Northern Ireland and the United Kingdom, 1974–1986

	Northern Ireland	United Kingdom
1974	33	29
1978	39	32
1979	39	33
1980	42	36
1981	45	37
1982	45	37
1983	44	37
1984	43	36
1985	43	36
1986	44	34
Annual average percentage increase 1974–86	2.4	1.3

Note: Public sector is defined to include SIC (1980), Division 1, Division 7 (elements of Classes 71, 72, 76 and 79) and Division 9 (elements of Classes 91–96) and equivalent Minimum List Headings from SIC (1968). Figures have been adjusted for privatisation over the period.
Sources: Census of Employment (various); NIAAS; ET.

PUBLIC EXPENDITURE/GDP RATIOS

The comparison of public expenditure with the value of GDP is perhaps the most popular and misunderstood measure of the importance of the public sector. Because of the way in which it is defined, public expenditure includes not only expenditure on goods and services but also expenditure on transfer payments such as unemployment benefits and social security payments. Since the latter represent transfers of purchasing power between different groups in society rather than payment for goods or services delivered they cannot legitimately be counted as part of GDP. In addition some public expenditure is spent on imported goods and services which by definition are not part of GDP. Both of these factors are particularly important at the regional level where per capita incomes may be considerably lower than the national average and the economy is unusually open. Despite this and other technical difficulties with the ratio it nevertheless provides an approximate guide to the significance of the public sector in an economy both in terms of the opportunity cost of public expenditure and the dependence of the private sector on government demand and the incomes generated by government activity.

Table 13.2 shows public expenditure/GDP ratios for Northern Ireland and Great Britain over the period from 1978/79 to 1986/87. For consistency the ratios for Great Britain are calculated on the basis of public expenditure on programmes comparable to those operating in Northern Ireland. Public expenditure on programmes which cannot meaningfully be attributed on a territorial basis such as defence and diplomatic representation have been excluded. In addition, GDP figures have been converted to a financial year basis to conform with public expenditure figures which are drawn from the planning total for each year.

The public expenditure/GDP ratio in Northern Ireland has varied over this period, reaching a high of 72 per cent in the recession years of 1981/82 and 1982/83. In Great Britain a similar cyclical upturn in the ratio is evident in the early 1980s and during this period there was some convergence in the ratios. From 1983 onwards the gap again opened due perhaps to a somewhat faster recovery of output in Great Britain allied to relatively stricter control of public expenditure on comparable programmes. When transfers to the personal and corporate sectors and subsidy payments are excluded from the figures, the public expenditure/GDP ratio in Northern Ireland presents a somewhat different picture. In 1978/79 the ratio calculated on this basis was about 36 per cent and in 1986/87 it was 33 per cent. To a considerable extent therefore public expenditure on goods and services (principally the wages of public sector

TABLE 13.2 Public expenditure as a percentage of GDP, Northern Ireland and Great Britain, 1978/79–1986/87

	Northern Ireland	Great Britain
1978/79	67	37.1
1979/80	67	37.7
1980/81	72	40.9
1981/82	72	42.3
1982/83	72	41.5
1983/84	71	40.5
1984/85	71	40.1
1985/86	69	37.8
1986/87	66	37.5

Note: Figures for Great Britain exclude public expenditure on defence, diplomatic representation overseas, EC contributions and national debt costs, GDP excludes the continental shelf.
Sources: Public Expenditure White Papers; NIAAS; AAS; ET November 1988.

employees) has served to provide an underlying stability to demand in the province over a period which has seen substantial decline in private sector activity. It should also be noted that pursuing a policy of parity in public expenditure per head between different regions will automatically produce a higher public expenditure/GDP ratio for regions where GDP per capita is relatively low. This effect has certainly operated in Northern Ireland though, as will be indicated later in this chapter, public expenditure per capita is considerably higher in Northern Ireland compared to other regions of the United Kingdom.

The comparison of public expenditure/GDP ratios within the United Kingdom is hindered by the lack of comprehensive information on public expenditure at the regional level. The only official series available are for 'identifiable public expenditure' which is expenditure which can be identified from official records as having been incurred in a particular region. In general this measure captures only about 80 per cent of total public expenditure in the United Kingdom in any year. In particular it excludes spending on defence, overseas aid and other overseas services which are considered to be for the benefit of the nation as a whole. Also included in identifiable public expenditure is government net lending to, and the market and overseas borrowings of, the public corporations as well as receipts from the sale of public sector assets. While it is possible to distinguish between these expenditures for Northern Ireland and Great Britain it is not possible to allocate this finance for expenditure in other regions.

Table 13.3 shows identifiable public expenditure/GDP ratios for the major areas of the United Kingdom from 1983/84 to 1986/87, the only period for which consistent data are available. In general all regions have seen a decline in the ratio over this period but the table stresses the importance of public expenditure for the economy of Northern Ireland and to a lesser extent for other areas of the United Kingdom apart from England.

By way of contrast it is interesting to note that public expenditure also accounts for a significant proportion of GDP in the Republic of Ireland which shares some of the economic and social problems of Northern Ireland but which is a sovereign country rather than a region. While exact comparisons are not possible because of differences in public expenditure and national accounts definitions, public expenditure on current and capital accounts by public authorities (central government and local authorities) in the Republic of

TABLE 13.3 Identifiable public expenditure as a percentage of GDP for major areas of the United Kingdom, 1983/84–1986/87

	England	Scotland	Wales	Northern Ireland
1983/84	36.5	49.1	49.6	70.3
1984/85	36.4	48.8	48.9	70.0
1985/86	34.8	47.3	45.8	68.1
1986/87	33.6	46.6	47.3	66.0

Sources: Hansard, 25 October 1988; ET November 1988.

Ireland excluding interest payments on the national debt amounted to 58.5 per cent of GDP at factor cost in 1980 and 58 per cent in 1986.[6]

PUBLIC SECTOR EMPLOYMENT

An obvious measure of the importance of the public sector in a regional economy is the share of total employment provided by public sector activities. Unfortunately consistent figures for public sector employment in Northern Ireland are available only from 1974 onwards. Estimates of public sector employment for earlier years can be obtained by combining employment totals in specific sectors, though this procedure unavoidably misapportions some private sector workers to the public sector.[7] In the 1950s the public sector share of employment in the province (employees in employment) averaged about 16 per cent. This was a considerably lower proportion than in Great Britain. Taking the average public sector share of employment in Great Britain during the 1950s to be 100, the share in Northern Ireland would have been approximately 86 for this period. In 1960 the estimated public sector employment in the province was 97,000 or 22 per cent of employees in employment but by 1970 the corresponding figures were 124,000 and 25 per cent. However, during the 1970s public sector employment growth accelerated very rapidly. Between 1970 and 1974, for example, total public sector employment rose by almost 40 per cent. Table 13.4 shows the composition of employment in the public sector in Northern Ireland since 1974. Overall the number of workers officially classified to the public sector grew on average by 1.3 per cent per annum during the period between June 1974 and June 1987

TABLE 13.4   Public sector employment in Northern Ireland, 1974 and 1987 (June)

	1974	1987	Average annual % change 1974–87
NI central government of which:	42,253	48,019	0.1
Government departments	33,139	29,161	−1.0
Police and prison services	9,114	18,858	5.7
Bodies under the aegis of NI central government of which:	88,853	119,868	7.2
Health and social services	44,731	64,035	2.8
Education services	40,244	52,493	2.1
UK central government	8,583	6,074	−2.6
Local government	7,424	10,577	2.8
Public corporations	25,956	20,029	−2.0
NI based	15,798	15,520	−0.1
UK based	10,158	4,509	−6.1
Total	173,069	204,567	1.3
Percentage of civil employment	30.5	37.5	1.6
Percentage of employees in employment	35.9	42.2	1.3

Sources: NIAAS No 1, 1982 and No 6, 1987.

but this figure disguises considerable variations within the sector. Employment in central government departments both Northern Ireland and United Kingdom based has declined over the period as has employment in the public corporations, particularly those based in the United Kingdom. To a large extent, however, the latter phenomenon is due to a classification change brought about by the privatisation of organisations such as British Telecom which operate in the province. Against these declines on the other hand there has been a substantial growth of employment in the various non-departmental public bodies in the province including those which provide health and social services and education services in Northern Ireland. Employment in health and social services increased by 43 per cent between 1974 and 1987 while employment in education services expanded by 30 per cent over the same period. Employment in the police and prison services in the province has more than doubled since 1974, growing on average by 5.7 per cent per annum.

The net result of this growth in public sector employment against a background of declining job opportunities in the private sector has been to considerably expand the proportion of total employment accounted for by the public sector in Northern Ireland. Thus between 1970 and 1987 the percentage of total employees in employment directly employed by public sector bodies has grown from about 25 per cent to over 40 per cent. However, these figures represent official classifications to the public sector and exclude some elements of the province's workforce which are nevertheless almost entirely dependent upon public expenditure for their jobs. Staff in Northern Ireland's two universities and general medical practitioners, for example, are classified as private sector employees and self-employed respectively despite the fact that their salaries are effectively paid from public funds. The same is true of other parts of the private sector such as the construction industry where employment is highly sensitive to expenditure on the public capital programme including public housing. Consequently, when account is taken of the nominally private sector employment which is indirectly dependent upon the level of public sector economic activity it is probable that well over half the total workforce in Northern Ireland are in one way or another dependent upon the public sector in the province.

The growth of public sector employment in Northern Ireland since the war has been considerably more rapid than in Great Britain, but, as Canning, Moore and Rhodes (1987) argue, this divergence did not become apparent until the late 1960s. By comparing the actual growth of employment in the sector with what would have happened if public sector employment in Northern Ireland had grown at the same rate as comparable areas of the public sector in Great Britain these authors conclude that by 1983 an additional 50,000 jobs had been created in the province. However, this technique must be used with care if misleading results are not to be obtained. Most of the public corporations in Northern Ireland, for example, are quite different in size, structure and scope of operations compared to their counterparts in Great Britain and it is a dubious exercise to attempt to compare employment growth in this area of the public sector. Figure 13.1, which uses consistent employment

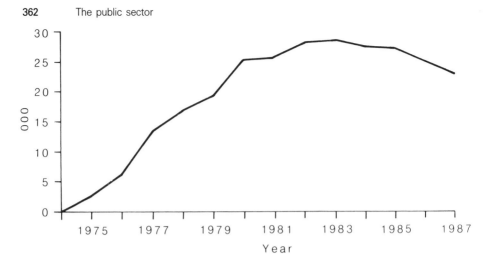

FIG 13.1   Actual minus expected employment in the public sector,[1] Northern Ireland, 1974–1987
[1] General government.

data for the public sector in Northern Ireland between 1974 and 1987, shows the difference between actual employment in general government (ie excluding the public corporations) in the province and what would have been expected if Great Britain rates of employment growth in similar areas had been experienced over this period.

What this figure shows is that employment in the public sector in Northern Ireland, which had already grown rapidly in the early 1970s, continued to expand faster than in Great Britain until the start of the 1980s when the disparity in employment growth effectively came to an end. Indeed, since 1983 there has been evidence that this process has been reversed with employment in general government in Great Britain growing more rapidly than in the province.

A closer examination of public sector employment statistics for the two areas indicates that the disparity in growth has been concentrated in particular categories. An important part of the explanation of more rapid public sector employment growth in the province was the deterioration in the security situation in Northern Ireland during the 1970s. This necessitated a rapid expansion of employment in both the police and prison services. However, in terms of numbers the most significant contribution to the disparity in employment growth rates in the public sector came from the social programmes and in particular health and social services and education. Overall, total employment in general government in Northern Ireland in 1987 was about 23,000 greater than if national trends had been followed since 1974 and of this number 15,000 jobs are accounted for by the more rapid expansion of health and education services than occurred in Great Britain. However, two important points need to be borne in mind when interpreting this type of analysis. The first is that the calculation of actual-minus-expected employment levels is sensitive to the initial date chosen as a starting point and the level of disaggregation at which the analysis is carried out. In practice, as the Canning, Moore and Rhodes analysis discovered, the level of disaggregation has little overall effect in the case of Northern Ireland and the discrepancy in employment persists (though not of course at the same level) for a wide variation in starting points. The second and more important point about an analysis of this type is that it makes no allowance for the relative need for public services between different regions. In effect the analysis is concerned only with the relative supply of public services and ignores demand-side factors which can vary quite significantly between regions. In Northern Ireland, for example, the rapid expansion in employment in public services during the 1970s partly reflected a process of catching up on standards of provision in Great Britain and was also influenced by the somewhat different structure of provision in both health care and the education system in the province relative to Great Britain. Differences in need, stemming largely from demographic distinctions, also contributed substantially to employment growth differentials. Table 13.5 shows the differences in some demographic and social indicators in Northern Ireland compared to Great Britain which on balance produce a higher demand for public services (and hence public sector employment) in the province.

The expansion of public sector employment in Northern Ireland during the 1970s was to a large extent paralleled in the Republic of Ireland. As Ross (1986) notes, public sector employment in the Republic of Ireland, not counting those employed in state sponsored bodies, rose from 138,000 in 1967 to 226,000 in 1983, an increase of more than 60 per cent. Moreover, there is some evidence that in both Northern Ireland and the Republic of Ireland growth of employment in the public sector was seen as a useful means of off-setting job losses in other parts of the economy and reducing unemployment though the consequences for the public finances of such a policy do not appear to have been fully appreciated at the time. In this respect Northern Ireland was in a more favourable position since the cost of additional public sector

TABLE 13.5   Demographic and social indicators, Northern Ireland and Great Britain, 1986 (1988)

	Northern Ireland	Great Britain
Percentage of population aged 15 and under	27 (25.1)	19 (18.7)
Percentage of population aged 65 and over*	14 (14.5)	18 (18.4)
Total period fertility ratio[1]	2.5 (2.41)	1.8 (1.82)
Standardised mortality ratio[2]:		
Males	110	100[3]
Females	107	100

[1] An enumeration of fertility which takes into account the age structure of the population.
[2] Mortality standardised for age structure of the population (1987).
[3] United Kingdom.
Source: Northern Ireland Commentary on Public Expenditure Plans 1988/89, DFP, 1988. Crown copyright.
* Females aged 60 and over, males aged 65 and over

employees could be met by transfers from the national exchequer, whereas in the Republic of Ireland they had ultimately to be carried by local taxpayers.

The growth of public sector employment in Northern Ireland from 1970 onwards had a significant influence upon the incidence of part-time working in the province and the provision of jobs for females. As O'Dowd (1987) points out: the number of part-time workers in Northern Ireland doubled between 1971 and 1983 and during the period from 1971 to 1978 when the expansion of public sector employment in the province was most rapid the part-time workforce increased on average by 5,644 each year. A substantial number of these part-time jobs were created in the public sector, particularly in the health and education services in the province. Moreover, the bulk of public sector jobs created during the 1970s and 1980s were taken by females. Of the 173,069 persons employed in the public sector in June 1974, 89,649 were male and 83,420 female. In June 1987 the equivalent total employment was 204,567 of which 90,465 were males and 114,102 females. Thus over this period total public sector employment for males increased by only 816 or less than 1 per cent whereas female employment in the sector expanded by 30,682 or almost 37 per cent. The majority of these new female jobs were again accounted for by expansions in health and education services.

Growth in public sector employment was also influential in terms of the spatial distribution of jobs in Northern Ireland. Most government offices, health and education facilities and headquarters for public utilities are located in the east of the province, particularly in the Greater Belfast area where the population density is greatest. As a consequence it is this area of Northern Ireland which has benefited most in employment terms from the expansion of the public sector. On the basis of 1981 Census of Population returns, O'Dowd estimates that the proportion of public sector employment relative to the economically active population is considerably higher in the east of the province (particularly around the provincial capital, Belfast) compared to the west. Taking the ratio of the proportion of total employment in an industry located in an area to the proportion of the economically active population in that area as a measure of the spatial distribution of employment, the ratio for the Belfast area in 1981 was 1.78 for employment in public administration and defence and 1.59 for employment in the category 'other services' (Census division 9) which is mainly health and education services. Comparable ratios for the west of the province in 1981 were 0.8 and 0.87 respectively. Since the east of the province already has a natural advantage as a location for manufacturing and private service employment the expansion of the public sector has to some extent exacerbated employment and unemployment differentials between different regions in Northern Ireland.

3. The public finances

Between 1920 and 1972 Northern Ireland was a largely self-governing province of the United Kingdom with a separate parliament and government structure closely resembling the Westminster model. The public finances of the province were originally established on a revenue basis so that Northern Ireland was expected to provide for its own public expenditure as well as making a contribution towards the cost of national services from revenues raised in or attributable to the province. However, given the paucity of the tax base in the province and the need for relatively higher levels of social expenditure because of unemployment and demographic factors, it quickly became apparent that these arrangements were untenable if parity of social provision was to be maintained with Great Britain. From 1926 onwards, therefore, when the contribution to national services – the 'Imperial Contribution' – was made a residual rather than a first claim on the local exchequer, a series of special financial arrangements were concluded between Northern Ireland and Great Britain which effectively converted the province's public finances to an expenditure basis. The most important milestone in this process was the acceptance of the principle of parity in 1938 by the then Chancellor of the Exchequer, Sir John Simon. This concept provided that, 'it would be equitable that means should be found to make good a deficit on the Northern Ireland Budget that was not the result of a standard of social expenditure higher than, or of a standard of taxation lower than, that of Britain'. In the 1950s this concept of parity was widened to permit additional expenditure in the province in order to make up 'lee-way' in substantial areas of social provision and to counter Northern Ireland's geographical disadvantage within the United Kingdom.[8]

Practical effect was given to these concepts by a series of agreements between the Treasury in London and the Ministry of Finance in the province. In financial terms the most important of these arrangements were in the areas of health and social services and national insurance. The Social Services Agreement of 1948 guaranteed that the United Kingdom government would cover 80 per cent of any excess of the cost of health and social services over and above 2.5 per cent of the total cost of similar services in the United Kingdom. A further agreement balanced resources between the Northern Ireland and Great Britain National Insurance Funds and the Redundancy and Industrial Injuries Funds. In the 1960s the United Kingdom agreed to meet the full cost of Selective Employment premia in the province and in 1971 this principle was extended to the services covered by the Social Services Agreement. At the same time a new Health Services Agreement was concluded on more generous terms than its 1948 predecessor.

Hence by 1972 when the local parliament was prorogued and direct rule instituted, public expenditure in Northern Ireland was effectively being determined by negotiation between the local Ministry of Finance and the Treasury and the necessary funds were subsequently being made available through *ad hoc* channels. However, constitutionally the public finances in the province were still presented as an exercise in matching expenditures to revenues and Northern Ireland appeared to be making a (nominal) contribution to the United Kingdom exchequer. This unreal situation was corrected by the 1973 Constitution Act which formally placed local public finance on an expenditure basis. The retention of a separate Consolidated Fund for Northern Ireland does however mean that financial transfers between the United Kingdom central government and the province are relatively transparent. This is not the case for any other region of the United Kingdom.

PUBLIC EXPENDITURE

Public expenditure in the United Kingdom is defined to include all expenditure on current and capital account by general government and the external financing requirements of public corporations and the nationalised industries. Since 1981 public expenditure in Northern Ireland has been treated as a single 'block' for control purposes within the annual Public Expenditure Survey (PES) for the United Kingdom. With the exception of social security expenditure, the resources for programmes within the Northern Ireland block are largely determined by comparability with similar programmes in Great Britain. As a starting point, Northern Ireland will normally receive 2.75 per cent (broadly the province's proportion of total United Kingdom population) of any change in expenditure on comparable programmes in Great Britain. However, the total level of public expenditure in the province may also reflect special circumstances which give rise to additional need for expenditure over and above the level determined by comparability. Expenditure on the social security programme is outside these arrangements and is automatically met according to the level of demand. As a corollary, however, any shortfall in social security expenditure is not available for re-allocation within the Northern Ireland block.

The Secretary of State for Northern Ireland has discretion to allocate expenditure between programmes included in the Northern Ireland public expenditure block (except for social security expenditure and some national agricultural support spending) but only within certain constraints. Firstly, the Northern Ireland block is divided into two cash limited components representing expenditure by the Northern Ireland Office and the Northern Ireland departments respectively. Resources can be freely transferred within each cash limited area but not between the two cash limits except with the express agreement of the Treasury. Secondly, public expenditure in Northern Ireland is broadly constrained by national policies and any change in expenditure priorities in the province which might have repercussions elsewhere in the United Kingdom would normally have to be agreed at the national level.

In the period between 1968/69 and 1987/88, total public expenditure in Northern Ireland approximately doubled in real terms (Table 13.6).[9] This represents an annual average increase of 3.4 per cent but the most dramatic period of growth was concentrated in the early 1970s. Between 1972/73 and 1975/76 real public expenditure grew by 33 per cent. This period coincided with the start of direct rule from Westminster and the reform of the public finances in the province contained in the Northern Ireland Constitution Act 1973. The rapid expansion in public expenditure at this time is evidence consistent with the well known 'displacement hypothesis' put forward by Peacock and Wiseman (1961) to explain the growth of public expenditure in national economies. Peacock and Wiseman argue that social crises or national upheavals associated with wars drive up public expenditure and weaken resistance to the taxation needed to finance this expenditure. In Northern Ireland the disturbances of the early 1970s exposed the need for additional public expenditure not only on law and order but also on social programmes such as health and housing. These new expenditures were mostly funded by increased fiscal transfers from central government. After the initial discontinuity, however, growth of public expenditure in real terms returned to more modest levels and since 1976/77 has averaged 1.6 per cent per annum. As Table 13.6 shows, the programmes which have expanded most since 1968/69 have been concentrated in the areas of law and order and social provision. These increases in expenditure were the driving force behind the growth of employment in the health and education programmes noted earlier and generated substantial employment in the local construction industry in the provision of public housing. It should also be noted, however, that real public expenditure on some programmes has declined or at best remained static since 1968/69. Expenditure on support for industry, for example, has stagnated principally because the substantial inflow of investment projects which was evident during the 1960s fell dramatically after 1973.

Table 13.6 also indicates that in terms of economic classification there has been a relatively steady decline in the proportion of public expenditure in Northern Ireland accounted for by capital expenditure since 1968/69. Capital expenditure includes both expenditure on fixed assets and loans and grants to

TABLE 13.6   Public expenditure by programme, Northern Ireland, 1968/69–1987/88 (£ million)

Programme	1968/69	1974/75	1979/80	1983/84	1987/88	Annual average % change 1968/69–1987/88 (constant prices)
Agriculture[1]	39	70	69	149	157	−2.4
Industry, energy, trade and employment	65	186	348	357	388	−0.3
Transport	24	54	113	124	123	−1.1
Housing	32	87	212	299	337	2.7
Environmental services	16	49	104	176	234	4.5
Law and order[2]	11	103	256	386	570	11.7
Education	61	165	388	580	788	3.8
Health and social services	54	147	381	634	810	4.6
Social security	98	214	590	1,085	1,461	4.6
Other public services	10	21	28	26	41	−2.2
Total public expenditure	410	1,096	2,489	3,816	4,909	3.4
Capital expenditure as a percentage of total	22	16	23	13	14	

[1] From 1981/82 includes expenditure in Northern Ireland by MAFF.
[2] Includes expenditure by the Northern Ireland Office.
Source: Public Expenditure White Papers, HM Treasury.

the private sector (including the net market borrowing of the public corporations). It should be noted, however, that within a relatively small total one or two large capital projects arising in any one year can seriously distort the overall distribution.

Comparisons between public expenditure in Northern Ireland and other regions of the United Kingdom is complicated by the paucity of information on expenditure (and revenue) flows in the regions of Great Britain. The only official expenditure figures which are available refer to identifiable expenditure and identifiable expenditure per head in the major regions of the United Kingdom. These figures are based upon the terms and definitions used in the annual Public Expenditure Survey and therefore change over time as the coverage of the Survey changes. As a result consistent series of identifiable public expenditure are only available for relatively short periods the most recent of which is 1983/84 to 1987/88. However, some information on public expenditure comparisons for earlier years is available from other sources though the figures are not strictly comparable on a year to year basis. Table 13.7 summarises how public expenditure per head in the major regions of the United Kingdom has changed for selected years from 1959/60 to 1987/88.

These figures suggest that public expenditure per head in Northern Ireland did not surpass corresponding levels in Scotland and Wales before the early 1970s. By the 1980s, however, identifiable public expenditure per capita in Northern Ireland was 50 per cent greater than in England though only 15 per cent larger than in Scotland. It should also be noted that the figures in Table 13.7 exclude the financing of expenditure by public corporations which it is not possible to apportion between the regions in Great Britain. Table 13.8

TABLE 13.7 Index of public expenditure per head in major areas of the United Kingdom, 1959/60–1987/88

	England	Scotland	Wales	Northern Ireland
1959/60[1]	100	105	95	88
1962/63[1]	100	118	99	92
1965/66[1]	100	111	94	97
1966/67	100	110	111	105
1968/69	100	125	115	109
1972/73	100	118	106	125
1974/75[1]	100	118	97	112
1977/78[1]	100	128	100	141
1982/83	100	127	111	147
1983/84	100	127	113	149
1984/85	100	126	110	149
1985/86	100	127	111	150
1986/87	100	129	115	150
1987/88	100	130	115	150

[1] Covers expenditure on only six main programmes.
Sources: 1966/67–1972/73 Northern Ireland: Finance and the Economy, HMSO 1974; 1959/60–1965/66 and 1965/66–1977/78 Needs Assessment Study, 1979; 1982/83–1987/88 Hansard 23 October 1987 and 25 October 1988.

TABLE 13.8   Identifiable public expenditure per head, absolute and relative, Northern Ireland and Great Britain, 1983/84–1987/88[1] (£ per head)

	Northern Ireland	Great Britain
1983/84	2,511 (144.3)	1,740 (100)
1984/85	2,697 (144.6)	1,865 (100)
1985/86	2,844 (147.0)	1,934 (100)
1986/87	2,976 (144.7)	2,057 (100)
1987/88	3,174 (147.4)	2,154 (100)

[1] Includes nationalised industries.
Source: Hansard 25 October 1988.

compares identifiable public expenditure per head between Great Britain and Northern Ireland including the financing requirements of public corporations for the period 1983/84 to 1987/88. Allowing for the inclusion of this expenditure reduces the differential in favour of Northern Ireland somewhat and this would probably fall further if it were possible to make comparisons with Scotland and Wales on this basis given the degree of investment by nationalised industries in these regions.

In addition to the official figures cited above, there have been a few unofficial attempts to compare public expenditure growth in Northern Ireland with other areas of the United Kingdom. Simpson (1980) using expenditure on similar services as a basis of comparison concludes that between 1967/68 and 1978/79 public expenditure in real terms grew significantly faster in the province than in the United Kingdom as a whole except for a brief period in 1975/76. At a more disaggregated level public expenditure comparisons for the regions of the United Kingdom have been exhaustively considered by Short (1978, 1981) and Short and Nicholas (1981). Short's analysis is particularly interesting because it attempts to embrace all public expenditure which is relevant to a region but the methodology adopted to allocate public expenditure on a territorial basis is controversial and the analysis is limited to the years between 1974/75 and 1977/78. For 1974/75 Short found that regionally relevant public expenditure per head in Northern Ireland was 28 per cent higher than for the United Kingdom as a whole but only 9.6 per cent greater than in Scotland. By 1977/78 the corresponding figures had grown to 41.6 per cent and 20 per cent respectively.

Within a unified state which aims for common standards in public service provision on a territorial basis, differences in the level of public expenditure between regions may largely be accounted for by differences in relative needs. In any comparison of public expenditure between Northern Ireland and other regions it is therefore essential to take account of relative need to ensure that like is being compared to like. However, this is an extremely difficult exercise and has only been officially attempted once in the United Kingdom. The 1979 Needs Assessment Study undertaken by the Treasury as part of the background work for devolved administrations in Scotland and Wales highlighted the disagreement which can arise over the selection of appropriate indicators of need.[10] In addition, this study was concerned only with those functions of government which were candidates for devolution and excluded, for example, expenditure on law and order services. Given Northern Ireland's special requirements in this area the result was to impart a downward bias to the province's apparent need for public expenditure relative to Scotland and Wales. On the basis of the programmes considered, the study concluded that the relative need for expenditure in each major region of the United Kingdom in 1976/77 was: England 100; Scotland 116; Wales 109; and Northern Ireland 131.

Several other unofficial attempts to assess actual expenditure relative to need have been made comparing Northern Ireland to Great Britain. Canning, Moore and Rhodes (1987), for example, conclude that in 1981/82 expected public expenditure (allowing for need) was 2.3 per cent greater than actual public expenditure in the province but by 1984/85 the reverse was the case and actual public expenditure in that year exceeded expected expenditure by 1.8 per cent. These results are broadly in line with calculations undertaken by the Northern Ireland Economic Council since 1980/81 which attempt to adjust actual public expenditure for a range of factors which distinguish the province from the rest of the United Kingdom. In the case of the energy and water industries, for example, different administrative arrangements in the province mean that subsidies appear as explicit public expenditure rather than being covered by transfer pricing within the industries. Equally, the cost of public housing in Northern Ireland is higher in part because of difference in land tenure compared to Great Britain. Migration from the province also results in a transfer of the benefit of public expenditure on education in Northern Ireland to Great Britain and distorts expenditure comparisons, as do other demographic and social factors such as the higher proportions of schoolchildren and unemployed in the local population. Further distortions are introduced because of the relatively greater importance of the agricultural sector in the province's economy and special needs with respect to housing and policing. Table 13.9 shows the effect on the per capita public expenditure differential between Northern Ireland and Great Britain when these matters are taken into account.

Assessing actual public expenditure against that justified by need is not an exact science and all such exercises must be treated with caution. Nevertheless, the studies cited above tend to indicate that public expenditure

TABLE 13.9 Adjusted and unadjusted per capita public expenditure differences between Northern Ireland and Great Britain, 1980/81–1985/86

	Unadjusted	Adjusted
1980/81	+30.5	+1.6
1981/82	+33.6	−1.6
1982/83	+35.8	−0.5
1983/84	+37.8	+1.1
1984/85	+37.9	+0.6
1985/86	+41.9	+1.7

Source: NIEC (1981a) updated.

in Northern Ireland, while substantially greater per head than elsewhere in the United Kingdom, is primarily a reflection of social and economic conditions in the province. What is not clear, however, is the degree to which these phenomena are interrelated. The existence of a large public sector in a region may be expected to have both beneficial and detrimental effects on economic activity in that region. The beneficial effects of public expenditure are relatively transparent – greater employment in the provision of public services and more demand for locally produced goods and services through multiplier effects are obvious examples – but the negative effects of a large public sector are less easily identified at the regional level. For the national economy there is a substantial literature on the hypothesis that the public sector tends to 'crowd out' the private sector through interest rate and wealth effects but these arguments do not easily convert to a regional context. However, one possible source of displacement in the labour market is the bargaining process for public sector wages and salaries which tend to be set at the national level and are essentially independent of local labour market conditions. This phenomenon also occurs in the private sector but is to some extent contained by the need for firms to maintain commercial viability – a constraint which is not operative in the public sector. It may therefore be argued that the public sector can set employment standards which the private sector, and in particular smaller companies, would find difficult to match while staying competitive. The counter-argument that high levels of unemployment in the region would ensure that wage levels and conditions in the private sector would not be significantly influenced by employment in the public sector depends on the existence of a strong correlation between employment and unemployment which does not generally appear to be the case in Northern Ireland.[11]

There are several other possible ways in which a large public sector might be detrimental to the development of the private sector in Northern Ireland. These include the promotion of a dependency culture among businesses in the province, the disproportionate share of the most able individuals in the workforce taken by the public sector – particularly those who might otherwise become entrepreneurs in their own right – and the general weakening of market disciplines in the local economy because of the scale of public sector support for industry. Many of these fears appear to underpin the government's 'Pathfinder' initiative (Department of Economic Development 1987) which is designed to revitalise the private sector in the province. It should be noted, however, that while these effects are frequently cited as contributing factors in the general decline of private industry in Northern Ireland quantitative evidence of their importance has not so far been produced.

PUBLIC REVENUE

For historical reasons Northern Ireland is the only region of the United Kingdom for which separate revenue accounts are maintained. This is a legacy of the revenue system of public expenditure which originally operated in the province but the present system of public finance is firmly expenditure based.

Under such a system public expenditure in Northern Ireland is determined in total by central government taking account of the particular needs of the province and sufficient funds are then made available from the exchequer to finance this expenditure. The popular view is that this system reduces the revenue side of the public finances in the province to an exercise in accounting with no direct influence on public expenditure decisions. However, this interpretation would seem to be at variance with some of the results which have recently appeared in the literature on grants in aid. We return to this point after discussing the sources of revenue available to Northern Ireland.

Northern Ireland has three main sources of revenue:

(a) Northern Ireland's share of United Kingdom taxes
(b) Northern Ireland non-tax revenue
(c) Payments from the United Kingdom central government

The Northern Ireland share of United Kingdom taxes (called the 'attributable share') represents that proportion of the total yield of nationally imposed taxes which is deemed to arise in the province, less the local cost of collecting these taxes and a sum representing Northern Ireland's share of the United Kingdom's contribution to the European Communities. Calculation of the attributable share is based upon proportional relations or the actual sum collected in the province, depending upon the tax involved.

Northern Ireland non-tax revenue consists of the proceeds of rates on property, land annuities, interest on advances and other miscellaneous receipts. Included in the latter is a sum representing the province's share of receipts from petroleum licences granted by the United Kingdom government in respect of the continental shelf. There are two rates on property levied in the province: a regional rate which contributes to the cost of services provided by central government in Northern Ireland which would be provided by local authorities in Great Britain, and a district rate which covers part of the cost of

TABLE 13.10 Northern Ireland public revenue (current), 1979/80–1987/88 (£m, current prices)

	1979/80	1983/84	1987/88
Revenue generated in Northern Ireland:			
NI attributed share of UK taxes (net)	1,021.7	1,576.8	2,154.8
National insurance contributions	270.9	407.3	504.0
Rates	109.4	170.7	251.3
Miscellaneous revenues	160.3	302.3	345.6
Sub-total	1,562.3	2,457.1	3,255.7
Receipts from the UK government:			
Grant in aid	590.0	775.0	855.0
National insurance fund transfers	73.8	77.0	155.0
Refund of VAT	11.7	27.3	30.8
Total current revenue	2,237.8	3,336.4	4,296.5

Source: Financial Statement.

services provided by district councils. For convenience, both rates are collected centrally and the proceeds of the district rate are passed on to local councils.

Payments from the United Kingdom government to Northern Ireland can be defined in various ways. On the narrowest interpretation these payments consist of a non-specific grant in aid which is paid to cover any gap between public revenue and public expenditure in the province; a balancing transfer between the Great Britain National Insurance Fund and the Northern Ireland National Insurance Fund and the refund of VAT payments by Northern Ireland government departments. Table 13.10 shows how the sources of Northern Ireland public revenue on current account have altered over the period from 1979/80 to 1987/88. It is clear from this table that revenue generated in Northern Ireland only accounts for between 70 and 75 per cent of total current revenue with the balance being made up of transfers from the United Kingdom central government. Relative to the total public expenditure programme in Northern Ireland, however, the revenue generated in the province has been sufficient to finance somewhere between 60 and 70 per cent as a comparison with Table 13.6 indicates. Moreover, this is only a partial picture of the extent of fiscal transfers to the province. A fuller analysis must take account of expenditure on behalf of Northern Ireland which falls upon the budgets of United Kingdom government departments. The latter include: expenditure by the Northern Ireland Office on law and order, the cost of operating the courts service in Northern Ireland which is covered by the Lord Chancellor's Department and local expenditure by the Ministry of Agriculture, Fisheries and Food. In addition the extra cost of army operations in Northern Ireland is met by the Ministry of Defence. The total transfer of funds to Northern Ireland needed to finance the difference between public expenditure in the province and revenue raised locally is generally termed the United Kingdom 'subvention' to Northern Ireland. Table 13.11 illustrates how the level of financial support for the province from central government has grown since the 1960s.

The table excludes expenditure by the Lord Chancellor's Department on the Northern Ireland courts system, which in 1987/88 amounted to about £30 million, and additional costs associated with army operations in the province, which are estimated to be about £200 million in 1987/88. When these expenditures are taken into account the real level of subvention to the province from the United Kingdom exchequer (measured in 1987/88 prices) has increased from £356 million in 1966/67 to approximately £1,860 million in 1987/88. The latter figure is equivalent to about £1,200 per head of population in Northern Ireland.

One consequence of this level of support is that a substantial proportion of capital expenditure in Northern Ireland has been funded by a surplus of current revenue over current expenditure. As a result the public sector borrowing requirement in the province has been maintained at very modest levels. This phenomenon was noted by Simpson (1980) and is explored further in Chapter 16. The low borrowing requirement of government in Northern Ireland, which is moreover protected against exchange rate risks by

TABLE 13.11   United Kingdom subventions to Northern Ireland, 1966/67–1987/88[1] (£m, current prices)

	1966/67	1972/73	1977/78	1980/81	1984/85	1987/88
Social Services Agreement	10	45	—	—	—	—
Health Services Agreement	—	25	—	—	—	—
Regional Employment Premium	—	11	11	—	—	—
Agricultural Remoteness Grant	2	2	—	—	—	—
MAFF expenditure in Northern Ireland	25	25	27	40	53	77
National insurance transfers	15	22	59	98	95	155
Grant in aid	—	51	432	640	905	855
Northern Ireland Office expenditure	—	—	175	308	401	512
VAT refunds	—	—	7	16	25	31
Total	52	181	711	1,102	1,479	1,630

[1] Excludes defence expenditure and expenditure by Lord Chancellor's Department.
Sources: NIAAS; Public Expenditure White Papers; Northern Ireland: Finance and the Economy, HMSO, 1974.

being denominated in sterling, is one of the most striking differences between the public finances in the province and those in the Republic of Ireland.

Northern Ireland is not unique among the regions of the United Kingdom in being a net recipient of funds from central government, though an analysis of such transfers is restricted by a lack of revenue information for the regions in Great Britain. The most comprehensive analysis available is that by Short (1981) for the limited period 1974/75 to 1977/78. For these years Short estimates that tax revenues exceeded expenditure for all of the English regions except the North and North West but Wales, Scotland and Northern Ireland all recorded substantial deficits. For Northern Ireland the net transfer amounted to 44 per cent of regionally relevant public expenditure during this period while the figure for Scotland was 28 per cent. Short's work also highlights the important fact that all taxes have some degree of regional bias which may or may not reinforce the more obvious policy of differential levels of public expenditure in the regions. The distribution of taxes collected by the Inland Revenue is broadly what might be expected since most of these taxes fall on income or capital and the base for such taxes is narrower in the underdeveloped regions. The same is true for national insurance contributions. For expenditure taxes, however, the above average incidence in Wales and Scotland which was revealed in Short's work would appear to run contrary to the objectives of regional policy.

Within the United Kingdom fiscal transfers from the central government to the regions serve the purpose of allowing broadly similar levels of public services to be provided independently of the local tax base. The implicit grant in aid represented by these transfers (in Northern Ireland it is an explicit grant in aid) has generally been seen as a residual repayment required to balance regional public income with regional public expenditure, with the latter being determined by need. However, this assumes that the transfer has no influence upon the demand for public expenditure in a recipient region. This view is increasingly being questioned in the literature on grants in aid (Topham 1983; King 1984). Transfers from central government reduce the 'price' which inhabitants of poorer regions have to pay for public services in the sense that without such transfers local tax rates would have to be substantially higher to finance the same level of services. In effect this suggests that block grants have a price as well as an income effect. Exploration of this hypothesis and its consequences is hampered in Great Britain by the lack of information on the extent of fiscal transfers to the regions and the structure of these transfers. For Northern Ireland, however, this information is generally available and the opportunity to investigate the behavioural relationships between financial transfers from the central government and local public expenditure is open.

A further and illuminating way of viewing the fiscal transfer between the United Kingdom government and Northern Ireland is provided by an analysis of the regional balance of payments position. However, this is not a straightforward process since there is a significant lack of information on trade flows and expenditures in the province but Rowthorn (1987) has presented a partial analysis based on a simplified regional balance of payments framework. By definition the regional balance of trade on current account must equal the difference between the value of regional output and regional expenditure. For Northern Ireland Rowthorn estimates that the trade balance has exhibited a growing deficit, from £158 million in 1970 to £1,548 million in 1984 at current prices. He also suggests that the method of financing this deficit has changed dramatically over the period. The surplus on capital account provided by foreign investment in the province has largely disappeared, leaving the burden of financing current account deficits to fiscal transfers from the central government which have risen accordingly. In the absence of such transfers, it is argued, balance of payments adjustment in Northern Ireland would require large falls in local income to reduce imports. While this is a suggestive analysis it essentially views the transfer from central government as an accommodating item, balancing the deficit on the trade and capital accounts. An alternative interpretation would be that the trade deficit for the province has in part been caused by increases in imports stimulated by the greater levels of central government activity in Northern Ireland since 1970.

Notes

1. See Department of Economic Development (1987).
2. For convenience some expenditure by United Kingdom central government departments in Northern Ireland is administered on an agency basis by Northern Ireland departments.
3. During 1989 both companies were returned to the private sector.
4. Strathearn Audio, a company producing hi-fi audio equipment, was established as

a state enterprise in 1975 but was closed in 1978. The HMSO (1976) suggested the development of a state manufacturing sector in the province to create a minimum of 1,500 jobs per year but this was never acted upon.

5. Beckett (1987) describes in detail the methods used to calculate GDP in the province.
6. National Income and Expenditure: 1987, Central Statistics Office, Dublin.
7. Northern Ireland Economic Council (1981b).
8. See Lawrence (1965) for a discussion of the arrangements governing public finance in Northern Ireland up until the 1960s.
9. Public expenditure deflated by the GDP deflator (1987–88=100).
10. The use of a mortality index as a proxy for morbidity was a matter of particular dispute in the group considering expenditure needs for health services.
11. Zabalza and Kong (1984) suggest that public sector pay settlements in the UK have a negligible influence on private sector pay.

References

Beckett, R (1987) *Northern Ireland Regional Accounts: Sources and Methods*, Policy Planning and Research Unit, Occasional Paper No 12, HMSO.

Buchanan, J M (1965) An economic theory of clubs, *Economica*, 32, 125, 1–14.

Canning, D, Moore, B and Rhodes, J (1987) Economic growth in Northern Ireland: problems and prospects, in Teague, P (ed), *Beyond the Rhetoric: Politics, the Economy and Social Policy in Northern Ireland*, Lawrence and Wishart, London.

Department of Economic Development (1987) *Building a Stronger Economy: The Pathfinder Process*, July.

Gibson, N J (1972) Note on the financial relationships between Britain and Northern Ireland, *Administration*, XX, 4, 136–39.

Gibson, N J and Spencer, J E (1981) Unemployment and wages in Northern Ireland, *The Political Quarterly*, 52, 1, 100–14.

HMSO (1976) *Economic and Industrial Strategy for Northern Ireland*. Report of a Review Team (the Quigley Report), Belfast.

King, D N (1984) *Fiscal Tiers: The Economics of Multi-Level Government*, George Allen and Unwin.

Lawrence, R J (1965) *The Government of Northern Ireland: Public Finance and Public Services, 1921–1964*, Oxford University Press.

Litvak, J M and Oates, W E (1970) Group size and the output of public goods: theory and an application to state local finance in the United States, *Public Finance*, 25, 42–58.

Musgrave, R A (1959) *The Theory of Public Finance*, McGraw-Hill, New York.

Northern Ireland Economic Council (1981a) *Public Expenditure Comparisons Between Northern Ireland and Great Britain*, Report 18, January.

Northern Ireland Economic Council (1981b) *Employment Patterns in Northern Ireland: 1950–1980*, Report 23, June.

O'Dowd, L (1987) Trends and potential of the service sector in Northern Ireland, in Teague, P (ed), *Beyond the Rhetoric: Politics, the Economy and Social Policy in Northern Ireland*, Lawrence and Wishart, London.

Peacock, A T and Wiseman, J (1961) *The Growth of Public Expenditure in the United Kingdom*, Allen and Unwin, London.

Ross, M (1986) Employment in the public domain in recent decades, *General Research Series*, 27, Economic and Social Research Institute, Dublin.

Rowthorn, R (1987) Northern Ireland: an economy in crisis, in Teague, P (ed), *Beyond the Rhetoric: Politics, the Economy and Social Policy in Northern Ireland*, Lawrence and Wishart, London.

Short, J (1978) The regional distribution of public expenditure in Great Britain, 1964–70 to 1973–74, *Regional Studies*, 12, 5, 499–510.

Short, J (1981) *Public Expenditure and Taxation in the UK Regions*, Gower, Farnborough.

Short, J and Nicholas, D J (1981) *Money Flows in the UK Region*, Gower, Farnborough.

Simpson, J V (1977) Public sector revenue and expenditure in Northern Ireland, *Administration*, XXV, 3, 338–48.

Simpson, J V (1980) The finances of the public sector in Northern Ireland: 1968–1978, *Journal of the Statistical and Social Inquiry Society of Ireland*, Vol XXIV, Part II, 1979–80, 99–118.

Tiebout, C M (1956) A pure theory of local expenditures, *Journal of Political Economy*, 64, 416–24.

Topham, N (1983) Local government economics, Ch 4 in Millward, R, Sumner, M T and Zis, G (eds), *Public Sector Economics*, Longman.

Treasury (1979) *Needs Assessment Study* – Report, The report of an inter-departmental study co-ordinated by HM Treasury on the relative public expenditure needs in England, Scotland, Wales and Northern Ireland, HMSO, London.

Zabalza, A and Kong, P (1984) Pay determination in the public and private sectors, *Centre for Labour Economics*, WP 574, London School of Economics.

CHAPTER FOURTEEN

The Social Services

Peter R Simpson and Mary P Trainor

1. Introduction

There is no unique definition of the Social Services. This chapter concentrates on the benefits of a tangible nature provided by the Government as opposed to social security benefits which are of a monetary nature. Social security benefits, as a form of income, are discussed in Chapter 9. All Social Services are provided primarily on the basis of need rather than on the basis of ability or willingness to pay. Although some of the services (such as law, order and protection) have a significant public good content, the majority benefit specific households. The following services are considered:

(i) Education
(ii) Health
(iii) Personal social services (eg residential accommodation for the elderly)
(iv) Housing
(v) Law, order and protective services

During the financial year 1986/87 expenditure on all Social Services, including social security benefits, accounted for 70.3 per cent of total public expenditure in the United Kingdom (see Table 14.1). The five Social Services considered in this chapter comprised 37.5 per cent of total public expenditure, just over half the total expenditure on all Social Services. Social security benefits are the largest single public expenditure category, accounting for 32.9 per cent of the total in 1986/87.

The twentieth century has seen increasing Government involvement in the provision of Social Services. This is largely due to the inability of the free market to provide either an efficient allocation of resources to the various Social Services or an equitable distribution of the services (see Le Grand and Robinson 1984; Culyer 1980).

In the case of efficiency, most of the evidence suggests that markets will allocate too few resources to the various Social Services. Most of the services are supplied to a specific geographical locality and so elements of monopoly power are often present. It is often tempting for monopolists to restrict their output in order to boost their profits. Also with many of the services any externalities present tend to be of a desirable consumption nature

TABLE 14.1   Public expenditure by function, United Kingdom, 1986/87

	£ million	% of total	£ per capita
Health and personal social services	22,267	16.0	392
Education and science	19,178	13.8	338
Housing	3,779	2.7	67
Law, order and protective services	6,904	5.0	122
Social Services excluding social security	52,128	37.5	918
Social security	45,805	32.9	807
Social Services including social security	97,933	70.3	1,725
Other functions	41,299	29.7	728
Total public expenditure	139,232	100.0	2,453

Note: Per capita figures based on a mid-year estimated UK population of 56.763 million in 1986.
Sources: The Government's Expenditure Plans 1988–89, HM Treasury, January 1988; AAS No 124, 1988.

rather than an undesirable production kind, so again, under-provision tends to result. With some services, like health care, there is much uncertainty about when an individual will require treatment, and free markets rarely operate efficiently under conditions of risk and uncertainty. Finally of course, any element of public goods present in the services is likely to result in under-provision by the market. Bearing this in mind, during the 1980s the Government has maintained state provision of Social Services, though it has been keen to see this public sector involvement supplemented wherever possible by active private sector provision.

However, the strongest arguments in favour of state provision of Social Services are probably based more on the inability of markets to achieve a fair distribution of services amongst the members of society. Although private charity is far from trivial in its effects, it is unlikely to achieve either the magnitude of redistribution thought necessary, nor the channelling of care to the most needy members of society. For example, in 1987 total voluntary donations within the United Kingdom to the Royal Society for the Prevention of Cruelty to Animals (£13.8 million) were almost as large as those to the National Society for the Prevention of Cruelty to Children (£15.9 million). This giving may well reflect the preferences of donors, but it is unlikely to reflect the preferences of society in general. Also because many members of society do not fully appreciate their need for Social Services, it is unlikely that society could rely simply on social security payments to achieve an equitable distribution of the services (as recipients of cash benefits may be reluctant to spend them on things like education). As a result the state tends to provide Social Services on a universal basis to those in most need. Those members of society who demand greater care can then boost or substitute public sector provision with private sector supply.

Clearly the Social Services are different from other goods and services provided in an economy, but they also need to be examined on a regional basis. This is because firstly, different regions have different levels of need for Social Services, and so public provision is likely to be of more importance to some regions than to others. Secondly, whilst much expenditure on the Social Services (particularly capital expenditure), has a significant multiplier effect, most of this effect is restricted to the local regional economy. Thus, although public policy on the Social Services may well be formulated at national level, the economic and social effects of this policy can vary from region to region.

The level of spending on Social Services in any particular region of the United Kingdom depends upon many factors including:

(i)   the size of the population of the region;
(ii)   the age-structure of the region's population;
(iii)   the composition of households in the region; and
(iv)   the general economic prosperity of the region.

Because of their remoteness from the geographical centre of economic activity, peripheral regions have a tendency towards a lack of economic prosperity and so, other things being equal, have a propensity to above average per capita expenditure on Social Services. Northern Ireland is no exception to this rule. According to all standard measurements, Northern Ireland is the poorest region of the United Kingdom, having for example, in 1987, a personal disposable income per head of only 83.6 per cent of the United Kingdom average (NIAAS No 7, 1988 Table 14.2 – see also Chapter 9). However Northern Ireland, unlike say Scotland or Wales, is not only an exceptional region of the United Kingdom in terms of economic prosperity, it is also exceptional in terms of age-structure and household composition. All of these factors compound to make the provision of the Social Services of disproportionate importance to the Northern Ireland economy.

This chapter commences with a study of the Northern Ireland population, paying particular attention to its age-structure, and some of the main characteristics of Northern Ireland households. The period under consideration starts in 1951, a date which is particularly suitable, since significant changes in the provision of Social Services were made in the immediate post-war period (eg the setting up of the National Health Service in 1948).

The chapter then considers each of the five Social Services mentioned above in turn. Surveys will be made of expenditure over the post-war period with particular attention being paid to the current position. Present policies and levels of expenditure on each of the services are assessed relative to needs, and comparisons made with the rest of the United Kingdom. As it is not straightforward comparing the provision of Social Services in Northern Ireland with provision in the Republic of Ireland, the latter is covered in Appendix 14.1, rather than within the main text.

Finally, the chapter looks to the future and examines the projected size and age-structure of the Northern Ireland population through to the year

2001. These estimates are contrasted with those for the United Kingdom as a whole and inferences made about future policies for the Social Services in the province. The Republic of Ireland also features in this final section, for when assessing future needs (as against institutional arrangements) a comparison with Northern Ireland can very usefully be made. Whilst at present, in terms of age-structure, the Northern Ireland population lies somewhere between that of the United Kingdom and the Republic of Ireland, this position is likely to change during the next fifteen years.

2. People and households in Northern Ireland and the United Kingdom, 1951 to 1986

Although the geographical area of Northern Ireland is 5.8 per cent of that of the United Kingdom as a whole, because the region has the second lowest population density of the eleven standard regions of the United Kingdom (Scotland having the lowest) its population forms a much smaller proportion of the United Kingdom total. The estimated population of Northern Ireland at mid-1986 was 1.567 million which is just 2.8 per cent of the 56.763 million people estimated to be usually resident in the United Kingdom. As Table 14.2 shows, this proportion has hardly altered over the thirty-five year period from 1951 to 1986.

TABLE 14.2   Population in Northern Ireland and the United Kingdom, 1951–1986 (million)

	Northern Ireland	United Kingdom	NI as % of UK
1951	1.371	50.225	2.73
1961	1.425	52.709	2.70
1971	1.536	55.515	2.77
1981[1]	1.532	55.089	2.78
1986	1.567	56.763	2.76

[1] Usually resident population – not strictly comparable with earlier data.
Sources: 1951–1971 NI COP, 1981 and 1986 NIAAS No 6, 1987; AAS No 124, 1988.

The stable picture painted by Table 14.2 is, however, somewhat misleading, as stocks are not good indicators of flows. In fact during the period, Northern Ireland experienced an above average rate of net natural increase accompanied by a high rate of net outward migration, and during the 1970s these two effects tended to cancel each other out, leaving the population size more or less unchanged. This consideration is even more important when one comes to examine the changing age-structure of the Northern Ireland population, because migration tends to be concentrated in the early years of adult life (see Chapter 6). Table 14.3 shows the changing age-structures of the

TABLE 14.3 Age-distribution in Northern Ireland and the United Kingdom, 1951–1986 (percentage)

Age-group	1951		1961		1971		1981		1986		Main needs of age-group for social services
	NI	UK	NI	UK	NI	UK	NI	UK	NI	UK	
Under 1	1.9	1.5	2.2	1.7	2.0	1.6	1.8	1.3	1.8	1.3	Maternity services Health visiting Preventive medicine
1 to 4	8.1	7.1	8.1	6.3	8.2	6.5	6.8	4.8	6.9	5.1	Day care Nursery education
5 to school leaving age	16.0	13.9	18.6	15.4	19.6	16.0	20.4	16.4	18.5	14.2	Compulsory education
Working age	62.0	63.9	58.5	61.9	56.9	59.7	56.6	59.9	58.4	61.3	Health care Housing
Pensionable age	12.0	13.6	12.6	14.7	13.3	16.2	14.4	17.6	14.4	18.1	Health care Home helps Sheltered housing Retirement homes

Note: School leaving age was 14 in 1951, raised to 15 in 1957, and to 16 in 1972. Working age is from school leaving age to pensionable age; pensionable age is 60 and over for females, 65 and over for males.
Sources: As for Table 14.2 and ST No 18, 1988.

Northern Ireland and United Kingdom populations from 1951 to 1986, and summarises the main needs of the various age-groups for Social Services.

After examining these changing age-structures, it is perhaps surprising to find that over this thirty-five year period the median ages of both the Northern Ireland and United Kingdom populations have remained remarkably constant, with the median age in Northern Ireland remaining between five and six years below that in the United Kingdom, as shown in Table 14.4. This table of course shows how misleading a single summary statistic can be, as a constant measure of central tendency in a distribution does not necessarily imply no change in dispersion or skewness.

TABLE 14.4   Median age in Northern Ireland and the United Kingdom, 1951–1986 (years)

	Northern Ireland	United Kingdom	Difference
1951	29.9	34.9	5.0
1961	30.1	35.5	5.4
1971	28.4	34.1	5.7
1981	29.3	34.5	5.2
1986	29.5	35.4	5.9

Source: As Table 14.2.

Throughout the period, Northern Ireland has persistently had the most atypical age-structure of any region of the United Kingdom. What is particularly interesting about Table 14.3, as far as the provision of Social Services is concerned, is that the age-group which tends to place the smallest demands on the Social Services (ie those of working age) has always formed a smaller proportion of the Northern Ireland population than of the United Kingdom population. Thus on grounds of age-structure, Social Services are likely to have been of particular importance in Northern Ireland, other things being equal. This idea will be explained in more detail in the next section where the various Social Services are examined in turn.

However, even ignoring the considerable regional variations in economic prosperity, other things are not equal. As Table 14.5 shows, the composition of households in Northern Ireland is atypical of the United Kingdom as a whole. During the period of study, although average household size has been falling, average household size in the province has remained about 20 per cent higher than in Great Britain.

The fall in average household size over time is important, since it implies that the number of households has been rising more rapidly than the population size. For example, as Table 14.2 shows, although between 1951 and 1986 the population of Northern Ireland only rose by 14 per cent, it is estimated that over this same period the number of households rose by 48 per cent. For some Social Services (most obviously housing), the number of households is of more relevance than the population size, whilst for others (say personal social services like home helps), a knowledge of the number of

TABLE 14.5   Average number of persons per household, Northern Ireland and Great Britain, 1951–1986

	Northern Ireland	Great Britain	Absolute difference	Relative difference (as % of GB)
1951	3.91	3.21	+0.70	+22
1961	3.70	3.00	+0.70	+23
1971	3.49	2.89	+0.60	+21
1981	3.20	2.71	+0.49	+18
1986	3.07	2.56[1]	+0.51	+20

[1] 1985.
Sources: COP 1951–81; GHS (GB) 1985; CHS (NI) 1986.

households of certain types (eg one person elderly) is vitally important when assessing the needs of a population. Not surprisingly, the fall in average household size has been accompanied by a rise in the proportion of one-person households. Although in 1951 it was estimated that only 9.3 per cent of all households in Northern Ireland were one-person households (11.0 per cent in the case of Great Britain) by 1985 this proportion had risen to 20.0 per cent (24.6 per cent for Great Britain). Table 14.6 shows some other ways in which household types in 1985 are estimated to have differed between Northern Ireland and Great Britain.

There is a tendency (other things being equal) for households of the first three types shown in Table 14.6 (all household members aged 16–59) to have the least need for Social Services. It is estimated that, in 1985, such households formed a smaller proportion of all households in Northern Ireland than in Great Britain.

The impression gained by this brief survey of the age-structure of the population and the composition of households in the region is that these two factors will combine with the effect of the relatively poor economic prosperity of the region to make the population of Northern Ireland have an above average dependence on the Social Services by United Kingdom standards. It is perhaps therefore not surprising to find that public expenditure on the Social Services in Northern Ireland is high by United Kingdom standards.

During the financial year 1986/87 expenditure on Social Services, including social security benefits, accounted for almost 80 per cent of total public expenditure in the province (30 per cent was on social security benefits and 50 per cent on Social Services excluding social security, see Table 14.7). It is not appropriate to compare these percentages of public expenditure with the national percentages (see Table 14.1) since different programmes of expenditure are included in the 'other functions' category in the two areas. It is much more appropriate to compare per capita expenditure in the different programmes.

In 1986/87 per capita expenditure on all the Social Services was higher in Northern Ireland than in the United Kingdom. Table 14.8 shows that

TABLE 14.6   Percentage distribution of households by type, Northern Ireland and Great Britain, 1985

Household type	Northern Ireland		Great Britain	
1 adult (16–59)	6	⎱	8	⎱
2 adults (16–59)	10	⎰ 30	15	⎰ 35
3 or more adults	14	⎰	12	⎰
Youngest aged 0–4	20		13	
Youngest aged 5–15	20		18	
2 adults, one or both aged 60 or over	15		17	
1 adult aged 60 or over	15		16	

Source: PPRU Monitor No 1/88, Table 2. Crown Copyright.

per capita expenditure on Social Services, excluding social security, was 61 per cent above the national average. Within this, housing and law, order and protective services stand out as exceptionally high, reflecting the much greater needs of the province for these two services. Social security benefits in Northern Ireland are only 10 per cent higher than the national average. This reflects, in part, higher need in the province but also the application of uniform rates of benefit payments throughout the United Kingdom. At the national level the 1970s was a period of rapid expansion but this was particularly the case in Northern Ireland where public spending grew much more rapidly to catch up on national levels of per capita expenditure relative to need (see NIEC 1981a). The 1980s saw a substantial reduction in the rate of growth of spending on the Social Services in Northern Ireland, a reflection of the restraint in national Social Service spending and also because per capita spending in the province relative to need had caught up with national levels.

TABLE 14.7   Public expenditure by function, Northern Ireland, 1986/87

	£ million	% of total	£ per capita
Health and personal social services	751	16.2	479
Education and science	729	15.7	465
Housing	333	7.2	213
Law, order and protective services	500	10.8	319
Social Services excluding social security	2,313	49.9	1,476
Social security	1,389	30.0	887
Social Services including social security	3,702	79.9	2,363
Other functions	931	20.1	594
Total public expenditure	4,633	100.0	2,957

Note: Per capita figures based on a mid-year estimated NI population of 1.567 million in 1986.
Sources: The Government's Expenditure Plans 1988–89, HM Treasury, January 1988; NIAAS No 6, 1987.

TABLE 14.8 Indices of per capita public expenditure by function, Northern Ireland
(UK = 100)

	1971/72	1981/82	1986/87
Health and personal social services	113	124	122
Education and science	98	124	138
Housing	124	201	318
Law, order and protective services	138	283	261
Social Services excluding social security	112	150	161
Social security	107	106	110
Social Services including social security	110	131	137
Other functions	81	77	82
Total public expenditure	98	113	121

Sources: As Tables 14.1 and 14.7.

The next section of the chapter examines spending on each of the five Social Services in turn, particularly over the period 1976–86, and pays much attention to capital expenditure. An attempt will also be made to consider more formally the needs of the Northern Ireland population for the various services, so that the case for higher per capita levels of provision in the region can be assessed.

3. Relative patterns of expenditure in relation to need

In December 1979, HM Treasury published its *Needs Assessment Study*. This was the report of an inter-departmental exercise coordinated by the Treasury on the relative public expenditure needs of England, Wales, Scotland and Northern Ireland. The survey covered six major areas of public expenditure in which it is realistic to consider each £1 of spending as benefiting people in a specific region of the United Kingdom. (It would obviously not be appropriate to look at public expenditure on, say, national defence or interest payments on the national debt in this way.) The survey considered public expenditure on: health and personal social services; education (excluding universities); housing; other environmental services; roads and transport (excluding railways); and law, order and protective services (excluding the police).

The study assumed 'the long-established principle that all areas of the United Kingdom are entitled to broadly the same level of public services and that the expenditure on them should be allocated according to their relative needs'. (For further information on this parity principle, see Northern Ireland Office 1974.) What it attempted to do was to estimate a 'needs index' for each of the six areas of spending in each of the four countries. The study considered the need both for recurrent expenditure and for capital expenditure. The needs index for both types of expenditure within each of the six areas of spending was given the value of 100 in England. If for example, the per capita need for recurrent expenditure on education in Northern Ireland was considered to be 25 per cent higher than in England, then the index for Northern Ireland would be 125. This implies that if recurrent expenditure in Northern Ireland (per capita) is set at levels 25 per cent above those in England, then the 'real' levels of educational service provided in the two countries should be broadly similar.

It is important to realise that the needs indices provided in the study should not be looked upon as being permanent. Relative needs will change over time and so the indices for recurrent expenditure will change. The same is true with the need for capital expenditure but here there is an added complication. Future needs indices will be dependent on levels of capital expenditure in earlier years. If a country has a high need for capital expenditure and this expenditure is made, then its future needs for capital expenditure will come more into line with those for the other countries in the United Kingdom. However, if the extra expenditure is not made, then other things being equal, its future needs for capital expenditure will presumably move more out of line from those of the other countries. The *Needs Assessment Study* in fact was based on data referring to the financial year 1976/77 and provided information on suggested levels of expenditure in that year if parity between the different countries was to be achieved. Some of the capital projects required to achieve parity would entail expenditure over many years, while other projects would entail expenditure over relatively few years.

What this of course means is that if parity in the provision of the various Social Services is to be achieved (ie expenditure is to be proportional to need), then the *Needs Assessment Survey* will need to be an on-going survey. Strictly this is not the case. In reality, little information is provided on how the published Public Expenditure Estimates are arrived at each year. These estimates show the funds which are to be provided by the Central Government for various purposes (including those which are the responsibility of local authorities) in England, Wales, Scotland and Northern Ireland. The amounts which are made available, for example, to the Secretary of State for Northern Ireland, are known to take into account how the age-structure of the Northern Ireland population differs from that of the United Kingdom. Estimates for 'equivalences' are made which reflect the effect of differences in population structure. In the area of health, it is well known that the elderly tend to make above average demands on the NHS (in 1984 the average person aged 75 or over was estimated to cost the NHS over four times the average for all ages); and in the area of education, the cost of educating a secondary school pupil tends to be higher than that for a primary school pupil (in England in 1985, almost 50 per cent more). The Government is known to use weights – or equivalences – to take this type of factor into account, but it is not at all clear from the published Public Expenditure Estimates how many of the other factors included in the *Needs Assessment Study* are considered on a routine basis. It is, however, clear that by no means all of the factors are, since information is not routinely collected on them all.

Although the survey is not strictly an on-going one, it is worthwhile considering it in some detail, since it is based on a year inside the period covered in this section, and so it will be possible to compare the relative levels of public expenditure in Northern Ireland which are shown in Table 14.8 with the levels recommended in the survey. Also, the survey sheds light on the factors which most affect the needs for recurrent and capital expenditure, and the results suggest that the demographic and household characteristics studied in the previous section (and which are known to be considered in the Public Expenditure Estimates) are particularly important.

The *Needs Assessment Study* considered two types of factors affecting the relative needs of a country – 'objective' and 'subjective'. The objective factors were defined as those outside the direct control of the public authority providing the service and included, for example, in the case of education, the proportion of the population of school age, and in the case of housing, the proportion of dwellings deemed to be substandard. On the other hand, the subjective factors considered to affect needs, flowed primarily from differences in policy in the four countries. In the case of education, subjective factors included bilingualism (important in Wales) and denominational schooling (particularly important in Northern Ireland).

The list of variables included in the study was impressive (and long!). However, an analysis of the survey results revealed that if only a limited number of objective factors had been considered the needs ratios would have been 'little' different from those actually estimated using the longer list of objective factors. (As it turned out, when the study was published in 1979, it was decided to merely list the subjective factors and not to use them in the estimation of the ratios.) In what follows, mention will only be made of the most important objective factors, though the needs ratios reported will be those based on the full list of objective factors.

The five Social Services are now considered in turn. The pattern of expenditure in Northern Ireland is examined in relation to national levels of expenditure, distinguishing between capital and recurrent expenditure. This expenditure is assessed in relation to the needs of the region as shown in the *Needs Assessment Study* and other more recent evidence of the public expenditure needs of Northern Ireland. Finally, the implications of this expenditure for the wider regional economy are considered.

EDUCATION

While education policy in Northern Ireland does differ in some respects from that in Great Britain (see Osborne et al 1987), it is similar in its major aim of developing the abilities of individuals for their own benefit and that of society as a whole. Much of the post-war period has been characterised by growth but 'recent years have seen increasing reassessment and consolidation with a view to making the best use of resources in the light of a substantial drop in the birth rate and the need to control public expenditure' (Central Office of Information 1988).

The fact that over the entire post-war period the province has had a relatively young population by national standards (see Tables 14.3 and 14.4) and is expected to continue as such for the remainder of this century (see Table 14.20) suggests that educational expenditure should be running at relatively high levels in the region, if public expenditure is allocated to the regions according to their relative needs. Although it is not simply the age-structure of a region's population which affects its needs for educational services, the *Needs Assessment Study* did show that in the case of current expenditure, the only two objective factors having a major effect on the needs ratio were the size of the school-age population and the age distribution of that population. In the case of the need for capital expenditure, the survey identified four major objective factors: lack of pupil places, overcrowding, substandard places and deprivation.

The estimated needs ratios in the case of education for the year 1976/77 were as follows:

	England	Wales	Scotland	Northern Ireland
Recurrent expenditure	100	103	106	125
Capital expenditure	100	111	116	173

The above estimates cover all forms of education (excluding universities) including libraries. The high ratio for current expenditure in Northern Ireland was largely due to the relatively high number of school-children in the province and the very high ratio for capital expenditure reflected the relatively high incidence of overcrowding, substandard places and pupils living in deprived neighbourhoods.

It is interesting to note that the indices of actual per capita expenditure on education and science given in Table 14.8 are not out of line with the ratios estimated in the *Needs Assessment Study*. In effect, Northern Ireland needs above average per capita expenditure on education, and at least in recent years, has received it. However, even if relative patterns of spending are about right, it does not follow that absolute levels of public expenditure on education in the province are in any sense optimal.

Table 14.9 shows that throughout the period 1976 to 1985 capital expenditure formed a greater proportion of total expenditure in Northern Ireland than in the United Kingdom and this is in line with the *Needs Assessment Study* which recommended more emphasis on capital expenditure in the region than at the national level. The relatively high levels of capital expenditure in Northern Ireland in the years 1976 to 1979 can partly be explained by the need to catch up on a backlog of building which had been delayed by a particularly severe period of the 'troubles' in the early 1970s (see McGill 1987).

Education is a very labour intensive industry and, as Table 14.10 shows, the number of teachers employed in grant-aided schools in Northern Ireland has risen far more rapidly over the post-war period than the number of

TABLE 14.9   Public expenditure on school education, Northern Ireland and the United Kingdom, 1976/77–1985/86 (current prices)

| | Northern Ireland | | United Kingdom | |
	Total expenditure (£m)	Capital expenditure as % of total	Total expenditure (£m)	Capital expenditure as % of total
1976/77	155	11.9	5,143	9.4
1977/78	177	12.2	5,412	7.7
1978/79	186	13.9	5,966	6.3
1979/80	214	11.0	6,750	5.8
1980/81	261	8.2	8,204	5.9
1981/82	289	6.0	8,902	4.4
1982/83	307	6.1	9,440	4.2
1983/84	324	5.6	9,882	4.0
1984/85	343	4.7	10,193	3.7
1985/86	351	5.4	10,731	3.8

Sources: AAS No 124, 1988; Northern Ireland Appropriation Accounts; Report and Accounts of Education and Library Boards.

TABLE 14.10   Number of full-time teachers and pupils in grant-aided schools, Northern Ireland

School year	Teachers	Pupils (000)	Pupil/teacher ratio
1951/52	7,664	236	30.7
1955/56	8,511	258	30.3
1961/62	10,645	289	27.1
1965/66	12,246	301	25.7
1971/72	15,294	357	23.8
1975/76	17,327	373	21.7
1981/82	18,721	358	18.9
1982/83	18,616	353	18.7
1983/84	18,483	350	18.7
1984/85	18,392	349	18.7
1985/86	18,333	345	18.6

Note: The pupil/teacher ratios include part-time teachers.
Sources: NIAAS; NIDS.

pupils, with the result that pupil–teacher ratios have fallen. Nevertheless, even in 1985/86, the pupil–teacher ratio in Northern Ireland was above that in the other three countries in the United Kingdom. Compared to the ratio of 18.6 for Northern Ireland, the ratio in England was 17.6, in Wales 18.2 and in Scotland 16.4. The ratio for the United Kingdom in this year was 17.5.

Looking at school leavers' examination achievements, Northern Ireland pupils are well qualified by national standards, as Table 14.11 shows. (Scottish school leavers are excluded from the table because Scotland has a different examination system from the remainder of the United Kingdom.) What

TABLE 14.11   Qualifications of school leavers by sex, regions of the United Kingdom, 1985/86 (percentage of school leavers)

	3 or more 'A' level passes		At least 5 'O' level passes[1]		No graded result[2]	
	Male	Female	Male	Female	Male	Female
North	9.0	7.6	24.8	24.5	10.2	8.9
Yorkshire and Humberside	9.4	8.0	23.6	24.5	12.5	10.0
East Midlands	9.3	7.6	23.8	25.6	9.9	6.9
East Anglia	10.1	7.6	26.7	27.5	12.0	8.0
South East	11.9	10.3	30.5	32.0	10.1	7.6
South West	10.6	8.9	30.8	31.8	6.3	4.8
West Midlands	9.4	8.4	24.4	26.6	12.4	9.0
North West	11.2	9.3	27.1	26.9	13.3	10.4
Wales	9.2	8.2	25.3	29.2	18.4	13.8
Northern Ireland	13.2	14.8	31.8	39.7	27.4	16.3

[1] This includes GCE 'O' level grades A to C, CSE Grade 1, an 'O' level grade on an 'A' level paper and those with one, two, three or more 'A' levels.
[2] No 'O' levels or CSEs (any grade).
Source: RT No 23, 1988.

is particularly interesting is how well qualified female school leavers are in Northern Ireland, particularly at 'A' level. Whilst in all the other regions shown in the table, a higher proportion of boys than girls leave school with three or more 'A' level passes – in Northern Ireland the reverse is true. The table however also shows that Northern Ireland has the highest proportion of male and female school leavers with no 'O' levels or 'A' levels. In 1985/86, 21.8 per cent of Northern Ireland school leavers had no graded results, compared with 9.5 per cent of English school leavers and 16.1 per cent of Welsh school leavers. So in a sense, in terms of educational achievements, the region is one of extremes. Although not shown in the table, there is some association in Northern Ireland between religious affiliation and educational qualifications. During the 1970s there was a tendency for Roman Catholics to leave school slightly less well qualified than Protestants (Murray and Osborne 1983).

The Northern Ireland Economic Council (NIEC) recently stated that

'the education programme plays a vital role in the Northern Ireland economy. It represents a large and important sector in resource terms and makes a major contribution to the welfare of the population in providing for their educational and leisure needs. Given the magnitude and intractability of the economic problems facing Northern Ireland, the education programme has another important contribution to make in the medium and longer term. It provides part of the investment in research and development, and in the development of skills at all levels, which are essential for an efficient and competitive economy. Against this background it is desirable that educational provision in Northern Ireland should not only be as good as elsewhere in the United Kingdom, but in many important respects should be much better.'   (NIEC 1982b)

In a report published in 1984 on Public Expenditure Priorities, the NIEC concluded 'that education is currently receiving the right order of priority in overall public expenditure terms' (NIEC 1984). This conclusion was influenced by a report of December 1983 by the Department of Education's (Northern Ireland) Inspectorate which stated that on the whole educational standards in schools have not been adversely affected by expenditure policies.

However, in a report published in March 1989, the NIEC stated that the Department of Education (Northern Ireland) had recently claimed that there had been a significant decrease in the quality of provision, in terms of equipment, for the educational sector as a whole. The Department claimed that more needed to be done in the areas of computer-assisted learning, electronics and technology systems. Nevertheless, the Council felt able to repeat its earlier verdict that current levels of expenditure on education in the province are about right (NIEC 1989).

In summary then, in the case of education, Northern Ireland stands out as a region with high expenditure, high needs and high achievement by national standards.

HEALTH

In its publication, *Britain 1988, an Official Handbook*, the Central Office of Information (1988) stated that:

> 'The National Health Service (NHS) is based upon the principle that there should be a comprehensive range of publicly provided services designed to help the individual to stay healthy and to provide effective and appropriate treatment and care where necessary. All taxpayers, employers and employees contribute to its cost so that those members of the community who do not require health care help to pay for those who do. Some forms of treatment, such as hospital care, are provided free of charge; others may be charged for.
>
> Growth in real spending on the Health Service is being used, in conjunction with other factors, to meet the needs of increasing numbers of elderly people and to remedy disparities in provision between the regions of Britain.'

The report of the Royal Commission on the National Health Service in 1979 claimed that 'a fundamental purpose of a national service must be equality of provision so far as this can be achieved without an unacceptable sacrifice of standards'. The Commissioners quoted from the 1976 report of the DHSS Resource Allocation Working Party (RAWP) which claimed: 'The methods used to distribute financial services to the NHS have, since its inception, tended to reflect the inertia built into the system by history. They have tended to increment the historic basis for the supply of real resources and, by responding comparatively slowly and marginally to changes in demography and morbidity, have also tended to perpetuate the historic situation.' The Commissioners doubted if there was a fair geographical distribution of resources.

The *Needs Assessment Study* identified five major objective factors which were considered to affect the needs of a country for recurrent expenditure and capital expenditure on hospitals and community health, namely: size of population, age and sex-structure of population, mobility of population, social deprivation and teaching responsibilities of hospitals. The per capita ratios of needs estimated for the year 1976/77 were as follows:

	England	Wales	Scotland	Northern Ireland
Recurrent expenditure	100	105	109	108
Capital expenditure	100	108	104	87

In the case of current expenditure, the higher prevalence of elderly people in England and Wales increased their relative needs. Greater morbidity acted to increase the needs of Scotland and Northern Ireland and, to a lesser extent, Wales. Teaching hospital responsibilities were relatively greater in Scotland and also in Northern Ireland (where in fact fertility was an additional point of importance). On the capital expenditure side, it was found that the number of hospital beds available in Scotland and Northern Ireland was relatively greater than elsewhere, although in Northern Ireland a higher proportion of these were of post-war construction, and so their needs for extra and more modern provision were correspondingly lower.

Turning to family practitioner services, the study considered four objective factors to be of most importance in influencing the need for (current) expenditure, namely: size of population, structure of population, morbidity and deprivation. The results of the study in the case of family practitioner services for the year 1976/77 were as follows:

	England	Wales	Scotland	Northern Ireland
Needs ratio	100	111	109	114

With family practitioner services, deprivation was found to be very important, and this was relatively greater in Scotland and Wales and even more so in Northern Ireland.

Table 14.12 shows that during the period 1976–86, capital expenditure in Northern Ireland was running at around 3.8 per cent of the United Kingdom total, and with the Northern Ireland population forming about 2.77 per cent of the national total (see Table 14.2) a per capita expenditure index of around 137 is obtained. This is somewhat above the per capita needs ratios estimated in the *Needs Assessment Study*, suggesting that Northern Ireland is relatively well-off in terms of public expenditure on the NHS. Indeed, a discussion paper published by Birch and Maynard (1986) suggested that the NHS in Northern Ireland was over-funded by about 27 per cent during each of the financial years 1984/85 and 1985/86.

In the NIEC report of May 1982 (NIEC 1982a), the Council pointed

TABLE 14.12 Public expenditure on the National Health Service, Northern Ireland and the United Kingdom, 1978/79–1986/87 (current prices)

	Northern Ireland		United Kingdom	
	Total expenditure (£m)	Capital expenditure as % of total	Total expenditure (£m)	Capital expenditure as % of total
1978/79	285	7.5	7,835	5.9
1979/80	346	7.3	9,195	5.7
1980/81	438	5.7	11,944	5.8
1981/82	502	5.1	13,267	6.3
1982/83	557	5.0	14,385	6.0
1983/84	600	5.0	15,383	5.8
1984/85	642	5.0	16,312	6.1
1985/86	675	5.0	17,344	6.3
1986/87	721	2.8	18,713	6.2

Sources: AAS No 124, 1988; NIAAS No 6, 1987.

to ways in which savings could be made without any deterioration in the quality of service. In September 1983 in its response to the draft regional strategic plan for the health and personal social services in the period 1983–88, the Council clearly questioned the wisdom of developing acute hospital services any further without a serious consideration of the opportunity cost of so doing (NIEC 1983). In March 1984 the Council spoke out more strongly on this point in its overall review of public expenditure priorities and recommended 'that the existing balance of health care should be switched away from hospitals towards more efficient forms of provision and brought more closely into line with standards in Great Britain' (NIEC 1984). Many of the statistics which follow support this recommendation.

Turning again to Table 14.12, in terms of capital expenditure, Northern Ireland commenced the period with a greater proportion of its expenditure devoted to capital works than was the case at the national level, though by the end of the period it devoted a smaller proportion. This change is in keeping with the low estimated needs ratio for capital expenditure in Northern Ireland. The large fall in the level of capital expenditure in Northern Ireland in the year 1986/87 is largely accounted for by the completion of the Belfast City Hospital tower block – a major new hospital building which took well over a decade to complete.

Table 14.13 shows trends in the provision of hospital beds, general medical practitioners and general dental practitioners for the populations of Northern Ireland and the United Kingdom over the period 1951 to 1986.

On comparing 1986 with 1951, it is noticeable that the number of hospital beds per thousand population in Northern Ireland is more or less unchanged, whilst the number in the United Kingdom as a whole fell by almost one-third. However, both in Northern Ireland and the United Kingdom, there were marked increases in the number of cases treated per bed. In 1951 there were on average only 7.4 cases treated per bed in Northern Ireland (7.1 in the

TABLE 14.13   Provision of hospital beds, general medical services and general dental services, Northern Ireland and the United Kingdom, 1951–1986

	Hospital beds per 1,000 population		Average number of patients per GP (000)		Average number of persons per dentist (000)	
	NI	UK	NI	UK	NI	UK
1951	10.6	10.7	1.72	2.37	4.14	4.45
1961	11.9	10.6	1.91	2.25	4.77	4.41
1971	11.6	9.5	2.08	2.39	4.65	4.47
1981	11.6	8.2	2.05	2.15	4.60	3.67
1986	10.5	7.2	1.83	2.01	3.78	3.29

Sources: NIDS; NIAAS; AAS; ST No 18, 1988.

United Kingdom), but by 1986 the number of cases treated had risen to 16.8 (19.5 in the United Kingdom). Interestingly enough, although the total number of cases treated per year in Northern Ireland and United Kingdom hospital beds has been rising fairly steadily, so have hospital in-patient waiting lists.

Turning to dental services, not only has the number of dentists in Northern Ireland and the United Kingdom risen more rapidly than the populations, but the average number of courses of treatment per dentist has also risen rapidly – from an average of around 940 for Northern Ireland dentists in 1951 (1,020 for United Kingdom dentists) to around 2,150 in 1986 (2,200 for United Kingdom dentists).

When the NHS was instituted in 1948, it was naïvely assumed that the demand on resources would fall after a few years as the population became more healthy. In reality the reverse was the case with the NHS consuming more and more resources almost every successive year. The population is nowadays a more healthy one than it was in 1948 and life expectancy is rising. An increasing proportion of the population is surviving past the age of 'three score years and ten', into 'old-age' when heavy demands tend to be placed on health services. Furthermore, people's expectations have risen and so almost every age-group is making greater, not less, use of health services. This is particularly true in the case of dental care where an increasing number of people are demanding conservative treatment so that they can retain the majority of their natural teeth into old age.

In all of these respects the population of Northern Ireland has followed the United Kingdom trend, though usually lagging somewhat behind. In fact once one has standardised for the relatively young population of Northern Ireland by national standards, one is left with a picture of a relatively unhealthy regional population. For example, life expectancy at birth for a male born in Northern Ireland in 1985 was 70.1 years (compared with 71.5 years in the United Kingdom), with the corresponding figure for females being 76.3 years (77.4 years in the United Kingdom). This point is supported by Table 14.14 which shows that in 1986, Northern Ireland had the second highest standardised mortality ratio of any United Kingdom region.

Although throughout the post-war period the mortality record of the province has been relatively poor, the few comparative statistics which are

TABLE 14.14   Regional standardised mortality ratios, 1986

Region	Male	Female
North	110	107
Yorkshire and Humberside	104	102
East Midlands	97	99
East Anglia	89	91
South East	92	94
South West	91	93
West Midlands	102	102
North West	109	107
Wales	103	100
Scotland	114	111
Northern Ireland	112	109

Note: The standardised mortality ratio shows the ratio of the actual number of deaths in a sub-group of the population to the number that would be expected if that group had experienced the age specific mortality rates of the population as a whole (multiplied by 100).
Source: RT No 23, 1988.

available on morbidity often point towards a relatively healthy (if short-lived) regional population. For example, for all the age-groups considered, in the case of both males and females, the Continuous Household Survey of Northern Ireland in 1985 showed lower prevalences of chronic sickness (reported long standing illness) than was revealed in the 1985 General Household Survey in Great Britain. However, this difference is in fact thought to be largely due to lower expectations about health amongst the region's population than amongst the national population.

In sum then, the general picture of health care in Northern Ireland since the setting up of the NHS in 1948, is that the province has been one of the most costly yet unhealthy regions of the United Kingdom. Yet, when evaluating expenditure on health care, one must realise that in addition to being undesirable in their own rights, illness and absenteeism lower productivity and efficiency and thus have effects on the wider economy; so that spending not only affects the health of individuals, it can also influence the health of the economy. Also, because the health service is such a labour intensive industry, the relatively high levels of spending have helped to improve the very poor employment record of the region.

Nevertheless, as the NIEC's March 1989 overall review of economic strategy states: 'the Department of Health and Social Services in Northern Ireland is now looking at the case for shifting resources from treatment to prevention' (NIEC 1989). The implications of such a change of policy on health service costs, community health, and the wider economy could well be far reaching over the years ahead.

PERSONAL SOCIAL SERVICES

The Central Office of Information, in its publication *Britain 1988: an Official Handbook*, stated:

'Responsibility for personal social services rests with the Social Services Authorities (Local Authority Social Services Departments in England and Wales, Social Work Departments in Scotland and Health and Social Services Boards in Northern Ireland). Their services are directed towards elderly people, children and young people, families, people with mental illness or with physical or mental handicap, young offenders and other disadvantaged individuals and their carers. The major services include residential care, day care, community care and various forms of social work.

Much of the care given to elderly and disabled people is provided in the community itself, by their families, self-help groups and through voluntary agencies. The statutory sector offers the skilled care needed in particular services. The importance of the contribution made by the voluntary organisations is recognised especially when economies are being made in public expenditure and the demand on the statutory services is heavy.'

The *Needs Assessment Study* identified five major factors which were considered to influence the needs of a country for personal social services, namely: the size of the population, the number of people aged 65 and over living alone, poverty (low income) amongst people aged 65 and over, the density of accommodation for people under 18 and poverty amongst people aged 18–64.

The results of the study in the case of personal social services for the year 1976/77 were as follows:

	England	Wales	Scotland	Northern Ireland
Needs ratio	100	103	101	103

Relative needs in Scotland were affected by the higher incidence of deprivation, partly offset by fewer elderly people. A similar situation existed in Northern Ireland, but the deprivation was much greater. The Welsh relativity reflected a greater incidence of deprivation than in England.

Two of the most important personal social services are child care services and residential care of the elderly. These services will be examined in a little more detail.

Authorities must receive into their care any child under the age of seventeen who has no parent or guardian, who has been abandoned, or whose parents are unable to provide for him or her, if they are satisfied that such intervention is in the best interests of the child. Of course the type of care given can take a wide variety of forms. Information on trends in child care services in Northern Ireland, and at the national level, during the period 1961–85 is given in Table 14.15.

In all years, the proportion of children in care in Northern Ireland has been below the national rate, although by 1985 the rate in the province was only slightly lower than the United Kingdom rate. During this period there has been a change in emphasis in the type of care given, particularly in the manner

TABLE 14.15 Proportions[1] of child population (aged under 18) in care, Northern Ireland and the United Kingdom, 1961–1985

	Northern Ireland	United Kingdom
1961	2.7	5.0
1971	3.3	6.6
1981	5.1	8.2
1985	5.2	6.6

[1] Rates per 1,000 children.
Sources: NIDS, AAS No 124, 1988; ST No 15, 1985.

of accommodation. Nowadays an increasing proportion of children in care are fostered in the community, rather than living in residential homes.

Trends in the care of the elderly have been somewhat different. Services for elderly people are provided by statutory and voluntary bodies to help them to live at home whenever possible. These domiciliary services include advice and help given by social workers, domestic help, the provision of meals in the home, sitters-in, night attendants and laundry services as well as day centres, luncheon clubs and recreational facilities. However, Social Services authorities also provide residential care for the elderly and infirm. The authorities also register and inspect homes run by voluntary organisations or private bodies. Table 14.16 provides some relevant details for the period 1974 to 1985.

During this period, Northern Ireland has seen a significant growth in the provision of residential care in statutory homes with little expansion in the voluntary and private sector, whilst the United Kingdom saw little growth in the public sector but extremely rapid growth in the private sector. As a result, whilst the rate of provision of all types of residential care for the elderly was much higher at the regional than at the national level in 1974, by 1985 this regional differential had virtually disappeared.

Clearly then, by 1985 the levels of provision of child care and residential care of the elderly were fairly equal at the regional and national levels, which is consistent with the expenditure ratios estimated in the *Needs Assessment Study*.

TABLE 14.16 Residential care of the elderly, Northern Ireland and the United Kingdom, 1974, 1981 and 1985

	Residents in statutory homes (000)		Residents in voluntary and private homes (000)		Rates per 1,000 population aged 65 and over[1]	
	NI	UK	NI	UK	NI	UK
1974	2.6	109.0	1.4	21.0	23.5	16.8
1981	3.5	121.7	1.3	65.3	25.9	22.9
1985	3.5	120.5	1.5	102.2	26.6	26.0

[1] Includes all types of old people's homes.
Sources: NIAAS; ST; AAS No 124, 1988.

In its March 1989 overall review of economic strategy, the NIEC commented on the need to have a reallocation of resources from institutional to community care. Such a policy is indeed being proposed on a national level, and this is hardly surprising given the projected increases in the number of elderly people (especially those aged 85 and over) which is considered in the next section of this chapter. A move towards community care will alter both the social costs and benefits of the personal social services, though recent evidence by Knapp (1984) suggests that at least in the case of care of the elderly, it is only at high levels of dependence that the net social benefit of residential care will exceed that of domiciliary care. It would therefore appear that any future expansion of personal social services in Northern Ireland should be concentrated on community based (domiciliary) services.

HOUSING

The figures presented in Table 14.8 show very high levels of public expenditure on housing in Northern Ireland by national standards throughout the 1980s. The Department of the Environment has overall responsibility for the formation and direction of housing policy in Northern Ireland and works closely with the Northern Ireland Housing Executive (NIHE) in implementing these policies in the public sector.

In 1985, the total housing stock in Northern Ireland consisted of 524,000 dwellings, 34.7 per cent of which were owned by the NIHE. In 1979, the NIHE conducted a House Condition Survey, similar to a survey which was completed in 1974, in order to provide information on the housing stock and to measure the net effect of housing policy in Northern Ireland since 1974. The results showed that in 1979, 30 per cent of the total housing stock, compared to 38 per cent in 1974, was estimated to require remedial action ranging from major repair to renewal. Between 1974 and 1979 the proportion of unfit dwellings in Northern Ireland declined from 19.6 per cent to 14.1 per cent and the number of dwellings lacking at least one basic amenity declined by about 30 per cent. Nevertheless, in 1979 over 140,000 dwellings still required remedial action. This action was needed not only because of the age and condition of the property but also as a result of the civil disturbances during the 1970s. In 1979, as in 1974, a high proportion of the dwellings needing action were concentrated in Belfast. The 1979 House Condition Survey showed that of the 112,000 dwellings in the Belfast City Council area, 17,000 (15 per cent) were unfit for human habitation, 27,000 (25 per cent) lacked an inside toilet, and 26,000 (23 per cent) of families lacked the exclusive use of a bath or shower (*Ulster Yearbook 1983*).

During the 1970s and early 1980s, Belfast suffered from problems of inner city decline similar to many other major United Kingdom cities. Over these years there was a large movement of population from the centre of Belfast, leaving behind a preponderance of the elderly, unskilled and unemployed. The decline of traditional industries, the 'troubles' and the economic recession all interacted over this period to intensify both the nature and the scale of Belfast's inner city decline.

The *Needs Assessment Study* identified three major factors affecting the need for public sector capital expenditure on housing: the household/dwelling balance, the proportion of substandard dwellings and the prevalence of overcrowding.

Given the information in the House Condition Surveys of 1974 and 1979, it is perhaps not surprising to learn that the *Needs Assessment Study* recommended relatively high levels of public spending in Northern Ireland, as the following needs ratios for the year 1976/77 show:

	England	Wales	Scotland	Northern Ireland
Capital expenditure	100	114	120	174

The study showed that Northern Ireland had a relatively high score on all three of the major factors, but particularly on the first. In Wales the proportion of substandard housing was particularly high, while in Scotland both overcrowding and unsatisfactory housing were proportionately greater than in England.

It should be noted that the indices of per capita public expenditure on housing in Northern Ireland during the 1980s (see Table 14.8) are considerably higher than this needs ratio would commend, suggesting that in recent years Northern Ireland has been treated very favourably in this respect. To a certain extent this is due to a need to 'catch up' in house building following a period of low investment in the early 1970s due mainly to the 'troubles'.

In May 1981, the NIEC called for a commitment by the Government to bring Northern Ireland's housing up to the national standard, claiming that the main deficiencies could be overcome in a decade (NIEC 1981b). Four years later, it noted a significant improvement, but still recommended that housing be given continued priority on grounds of parity (NIEC 1985). By March 1989, however, the Council reported that

> 'in recent years, housing appears to have been downgraded in the Government's priorities. The 8 per cent share of total public expenditure devoted to housing in 1983/84 has fallen to 7 per cent in 1987/88 and is planned to fall to about 4 per cent in 1991/92. As a result, the Housing Executive has been required to reduce new public housing starts significantly from 1,750 to 1,500 in 1988/89, falling to a projected 1,300 in 1991/92, and to place greater emphasis on the rehabilitation and maintenance of public sector dwellings.'   (NIEC 1989)

It felt that this cut-back was regrettable given the improvements achieved during the early 1980s. For example, the mini-House Condition Survey of 1987 suggested a reduction in unfitness levels from 14.1 per cent in 1979 to 8.4 per cent in 1987 (the corresponding rate for England and Wales being less than 5 per cent).

TABLE 14.17 New houses under construction, Northern Ireland and the United Kingdom, 1976–1986

End of year	Northern Ireland		United Kingdom	
	Total houses (000)	Public sector as % of total	Total houses (000)	Public sector as % of total
1976	16.8	59.9	462.1	54.2
1977	14.6	49.3	423.5	51.4
1978	13.5	36.6	407.4	47.2
1979	12.6	28.0	387.2	43.4
1980	12.6	29.3	299.1	39.0
1981	12.5	30.1	254.0	27.3
1982	13.9	31.0	274.9	26.4
1983	16.1	28.4	300.6	23.4
1984	16.6	23.9	292.6	20.5
1985	15.8	18.0	297.7	17.9
1986	15.3	15.2	309.4	16.6

Sources: NIHS 1987; UKHS 1976–86.

This proposed cut-back in public expenditure will also have effects on the wider economy. Public expenditure on housing has generated much employment in the construction and related industries over the past few years. Not only will this valuable social benefit be reduced by the cuts, but external diseconomies arising from poor housing will not be reduced as much as would otherwise have been the case.

The statistics on house building in Northern Ireland over the period 1976–86 are rather different from the corresponding figures at the national level Table 14.17 shows that, although the proportions of houses being built in the public sector have been fairly similar throughout the period at both the regional and national levels, with proportions clearly declining, the total level of house building in Northern Ireland has been relatively constant in comparison with the definite decline in house building in the United Kingdom as a whole. As a result, the public sector has withdrawn from house building at the national level in a more dramatic way than it has at the regional level.

The effects of these differences in the levels of public sector house building at regional and national levels are partly reflected in the statistics shown in Table 14.18. The changes in the housing stocks shown in this table

TABLE 14.18 Public sector and private sector houses, Northern Ireland and the United Kingdom, 1971, 1981 and 1985 (per 1,000 households)

	Northern Ireland		United Kingdom	
	Public sector	Private sector	Public sector	Private sector
1971	370	695	319	717
1981	421	677	358	729
1985	364	684	316	741

Source: As Table 14.17.

reflect not only the rates of house building in the two sectors, but also the rates of demolition and transfer from the public to private sectors, together of course with changes in the numbers of households over the period. The table, however, clearly demonstrates that throughout the period, public sector housing remained more prominent in Northern Ireland than it did at the national level.

LAW, ORDER AND PROTECTIVE SERVICES

The *Needs Assessment Study*, when considering law, order and protective services, excluded the police service. It considered that the three most important objective factors affecting the need of a country for public spending to be: the age-structure of the population, the number and types of crime (in particular crimes of violence) and the numbers of buildings and other installations in the various categories of high fire risk.

Taking all relevant objective factors together the results of the *Needs Assessment Study* expressed as per capita ratios for the year 1976/77 were:

	England	Wales	Scotland	Northern Ireland
Needs ratio	100	103	108	123

The much higher Northern Ireland figure reflected the considerably larger relative number of people committed to prison in the province. Likewise, the higher Scottish figure relative to England was also attributable to the greater prison population (which in part reflects relative incidence of crime). Also (though this was not a major factor), both Northern Ireland and Wales had relatively larger numbers of families of low or moderate means in comparison with England. That is the category representing potential beneficiaries of legal aid.

Of course, in recent years the need for public expenditure on law, order and protective services in Northern Ireland has been much larger than the above ratio suggests. As explained, the ratio excludes the police, and during the years of the 'troubles' the province's need for policing has been much greater than that of any other region of the United Kingdom.

The present situation in Northern Ireland had its beginnings in the summer of 1969 when the reactions and counter-reactions to the civil rights campaign, which had gathered momentum during the year, culminated in severe and prolonged communal riots. At the heart of the Government's security policy is a determination to develop the effectiveness of the police (the Royal Ulster Constabulary – RUC) to the point where military involvement in the maintenance of law and order in Northern Ireland is no longer required. Between 1977 and 1986, the full-time strength of the RUC increased by 102 per cent, compared with growth rates of the full-time police force in England and Wales of 25 per cent and in Scotland of 24 per cent. Total expenditure (at current prices) on law, order and protective services in Northern Ireland rose from £17 million (£11 per head of population) in the year 1968/69 to a level of £500 million (£319 per capita) in the year 1986/87. The corresponding increase in per capita expenditure for the United Kingdom was from a level of £13 in 1968/69 to £122 in 1986/87. Expressed in terms of per capita indices for Northern Ireland (with UK = 100), this is an increase from an index of 85 in 1968/69 to an index of 261 in the year 1986/87, as shown in Table 14.19.

This table shows a total of 2,524 deaths over the eighteen year period (an average of 140 deaths a year) and a total of 29,114 injuries connected with the 'troubles'; 1972 stands out as being the worst year at least in terms of the statistics, and soon after per capita expenditure on law, order and protective services rose to between three and four times the United Kingdom level and remained as such through to the financial year 1980/81. Since then the relative level of expenditure has fallen back somewhat, reflecting the slight easing off of the 'troubles' in the 1980s together with greater civil unrest in Great Britain.

In its March 1989 overall review of economic strategy, the NIEC stated that it agreed that the maintenance of law and order in the province must be afforded a high priority by Government. However, it expressed

TABLE 14.19 Deaths and injuries connected with the civil disturbances, Northern Ireland, 1968–1986

Year[1]	Total people killed	Total people injured	Relative per capita expenditure on law, order and protective services in NI (UK = 100)
1968	na[2]	na[2]	85
1969	13	711	100
1970	25	1,056[3]	90
1971	174	2,543	138
1972	467	4,876	269
1973	250	2,651	294
1974	216	2,398	313
1975	247	2,474	365
1976	297	2,729	370
1977	112	1,398	369
1978	81	985	319
1979	113	875	305
1980	75	801	304
1981	101	1,350	283
1982	97	525	273
1983	77	510	260
1984	64	866	250
1985	54	916	263
1986	61	1,450	261

[1] The per capita expenditure index is calculated on a financial year basis; deaths and injuries are on a calendar year basis.
[2] This is the year prior to the start of the 'troubles'.
[3] Includes substantially more minor injuries than those for later years.
Sources: NIAAS No 6, 1987; Public Expenditure White Papers, HM Treasury; AAS No 124, 1988.

concern that increases in expenditure on law and order might be at the expense of other programmes and announced an intention to monitor the general influence of the law and order budget on the allocation of resources within the Northern Ireland public expenditure block and its effect on the economy (NIEC 1989).

Once more, this recognises the external benefits of spending on the Social Services, not least in the area of job creation. Clearly, all the services have important effects on the wider economy, although it is difficult to estimate the net effect of the 'troubles' on jobs in the province (see Chapter 6). On the negative side, the 'troubles' have obviously deterred firms from investing in the province, but many people are employed as a result of the 'troubles' (either directly as in the RUC, or indirectly as in the building industry, repairing and replacing damaged property). Sadly, at the time of writing there is no end to the present episode of civil disturbances in sight, and public expenditure on this function in the province is likely to remain relatively high into the 1990s.

4. Projected population to 2001 and implications

The second section of this chapter showed that over the period 1951 to 1986 the population of Northern Ireland was atypical of the United Kingdom population, with the median age in Northern Ireland being a little over five years below that in the United Kingdom. The third section of the chapter showed that this relatively young age-structure was an important factor when explaining the high levels of spending on the Social Services in the region over the post-war period. This final section of the chapter looks to the future through to the year 2001. It compares the population projections for Northern Ireland with those for the United Kingdom and the Republic of Ireland. It shows that the common belief that the experience of Northern Ireland will lie somewhere between that of the United Kingdom and the Republic of Ireland is likely to be incorrect and that over the remaining years of the twentieth century, as far as population is concerned, Northern Ireland is expected to become increasingly different from other United Kingdom regions. Needless to say, this has important implications for the provision of Social Services in the province over the next few years.

Table 14.20 shows the projected size and age-distributions of the Northern Ireland, United Kingdom and Republic of Ireland populations over the period 1986–2001, and together with Table 14.3 provides demographic information for a half century.

The projections given in Table 14.20 suggest an average annual rate of change for the Northern Ireland population of +0.45 per cent as against +0.25 per cent for the United Kingdom and −0.10 per cent for the Republic of Ireland. The figures for 1986 tend to support the view that in terms of its age-structure the Northern Ireland population lies somewhere between that of the

TABLE 14.20 Projected population size and age distribution, Northern Ireland, United Kingdom and the Republic of Ireland, 1986–2001 (percentage)

Age group	1986			1991			1996			2001		
	NI	UK	RI	NI	UK	RI	NI	UK	RI	NI	UK	RI
Under 5	8.7	6.4	9.2	8.6	6.9	8.1	8.5	7.1	7.4	7.9	6.7	7.3
5 to school leaving age	18.5	14.2	19.8	17.9	13.5	18.9	17.9	14.2	17.2	17.8	14.9	15.5
Working age	58.4	61.3	58.1	59.1	61.3	59.9	59.2	60.5	62.2	60.0	60.4	63.8
Pensionable age to 74	9.6	11.7	8.8	9.3	11.4	8.7	9.0	11.0	8.5	8.8	10.5	8.6
75–84	3.9	5.2	3.4	4.1	5.4	3.6	4.1	5.4	3.8	4.1	5.5	3.8
85 and over	0.9	1.2	0.7	1.0	1.5	0.8	1.3	1.8	0.9	1.4	2.0	1.0
Population (m)	1.57	56.8	3.54	1.61	57.5	3.54	1.65	58.3	3.50	1.68	59.0	3.49
Median age	29.5	35.4	27.5	30.2	35.8	29.3	31.3	36.4	31.5	32.4	37.5	33.4

Note: In 1986, the school leaving age in the Republic of Ireland was 15 years, one year below that in the United Kingdom. Pensionable ages were the same. It is assumed that there will be no changes prior to 2001.
Sources: Population Projections 1985–2025, OPCS Series PP2 No 15, 1987; Population and Labour Force Projections 1991–2021 (CSO, Dublin).

United Kingdom and the Republic of Ireland. However, what is perhaps surprising is the fact that the projections through to 2001 suggest that in many respects the Northern Ireland population will become even more distinct from that of the United Kingdom, whilst the population of the Republic of Ireland will become more similar to that of the United Kingdom.

The unique demographic position of Northern Ireland is well understood (Compton 1987). During the 1980s (and indeed over most of this century) a little over one-third of the population has been Roman Catholic and a little under two-thirds has been Protestant (or more correctly, non-Roman Catholic). The Protestant population has tended to closely resemble the population of Great Britain in its marriage and child-bearing habits whilst the Roman Catholic population has tended to resemble the population of the Republic of Ireland in these respects. The main explanation for the very slow rise in the proportion of Roman Catholics in the population during this century is the higher rate of celibacy among Roman Catholics and the tendency to marry at an older age than Protestants, though these factors are partly offset by higher fertility rates among Roman Catholics. Migration has also affected the situation with Roman Catholics having a higher propensity to leave the province than Protestants (Compton 1987).

The population projections through to 2001, however, suggest that this established pattern will not continue into the future. This is reflected in the figures given in Table 14.21 which show the total period fertility rate (TPFR) for Northern Ireland, the United Kingdom and the Republic of Ireland over the period 1971–86 along with projections through to the year 2001. The TPFR is the average number of children which would be born per woman, if women experienced the age-specific fertility rates of the period in question, throughout their child-bearing years.

During the 1970s the TPFR for Northern Ireland lay almost mid-way between the low United Kingdom figure where around 10 per cent of the population are Roman Catholic and the high Republic of Ireland figure where over 90 per cent are Roman Catholic. The most interesting aspect of the projections through to 2001 is the marked decline in the Republic of Ireland's

TABLE 14.21   Total period fertility rates, Northern Ireland, United Kingdom and the Republic of Ireland, 1971–2001

	Northern Ireland	United Kingdom	Republic of Ireland
1971	3.23	2.41	3.98
1976	2.53	1.74	3.31
1981	2.59	1.81	3.07
1986	2.41	1.78	2.39
1991	2.35	1.90	2.16[1]
2001	2.23	1.99	1.91[1]

[1] CSO (Dublin) assumes a TPFR of 2.10 from 1991 onwards in its population projections (this being the population replacement level) – see CSO April 1988, Population and Labour Force Projections 1991–2021.
Sources: ST No 18, 1988; RT No 23, 1988; Ireland's Changing Population Structure, DMK Ltd, 1987, Dublin.

TPFR to a level more typical of other European countries, including the United Kingdom. (The 1986 Demographic Statistics prepared by the Statistical Office of the European Communities reveal a TPFR in 1981 of 2.14 for Portugal, 2.06 for Spain, 1.94 for France, 1.57 for Italy and 1.81 in the United Kingdom.) In contrast, the estimates would appear to suggest that the TPFR of the minority Roman Catholic community in Northern Ireland will remain high. This taken together with the expected rise in the British TPFR (which the majority Protestant community in the province is assumed to follow) results in a projected TPFR for Northern Ireland in 2001 higher than either the United Kingdom or Republic of Ireland rates.

As Table 14.20 shows, the expected outcome of all the demographic influences over the period 1986–2001 is an ageing population. The median age of the population is expected to rise by 2.9 years in Northern Ireland, 2.1 years in the United Kingdom and 5.9 years in the Republic of Ireland. In 1986, the median age in Northern Ireland was estimated to be two years higher than that in the Republic of Ireland, but by the year 2001 it is predicted to be one year lower. Whilst in 1986 Northern Ireland had a population which in terms of growth and age-structure lay between the populations of the United Kingdom and the Republic of Ireland, by the year 2001 it is predicted that not only will Northern Ireland have the youngest and fastest growing population of any of the eleven standard regions of the United Kingdom, it will also have a younger and faster growing population than that of the Republic of Ireland.

This has important implications for the provision of Social Services in the region through to the end of the century since it appears that Northern Ireland will continue to be an exceptional region of the United Kingdom with above average needs per capita for the Social Services. It is unlikely that the general economic prosperity of the region relative to the national economy will improve significantly over the remaining years of this century and so, with the continuing atypical age-structure predicted for the region's population, national estimates for public spending on the various Social Services may be of little relevance to the province.

As explained at the beginning of this chapter, the composition of households in the region is also important when considering provision of the Social Services. For services such as housing, the number of households is more important than the size of the population. For 1951–86, it was noted in Section 2 above, that although the population of Northern Ireland rose by 14 per cent, the number of households rose by some 48 per cent. Unfortunately there are no reliable estimates for the projected increase in the number of households in Northern Ireland through to the year 2001, though estimates for Great Britain and the Republic of Ireland are shown in Table 14.22.

This table predicts a 9 per cent increase in the number of households both in Great Britain and the Republic of Ireland over the fifteen years up to the year 2001. The percentage increase for Northern Ireland is likely to be higher. The table suggests a 6 per cent fall in average household size in Great Britain over the period and the information presented in Table 14.5 which covers the period 1951–86 suggests that it might not be unreasonable to apply

TABLE 14.22   Projected number of households and average household size, Great Britain and the Republic of Ireland, 1986–2001

	Households (million)		Average household size	
	Great Britain	Republic of Ireland	Great Britain	Republic of Ireland
1986	20.8	1.00	2.60	3.44
1991	21.7	1.03	2.50	3.33
1996	22.4	1.06	2.45	3.20
2001	22.7	1.09	2.44	3.08

Sources: ST No 18, 1988; Ireland's Changing Population Structure, DMK Ltd, 1987, Dublin.

this fall to Northern Ireland households over the period 1986–2001. This gives an estimated average number of persons per household in Northern Ireland in the year 2001 of 2.88 which, together with the projected population of 1.68 million, gives an estimated number of households of 0.583 million in 2001. This is approximately a 17 per cent increase over the 0.500 million households estimated for Northern Ireland in 1986. Thus, although there are no official estimates, the available evidence suggests that the increase in the number of households in Northern Ireland over the period 1986–2001 will be considerably higher than the 9 per cent increases predicted for Great Britain and the Republic of Ireland. Given the lack of information on the subject, it is not possible to provide a projected table through to 2001 on household types to correspond with the historical information given in Table 14.6.

In sum, it can be assumed (with a fair degree of confidence) that over the remaining years of this century, as long as the Government allocates public spending on the Social Services primarily on the basis of need (as assumed for example in the Treasury's *Needs Assessment Study*), a disproportionately large amount of expenditure will have to be allocated for the provision of Social Services to the population of Northern Ireland.

5. Conclusion

From 1951 to date, the Social Services have been of much importance to the Northern Ireland economy. During much of this period, the well-documented high level of public expenditure in the region in relation to the United Kingdom can be explained chiefly in terms of the high per capita levels of spending on the five main Social Services considered in this chapter. The studies of the individual services made in the third section of the chapter showed that this high level of dependence on the Social Services is hardly surprising.

Since the end of the Second World War, Northern Ireland has tended to be the most atypical region of the United Kingdom, marked by a relative lack of general economic prosperity, with a relatively young population living in relatively large households. These factors have combined to place heavy demands on the Social Services. In terms of material well-being, the region's population has been a relatively poor one, but there can be no doubt that but for the high levels of public spending on the Social Services, it would have been even poorer, at least in the short run. The question must be asked, however, of whether greater public spending aimed at reducing the economic problems of the region might in the long run reduce the levels of public spending required to deal with the social problems of the region. Undoubtedly the present episode of civil unrest in the province is doing much to contribute to the economic problems of the region, but it is also clear that much of the expenditure on Social Services in Northern Ireland is merely treating the economic ills of the community and doing little to cure them.

Turning to the future, the data presented in the previous section would suggest that levels of spending on Social Services in the region will continue to be high by national standards and that the Social Services are destined to go on playing an important part in the lives of the region's population for many years to come.

Appendix 14.1 Republic of Ireland

It would be of interest to compare the Northern Ireland Social Services with those in the Republic of Ireland which are also well developed. However, because of the different organisational structures it would require more space than is available here. This appendix provides some information on the Irish health, education and housing sectors.

HEALTH

The development of the health care system in the Republic of Ireland is well documented (Hensey 1979). The structure of the present system is based on entitlement to benefits (established by means-testing) as opposed to the universalist National Health Service in the United Kingdom. All residents are 'eligible for free or subsidised care in a complex three-tiered system' (Tussing 1985, 3). The services provided under this system are, in brief, the free provision of all medical care, including general practitioner services, for those with category I eligibility; free provision of specialist care (both in-patient and out-patient) and free hospital accommodation in a public ward is available to those with category II eligibility; whilst the rest (those with category III eligibility) are only entitled to free hospital accommodation in a public ward.[1] The proportion of the population included in categories I and II rose from 74 to 85 per cent between 1973 and 1987. This change in the composition of entitlement has affected most occupational groups, although some groups (eg large farm households) have benefited more than others.[2]

Unlike most other European countries,[3] the Irish health service is financed predominantly from the Exchequer. In 1986, 85.7 per cent of health service income came directly from this source, 6.2 per cent from health contributions[4] and the remaining 8.1 per cent from charges and other sources.[5]

Total expenditure on the health service contains both private and public components and whilst a detailed analysis of the latter is readily available, information on private expenditure can only be estimated.[6] During the 1970s, public spending on health care (current plus capital) rose dramatically (see Table 14.1A). This phenomenal growth reflects the increase in price and quantity of services combined with the transfer of some services from the private to the public sector. In 1983 public expenditure controls were introduced because of the serious nature of the National Debt problem (see Chapter 16). Since then these controls have led to a curtailment of health care expenditure and are expected to continue for the foreseeable future (Tussing 1987).

TABLE 14.1A   Public expenditure per person on health care and education, Republic of Ireland, 1972, 1980 and 1986 (£ sterling)

	Health care[1]		Education	
	Current prices	Constant 1980 prices[2]	Current prices	Constant 1980 prices[2]
1972	35	107	37	113
1980	195	195	147	147
1986	330	178	242[3]	136[3]
Annual average growth rate (%)				
1972–80	23.9	7.8	18.8	3.3
1980–86	9.2	−1.5	10.5[3]	−1.5[3]

[1] Includes spending on personal social services.
[2] Deflated by the Consumer Price Index, hence no account is taken of any relative price effect.
[3] 1985 figure; rate 1980–85.
Sources: National Income and Expenditure (CSO, Dublin); Health Statistics 1987 (Department of Health, Dublin).

Although it is difficult to compare health care in the Republic of Ireland with other countries[7] because of the different systems, indicators of health care provision show that Irish standards are relatively high. For example, in 1986, the ratio of hospital beds per 1,000 population was 9.5 which, although slightly lower than the equivalent Northern Ireland figure (10.5), was higher than that for the United Kingdom (7.2). In 1987, the number of general practitioners per 100,000 population in the Republic of Ireland was 58, the same as for Northern Ireland and above that of the United Kingdom (54).[8]

A major review of the health care system is currently in progress. Besides considering the problems associated with the present methods of funding[9] certain policy issues are also being examined (eg more emphasis on preventive care) with the ultimate aim of reforming the system to produce a more equitable and cost effective service.

EDUCATION

Since the mid-1960s the two main objectives of educational policy have been to provide equality of educational opportunity irrespective of location and to prepare young people for entry into the labour market. The latter objective is the result of the influential government report 'Investment in Education' (1965) which has since formed much of the basis of Irish educational policy.

The educational system provides compulsory schooling for all children between the ages of 6 and 15 years. Provision for non-compulsory schooling, for children under 6 years, is available in the primary sector[10] whilst an increasing number of pupils remain at school beyond the minimum school leaving age. Throughout the period 1966–85 participation rates[11] for those aged 15 to 17 years have increased. In 1966, 54 per cent of those aged 15 remained at school; the raising of the school leaving age to 15, in 1972, increased the rate to 94 per cent by 1985. The population aged 16 and 17 years have experienced similar increases. For the former age the rate rose from 39 to 80 per cent whilst for those aged 17 years the rate increased from 27 to 63 per cent. The increases in participation rates reflect policy changes[12] introduced in 1967/68 combined with rising real incomes and changes in unemployment throughout the period (see Joyce and McCashin 1982, Chapter 6). Opportunities for further and higher education[13] are available for suitably qualified school leavers.

During the period 1972–85 per capita growth in total public expenditure on education (see Table 14.1A) was similar to that for the health service. The high growth levels, particularly between 1972 and 1980, were partly due to demographic and participation rate changes but mainly the result of substantial increases in total costs per pupil. O'Hagan and Kelly (1984) concluded that the most important factor explaining the increase in the ratio of expenditure on education to total public expenditure during the 1970s was the increase in the cost ratio.[14]

Since education is a labour intensive industry a major element of total educational expenditure is salaries.[15] Thus, the rise in costs per pupil can be related to an increase in the number of teachers employed combined with rising salaries.[16] This increase in the number of teachers has been paralleled by rising enrolments but to a lesser degree, so that pupil–teacher ratios at both primary and secondary level have been declining. In 1984/85 the ratio at the primary level was 26.5 which was higher than that in both Northern Ireland (23.3) and the United Kingdom (22.0). However, the secondary level ratio of 15.5 (17.2 in 1961/62) lay between that of Northern Ireland (15.4) and the United Kingdom (15.9). The Republic of Ireland is currently experiencing falling fertility rates and the future demand for both primary and secondary level education will therefore decline.

HOUSING

Housing policy in the Republic of Ireland is formulated by the Department of the Environment and administered jointly with the local authorities. Irish housing policy operates on the principle that the responsibility for the provision of housing rests with the individual. Those who can afford to house themselves are encouraged to do so and an extensive range of financial incentives[17] from central and local authorities are available to help achieve home ownership. The local authorities are responsible for housing those persons unable to house themselves from their own resources.

This emphasis on home ownership combined with a relatively high proportion of the housing stock in rural areas, which tend to have high rates of owner occupation, has resulted in the Republic of Ireland having one of the highest rates of owner occupation in the world. In 1987, 78 per cent of all occupied dwellings were owner occupied (Comprehensive Public Expenditure Programmes 1988, 368). This contrasts with the position in both Northern Ireland and the United Kingdom where, in 1986, the rate of owner occupation was 61 and 63 per cent respectively. The proportion of dwellings rented from local authorities in the Republic of Ireland (12 per cent) was substantially lower than in either Northern Ireland (34 per cent, including NIHE houses) or the United Kingdom (27 per cent).

The national housing stock grew from 676,000 units in 1961 to an estimated 950,000 units by 1984. Most of this growth (82 per cent) has occurred since 1972; an average of 25,000 dwellings were completed annually, a quarter of which were local authority houses. This growth in the housing stock has been paralleled by an improvement in the quality of housing (see Table 14.2A). However, the rate of improvement in amenities was greater in urban that rural areas (Joyce and McCashin 1982, Ch 5, 56). A major factor contributing to the improvement in the quality of the housing stock has been the generous improvement grant scheme which operated from the mid-1970s to the late 1980s.

TABLE 14.2A   Housing quality indicators, Republic of Ireland, 1961, 1971 and 1981 (percentage)

	1961	1971	1981
Dwellings erected pre-1919	57.9	44.8	28.2
Housing units with piped water inside	51.0	73.2	92.3
Housing units with indoor toilet	42.7	62.9	84.3
Housing units with fixed bath/shower	33.2	55.4	81.8
Persons in private households having more than two persons per room[1]	11.5	9.3	3.2
Average number of persons per room	0.90	0.86	0.74

[1] Measure of overcrowding.
Source: Statistical Abstract 1965, 1981, 1985 (CSO, Dublin).

Currently there are approximately 110,000 houses rented from the local authorities. During the last ten years, local authority housing waiting lists have been declining due to the relatively high level of local authority building, combined with increased accessibility to home ownership for lower income groups under publicly funded house purchase loan schemes. In 1987, there were 18,560 applicants for local authority houses, the lowest level since 1976.

During the period 1980–85, capital expenditure on housing accounted for 20 per cent of all public capital expenditure and 70 per cent of social capital expenditure.[18] Like health and education, the housing sector has been affected by public expenditure constraints; three housing grant schemes were terminated on 27 March 1987. The schemes affected were the House Improvement Grant Scheme (referred to above), the IR£2,250 builders' grant for new houses and the IR£5,000 surrender grant payable to local authority tenants who move to the private sector. Thus the cost of non-essential home improvements will now have to be borne completely by the home owner and movement of local authority tenants into the private sector, thereby freeing their local authority houses for reletting, will be financially less attractive. However, the tax system favours owner occupation in a pronounced manner and this may prove to provide sufficient financial incentive.

Notes

1. Details on eligibility status and the role of the Voluntary Health Insurance Board, for those not in category I, are discussed in Gormley (1980). The Department of Health's annual publication, *Health Statistics*, provides details on income levels

required for entitlement to benefits.

2. For a detailed analysis of the changing distribution to entitlement, for the period 1973–80, see NESC Report 85, June 1988, Ch 3.

3. Many European countries finance a significant proportion of the public health service through social insurance contributions (Maynard 1975).

4. A flat rate contribution levied on those with category II and III eligibility. In 1988 the rate was 1.25 per cent of income up to a maximum of IR£15,500.

5. NESC Report 83, November 1986, 210.

6. Data on private expenditure are available from the HBS and an ESRI survey (Tussing 1985, Ch 5). The latter estimates that, in 1980, IR£107.4 million was spent on medical care.

7. Comparisons with the United Kingdom, for 1979, can be found in NESC Report No 73, November 1983, Ch 4.

8. Republic of Ireland figure based on an estimate from the Department of Health, Northern Ireland and the United Kingdom figures from Annual Abstract of Statistics, 125, 1989.

9. A Government Commission is currently examining the funding of health care (Programme for National Recovery 1987, Section 4, point 9) and the debate on privatisation has begun (Nolan 1988).

10. In the academic year 1984/85 the participation rate for children aged 4 and 5 years was 79.4 per cent (Department of Education, Statistical Report). Participation rates are the number in full-time education, in a particular age group, divided by the population in that age group, expressed as a percentage.

11. See previous note.

12. Abolition of school fees in most secondary schools and the introduction of free school transport.

13. Third level education is dominated by the universities although regional technical colleges and colleges of technology have grown in importance since the mid-1970s.

14. The cost ratio is defined as the ratio of total expenditure on education per student to nominal GDP per capita. It consists of a relative price effect and real relative inputs.

15. Primary and secondary level pay accounts for 68 per cent of total expenditure (current and capital) – NESC (1986), 218.

16. In 1974 the introduction of the Anti Discrimination (Pay) Act led to the abolition of the married man/single man/woman salary differential. A single pay rate, the married man's, was introduced for all teachers leading to substantial growth in current expenditure during the mid-1970s.

17. Details of incentives available for purchasers are published in the Annual Report of the Department of the Environment.

18. Social capital expenditure comprises capital expenditure on health, education and housing.

References

Birch, S and Maynard, A (1986) *The RAWP Review*. University of York Centre for Health Economics Discussion Paper 19.

Central Office of Information (1988) *Britain 1988, an Official Handbook*, HMSO, London.

Compton, P A (1987) Population, in Buchanan, R H and Walker, B M (eds) *Province, City and People*, Greystone Books Ltd, Antrim, 237–61.

Culyer, A J (1980) *The Political Economy of Social Policy*, Martin Robertson, Oxford.

Gormley, M (1980) *Guide to the Irish Health Service*, Emerald Printers, Galway.

Hensey, B (1979) *The Health Services of Ireland*, Institute of Public Administration, Dublin.

HM Treasury (1979) *Needs Assessment Study*, HMSO, London.

Joyce, L and McCashin, A (1982) *Poverty and Social Welfare*, Institute of Public Administration, Dublin.

Knapp, M (1984) *The Economics of Social Care*, Macmillan, London.

Le Grand, J and Robinson, R (1984) *The Economics of Social Problems*, Macmillan, London.

McGill, P (1987) The financing of education in Northern Ireland, in Osborne, R D, Cormack, R J and Miller, R L (eds) *Education and Policy in Northern Ireland*, Policy Research Institute, Belfast, 281–96.

Maynard, A (1975) *Health Care in the European Community*, Croom Helm, London.

Murray, R C and Osborne, R D (1983) Educational qualifications and religious affiliation, in Cormack, R J and Osborne, R D (eds) *Religion, Education and Employment*, Appletree Press, Belfast, 118–45.

NESC 73 (1983) *Health Services: The Implications of Demographic Change*, National Economic and Social Council, Report 73, Dublin.

NESC 83 (1986) *Strategy for Development 1986–1990*, National Economic and Social Council, Report 83, Dublin.

NESC 85 (1988) *Redistribution Through State Social Expenditure in the Republic of Ireland 1973–1980*, National Economic and Social Council, Report 85, Dublin.

NIEC (1981a) Report 18, *Public Expenditure Comparisons Between Northern Ireland and Great Britain*, Northern Ireland Economic Council, Belfast.

NIEC (1981b) Report 22, *Public Expenditure Priorities: Housing*, Northern Ireland Economic Council, Belfast.

NIEC (1982a) Report 31, *Public Expenditure Priorities: Health and Personal Social Services*, Northern Ireland Economic Council, Belfast.

NIEC (1982b) Report 33, *Public Expenditure Priorities: Education*, Northern Ireland Economic Council, Belfast.

NIEC (1983) Paper 4, *Response to Draft Regional Strategic Plan for the Health and Personal Social Services in Northern Ireland 1983–1988*, Northern Ireland Economic Council, Belfast.

NIEC (1984) Report 42, *Public Expenditure Priorities: Overall Review*, Northern Ireland Economic Council, Belfast.

NIEC (1985) Report 48, *Review of Recent Developments in Housing Policy*, Northern Ireland Economic Council, Belfast.

NIEC (1989) Report 73, *Economic Strategy: Overall Review*, Northern Ireland Economic Council, Belfast.

Nolan, B (1988) *Financing the Health Care System: Is Private Financing an Alternative?* ESRI, Policy Research Series, Paper No 9, Dublin.

Northern Ireland Information Service (1983) *Ulster Year Book 1983*, HMSO, Belfast.

Northern Ireland Office (1974) Northern Ireland Discussion Paper: *Finance and the Economy*, HMSO, London.

O'Hagan, J and Kelly, M (1984) Components of growth in current public expenditure on health and education, *The Economic and Social Review*, 15, 87–93.

Osborne, R D, Cormack, R J, and Miller, R L (1987) *Education and Policy in Northern Ireland*, Policy Research Institute, Belfast, 1–27.

Royal Commission on the National Health Service (1979) *Report*, HMSO, London.

Tussing, A D (1985) *Irish Medical Care Resources: An Economic Analysis*, ESRI, Paper 126, Dublin.

Tussing, A D (1987) The recent cuts in Irish health expenditure, *Irish Medical Journal*, 80, 12, 342–5.

CHAPTER FIFTEEN

The impact of the European Community

Martin J Trimble

1. Introduction

The accession of the United Kingdom of Great Britain and Northern Ireland to the European Community (EC) in 1973 was the culmination of years of tortuous and sometimes acrimonious political and economic debate. The arguments in favour of entry were primarily political and the economic case appeared to be somewhat tenuous and difficult to substantiate in a meaningful and quantitative manner. If the residents of Great Britain were uncertain about the objectives of EC membership, or indeed, divided as to its desirability, then this division was even more pronounced in Northern Ireland where a significant proportion of the electorate opposed Community membership on any grounds.

The Northern Ireland Government White Paper published in 1971 stated that:

> 'Accession to the EEC will require us to make certain changes and adjustments. It will, however, also give us new rights, privileges and opportunities in the other Member States which we do not possess today . . . We must ensure that these opportunities are fully exploited so that the standard of living of our people benefits as much as possible from accession to the Community.'

This chapter is an attempt to estimate the extent to which these opportunities have been fully exploited in fifteen years of Community membership. As Northern Ireland is a relatively depressed, peripheral region of the United Kingdom, accession to the European Community introduced the possibility that the regional isolation, already experienced by the province, might be exacerbated in a wider EC context and the adverse effects of this peripherality be more clearly emphasised.

Section 2 of this chapter details the financial flows from the EC General Budget to Northern Ireland, other regions within the United Kingdom and the Republic of Ireland. The relative socio-economic position of Northern Ireland as an EC region is examined in Section 3 and attempts are made to ascertain whether or not Community membership has resulted in a tendency towards regional economic convergence. The fourth section traces the development of EC regional policy and its impact on the province, while the fifth section examines the role played by the United Kingdom central

TABLE 15.1(a) Northern Ireland attributed contributions to and receipts from the European Community budget, 1973/74–1986/87 (£m)

	UK gross contribution (1)	NI attributed share (2)	NI as % of UK (3)	ERDF (4)	ESF (5)	FEOGA Guidance[1] (6)	Urban renewal (7)	Supplementary Measures, UK (8)	Total (9 = 4 + 5 + 6 + 7 + 8)
1973/74	200	1.0	—	—	—	—	—	—	—
1974/75	197	5.6	2.8	—	3.4	0.3	—	—	3.7
1975/76	370	7.9	2.1	2.9	—	0.7	—	—	3.6
1976/77	544	12.7	2.3	7.2	6.4	2.4	—	—	16.0
1977/78	941	16.0	1.7	6.4	8.0	2.9	—	—	17.3
1978/79	1,323	23.9	1.8	4.0	15.0	3.4	—	—	22.4
1979/80	1,665	28.1	1.7	16.0	15.0	4.7	—	—	35.7
1980/81	1,900	28.2	1.5	21.0	23.0	6.3	—	23.6	73.9
1981/82	2,330	50.3	2.2	16.4	25.0	6.2	—	100.0	147.6
1982/83	2,820	65.6	2.3	17.6	35.0	6.8	—	108.7	168.1
1983/84	3,097	65.6	2.1	12.7	38.0	16.6	14.9	62.3	144.5
1984/85	3,611	93.8	2.6	15.6	38.0	14.5	14.2	—	82.3
1985/86	3,745	102.0	2.7	16.9	25.0	15.4	23.3	—	80.6
1986/87	5,121	107.4[2]	2.1	23.0	54.0	8.8	—	—	85.8
1973–87	27,864	608.1		159.7	285.8	89.0	52.4	294.6	881.5

[1] Direct measures only.
[2] Estimate.
Sources: White Paper on Government Expenditure Plans, HMSO; Finance Accounts of Northern Ireland, HMSO; DED; DFP.

government in the handling and official justifiable usage of EC finances. Finally, Section 6 analyses the Community's integrated approach to regional development and the implications of the current reform of the Structural Funds, the rules of which were finally agreed in Brussels on 21 November 1988 and became effective on 1 January 1989.

2. Financial analysis

Northern Ireland's attributed contributions to and receipts from the EC budget are detailed in Tables 15.1(a) and (b) and from this we can see that, over the period of Community membership, the province in an accounting sense has been the recipient of a net transfer of funds totalling £850 million. The derivation of Northern Ireland's attributed share is rather obscure, but it is identified in the *Finance Accounts of Northern Ireland* and would appear to be an approximation of national tax revenue attributed to the province, ie circa one-fortieth of that for the United Kingdom as a whole.

The major source of Community funding is that emanating from the European Agricultural Guidance and Guarantee Fund (FEOGA) which accounted for 46 per cent of the total. An estimate has been made for the

TABLE 15.1(b)   Net gain to Northern Ireland from the European Community, 1973/74–1986/87 (£m)

	Total[1]	As % of NI public expenditure[2]	FEOGA Guarantee estimate[3]	Total receipts	Net gain[4]
1973/74	—	—	5.3	5.3	4.3
1974/75	3.7	0.4	12.3	16.0	10.4
1975/76	3.6	0.3	19.2	22.8	14.9
1976/77	16.0	1.1	10.6	26.6	13.9
1977/78	17.3	1.1	16.3	33.6	17.6
1978/79	22.4	1.2	21.3	43.7	19.8
1979/80	35.7	1.6	22.8	58.5	30.4
1980/81	73.9	3.0	38.1	112.0	83.8
1981/82	147.6	5.1	38.3	185.9	135.6
1982/83	168.1	5.2	65.3	233.4	167.8
1983/84	144.5	4.2	78.7	223.2	157.6
1984/85	82.3	2.2	78.0	160.3	66.5
1985/86	80.6	2.1	105.1	185.7	83.7
1986/87	85.8	2.1	65.5	151.3	43.9
1973–87	881.5		576.8	1,458.3	850.2

[1] Column 9 Table 15.1(a).
[2] NI Departments only.
[3] The ratio of NI gross agricultural output to that of the UK, for the period 1973 to 1986, was in the range 5.7% to 6.8%. Since this is only an approximation, an annual average figure of 6.18% was used to estimate NI's share of FEOGA Guarantee expenditure.
[4] Total monies to NI less NI attributed share (col 2, Table 15.1(a)).
Sources: As Table 15.1(a).

Guarantee Section, based on Northern Ireland's share of United Kingdom national agricultural output, since Guarantee expenditure is only available on a national basis. The European Social Fund (ESF) and the European Regional Development Fund (ERDF) contributed 20 per cent and 11 per cent respectively, while the balance was made up of exceptional financial instruments relating to Northern Ireland, such as the Urban Renewal Regulation[1] and the province's share of the Supplementary Measures (SMUK) negotiated for the United Kingdom as a whole. As well as the grants and subsidies outlined in Table 15.1, the Department of Finance and Personnel have confirmed that European Investment Bank (EIB) loans to the value of £190.4 million were also made available to the province, including £59.5 million to British Telecom (1977 and 1980), £43.3 million to Northern Ireland Electricity (1979 and 1986), £20.0 million to the Department of Finance and Personnel for road improvements in Belfast and Londonderry (1979 and 1981) and £50.0 million to Short Bros plc (1983, 1984 and 1986).

Northern Ireland has been singularly well placed to benefit from ESF funding and Table 15.2 shows that the province received 17 per cent of the United Kingdom's share from this source. The amounts for the ERDF and FEOGA were 10 per cent and 7 per cent respectively. Unfortunately, with the exception of Northern Ireland, the regional allocation of ESF aid to the United Kingdom is not available, although grant commitments from the ERDF, as distinct from receipts, can be readily identified and are shown in Table 15.3. Northern Ireland has received 10 per cent of the British allocation of ERDF commitments over the period 1975–86, a figure that corresponds closely with that in Table 15.2, when due allowance is made for the inevitable time lag between commitments and payment receipts. The comparable figures for Scotland and Wales were 24 per cent and 18 per cent respectively.

Table 15.4 shows the per capita distribution of the ERDF commitments and the province is seen to have the highest allocation with £158 per head, compared to the Scottish, Welsh and Northern totals of £112, £147 and £62. In view of the fact that Northern Ireland accounts for less than 3 per cent of the United Kingdom population, it would appear that the province has received a disproportionate share of British Community funds. However, on balance, the flow of Community monies to Northern Ireland must be regarded as relatively modest, since with the exception of the years when the

TABLE 15.2 Northern Ireland's share of total United Kingdom receipts from Structural Funds, 1973/74–1986/87

	United Kingdom (£m)	Northern Ireland (£m)	NI as % of UK
FEOGA[1]	9,144	665.8	7.3
ESF	1,688	285.8	17.0
ERDF	1,668	159.7	9.6

[1] Includes Guarantee and Guidance receipts.
Sources: As Table 15.1(a).

TABLE 15.3   Regional allocation of ERDF grant commitments to the United Kingdom, 1975–1986 (percentage)

NI	Scotland	Wales	North[1]	Midlands[2]	South[3]	UK (£m)
10.4	24.0	17.5	37.5	6.3	4.3	2,378.7

[1] North consists of North, Yorkshire and Humberside, North West.
[2] Midlands consists of East and West Midlands.
[3] South consists of East Anglia, South East, South West.
Sources: 1975–82, Commission of the European Communities, UK Introduction to regional briefs, DG X, Brussels, February 1984; 1983–86, ERDF Annual Reports.

TABLE 15.4   Per capita regional allocation of ERDF grant commitments to the United Kingdom, 1975–1986 (£)

	NI	Scotland	Wales	North[2]	Midlands[2]	South[2]
Per capita	158	111.6	147.2	62.1	16.5	4.3

[1] Based on mid-1986 population figures.
[2] As defined in Table 15.3.
Sources: As Table 15.3.

TABLE 15.5   European Community receipts to Northern Ireland and the Republic of Ireland, 1973–1986

	Northern Ireland		Republic of Ireland[2]	
	Receipts (£m)	Per capita[1] (£)	Receipts (£m)	Per capita[1] (£)
FEOGA Guarantee	538.6	343.1	4,544.4	1,283.7
FEOGA Guidance	86.8	55.3	329.2	93.0
ESF	273.6	174.3	579 7	163.8
ERDF	150.1	95.6	427.0	120.6
SMUK[3]	294.6	187.6	—	—
Urban Renewal[3]	52.4	33.2	—	—
Total	1,396.1	889.1	5,880.3	—

[1] Based on mid-1986 population figures.
[2] £ sterling.
[3] These measures do not apply to the Republic of Ireland.
Source: Derived from Tables 4.6 and 4.10 in NIEC and NESC 'Economic Implications for Northern Ireland and the Republic of Ireland of recent developments in the European Community', Belfast, February 1988.

Supplementary Measures were in force, Community receipts, as a proportion of Northern Ireland public expenditure, averaged around 2 per cent (Table 15.1(b)).

In comparison with the Republic of Ireland, however, Northern Ireland has not received a pro rata distribution of Community receipts and Table 15.5 illustrates the magnitude of the differential, even allowing for the difficulties associated with summing over time. But it should be noted that this table is not directly comparable with Tables 15.3 and 15.4, since the former refers to EC receipts and the latter to EC commitments. From Table 15.5 we can see that, with the exception of ESF receipts, the Republic of Ireland has fared significantly better than Northern Ireland in attracting EC monies. While one would expect the Republic of Ireland to receive proportionately more assistance than Northern Ireland from FEOGA (see Chapter 2), it is not immediately apparent why the Republic should have a per capita ERDF expenditure of £121 over the period, in comparison to a figure of £96 per head for Northern Ireland.

3. Northern Ireland's relative economic position in the European Community

Northern Ireland, for various reasons, has for some considerable time been recognised as a region with unique and specific problems not normally present in the rest of the Community. The revised regional guidelines of 1977[2] first identified the province as one which would require '. . . massive Community aid for a long time to come' and subsequent European Parliament reports[3] have confirmed this designation.

The Commission, in attempting to gauge the relative severity of Community regional problems, has developed a Synthetic Index which purports to do just that. The first of these indices[4] published in 1984, based on productivity and unemployment differences, placed Northern Ireland second bottom out of a total of 131 Level II regions[5] in the Community of Nine (Table 15.6). This index showed that the most prosperous regions were found in Germany, France, the Netherlands and northern Italy, while the least prosperous were situated in the south of Italy, Northern Ireland and the Republic of Ireland. If EUR 9 = 100 is taken as a convenient dividing line, then the core regions with a Synthetic Index value greater than 100 were all positioned in a central EC location, approximately bounded by an equilateral triangle, the corners of which were located in northern Italy, western Denmark and southern England.

In 1987, the Commission published a more sophisticated Synthetic Index[6] for the enlarged Community of Twelve and its 160 Level II regions. This index calculated a region's economic strength by reference to GDP per head of population and persons employed, and also incorporated a labour market component by utilising unemployment rates adjusted for under-employment and an estimate of the prospective labour force changes to the year 1990. Table 15.7 lists those regions which have a Synthetic Index value more than one standard deviation (32.9 points) below the Community average of 100, ie less than 67.1 points. Thus certain areas which have the highest intensity of regional problems can be identified: Greece, Republic of Ireland, the Mezzogiorno, Portugal, Spain and Northern Ireland.

Northern Ireland's relative position in the Community of Twelve would appear to have improved as a result of the recent enlargements, since 32

TABLE 15.6   Selected regions from the European Community Synthetic Index (average of 1977, 1979, 1981) (EUR 9 = 100)

Rank	Region	Country	Value	Rank	Region	Country	Value
1	Calabria	I	30.3	77	Bourgogne	F	105.0
2	Northern Ireland	UK	35.4	91	Greater London	UK	110.8
3	Sardegna	I	40.5	93	Lombardia	I	113.6
4	Ireland	Irl	41.8	101	Arnsberg	D	119.3
5	Merseyside	UK	43.8	107	Koblenz	D	123.0
9	Strathclyde	UK	54.7	115	Koeln	D	128.4
14	Abruzzi	I	63.7	128	Ile de France	F	135.3
21	West Midlands	UK	71.5	129	Darmstadt	D	144.0
31	Lancashire	UK	80.7	130	Oberbayern	D	146.8
56	Auvergne	F	93.3	131	Stuttgart	D	147.7
66	Picardie	F	97.1		Hamburg	D	154.4

Note: The most serious regional problems are shown by the lowest values of the index and vice versa.
Source: Commission of the European Communities, Second periodic report on the social and economic situation and development of the regions of the Community, COM (84) 40 Final/2, Brussels 1984.

regions (including the Republic of Ireland) are now deemed to have economic problems more severe than those which exist in the province. But closer inspection of Table 15.7 reveals that, with the exception of the Republic of Ireland, all these regions are located in the southern Mediterranean periphery. The accession of the Iberian countries in 1986 statistically lowered the average income in the Community and hence improved the relative position of Northern Ireland. There has been a relative, as distinct from an absolute, improvement in the province's economic performance. The entry of Greece, Spain and Portugal merely introduced peripheral regions with socio-economic problems even more acute than those of Northern Ireland.

A recent study undertaken at Cambridge University (Walker and Keeble 1987) showed that the EC peripheral regions were significantly differentiated from central regions not only by geographical location, but also by a range of demographic, economic and labour market attributes. There were marked differences in income per head, dependence on agriculture and manufacturing industry, manufacturing structure, services structure and unemployment rates, especially for the under-25s and women. However, some positive developments in the economic performance of the peripheral regions (excluding Spain and Portugal) since the late 1970s were identified, in contrast to the trends exhibited in the early 1970s. For example, manufacturing employment losses between 1979 and 1983 were much faster, and greater in volume, in central regions than in the EUR 10 periphery. Unfortunately, empirical evidence in Northern Ireland does not substantiate this finding since over the period 1979–85 the manufacturing sector shed 44,000 employees, a decline of 30 per cent, compared to one of 25 per cent in Great Britain over the same period.

TABLE 15.7 Selected regions from the European Community Synthetic Index (average of 1981, 1983, 1985) (EUR 12 = 100)

Rank	Region	Country	Value
1	Basilicata	I	36.9
2	Calabria	I	38.0
3	Andalucia	ESP	38.8
4	Extramadura	ESP	39.2
5	Canarias	ESP	46.1
6	Ireland	IRL	47.6
7	Sardegna	I	49.4
8	Castilla Mancha	ESP	50.0
9	Thrakis	GR	50.5
10	Molise	I	50.6
11	Murcia	ESP	51.3
12	Galicia	ESP	53.8
13	Ipirou	GR	54.4
14	Comm Valenciana	ESP	54.6
15	Sicilia	I	54.9
16	Castilla Leon	ESP	55.0
17	Campania	I	55.7
18	Pelop and Dit Ster Ell	GR	56.9
19	Puglia	I	57.2
20	Thessalias	GR	57.2
21	Cataluna	ESP	57.7
22	Pays Vasco	ESP	58.3
23	Asturias	ESP	58.4
24	Portugal	POR	58.4
25	Kritis	GR	58.4
26	Anatolikis Makedonias	GR	59.0
27	Aragon	ESP	59.5
28	Cantabria	ESP	59.7
29	Madrid	ESP	59.8
30	Navarra	ESP	59.9
31	Anat, Stereas Ke Nison	GR	61.9
32	Kent ke Dit Makedonias	GR	63.0
33	Northern Ireland	UK	64.4
34	Rioja	ESP	65.9
35	Balearas	ESP	66.8
36	Nison Anatolikou Egeou	GR	67.1

Note: The most serious regional problems are shown by the lowest values of the index and vice versa.
Source: Commission of the European Communities, Third periodic report from the Commission on the social and economic situation and development of the regions of the Community, COM (87) 230 final, Brussels, 21/5/87.

4. Development of EC regional policy

The preamble to the Treaty of Rome (1957) stated that the contracting parties were 'anxious to strengthen the unity of their economies and to ensure their harmonious development by reducing the differences existing between the various regions and the backwardness of the less-favoured regions'. Yet in the period prior to the first Community enlargement in 1973, Member States were preoccupied with the establishment of a free trade area, tariff negotiations and the implementation of the Common Agricultural Policy (CAP). The negotiations which preceded the accession of the United Kingdom, the Republic of Ireland and Denmark focused attention on the consequential regional difficulties which might emerge and in 1973 the Commission published the results of a study[7] which examined the embryonic development of a Community regional policy. This study was significant for a number of reasons (Mawson, Martins and Gibney 1985) but mainly because it examined the regional distribution of the ESF and FEOGA. The conclusion which emerged from the report was that the Community possessed a diverse collection of largely unrelated financial instruments and 'the regions which benefited the most from Community financing were not always the ones most in need of regional development assistance'.[8]

Article 3 of the Treaty of Rome, which outlined the future policies to be developed by the Community, made no specific reference to regional policy, but provision was made for the creation of certain Funds which could, albeit indirectly, contribute to regional development. The largest of these Funds still remains FEOGA and the Guidance Section of it began effective operations in 1964 (see Chapter 2).

The European Social Fund was established by Articles 123–128 of the Treaty of Rome 'to render the employment of workers easier by increasing their geographical and occupational mobility within the Community'. It provides financial assistance towards eligible training and retraining schemes carried out by government departments, public authorities and private bodies and these schemes must be wholly or partly financed by public funds. The grants from the ESF are given within the framework of the Member States' own employment policies, and the Fund neither evaluates established, government-sponsored training schemes nor initiates new ones. The ESF was reformed in 1971,[9] 1977[10] and 1983[11] (Collins 1983) in an attempt to make its role more effective in combating a Community-wide deterioration in employment opportunities. The 1977 amendment directed assistance more explicitly to those with long-term unemployment problems and to young persons under the age of 25. The 1983 revision strengthened the latter objective and enabled 75 per cent of ESF resources to be devoted to vocational training and job-creation schemes for young persons. The geographical concentration of the Fund in the less favoured areas was increased to 40 per cent (ie Greece, Ireland, the Mezzogiorno, Northern Ireland and the French Overseas Departments) and, following the 1986 enlargement, this list was extended to include certain parts of Spain and all of Portugal, with the proportion of total ESF resources allocated to these regions rising to 44.5 per cent.

Table 15.8 shows the individual region in each Member State with the most severe youth unemployment problem and although the Republic of Ireland and Northern Ireland have significant difficulties with rates of 26.9 per cent and 26.6 per cent, these problems are much less severe than those encountered in the Spanish region of Noreste (53.2 per cent) or the Italian

TABLE 15.8   Selected European Community regional youth unemployment rate[1], 1986 (percentage)

Country	Region	Rate
Belgium	Hainaut	30.8
Denmark	Ost for Storebaelt	11.7
Germany	Bremen	27.2
Greece[2]		23.2
Spain	Noreste	53.2
France	Languedoc-Roussillon	31.1
Ireland[2]		26.9
Italy	Sardegna	53.0
Luxembourg[2]		5.3
Netherlands	Groningen	20.8
Portugal[2]		19.7
United Kingdom	Northern Ireland	26.6

[1] Under 25s.
[2] No regional breakdown available.
Source: Eurostat, Regions – Statistical Yearbook, 1987.

island of Sardegna (53.0 per cent). Indeed no region exists in Spain with a youth unemployment rate less than that found in Northern Ireland and only 7 are present in Italy. The comparable figures for the other British regions are shown in Table 15.9 and Scotland, Wales and the North have a problem similar to that of Northern Ireland. If, as seems probable, future developments in the ESF progressively favour schemes aimed at improving the unemployment rate in the young persons' category, this does not augur well for a region such as Northern Ireland, which is currently a major beneficiary of the United Kingdom's allocation from the Fund.

TABLE 15.9   Selected United Kingdom regional youth unemployment rates,[1] 1986 (percentage)

Scotland	Wales	North[2]	Midlands[2]	South[2]	UK
22.3	23.4	23.4	18.7	13.4	18.2

[1] Under 25s.
[2] As defined in Table 15.3.
Source: Eurostat, Regions – Statistical Yearbook, 1987.

Table 15.10 details the allocation of ESF grants to the various Member States for selected years in the period 1978–87 and although the Fund's budget is not, in theory, distributed according to pre-determined national quotas, sufficient evidence would appear to exist that political considerations dictate national shares. However, the accession of Greece and the Iberian countries will have an influence on the future distribution of ESF grants and this, in turn, will have fundamental implications for Northern Ireland.

TABLE 15.10 National allocation of ESF grants, 1978, 1981, 1984 and 1987 (percentage of annual total)

Country	1978	1981	1984	1987
Belgium	2.0	2.3	4.8	1.8
Denmark	2.5	2.4	5.1	1.1
France	15.2	14.1	11.5	12.3
Germany	10.1	7.4	4.4	5.1
Greece	—	3.0	5.0	5.8
Ireland	7.8	10.6	11.8	6.6
Italy	41.0	34.1	22.4	20.6
Luxembourg	0.0	0.1	0.0	0.1
Netherlands	1.7	1.3	2.8	2.2
Portugal	—	—	—	11.3
Spain	—	—	—	14.4
United Kingdom	19.7	24.9	32.1	18.8
Total (£m)	396.1	553.2	1,098.0	2,175.5

Source: ESF Annual Reports.

The existence of FEOGA and the ESF since the signing of the Treaty of Rome did not constitute a coherent or comprehensive EC regional policy, and various factors combined to provide further impetus in the search for an acceptable policy (Armstrong 1978). Thus the ERDF together with the Regional Policy Committee were established in 1975. The former assumed the role of the Community's main regional policy instrument, charged with assisting in the development and structural adjustment of the less prosperous areas. It was empowered to finance infrastructure projects such as industrial estates, roads, power stations, etc, as well as industrial, craft and service activities, which create or maintain employment opportunities.

The contribution usually amounts to 50 per cent of the public expenditure, but may increase to 55 per cent in cases of particular importance for the regions in which they are located. It also provides firms, particularly small and medium-sized ones and local/regional authorities, with access to advice on marketing, management and innovation.

From the inception of the ERDF, allocations were determined on a national quota basis and the United Kingdom's quota in 1981 was set at 23.8 per cent. Northern Ireland has received 10 per cent of the British allocation of commitments over the period 1975–86 (Table 15.3) and the highest per capita commitment allocation in the United Kingdom (Table 15.4). However, the activities of the ERDF were severely handicapped from the outset by limited finances, in that the initial commitment appropriations, allocated to the Fund from the General Budget of the EC, were less than 5 per cent in 1975 (£145 million), rising to 7.3 per cent (£852 million) in 1981, the year Greece joined the Community and 8.6 per cent (£2,080 million) in 1986, to take account of the accession of Spain and Portugal.

In 1979 the Council adopted a Commission proposal advocating the introduction of a non-quota section to finance specific actions and by 1981 the first Regulations instituting specific regional development measures under the non-quota section had been adopted.[12] But even the non-quota measures, which were designed to cope with the regional consequences of Community policies and, thus, were the most Community-oriented element of the ERDF, had minimal funding and were limited to 5 per cent of the total ERDF allocation.

The Stuttgart European Council of June 1983 reached a unanimous conclusion that measures were necessary to relaunch the EC, including the identification of ways of improving the effectiveness of Community Structural Funds, such as the ERDF. A report was subsequently produced and this formed the basis of new proposals for revising the ERDF and these were adopted by the Council[13] and came into force on 1 January 1985. The new Regulation replaced the non-quota section of the Fund, it advocated a system of programme-financing, the concentration of aid effort on internally generated developments, as well as the coordination of ERDF grants with other EC financial instruments. The objective was to give the Commission more influence in the disbursement of ERDF assistance and to coordinate aid within the framework of an overall programme, as distinct from an individual project. Indicative ranges of assistance for each Member State were introduced (Table 15.11), with the lower limit of the range being the minimum amount of resources guaranteed to a Member State, on submission of sufficient eligible applications. Allocation of resources above the lower limit depends on the extent to which grant applications satisfy the priorities and criteria laid down by the Regulation.

The foregoing instruments (FEOGA Guidance, ESF, ERDF) are solely concerned with grants and subsidies but, in addition, there exists certain important Community lending institutions, which have progressively endeavoured to dovetail their activities to complement the efforts of the other

TABLE 15.11   National ranges for ERDF assistance, 1985 and 1986

Country	% of total funds	
	1985	1986
Belgium	0.90–1.20	0.61–0.82
Denmark	0.51–0.67	0.34–0.46
France	11.05–14.74	7.48–9.96
Germany	3.67–4.81	2.55–3.40
Greece	12.35–15.74	8.36–10.64
Ireland	5.64–6.83	3.82–4.61
Italy	31.94–42.59	21.62–28.79
Luxembourg	0.06–0.08	0.04–0.06
Netherlands	1.00–1.34	0.68–0.91
Portugal		10.66–14.20
Spain		17.97–23.93
United Kingdom	21.42–28.56	14.50–19.31

Note: For each year the first figure denotes the lower limit available, the second figure denotes the upper limit available.
Source: ERDF, Eleventh Annual Report, 1985.

financial instruments. The European Investment Bank was set up by Article 130 of the Treaty of Rome to contribute to the balanced development of the Community. It finances regional development projects, schemes of common interest to several Member States and also helps alleviate the difficulties associated with structural problems. The New Community Instrument (NCI), administered by the EIB, was established in 1978 to finance investment projects which contribute to the integration of Member States' economic policies and also serve priority Community objectives in the energy, industry and infrastructure sectors, particular consideration being given to the regional impact of projects and the need to combat unemployment.

Thus, over the years, the European Community has developed an impressive, if somewhat heterogeneous, collection of financial instruments, employing both loans and grant subsidies, to implement a Community regional policy. It had come some way in this respect from the period when its efforts had been dismissed as 'this motley collection of qualifications, derogations and exhortations' (Nevin 1980). However there still existed in the Commission an awareness of certain underlying weaknesses in the implementation of regional policy, as well as a more realistic assessment of the magnitude of the problem itself. For example, the ERDF reforms of 1985 no longer referred to 'correcting the principal regional imbalances within the Community' but rather that the Fund should, in future, 'contribute' to the correction of those imbalances. The experience of the Community's main policy instrument (ERDF) in Northern Ireland would substantiate this new awareness, insofar as its impact has been supportive of, as distinct from additional to, the existing job creation activities of the Industrial Development Board and the Local Enterprise Development Unit. Table 15.12 compares the record of the IDB and the ERDF over the period 1975–86 and shows that while more than half of

TABLE 15.12   Job promotion and maintenance – a comparison of IDB and ERDF, 1975–1986

Calendar year	Jobs promoted		Jobs maintained	
	IDB	ERDF	IDB	ERDF
1975–76	6,376	4,516	23,167	633
1977	4,647	3,100	14,341	nil
1978	6,413	1,700	19,565	700
1979	5,472	2,610	21,642	112
1980	5,545	2,100	10,458	nil
1981	2,476	3,143	8,035	500
1982	3,420	998	9,386	1,017
1983	2,658	1,141	6,379	901
1984	5,189	1,288	4,629	1,882
1985	3,966	2,252	3,400	1,825
1986	2,331	2,842	2,480	2,702
Total	48,593	26,552	123,482	12,192

Source: Harris (1988).

the jobs promoted by the IDB were supported by grants from the ERDF, a much smaller proportion of jobs maintained were aided by the ERDF. However an element of double counting exists since one cannot assert that ERDF intervention has resulted in the promotion of 26,552 jobs, since all these projects were already in receipt of state aid. Thus even if all the ERDF aid were strictly additional, only a proportion of jobs may be attributed to ERDF assistance. For some time, suspicions had existed that Member States simply utilised receipts from the Structural Funds in a 'claw-back' capacity, with the intention of minimising national contributions to the EC Budget,[14] ie the transfer of monies from the various Funds was not used in the 'additional' sense defined by the Commission.[15] It was this line of reasoning which led the Commission to explore new approaches to structural funding and finally to the reforms agreed at the European Council meeting in Brussels in February 1988.

5. Principle of additionality

The principle of additionality is, in essence, a political commitment by the governments of the Member States to ensure that EC expenditure, deployed in parallel to national programmes, is used to supplement rather than replace national expenditure. The preamble to Council Regulation 724/75, establishing the ERDF, stipulates explicitly that the Fund's assistance should not lead Member States to reduce their own regional development efforts, but should complement those efforts and Article 19 of this Regulation requires Member States to adopt the necessary measures to indicate separately, according to the special characteristics of national budget systems, the sums received from the Fund.

In the United Kingdom, official spokesmen[16] have consistently argued that the government takes into account the anticipated Community contribution in determining the level of expenditure on various programmes, and expenditure ceilings are higher, as a consequence, than they would otherwise be. In the case of ERDF industrial grants, they assert that these grants allow the level of regional industrial support to be maintained, if not increased, although they concede that receipts for such projects are used to provide partial reimbursement of aid already paid by the United Kingdom. This interpretation is broadly in agreement with Article 36 of Council Regulation 1787/84[17] and would appear to be a loophole for Member States, so inclined, to circumvent the Commission's endeavours to ensure the genuine additionality of Community expenditure. Similarly for infrastructure projects: the government admits to a curtailment of national resources devoted to regional policy, but insists that the reductions would have been greater without ERDF assistance.

Table 15.13 shows the United Kingdom's net payments to EC institutions for the financial year 1986/87. The total gross payment to the Community (VAT, customs duties, agricultural levies, etc) were £5,121 million, offset by public sector receipts of £2,557 million and VAT

TABLE 15.13   United Kingdom net payments to the European Community, 1986/87 (£m)

Gross payments	5,121
Public sector receipts	−2,557
VAT abatements	−1,343
Net payments to EC budget	1,221
Miscellaneous receipts/payments	−143
Total net payments to EC institutions	1,078
Composition of receipts:	
FEOGA	1,567
ESF	413
ERDF	329
Refund of collection costs	168
Other	80
Total receipts	2,557

Source: White Paper on Government Expenditure Plans, 1988, HMSO.

abatements[18] of 1,343 million. Various other receipts and payments, such as grants from the ECSC and contributions to the Community aid programme, combined to show that the net cost to the United Kingdom, in public expenditure terms, of membership of the EC was approximately £1.1 billion. It is this total which determines the British government's attitude towards the principle of additionality and it rests crucially on the assumption that £2,557 million would be forthcoming from the Community and utilised to finance existing public sector expenditure plans. If some of these receipts were to be attributed to the private sector or, alternatively, were to be used to finance new projects in the public sector, then this would result in a rise in the attributed cost of Community membership which, in turn, would increase overall United Kingdom public expenditure. As a consequence of the British government's perception of Community finances, there exists no incentive to embrace innovative Community projects which fall outside existing public expenditure priorities. The paramount consideration must ultimately be the maximisation of EC receipts, which are then used to finance existing public expenditure programmes rather than additional or private sector programmes. This approach would appear to be incompatible with the objectives and aspirations contained in the joint declaration by the Council, the Commission and the European Parliament (19/6/84) which stated that: 'The three institutions agree on the advantages . . . of more efficient relations between the Commission of the Communities and regional or, where applicable, local authorities. This will enable regional interests to be better taken into account when regional development programmes and assistance programmes are drawn up. ERDF aid will, in general, be an additional overall source of finance for the development of beneficiary regions and areas.'

The consequences for a region, such as Northern Ireland, of the

United Kingdom government's policy on EC expenditure means that the province would not, as a result of an increase in Community funding, experience an increase in total expenditure from national and Community sources, over the level which would prevail in the absence of increased Community funding.

However, the United Kingdom is not unique in its interpretation or implementation of the principle of additionality and even the Federal Republic of Germany, with its clearly defined semi-autonomous, subnational regions (the *Länder*), does not behave in a manner which demonstrates unequivocally that additionality is being applied.[19] In France, DATAR (*Délégation à l'Aménagement du Territoire et à l'Action Régionale*) is responsible for the preparation of ERDF applications and payments are made directly to the national treasury and then placed on the account of the public agency involved as reimbursement for expenditure incurred. Theoretically, DATAR consults the regional authorities on projects being considered in their areas, but in practice this consultation may be little more than a formality. The Republic of Ireland, together with Portugal, is exceptional among the Member States in that the entire country is treated as one region by the Commission and hence, by definition, the transfer of ERDF resources to Ireland are inter-governmental transfers. These difficulties, among the various Member States, has led the European Parliament to conclude that the exercise of central government control is pernicious in varying degrees to the achievement of reducing economic disparities between the regions of the European Community – a major objective of the Treaty of Rome.

6. An integrated approach to regional development

The integrated approach to regional development was first advanced by the Commission, at the end of the 1970s, as a way to increase the effectiveness of both Community and national regional policies and by 1979 the Commission had committed itself to the active promotion of integrated initiatives. To date, this approach has manifested itself in three specific ways, namely the development of (a) Integrated Operations schemes, (b) Integrated Development Programmes (IDPs) and (c) Integrated Mediterranean Programmes (IMPs). Although interrelated, the diversity of these developments has led to some initial confusion among the Member States.

Essentially, Integrated Operations schemes have concentrated on urban areas, such as Naples, where at the end of 1986, some 170 investment projects totalling almost £4 billion had been selected for an Integrated Operation. These grants were, in the main, directed at the problems associated with inadequate sanitation, transport and road networks. The IDPs,[20] on the other hand, are mostly agricultural initiatives designed to offset or overcome a region's natural handicaps and, in 1981, three of these were adopted for the south-east of Belgium,[21] the French department of Lozère[22] and the Western Isles of Scotland.[23] The final category of IMPs, as their name implies, are directed solely at the Mediterranean regions and embrace all aspects of economic activity from agriculture to manufacturing industry. In July 1985, the Council adopted the Regulation concerning these programmes[24] and the relevant Member States submitted their proposals to the Commission. France and Greece each presented 7 programmes and Italy 17, resulting in a total of 31 IMPs which will receive £2,415 million from the EC Budget – £1,473 million from the Structural Funds and the balance of £942 million in the form of an additional budgetary allocation.

The confusion associated with this new approach to regional development first evidenced itself in Northern Ireland, when in May 1981, the United Kingdom government presented a draft document[25] to the Commission which detailed an integrated plan for the economic development of Belfast. This document contained a series of measures in the areas of urban transport, infrastructure and vocational training, valued at almost £500 million over a 5-year period. For various reasons, the format was unacceptable to the Commission and, ultimately, the Integrated Operations plan was redrafted and submitted a second time on 21 February 1985. This new plan was more ambitious and comprehensive, providing for some 800 projects at a cost of £763 million. But there still remains a suspicion that the Integrated Operations scheme for Belfast is nothing more than a collection of diverse projects, lacking in overall coordination, the bulk of which would be eligible for EC aid through the normal procedures. Indeed a recent HMSO publication[26] does not even list Belfast as one of the 11 areas within the United Kingdom which have either submitted, or have indicated that they will be submitting, an Integrated Operations programme. It would appear that the Belfast initiative with regard to Integrated Operations has either been overtaken by events or relegated to limbo.

However, the Commission's disenchantment with certain aspects of regional policy implementation did lead it to initiate a unique approach to Community financing in the case of Northern Ireland, which operated alongside the more general objectives of the integrated approach. In November 1981, the Commission submitted a proposal to the Council of Ministers instituting a specific measure to promote housing in the province, within the broad framework of the initial Integrated Operations scheme for the city of Belfast. This proposal was the result of a European Parliament resolution on Community regional policy and Northern Ireland.[27] The proposal was rejected by the Council in June 1982, owing to the reservations felt by certain Member States with regard to Community financing of housing projects. An amended, compromise proposal was drafted and subsequently adopted by the Council in June 1983.[28]

This Urban Renewal Regulation specified explicitly that the granting of circa £60 million over a 3-year period was conditional on the fact that 'the UK government shall also provide the Commission with all the information it needs to satisfy itself that the Community aid is additional to the total volume of national expenditure allocated to the investment projects necessary for urban renewal, including the infrastructure projects benefiting from this Community aid. The granting of the aid shall be subject to a finding that it is indeed additional thereto' (Article 5). This was the first occasion that the legal commitment to additionality had been written into Community law and by March 1987 receipts to the value of £52.4 million had been released to the relevant authorities (Table 15.1(a)). The United Kingdom had conceded that exceptional aid for Northern Ireland must be transparently additional, in return for a controversial quid pro quo, namely that the additional finance should go towards a housing programme.

Thus, on balance, the conclusion would seem to be that the integrated approach to regional development has had a very minimal degree of success in the province and the absence of a legislative framework for Integrated Operations, such as that in Belfast, places the onus of action on the United Kingdom government – a government whose policy parameters are determined by rigid, public expenditure considerations. Similarly, there has been a singular lack of interest shown in the United Kingdom in the adoption of agricultural IDPs, perhaps not totally surprising given that agricultural employment is less than 3 per cent of total employment and the sector contributes less than 2 per cent of GDP.[29] But this is not the case in Northern Ireland, where agriculture represents 8 per cent of total employment and 4 per cent of GDP.[30] The European Parliament has given a lead in this respect and, in 1986, it adopted a resolution calling for the introduction of an integrated rural development programme for the less favoured areas in Northern Ireland. This resolution was based on the Maher Report[31] which had advocated this action and, in addition, requested that the Commission undertake a thorough appraisal of the socio-economic situation in the province and also review all current and planned projects by the Community and the British government therein. The Commission is yet to respond to this request although a precedent has been set in the United Kingdom with the adoption of the IDP for the Western Isles of Scotland in 1981.

7. Current reforms

The Single European Act which came into force in July 1987, is primarily an updating of the original EC Treaties and contains among its major economic objectives the attainment of greater economic and social cohesion among the regions of the Community. An integral part of this goal is the complete reorganisation of the Structural Funds, an increase in EC budgetary 'Own Resources' and the consequential reform of the CAP. The fiscal implications of indirect tax harmonisation, as part of the measures currently being undertaken to complete the internal market by 1992, are considered in Chapter 16 and the future prospects for the agricultural sector are dealt with in Chapter 2.

As part of the Council Agreement of February 1988,[32] it was decided that henceforth the Structural Funds, the EIB and the other financial instruments, as part of a coordinated approach, would pursue five priority objectives:

1) promoting the development and structural adjustment of the less developed regions (ERDF, ESF, FEOGA Guidance);
2) converting the regions, border regions or part regions seriously affected by industrial decline (ERDF, ESF);
3) combating long-term unemployment (ESF);
4) facilitating the occupational integration of young people (ESF);
5) with a view to the reform of the CAP, speeding up the adjustment of agricultural structures and promoting the development of rural areas (FEOGA Guidance, ESF, ERDF).

The regions to be included in the first objective were:

– those regions with a per capita GDP lower than 75 per cent of the EC average, taking the figure for the last 3 years;
– Northern Ireland and the French Overseas Departments;
– other regions whose GDP per capita is close to that of the regions mentioned in the first indent and for which particular reasons exist for their inclusion on the list.

The list of regions would be valid for 5 years and on expiry of the 5-year period the Council, acting by qualified majority on a Commission proposal, would decide on a new list.

It was also agreed that the contribution of the Structural Funds to the regions covered by the first objective would be doubled and by 1992 two-thirds of all Structural Funds' resources would be concentrated on those regions. The budget estimates were determined and are shown in Table 15.14 below. A minimum of £11 billion has been set aside for the various policies of the Structural Funds in 1992, out of a budgetary total of £37 billion.

From the point of view of future Community assistance to Northern Ireland, the critical consideration in all these reforms must necessarily be the intended concentration of two-thirds of the resources of the Structural Funds in

TABLE 15.14   EC budget estimates, 1988 and 1992 (£b, 1988 prices)

	1988	1992
FEOGA Guarantee	19.38	20.86
Destocking, set-aside etc	0.85	1.34
Structural Funds	6.56	10.92
Other policies (incl IMPs)	1.20	1.97
Administration	2.47	1.41
Monetary reserve	0.70	0.70
Total budget	31.16	37.20

Note: ECU 1 = £0.7047.
Source: Council Communication, No SN 517/88, Overall Compromise, Brussels, February 1988.

TABLE 15.15 GDP per head of population in selected regions of the European Community, 1985 (EUR 12 = 100)

Rank	Region	Country	GDP/head
1	Thrakis	GR	43.2
3	Extramadura	ESP	46.6
5	Calabria	I	54.4
11	Andalucia	ESP	58.3
15	Sicilia	I	63.0
22	Ireland	Irl	69.5
25	Corse	F	73.0
27	Abruzzi	I	74.3
32	Lueneburg	D	79.3
33	Hainaut	B	80.9
37	Friesland	NL	82.4
40	Salop, Staffs	UK	85.7
46	Humberside	UK	89.0
49	Northern Ireland	UK	89.7[1]

[1] The 1985 Northern Ireland GDP figure has been revised upwards by 8.3% (NIAAS No 7, 1988) and this will have a consequential effect on the relative ranking.
Source: As Table 15.7.

certain designated regions. The criterion adopted by the Commission is that those regions with a per capita GDP lower than 75 per cent of the EC average will be so designated – a definition which excludes the province. At the moment in the Community of 12, there are 27 Level II regions with a per capita GDP of less than three quarters of the Community average, and, with the exception of the Republic of Ireland, they are exclusively Mediterranean regions. Table 15.15 shows a selection of the 160 Level II regions in the Community and Northern Ireland is ranked forty-ninth in terms of per capita GDP. On this basis, there are other more deserving British regions than Northern Ireland, as well as some regions in Member States not normally associated with relative poverty, such as Lueneburg in Germany, Friesland in the Netherlands and Hainaut in Belgium. However, the Commission in its deliberations decided to include the province in the designated list owing to 'the special situation there',[33] but considering that this list is only valid for 5 years and could be changed at the end of this period by a majority vote in the Council of Ministers, there is no guarantee that Northern Ireland will continue to be regarded as a special case. Unanimity is not required for a re-definition of designated regions and the province's current privileged position could be reversed in favour of political expediency. The predominance of impoverished Mediterranean regions could, yet again, threaten the position of the poorer, northern peripheral areas in any future reallocation of Community priority funding.

8. Conclusion

Northern Ireland's membership of the European Community has not resulted in a significant change in the economic environment of the province. Factors other than Community membership have largely determined the performance of the local economy, and the energy crisis, the world recession and political instability must feature more prominently in any objective analysis of recent trends than the signing by the United Kingdom government of the Treaty of Accession. Unlike the assertions on behalf of the Republic of Ireland (Blackwell and O'Malley 1984), industrial growth in Northern Ireland was not stimulated by Community membership. The 1979 recession caused a downturn in output in the province, which was both more severe and of longer duration than the United Kingdom average and though industrial production in Great Britain had, by 1985, returned to its 1979 level, the corresponding figure for Northern Ireland was 9 per cent below the 1979 level.

Orthodox economic theory outlines a number of advantages associated with the formation of a customs union, such as a more efficient allocation of production and consumption between Member States on the basis of production costs, as well as the dynamic considerations of economies of scale and the gains from enforced competition, but these are primarily long-term, national objectives and do not readily lend themselves to analysis on a regional basis. The issue is further complicated by the fact that sectoral decline, in the strict sense, need not necessarily be synonymous with regional decline. The whole range of quotas, co-responsibility levies, stabilisers, etc, designed to curb the output of grassland, agricultural produce, is equally applicable to Northern Ireland as it is to the relatively prosperous Haute-Normandie, notwithstanding the fact that climate and factor endowment dictate that the province's agricultural sector has little alternative output. Similarly, the world slump in the shipbuilding industry has not, as yet, had the terminal impact on Northern Ireland's shipbuilding industry which might reasonably have been anticipated. Indeed, the Sixth Directive[34] on the future aid strategy for shipbuilding, approved by the Council of Ministers and valid for 4 years, emphasises 'the need to take social and regional problems into account'. In light of the Commission's awareness of, and sympathetic attitude to, the particular needs of Northern Ireland, there is no reason to anticipate that the favourable Community attitude to the Northern Ireland shipbuilding industry will not continue in the medium term. As well as this, the government's industrial development policies have not contravened the regional aids criteria of the Commission, and generous industrial assistance should continue to be readily available.

If one were to attempt to isolate a yardstick by which to judge the efficacy of Community policies in Northern Ireland, then perhaps the simplest criterion to apply would be the extent to which Northern Ireland's position, in relation to Community regional disparities, has improved or deteriorated since 1973. Unfortunately the empirical evidence, reflected in the EC Synthetic Indices (1984 and 1987), does not indicate any significant improvement in the position of the province. Moreover, the enlargement of the Community in 1981 and 1986, has introduced other regions, located in the southern periphery, with socio-economic problems at least as severe as those which appear to be endemic in Northern Ireland. As a consequence, the United Kingdom has already experienced a reduction in its relative share of commitment appropriations from both the ESF and the ERDF, and the current reforms do not guarantee that the province will continue to receive preferential treatment.

The major source of EC receipts to the United Kingdom was from the FEOGA Guarantee Section. In the financial year 1986/87, funds emanating from this source were more than double those of the ESF and ERDF combined (Table 15.13). The pressure on the EC budget and the unwillingness to raise significantly more revenue must imply a future reduction in support of the CAP. Since the CAP provides regional support, albeit in an inefficient manner, this also implies a reduction in regional support for Northern Ireland.

The current reforms are designed to concentrate funding on disadvantaged regions and a central role is envisaged for integrated programmes. To date, the United Kingdom government has shown scant interest in the introduction of these programmes. All EC funds to Northern Ireland are second-stage transfers, regulated by the Treasury, the only possible exceptions being ERDF awards to charitable projects and private sector ports, as well as ESF grants to voluntary organisations and industrial training boards – categories outside the control of the government departments. As a result of this procedural arrangement and, given the United Kingdom's perception of Community finances, one must inevitably concur with the view of the European Parliament, namely that the exercise of central government control is pernicious to the objective of realistically reducing economic disparities between the regions of the European Community.

Notes

1. Council Regulation, No 1793/83, OJ L 171 of 29/6/83.
2. *Bulletin of the European Communities*, Supplement 2/77. *Community Regional Policy: New Guidelines*, Brussels, 3/6/77, p 11.
3. European Parliament Working Document 1–177/81, *Community Regional Policy and Northern Ireland*, Rapporteur: Mrs S Martin, 4/5/81. European Parliament Working Document 1–1526/83, *The Situation in Northern Ireland*, Rapporteur: Mr N J Haagerup, 19/3/84.
4. Commission of the European Communities, COM (84) 40 Final/2, *The Regions of Europe: Second Periodic Report on the Social and Economic Situation and Development of the Regions of the Community*, Brussels, 1984.
5. Level II regions conform to the Nomenclature of Territorial Units for Statistics (NUTS) agreed between Eurostat and EC Member States, with the purpose of providing a uniform reference framework for regional statistics. This nomenclature distinguishes three levels of regional disaggregation in EUR 12:
   I   : 64 regions
   II : 167 basic administrative regions
   III : 824 subdivisions of Level II regions
6. Commission of the European Communities, COM (87) 230 final, *Third Periodic Report from the Commission on the Social and Economic Situation and Development of the Regions of the Community*, Brussels, 21/5/87.
7. Commission of the European Communities, *Final Report on the Study of*

Community Financing for Regional Policy Purposes (1954–72), Battelle-Genève Research Centre, Brussels 1972.

8. Commission of the European Communties, op cit, (1972), p 15.

9. Council Regulation, No 2396/71, OJ L 249 of 10/11/71.

10. Council Regulation, No 2895/77, OJ L 337 of 27/12/77.

11. Council Regulation, No 2950/83, OJ L 289 of 17/10/83.

12. First 5-year programme, 1981–85, £35 million granted to UK to provide alternative employment opportunities in shipbuilding and steel regions and also to improve the economy in the border areas of Northern Ireland. Second 5-year programme, 1985–90, £89 million granted to UK to continue its activities in those regions, plus the textile closure areas. NI is included in both the shipbuilding and textile categories.

13. Council Regulation, No 1787/84, OJ L 169 of 28/6/84.

14. Northern Ireland Assembly, Finance and Personnel Committee, *Report on the Additionality of Receipts from European Funds*, NIA 46, Belfast, 5/10/83.

15. Commission of the European Committee, COM (87) 521 Final, *ERDF Twelfth Annual Report*, Brussels, 1/12/87, p 6.

16. See House of Commons, *Official Report*, Sixth Series, Vol 59, Cols 821–829, 8/5/84.

17. Article 36: Assistance from ERDF may, in accordance with a decision of the Member State concerned communicated at the same time as the request for assistance, either supplement aid granted to the relevant investment by the public authorities or remain in the hands of those authorities as a partial reimbursement of such aid.

18. The Fountainebleau European Council (June 1984) agreed, *inter alia*, that:
    (a) the *ad hoc* UK budgetary refunds (SMUK) would be terminated;
    (b) from 1986, the UK would receive instead, an annual sum equivalent to two-thirds of the difference, in the previous year, between its share in the EC's VAT own resources and its share in expenditure from the EC Budget;
    (c) these refunds were to be effected by an automatic, legally binding abatement of the UK's VAT payments to the General Budget.

19. European Parliament, Directorate-General for Research, *Application of the Principle of 'Additionality' in the Use of ERDF Resources by some Countries of the European Communities*, Luxembourg, 19/8/86.

20. Commission of the European Communities, *Information on Agriculture*, No 89, *Integrated Development Programmes*, Brussels, July 1983.

21. Council Regulation, No 1941/81, OJ L 197 of 20/7/81.

22. Council Regulation, No 1940/81, OJ L 197 of 20/7/81.

23. Council Regulation, No 1939/81, OJ L 197 of 20/7/81.

24. Council Regulation, No 2088/85, OJ L 99 of 22/7/85.

25. Department of the Environment (NI), *Belfast Integrated Operations – Belfast Urban Area*, Belfast, May 1981.

26. *Employment Gazette*, HMSO, London, August 1988, pp 456–457. The United Kingdom areas cited are Birmingham, Bradford, Clwyd, Durham/Cleveland, Dyfed/Gwynedd/Powys, industrial South Wales, Manchester/Salford/Trafford, Merseyside, South Yorkshire/Scunthorpe, Strathclyde, Tyne/Wear/South East Northumberland.

27. European Parliament Resolution, OJ C 172 of 13/7/81.

28. Council Regulation No 1793/83, op cit.

29. Northern Ireland Economic Council and the National Economic and Social

Council, *Economic Implications for Northern Ireland and the Republic of Ireland of Recent Developments in the European Community*, Belfast, February 1988, pp 5.4 and 5.7.

30. Ibid.

31. European Parliament Working Document 2–105/86, *Report Drawn up on Behalf of the Committee on Regional Policy and Regional Planning on an Integrated Rural Development Programme for the Less-favoured areas of Northern Ireland*, Rapporteur: Mr J Maher, 25/9/86.

32. Council Communication, No SN 517/88, *Overall Compromise*, Brussels, February 1988. Council Communication, No SN 461/88, *Note from the Presidency, Making a Success of the Single European Act – Draft Conclusions of the European Council*, Brussels, 9/2/87.

33. Commission of the European Communities, COM (87) 376 final 2, *Reform of the Structural Funds*, Brussels, 24/8/87, p 6.

34. Commission of the European Communities, COM (86) 531 final, *Proposal for a Council Directive on Aid to Shipbuilding*, Brussels, 17/10/86.

References

Armstrong, H W (1978) Community regional policy: a survey and critique, *Regional Studies*, 12, 5, 511–28.

Blackwell, J and O'Malley, E (1984) The impact of EEC membership on Irish industry, in Drudy, P J and McAleese, D (eds), *Ireland and the European Community*, Cambridge University Press.

Collins, D (1983) *The Operations of the European Social Fund*, Croom Helm.

Harris, R I D (1988) European regional policy in relation to Northern Ireland, in Simpson, J V (ed), *Northern Ireland and the European Community: An Economic Assessment*, Commission of the European Communities.

Mawson, J, Martins, M R and Gibney, J T (1985) The development of the European Community regional policy, in Keating, M and Jones, B (eds), *Regions in the European Community*, Clarendon Press, Oxford.

Nevin, E T (1980) Regional policy, in El-Agraa, A M (ed), *The Economics of the European Community*, Philip Allan, St Martin's Press.

Walker, S and Keeble, D (1987) *Peripheral Regions and the Twelve-member European Community: an Overview*, Annual Conference of the British Association for the Advancement of Science, The Queen's University of Belfast, 27/8/87.

The Irish economies: some comparisons and contrasts

James F Bradley

1. Introduction

This chapter examines three important areas where major differences exist between the economies of the Republic of Ireland and Northern Ireland: the financing of shortfalls between public expenditure and revenue, the tax system, and the exchange rate.

The Republic of Ireland's failure to raise sufficient revenue to finance public expenditure during the 1970s and 1980s resulted in very substantial borrowing at home and abroad. In Northern Ireland the British transfer ensured that public expenditure was financed without the need for either additional taxation or large increases in borrowing. The dramatic increase in the Republic of Ireland's national debt has constrained severely the operations of fiscal policy and the increased reliance on foreign borrowing has increased the exposure of the economy to international fluctuations in interest rates and revaluations of the debt due to exchange rate changes. Had the Northern Ireland economy to rely on receipts generated from its own economic activity it too would have operated with budget deficits and levels of borrowing not too dissimilar from those experienced in the Republic of Ireland, assuming the level of economic activity and all other factors remained unchanged. While the British transfer has often been compared to foreign borrowing in the Republic of Ireland the major difference concerns interest costs and repayments which in the case of the transfer are zero but in the case of foreign borrowing have been very considerable.

A comparison of the tax systems reveals sharp differences between the Republic of Ireland and Northern Ireland. An important distinguishing feature of the tax system of the Republic of Ireland is the narrowness of its tax base which relies heavily on the taxation of goods, services and incomes. The resultant widening of the gap between the after-tax wage of an average employee and the cost of his employment is regarded by OECD (1987) as the most important factor in explaining the country's poor record in creating jobs. Compared to the United Kingdom the yield from corporation tax and property taxes is extremely low. By Northern Ireland standards the income tax system in the Republic of Ireland is steeply progressive and higher indirect taxes in the Republic of Ireland have been the main contributing factor to price differentials between the two economies and to the increase in cross-border trade which occurred throughout the 1980s. The abolition of border controls and the tax harmonisation proposals for 1992 will therefore have major implications for both economies with considerable reductions in revenue expected in the Republic of Ireland.

Since 1979 the Republic of Ireland has participated in the Exchange Rate Mechanism of the European Monetary System (EMS) and in contrast to Northern Ireland the Irish pound floats against sterling. Differences between prices in Northern Ireland and the Republic of Ireland, which affect cross-border trade, are now dependent on exchange rate fluctuations. The extent to which exchange rate uncertainty has enabled the Irish authorities to pursue an independent domestic monetary policy and to exert some influence on domestic interest rates is still an open question.

Justification for the selection of these three aspects of the Irish economies is provided by, among others, the recent medium term plans for the economy of the Republic of Ireland. *A Strategy for Development 1986–90* (NESC 1986) analyses the major developments in the economy of the Republic of Ireland over the first half of the 1980s and puts forward an overall strategy for economic and social development for the medium term. This strategy and the underlying principles have been accepted by government (Budgets 1987 and 1988) and form the blueprint for the *Programme for National Recovery* (Stationery Office 1987) which outlines policy priorities for the period 1987–90 agreed between the government and all the major interest groups in the Republic of Ireland. In these documents the macro-economic proposal is paramount and its central focus is on fiscal policy accompanied by compatible exchange rate and incomes policies. Stabilisation of the national debt/GNP ratio is regarded as an imperative of fiscal policy and the overriding target for the public finances; it is seen as the first step to reducing the debt ratio.

Fundamental reform of the Republic of Ireland's tax system is the second major element of the NESC strategy and the *Programme for National Recovery*. The NESC concluded that tax reform may be the most powerful instrument at the government's disposal to promote faster output and employment in the short to medium term (Chapter 10). While recognising the importance of weak demand and rigid labour markets in the Republic of Ireland the recent OECD survey (1987) lists the substantial increase in taxation and the distortion of relative factor prices by the tax system in favour of capital and against labour as two very important reasons for the economy's poor record in job creation. In concluding her survey of the Republic of Ireland for *The Economist* (16 January 1988) Frances Cairncross puts the need for tax reform more forcefully when she states that 'no durable recovery will be possible in Ireland unless it tackles the lunacies of its tax system'.

2. Imbalances in the public finances

REPUBLIC OF IRELAND

A comprehensive analysis of fiscal policy in the Republic of Ireland for the period 1967 to 1980 by Bradley et al (1985) concluded that while policy had some favourable effects in the short run it had no long term beneficial consequences. One fiscal policy stance frequently adopted in the Republic of Ireland during the 1970s aimed to promote economic growth and indirectly employment growth through increased government expenditure. The hope was that the expected expansion in economic activity would generate sufficient tax revenue to help finance the borrowing incurred by the initial increase in expenditure. However, the 1973 and 1979 oil price shocks and the contraction in world demand which followed were greatly at variance with the expectations of buoyant world demand conditions assumed in the budgets of the 1970s. The expected revenue growth failed to materialise and government debt increased. Bradley et al (1985) regarded the massive national debt, which was to constrain severely fiscal policy for years to come, as the long term effect of aggregate fiscal policy for the period 1967 to 1980. They were of the opinion that even if expectations of world demand growth had been realised tax revenues would have been insufficient to repay the initial debt incurred owing to government underestimation of leakages from the economy in the form of increased imports and savings.

An examination of the public finances of the Republic of Ireland over the past decade is given in Table 16.1. Between 1977 and 1986 the budget deficit as a per cent of GNP more than doubled and the Exchequer Borrowing Requirement[1] (EBR) climbed from 9.7 to 13.2 per cent of GNP. Over the same period the growth in the national debt/GNP ratio was dramatic, rising from 75.6 per cent to 130 per cent (see Table 16.2). This is among the highest debt/GNP ratios in the OECD and by the end of 1986 it was equivalent to marginally more than IR£21,000 per employed person. Growth in the ratio between 1981 and 1986 was particularly pronounced. As a result, the correction of the imbalances in the public finances has dominated economic policy discussions since 1981. Targets for the budget deficit and the EBR have been central to the medium term plans proposed by governments[2] over this period. The Fianna Fail government's plan outlined in *The Way Forward* (Stationery Office 1982) sought to eliminate the deficit on current account and to reduce the EBR to 5 per cent of GNP by 1986. *Building on Reality* (Stationery Office 1984), the Fine Gael government's medium term plan, aimed to reduce the deficit to 5 per cent of GNP and the EBR to 9.75 per cent of GNP by 1987: the first explicit target for the debt/GNP ratio appeared in this plan which also sought to halt its growth by 1987. The current Fianna Fail government's medium term plan, *Programme for National Recovery* (Stationery Office 1987) seeks to reduce the EBR to between 5 and 7 per cent of GNP by 1990 and to stabilize the debt/GNP ratio.

A standard Domar-type dynamic model of an economy where deficits are financed by issuing debt can help explain the preoccupation with the debt/GNP ratio in the Republic of Ireland since the early 1980s. In such a model the debt/GNP ratio will explode for any primary deficit[3] if the nominal interest rate exceeds the nominal rate of growth in GNP (see OECD 1987). Historically, with the exception of periods of high inflation, nominal interest rates have exceeded nominal GNP growth rates (OECD 1987, p 106). Only during the late 1970s and very early 1980s did nominal GNP growth rates in the Republic of Ireland exceed the nominal interest rate.[4] Although the nominal interest rate has exceeded the growth rate since 1983 (O'Leary 1987) the Republic of Ireland continued to run a primary deficit up to 1987 (see Table 16.1). The conditions for a dynamically unstable debt/GNP ratio, therefore, existed in the Republic of Ireland between 1983 and 1987 with the resultant growth in the ratio shown in Table 16.2.

To stabilise the debt/GNP ratio in these circumstances would have required a primary surplus equal to the product of the initial debt/GNP ratio and the difference between the nominal interest rate and the nominal GNP growth rate (OECD 1987, Annex 11). Row 5 of Table 16.1 shows that progress has been made; the primary deficit has fallen from 8.5 per cent of GNP in 1981 to 2 per cent in 1986 and the figures since 1987 show a surplus. This improvement has been due to the steadily rising surplus on the non-interest current account[5] since 1982 and the steady decline in exchequer borrowing for capital purposes which fell from 8.5 per cent of GNP in 1981 to 4.6 per cent in 1986 and is expected to decline further to 1.2 per cent in 1989. The marked improvement in the non-interest current account has been due to the sharp increase in tax revenues from 32.5 per cent of GNP in 1982 to 37.4 per cent in 1986 and the curbing of current government expenditure over the period.

Despite the considerable improvement since 1982 in the non-interest current account balance and the non-interest EBR the conventional indicators of fiscal stance such as the budget deficit and the overall EBR show little improvement prior to 1987 (see Table 16.1). The improvement in the non-interest current account and EBR was not reflected in these conventional measures because of the increase in interest payments on the national debt since 1981 (see row 6, Table 16.1). Interest payments as a percentage of GNP more than doubled between 1977 and 1986 with the increase in the 1980s being particularly pronounced. The magnitude of the interest burden is also apparent from the final columns of Table 16.2. Since 1982 around 30 per cent of total tax revenue or over 70 per cent of income tax revenue went on servicing the national debt. Interest payments in 1988 accounted for 25.1 per cent of current expenditure compared to 14.2 per cent in 1977. This interest burden has seriously affected the fiscal manoeuvrability of the authorities in recent years. Since 1987 there is evidence of some marginal decline in interest payments as a per cent of GNP which when combined with the primary surpluses has resulted in downward movements in the EBR and budget deficit (see Table 16.1). The actual budget deficit, adjusted for the one-off increase in revenue from the tax amnesty introduced in January 1988, fell to 4.4 per cent of GNP in 1988 and the EBR declined to 6.0 per cent: the post-budget estimates for 1989 expect a budget deficit of 4.1 per cent and an EBR of 5.3 per cent of GNP (see Table

TABLE 16.1 Components of public finances, Republic of Ireland, 1977–1988 (% of GNP)

	1977	1978	1979	1980	1981	1982	1983	1984	1985	1986	1987	1988[1]	1989[2]
1 Current revenue	31.40	30.97	31.23	35.05	36.60	39.41	42.30	40.60	41.31	41.21	40.00	38.72	36.70
2 Non-interest current spending	30.16	31.53	32.17	34.65	36.66	38.17	39.57	37.01	37.77	38.61	35.77	32.56	30.55
3 Non-interest current balance (3 = 1 − 2)	1.24	−0.54	−0.94	0.40	−0.06	1.24	2.73	3.59	3.54	2.60	4.23	6.16	6.15
4 Exchequer capital borrowing	6.00	6.33	6.38	7.44	8.48	7.68	5.90	5.36	4.77	4.61	3.39	1.60	1.18
5 Non-interest exchequer borrowing requirement (5 = 4 − 3)	4.76	6.87	7.32	7.04	8.54	6.44	3.17	1.77	1.23	2.01	−0.84	−4.56	−4.97
6 Interest payments	4.98	5.54	5.89	6.47	7.33	9.18	9.85	10.68	11.92	11.17	10.82	10.57	10.25
7 Exchequer borrowing requirement (7 = 5 + 6)	9.74	12.41	13.21	13.51	15.87	15.62	13.02	12.45	13.15	13.18	9.98	6.01	5.28
8 Budget deficit (8 = 6 − 3)	3.74	6.08	6.83	6.07	7.39	7.94	7.12	7.09	8.38	8.57	6.59	4.41	4.10

[1] The 1988 figures exclude the one-off impact of the tax amnesty which boosted tax receipts by an estimated IR£500m in 1988.
[2] The 1989 figures are based on the post-budget estimates contained in budget 1989.
Sources: Budget Statements, 1977 to 1989; OECD (1987), Table A, p 119.

TABLE 16.2 The national debt and interest payments on national debt, Republic of Ireland, 1977–1986

	Total national debt (% of GNP)	Foreign debt (% of GNP)	Foreign debt (% of total national debt)	Interest payments on national debt (as percentage of)		
				Current budget expenditure	Total tax revenue	Income tax revenue
1977	75.6	18.6	24.6	14.2	18.8	53.4
1978	79.1	16.3	20.6	14.9	20.9	59.7
1979	85.7	20.2	23.6	15.5	22.4	61.5
1980	87.7	24.5	28.0	15.7	22.2	57.4
1981	93.9	35.0	37.2	16.7	24.0	64.0
1982	93.3	42.0	45.0	19.4	28.2	78.3
1983	106.4	51.0	47.9	19.9	28.4	79.9
1984	113.3	53.3	47.0	22.4	29.5	79.7
1985	118.2	51.8	43.8	24.0	32.7	86.9
1986	130.1	55.5	42.7	22.4	29.8	76.1
1987	132.5	54.2	40.9	24.5	29.8	71.3
1988	132.5	51.1	38.6	25.1	28.8[1]	64.2[2]

[1] Excludes receipts from tax amnesty.
[2] Inclusive of receipts from tax amnesty.
Source: As Table 16.1.

16.1). The indications are that the key target of stabilising the national debt as a percentage of GNP has been achieved (see Table 16.2).

The increased reliance on foreign borrowing is evident from Table 16.2: exchequer foreign debt was equivalent to 55.5 per cent of GNP and 42.7 per cent of the total national debt in 1986 compared to 18.6 per cent and 24.6 per cent respectively in 1977. The pronounced growth which occurred in foreign debt up to 1986 has stopped and figures for 1987 and 1988 show a decline in the foreign debt/GNP ratio (see Table 16.2). During the late 1970s and early 1980s, when outstanding foreign debt was relatively low, reliance on this type of borrowing provided the economy with additional resources because the cost of servicing the debt was also relatively modest. Between 1979 and 1982 net external government borrowing amounted to IR£3,508 million against interest payments on foreign debt of IR£1,033 million. The demand stimulus from this high level of foreign borrowing over those four years, however, was relatively short-lived due to the build-up of foreign debt which then required servicing. Interest payments on government external debt climbed to IR£761 million or 4.2 per cent of GNP in 1986 from IR£193 million or 2.1 per cent of GNP in 1980 (see Table 16.8). Net external government borrowing was dramatically reduced in 1983 and since then it has remained at a level which only marginally exceeds interest payment on past debt. Net external borrowing by government amounted to IR£3,060 million between 1983 and 1986 compared to interest payments on past external borrowing of IR£2,873 million.

The rapid growth in outstanding debt during the 1980s only partially explains the pronounced increase in interest payments in the Republic of Ireland; interest rates also played an important role. In sharp contrast to the 1970s, when average real rates in many countries were negative, the 1980s witnessed a return to positive real rates. Increased domestic borrowing in the Republic of Ireland exerted upward pressure on rates (OECD 1987; FitzGerald 1986): the average real interest rate increased from −2.7 per cent for the period 1970–80 to 2.9 per cent for the period 1981–85.[6] Those countries which financed most of the Republic of Ireland's borrowing also experienced substantially higher real interest rates in the early 1980s; real interest rates in Germany and the USA averaged 4.5 per cent and 6.2 per cent respectively for the period 1981–85 compared to 2.8 and −0.6 per cent respectively for the period 1970–80.[7] Since 29 per cent of the Republic of Ireland's external debt was denominated in dollars and 28 per cent in deutschmarks at the end of 1986 these relatively high rates contributed significantly to the high levels of foreign interest payments throughout the 1980s. FitzGerald (1986) has shown that if foreign real interest rates had remained at 2 per cent between 1980 and 1985 the current budget deficit as a per cent of GNP would have been at least 2 percentage points lower in 1985. The operation of fiscal policy during the 1980s in the Republic of Ireland has, therefore, been seriously constrained by factors which have affected the cost of finance in countries such as the USA and Germany.

The effect of changes in the exchange rate on the value of outstanding exchequer debt has resulted in sizeable revaluations during the

1980s. At the end of 1986 about 83 per cent of total foreign debt was held in dollars, deutschmarks, Swiss francs and yen. Since 1981, with the exception of 1985 when the value of average outstanding exchequer debt declined by 3.4 per cent owing to the sharp fall of the dollar, the Irish pound has depreciated against a weighted average of these currencies. Capital appreciation of the national debt due to exchange rate changes over the six year period 1981–86 has been equivalent to around 2.2 per cent of average outstanding debt per annum.[8] These revaluation effects have been considerable, bearing in mind that the nominal annual interest rate on average outstanding debt for this period was around 10 per cent.[9] Since accounting practices in many countries, including the Republic of Ireland, exclude the capital appreciation from government income and expenditure accounts the figures for government deficits underestimate the actual situation.

NORTHERN IRELAND

In contrast to the Republic of Ireland, Northern Ireland receives a large transfer annually from the British Exchequer in the form of the British subvention (see Chapter 13). This transfer, excluding the extra cost of the army in Northern Ireland, was equivalent to 8.4 per cent of GDP[10] in 1970/71, 26 per cent in 1976/77 and 21.8 per cent in 1986/87. In recent years it has raised disposable income in the province by around 25 per cent annually.[11] Its major components are the contribution to the Northern Ireland Consolidated Fund (grant-in-aid), the expenditure of the Northern Ireland Office which, as a United Kingdom department, is regarded as being funded directly from Britain and the contribution to the Northern Ireland Insurance Fund[12] from the British National Insurance Fund. These three elements constituted 24.3 per cent of GDP in 1976/77 and the percentage has remained relatively stable over the past ten years.

The grant-in-aid has been the most significant element of the transfer. With the exception of 1977/78 when it stood at 24.8 per cent of GDP, owing to expenditure on the redemption of debt of the Northern Ireland Electricity Service, the grant-in-aid has ranged from 11.6 to 18.3 per cent of GDP (see Table 16.3). It acts as a residual receipt from the United Kingdom government to ensure that the expenditure of Northern Ireland departments is financed. This expenditure is determined by the principle of parity with the rest of the United Kingdom which requires the uniform provision of health, welfare, education and other services (see Chapter 13). For any given expenditure on services in Northern Ireland the grant-in-aid would decline as revenue raised in Northern Ireland increased. The size of the grant-in-aid therefore depends upon Northern Ireland's ability to generate tax revenue and other receipts which in turn depend upon the buoyancy of the local economy.

Northern Ireland's attributed share of United Kingdom taxes is assessed in accordance with legislation and is paid from the United Kingdom Consolidated Fund to the Northern Ireland Consolidated Fund, after deducting the collection costs and Northern Ireland's share of the United Kingdom

TABLE 16.3 Aspects of public finances, Northern Ireland, 1975/76–1987/88

	NI net share of UK taxes[1]		Grant-in aid to NI from the UK government		Interest on borrowing by Northern Ireland departments	
	£m	% of GDP[2]	£m	% of GDP[2]	£m	% of GDP[2]
1975/76	567.7	27.4	351	16.9	70.0	3.2
1976/77	622.7	25.8	360	14.9	77.6	2.9
1977/78	710.8	25.9	682	24.8	79.3	2.9
1978/79	813.7	26.6	560	18.3	64.1	2.1
1979/80	1,021.7	28.9	590	16.7	87.3	2.5
1980/81	1,254.7	31.1	640	15.8	104.6	2.6
1981/82	1,417.1	32.2	585	13.3	108.8	2.5
1982/83	1,485.1	30.6	630	13.0	112.0	2.3
1983/84	1,576.8	29.8	775	14.6	113.0	2.1
1984/85	1,795.8	31.8	905	16.0	126.1	2.2
1985/86	1,885.1	30.6	955	15.5	189.0	3.1
1986/87	1,938.0	28.3	845	12.4	152.3	2.2
1987/88	2,154.8	29.2	855	11.6	147.1	2.0

[1] Figures include subsequent adjustments.
[2] GDP current prices at factor cost.
Source: HMSO, Financial Statement, various years.

TABLE 16.4   National accounts classification of Northern Ireland departments (estimates), 1975/76–1988/89

| | Assuming receipts include the British contribution to the Northern Ireland Insurance Fund and the Grant-in-aid | | | Assuming receipts are confined to revenue and other receipts generated from Northern Ireland's own economic activity | | |
| | Current surplus | | Borrowing requirement | Current deficit | | Borrowing requirement |
	£m	% of GDP^2	(% of GDP^2)	£m	% of GDP^2	(% of GDP^2)
1975/76	219.2	10.6	6.3	57.2[1]	2.8	19.6
1976/77	248.2	10.3	6.0	139.1[1]	5.8	22.0
1977/78	269.7	9.8	5.0	126.7	4.6	19.5
1978/79	244.6	8.0	5.8	241.0	7.9	21.7
1979/80	397.3	11.3	3.6	259.6	7.4	22.2
1980/81	368.3	9.1	3.0	402.0	10.0	22.1
1981/82	457.4	10.4	1.4	374.7	8.5	20.3
1982/83	441.2	9.1	2.4	376.2	7.7	19.2
1983/84	362.3	6.8	2.9	502.6	9.5	19.2
1984/85	423.5	7.5	1.8	536.5	9.5	18.8
1985/86	451.7	7.3	1.5	577.5	9.4	18.2
1986/87	422.0	6.2	2.1	628.1	9.2	17.4
1987/88	469.4	6.4	1.2	517.8	7.0	14.9
1988/89	532.0	na	na	576.1	na	na

Note: These calculations are based on estimates for the Northern Ireland central government contained in the annual Financial Statement.
[1] Receipts also exclude payments under the Agricultural Acts 1957 and 1970.
[2] GDP current prices at factor cost.
Source: As Table 16.3.

contribution to the EC. In deriving Northern Ireland's share of United Kingdom taxes certain rules and conventions are used. Income tax estimates are derived by applying a proportionate rate to total United Kingdom income tax receipts. This rate is equal to the total income of individuals resident in Northern Ireland as a proportion of the total income of individuals resident in the United Kingdom. Corporation profits tax estimates are calculated by applying a proportionate rate to United Kingdom corporation tax receipts. In this case the rate is Northern Ireland profits as a proportion of total United Kingdom profits. For customs and excise duties Northern Ireland is also attributed a proportion of United Kingdom total customs and excise duties. This proportion is the province's share of total United Kingdom purchases of goods subject to these duties or Northern Ireland's share of United Kingdom population where data are unavailable. Only a limited number of duties, such as stamp duties and vehicle excise duties, are based on actual amounts collected in the province. Northern Ireland's share is biased upwards because it includes an element of United Kingdom revenue from North Sea oil and gas although these products are not produced in the province. The share of United Kingdom taxes attributed to the province since 1975/76 is given in Table 16.3. Since 1980/81 its share has remained at around 30 per cent of GDP.

Had the Northern Ireland central government been forced to rely on this revenue and other receipts generated from the province's own economic activity to finance expenditure, assuming the level of economic activity and all other factors remained unchanged, the result would have been a series of current budget deficits and substantial borrowing, as shown in Table 16.4. Indeed these figures would clearly understate the position as interest payments on accumulated debt are ignored. With the exception of 1987/88 the estimated budget deficit since 1978/79 would have exceeded 7 per cent of GDP and the borrowing requirement to finance this deficit and capital expenditure would have averaged over 17 per cent of GDP annually. In most instances these figures exceed those for the Republic of Ireland given in Table 16.1. Such calculations exclude the grant-in-aid and the British contribution to the Northern Ireland Insurance Fund. Classification of these transfers within the national accounts as current receipts produces a current account surplus. Estimates of the current surplus since 1975/76 are given in Table 16.4. Over this period it ranged from 11.3 per cent of GDP in 1979/80 to 6.2 per cent in 1986/87. The grant-in-aid has not only ensured that current expenditure has been fully financed, it has also financed a substantial amount of capital expenditure. As a result, the need for borrowing has been reduced considerably. Estimates of the borrowing requirement are given in Table 16.4. Since 1980/81 the estimated borrowing requirement has not exceeded 3 per cent of GDP, very considerably below the borrowing which would have been required without these transfers (see final column of Table 16.4). Actual interest payments on borrowing by Northern Ireland departments have been remarkably stable (see Table 16.3). This is in sharp contrast to the experiences of the Republic of Ireland and shows that it is invalid to draw a parallel between the transfer to Northern Ireland which is free of future interest charges and foreign borrowing by the Republic of Ireland where the interest costs have been sizeable throughout the 1980s. In addition, the Northern Ireland economy is sheltered from exchange rate fluctuations since virtually all of its borrowing is denominated in sterling.

3. Tax systems

The Irish government's preoccupation with stabilising the debt/GNP ratio throughout the 1980s has meant that options such as reducing the overall burden of taxation or increasing government expenditure in order to stimulate economic activity in the medium term have not been available. The NESC have stressed the importance of tax reform, through a restructuring of the burden of taxation, as a way of increasing output and employment growth in the medium term. The extent to which the present tax system in the Republic of Ireland militates against job creation has been emphasised by OECD (1987). This section examines aspects of the Republic of Ireland's tax system which distinguish it from the system operating in Northern Ireland and explores some of the implications of these differences. In many instances comparisons will be drawn between the Republic of Ireland and the United Kingdom because United Kingdom rates and allowances apply to Northern Ireland and because revenue figures for customs and excise, income tax and corporation tax are not based on actual amounts collected in Northern Ireland.

COMPARISON OF TAX SYSTEMS

A comparative analysis of the structure of tax revenue reveals sharp differences between the Republic of Ireland and other EC countries, particularly the United Kingdom (see Tables 16.5 and 16.6). Total tax revenue as a proportion of GDP in the United Kingdom exceeded that in the Republic of Ireland until the 1980s when the growing crisis in the Irish public finances resulted in a pronounced increase in the country's tax burden. By 1985 this percentage had risen to 44.2 compared to 38.4 in the United Kingdom. This increase is reflected both in the growth of personal income taxes and in indirect taxes. The dependence of the Republic of Ireland on taxes levied on goods and services is particularly heavy; these taxes accounted for over 45 per cent of total tax revenue in 1984 compared to an EC average of around 31 per cent.

Tables 16.5 and 16.6 indicate that taxes on incomes and profits have been moving towards the EC average since 1970. However, while the total exhibits convergence, the components have diverged sharply over the period. Whereas taxes on personal incomes as a proportion of GDP remained fairly stable in the United Kingdom during the 1970s and have declined in the recent past, the trend in the Republic of Ireland has been in the upward direction. However, it is in the area of corporate taxation that the divergence from the United Kingdom and EC average is most pronounced. Corporate income taxes accounted for only 1.3 per cent of the Republic of Ireland's GDP in 1984,

TABLE 16.6 Sources of tax revenue as a percentage of total tax revenue,[1] Republic of Ireland, United Kingdom and the European Community

	1970			1975			1980			1984		
	RI	UK	EC	RI	UK	EC	RI	UK	EC	RI	UK	EC
Total taxes on goods and services of which:	52.4	28.8	36.2	46.5	25.4	31.5	43.7	29.2	30.8	45.1	30.5	31.0
Taxes on specific goods and services (excise)	36.4	19.9	18.3	30.0	14.8	14.2	28.3	13.1	12.2	22.1	14.1	12.4
General taxes on production and sales (VAT)	13.1	6.5	15.8	14.7	8.8	15.4	14.8	14.4	17.2	21.3	14.7	16.8
Total taxes on income and profits of which:	27.1	40.4	30.7	30.0	44.5	33.9	36.5	37.9	35.1	34.0	38.2	34.4
Taxes on personal income	18.3	31.1	23.3	25.2	38.3	27.3	32.0	30.0	28.1	30.8	26.7	27.2
Taxes on corporate income	8.8	9.3	7.4	4.8	6.3	6.4	4.5	7.8	6.7	3.3	11.5	6.9
Taxes on property	12.2	12.4	6.8	9.7	12.7	5.9	5.3	12.1	5.1	3.8	12.2	4.4

[1] Total tax revenue includes compulsory social security contributions.
Source: Revenue Statistics of OECD Member Countries 1965–1985, OECD, Paris, 1986.

TABLE 16.5 Sources of tax revenue as a percentage of GDP, Republic of Ireland, United Kingdom and the European Community

	1970			1975			1980			1984		
	RI	UK	EC	RI	UK	EC	RI	UK	EC	RI	UK	EC
Total tax revenue[1]	31.2	37.2	33.2	31.5	35.5	35.8	34.0	35.3	38.9	39.5	38.5	41.9
Total taxes on goods and services of which:	16.4	10.7	11.9	14.7	9.0	10.9	14.9	10.3	11.8	17.8	11.7	12.9
Taxes on specific goods and services (excise)	11.4	7.4	5.9	9.4	5.2	4.8	9.6	4.6	4.6	8.7	5.4	5.1
General taxes on production and sales (VAT)	4.1	2.4	5.3	4.6	3.1	5.5	5.0	5.1	6.7	8.4	5.7	7.1
Total taxes on income and profits of which:	8.5	15.0	10.6	9.5	15.8	12.6	12.4	13.4	13.9	13.4	14.7	14.6
Taxes on personal income	5.7	11.6	8.1	7.9	13.6	10.2	10.9	10.6	11.3	12.1	10.3	11.6
Taxes on corporate income	2.8	3.5	2.4	1.5	2.2	2.4	1.6	2.8	2.6	1.3	4.4	2.9
Taxes on property	3.8	4.6	2.2	3.1	4.5	2.0	1.8	4.3	1.9	1.5	4.7	1.8

[1] Total tax revenue includes compulsory social security contributions.
Source: Revenue Statistics of OECD Member Countries 1965–1985, OECD, Paris 1986.

substantially below the United Kingdom at 4.4 and the EC average of 2.9 per cent. As a proportion of total tax revenue it was less than one-third of the United Kingdom figure and less than half the EC average in 1984.

Until the 1970s property taxes were an important source of revenue in both the United Kingdom and the Republic of Ireland: as a proportion of GDP or total tax revenue these figures were substantially above the EC average (see Tables 16.5 and 16.6). Since the mid-1970s the yield from property taxation in the Republic of Ireland has fallen relative to the United Kingdom and the EC average: this has been due to the abolition of domestic rates in 1978 and to the decision of the Irish High Court in 1982 (confirmed by the Supreme Court) that rates on agricultural land were unconstitutional. Unlike Northern Ireland, rates in the Republic of Ireland are currently payable only on industrial and commercial property.

Widening the tax base

The narrowness of the Republic of Ireland's tax base is evident from Tables 16.5 and 16.6. Taxes on goods and services and on personal incomes accounted for over 75 per cent of total tax revenue in 1984; the comparable figure for the United Kingdom was 57.2 per cent which was close to the EC average. Taxes on corporate income and property yielded 7.1 per cent of total tax revenue in 1984 compared to 23.7 per cent in the United Kingdom and an average of 11.3 per cent in the EC.

The need for a broader base for tax liability has been generally recognised. Widening of the tax base and the simultaneous reduction of tax rates is regarded by the NESC (1986) as the priority of taxation policy in the medium term. OECD (1987) argues that tax reform should not be used to increase the overall burden of taxation and implicitly suggests a wider tax base with lower rates. The general thrust of government policy is also towards a wider tax base and more effective collection (Stationery Office 1988).

BUSINESS TAXATION

The relatively low yield from corporation tax in the Republic of Ireland, accounting for 3.3 per cent of total tax revenue in 1984 compared to 11.5 per cent in the United Kingdom, is indicative of the favoured position of companies within the tax system; the revenue yield in 1987 was a mere IR£257 million or 3.1 per cent of total tax revenue. The major difference between the corporate tax structure of the Republic of Ireland and that of the United Kingdom, which applies to Northern Ireland, lies in the rate of tax on profits in manufacturing industry. Prior to 1981 the Republic of Ireland operated an export profits tax relief scheme which exempted profits from export sales from corporation tax and taxed profits from domestic sales at rates between 35 and 45 per cent. Since 1981 the tax rate for all manufacturing industry in the Republic of Ireland has been 10 per cent with an imputation rate[13] of just over 5 per cent compared to 25 per cent in Northern Ireland. In contrast to the

United Kingdom, where the imputation rate is always set equal to the basic income tax rate, this system clearly favours profit retention as no further tax is paid if profits are retained, whereas distributions are taxed at the normal income tax rates. The 1980 Finance Act in the Republic of Ireland allows tax relief on profits from exports to continue for firms in existence prior to January 1981, subject to a maximum of 20 years' relief. In its review of industrial policy the NESC (1982) found that a number of the multinational companies indicated that such tax incentives would have been sufficient to entice them to the Republic of Ireland and that capital grants were 'extra icing on the cake'.[14]

Before 1983 the most important industrial incentive in Northern Ireland took the form of a cash grant rather than a tax concession on profits as in the Republic of Ireland. However, with the introduction of the Corporation Tax Relief Grant (CTRG) in Northern Ireland in 1983 the similarity of the incentive packages offered in both jurisdictions appeared to increase. The CTRG, in theory, reimburses up to 80 per cent of corporation tax paid on profits from a project for which companies negotiated assistance with the IDB. Payment of the grant is conditional on the company creating additional employment in new or expanding industry and the IDB determines the proportion of total corporation tax paid which would qualify for CTRG; payment of the grant is related to the achievement of agreed employment targets and to the extent to which the company's profits are related to the assessed part of its activities. In practice the IDB does not promote the CTRG and the uptake of the scheme has been extremely poor; it is difficult to implement a scheme which operates for a twenty year period and requires the company to provide forecasts of profits for this period.

Industrial policy in both the Republic of Ireland and Northern Ireland has relied heavily upon substantial capital grants and generous depreciation and initial allowance provisions to encourage investment. While these allowances undoubtedly reduce the corporate tax base they also distort relative factor prices by lowering the cost of capital (Geary et al 1975; Ruane and John 1984). This thesis is supported by the findings of an OECD survey (McKee at al 1986) which showed that the tax system in the Republic of Ireland was more highly biased against the use of labour than any other OECD country: this study also concluded that the tax system in the United Kingdom had a similar bias prior to the major reform programme for corporation tax announced in the 1984 United Kingdom budget (Edwards 1984). These United Kingdom reforms, which apply to Northern Ireland, abolished stock relief[15] and introduced phased reductions in the standard corporation tax rate to 35 per cent together with the phased abolition of initial allowances for investment. The government of the Republic of Ireland recognises that investment incentives have been exceptionally high and have favoured investment in fixed assets at the expense of jobs.[16] Stock relief in the Republic of Ireland was abolished in 1986 and the 1988 budget contains proposals which, like the United Kingdom reforms, aim to broaden the corporate tax base through less generous reliefs and to lower the standard tax rate. First year accelerated capital allowances for plant, machinery and industrial buildings will fall from

100 per cent to 50 per cent by April 1989 and the standard corporation tax rate will fall from 50 to 43 per cent.[17]

Profits from export sales have been exempt from tax in the Republic of Ireland but this scheme is due to end in April 1990. Since most foreign companies use the Republic of Ireland as a base for exporting this seriously militated against the use of labour by these companies. Labour costs cannot be offset against profit taxes if almost all profits are exempt from tax; other things being equal, it is thus tax efficient for foreign companies to incur labour costs in countries where these costs can be offset against profit taxes. The Irish tax system may, therefore, have encouraged the location of profits rather than employment.

Some indication of the contribution of foreign companies to domestic value added in the Republic of Ireland can be gained from Table 16.7. Although the net output of foreign companies was substantially higher than that from Irish companies their contribution to domestic employee income was relatively low. Less than 25 per cent of the net income of foreign companies was spent on wages and salaries compared to over 50 per cent by Irish companies. The contribution of non-EC companies to wages and salaries was below 20 per cent of total net income and in pharmaceuticals it was as low as 7.6 per cent. Profits, therefore, accounted for the major part of net output by foreign companies.

The rapid expansion in the exports of foreign firms during the 1980s resulted in rising net output which when combined with relatively low employment growth and favourable movements in prices yielded a steep rise in their tax exempt profits.[18] However, the contribution of this increase in profits to the economy of the Republic of Ireland has been limited due to the

TABLE 16.7   Net output in manufacturing, Republic of Ireland, 1983

	Net output[1]	Wages and salaries	
	(IR£m)	IR£m	% of net output[1]
Foreign companies by industry group:			
Office and data processing equipment	427	53	12.4
Pharmaceuticals	512	39	7.6
Electrical engineering	302	94	31.1
Instrument engineering	179	56	31.3
Total foreign companies	2,631	655	24.9
of which:			
EC	625	255	40.8
Non-EC	2,006	400	19.9
Irish companies	1,806	922	51.1

[1] Net output corresponds to gross value added and includes profits, wages, non-industrial inputs and non-wage remuneration.
Sources: Census of Industrial Production 1983, CSO (Dublin), May 1987; OECD (1987), December.

TABLE 16.8 Outflow of trading and investment income from the Republic of Ireland, 1980–1986

	Interest payments on government external debt		Other interest payments[2]		Outflow of profits, dividends and royalties		Total net outflow	
	IR£m	% of GDP[1]	IR£m	% of GDP[1]	IR£m	% of GDP[1]	IR£m	% of GDP[1]
1980	193	2.1	381	4.1	258	2.8	358	3.8
1981	266	2.3	455	4.0	362	3.2	504	4.4
1982	526	3.9	498	3.7	499	3.7	928	6.9
1983	597	4.1	490	3.3	659	4.5	1,184	8.1
1984	720	4.4	598	3.7	983	6.0	1,660	10.2
1985	795	4.6	612	3.5	1,321	7.6	1,992	11.5
1986	761	4.2	588	3.2	1,346	7.4	2,032	11.1

[1] GDP at current market prices.
[2] Includes semi-state bodies and interest flows of banks.
Sources: Economic Review and Outlook 1987; O'Malley and Scott, 'Determinants of Profit Outflows from Ireland' in Medium Term Review 1987–1992 by Bradley et al, ESRI December 1987; OECD (1987).

repatriation of most of these profits overseas. Table 16.8 shows that the outflow of profits for the Republic of Ireland increased from 2.8 per cent of GDP in 1980 to 7.6 per cent in 1985. Profit outflows increased faster than any of the other outflow components of the Republic of Ireland's trading and investment income during the 1980s (see Table 16.8). This increase has contributed significantly to the pronounced growth in the deficit of the 'trading and investment income' transactions within the balance of international payments since inflows have remained fairly stable over the period. The total net outflow, shown in the final column of Table 16.8, increased more than fivefold between 1980 and 1986 and was equivalent to 11.5 per cent of GDP in 1985. This has resulted in very sizeable differences between the economy's GNP and its GDP and has serious implications for overall well-being since GNP is preferable to GDP as a measure of a country's economic welfare. Between 1984 and 1986 more than 10 per cent of the value of goods and services produced in the Republic of Ireland left the country.

Rates of taxation

A restructuring of the tax system in the Republic of Ireland which would redistribute the burden of direct taxes from wages and salaries towards corporate profits, property and income from self-employment has been inhibited throughout the 1980s because of the government's preoccupation with the debt crisis. Fundamental reform of this nature would have involved unacceptable risks with respect to the flow of revenue. Because of the Republic of Ireland's very narrow tax base, rates of tax on personal incomes and goods and services are high by international standards.

In the 1986/87 tax year 42 per cent of income tax payers were liable at rates above the standard rate compared to 15 per cent in 1981/82 and 1 per cent in 1973/74. The *Programme for National Recovery* contains a commitment to reduce income tax and the aim is to have two-thirds of taxpayers on the standard rate by the end of 1990. As a result of the increases in personal allowances, PAYE allowance and the widening of tax bands proposed in the 1988 Budget, nearly 63 per cent of taxpayers are expected to pay tax at the standard rate in 1988/89. However, despite the 1988 Budget proposals the Republic of Ireland still has an income tax system which is seriously out of line with that in Northern Ireland. Basic income tax allowances, tax bands and tax rates in the Republic of Ireland and Northern Ireland are compared in Table 16.9. Distinguishing features include the PAYE and Pay Related Social Insurance (PRSI) allowances which were introduced in the Republic of Ireland in 1980 and 1983 respectively: the PAYE allowance was instituted to reduce tax progressivity for the PAYE taxpayer in order to compensate for the fact that the self-employed pay tax on a previous year basis and the PRSI allowance was introduced to improve the take home pay of those paying the higher rate of contribution, ie the normal private sector employee. A substantial number of taxpayers are not entitled to either of these allowances.

By Northern Ireland standards the income tax system in the Republic of Ireland is steeply progressive. A single taxpayer in the Republic of Ireland moves on to the top marginal tax rate of 58 per cent on taxable income over £7,478; his Northern Ireland counterpart is taxed at 25 per cent on taxable income up to £19,300. The single personal allowance is also substantially below that in Northern Ireland unless the taxpayer is entitled to PAYE and PRSI allowances. For a single taxpayer on £8,696 (IR£10,000), around average industrial earnings in the Republic of Ireland, and availing of all allowances outlined in Table 16.9, the average tax rates are 25.5 per cent in the Republic of Ireland and 17.5 per cent in Northern Ireland. However, the taxpayer's marginal rate of 48 per cent in the Republic of Ireland is almost twice that for his Northern Ireland counterpart. The steep progressivity of the Republic of Ireland's system manifests itself more clearly when a single taxpayer on £21,739 (IR£25,000) per annum is considered: average tax rates are 44.3 per cent in the Republic of Ireland and 22.0 per cent in Northern Ireland and marginal tax rates are 58 per cent and 25 per cent respectively.

For a married couple with one working spouse the tax allowances are fairly similar: allowances in the Republic of Ireland exceed those in Northern Ireland if the taxpayer is entitled to PAYE and PRSI allowances. This is due to changes introduced in the 1980 Budget whereby all married couples, whether with one or two incomes, receive the benefits of double the single allowance and double the tax bands applicable to single taxpayers. Despite this, however, the average tax rate for such a couple on IR£25,000 is 33.2 per cent against 20.3 per cent in Northern Ireland, assuming all allowances given in Table 16.9 apply; the corresponding marginal tax rates are 58 per cent and 25 per cent. When both spouses are working the tax allowances in the Republic of Ireland are considerably lower than those in the United Kingdom but if both are entitled to PAYE and PRSI allowances the difference is marginal. Sharp divergences between average tax rates emerge, however, as taxable income increases due to high tax rates combined with relatively narrow tax bands.

OECD (1987) concluded that the system of taxation in the Republic of Ireland distorts economic incentives, encourages evasion and contributes to emigration, particularly among young qualified workers which further erodes the tax base.[19] However, Irish evidence[20] on the likely supply-side contribution of income tax cuts to economic growth is inconclusive and the extent to which tax-induced emigration is a serious issue within the context of total emigration is also an open question. In its discussion of lower income taxation the *Programme for National Recovery* (Stationery Office 1987) emphasised efficiency and equity considerations but it also stressed the relation between lower taxation and moderate pay expectations which it regarded as essential for the success of the programme. While the efficiency arguments for a reduction in the higher marginal tax rates are unclear, there are strong equity arguments against such a measure. Raising tax thresholds and tax bands would seem preferable on equity grounds and the resultant reductions in average tax rates rather than marginal rates might have a greater effect on tax-induced emigration.

Tables 16.5 and 16.6 show that taxes on goods and services in the

TABLE 16.9 Tax bands and tax allowances, Northern Ireland and the Republic of Ireland,[1] 1988/89

	Northern Ireland		Republic of Ireland[4]			Allowances[2]	
	Taxable income (£)	Tax rate (%)	Taxable income (£)	(IR£)	Tax rate (%)	Northern Ireland (£)	Republic of Ireland (£) (IR£)
Single person	First 19,300 Over 19,300	25 40	First 4,957 Next 2,522 Over 7,478	(5,700) (2,900) (8,600)	35 48 58	2,605	1,783 (2,050)
Married couple one spouse working	First 19,300 Over 19,300	25 40	First 9,913 Next 5,043 Over 14,957	(11,400) (5,800) (17,200)	35 48 58	4,095	3,565 (4,100)
Married couple both working	Up to 38,600[3] Over 38,600	25 40	First 9,913 Next 5,043 Over 14,957	(11,400) (5,800) (17,200)	35 48 58	6,700[3] or 5,210	3,565 (4,100)

[1] Irish pound values are given in brackets. Exchange rate as on British Budget day, 15 March 1988, £1 = IR£1.15.
[2] In addition to personal allowances there is in the Republic of Ireland a PAYE allowance of £696 (IR£800) for those paying tax under PAYE, and a pay-related social insurance (PRSI) allowance of £249 (IR£286), for those who are paying PRSI at the full rate.
[3] A working couple may opt for separate taxation or the married allowance plus the wife's earned income allowance and one set of tax bands.
[4] In addition to these taxes the Republic of Ireland operates a Youth Employment levy of 1 per cent on the gross income of all taxpayers. Social insurance rates are also excluded from this table.
Source: Budget Statements 1988, United Kingdom and Republic of Ireland.

Republic of Ireland are also seriously out of line with those in the United Kingdom and other EC countries. The rapid rise in rates of indirect taxation in the Republic of Ireland, particularly in the 1980–85 period, is evident from Table 16.10 which compares the main VAT rates in the Republic of Ireland since its introduction in 1972 with the single United Kingdom rate introduced in 1973. Both countries zero rate a range of goods including food. While the United Kingdom rate has been stable at 15 per cent since 1979 the main rates in the Republic of Ireland increased rapidly between 1980 and 1983. These sharp differences in VAT rates are compounded by higher excise taxes in the Republic of Ireland (see Table 16.11). Excise duties on beer, which were just over twice the United Kingdom rate in 1970, were nearly four times the United Kingdom rate in 1987.

American studies by Ballard et al (1985) and Stuart (1984) show that the deadweight loss of taxation, which results in the distortion of private decisions, increases approximately with the square root of the tax rate. Because of the very narrow tax base in the Republic of Ireland and the resultant high tax rates on incomes and goods the distortionary effects of the tax system are therefore likely to be relatively high. Honohan and Irvine (1987) have attempted to estimate, using a partial equilibrium approach, the deadweight loss associated with taxation in the Republic of Ireland. Their study, which concentrates on labour market and commodity market taxation, shows that welfare losses are particularly sensitive to supply and demand elasticities because of high tax rates. Marginal welfare losses can be several times the increased tax revenue when elasticities are high. Their findings support the case for a tax on property in the Republic of Ireland as deadweight losses associated with such a tax, particularly on land and residential property, would be low owing to their relatively low supply and demand elasticities (Mayo 1981; White and White 1977). Substitution of property taxation for

TABLE 16.10   Main VAT rates, Northern Ireland and the Republic of Ireland, 1 March 1988

| | Northern Ireland | Republic of Ireland | | |
	VAT rate	Low rate	Normal rate	Luxury rate[1]
1972	—		5.26	16.37
1973	10		6.75	19.5
1976	8		10	20
1980	15		10	25
1981	15		15	25
1982	15		18	30
1983	15	8	23	35
1984	15	8	23	35
1985	15	10	23	
1986	15	2.4 and 10	25	
1987	15	2.4 and 10	25	
1988	15	1.4 and 10	25	

[1] The luxury rate was abolished in 1985.
Sources: Budget Statements; FitzGerald et al (1988), Table 3.2.

TABLE 16.11   Rates of excise tax, Northern Ireland and the Republic of Ireland, 1 March 1987

Commodity	Unit	Northern Ireland (£)	Republic of Ireland (£)	(IR£)
Spirits	£ per litre	15.77	17.96	(19.52)
Beer	£ per hectolitre	42.22	137.39	(149.35)
Petrol	£ per hectolitre	19.38	25.18	(27.37)
TV sets	17 inch to 24 inch	0.0	45.08	(49.00)

Source: FitzGerald et al (1988), Table 3.3.

some of the existing income and expenditure taxes in the Republic of Ireland would, therefore, result in considerable reductions in deadweight losses.

The NESC regards the system of taxation in the Republic of Ireland as the most notable influence on the evolution of incomes over the recent past.[21] Because of the substantial growth during the 1980s in income taxes and indirect taxes the gap between the after-tax wage of an average employee and the cost of his employment has widened considerably. Between 1979 and 1986 real labour costs rose by around 20 per cent but post-tax wages fell by over 10 per cent owing to higher income and indirect taxes. The OECD (1987) regards this trend as an important factor in explaining the relatively poor job creation record of the Republic of Ireland.[22]

CROSS-BORDER SHOPPING

Whereas rates of indirect taxes have risen very slowly in Northern Ireland since 1980, tax rates in the Republic of Ireland have increased rapidly and this has been the major contributing factor to the price differentials which exist between the two economies (FitzGerald et al 1988). Consequently, high indirect taxes in the Republic of Ireland have been one of the main factors which contributed to the substantial growth in cross-border consumer trade and smuggling during the 1980s.

Various comparative surveys of price levels in Northern Ireland and the Republic of Ireland were carried out by the National Prices Commission between 1976 and 1985 and the Economic and Social Research Institute (ESRI) in 1987. The results of these surveys show that while prices in Northern Ireland and the Republic of Ireland were very similar during the 1970s, by 1983 tax inclusive prices were substantially higher in the Republic of Ireland. Although the difference narrowed somewhat by early 1985, tax inclusive prices in the Republic of Ireland were over 20 per cent higher than those in Northern Ireland by early 1987. These trends are confirmed by Eurostat purchasing power parity data on the assumption that Northern Ireland price behaviour can be proxied by movements in the United Kingdom price level. Overall, the ESRI findings[23] (FitzGerald et al 1988) show that consumer prices in the Republic of Ireland rose by 23 percentage points more than in Northern Ireland between early 1980 and the end of 1987 and that 16 percentage points of this excess could be attributed to the rise in indirect taxation.

While the principal reason for the increasing differential between the prices of excisable goods during the 1980s has been the rise in indirect taxation the tax exclusive prices of these commodities are generally higher in the Republic of Ireland. The Restrictive Practices Commission (1987) reviewed the results of a number of surveys concerning net of tax price differences between the Republic of Ireland and the United Kingdom but particularly Northern Ireland. Replies from many firms suggested that transport costs contributed to the higher tax exclusive prices in the Republic of Ireland. Transport costs to Northern Ireland are often subsidised by producers in Great Britain who charge a fairly uniform price throughout the United Kingdom. This suggests that United Kingdom manufacturers enjoy higher profits when selling to the Republic of Ireland. In some cases the additional distribution layer in the form of the importer in the Republic of Ireland was found to exert upward pressure on prices. The Commission also produced evidence that retail margins are calculated as a percentage of the buying-in price of a good which includes excise taxes so that goods subject to relatively high excise taxes, as in the Republic of Ireland, will have higher absolute retail margins. The important effect of changes in the exchange rate on net of tax prices will be dealt with later.

Because of price differences cross-border trade has grown despite a range of restrictions on the total value of goods and the maximum worth of any single item which may be brought into the Republic of Ireland exempt from domestic indirect taxes. Since April 1987 these allowances are available only to those living more than 15 km from the border provided they remain in Northern Ireland for at least 48 hours. These regulations have been challenged by the European Commission and the matter has been referred to the European Court.

The ESRI study (FitzGerald et al 1988) suggests that during the latter 6 months of 1986 about 12 per cent of households in the Republic of Ireland made a total of over 800,000 shopping trips to Northern Ireland; the percentage of households living in border counties who made trips was substantially higher. Combining survey and time series evidence the ESRI findings show that the amount spent on cross-border trade in consumer goods by shoppers from the Republic of Ireland in 1986 could lie within the range of IR£150 million to IR£250 million, equivalent to around 2 per cent of personal consumer expenditure in the Republic of Ireland. Cross-border shopping in Northern Ireland by households in border areas accounted for nearly 10 per cent of their total expenditure in 1986. A Customs and Excise survey (1986) estimated that cross-border shopping in Northern Ireland in 1986 was over IR£300 million but the ESRI paper argues that because the survey was based entirely on information from Saturday shoppers, Saturday being the peak shopping day, it is not representative and is likely to exaggerate the volume of such shopping. The ESRI study also shows that shoppers from Northern Ireland spent only IR£7.0 million in the Republic of Ireland in 1986, mostly on clothing which is subject to 15 per cent VAT in Northern Ireland compared to

10 per cent in the Republic of Ireland.

These distortions in trade, due mainly to differences in indirect tax rates, have serious implications for the development of border counties in the two jurisdictions and for general budgetary policy in the Republic of Ireland because of the loss in tax revenue. The ESRI study argues that there is some evidence that a reduction in the tax rates on spirits and television sets in the Republic of Ireland would be close to self-financing since the reduction in indirect taxes on these commodities in 1984 resulted in considerable increases in domestic sales. This was disputed by the Department of Finance[24] on the grounds that it would require a fivefold increase in sales of television sets to compensate for an equalisation of tax levels and a 20 per cent increase in sales of spirits. The indications were, according to the Department, that markets would not expand by this amount.

TAX HARMONISATION

The abolition of border controls and the proposals for tax harmonisation contained in the EC Commission's White Paper on Completing the Internal Market (1985) will have important implications for the Irish economies. Indirect taxation and company taxation are seen as the most important areas necessitating further tax harmonisation in the Community.

The Republic of Ireland's scope for using indirect taxation as an independent policy instrument for demand management is already limited because of the prospect of increased cross-border trade and smuggling and the resultant loss of revenue when tax structures in the two economies diverge. Since tax exclusive prices are generally higher in the Republic of Ireland, the harmonisation of the indirect tax system need not necessarily lead to the approximation of tax exclusive prices in the short run. However, with the abolition of economic frontiers it would be possible for retailers in the Republic of Ireland to purchase from wholesalers in Northern Ireland. This would lead to reduced prices in the Republic of Ireland if, as the Restrictive Practices Commission report (1987) suggests, tax exclusive prices are higher partly because of exporters in Britain taking higher profit margins. If manufacturers and distributors in the Republic of Ireland are currently the beneficiaries of higher tax exclusive prices then reduced prices for consumers could lead to a contraction in profits with possible implications for employment. The Confederation of Irish Industry[25] estimates that the general price level in the Republic of Ireland will fall by 3 per cent as a result of completing the internal market.

The Commission's proposal for a two-tier system for VAT with a standard rate between 14 and 19 per cent and a reduced rate within the 4 to 9 per cent range will have serious implications for revenue in the Republic of Ireland where the standard rate is currently 25 per cent. The alignment of excise duties with the EC average will also involve substantial reductions in revenues for the Republic of Ireland since its dependence on excise revenues is currently well above the EC average. Although lower than in the Republic of

Ireland, excise duty on drink and tobacco in Northern Ireland is also significantly above the EC average and substantial reductions in revenue can be expected. Many of the goods which are currently zero rated in both jurisdictions are the same and include food, books, children's clothing and footwear. The charging of these basic necessities at the reduced VAT rate will lessen the expected revenue losses. While no figures are available for Northern Ireland, the Minister for Finance in the Republic of Ireland has stated[26] that the gross cost to the exchequer of harmonisation could be IR£470 million in the first year, equivalent to 7.2 per cent of total tax revenue in 1987 or 15.8 per cent of revenue from excise duties and VAT, and IR£350 million in each succeeding year. Although the Republic of Ireland has agreed in principle to tax harmonisation and has accepted two bands for VAT it is seeking a revision of the proposals on excise duties. The United Kingdom remains the only state which refuses to endorse indirect tax harmonisation in principle and is opposed to the abolition of a zero VAT rate despite offers of a derogation for some years after 1992.

In addition to the revenue gain, the imposition of VAT on goods which are currently zero rated will have important redistributive effects. Harmonisation will cause a change in the structure of relative prices, even if tax changes are not fully passed to consumers, and will affect the pattern of consumer expenditure: alcohol and tobacco consumption in the Republic of Ireland and Northern Ireland will be encouraged with resultant social costs.

Thom (1988) has attempted to take account of the effects of tax induced price changes on the pattern of consumer demand in his estimation of the revenue implications for the Republic of Ireland. Estimates of potential revenue changes are based on prior estimates of a demand system which relies on aggregate expenditure data. Since the imposition of utility maximising restrictions could yield erroneous results when using aggregate data, Thom provides two sets of estimates for possible revenue change: one set from a model which satisfies utility maximising restrictions and another set from an unrestricted model which ignores these properties. Projected revenue changes are based on VAT rates at 19 per cent on all goods and services except food, fuel, clothing and rent which are subjected to VAT at 4 or 9 per cent; excise duties are based on EC averages on 1 August 1987. The data relate to personal expenditures only and exclude revenue from expenditures by businesses and the results clearly depend on how well the demand system's parameters approximate to the true values. The estimated effects of harmonisation are given in Table 16.12. The greatest effect of harmonisation of indirect taxes on consumer prices occurs in the price of alcohol which is expected to decline by 34 per cent, followed by a decline of 6.1 per cent in petrol and 5.4 per cent in tobacco. Food prices show an increase of 7.6 per cent when the reduced VAT rate is 9 per cent. When these consumer price changes are weighted by expenditure shares, the average expected price reduction is 3.5 per cent with a reduced VAT rate of 9 per cent or 5.6 per cent with a reduced VAT rate of 4 per cent.

The predicted annual reductions in revenue range from IR£191.3

TABLE 16.12 Implications of tax harmonisation, estimated price and revenue changes, Republic of Ireland

| | Consumer price changes (%) | | Revenue changes (IR£m) | | | |
| | | | Restricted model | | Unrestricted model | |
	Reduced VAT = 4%	Reduced VAT = 9%	Reduced VAT = 4%	Reduced VAT = 9%	Reduced VAT = 4%	Reduced VAT = 9%
Food	2.55	7.64	65.9	188.2	58.6	174.2
Alcohol	−34.00	−34.00	−375.0	−379.9	−395.0	−399.9
Tobacco	−5.44	−5.44	18.4	13.3	58.3	54.1
Clothing	−4.00	0.67	15.0	14.5	10.9	9.6
Fuel	0.00	4.19	23.4	23.1	21.2	20.4
Petrol	−6.06	−6.06	3.0	10.7	−51.7	−57.5
Rent	4.32	9.62	21.8	45.9	22.4	47.7
Durables	−3.27	−3.27	5.4	7.7	−7.6	−4.9
Transport equipment	−3.04	−3.04	10.4	8.1	−23.8	−12.6
Services	−3.33	−3.33	−116.9	−116.9	−32.7	−34.4
Other goods	−2.92	−2.92	−4.9	−6.2	−11.9	−13.6
Weighted average	−5.58	−3.47	—	—	—	—
Total	—	—	−333.5	−191.3	−351.3	−216.9

Source: Thom (1988).

million to IR£351.3 million; considerably less than the IR£470 million estimate given by the Minister for Finance. Table 16.12 shows that the predicted reductions in revenue are dominated by alcohol. This is due to the importance of alcohol as a revenue source in the Republic of Ireland and the substantial price reduction which harmonisation would imply. The combination of an own-price elasticity of −0.48 and a 34 per cent reduction in price would reduce expenditure on alcohol by 18 per cent. It should be emphasised that the revenue loss will be extremely sensitive to minor changes in elasticities and the elasticity measure depends on how well the parameter estimates of the demand system approximate to the true values. The dramatic reduction in the price of alcohol is likely to increase the revenues from complementary goods even if the cross-price elasticities of these goods with respect to the price of alcohol are low: this explains the expected revenue increase from tobacco despite a fall in price and a relatively low own-price elasticity. Food could compensate for nearly half the revenue loss from alcohol if subjected to a VAT rate of 9 per cent. With an own-price elasticity less than one and a rise in price, expenditure on food will increase; the combination of increased expenditure and a higher tax rate boosts revenues.

Although less attention has been given to the harmonisation of corporate tax systems the Commission has argued that all enterprises be treated in the same way for corporation tax purposes and it also envisages that national state aid to industry will be tightly controlled.[27] It is not likely that harmonisation of the systems with respect to types of allowances and definition of the tax base would involve major upheavals in the tax system of the United Kingdom or the Republic of Ireland; although it would almost certainly require further reductions in allowances particularly in the Republic of Ireland. The 1988 Budget proposals in the Republic of Ireland and the recent changes announced with respect to state aid for industry are in line with trends in the United Kingdom and other EC countries. If the Commission's 1975 proposal for the harmonisation of tax rates within a 45 to 55 per cent range were implemented, however, it would seriously affect firms in the manufacturing sector now subject to a 10 per cent rate in the Republic of Ireland. A significant increase in this tax rate would discourage new investment, since this has been one of the most important incentives for foreign firms locating in the Republic of Ireland, and would seriously affect the revenue base for all taxes.

4. The exchange rate

The Republic of Ireland's decision to participate in the Exchange Rate Mechanism (ERM) of the European Monetary System (EMS) in 1979 ended a long-standing relationship between the Irish pound and sterling: the fixed exchange rate between the two currencies which had existed for over 150 years was abandoned and the free movement of capital between the two countries gave way to exchange controls with respect to the United Kingdom. While the introduction of exchange controls has not been effective in preventing capital outflows, the introduction of uncertainty regarding the sterling exchange rate has serious implications for the Republic of Ireland, given the importance of the United Kingdom in its trading relations and financial arrangements. This section examines (1) how a volatile Irish pound/sterling exchange rate implicitly affects cross-border trade through its effect on the net of tax price differential between Northern Ireland and the Republic of Ireland and (2) how the relationship between Irish and United Kingdom interest rates has changed since the Republic of Ireland joined the EMS. The comparison with Northern Ireland is implicit since Northern Ireland interest rates are closely aligned to United Kingdom rates.

THE EXCHANGE RATE AND PRICES

The economic theory of the small open economy predicts that inflation in such an economy, operating a fixed exchange rate with a dominant trading partner, will be very similar to that of its major trading partner. Studies of price determination in the Republic of Ireland during the 1970s, using pre-1978 data, show that inflation was determined by, and roughly equal to, inflation in the United Kingdom (Honohan and Flynn 1986). The trends in Irish and British consumer prices over the entire period between 1922 and 1978, when the link with sterling was broken, have been extremely close (Kennedy et al 1988). This contrasts sharply with the deviations which have occurred between prices in the United Kingdom and the Republic of Ireland following the break with sterling. Since joining the EMS the pattern of inflation in the Republic of Ireland cannot be explained by the standard small open economy model of price determination because the close relation with United Kingdom inflation no longer holds and the expectation that Irish inflation would be determined by German inflation has not materialised.

In an earlier discussion of possible explanations for differences in net of tax prices in the Republic of Ireland and Northern Ireland, which follow closely those in the rest of Britain, the possible effect of exchange rate changes on net of tax prices was not explored. In principle one would expect that changes in the sterling/Irish pound exchange rate would result in changes in output prices in the Republic of Ireland to match United Kingdom competitors. If a mark-up model of pricing is assumed, a downward movement in Irish prices could result from an appreciation of the Irish pound *vis-à-vis* sterling through its effect on the cost of imported inputs. However, evidence suggests that whereas Irish producers are quick to follow foreign competitors when their prices, in foreign currency terms, are raised they are relatively slow to adjust their prices to changes in the exchange rate.

The April 1985 survey of the National Prices Commission found that net of tax prices in the Republic of Ireland were 1.8 per cent lower than in Northern Ireland, whereas the ESRI survey (FitzGerald et al 1988) of February 1987 showed net of tax prices in the Republic of Ireland to be some 10 to 11 per cent higher than in Northern Ireland. The reason advanced in the ESRI survey for this change in net of tax price differentials was the failure of prices in the Republic of Ireland to adjust to the higher value of the Irish pound *vis-à-vis* sterling which occurred over this period: the Irish pound appreciated significantly from £0.82 per IR£1.00 in April 1985 to £0.92 per IR£1.00 in February 1987.

Using quarterly data for the period 1979–87, FitzGerald et al (1988) attempted to estimate how prices in the Republic of Ireland adjust to exchange rate changes by regressing the net of tax Irish consumer price index on the United Kingdom consumer price index in sterling and the sterling/Irish pound exchange rate. Although lagged values of the dependent variables of up to eight quarters were tried, the estimated equation was unable to capture adequately the effects of exchange rate changes on consumer prices in the Republic of Ireland, suggesting that the adjustment lags are longer than two years and that purchasing power parity fails to hold in the short run. Callan and FitzGerald (1989) used quarterly data on wholesale prices of manufacturing output in the Republic of Ireland in their analysis of the reaction of Irish prices to short-run changes in the exchange rate and in foreign currency prices. Their findings confirm that while Irish prices quickly follow foreign currency price changes the adjustment of prices to exchange rate changes is considerably slower. There is no evidence of an asymmetrical response to appreciation and depreciation of the Irish pound *vis-à-vis* sterling but it is questionable if the number of post-EMS observations is adequate to test this hypothesis properly.

The findings of the Restrictive Practices Commission (1987) show that firms use forecasts of exchange rates rather than the current exchange rate for pricing purposes; exchange rate expectations are therefore crucial for price determination. Nearly all of the firms interviewed indicated that it was incorrect to compare prices in the Republic of Ireland and Northern Ireland at a particular point in time using the current exchange rate. Because of the uncertainty involved in forecasting exchange rates, firms are reluctant to react to changes in the exchange rate until they are satisfied that it will not be reversed in the immediate future. Surveys by the National Prices Commission show that, with some exceptions, net of tax prices in Northern Ireland and the Republic of Ireland were fairly similar up to 1985. The appreciation of the Irish pound against sterling during the period 1985–87 resulted in significantly higher net of tax prices in the Republic of Ireland at the time of the ESRI survey in 1987 because of this slow rate of adjustment of prices to exchange rate changes, thereby increasing the incentive for residents of the Republic of Ireland to shop in Northern Ireland. With stable exchange rates the expectation would be that net of tax prices in the two jurisdictions would slowly adjust into line again. This relatively slow adjustment to exchange rate changes could have serious implications for cross-border trade flows following the completion of the internal market in 1992 if the United Kingdom does not participate in the Exchange Rate Mechanism of the EMS.

INTEREST RATES

In their pre-EMS analysis of the degree of integration between Irish and United Kingdom financial markets, Browne and O'Connell (1978) found a close relationship between Irish interest rates on similar assets when denominated in sterling and Irish pounds. In the absence of exchange rate uncertainty, the United Kingdom market was paramount in the determination of rates of return on Irish government securities, exchequer bills and other financial assets; inadequate domestic demand for these assets in the Republic of Ireland resulted in an inflow of United Kingdom funds which maintained the rates of return at United Kingdom levels. Free movement of capital implied that since the Irish authorities could not control the supply of money in the economy they could not control domestic interest rates. With no risk premiums, discrepancies between United Kingdom and Irish interest rates led to inflows or outflows from the Republic of Ireland until rates were realigned.

The Republic of Ireland's participation in the ERM since 1979 has resulted in exchange rate uncertainty not only with respect to sterling but also with respect to its EMS partners. The extent to which the Republic of Ireland was replacing a fixed exchange rate regime for an uncertain relation with the deutschmark and other EMS currencies was not fully appreciated when the decision to join the ERM was taken in late 1978; the presumption was that Irish interest rates in the post-1979 period would be determined by German rates just as they had been determined by United Kingdom rates in the pre-1979 period. However, exchange rate uncertainty allows interest rate differentials to exist since investors will not treat domestic and foreign financial assets as perfect substitutes. Some role can therefore be established, in theory at least, for an independent domestic monetary policy in the Republic of Ireland which could determine domestic interest rates.

The consequences for Irish interest rates of exchange rate volatility have been examined by O'Connell (1982), FitzGerald (1986) and O'Connor (1987). While a distinction is drawn between domestic policy and exchange rate expectations, it is recognised that domestic policies are likely to have a significant effect on the formation of expectations about the exchange rate. The evidence for the early 1980s shows that domestic policy action in the Republic of Ireland, such as the government's policy on debt, did influence domestic interest rates (FitzGerald 1986). During 1985 and 1986, however, expectations of the sterling/Irish pound exchange rate exerted a dominant influence on Irish interest rates. In anticipation of an expected devaluation of the Irish pound in an EMS realignment, which occurred in April 1986, speculative outflows caused a liquidity shortage which put pressure on Irish interest rates from late in 1985. During 1986 speculative foreign exchange outflows from the Republic of Ireland due to the appreciation of the Irish pound against sterling resulted in a sizeable uncertainty premium in Irish interest rates relative to United Kingdom rates.

Up to 1987 the influence of German interest rates on Irish money markets appeared to be no greater than before the Republic of Ireland joined the ERM: indeed, there had been a total lack of convergence between Irish interest rates and EMS rates. There is some evidence (Bacon 1988), however, of a fundamental adjustment in the structure of Irish interest rates and yields on government securities since 1987. Short-term interest rates have fallen steadily in the Republic of Ireland since early 1987 to levels below those in the United Kingdom in 1988. A comparison of long dated gilt yields in the Republic of Ireland and the United Kingdom also shows a steady decline in Irish rates since August 1987 with rates below those in the United Kingdom throughout 1988.

A contributory factor to this adjustment in the structure of Irish interest rates may have been the relative stability of sterling *vis-à-vis* the deutschmark and indirectly the Irish pound. This would suggest that the Republic of Ireland would benefit from United Kingdom membership of the ERM. The implications of United Kingdom membership for the Republic of Ireland, however, are not clear: it would certainly increase the stability of Irish financial markets by reducing the short-term volatility of sterling but it could also decrease the stability of the system by increasing the frequency of realignments. Another interpretation of this adjustment in the structure of Irish interest rates is that the Republic of Ireland is now realising the benefits of EMS membership in the form of low interest rates which are converging to EMS levels. Such an outcome is attributed to the improvements in the fundamental imbalances which characterised the economy up to 1985/86: the current balance of payments has moved from deficit into surplus, imbalances in the public finances are being successfully tackled, the decline in GNP has been reversed, and inflation is no longer in excess of the average rate for EMS countries. Undoubtedly the improvement in the balance of payments has increased liquidity and contributed to lower interest rates. This has been augmented by the considerable increase in non-resident investment in Irish government securities and the pronounced reduction in unidentified capital outflows: signs of renewed confidence in the country's economy.

Notes

1. The Exchequer Borrowing Requirement (EBR) is the sum of the current budget deficit and the net exchequer borrowing for capital purposes by central government. The difference between the Public Sector Borrowing Requirement (PSBR) and the EBR is the extent of borrowing by state-sponsored bodies and local authorities.

2. Fine Gael and Labour Coalition government: June 1981–February 1982. Fianna Fail government: February 1982–December 1982. Fine Gael and Labour Coalition government: December 1982–February 1987. Fianna Fail government: February 1987–June 1989. Fianna Fail and Progressive Democrats coalition: June 1989.

3. The primary surplus/deficit is the EBR excluding interest payments on the national debt.

4. The nominal interest rate is computed by dividing interest payments on the national debt by the stock of outstanding debt.

5. The non-interest current account is the difference between central government revenue and expenditure on current account when interest payments are excluded from current expenditure.

6. FitzGerald (1986), Table 3.3.

7. Ibid 5.
8. OECD (1987), Table 17.
9. Ibid 8.
10. GDP current prices at factor cost.
11. See *New Ireland Forum*, May 1984, 11.
12. The Northern Ireland Insurance Fund consists of three main elements: contributions from employees, employers and the Northern Ireland Consolidated Fund. The deficit in the Northern Ireland Insurance Fund is made up by payments from the British National Insurance Fund.
13. Company taxation in Ireland and the United Kingdom is based on the imputation system: shareholders are given credit for tax paid by the company, and this credit can be used to offset their income tax liability on dividends received. Company profits are taxed at the corporation tax rate and any distributions are regarded as having already paid tax at a certain rate called the imputation rate. Shareholders pay additional income tax on their dividends if their marginal income tax rates exceed the imputation rate.
14. NESC (1982), 198.
15. In the early 1970s, with most United Kingdom firms using historic cost accounting, it was not possible to exempt stock appreciation from tax and in order to alleviate the serious liquidity problems faced by companies an arbitrary form of relief, stock relief, was introduced in 1974. Stock relief enabled companies to deduct for tax purposes a proportion of the increase in the book value of stocks in any year.
16. Stationery Office (1988), 31.
17. The reduced corporation tax rates for profits up to £35,000 will also be abolished from April 1989. These currently stand at between 40 and 50 per cent for profits taxed at the normal rate and between 8 and 10 per cent for manufacturing companies.
18. OECD (1987), diagram 1.
19. OECD (1987), 62.
20. O'Hagan (1987), 152, 154; ESRI, *Quarterly Economic Commentary*, October 1988, 31.
21. NESC (1986), 309–10.
22. OECD (1987), 46–48.
23. The ESRI study does not include the legal import of goods by retailers in the Republic of Ireland who may bypass domestic distribution outlets due to higher tax exclusive prices. Also excluded from the study are the distortions in the patterns of trade in agriculture produce induced by the EC system of MCAs.
24. *The Irish Times*, March 31, 1988, 12.
25. Statement from the Director-General of the Confederation of Irish Industry, April 26, 1988. See *The Irish Times*, April 27, 1988, 14.
26. Dail Eireann, Parliamentary Debates, May 19, 1988. The minimum annual loss to the Irish Exchequer is estimated at £350 million with an additional loss of £120 million arising in one year as a result of the elimination of VAT at the point of entry.
27. Report on the scope for convergence of tax systems in the Community, *Bulletin of the European Communities*, Supplement 1/80.

References

Bacon, P (1988) The European Monetary System – sterling and the Irish pound, *The Irish Banking Review*, Autumn, 3–20.

Ballard, C L, Shoven, J B and Whalley, J (1985) General equilibrium computations of the marginal welfare costs of taxes in the US, *American Economic Review*, 75, 1, 128–38.

Bradley, J, Fanning, C, Prendergast, C and Wynne, M (1985) *Medium-term Analysis of Fiscal Policy in Ireland: a Macroeconomic Study of the Period 1967–1980*, ESRI, 122, Dublin.

Browne, F X and O'Connell, T (1978) A quantitative analysis of the degree of integration between Irish and United Kingdom financial markets, *The Economic and Social Review*, July, 9, 4, 283–300.

Cairncross, F (1988) Republic of Ireland, *The Economist*, 16 January, 3–26.

Callan, T and FitzGerald, J D (1989) Price determination in Ireland: effects of changes in exchange rates and exchange rate regimes, *The Economic and Social Review*, January, 20, 2, 165–188.

Commission of the European Communities (1985) *Completing the Internal Market*, White Paper from the Commission to the European Council, June, Luxembourg.

Davy Kelleher McCarthy Ltd (1984) *New Ireland Forum: the Macroeconomic Consequences of Integrated Economic Policy, Planning and Co-ordination in Ireland*, Stationery Office, Dublin.

Edwards, J (1984) The 1984 corporation tax reform, *Fiscal Studies*, 5, 2, 30–44.

FitzGerald, J D (1986) *The National Debt and Economic Policy in the Medium Term*, ESRI Policy Research Series 7, Dublin.

FitzGerald, J D, Quinn, T P, Whelan, B J and Williams, J A (1988) *An Analysis of Cross-Border Shopping*, ESRI, 137, Dublin.

Geary, P T, Walsh, B M and Copeland, J (1975) The cost of capital to Irish industry, *The Economic and Social Review*, April, 6, 3, 299–312.

Honohan, P and Flynn, J (1986) Irish inflation in EMS, *The Economic and Social Review*, April, 17, 3, 175–91.

Honohan, P and Irvine, I (1987) The marginal social cost of taxation in Ireland, *The Economic and Social Review*, October, 19, 1, 15–41.

Kennedy, K A, Giblin, T and McHugh, D (1988) *The Economic Development of Ireland in the Twentieth Century*, Routledge, London and New York.

McKee, M, Visser, J C and Saunders, P G (1986) Marginal tax rates on the use of labour and capital in the OECD countries, *OECD Economic Studies*, Autumn, Paris.

Mayo, S (1981) Theory and estimation in the economics of housing demand, *Journal of Urban Economics*, 10, 95–116.

National Economic and Social Council (1982) *A Review of Industrial Policy*, 64, P1 409, Dublin.

National Economic and Social Council (1986) *A Strategy for Development, 1986–1990*, 83, P1 4450, Dublin.

OECD (1987) *Economic Surveys – Ireland 1987/88*, Paris.

O'Connell, T (1982) What determines Irish interest rates? *The Irish Banking Review*, June, 15–24.

O'Connor, P (1987) Exchange rate volatility and consequences for Irish interest rates, *The Irish Banking Review*, Spring, 3–14.

O'Hagan, J W (ed) (1987) *The Economy of Ireland: Policy and Performance*, Irish Management Institute, Dublin, 5th edition.

O'Leary, J (1987) The national debt: implications for fiscal policy, *The Irish Banking Review*, Autumn, 3–20.

O'Malley, E and Scott, S (1987) Determinants of profit outflows from Ireland, *Medium-Term Review: 1987–1992*, ESRI, 2, Dublin.

Restrictive Practices Commission (1987) *Report on Alleged Differences in Retail Grocery Prices between the Republic of Ireland and the United Kingdom (including particularly Northern Ireland)*, Stationery Office, P1 5236, Dublin.

Ruane, F P and John, A A (1984) Government intervention and the cost of capital to Irish manufacturing industry, *The Economic and Social Review*, October, 16, 1, 31–50.

Stationery Office (1982) *The Way Forward: National Economic Plan, 1983–1987*, P1 1061, Dublin.

Stationery Office (1984) *Building on Reality, 1985–1987*, P1 2648, Dublin.

Stationery Office (1987) *Programme for National Recovery*, P1 5213, Dublin.

Stationery Office (1988) *Budget 1988*, Dublin.

Stuart, C (1984) Welfare costs per dollar of additional tax revenue in the US, *American Economic Review*, 74, 3, 352–62.

Thom, R (1988) *The Revenue Implications of Tax Harmonisations*. Report prepared for the European League for Economic Co-operation.

White, M J and White, L J (1977) The tax subsidy to owner-occupied housing: who benefits? *Journal of Public Economics*, February, 7, 111–26.

Index